DIARY, REMINISCENCES,

AND

CORRESPONDENCE

OF

HENRY CRABB ROBINSON,

BARRISTER-AT-LAW, F. S. A.

SELECTED AND EDITED BY

THOMAS SADLER, PH.D.

IN TWO VOLUMES.

VOL. I.

BOSTON:

FIELDS, OSGOOD, & CO.,

SUCCESSORS TO TICKNOR AND FIELDS.

1870.

"A Man he seems of cheerful yesterdays
And confident to-morrows ; with a face
Not worldly-minded, for it bears too much
Of Nature's impress, — gayety and health,
Freedom and hope ; but keen withal, and shrewd.
His gestures note, — and hark ! his tones of voice
Are all vivacious as his mien and looks."
The Excursion, Book VII.

From Advance Sheets.

UNIVERSITY PRESS : WELCH, BIGELOW, & CO.,
CAMBRIDGE.

PREFACE.

THE materials placed in the hands of the Editor, from which to make selections for the following work, were : 1. Brief journals reaching as far as 1810, inclusive ; 2. A regular and full home Diary, begun in 1811, and continued till within five days of Mr. Robinson's death, forming thirty-five closely written volumes ; 3. About thirty volumes of Journals of tours ; 4. Reminiscences, reaching down to the year 1843, inclusive ; 5. Miscellaneous papers ; 6. A large number of letters. It was Mr. Robinson's intention to very materially reduce the number of letters, and to leave only those which were valuable. This sifting he regarded as a chief work of his later years, and he was fond of quoting respecting it the saying of Dr. Aikin when struck by paralysis : "I must make the most of the salvage of life." But although he destroyed a vast number of letters, the work of selection and arrangement was very far from completed.

The part of his papers of which he himself contemplated the posthumous publication, was a selection from his Reminiscences, with some letters. Many friends repeatedly urged him to make the necessary preparation for such a publication. Among these were Rogers and Wordsworth. On the recommendation of the latter, Mr. Robinson laid special stress, for he said : "Wordsworth must be aware that there are many interesting particulars respecting himself, which I should wish to preserve, if I preserved anything." And the recommendation was, therefore, interpreted as a sanction to including these particulars with those relating to Goethe, Wieland, and others. To his executors, Mr. Robinson used to say: "If you were to print all that you find" (referring to the Reminiscences), "I should think you would show great want of judgment; and I should think the same if you came to the conclusion that there is nothing worth printing." About six weeks before his death, he met Mr. Macmillan, the publisher of these volumes, who, as they were going down to lunch, gave him his arm, and on the stairs said: "Mr. Robinson, I wonder that you have never been induced to undertake some great literary work." Mr. Robinson stopped, and, placing his hand on Mr. Macmillan's shoulder, answered: "It is because I am a wise man. I early found that I had not the literary ability to give me such a place among English authors as I should have desired; but I thought that I had an opportunity of gaining a knowledge of many of the most distinguished men of the age, and that I might do some good by keeping a record of my interviews with them." And writing to his brother in 1842, he said: "When you complain of my not being so copious as I ought on such occasions, you only remind me of what I am already sufficiently aware, and that I want in an eminent degree the Boswell faculty. With his excellent memory and tact, had I early in life set about following his example, I might, beyond all doubt, have supplied a few volumes superior in value to his 'Johnson,' though they would not have been so popular. Certainly the names recorded in his great work are not so important as Goethe, Schiller, Herder, Wieland, the Duchesses Amelia and Louisa of Weimar, and Tieck, — as Madame de Staël, La Fayette, Abbé Grégoire, Benjamin Constant, — as Wordsworth, Southey, Coleridge, Lamb, Rogers, Hazlitt, Mrs. Barbauld, Clarkson, &c., &c., &c., for I could add a great number of minor stars. And yet what has come of all this? Nothing. What will come of it? Perhaps nothing."

From the year 1811 the Diary is entitled to the most prominent place. The Reminiscences were not begun till Mr. Robinson had nearly reached threescore years and ten; and even if they had been written in the freshness of his memory, and in the fulness of his mental vigor, they would still hardly have had equal value with the daily record, which breathes the air of the scenes and incidents to which it relates.

In the execution of his task, the Editor has kept two objects especially in view : first, to preserve interesting particulars respecting distinguished men, both in England and on the Continent; and, secondly, to keep unbroken the thread of Mr. Robinson's own life. One reason why the materials were put into his hands rather than those of one possessing more literary experience was, that he had been himself a student at German Universities, and was interested in German literature ; but the chief reason was that, from various circumstances, he was likely to give due prominence to Mr. Robinson's own modes of thinking and mental characteristics, his independent unconforming ways, without which those who knew him best would feel that they had not a faithful portrait of their friend. If this were not secured, the executors would consider that they were not carrying out his own aim, in leaving the selection of editor to them, without guidance or restraint. The Editor has, therefore, felt it to be his duty to take all the care he could that the unpopular, or commonly uninteresting, subjects of Mr. Robinson's thought and interest should not be suppressed, in order to make the book more in accordance with the public taste.

The Editor cannot venture to hope that, in the first edition of the work, there will not be many mistakes. Mr. Robinson often excited surprise by his wonderful memory in the narration of personal incidents ; but in regard to dates and names, it was not altogether without grounds that he called himself an incorrigible blunderer.

Of the mass of MS. which remains after selection, it will be enough to say, that it, for the most part, refers simply to the ordinary matters of private life, but that there are some parts which, though they could not, with propriety, be published now, may in time have a public interest and value.* It may, perhaps, not be out of place to give very

---

* Mr. Robinson's papers will be carefully preserved with a view to any historical value they may acquire by the lapse of time. It may be stated, as a rough guess, that the selections, not taking into account the letters, do not amount to more than a twenty-fifth or thirtieth part of the whole.

briefly some of the most marked impressions of Mr.
Robinson, which have been left on the Editor's mind,
after reading the whole.

In Holcroft's "Hugh Trevor" there is a passage in
which Mr. Robinson was greatly interested, because he
felt it to be singularly applicable to himself: " I was possessed of that hilarity which, when not regulated by a
strong desire to obtain some particular purpose, shows
itself in a thousand extravagant forms, and is then called
animal spirits ; but when once turned to an attainment
of some great end, assumes the more worthy appellation
of activity of mind." Of this passage Mr. Robinson says :
" I have through life had animal spirits in a high degree.
I might, under certain circumstances, have had more."
When he was in his seventieth year, Mrs. Clarkson said
of him, that he was " as much a boy as ever." Wordsworth called him " a healthy creature, who talked of coming again in seven years as others would of seven days."
And the first line of the Dedication to H. C. R. of the
" Memorials of the Italian Tour " is : —

> " Companion! By whose *buoyant* spirit cheered."

This was, doubtless, in some measure owing to a healthful and vigorous constitution. Very rarely does so long
a life pass with so little interruption from illness. Even
so late as 1831, when he was in Italy, he made an excursion with three gentlemen, one of whom, before their
return, volunteered this confession : " When I heard that
you were to be of the party, I, at first, refused to go ; ' For,'
I said, ' Mr. Robinson is an old man, and the rest of us
shall have to accommodate ourselves to his infirmities ' ;
but you have already knocked up two of us, and all but
me also."

Mr. Robinson was a voracious devourer of books. He
read before he got up, and after he went to bed. On his
journeys, whether on foot or on a stage-coach, he was in
the habit of spending much of his time in reading. The
most attractive scenery had to share his attention with a
book. He said : " I could have no pleasure at the seaside
without society. That is the one great want of my life,
or rather the second, — the first being books." In a

Christmas visit to Rydal, for a month or five weeks, he would read from ten to twenty volumes of such works as those of Arnold, Whately, and Isaac Taylor. Nor was he one of those who think they have read a work when they have only skimmed through it, and made themselves acquainted with its general contents. Sometimes he gives, in the Diary, an account of what he read, and there is a large bundle of separate papers, containing abstracts of books, plots of stories, and critical remarks.

In his case, however, there was no danger of becoming so absorbed in literature as to lose his interest in men. He was eminently *social.* But he liked to have to do with persons who had some *individuality.* It was an affliction to him to be obliged to spend several hours with one of those colorless beings who have no opinions, tastes, or principles of their own. Writing from Germany to his brother, he said, " I love *characters* extremely." The words, " He is a character," are frequently the prelude to an interesting personal description. Of one whom he knew, he says : " All his conversation is ostentatious egotism ; and yet it is preferable to the dry talk about the weather, which some men torment me with. The revelations of character are always interesting." This interest in character seems to have given him an intuitive power of finding out noticeable men. Wherever he was, — in London, Germany, or Rome, — a secret affinity was almost sure to bring him into contact with those who were most worth knowing, and to lead to a lasting acquaintance with them. When compelled, by Napoleon's soldiers, to fly from Hamburg, and to take refuge in Stockholm, he formed a friendship with the veteran Arndt, and there was no diminution in the warmth of their greeting after an interval of twenty-seven years.

Mr. Robinson's name is widely known as that of a capital talker. There is a saying that a man's strength is also his weakness, and in this case there are not wanting jokes about his taking all the conversation to himself. It is reported that one day at a breakfast-party at Sam Rogers's, the host said to those assembled : " O, if there is any one here who wishes to say anything, he had bet-

ter say it at once, for Crabb Robinson is coming." But
there is no subject on which he more frequently reproaches himself, than with this habit of taking too large
a share of the talk.   When his strength was beginning to
fail, his friend Edwin Field urged him in a letter to refrain from talking " more than two hours consecutively."
He notes this in the Diary, and adds : " Is this satire ?   It
does not offend me."   Yet he was too candid not to acknowledge that conversation was the one thing in which,
in his own estimation, he excelled.   It was, he said, his
power of expression which enabled him to make his way
as a barrister, notwithstanding his deficiencies in legal attainment.*   He not only had a copious vocabulary, but
could also convey much meaning by his manner, and by
a playful exaggeration in his words.

Of this last use of speech he says in a letter to his
brother : " What I wrote about the parson's alleging
that he had never seen me at church, was not altogether
a joke, but was a real feeling, exaggerated into a joke,
which is very much my habit in company, and, I may
say, is one of the secrets of conversational tact.   There
is not a better way of insinuating a wholesome but un-
palatable truth, than clothing it in language wilfully beyond truth, so that it may be taken as a satire on those
who gravely maintain the same doctrine, by all who perhaps would not tolerate a sober and dry statement of it.
I have the vanity to think I know how to do this, but I
may sometimes fail, of course.   The intelligent always
understand me, and the dull are puzzled."   It is not too
much to say, that to the great majority of those who
were in the habit of meeting him his conversation was a
real delight.   The Editor well remembers the secret pleasure with which he invariably saw him come into the
room, and the feeling which the announcement of his
death caused, as of a loss which, in kind, could never be
made up.   There were veins in his conversation, from which
more good was to be gained in a pleasant hour after dinner, than from many a lengthened serious discourse.

---

* Whatever amount of truth there may be in Mr. Robinson's own idea of
his legal attainments. he, at all events, as the Diary shows, was a great reader
of legal books, while he was in practice at the bar.

Throughout life Mr. Robinson was a man of unusual activity. He himself would hardly have admitted this. A title that suggested itself to him for his Reminiscences was, " Retrospect of an Idle Life." When on one occasion he was told by his medical attendant that he had been using his brain too much, he exclaimed, "That is absurd." He would say of himself, that while he talked too much he *did* nothing. But, in truth, men "who have nothing to do" are very serviceable members of society, if they only know how to employ their time.

Those who knew him best, protested against the self-reproaches he heaped upon himself for not being of more use. Miss Denman says in a letter : "I must scold you in good earnest. What can you mean by complaining of being useless in the world, when you must be conscious that every human being you ever called friend has found you one in any and every emergency where your kindness and services could be made available ? Do we not all feel and acknowledge this, and are you the only forgetful person ? I 'll tell you what you should do. When the uncomfortable discouraging idea is taking hold of your mind, call over the names of the persons you have been most intimate with, and ask yourself before you dismiss each name, Have I never done a service, given useful advice or pecuniary aid, to this person ? Try this, and I think your mind will be relieved from the fancied evil." He was, as he himself expressed it, " a busy idle man."

In the early part of his life, simple habits and a very limited expenditure were necessary to " make both ends meet." But when his means became considerable he had no desire to alter, materially, his mode of living. He did not covet the kind of rank and station which are attained by a costly establishment and a luxurious table. He had not a single expensive habit ; but he said, " My parsimony does not extend to others." He would rather help some widow to bring up her children, or some promising young man to obtain superior educational advantages. But he had his own method of giving. It was rather in the spirit of *generosity*, than of charity, in the narrower sense of that word. He had his pensioners among the poor, but he had a wholesome fear of encouraging a spirit of dependence, and was conscientiously on his guard against that kind of liberality which is easily taken in. There were friends to whom he used to say, "If you know of any case in which money will do good, come to me!" * And he did not like to be much thanked; he felt humiliated by it, when he had simply followed the natural dictates of kindness and good-will. He was especially fond of promoting the enjoyment of the young. "In the happiness of the young," he said, in a letter to his brother, "we, the aged, if we are not grossly selfish, shall be able to take pleasure." If it were rumored that the students of University Hall wanted the relief of a dance, towards the close of a session of hard study, they would presently hear that an anonymous friend had presented £ 50 for the purpose. He took great *pains* with his gifts. He would often get some friend to choose a wedding present, and the value was "not to be less than a sum named," — always a handsome amount. With a book-gift, he would sometimes send a long and valuable letter about the best way to read it. In Rome, on the birthday of Pepina, Miss Mackenzie's adopted child, he put into her hands a present of money, with a kind letter of advice, which he hoped would be valuable to her in after life. There was often peculiar delicacy in his acts of generosity. In one of his tours, he found his old friend Charlotte Serviere somewhat narrowed in her circumstances, and, calling at Frankfort on his way back, he begged her to do him the favor of relieving him of a part of the too large balance which his tour had left in his hands, and to excuse a pecuniary gift from an old friend. He would not let her express the gratitude she felt ; but on leaving the house, on a subsequent visit, he could not prevent the old servant from seizing him by the hand and saying, "I thank you for the great joy you have given to the Fräulein." Some who are now thriving in fortune, and holding a prominent place in the literary world, will remember the little " sealed

---

* Mr. Robinson often said to E. W. Field: " You cannot think what a trouble it is to me to spend a shilling on myself; but if you know of any good way of using my money, come to me."

notes," containing a valuable enclosure, for which he would fain have it believed that a volume or two of the author's works, or a ticket to a course of lectures, was ample return. Nor was his generosity by any means confined to pecuniary gifts and personal exertions.

Not a few of his best anecdotes have got, prematurely, into print. This was inevitable with a good talker. And he would not have avoided it, if he could, by putting a restraint on the sociability of his nature, though he *did* like to have his anecdotes told as they ought to be. Not only, however, did some of his best anecdotes get abroad, if sometimes in an imperfect form, but he seems to have had no disposition to keep back other matter, though strictly under his own control. When he heard that Moore was preparing a " Life of Byron," he wrote a letter, which, it appears, never reached its destination, giving a full account of those highly interesting interviews, in which Goethe's opinions of Byron were expressed. Mrs. Austin, in her " Characteristics of Goethe," and Mr. Gilchrist, in his " Memoirs of Blake," not to mention others, received valuable contributions from Mr. Robinson ; and this, notwithstanding that recollections of his own would, in all probability, be some day published.

His love for the young showed itself, not only in his thoughtfulness for their pleasure, but also in the allowance he made for their faults.* Jean Paul says, that in the young man the wing feathers (the impulsive energies) are chiefly developed, and that the tail feathers (the balancing power, or judgment) are the growth of later years. Accordingly, Mr. Robinson, though himself of the widest toleration, thought " intolerance not inexcusable in a young man. Tolerance comes with age." His own large experience of diversity of opinion, taste, and feeling, combined with excellence of character, had made him thoroughly catholic in spirit ; and with his tendency to self-depreciation, he was (to borrow Dr. King's expression) " too modest to be tolerant." But there were two

---

* Not indeed for the faults of the young only. " Dr. E. spoke with spirit about T. I defended poor T. as well as I could, with more love than logic. He is indefensible. Amyot cheered me on, who loves all his old friends ; he gives up none." — H. C. R., October 22, 1832.

classes of persons who formed exceptions. One consisted of those who spoke disrespectfully of his demigods ; the other class is indicated by his own words : " I cannot tolerate the toleration of slavery." Of these two forms of intolerance, the first, which cost him some friendships, he acknowledged as a fault, and, on various occasions, expressed his deep regret at it, as arising from a want of control over his temper ; the second he felt to be a virtue. To one who was satirical on the subject of slavery, he said : " Lord John is fair game, and the *Times,* and the Whigs too, if by Whigs you mean the great Whig families ; but *humanity* is too sacred a subject for irony."

Mr. Robinson used to lament that he had not the faculty of giving a graphic account of the illustrious men with whom he came into contact. He had, at all events, one qualification for interesting. others, — he was interested himself. The masters of style have no arts which can take the place of a writer's own enthusiasm in his subject. Mr. Robinson's descriptions are often all the more effective from their very naturalness and simplicity. The Italian tour, with Wordsworth, may be cited as an example. What was written on the journeys is, on the whole, hardly equal to the ordinary home Diary. Nor is that tour one of the best, so far as the record is concerned. And yet the few notes jotted down day by day are admirably illustrative of Wordsworth's mind and character, and are strikingly confirmed by the " Memorials " written by him afterwards. The poet's love for natural beauties rather than works of art, for the country rather than the towns, for fresh life in bird, or flower, or little child, rather than for the relics of the things of old, — his annoyance at the long streets of Bologna, — his eagerness to depart from the fashionable watering-place of Ischl, — the wide difference in his interest in those places which have influenced the character and works of a great man, and those which have only been outwardly associated with him, — his being allured by the sound of a stream, and led on and on till midday, notwithstanding that he was expected back to breakfast, and the relief his anxious friend felt as soon as he heard the same sound, knowing that it would be likely to be irresistible to the truant, and tracking him out by this clew, — these and kindred touches of character have in them the material and coloring of genuine biography.

The time spent by Mr. Robinson in Germany, as a young man, was a turning-point in his life. And he did not derive the advantage of between four and five years' study there, in the best society, without leaving a very favorable impression on many, whose esteem and friendship were, in the highest degree, honorable to him, as well as a rich possession. He must have been a tolerable German scholar to have been able to personate Professor Fichte to the lionizing landlord and the confidential priest. What warm greetings he invariably received at Jena and Weimar, Frankfort and Heidelberg! So thoroughly had he entered into the thoughts and customs of his German friends, that they felt themselves to be understood by him, and fully trusted him to represent them on his return to his native country. And certainly if he were a "missionary of English poetry in Germany," he was also a missionary of German literature in England. This is amply acknowledged in the "Memoirs of Frederick Perthes." * Besser, the partner of Perthes, writing from England in 1814, says: "Such men as Robinson are of rare occurrence in England. A better medium than this remarkable and most attractive man it would be impossible for Germany to find. I unconsciously place him, in my mind, by the side of Villers, and then the different influence which a thorough German education has had on the Frenchman and on the Englishman is very striking."

Mr. Robinson's breakfast and dinner parties were characteristically interesting. He did not seek to gather about him either the lions or the wits of the day. There were witty men and eminent men at his table, but not *as such* were they invited. None were allowed to come there who showed themselves to be either intolerant or subservient. He liked to gather around him cultivated and earnest representatives of various phases of political and

* Vol. I., ch. xix., p. 258.

religious thought. "His house" (Mr. Taylor said in his
address at Highgate) "was a centre of attraction for
minds from the most opposite points in the wide horizon
of opinion. Softened by his genial spirit, and animated
by his cheerful flow of kindly and interesting talk, Tories
and Liberals, High-Churchmen and Dissenters, found
themselves side by side at his hospitable board, without
suspecting that they were enemies, and learned there, if
they had never learned it before, how much deeper and
stronger is the common human heart, which binds us all
in one, than those intellectual differences which are the
witness of our weakness and infallibility, and sometimes
the expression of our obstinacy and self-will." It was,
indeed, no small privilege to hear the passing topics of
the day, and the chief questions of literature, talked over
by able men of such widely differing points of view, and
in a spirit of mutual respect and kindness. And the
host, who was as free in the expression of his own opinions as he was ready to listen to the opinions of others,
seldom failed to bring to bear on the question under consideration some recollection from Weimar or Highgate, a
walk with Wordsworth at Rydal, or an evening with
Charles Lamb.

To those who were not intimate with Mr. Robinson
what he says respecting religion may sometimes be puzzling. There are occasions when his words seem to imply
that with him belief was rather hoped for than an actual
possession. He thought there was more real piety in the
exclamation of the anxious father in the Gospels, "Lord,
I believe; help thou mine unbelief," than in the confident
and self-satisfied assertion of the longest creed. His
sympathy in opinions was with those who have exercised
the fullest liberty of thought. He had traversed far and
wide the realms of theological speculation, and in every
part he had found sincere and devout men. But he was
always interested and touched by genuine religious feeling, wherever he found it, — whether in the simple and
fervent faith of the Moravians at Ebersdorf, or in the
blessings which the old Catholic woman at Bischoffsheim *

* Where Christian Brentano had been at school.

poured upon Christian Brentano, or in the vesper service
at the wayside inn in the Tyrol, or in the family worship
at Ambleside, where "sweet Jessie" Harden "read the
prayers." He thoroughly entered into the sentiment of
the author of the "Religio Medici," — "I cannot laugh at,
but rather pity, the fruitless journeys of pilgrims, or condemn the miserable condition of friars ; for though mis-
placed in circumstances, there is something in it of devotion. I could never hear the Ave Mary bell without an
elevation, or think it a sufficient warrant, because they
erred in one circumstance, for me to err in all, — that is,
in silence and contempt. Whilst, therefore, they directed
their devotions to her, I offered mine to God, and recti-
fied the errors of their prayers by rightly ordering mine
own." Looking to the church of the future, he hoped
there would be found in it "the greatest quantity of religion founded on devotional sentiment, and the least quantity of church government compatible with it, and consistent with order." The concluding paragraph of his
obituary of his friend Anthony Robinson, written in
1827, is strikingly applicable to himself: "Could Mr.
Robinson be justly deemed a religious man ? If religion
be a system of confident conclusions on all the great
points of metaphysical speculation, as they respect the
universe and its author, — man and his position in the
one, and relation to the other, — it must be owned Mr.
Robinson laid no claim to the character. But if the religious *principle* be that which lays the foundations of all
truth deeper than the external and visible world ; if religious *feeling* lie in humble submission to the unknown
Infinite Being, who produced all things, and in a deep
sense of the duty of striving to act and live in conformity with the will of that Being ; if, further, Christianity
consist in acknowledging the Christian Scriptures as the
exposition of the Divine will, and the guide of human
conduct, — then, surely, he may boldly claim to be a
member of that true Christian Catholic Church, according
to his own definition of it, — 'An association of men for
the cultivation of knowledge, the practice of piety, and
the promotion of virtue.' " *

* *Monthly Repository*, 1827, p. 293.

Mr. Robinson was an earnest thinker on the profoundest and most difficult religious subjects. This was especially the case in his old age. As we like to look up to the stars, though we may not be able to tell their magnitude or their distance, and to behold the majesty of the sea, though we may not be able to fathom its depths, so he seemed to be attracted to the great problems of religion, as if he liked to feel their infinitude, rather than hoped to find their solution. He stated as his experience, that " Religion in age supplies the animal spirits of youth." His old age had its pathetic side, as, indeed, every old age must have.

Those who, in his later years, met him in society, and saw how full of life he was, with what zest and animation he told his old stories, merely requiring, now and then, help as to a name or a date, may easily have imagined his strength greater than it really was.

But though few, perhaps, have ever so closely watched the approach of infirmity, and though he was in the habit of saying, " Growing old is like growing poor, a sort of going down in the world," his frequent expression was, " This does not make me melancholy." And when, at last, " everything seemed to tire," there was, with this feeling of mortal weariness, another feeling, which was that he was

" On the brink of being born."

T. S.

HAMPSTEAD.

The Editor desires to acknowledge the valuable assistance he has received ; and would especially mention James Gairdner, Esq., of the Record Office ; George Scharf, Esq., one of Mr. Robinson's intimate and highly valued friends ; and J. Morley, Esq., author of " Burke : a Historical Study," &c. Mr. Gairdner made the selections in some of the years. The proofs have had the advantage of additional notes, especially in connection with art, by Mr. Scharf, and of excellent suggestions by Mr. Morley. Dr. Wagner has rendered a like service, in regard to those parts which relate to Germany. The admirable paper by Mr. De Morgan, at the end of the second volume, speaks for itself. In acknowledging the kindness of Lady Byron's relatives, in regard to the letters by her, the Editor cannot but add the expression of a hope, that, before long, the public may have the opportunity of a fuller acquaintance with the correspondence of one capable of writing such letters.

CONTENTS OF VOL. I.

CHAPTER XXIV. 1820.

CHAPTER XXV. 1821.

CHAPTER XXVI. 1822.

CHAPTER XXVII. 1823.

REMINISCENCES

OF

HENRY CRABB ROBINSON.

CHAPTER I.

FAMILY AND CHILDHOOD.

IT is one of the evidences, or shall I say consequences, of a happy frame of mind, that I am capable of deriving pleasure from things, the absence or even loss of which does not give me pain. I should have rejoiced had I been *well* born, could I have reckoned historical characters among my ancestors; but it has never occasioned me any serious uneasiness that my family are of as insignificant a class as can be imagined. Among the Robinsons I cannot find a single individual who appears to have acquired any distinction, and among the Crabbs only a remote probability of an affinity to a single individual of the name, who has ever been heard of, — and that is the Poet.

My father used to say that his great-grandfather was a tanner at Bildeston in Suffolk, and that his name was Henry. *My* great-grandfather was Thomas. He was a tanner at Sudbury, where he is said to have attained the dignity of Mayor.

Some circumstances concerning the marriage of my father and mother are worth writing down. I have forgotten from whom I heard them. My mother, Jemima Crabb, was the eldest daughter of a large family, and when of an age to be useful she left her father's crowded house to reside at Bury with a family very intimate with her own. Mr. Bullen, the head of this family, being a Dissenter, it was quite a matter of course that Miss Crabb should be known to the Robinsons. My grandfather was reputed wealthy, and was certainly one of the most respectable of the Dissenters. Jemima Crabb could have very little fortune, and my grandfather did not consent to a love-match between her and his second son Henry.

She therefore returned to Wattisfield.   One day her brother
Zachariah seeing Henry Robinson in the market-place, said to
him, " Not yet married, Master Henry ?   I expected to hear
of your marriage before this time."   Henry answered, " No,
Mr. Zachary, as I cannot have your sister Mimie I won't
marry at all."   A few days after this, a letter came to him
from Miss Crabb, in which she said she was sorry for what she
had heard from her brother, — that it would be sinful in him
not to marry, for it is God's ordinance, and he should not refuse to do so because he could not have the first woman he
had taken a liking to.   It would be undutiful to his father
also, who did not approve of his marrying her.   She hoped
to hear that he had thought better of this, and that he would
make a happy marriage in conformity with his father's wishes.
This letter Henry showed to his brother Thomas, who carried
it to his father.   The old gentleman was so pleased with its
tone that he withdrew his objection.   Henry immediately went
over to Wattisfield with the good news, and the marriage soon
followed.   It took place in 1766.

There were born two children, who died in infancy ; and
besides these, Thomas, born January 25, 1770 ; Habakkuk,
born June 4, 1771, and Henry Crabb, the writer of these
Reminiscences, born May 13, 1775.

When I was about twenty-one years of age, I met on a
stage-coach a very gentlemanly man, who, hearing my name,
asked me whether my father was not a tanner, and whether
my mother's name was not Crabb.   Surprised at the question
from a stranger, I inquired why he asked.   He thus explained
himself : " More than twenty years ago I attended the
Gentlemen's Club at the Angel, when the chairman gave as a
toast, ' The Handsome Couple ' ; I was from the country, and
it was then related to me that that morning there had been
married a couple said to be the handsomest pair ever known
to have lived at Bury.   I recollect that the names were Robinson and Crabb, and that he was a young tanner."

In general, it is not easy to fix a date to the earliest recollections.   My mother's pocket-books supply a few.   The very
earliest that I am aware of is the being taken out one night
in the arms of the nurse to see an illumination.   I recollect
being frightened at the report of a gun, or some fireworks, and
that advantage was taken of my crying to carry me home.
Now my mother writes under February 15, 1779, " The
town (Bury St. Edmunds) illuminated in honor of Admiral

Keppel." I was then three years and nine months old, being born May 13, 1775.

I recollect going to a dame's school, to a Mrs. Bard who lived in a very small house in the South Gate Street. I find a payment of five shillings to Mrs. Bard, — one quarter, for H. C. R. This was in July, 1780.

I have a very clear recollection of seeing my aunt Williamson enter the keeping-room one morning and lift up her hands in a melancholy way, on which my mother exclaimed, " My father's dead !" In her pocket-book she has written, February 25, 1781 : " My dear father died. 26th, Sister here by break-fast." This same aunt Williamson had a doleful tone of voice which I used to make game of ; I recollect being reproved for crying out on her coming one day from Wattisfield, " Behold, the groaner cometh."

I find that these are not the very earliest recollections, for it appears that my grandmother Crabb died June 22, 1779 ; now I very well recollect hearing it discussed with my mother whether the departed would be known in the other world, and saying, " I shall know my grandmamma in heaven by the green ribbon round her cap."

Another very early, but also faint recollection is of going with my mother to see the camp on Fornham Heath, of being lost there, and taken into a tent by some officers and feasted, and while there seeing my mother pass, and calling out to her with great joy. This must have been in the summer of 1778.

Of early education and religious instruction I recollect next to nothing. I was an unruly boy, and my mother had not strength to keep me in order. My father never attempted it. I have a faint impression of having learnt a catechism, in which there was this : " Dear child, can you tell me what you are ?" A. " I am a child of wrath like unto others." I have never found this precisely in any catechism, — but I was brought up with Calvinistic feelings.

It appears from my mother's pocket-book that I went to school in the year 1781 to *old* Mr. Blomfield. He was the grandfather of the present Bishop of London. My brothers went with me for a short time. They went to a boarding-school in 1782, and then, I incline to think, I was removed to an inferior English and Writing School kept by a Mr. Lease.

One really interesting occurrence I recollect which I have often thought of as significant. There used to be given to the

boy who was at the head of his class a box and ring, and he
had a present if he could keep it a certain number of days.
On one occasion I lost it, to my great sorrow, and as I thought,
very unjustly; therefore next day I went boldly to young
Blomfield, who was an usher under his father, and with a book
in my hand, and with a consciousness of injured innocence, said,
"Sir, you turned me down for spelling the word —— so, but
I was right after all. There, see! I was right." Mr. Blomfield smiled, patted me on the head, and said : "Well, Henry,
as you read it in a printed book you are not to blame, but
that's printed wrong." I was quite confounded, I believed as
firmly in the infallibility of print as any good Catholic can in
the infallibility of his church. I knew that naughty boys
would tell stories, but how a book could contain a falsehood
was quite incomprehensible.

I will here mention what is the most important of all my
reminiscences, viz. that in my childhood my mother was to
me everything, and I have no hesitation in ascribing to her
every good moral or religious feeling I had in my childhood or
youth. Had she possessed more knowledge and more activity
she might have made a much better character of me. But she
was guided by the instinct of motherly love and pious feelings.
It was, I dare say, with a purpose, that when I had one day
brought home a pin from Mrs. Ling's (an old lady with whom
she used to drink tea) she made me carry it back with an apology, my excuse being that I did not think it was of any value :
she thus gave me a respect for property. This same Mrs. Ling
had an engraving in her parlor. She told me it was Elisha
raising the Shunamite's son. And what story was that, I
asked her. "I thought, Master R., you had been better educated," she replied, very formally. I was much affronted, but
set about reading the Bible immediately.

My mother's mantua-maker was a Roman Catholic. I was
one day told to go to her, but was unwilling to do so; I said I
was afraid of her, I was told she was a Pope and would do me
a harm. My mother scolded me as a silly boy and forced me
to go. I believe she gave Mrs. Girt a hint, for the latter bribed
me to religious tolerance by giving me shreds of silk and satin
to clothe pictures with, which was a favorite employment.
This reminds me that I had very early a great horror of
Popery, my first notions of which were taken from a ballad
relating how

"As Mordecai the Jew one day
Was skating o'er the icy way,"

he fell in, and would have been drowned, but a Popish priest came by. The Jew called for help. "You, a Jew! I won't help a Jew." "If you will help me out I will be baptized." "You must be baptized first." The Jew consented, and then begged to be taken out. "No," said the priest, "if I let you out you will relapse into Judaism and so be damned. I will rather save your soul."

> "And saving this he in a trice
> Clapped Mordecai beneath the ice."

Could and would men closely examine they would probably find that their most inveterate religious prejudices, which they think their most valuable religious convictions, are of such origin. But Mrs. Girt's bits of silk went far to counteract the ballad.

When a child, like other children, my faith was implicit in what I was told to be true by my mother, and I have no sense of devotion now, which I did not catch from her.

The name of the minister whose religious services my father and mother attended was Lincolne. He was a gentlemanly person and inspired respect, especially by a very large white wig. He was often at our house, and his two daughters were my mother's very great friends. When he came I used to be kept at a distance, for I was always running about as well as talking, and he was afraid for his gouty toes. When I set about reading the Bible I used to ask my mother questions. Her prudent answer frequently was, "Ask the minister, my dear." I recollect hearing some anecdotes told of me and the minister, and some I seem to recollect myself, one especially. I had taken a great fancy to the Book of Revelation ; and I have heard, but this I don't recollect, that I asked Mr. L. to preach from that book, because it was my favorite. "And why is it your favorite book, Henry ? " " Because it is so pretty and easy to understand."

I had a happy childhood. The only suffering I recollect was the restraint imposed upon me on Sundays, especially being forced to go twice to meeting ; an injurious practice I am satisfied. To be forced to sit still for two hours, not understanding a word, was a grievance too hard to be borne. I was not allowed to look into a picture-book, but was condemned to sit with my hands before me, or stand, according to the service. The consequence was that I was often sent to bed without my supper for bad behavior at meeting. In the evening my father used to read aloud Mr. Henry's Commentary, and in winter it was my agreeable occupation to turn the apple-pie that was in a Dutch-oven before the fire, which was a great relief from Mr. Henry. Once I recollect being whipped by my mother for being naughty at meeting. A sad preparation for a religious life.

Now and then, by way of treat or reward for good behavior, I was allowed to go to the Independent meeting to hear Mr. Waldegrave preach. Mr. W. as I afterwards knew, was an ignorant, noisy, ranting preacher; he bawled loud, thumped the cushion, and sometimes cried. He was, however, a kind man, and of course he was a favorite of mine. It belongs perhaps to a later time, but I well recollect he repeatedly used the phrase, "But as the 'Postle Paul say " (say is Suffolk grammar). And after all I could carry away a thought now and then from him.

To return to my mother's instructions; I recollect a practice of hers, which had the best effect on my mind. She never would permit me (like all children, a glutton) to empty the dish at table if there was anything particularly nice, such as pudding or pie. "Henry, don't take any more; do you not suppose the maids like to have some?" A respect and attention to servants and inferiors was a constant lesson; and if I have any kindness and humanity in my ordinary feelings I ascribe it all to her, and very much to this particular lesson.

Of my schooling at Mr. Lease's I have little or nothing to say. I was an ordinary boy and do not recollect acquiring any distinction at school. The sons of Mr. Lease I knew and the children of some other Dissenters who went there; but some others of my acquaintance went to the grammar school. This set them above the rest of us, and I believe I should have wanted to go to the grammar school too, but I had heard that Mr. Lawrence was a flogging master, and I was therefore glad to escape going there.

It was either in 1782 or 1783, the Annual Register of the year will say which, that there was a very hard winter throughout the country. To raise a fund for the poor of the town, the grammar-school boys were induced to act plays at the theatre. I have a distinct recollection of some of the boy actors; the principal play was Venice Preserved. There is nothing worth noticing in the acting of the tragedy, but it is a significant circumstance, and one that belongs to the state of moral and religious feeling in the country between sixty and seventy years ago,* that the farce acted with Venice Preserved was

---

* This was written in 1845.

Foote's Minor, the performers being school-boys! It would seem impossible, but it becomes less surprising when one recollects that the hatred of the clergy was still active against the Methodists, that Dr. Squintum (Whitfield) was vigorously satirized, and that the religious classes were the object of derision to all the genteel part of the community, especially to the clergy. I only wonder that I was allowed to be present, but probably the Dissenters, certainly my parents, knew nothing about such plays.

How much I understood of the farce I cannot now tell. Perhaps little clearly. But children are content with confused and obscure perceptions of a pleasurable character.

When very young indeed, my mother delighted me by singing a ballad which must be in some of the popular collections. It was about the rich young lady who lived " in the famous town of Reading," and fell in love with a poor lawyer. She challenges him and he is forced to fight or marry her in a mask. He consults a friend who answers : —

> " If she 's rich you are to blame,
> If she 's poor you are the same."

Of course it ends happily. I used to delight in this story. Children's moral feelings are not more delicate than those of the people or their poets.

I recollect too the coming out of John Gilpin, and rather think I had a sixpence given me for learning it by heart.

My mother's sister married a Dissenting minister, Mr. Fenner, who kept a boarding-school at Devizes. I was accordingly sent to his school, where I remained three years. The time passed pleasantly enough, but I have often regretted that my educational advantages were not greater at this period of my life. Among the places in the neighborhood where I spent some happy days was a gentleman's seat called Blacklands. At that time it was occupied by an old gentleman named Maundrel, one of whose sons was at the same school with me. The old gentleman was burly and bluff, very kind and generous, but passionate ; once or twice he did not scruple to box the ears of his young visitors. Not far from the house was a horse cut out of the chalk hill. I believe it exists still. Maundrel set us boys — there were some seven or eight of us — to weed it, and very good workmen we were. He used also to make us carry logs of wood for the fires up stairs, telling us that we must work for our living. But he fed us well.

During my school life I obtained among my school-fellows

the reputation of being a good talker, and was put forward as
a speaker on public matters in school, such as a combination
against a head-boy.   And I was also noted as an inventor of
tales, which I used to relate to the boys in bed ; but this faculty did not grow with me, and has utterly died away.   I had
no distinction in any branch of school exercise but one, and
this was French.   I did not like learning it at first, and wrote
to my mother to beg that I might be relieved from the task ;
but she wisely took no notice of my letter.   Before I left school
I liked French above everything, and was quite able to read
with pleasure the French classics, as they are called.

I did not once go home during the three years of my school
life at Devizes, but in the summer of the second year my
mother came to see me.   The sensation which I most distinctly recollect is that of seeing her at the Turnpike gate of the
Green.   I thought her altered, or rather for a moment did not
know her, and that pained me ; but she gradually became to
me what she had been.

Though Mr. Fenner was a minister I received no religious
instruction at his school.   What I fancied to be religion was
of my own procuring.   I had fallen in with De Foe's Family
Instructor, and I became at once in imagination a religious
teacher.   I had an opportunity of trying my power, for during
one of my last holidays I was left with a few Irish boys when
Mr. and Mrs. Fenner went a journey.   I was the older and
placed in authority over the other boys, and I was not a little
pleased with myself for my mode of governing them.   On the
Sunday I read a sermon to them, and I made the boys and
servants attend prayers.   But I scorned *reading* a prayer ; I
prayed extempore, and did not hold my gift in low estimation.

In the summer of 1789 I returned home with Mr. Fenner
and my aunt.   My uncle Crabb had a few years before accepted the office of pastor at the Wattisfield meeting, and as he
intended to open a school there, I went to him for the next
half-year.   Our numbers were so few that we were subject to
little of the ordinary restraint of school.

It was while here that I had a letter from my brother
Thomas directed to " Mr. Robinson, Attorney at Law."   I had
to ask Mr. Crabb to explain to me the nature of an attorney's
profession, which had been chosen for me without my knowledge.

So entirely have I lost all recollection of the few months
spent at Wattisfield that I cannot call to mind anything

I studied or read. I only recollect having a sentiment of respect and regard towards Mr. Crabb.

I recollect too that it was while I was with Mr. Crabb that the French Revolution broke out, that every one rejoiced in it as an event of great promise, and that Popery and absolute government were both to be destroyed. Though I had no proper political knowledge, yet I had strong party feelings. In my childhood I had always heard the Church spoken of as an unjust institution, and thought Dissenters a persecuted body.   .

I can testify to this fact, that very strong prejudice may be raised without any degree or sort of knowledge in justification of the sentiment. I knew too I was, or rather that my friends were Presbyterians, and I had a vague notion that the Independents were more orthodox than was reasonable, and that there was a degree of rationality compatible with sound doctrine. Mr. Lincolne, too, our minister, was much more of a gentleman and scholar than Mr. Waldegrave, the Independent minister.

Among my letters are a number by my dear mother. Her memory is very dear to me, but I would not have these letters survive me. They would not agreeably impress a stranger, but they express the warm affections of a fond mother, full of anxiety for the welfare of her children. Her mother-love was combined with earnest piety. She had no doctrinal zeal, and seems, though educated in a rigidly orthodox family, to have had very little knowledge of religious controversy.

It is worth mentioning that I have found my mother's *Experience*, that is the paper she delivered in before she was admitted a member of the church at Wattisfield. The paper is in one respect curious ; it shows that at that time even among the Independents, doctrinal faith was not the subject of a formal profession, though of course inferred. In this paper there is no allusion to the Trinity, or any other disputed doctrine. Indeed, the word *belief* scarcely occurs. The one sentiment which runs throughout is a consciousness of personal unworthiness, with which are combined a desire to be united to the Church, and a reliance upon the merits of Christ. Therefore her orthodoxy was indisputable. But when in after life her brother (the minister, Mr. Habakkuk Crabb) became heretical, either Arian or Unitarian, and his son also professed liberal opinions, she was not disturbed by these things of which she had a very slight knowledge.

1 *

CHAPTER II.

AN ARTICLED CLERK AT COLCHESTER.

WHILE I lived as an articled clerk with Mr. Francis of Colchester, I learned the ordinary routine of an attorney's office and was absorbed in newspaper and pamphlet reading, in which religious controversy was included.

On religious subjects I seem very quietly to have given up my orthodoxy, and to have felt strongly for Dr. Priestley on account of the Birmingham riots ; but even the orthodox Dissenters became sympathizing on that occasion. I attended a meeting of Dissenters at Chelmsford to appoint deputies to go to London to concert measures for the repeal of The Corporation and Test Act ; we dined together, and among the toasts given was one in honor of Dr. Priestley and other Christian sufferers. I recollect that I was irritated by the objection of one who was present that he did not know Dr. Priestley to be a Christian. I replied that if this gentleman had read Priestley's Letter to the Swedenborgians he would have learned more of real Christianity than he seemed to know. I had myself, however, not formed any distinct religious opinions, but felt deeply the importance of religious liberty and the rights of conscience.

Through Mr. Dobson, who afterwards became a distinguished mathematician at Cambridge, I formed an acquaintance with a number of French emigrants on their escape from France during the horrors of the Revolution, and my compassion for them modified my Jacobinical feelings. I was, however, a Jacobin notwithstanding, and felt great interest in one Mr. Patmore, who was indicted for selling some of Paine's works, and ultimately escaped through a defect in the indictment. But my Journal records my shock at the death of the King of France. My French attachment expired with the Brissotine party, though in my occasional pious moods I used to pray for the French.

At the spring assizes of 1791, when I had nearly attained my sixteenth year, I had the delight of hearing Erskine. It was a high enjoyment, and I was able to ·profit by it. The subject of the trial was the validity of a will, — Braham *v.*

Rivett. Erskine came down specially retained for the plaintiff,
and Mingay for the defendant. The trial lasted two days.
The title of the heir being admitted, the proof of the will was
gone into at once. I have a recollection of many of the circumstances after more than fifty-four years ; but of nothing do
I retain so perfect a recollection as of the figure and voice of
Erskine. There was a charm in his voice, a fascination in his
eye, and so completely had he won my affection that I am sure
had the verdict been given against him I should have burst
out crying. Of the facts and of the evidence I do not pretend
to recollect anything beyond my impressions and sensations.
My pocket-book records that Erskine was engaged two and a
half hours in opening the case, and Mingay two hours and
twenty minutes in his speech in defence. E.'s reply occupied
three hours. The testatrix was an old lady in a state of imbecility. The evil spirit of the case was an attorney. Mingay
was loud and violent, and gave Erskine an opportunity of
turning into ridicule his imagery and illustrations. For instance, M. having compared R. to the Devil going into the
garden of Eden, E. drew a closer parallel than M. intended.
Satan's first sight of Eve was related in Milton's words,

> " Grace was in all her steps, heaven in her eye,
>   In every gesture dignity and love " ;

and then a picture of idiotcy from Swift was contrasted. But
the sentence that weighed on my spirits was a pathetic exclamation, " If, gentlemen, you should by your verdict annihilate an instrument so solemnly framed, *I should retire a troubled
man from this court.*" And as he uttered the word *court*, he
beat his breast and I had a difficulty in not crying out. When
in bed the following night I awoke several times in a state of
excitement approaching fever, the words *" troubled man from
this court "* rang in my ears.

A new trial was granted, and ultimately the will was set
aside. I have said I profited by Erskine. I remarked his
great artifice, if I may call it so ; and in a small way I afterwards practised it. It lay in his frequent repetitions. He had
one or two leading arguments and main facts on which he was
constantly dwelling. But then he had marvellous skill in
varying his phraseology, so that no one was sensible of tautol-
ology in the expressions. Like the doubling of a hare, he was
perpetually coming to his old place. Other great advocates I
have remarked were ambitious of a great variety of arguments.

About the same time that I thus first heard the most perfect of forensic orators, I was also present at an exhibition equally admirable, and which had a powerful effect on my mind.   It was, I believe, in October, 1790, and not long before his death, that I heard John Wesley in the great round meeting-house at Colchester.   He stood in a wide pulpit, and on each side of him stood a minister, and the two held him up, having their hands under his armpits.   His feeble voice was barely audible. But his reverend countenance, especially his long white locks, formed a picture never to be forgotten.   There was a vast crowd of lovers and admirers.   It was for the most part pantomime, but the pantomime went to the heart.   Of the kind I never saw anything comparable to it in after life.*

The following letter enters a little more into particulars respecting this interesting occasion : —

October 18, 1790.

DEAR BROTHER : —

. . . . I felt a great Satisfaction last Week, on Monday, in hearing (excuse me now) that veteran in the Service of God, the Rev. John Wesley.   I was informed in the Afternoon that he was in Town and would preach that Evening.   Unfortunately a sick Man had sent to have his Will made directly, and it was given to me to write.   But Mr. Francis, seeing how mortified I appeared, gave it to some one else, and I went to the Chapel.   At another time, and not knowing the Man, I should almost have ridiculed his figure.   Far from it now.   I lookt upon him with a respect bordering upon Enthusiasm. After the people had sung one Verse of a hymn he arose, and said : " It gives me a great pleasure to find that you have not lost your Singing.   Neither Men nor Women — you have not forgot a single Note.   And I hope that by the assistance of the same God which enables you to sing well, you may do all other things well."   A Universal Amen followed.   At the End of every Head or Division of his Discourse, he finished by a kind of Prayer, a Momentary Wish as it were, not consisting of more than three or four words, which was always followed by a Universal Buzz.   His discourse was short — the Text I could not hear.   After the last Prayer, he rose up and addressed the People on Liberality of Sentiment, and spoke much against refusing to join with any Congregation on ac-

---

* I have heard Mr. R. tell this more than once at his own table, with the interesting addition that so greatly was the preacher revered that the people stood in a double line to see him as he passed through the street on his way to the chapel. — G. S.

count of difference of Opinion.   He said, " If they do but fear
God, work righteousness, and keep his commandments, we
have nothing to object to."   He preached again on Tuesday
Evening, but I was out of Town with Mr. Francis all day, holding a Court Baron. . . . .

I remain, &c.,

H. C. R.

1793.

On the 8th of January in this year died my dear mother,
an excellent woman I firmly believe, though without any superiority of mind or attainments.   Her worth lay in the warmth
of her domestic affections, and in her unaffected simple piety.
After fifty-two years I think of her with unabated esteem
and regard.

1794.

Among my Colchester acquaintance there is one man of
great ability whom I recollect with pleasure, though I was
but slightly acquainted with him.   This is Ben Strutt.   He
was a self-educated man, but having been clerk to a provincial
barrister, the Recorder of the town, where he had a great deal
of leisure, he had become a hard reader and so acquired a great
deal of knowledge.   He was a man of literature and art, and without being an attorney knew a great deal of law.   He was a sort
of agent to country gentlemen, particularly in elections.   He
published an edition of the poems of Collins, whom he praised
and declared to be much superior to Gray.   And I think (though
I have lost the book) that it contains additional stanzas by himself to the Ode on Superstition.   Strutt also painted in oil, and
was skilful as a mechanic.   I recollect once having a peep into
his bedroom, in which were curious figures and objects which I
beheld with some of the awe of ignorance.   I looked up to him,
and his words made an impression on me.   One or two I recollect.   When I went to Colchester I was very desirous of studying, but I had no one to direct me, and therefore followed the
routine practice and advice given to all clerks.   I bought a
huge folio volume to be filled with precedents, and copied
therein my articles of clerkship.   One evening I was writing
very industriously in this volume when Ben Strutt came in.
" I 'm sorry to see you so lazy, young gentleman ! "   " Lazy !
I think I 'm very industrious."   " You do ?   Well now, whatever you think, let me tell you that your writing in that book

is sheer laziness. You are too lazy to work as you ought with your head, and so you set your fingers at work to give your head a holiday. You know it is your duty to do something, and try to become a lawyer, and just to ease your conscience you do that. Had you been really industrious you would have studied the principles of law and carried the precedents in your head. And then you might make precedents, not follow them." I shut up the book and never wrote another line; it is still in existence,* a memorial of Strutt. Yet Mephistopheles might have given the advice, for in my case it did harm, not good. S. was cynical, a free-thinker, I think an unbeliever. Yet one day he said something that implied he was a churchman. " What ! " I exclaimed, " you a churchman ! " He laughed : " Let me give you a piece of advice, young man. Whatever you be through life, always be of the Act of Parliament faith."

I recollect a wise word of Strutt's about law. I had been repeating to him some commonplace saying that governments ought to enounce great principles, and not to interfere with men's actions or details. " Just the contrary," growled Strutt, " government has to do with nothing but details ; of course it ought to do the right, not the wrong thing, and it makes many blunders. There is no use in prating about abstract rights. It is the business of government to counsel people to do what is right." In the same spirit at another time he said, I having uttered some commonplace saying as if Locke's principles had produced the Revolution : " That 's all nonsense, Locke's book was the effect, not the cause of the Revolution. People do not rebel and overset governments because they have any ideas about liberty and right, but because they are wretched, and cannot bear what they suffer. The new government employed Locke to justify what they had done, and to remove the scruples of weak, conscientious people." I believe I owe a great deal to Strutt, for he set me thinking, and had he been my regular instructor might have really educated me. But I saw him only now and then. I once saw him by accident in London a few years after I had left Mr. Francis. He was going to the Opera ; I mentioned that I had no ear for music, least of all for Italian music. " Get it as soon as you

---

* Yes. It was found among his books by his executors after his death. It gives evidence of great industry, accuracy, and neatness as well as order and method. On page 76 of the book is the following memorandum at the end of one of the precedents : " Wrote this April 1st, 1791, the first year of my clerkship being then finished." The book is continued to page 120, and finally stops in the middle of a precedent.

can. You must one day love Italian music, either in this or another life. It is your business to get as much as you can *here*, — for, as you leave off here you must begin *there.*" This, if seriously said, implied a sort of hope of immortality very much like that of Goethe.

Ben Strutt has been many years dead. He had a son who survived him and became a painter. He made a portrait of me, a disagreeable but a strong likeness.

On my becoming clerk at Colchester, only thirteen miles from Witham, I had frequent opportunities of visiting my relatives, the Isaacs, and through them I became acquainted with others. Among these was Mr. Jacob Pattisson. He had a wife whom he married late in life, — a cousin, deformed in person and disfigured by the small-pox, but there was a benignity and moral beauty in her face which rendered her a universal favorite. Mr. Pattisson had only one child, who became my most intimate friend for many years, and our regard has never ceased. He is a few months younger than myself. His education had been much better than mine ; when young he was at Mr. Barbauld's school. But his Dissenting connections had not been favorable to his forming acquaintance superior to himself, though his own family were wealthy. So that when he and I met at Witham, each thought the other a great acquisition. Being of the same profession, having alike an earnest desire to improve, and being alike ignorant how to set about it, we knew no better expedient than to become correspondents, and I have preserved a formidable bundle of his letters, with copies of my own. I have glanced over those of the first year, — we began to write in the spring, — I had hoped to find in them some references to incidents that occurred, but there is nothing of the kind. They are mere essays on abstract subjects, mine at least very ill-written and evincing no original thought whatever ; law questions are discussed and criticisms on style fill many a dull page. There are also occasional bursts of Jacobin politics. It was this friend who drew my attention to the *Cabinet*, a Norwich periodical, and set me on fleshing my maiden sword in ink.

It was in December, 1794, that my vanity was delighted by the appearance in print of an essay I wrote on Spies and Informers. It was published in the *Cabinet*, which had been got up by the young liberals of the then aspiring town of Norwich, which at that time possessed two men of eminent abilities, — William Taylor and Dr. Sayers. They, however, took very little, or no part, in the *Cabinet*. Charles Marsh, Pitchford, Norgate and Amelia Alderson were its heroes. My essay is very ill written, only one thought rather pompously expanded, viz. that the shame of being an informer ought to be transferred to the *Law;* for the detection of the breach of good laws ought to be honored. My friend Will Pattisson was also a contributor to this periodical, under the signature of Rusticus.

Another friend of this period, with whom I have ever since retained an intimate acquaintance, was Thomas Amyot. At the time of my beginning a correspondence with Pattisson he was already the correspondent of Amyot. He communicated the letters of each to the other, and from first writing on Pattisson's letters we began to write to each other directly, and became correspondents without having seen each other. Amyot's letters are far the best of the whole collection, as in ability and taste he was far the superior of the three. He was the son of a watchmaker in Norwich, and clerk in the house of some eminent solicitors in that town. Our correspondence had led to an invitation to visit Amyot, and Pattisson joining me in the visit, we met at the house of Amyot's father on the 5th of December and remained there till the 9th. Within a few years of this time, Amyot married the daughter of Mr. Colman, a Norwich surgeon. He was fortunate enough to become the law agent of Mr. Windham, and when the latter became War and Colonial Minister, he offered Amyot the post of private secretary. This was readily accepted, and when after the death of his patron this place was wanted for some one else, he was appointed Registrar in London of the West India Slaves, an office which still remains, though slavery has been long abolished. Why this should be I could never learn. He became an active F. S. A., and is now (1846) treasurer of that learned and very dull body.

My visit to Norwich made me also acquainted with Mrs. Clarkson, and that excellent couple Mr. and Mrs. John Taylor, the parents of a numerous family, among whom is Mrs. Austin. With several of the sons I am now in very friendly, not to say intimate relations. I was also very civilly received by Dr. Alderson, the father of Amelia, who afterwards became Mrs. Opie. I even now retain a lively recollection of this young lady's visit to Bury, and of the interest excited by her accomplishments and literary celebrity. Another person with whom I became acquainted was William Taylor, of whom I shall have occasion to write hereafter.

The perusal of my Journal for the year 1794 has brought a

few facts to my recollection that deserve to be briefly mentioned. The chief of these are the famous State Trials of
Hardy, Horne Tooke, and Thelwall. I felt an intense interest
in them. During the first trial I was in a state of agitation
that rendered me unfit for business. I used to beset the post-
office early, and one morning at six I obtained the London
paper with "NOT GUILTY" printed in letters an inch in
height, recording the issue of Hardy's trial. I ran about the
town knocking at people's doors, and screaming out the joyful
words.

Thomas Hardy, who was a shoemaker, made a sort of circuit, and obtained, of course, many an order in the way of
his trade. In 1795 he visited Bury, when I also gave him an
order, and I continued to employ him for many years. His
acquaintance was not without its use to me, for his shop was
one in which obscure patriots (like myself) became known to
each other. Hardy was a good-hearted, simple, and honest
man. He had neither the talents nor the vices which might
be supposed to belong to an acquitted traitor. He lived to an
advanced age and died universally respected.

Thelwall, unlike Hardy, had the weakness of vanity, but he
was a perfectly honest man, and had a power of declamation
which qualified him to be a mob orator. He used to say that
if he were at the gallows with liberty to address the people
for half an hour, he should not fear the result; he was sure
he could excite them to a rescue. I became acquainted with
him soon after his acquittal, and never ceased to respect him
for his sincerity, though I did not think highly of his understanding. His wife, who was his good angel, was a very
amiable and excellent woman. He was many years a widower,
but at last married a person considerably younger than himself. Thelwall's two sons, Hampden and Sydney, became
clergymen.

CHAPTER III.

INTERVAL AT BURY.

AFTER leaving Colchester at midsummer, 1795, I remained at Bury till April in the next year. During
this time I had serious thoughts of being called to the bar;
it was I believe Mr. Buck who put this into my head. He
had always a good opinion of me. My vivacity in conversation pleased him, and others like him entertained the very
false notion that the gift of words is the main requisite for a barrister, — a vulgar error, which the marvellous success of such
men as Erskine and Garrow had encouraged. I was invited
to meet Mr. Capel Lofft at dinner, that I might have the benefit of his opinion. He was against my being called. My
acquaintance in general — among others not yet named, Walter Wright — concurred in this view, and the effect was that I
neglected being entered a member of an Inn of Court; nevertheless I was averse to being an attorney, for which I was as
little qualified as to be a barrister. I determined, however, to
read law and occupy myself as well as I could, living mean-
while with the utmost economy. With youth, health, high
spirits, and, alternating with a very low opinion of myself, a
vanity which was gratified by perceiving that I could readily
make my way in society, I was able to lead a busy idle life.
In me was verified the *strenua inertia* of Horace. And in society I verified a line of the French Horace, as his countrymen term him, —

> " Un sot trouve toujours un plus sot qui l'admire."

I was now, as it were, entering society, and before I relate
the few incidents of the year, I will review the more remarkable of the persons I then knew.

The most noticeable person I had ever been in company
with was Capel Lofft, — a gentleman of good family and
estate, — an author on an infinity of subjects; his books were
on Law, History, Poetry, Antiquities, Divinity, and Politics.
He was then an acting magistrate, having abandoned the profession of the bar. He was one of the numerous answerers
of Burke; and in spite of a feeble voice and other disadvan-

tages, an eloquent speaker. This faculty combined with his rank and literary reputation made him the object of my admiration.

Another of my acquaintances was Walter Wright. He was rather older than myself, and the object of my envy for having been at Cambridge. He had been trained for the bar, but accepted a colonial appointment, first at Corfu and afterwards at Malta. Wright published a small volume of poems entitled Horæ Ionicæ, which Lord Byron praised warmly in his first satire. It was from his friend I used to hear of Lord Byron when his fame first arose. W. was the friend of Dallas, a barrister, and told me one day (this is anticipation) that he had been reading a MS. poem, consisting of two cantos, entitled "Childe Harold's Pilgrimage," which Lord B. offered to present to Dallas if he thought it worth his acceptance. " I have told him," said Wright, " that I have no doubt this will succeed. Lord B. had offered him before some translations from Horace, which I told him would never sell, and he did not take them."

Walter Wright was Recorder of Bury.* He always expressed a great interest in me ; and though at this time he discouraged my going to the bar he approved of my doing so some years later.

But of far greater influence over me was the family of Mr. Buck. And among these the one to whom I was most devoted was his eldest daughter, Catherine. She was three years older than I. Being the playfellow of her brother John, who was of my own age, I soon became intimate at the house ; as I was perhaps the most promising of her brother's playfellows, Catherine took me in hand to bring me forward. I have very severe letters from her, reproaching me for slovenliness in dress, as well as rudeness of behavior. But at the same time she lent me books, made me first acquainted with the new opinions that were then afloat, and was my oracle till her marriage with the then celebrated Thomas Clarkson, the founder of the society for the abolition of the slave-trade. After her marriage she quitted Bury, but our friendship never ceased, and her name will frequently occur in these reminiscences. Catherine Buck was the most eloquent woman I have ever known, with the exception of Madame de Staël. She had a quick apprehension of every kind of beauty, and made her

* This seems to be an error. John Symonds, LL.D., was Recorder at this period.

own whatever she learned.   She introduced me to Lamb, Coleridge, Wordsworth, &c.*

Catherine Buck had an intimate friend in Sarah Jane Maling, a person rather older than herself and of much originality of mind and character.   She was also one of my friends.

It was in the spring of this year and before I left Colchester that I read a book which gave a turn to my mind, and in effect directed the whole course of my life, — a book which, after producing a powerful effect on the youth of that generation, has now sunk into unmerited oblivion.   This was Godwin's Political Justice.   I was in some measure prepared for it by an acquaintance with Holcroft's novels, and it came recommended to me by the praise of Catherine Buck.   I entered fully into its spirit, it left all others behind in my admiration, and I was willing even to become a martyr for it ; for it soon became a reproach to be a follower of Godwin, on account of his supposed atheism.   I never became an atheist, but I could not feel aversion or contempt towards G. on account of any of his views.   In one respect the book had an excellent effect on my mind, — it made me feel more *generously*.   I had never before, nor, I am afraid, have I ever since felt so strongly the duty of not living to one's self, but of having for one's sole object the good of the community.   His idea of justice I then adopted and still retain ; nor was I alarmed by the declamations so generally uttered against his opinions on the obligations of gratitude, the fulfilment of promises, and the duties arising out of the personal relations of life.   I perceived then the difference between principles as universal laws, and maxims of conduct as prudential rules.   And I thought myself qualified to be his defender, for which purpose I wrote a paper which was printed in Flower's Cambridge Intelligencer.   But

* She felt it to be, as she herself expresses it, "a prodigious disadvantage to a man not to have had a sister."   But in Mr. Robinson's case she did her utmost to make up the deficiency.   Indeed, few elder sisters have done more for her brother than she seems to have done for her friend.   He had so much esteem for her judgment and such a perfect reliance on the genuine kindness which actuated all her conduct towards him that there was no danger of offence or misunderstanding when she pointed out his weakness or faults, and expressed her anxiety as to the effect of any pursuit on his character or on his health.   "There are many points," she says, "in which from the circumstances in which you have been placed, the habit of feeling you have acquired is not like that of other people"; but she adds, "of all those whom I knew in childhood or youth you are the only one who has retained any likeness to myself; and you are so like that I wonder how it is possible that you can be so different."

one practical effect of Godwin's book was to make me less inclined to follow the law, or any other profession as a means of livelihood.   I determined to practise habits of rigid economy, and then I thought my small income would suffice with such additions as might be gained by literature.

In the autumn of this year I was led to take a part in public matters, and from its being the first act of the kind, I may here relate it.   In consequence of Kyd Wake's * attack upon the King, two Acts were introduced, called the Pitt and Grenville Acts for better securing the King's person.   They were deemed an infringement on the Constitution, and in every part of the kingdom petitions were prepared against them and public meetings held.   The drawing up of the petition and obtaining signatures at Bury were intrusted to Walter Wright and myself.   I was very active, but nevertheless impartial enough to see all that was foolish in the business, and it is a satisfaction to me to recollect the great glee with which I read Johnson's admirable satirical account of a petition in his "False Alarm."   I have pleasure also in remembering that even while I was a partisan of the French Revolution I was an admirer of Burke, not merely for his eloquence, but also for his philosophy.   It was after the Bury petition had been prepared that a county meeting was held at Stowmarket.   Mr. Grigby was in the chair ; the Whig Baronets Sir W. Middleton and Sir W. Rowley attended ; but the hero of the day was Capel Lofft.   He spoke at great length, and as I thought, very admirably.   His voice was sweet, though feeble.   He was the only orator I had heard except at the bar and in the pulpit. The Whig gentry became impatient and at length retired, but by way of compromise, after Mr. Lofft's resolutions had been passed, the Bury petition was clamorously called for.   Towards the end of the proceedings, I got upon the wagon and was endeavoring to prompt Mr. Lofft to move a vote of thanks, when he suddenly introduced me to the meeting, as one to whom the county was greatly indebted as the author of the petition.   This little incident served as a sort of precocious introduction to public life.

---

* Kyd Wake, a journeyman printer, was convicted for insulting the King in his state carriage, and sentenced to stand an hour in the pillory each day for three months and to be imprisoned for five years.   The "Treason" and "Sedition" Bills were laid before Parliament November 6 and November 10, 1795.

See Stanhope's "Life of William Pitt," Vol. II. p. 358.

CHAPTER IV.

1796–1800. — UNSETTLED LIFE IN LONDON.

ON the 20th of April I went to London with the intention of entering an attorney's office in order to qualify myself for practice. This step was taken, not on account of my having less dislike to the law as a profession, but because friends urged me, and because I was unwilling to remain idle any longer. My lodgings were of a simple kind, in Drury Lane, and my expenses not more than about a guinea a week ; but a first residence in London cannot be otherwise than a kind of epoch in life.

Among the new acquaintance which I formed there is one of whom I was proud, and to whom I feel considerable obligation, — John Towill Rutt. He was the son of an affluent drug-grinder, and might possibly have himself died rich if he had not been a man of too much literary taste, public spirit, and religious zeal to be able to devote his best energies to business. He was brought up an orthodox dissenter, and married into a family of like sentiments. His wife was an elder sister of Mrs. Thomas Isaac, daughter of Mr. Pattisson of Maldon and first cousin of my friend William Pattisson. I was therefore doubly introduced to him. I had the good fortune to please him, and he became my chief friend. He had become a Unitarian, and was a leading member of the Gravel Pit congregation, Hackney, of which Belsham was the pastor. Mr. Rutt was the friend and biographer of Gilbert Wakefield and of Priestley. He also edited the entire works of the latter. He was proud of having been, with Lord Grey, an original member of the Society of the Friends of the People. The eldest daughter of his large family is the widow of the late Sir T. N. Talfourd.

My days were spent in attending the courts with very little profit. I heard Erskine frequently, and my admiration of him was confirmed ; but I acquired no fresh impression concerning him.

I tried to procure a suitable situation but without success ; and this, with an almost morbid feeling of my own ignorance, made me more unhappy than I had been before, or ever was afterwards. Thus discouraged, I returned to Bury in the summer. My brother's marriage, which took place soon afterwards, was the cause of my being introduced to an entirely new connection, — the Fordhams and Nashes of Royston. The most prominent of the former for wealth and personal character was Edward King Fordham, a remarkable man, who retained his bodily and mental vigor to a great age. Of all these new friends the one to whom I became most indebted was Mr. William Nash, an eminent solicitor and a first-rate character in the sphere in which he moved. Both of these families were liberal in religious opinion and zealous for political reform. There had been established at Royston a book-club, and twice a year the members of it were invited to a tea-party at the largest room the little town supplied, and a regular debate was held. In former times this debate had been honored by the participation of no less a man than Robert Hall. My friend J. T. Rutt and Benjamin Flower, the ultra-liberal proprietor and editor of the *Cambridge Intelligencer*, had also taken part. To one of these meetings my brother was invited and I as a sort of satellite to him. There was a company of forty-four gentlemen and forty-two ladies. The question discussed was, "Is private affection inconsistent with universal benevolence?" Not a disputable point, but it was meant to involve the merits of Godwin as a philosopher, and as I had thought, or rather talked much about him, I had an advantage over most of those who were present. I have no doubt that what I said was, in truth, poor stuff, but I was very young, had great vivacity and an abundance of words. Among the speakers were Benjamin Flower, Mr. Rutt, and four or five ministers of the best reputation in the place ; yet I obtained credit, and the solid benefit of the good opinion and kindness of Mr. Nash. He was told of my unsettled state and my want of an introduction in London. He did not offer to be of any practical use, perhaps had not the means, but his advice was emphatically given in the words, Fag, fag, fag." By laborious fagging he had raised himself to wealth and distinction.

On my return to my old London quarters in October I entered a solicitor's office on the condition of nothing being paid on either side. This was Mr. White's office in Chancery Lane. My occupation was almost entirely mechanical, and therefore of no great advantage to me. My leisure was devoted partly to legal and miscellaneous reading, from which I derived little profit, and partly to attending debating societies, which afforded me practice in public speaking, and thus materially contributed to my moderate success in life. At the meetings of one of these societies I frequently had, as an adversary, John Gale Jones. At those of another, to which Mr. Rutt introduced me, and which was presided over by Belsham, I formed a lifelong friendship with Mr. Anthony Robinson, whose powers of conversation were far greater than those of any other of my acquaintance.

1797.

THE SERVILE YEAR.

I have spent several days in deciphering a short-hand journal, and looking over a collection of letters belonging to this year; an employment that must have humiliated me, if after half a century it were possible to have a strong sense of personal identity. Thus much I must say, that if " the child " (in this instance the youth) be " father of the man," I must plead guilty to the impiety of despising my parent.

How long I should have gone on in my mechanical work there is no guessing, had not an accident relieved me.

There came to the office one day a clerk who was going to leave his situation at Mr. Hoper's (Boyle Street, Saville Row), and he advised me to apply for it, which I did, and was accepted as a conveyancing clerk at a guinea a week. I went on the 5th of April. At the end of three weeks, however, my employer told me he should no longer need my services, but had recommended me to a better place than his. This was in the office of Mr. Joseph Hill, of Saville Row, with whom I remained from the 28th of April till my uncle's death at the close of the year. Mr. Hill's name appears in the Life of Cowper, whose particular friend he was. He had no general law practice, but was steward to several noblemen. All I had to do was to copy letters, make schedules of deeds, and keep accounts. My service was light but by no means favorable to my advancement in legal knowledge. I attended from half past nine or ten till five, and had therefore leisure for reading. The treatment I received was kind, though I was kept at a distance. Mr. Hill seemed to have an interest in my welfare, and gave me good counsel. He had a country-house at Wargrave, on the Thames, and was frequently absent for weeks together in the summer. When he was in London he sent me very nice meat luncheons, which usually served me for dinner. On the whole I was not at all uncomfortable, and

should have been even happy if I could have kept out of my
thoughts the consideration that I was, after all, it was to be
hoped, fit for something better than to be a writing-clerk at a
guinea a week.

On going to Mr. Hoper's I removed from Drury Lane to
small and neat rooms on the second floor at 20 Sherrard
Street. One of my principal amusements was the theatre.
I had great pleasure in the acting of Mrs. Jordan and others,
but my admiration for Mrs. Siddons was boundless. One little anecdote concerning her effect upon me has been printed in
Campbell's life of her. I had told it to Charles Young, and
he thought he was at liberty to repeat it for publication.

The play was "Fatal Curiosity," acted for her benefit. In
the scene in which her son having put into her hands a casket
to keep, and she having touched a spring it opens and she
sees jewels, her husband (Kemble) enters, and in despair exclaims, "Where shall we get bread?" With her eyes fixed
on the jewels, she runs to him, knocks the casket against her
breast, and exclaims, "Here! Here!" In Mrs. Siddons's tone
and in her look there was an anticipation of the murder which
was to take place. I burst out into a loud laugh, which occasioned a cry of "Turn him out!" This cry frightened me,
but I could not refrain. A good-natured woman near me
called out, "Poor young man, he cannot help it." She gave
me a smelling-bottle, which restored me, but I was quite
shaken, and could not relish the little comedy of "The Deuce
is in him," though Mrs. Siddons played in it. I thought her
humor forced, and every expression overdone. By the by,
the title of the piece may have been "Diamond cut Diamond." It is the only piece in which I did not admire Mrs.
Siddons.

The Forums were a source of great enjoyment to me. They
exercised my mind, and whatever faculty of public speaking I
afterwards possessed I acquired at these places. If the attention my speeches received from others may be regarded as
a criterion, my progress seems to have been very considerable.
In general the speakers were not men of culture or refinement. There was one, however, of extreme liberal opinions,
who was distinguished from all others by an aristocratic air.
His voice was weak but pleasing, and his tone that of a high-
bred gentleman. Some compliments paid me by him were
particularly acceptable. He was accompanied by his wife,
one of the most beautiful women I had ever seen. On one

occasion I chanced to sit next to her and a very lively and agreeable lady who accompanied her. No gentleman was with them. She asked me whether I did not know Hardy the patriot; and as she seemed to know me, I ventured to offer my services in procuring them a carriage. But none was to be had, and so I saw them safely home. In a few days I had a call from her husband, Mr. Collier, to thank me for my attention. Thus began an acquaintance, which lasted through life, and was to me of inestimable value. The Colliers passed through great changes of fortune, but if I had it in my power to render them any service or kindness I have always felt it to be very far below what they rendered to me. Perhaps they thought otherwise, — it is well when persons can so estimate their relation to each other.

In some money transactions that passed between Mr. C. and me, the only dispute we ever had was that each wished to give the other some advantage which he would not take. The eldest son, John Payne Collier, the editor of Shakespeare, is now one of my most respected friends. The parents have long been dead.

At the Westminster Forum late in the year I made a successful speech on the French Revolution, and among those present was one of the most respectable inhabitants of Bury, Gamaliel Lloyd, a gentleman of fortune, — a Whig of the old school, a friend of Cartwright and Wyvill as well as Capel Lofft. I knew him merely by meeting him at the Bury Library. He complimented me on this occasion, and an invitation to his lodgings was the origin of an acquaintance of which I was proud. He was a fine specimen of the Yorkshire gentry. He has long been dead, leaving as his present representative William Horton Lloyd, a most respectable man. Leonard Horner is the husband of G. L.'s second daughter. One of her daughters will probably be hereafter Lady Bunbury; another is married to Sir Charles Lyell.

My old friend Pattisson lodged in Carey Street. We saw each other daily, and in order to avoid missing each other we agreed always to pass through certain streets between our two abodes. I recollect with tenderness how many hours of comfort and enjoyment I owed to his companionship. At his apartments I became acquainted with Richard Taylor, the eminent printer and common-council man.

1798.

On the first of January in this year I received the news of the death of my uncle Robinson. He was good-natured and liberal, and richer than any other relation. His property was left to my brothers and myself. I soon ascertained that I should have about a hundred pounds per annum. A very poor income for a student aspiring to the bar; a comfortable independence to fall back upon for one content to live humbly as a literary man. Between a legal and a literary occupation I was unable at once to determine. All I resolved on for the present was to quit Mr. Hill. With him I was idling away my time and learning nothing. I remained with him till the 5th of March, when he was able to procure a successor. He dismissed me with good advice, counselling me to lead a life of business, and warning me against indulging in habits of speculation. This he said in a parental way. I met him afterwards in the streets, but was never recognized by him.

On the 6th of May I went down to Bury and did not return till October. In the interval I made a visit to Norwich and Yarmouth. At the latter place I stayed four weeks. My main inducement was to read to Harley, a blind man I became acquainted with through Miss Maling. An interesting man in humble circumstances. At Yarmouth also I fell in with two young men about to go to Germany to study. One afterwards became famous, Captain Parry, the traveller and discoverer in the Polar regions.

But the most eventful occurrence of the year was an introduction to William Taylor of Norwich, who encouraged in me a growing taste for German literature.

I had already thought of a visit to Germany, and my desire to go was very much strengthened. But it proceeded chiefly from dissatisfaction with my present pursuits, and from a vague wish to be where I was not.

What I have written about my general occupations in 1797 is applicable to a large part of this year. I went on reading in a desultory way. Books were oddly jumbled together in my brain. I took a few lessons in German.

In my visit to Bury I found I had already acquired a bad character for free thinking. This led to a correspondence between the famous Robt. Hall and me. I heard that he had told Mr. Nash it was disgraceful to him as a Christian to admit me into his house. I remonstrated with Mr. Hall for this officious interference, and asked him why he had defamed me. He answered me in a letter which I have preserved as a curiosity. It is an excellent letter of the kind. He said he ·believed me to be a professor of infidelity, of pantheism, and therefore as became him he warned a Christian brother of the peril of intercourse with me. On his own principles he was right. My letter I have also preserved. It is as ill as his is well written.

To the Rev. R. Hall.

YARMOUTH, 30th August, 1798.

SIR, — Your own good sense will suggest every apology necessary for troubling you with this unpleasant letter. Unpleasant it certainly is for me to write, and it will be more or less so for you to receive, as your recollection may echo the observations I have to make. I am informed that you have of late distinguished yourself by displaying much zeal against certain very prevalent speculative opinions. And I am also told that in connection with such subjects you have thought proper frequently and generally to introduce my name and character. Recollecting probably the great secret of poetry, where beauty and effect consist in the lively representation of individual objects, you have, it seems, found it convenient to point the sting of your denunciation by setting the mark of censure and reprobation on my forehead. I hear too that you have travelled amongst my friends in a neighboring county, urging them no longer to honor me with their friendship, and declaring it to be a disgrace to them to admit me into their houses. I will name but one person, and that a gentleman for whom I feel the warmest sensations of esteem and love ; and the loss of whose good opinion I should consider as a very serious privation, Mr. Nash, of Royston. And this style I understand you scruple not to hold in large and mixed companies, where I am of course unknown, and where only, I flatter myself, your labors could be successful. Indeed, sir, I as little deserve the honor of such notice from you as I do the disgrace of so much obloquy. But not having so much of the childish vanity of being talked about, as of the honorable desire to be esteemed by the truly respectable, I am compelled to remonstrate with you, and call upon you for some reason why you have thus made an attack, in its possible consequences incalculably injurious to the reputation of a young man, who is an entire stranger to you. Were I addressing a

man of the world, I know that what I have written is vague
enough to allow room for evasion and prevarication, for a
denial of having used the precise terms stated, and for a demand of my authors. But I recollect that you have adopted
a profession of high pretensions, and that it is probable you
will excuse yourself on the ground of performing a religious
duty. As such you cannot scruple to inform me what more
and worse things you have said, — particularly what opinions
they are which excite so much anger, and what authority you
have for imputing them to me. I do not accuse you of personal malignity, but I charge you with wantonly casting
arrows and death. And it matters not to the sufferer whether
sport or false zeal direct the aim. I do not think you capable
of inventing calumny; but it seems that you have heedlessly
built opinions on vague report, drawn unwarrantable inferences
from general appellations, and carelessly trifled with the happiness of others as objects below your regard. Constitutional-
ly enthusiastic, I have warmly expressed, perhaps without
enow limitations, my high admiration of the "Political Justice."
Hence, I suspect, all the misapprehension. I was told by a
gentleman who knows you well, that so inveterate was your
rage against Mr. Godwin, that when any incident of unnatural
depravity or abandoned profligacy was mentioned, your exclamation has been, "I could not have supposed any man capable
of such an action, except Godwin." Excuse me when I add,
that had this been told me of a stranger, I should have felt
great contempt for him. I could not despise Mr. Hall; and
therefore it only added one more to the list of examples which
prove a most important truth, that the possession of the greatest talents is no security against the grossest absurdities and
weaknesses. I do not choose to consider this as an exculpatory
letter, and therefore I will not state why I admire the "Political Justice"; but as I understand that the sprinkling I have
felt is but a spray of the torrent cast on poor Godwin, it is hardly
irrelevant for me to remark, that such intemperate abuse will
be received by some with stupid and vulgar applause, and by
others with pity and regret. I am anxious you should not
mistake me. I believe your motives, so far as you could be
conscious of them, were good; that zeal (always respectable
whatever be its object) alone impelled you; but I fear that,
like most zealots, your views were confined and partial, and
that, eager to do your duty towards your God, you forgot what
you owed to your neighbor; that your imagination, forcibly

excited by passion, waited not for the dull inquiry, the tedious discrimination of your judgment ; and that you reasoned absurdly, because you felt passionately.   R. is a Godwinite — therefore an atheist — therefore incapable of virtuous habits or benevolent feelings — therefore disposed only to commit crimes and make proselytes — therefore I ought to use my appropriate weapons of excommunication by exciting against him both his friends and strangers, and deprive him of all power to do injury by blasting his reputation, and making him an object of hatred and contempt.   Thus, by the ruin of one, I shall save many.   Something of this kind, though certainly short of its extent, has probably influenced you.   However, giving you credit for integrity and benevolence, of which I shall be better able to judge hereafter, I remain, without enmity, and with respect for your general character,

Yours, &c.,

H. C. R.

To MR. HENRY ROBINSON.

October 13, 1798.   CAMBRIDGE.

SIR, — That I have not paid to your frank and manly letter the prompt and respectful attention it deserved, my only apology is a variety of perplexing incidents which have left me till now little leisure or spirits.

Before I proceed to justify my conduct, I will state to you very briefly the information on which it was founded, not doubting that where I may seem to usurp the office of a censor you will attribute it to the necessity of self-defence.

I have been led to believe you make no scruple on all occasions to avow your religious scepticism, that you have publicly professed your high admiration of the " Political Justice," even to the length of declaring, I believe at the Royston Book Club, that no man ever understood the *nature* of virtue so well as Mr. Godwin ; from which I have drawn the following inference, either that you disbelieve the being of God and a future state, or that admitting them to be true, in your opinion they have no connection with the nature of virtue ; the first of which is direct and avowed, the second *practical* atheism.   For whether there be a God is merely a question of curious speculation, unless the belief in him be allowed to direct and enforce the practice of virtue.   The *theopathetic* affections, such as love, reverence, resignation, &c., form in the estimation of all theists a very sublime and important class of vir-

tues. Mr. Godwin as a professed atheist is very consistent in
excluding them from his catalogue ; but how he who does so
can be allowed best to understand the nature of virtue, by
any man who is not himself an atheist, I am at a loss to conceive.

A person of undoubted veracity assured me that on being
gently reprimanded by a lady for taking the name of God in
vain in a certain company, you apologized by exhibiting such
an idea of God as appeared to him to coincide with the system
of Spinoza, in which everything is God, and God is everything.
Since the receipt of your letter I applied to this gentleman,
who confirms his first information, but is concerned at having
mentioned the circumstance, as it might be construed into an
abuse of the confidence of private conversation. You will
oblige me by not compelling me to give up his name. Of this
you may rest satisfied, he will make no ungenerous use of this
incident, and that his character is at the utmost removed from
that of a calumniator. He will not affirm the sentiments
you uttered were serious ; they might be a casual effort of
sportive ingenuity, but their coincidence with other circumstances before mentioned strengthened my former impressions.

More recently I have been told your chief objection to the
system of Godwin is an apprehension of its being too *delicate*
and *refined* for the present corrupt state of society ; which
from a person of your acknowledged good sense surprised me
much, because the most striking and original part of his system, that to which he ascends, through the intermediate stages,
as the highest point of perfection, — the promiscuous intercourse of the sexes, — has been uniformly acted upon by all
four-footed creatures from the beginning of the world.

In another particular I am sincerely glad to find myself mistaken. From a late conversation with Mr. Ebenezer Foster, I
was induced to suppose you had been at pains to infuse into
his mind atheistical doubts. I retract this opinion with pleasure as founded on misapprehension. Having no reason to
doubt of your honor, your disavowal of any opinion will be
perfectly satisfactory. I will repeat that disavowal to any
person whom I may have unintentionally misled.

In exonerating me from the suspicion of being actuated by
personal malignity, you have done me justice ; but you have
formed an exaggerated idea of those circumstances in my conduct which wear the appearance of hostility. Your moral

character has been unimpeached.   I have neither invented nor
circulated slander.   On the contrary, when I have expressed
myself with the greatest freedom, I have been careful to pre-
mise that I had no personal acquaintance with you, that your
manners might for anything I knew be correct, and that all
the censure attached or fear expressed was confined to the licentious opinions I understood you to embrace.   I have never
travelled a mile on your account.   My efforts have been confined to an attempt within a very limited circle (for it is in a
very limited circle I move) to warn some young people against
forming a close intimacy with a person who by the possession
of the most captivating talents was likely to give circulation
and effect to the most dangerous errors.   As you allude to a
conversation with Mr. Nash (whom in common with you I
highly esteem), I will relate it to you as nearly as my recollection will serve.   After a sort of desultory debate on heresy and
scepticism, he told me he designed at your next visit to Royston to request you. to make his house your home.   Warmed
in a degree, though not irritated by the preceding dispute, I
replied it was all very proper considering him as a man of the
world, but considering him as a Christian it was very unprin-
cipled, — an expression of greater asperity, I will allow, than
either politeness to him or delicacy to you will perfectly justify.   I conceived myself at liberty to express my sentiments
the more freely to Mr. Nash because he is a member and an
officer in our Church.

I have ventured repeatedly to express my apprehension of
baneful consequences arising from your attendance at the
book club, where if your principles be such as I have supposed,
you have a signal opportunity, from the concourse of young
people assembled, of extending the triumph of the new philosophy.

Such, as far as my recollection reaches, is the faithful sketch
of those parts of my conduct which have provoked your displeasure.

To make an attack in its possible consequences incalculably
injurious, to seek the salvation of others by your ruin, are
the gigantic efforts of a powerful malignity, equally remote
from my inclination and ability.   The rapid increase of irreligion among the polite and fashionable, and descending of
late to the lower classes, has placed serious believers so entirely on the defensive, that they will think themselves happy if
they can be secure from contempt and insult.

How far a regard to speculative opinion ought to regulate the choice of our friendships is a delicate question never likely to be adjusted harmoniously by two persons who think so differently of the importance of truth and the mischief of error. Principles of irreligion, recommended by brilliant and seductive talents, appear to me more dangerous in the intercourse of private life than licentious manners.

Vice is a downcast, self-accusing culprit ; error often assumes an appearance which captivates and dazzles. The errors — or rather the atrocious speculations — of Godwin's system are big with incalculable mischief.   They confound all the duties and perplex all the relations of human life : they innovate in the *very substance* of virtue, about which philosophers of all sects have been nearly agreed. They render vice systematic and concerted ; and by freeing the conscience from every restraint, and teaching men to mock at futurity, they cut off from the criminal and misguided the very possibility of retreat.   Atheism in every form I abhor, but even atheism has received from Godwin new degrees of deformity, and wears a more wild and savage aspect.   I am firmly of opinion the avowal of such a system, · accompanied with an attempt to proselyte, ought not to be tolerated in the state, much less be permitted to enter the recesses of private life, to pollute the springs of domestic happiness or taint the purity of confidential intercourse. For the first of these sentiments, Mr. Godwin's disciples will doubtless regard me with ineffable contempt ; a contempt which I am prepared to encounter, shielded by the authority of all pagan antiquity, as well as by the decided support of Mr. Locke, the first of Christian philosophers and political reasoners.

I appeal to a still higher authority for the last, to those Scriptures which as a Christian minister I am solemnly pledged not only to explain and inculcate, but to take for the standards of my own faith and practice.

The Scriptures forbid *the disciples of Christ* to form any near relation, any intimate bond of union, with professed infidels. " Be ye not unequally yoked together with *unbelievers ;* for what fellowship hath righteousness with unrighteousness, and what communion hath light with darkness, and what concord hath Christ with Belial, and what part hath *he that believeth* with *an infidel ?* Wherefore come out from amongst them and be ye separate, saith the Lord." If it be urged that this precept primarily respects the case of marriage with an infidel, it is obvious to reply that the reason of marriage with such

2 *   c

persons being prohibited is the *intimate friendship* which such union implies.

> I am, sir,
>
>> Your humble servant,
>>
>>> R. HALL.

1799.

When I became a professed follower of Godwin as a moral philosopher I could not but be also an admirer of his ally Holcroft, whose novels "Anna St. Ives" and "Hugh Trevor" I had read with avidity; and I had thought his conduct noble in surrendering himself in court when the trial of Thomas Hardy began. I was introduced to Holcroft by Collier, but the acquaintance never flourished. I was present, however, at a remarkable dinner at his house (14th March). Aicken, of the Drury Lane company, highly respectable both as a man and an actor, and Sharp the engraver, were there. The latter is still named as one of the most eminent of English engravers; he is at the head of the English school. I possess one of his works which is a masterpiece, — "The Doctors of the Church," by Guido. I am no connoisseur certainly, and perhaps have no delicate sense of the beauty of engraving; but I never look on this specimen without a lively pleasure. Sharp was equally well known in another character which I will exemplify by an anecdote from the lips of Flaxman. "After Brothers had rendered himself by his insanity the object of universal interest, to which publicity had been given by the motion of Halked in the House of Commons, I had a visit from my old friend Sharp. 'I am come,' said he, 'to speak to you on a matter of some importance. You are aware of the great mission with which the Lord has intrusted Brothers?' I intimated that I had heard what everybody else had heard. 'Well,' he continued, 'perhaps you have not heard that I am to accompany the Children of Israel on their taking possession of their country, the Holy Land. Indeed, I think I shall have much to do in the transplanting of the nation. I have received my instructions, and I have to inform you that you also are to accompany them. I know from authority that you are of the seed of Abraham.' I bowed and intimated my sense of the honor done me by the invitation, but said it was quite impossible. I had other duties set out for me. On my return from Rome I bought this house, and established myself here, and here I must maintain myself and my family. ' I am aware of all that, said Sharp, ' and I have arranged everything. I know very well you are a great artist, I know too that you are a great architect as well as a great sculptor. I shall have intrusted to me the office of making all the chief appointments on this journey, and I pledge myself that you shall have the rebuilding of the Temple.'" The same mental delusion showed itself at the dinner at Holcroft's. On leaving the table Sharp called his host out of the room to say that Buonaparte was quite safe, — it was communicated to him last night by authority. There had been a great battle yesterday in Germany. Sharp was one of the objects of suspicion to the English government during the famous trials of 1794. He was a violent Jacobin and an extreme and passionate partisan of the Republicans. There is to be met with in the cabinets of the curious an admired engraving by him of Thomas Paine, as also of Brothers, whom he regarded as the messenger and sent of God.*

It is well known that the French Revolution turned the brains of many of the noblest youths in England. Indeed, when such men as Coleridge, Wordsworth, Southey, caught the infection, no wonder that those who partook of their sensibility but had a very small portion of their intellect were carried away. Many were ruined by the errors into which they were betrayed ; many also lived to smile at the follies of their youth. " I am no more ashamed of having been a republican," said Southey, " than I am of having been a child." The opinions held led to many political prosecutions, and I naturally had much sympathy with the sufferers. I find in my journal, February 21, 1799, " An interesting and memorable day." It was the day on which Gilbert Wakefield was convicted of a seditious libel and sentenced to two years' imprisonment. This he suffered in Dorchester jail, which he left only to die. Originally of the Established Church, he became a Unitarian, and professor at the Hackney College. By profession he was a scholar. His best known work was an edition of " Lucretius." He had written against Porson's edition of the " Hecuba of Euripides." † It is said that Porson was at a dinner-party at which toasts were going round ;

---

* Sharp's engraving of " Richard Brothers, Prince of the Hebrews," is a small square, dated 1795. Below it is inscribed: " Fully believing this to be the Man whom GOD has appointed, I engrave his likeness. — WILLIAM SHARP."
† In Euripidis Hecubam Londini nuper publicatam Diatribe Extemporalis. 1797.

and a name, accompanied by an appropriate sentence from
Shakespeare, was required from each of the guests in succession. Before Porson's turn came he had disappeared beneath the table, and was supposed to be insensible to what
was going on. This, however, was not the case, for when a
toast was required of him, he staggered up and gave, "Gilbert
Wakefield! — what's Hecuba to him, or he to Hecuba?"
Wakefield was a political fanatic. He had the pale complexion and mild features of a saint, was a most gentle creature in domestic life, and a very amiable man ; but when he
took part in political or religious controversy his pen was
dipped in gall. The occasion of the imprisonment before
alluded to was a letter in reply to Watson, the Bishop of
Llandaff, who had written a pamphlet exhorting the people to
loyalty. Wakefield asserted that the poor, the laboring
classes, could lose nothing by French conquest. Referring
to the fable of the Ass and the Trumpeter he said, "Will
the enemy make me carry two panniers?" and declared that
if the French came they would find him at his post with the
illustrious dead.

The prosecution was not intemperate, but he gloried in
what he had done, and was actuated by the spirit of martyrdom. Nothing could be more injudicious than his defence,
though in a similar trial an example had been set him just
before by Erskine of what such a defence should be. My
friend Rutt was one of Wakefield's bail. On being brought
up for judgment he spoke in mitigation, but in a way which
aggravated the offence. I accompanied him in a hackney-
coach to the King's Bench prison. While his friends were
arranging with the Governor about rooms there were brought
to the prison two young men named Parry, editors of *The
Courier* newspaper, who had been sentenced to six weeks' imprisonment for a libel on the Emperor of Russia. The libel
consisted in a single paragraph, stating that the Emperor had
acted oppressively and made himself unpopular with the
nobility by a late decree prohibiting the importation of tim-
ber. Such was the liberty of the press in the days of William
Pitt !

H. C. R. TO T. ROBINSON.

(No date.)

DEAR THOMAS, —
   . . . . One of the most interesting occurrences here has
been Wakefield's trial. How I wished that you had been

here then! My acquaintance with him perhaps heightened the effect; but I think to a mere stranger his delivery of his own defence must have been one of the most gratifying treats which a person of taste or sensibility could enjoy. His simplicity quite apostolic, his courage purely heroic. The energy and dignity with which he conducted himself have certainly had no parallel of late years. You saw a report of his speech in *The Courier*. It certainly was not a good defence, but as Anthony Robinson observed, something better than any defence, — a noble testimony. I dined in company with him on Monday and yesterday. His spirits are not in the least depressed.

Johnson, the Unitarian publisher in St. Paul's Churchyard, was convicted of a libel for selling Wakefield's pamphlet; he was imprisoned in the King's Bench for a few months. For a consideration he was allowed to occupy apartments within the rules. My first visit to him in prison was in company with Mary Hays,* a very zealous political and moral reformer, a friend of Mary Wollstonecraft, and author of a novel called "Memoirs of Emma Courtney." I called on Johnson several times and profited by his advice. He was a wise man, and his remarks on the evil of indulging in melancholy forebodings were applicable to a habit of my own. He described them as the effect of dreamy indolence, and as liable to increase from the unhealthy state into which they bring the mind. Though he did not cure me of my fault, some of its consequences were mitigated. I was especially unhappy from my inability to come to any satisfactory conclusion as to my plan of life. I hated the law, yet I knew not how otherwise to attain any social station. I was ambitious of literary distinction, but was conscious that I could never attain any reputation worth having. My desire to go to Germany was rather a *pis aller*, than from any decided preference of the comparative advantages of such a course.

One other political prisoner occasionally visited by me was Benjamin Flower, who had been committed to Newgate by the House of Lords for a breach of privilege.

---

* She professed Mary Wollstonecraft's opinions with more zeal than discretion. This brought her into disrepute among the rigid, and her character suffered, — but most undeservedly. Whatever her principles may have been, her conduct was perfectly correct. My acquaintance with her continued till her death. — H. C. R.

H. C. R. TO HIS BROTHER.

(About) June, 1799.

MY DEAR BROTHER, —

. . . . I suppose the fame of "Pizarro" has already reached you. It is unquestionably the most excellent play I ever saw for variety of attractions. The scenery and decorations are splendid and magnificent without being tawdry or puerile, and these ornaments are made to heighten, not supersede, real dramatic merit. The tragedy possesses scenes of the most tender and pathetic kind, and others highly heroic. Mrs. Siddons displays her usual powers in the character of the mistress of Pizarro, — proud, haughty, with a true sense of honor and a romantic passion for glory : in love with Pizarro because he was great, she hates him when he degrades himself by acts of meanness, — herself a criminal, her passion for humanity leads her to acts of heroism and desperation. Kemble plays the Peruvian Chieftain in his very best style. The lover of Cora, he voluntarily yields her to Alonzo, and when they are married, devotes his life to their happiness ; brave, generous, and pious, he is a kind of demi-god, — and you know with what skill Kemble can " assume the god and try to shake the spheres." The incidents are in themselves so highly interesting and extraordinary that far less superiority of acting and pomp of machinery would have given ordinary effect to the piece ; but, when united with the utmost efforts of the painter and machinist, they produce a drama absolutely without parallel. Were you a little richer I should recommend a journey to London on purpose to see it.

I have also been greatly amused by hearing one of Mackintosh's lectures. It was on the British Constitution. Though his praise of the British Constitution was extravagant, he was far from being uniformly favorable to the cause of government. His favorite notion concerning the Constitution is, that it is the most truly democratic of any that has ever existed. He defines a real democracy to be a government where the *opinion* of the body of the people influences and governs the state, whatever the nominal legislature may be. And he boldly asserts that a more formal democracy would lessen the real democracy, because it is the nature of all mobs and public assemblies to be under the secret guidance of factious demagogues ; and that the people in such states never act, precisely because they are the *direct* actors, and have a power nominally given them which they cannot exercise. He urged the common argument in favor of Monarchy, that it took from the ambitious the motives to be factious and breed dissension in order to procure the principal stations ; and that the king, sharing the honor of victory and the affections of the soldiery with the General, was not likely to become a military tyrant. He defended Coalitions, Parties, and moderation towards ex-Ministers, was eloquent against the French, but likewise hinted at the danger to public liberty from not watching the government. On the whole I was much pleased with the lecture, which was well adapted to secure popularity. As to his politics, they are certainly moderate, nor do I know that he has gone an inch beyond pure Whiggism.

Horne Tooke has never been a favorite of mine, but I never thought so well of his heart as I have done from his behavior to Wakefield, which was kind and respectful ; and when we consider, not how like, but how unlike their characters are, his attentions do him the greatest honor. The day sentence was passed he sent to Wakefield, and, in his jocular way, comforted him by observing that probably a year hence he and Mrs. Wakefield would be congratulating each other on his situation, — " For, my dear, it has saved you," Mrs. Wakefield will say ; " you see Tooke and the rest of them are half-way on their voyage to Botany Bay." Horne Tooke promised too, old as he was, to visit him at Dorchester, though he said he had not thought he should travel seven miles from Wimbledon again. This looks well. You have heard, I dare say, that Tooke's friends have lately raised him an annuity for life of £ 600. This following Dr. Parr's and Fox's seems to show that all regard for public characters is not at an end. . . . .

Adieu.   In haste,

Yours, &c.,

H. C. R.

I became acquainted about this time with George Dyer. He was one of the best creatures morally that ever breathed. He was the son of a watchman in Wapping, and was put to a charity school by some pious Dissenting ladies. He afterwards went to Christ's Hospital, and from there was sent to Cambridge. He was a scholar, but to the end of his days (and he lived to be eighty-five) was a bookseller's drudge. He led a life of literary labor in poverty. He made indexes, corrected the press, and occasionally gave lessons in Latin and Greek.

When an undergraduate at Cambridge he became a hearer of
Robert Robinson, and consequently a Unitarian.   This closed
the ·Church against him, and he never had a Fellowship.   He
became intimate with the Nashes, Fordhams, and Rutt, and
was patronized by Wakefield and Mrs. Barbauld.   He wrote
one good book, " The Life of Robert Robinson," which I
have heard Wordsworth mention as one of the best works of
biography in the language.   Dyer also put his name to several
volumes of poetry ; but on his poems my friend Reid made an
epigram that I fear was thought just : —

> " The world all say, my gentle Dyer,
> Thy odes do very much want fire.
> Repair the fault. my gentle Dyer,
> And throw thy odes into the fire."

Dyer had the kindest heart and simplest manners imaginable.
It was literally the case with him that he would give away his
last guinea.   He was not sensible of any impropriety in wear-
ing a dirty shirt or a ragged coat ; and numerous are the tales
told in illustration of his neglect of little every-day matters
of comfort.   He has asked a friend to breakfast with him, and
given him coarse black tea, stale bread, salt butter, sour milk,
and has had to run out to buy sugar.   Yet every one loved
Dyer.   One day Mrs. Barbauld said to me, " Have you heard
whom Lord Stanhope has made executor ? " — " No !   Your
brother ? " — " No, there would have been nothing in that.
The very worst imaginable." — " O, then it is Buonaparte." —
" No, guess again." — " George Dyer ? " — " You are right.
Lord Stanhope was clearly insane ! "   Dyer was one of six
executors.   Charles James Fox was another.   The executors
were also residuary legatees.   Dyer was one of the first to
declare that he rejected the legacy and renounced the execu-
torship.   But the heir insisted on granting him a small annuity ; his friends having before settled another on him, he
was comparatively wealthy in his old age.   Not many years
before his death, he married his laundress, by the advice of
his friends, — a very worthy woman.   He said to me once,
" Mrs. Dyer is a woman of excellent natural sense, but she is
not literate."   That is, she could neither read nor write.   Dyer
was blind for a few years before his death.   I used occasionally
to go on a Sunday morning to read to him.   At other times a
poor man used to render him that service for sixpence an hour.
After he came to London, Dyer lived always in some very
humble chambers in Clifford's Inn, Fleet Street.

Another interesting acquaintance I made at this period was with William Hazlitt, — a man who has left a deservedly high reputation as a critic ; but at the time I first knew him he was struggling against a great difficulty of expression, which rendered him by no means a general favorite in society. His bashfulness, want of words, slovenliness of dress, &c., made him sometimes the object of ridicule. It will be better, perhaps, if I confine myself at present to describing him as he was at this early period of our acquaintance. He was the younger brother of John Hazlitt, the miniature painter. His first design was to be a Dissenting minister ; and for that purpose he went to the Unitarian New College, Hackney. He afterwards thought of becoming a painter, and lived with his brother. At our first interview I saw he was an extraordinary man. He had few friends, and was flattered by my attentions. We were about the same age, and I was able to render him a service by introducing him to Anthony Robinson, who induced Johnson to publish Hazlitt's first work, "The Eloquence of the British Senate." Late in life, when our intimacy had been broken off, he said to Mary Lamb, "Robinson cuts me, but I shall never cease to have a regard for him, for he was the first person who ever found out that there was anything in me." I was alone in this opinion at the time of which I am speaking. I recollect saying to my sister-in-law, "Whom do you suppose I hold to be the cleverest person I know ? " — " Capel Lofft, perhaps ? " — " No." — " Mrs. Clarkson ? " — " O no." — " Miss Maling ? " — " No." — " I give it up." — " William Hazlitt." — " O, you are joking. Why, we all take him to be just the reverse." At this time he was excessively shy, especially in the company of young ladies, who on their part were very apt to make fun of him. The prettiest girl of our parties about this time was a Miss Kitchener, and she used to drive him mad by teasing him.

I was under great obligations to Hazlitt as the director of my taste. It was he who first made me acquainted with the Lyrical Ballads and the poems generally of Wordsworth, Coleridge, Lamb, and Southey.

Among those to whom Mary Hays introduced me was the free-thinking, ultra-liberal Roman Catholic priest, Dr. Geddes, translator of the Old Testament, — a man of fine person and very amiable manners. His wit was exhibited in macaronic verses. He was a patron of two young ladies, the Miss Plumptres. Anne Plumptres made herself known as one of the first

introducers of German plays, — she translated many of Kotzebue's.

During this summer my friend Miss Maling was in London,
living in the same house with the Archbishop of Aix, — a man
known to history ; he pronounced the oration at the coronation of Louis XVI., and afterwards by the favor of Napoleon
obtained a cardinal's hat.* He was a zealous emigrant at this
time. Having conceived a great respect for Miss Maling, he
had destined for her the post of *Lectrice* to the Duchess of Orleans, had the Revolution succeeded, which was projected this
year. He was a man of letters and a poet. I had the honor
of an introduction to him, but a mere introduction. I had
only time to admire his majestic figure. His preaching I
thought magnificent.

I made in this year a pedestrian tour in Wales. On my
way I visited Stonehenge, — the first place I ever went to see
as an object of curiosity ; and I had all the enjoyment that
was to be derived from so novel and so sublime a scene. This
tour, of which I shall write little, afforded me the opportunity
of visiting two men, who suffered for political opinions, —
Gilbert Wakefield and John Thelwall ; the former was in prison at Dorchester. A subscription of £ 3,000 had been raised.
by his friends, who were thereby enabled to supply Mrs. Wakefield with a very comfortable house in the vicinity of the
prison. Here she and the children dwelt, and a spare room
was always ready for some friendly visitor. During Wakefield's
imprisonment this room was almost always in use. I occupied it several days, and found him suffering more in his spirits
than was expected. The distress he witnessed in jail, and
the presence of physical and moral evil, preyed on his mind
and seemed to crush him.†

John Thelwall, to whom I have already alluded, as having
had a narrow escape of conviction for high treason, had settled
down in a farm in a beautiful place near Brecon. His history
is known to all who care to inform themselves of the personal
occurrences of this eventful period. He had left his shop (that
of a silk mercer) to be one of the Reformers of the age. After
his acquittal he went about the country lecturing, and was ex-

---

* On the copy of a letter by the Archbishop, Mr. Robinson has written :
. " Afterwards Cardinal Boisgelin, an emigrant nobleman who made his peace
with Buonaparte, and had his due reward in a cardinal's hat for preaching a
sermon on the Emperor's marriage."
† He was released from prison May 30, 1801, and died on the 9th of September in the same year.

posed to great varieties of fortune. Sometimes he was attended by numerous admirers, but more frequently hooted and pelted by the mob. In order to escape prosecution for sedition he took as his subject Greek and Roman History, and had ingenuity enough to give such a coloring to events and characters as to render the application to living persons and present events an exciting mental exercise. I had heard one or two of these lectures, and thought very differently of him then from what I thought afterwards. When, however, he found his popularity on the wane, and more stringent laws had been passed, to which he individually gave occasion, he came to the prudent resolution of abandoning his vagrant habits and leading a domestic life in the country. It was at this period that my visit was paid, and I received a most cordial welcome. His wife was a very pleasing woman, a great admirer of her husband, — never a reproach to a wife, though the kind of husband she has chosen may sometimes be so. But Thelwall was an amiable man in private life ; an affectionate husband, and a fond father. He altogether mistook his talents, — he told me without reserve that he believed he should establish his name among the epic poets of England ; and it is a curious thing, considering his own views, that he thought the establishment of Christianity and the British Constitution very appropriate subjects for his poem.

After a stay of a week, I left my friends with a strong sense of their personal kindness. I may add here that when farming had succeeded as ill as political agitation, he took to the teaching of oratory as a profession, and for a time succeeded in it. For some years he had an establishment in Upper Bedford Place, where he received boarders. But gradually his didactic talents were directed more especially to the correction of defects arising from the malformation of the organs of speech.

At Haverfordwest an unexpected pleasure awaited me. I fell in with Robert Hall. He received me with apparent pleasure, and was kind without being flattering. His countenance indicated a powerful intellect and strong sensibility. In disputation he expressed himself with his characteristic point, and sometimes with virulence. He spoke of my sister-in-law with unusual seriousness, and said she was the most extraordinary instance he had ever known of a woman of superior talents preserving universal respect ; abilities being so rare among women, and when found so rarely accompanied by amiable qualities. The only allusion he made to our correspondence was by saying of one who thought himself ill treated : " He ought at once to have come forward, and in a manly way, as you did, have made his complaint."

In passing through Wem in Shropshire I saw a very worthy old Presbyterian minister, — not worse than an Arian, I presume, — the father of the Hazlitts. William, who had become my friend, was not there, but John, the miniature-painter, was.* I liked the good old man and his wife, who had all the solidity (I do not mean stolidity) and sober earnestness of the more respectable Noncons. There was also a maiden sister. Altogether an amusing and agreeable group in my memory.

On my return from Wales I took Bath in my way. Seven years had elapsed since I attended my mother in her last illness, and my desire to see the place of her interment was increased by something Mrs. Fenner had related to me. My mother had expressed pain at being buried at so great a distance from her children. She feared they would never see her grave. " But," she added, " I have no doubt Henry will come though he walk." I did not need this stimulus, for my mother was the sole object of my fondness as a child. It was a substantial gratification to me to find my mother's grave in one of the most beautifully situated churchyards I ever saw, — a long slip of land near Whitcomb Church. I have often visited it since, and always with a sort of pleasure.†

CHAPTER V.

GERMANY. — 1800 AND 1801.

I AM now come to an incident, which had a great influence on my tastes and feelings, and therefore, I have no doubt, on my character. In the course of this year I went to Germany, where I remained more than five years, and pursued something like study, and where I was brought into contact with some of the most distinguished men of the age.

Mr. Aldebert, a German merchant with whom I had become

* An interesting but weakly painted portrait of Joseph Lancaster by John Hazlitt is in the National Portrait Gallery. It is in oil, the size of life, and evidently the production of an artist accustomed to work on a smaller scale with different materials. — G. S.

† This part of the Reminiscences was written in 1845 and 1846.

acquainted, undertook to convoy me as far as Frankfort. The journey, which now may be accomplished easily and in a very short time, was comparatively formidable at the beginning of this century. We embarked at Yarmouth, on the 3d of April, and on Friday evening I beheld that dismal fortress Heligoland, a scene which in my imagination might be appropriately connected with Goethe's " Natürliche Tochter." On the morning of the 6th we landed at Cuxhaven, and proceeded by land to Hamburg. I have still a clear recollection of the flat, cold, colorless country, which an instinctive feeling had led the inhabitants to make as lively as possible by the bright green on the scattered houses.

H. C. R. TO HIS BROTHER T. R.

We remained twelve days at the Kaiserhof, where we paid 7 s. a day for a dirty room on a second floor, 4 s. to the man who waited on us at the hotel and attended us in the town, and 1 s. 4 d. for breakfast ; in short, where, though we lived in the plainest and most economical style, our daily bill was nearly a guinea apiece. We then removed to private lodgings, where the civility and honesty of the good family reminded us of the family of Lot.

The houses at Hamburg perpetually suggest the idea that you are looking at England as it was a century ago. The original model of a farm-house (and farm-houses were the primitive houses) as I have seen it in the wild parts of Hanover, is that of one immense room, without chimney or division, — the various parts being allotted, as a farmer lays out his different seeds or fruits. At one corner the fire, — here the beds, — there the piggery, — there some furniture, — and a good carriage-way all through. Now the progress of refinement is this : after a time the sides are separated (like the King's Bench and Common Pleas in Westminster Hall), glazed, and adorned, for the women and children, — but still the centre is unpaved. I have seen several respectable houses of this kind in the country near Hamburg. Refinement increases, but still the old hall remains as in ancient English mansions. Perhaps we have gone beyond the exact mark of propriety through our proud love of retirement, and by converting our halls into narrow passages and large parlors, have injured our houses as summer retreats and promoted the natural shyness

of our tempers.   In the houses near Hamburg the genteelest
families dine or drink coffee in their halls, and with the doors
open to observation and curiosity.   In the town, too, most of
the houses have the narrow or gable end in front, which necessarily precludes the elegant uniformity of a Bath street,
but at the same time allows of an infinite variety of ornament,
which gives an idea of distinctiveness, and is, I think, an advantage.   As the stories rise, the curtain, if it may be so
called, is narrowed till it terminates in a pyramid.   There is,
it must be confessed, a great waste of room in the lofty halls
and shops which you see in the front of the Hamburg houses.
But perhaps it is more pleasing to witness resources and means
of future improvements, as necessities may arise, than to behold, as in London, every inch occupied, and management and
economy put to their last shifts.   The dress of the lower classes confirms the suggestion that Germany is now what England
was.   Many a poor woman wears a tight black velvet bonnet
like that in which Mary Queen of Scots is painted.   The Lutheran clergy appear to wear the cast-off ruffs of Queen Elizabeth.

After remaining a few weeks at Hamburg, we proceeded to
Frankfort, where Mr. Aldebert procured me lodgings near his
own house, and introduced me to his relations and partners.
I set about reading as hard as I could, dining at the various
hotels in the city, which were famed for their excellence.   My
first object was to acquire a knowledge of the German language, and I took lessons of an old man named Peile, who
confided to me that he had been when young a member of the
Illuminati, an order of which he gave me a better opinion than
I previously had, both in regard to their intentions and their
practical ability.

Frankfort was then a fortified town, much to its disadvantage in regard to air and comfort, and without any adequate
compensation, for the fortification was next to useless.   *Now*,
in the place of the walls and ditches, there are beautiful walks
which render the place as agreeable as it was formerly dismal.
Though professedly neutral, its neutrality was violated on the
6th of July.

H. C. R. to T. R.

I believe were a cracker or squib to be let off in any town
in Great Britain, and were it thought to come from a French

hand, half the old women would be in fits. Now, I had so much of the old woman in me that one day when I was sleeping over my German grammar, and the maid burst into the room, crying, "The French are at the gates," I made but two skips down stairs, and flew into the principal street. It was a false alarm, but I found all in confusion, — a body of Mayençois troops had demanded entrance, and were then on their march to support their allies, whom the French were attacking a few miles off. They had cannon, with lighted matches. The men were fine fellows, and without being sad were grave. I knew they were going into the field, and I felt that sinking within the breast which betrays the coward, — but they passed away and my sinking too. The rest of the day nothing was known. On the morrow we learnt that the French had been thrice beaten back, but that early in the morning they had renewed the attack, and were now in the midst of the engagement. I left my books, and hastened to the ramparts, which were covered with idlers. Couriers passed backwards and forwards, but nobody knew what was going forward. Citizens are mob, and soldiers are gentlemen at such times; and Sterne's remark concerning Susanna and the women at a groaning might be parodied here. Our curiosity was not left, however, to starve for want of nourishment; every now and then a wagon slowly entered the town, and though covered with straw or cloth, we generally could perceive something moving underneath, — it was only a wounded man, — nothing more! By and by I ventured, with the doctor of the house, to make an excursion. We walked up a hill, and were near enough to hear the discharge of musketry, and see the smoke and flash of the cannons, but that was all. And I was half angry with myself for being so composed. It was probable that every instant some horrid wound was inflicted, or some wretch suddenly carried off, and yet I ate cherries! And how could it be otherwise? We are sympathetic; and indifference, or the want of passion, is catching as well as passion itself. The persons around me were at their ease, and that made me so in a great degree. I cannot forbear to make· a remark, which though simple is important. From the modern system of war and politics, by which the civil and the military state are so much separated, and the subject is so much distinguished from the prince, this consequence has arisen, — that war has ceased to be a matter of national passion, and has become in a great degree a professional business. At least in this neighborhood it is so.

Next day in the evening the French actually came, and I, standing on the walls, witnessed their entrance. The general indifference at the event confounded me ; but it was in reality an affair of money. They came not as an enemy. The soldiers were billeted in the town ; and a gentlemanly young officer was in the house in which I lodged. With him I soon became acquainted. He loved poetry, and we talked on various subjects. Nor did he take any exception to my being an Englishman. At this moment the war was flagging.

Of those to whom I was introduced, there is one of whom it is necessary that I should write a few words. This was Sophia de la Roche, a sentimental novelist, and in her youth a friend of Wieland, under whose auspices she became known as an authoress. Her daughter married Brentano, a wealthy merchant, who died young; and among her grandchildren were several with whom I had much to do during my residence in Germany. She herself was never tired of talking of England, of which she was a passionate admirer. An amusing account of her is given in Madame d'Arblay's Memoirs.* In extravagant language she poured out to me her love of this country, declaring that on her death-bed she should thank God for her journey hither, and expressing the wish that she could offer up her soul to God in Richmond vale !

My journal mentions a circumstance worth recording in connection with the drama in the wealthy city of Frankfort. I saw the play of "Hamlet" performed by actors of repute ; but the catastrophe was changed. As Hamlet is about to drink the poison the Queen's illness is perceived, — his hand is stayed, — he rushes on the King and slays him, — he is attacked, — thunder is heard, — the Queen confesses, — he forgives Laertes, — and all's well that ends well. This I have told to Germans, who have wished to deny the fact.

In July I wrote to my brother : "My last letter told you that I had ceased to be a traveller. The effect produced on the mind by the knowledge that you are but the inhabitant of a day is really astonishing. It quickens the observation and animates the spirits exceedingly. While I was on my journey nothing escaped me. It was a second childhood. I was once more gay, impetuous, inquisitive, and adventurous ; but as soon as I had fixed myself I became the same dull, phlegmatic, and sometimes hyppish soul, which I was often in

---

* Diary and Letters of Madame d'Arblay. September, 1786. Vol. III. p. 136.

my lodgings in London. I am now so domesticated, so reconciled to the slight varieties of manners, that nothing but the language reminds me I am out of Old England."

In September I give this account of my life at Frankfort : —

"I breakfast at half past seven, and dine at twelve ; then I go to a reading society, where I meet with a profusion of German magazines (which are something between the English magazines and periodical essayists), the *Moniteur* and French journals, and the English *Chronicle*. This is an agreeable addition to what my sister properly calls 'my comforts,' and is my after-dinner dessert. Three times a week I go to a respectable old gentleman who corrects my translations into German, and from him I try to get an idea of German literature. It is, however, too soon to talk about it. I take solitary walks about the town, which are pleasant, and generally on the Sunday accompany some friends to one of the neighboring villages, where we drink coffee or wine. This is the universal custom, and I do not dislike it. These little parties are not expensive. The company is very mixed, and there is often music and dancing, — but the dancing is unlike anything you ever saw. You must have heard of it under the name of waltzing, — that is, rolling or turning, though the rolling is not horizontal but perpendicular. Yet Werter, after describing his first waltz with Charlotte, says, — and I say so too, — 'I felt that if I were married, my wife should waltz (or roll) with no one but myself.' Judge, — the man places the palms of his hands gently against the sides of his partner, not far from the arm-pits. His partner does the same, and instantly with as much velocity as possible they turn round and at the same time gradually glide round the room. Now, as Sir Isaac Newton borrowed his notion of attraction from an apple falling, why might not Copernicus, who was a German,* conceive his theory of the twofold motion of the earth from a waltz, where both parties with great rapidity themselves turn round and yet make the circuit of the room ? "

It was my habit to make occasional excursions when I found a suitable companion. On one of these occasions, when Mrs. Aldebert was following her husband to England, I accompanied her to the gates of Castel, a suburb of Mainz, and was left without a passport.

At the inn at Hochheim I found three French officers. I

* Copernicus was a Pole.

was startled, but as there was an armistice (it was the 16th
of August) I thought frankness the safest policy. I joined
them at the dinner-table. "A hot day, sir." — " Yes, sir."
(N. B. The French, like the Quakers, do not like to be called
" Citizen " but by a citizen, though, unlike the brethren, they
preserve the old forms of civility, and use " Sir " as much as
formerly to strangers.) I immediately told of my ride from
Frankfort, of my friends who were at Mainz, and of my incapacity to follow them. "It is mortifying," said I, "to see a
fine town and rich country shut against one." — " Yes, to be
sure ; but it is not difficult to get a pass. You are a German ? " — " No." — " Pray what countryman are you, then ? "
— " Can I answer with safety ?   If, now, I should be an
unlucky enemy by birth, are you bound officially to arrest
me ? " — " O no ! " said they, and laughed ; and I found
that the Englishman was very welcome. So I stayed several
hours with them, and debated on politics. I found in these
and several other officers more respect than I should. have expected for Mr. Pitt, who individually is fancied to be all in all
in the Cabinet ; they had a warm zeal for France as France,
without much care about its immediate government.

This spirit of patriotism unquestionably saved the nation.
Could Mr. Burke have persuaded the people of France that
" France was out of itself," the affair would have been over.
And the Revolution owed its success to the early creation of a
power which the people looked up to as its head. The first
Assembly, by calling itself the *National*, gained the nation by
the word.

In the progress of familiarity I begged the officers to tell me
how I stood as to personal safety. They said unquestionably
liable to be arrested every moment, but not in any great
danger ; there were parties on the scout to pick up deserters
and examine travellers. Being on foot I should likely enough
be considered a native, but if questioned, as I had no passport,
I should certainly be taken before the Commandant at Mainz,
and they did not advise my going farther.

I did not, however, take alarm, and went on to the little
town of Biebrich, the residence of the Prince of Nassau. Here
I was very civilly treated at the only inn in the place. Next
day I made a circuitous walk back, taking in my way Wiesbaden, a small neat dull curious old German town, famous
only for its hot spring. It is noteworthy that this has become
one of the most fashionable watering-places in Germany, much

frequented by English guests, with elegant gambling-houses which have been a source of great wealth to the Prince.

The following letters will give some idea of the condition of England at the close of the eighteenth century : —

T. R. TO H. C. R.

BURY, December 18, 1800.

I cannot forbear speaking a word or two on the situation of our own country. You cannot be aware, I think, to the extent in which it exists, of the distress of all orders of people amongst us on account of the high price of provisions. The poor-rates have risen to an unexampled height, — they have nearly doubled since you left England. The present rate at Bury for the *quarter* is seven shillings in the pound, upon an assessment of two thirds of the rental, — in short, as much is paid to the poor as to the landlord. At the commencement of the war the rate with us was not more than 1 *s.* 9 *d.* or 2 *s.* in the pound. The burden which the circumstances have laid upon the people will, I imagine, be scarcely credited in Germany, and yet the situation of Bury is much less lamentable than that of many other towns in the kingdom. The alarm respecting a scarcity is so great that Parliament is now assembled by special proclamation to take into consideration the best means of relieving the nation in the present dearth. High bounties are accordingly offered to encourage the importation of grain, and various plans of economy are recommended to diminish the consumption of bread. The causes of the distressed state of the country are a subject of controversy both within and out of Parliament. The Administration are, of course, very strenuous in maintaining that the *war* has no share in it, while the Opposition as loudly attempt to prove it is the principal cause. The seasons have unquestionably been very unfavorable. But besides these palpable reasons an idea has been set afloat, and very eagerly caught at by vast numbers of people, that the scarcity is to be chiefly attributed to monopoly. As a disciple of Adam Smith, you will probably recollect his sentiments on the subject. He compares the dread of monopoly, when a free trade is allowed in so bulky a commodity as corn, to the terror of witchcraft. This opinion, it is understood, has been adopted by our leading statesmen, both on the Ministerial and Opposition side. And so much has this opinion prevailed till of late, that I understand the old statute laws relating to forestalling, regrating, &c., were some few years since repealed. The common law, however, still remaining in force, a prosecution grounded upon it was a few months since commenced against Waddington, a great hop-merchant, for monopoly, and another against a contractor for regrating. On one of their trials Lord Kenyon combated the doctrine of Adam Smith ; and on the defendant being convicted, warmly applauded the jury for their verdict, and said the country was much indebted to them. He was followed in this opinion by the greater part of the judges, who, on the ensuing circuit, declaimed against those hard-hearted persons who made a prey of their fellow-creatures by withholding from them the necessaries of life, and strongly urged the magistrates to be vigilant to prevent the markets being forestalled. In consequence of this recommendation associations were formed in almost every county to carry it into effect.

Owing to these proceedings a violent clamor was excited against corn-dealers and farmers, which being joined in by the mob, artificial scarcity became the cry. Farmers were threatened, and their barns and ricks in many places were set on fire ; this has been particularly the case in the neighborhood of Bocking, where several wilful conflagrations have taken place. . . . .

January 27, 1801.

. . . . The times continue excessively hard with us, — indeed the cloud of evil seems to threaten more and more every day. Corn rises every market-day, and indeed alarm is spreading in all directions, and not least among the friends of the administration. I wish not to dwell upon political topics, but distress has brought them home to everybody's bosom, and they now produce all the interest of domestic incidents. With the Funds falling, and trade very precarious, Mary and I sometimes talk of emigration, — but where to go is the question. France is the only country which to my mind presents any temptation. The language, however, is an insuperable objection. Buonaparte seems as if he would make the assumed title of *great nation* a valid claim, and I fear it is as clear that the sun of England's glory is set. Indeed I am become quite an alarmist, which I believe is equally the case with the democrat and the aristocrat. Such is the state of the country in the prime article of life, flour, that the millers are prohibited under very heavy penalties from making any but coarse flour,

and instead of any restraint being laid upon them against mix-
ing of grains, encouragement is given them to do it. Speaking
on the state of the country the other day to Garnham, he exclaimed, "A very pretty state we are reduced to, — our pockets
filled with paper and our bellies filled with chicken's meat!"

March 9, 1801.

. . . . If you have noticed in the papers you are no doubt interested in the circumstances of Horne Tooke having obtained
a seat in the House of Commons as representative of the famous borough of Old Sarum. This he effected through the
patronage of the eccentric Lord Camelford. A very interesting debate is expected to-morrow on a motion of Lord Temple
to inquire into the eligibility of a priest to a seat in Parliament. Lord Camelford, it is said, told Lord Grenville that if
the black coat were rejected he would send a black *man*, referring to a negro servant of his, born in England, whom he
would qualify to take a seat.

. . . . When we were in London Mary and I had lodgings in
Newgate Street. The theatre was the only amusement which
interested me. We were, of course, desirous of seeing the
present *nine days' wonder*, Mr. Cooke. We were so lucky as
to see him in Richard, his favorite character. Nature has assisted him greatly in the performance of this part, — his features being strongly marked and his voice harsh. I felt at the
time that he personated the ferocious tyrant better than
Kemble could have done. There is besides a sort of humor
in his manner of acting which appeared very appropriate, and
which I think Kemble could not have given; and I think it
likely the latter would be surpassed in Shylock. Cooke's powers of expression are strong and coarse. I am persuaded that
in dignified and refined character, — in the philosophical hero,
— he would fall infinitely short of Kemble. He had the
effrontery to play the Stranger, but, if I mistake not, he appeared in it but once. . . . .

Early in 1801 I became acquainted with a very interesting
and remarkable person, — Baron Hohenfels, the Dom-dechant
von Speyer. He had a somewhat quixotic figure, — tall and
gaunt, with marked features. Though careless about his dress,
he had a distinguished gait. He was an elderly man who had
been for many years chancellor of the Elector of Treves, and
as such, had he continued in office, would have been the Elec-

tor's successor. He was also, as he used to tell me, a bishop *in partibus*. But he was a very liberal and philosophic churchman, and preferred a life of literary leisure. He had been in England, to which he was warmly attached, and had a strong liking for Austria. Everything French and Prussian he hated in an equal degree. To the Austrian state and the Romish Church he was attached politically. He was living an idle life, and in order therefore to gratify as well his indolence as his taste for everything English, — he loved our poets not less than our politicians, — he was glad to have even my acquaintance. We frequently walked together, and he taught me much by the questions he was in the habit of putting to me. On one occasion he was very particular in inquiring what the Unitarians believed. What did Priestley believe? On my mentioning some orthodox doctrines rejected, he asked " Did Priestley believe the resurrection ? " — " Yes." On this, with a very significant expression, he said : " This reminds me of an anecdote of Ninon de l'Enclos. Being asked one day by a Parisian lady, whether she believed that St. Denys walked *all* the way to Paris with his head under his arm, ' Pourquoi pas, Mademoiselle ? ' Ninon said ; ' ce n'est que le premier pas qui coûte.' "

The Baron was more fond of asking than of answering questions ; but when I pressed him, he did not shrink from a reply which, without compromising himself, seemed to me intelligible. I had before drawn from him the remark that Christianity is a great fact, — that the fact being admitted it allowed neither of criticism nor of argument ; and now in reference to the claims of Roman Catholicism, I asked whether the evidence of the later miracles was as strong as that of the earlier. His answer was again in the form of an anecdote : " In the time of Pope ―― there were some saints who were called the new saints. On one occasion his Holiness exclaimed, ' These new saints make me doubt the old.' You will excuse my not giving a more direct reply." I ought to add that some years afterwards, when the Baron died, he left all his property to the Roman Catholic church at Frankfort.

I had not known this interesting man many days before he said he would introduce me to two young ladies " *qui petillaient d'esprit*." These were Charlotte and Paulina Serviere. They were persons of small fortune and carried on a little business, but lived on terms of intimacy with one of the most distinguished families in Frankfort, — that of Brentano. Char-

lotte Serviere was not handsome, but was attractive to me by
singular good sense and sweetness of disposition, though the
latter quality was generally assigned in a higher degree to the
younger sister, Paulina, who was a joyous, kind creature,
naïve, sportive, voluble, — liked by every one.　In their house
I became intimate, and there I soon saw the ladies of the
Brentano family, — to whom I was introduced on the very
same day by Mad. de la Roche.　By them also I was received
as a friend.　Mad. Brentano, a beautiful Viennese, the eldest
daughter Kunigunda, — afterwards the wife of Savigny, the
great Prussian lawyer and statesman, — were my present companions.　They proposed that I should read English to them,
and that they should initiate me into German poetry, in other
words into Goethe, with whom they were personally acquainted,
and of whom they were all devoted worshippers.　During the
first four months of 1801 I made considerable progress in the
study of Goethe, and imbibed a taste for German poetry and
literature, which I have always retained.

H. C. R. TO T. R.

Goethe is the idol of the German literary public.　The
critics of the new school assert that since the existence of
letters there have been only four of those called geniuses, on
whom Nature and Art seem to have showered down all their
gifts to form that perfection of intellect, — a Poet.　Virgil,
Milton, Wieland, Klopstock, Ariosto, Ossian, Tasso, &c., &c.,
are singers of various and great excellence, but the sacred
poetic fire has been possessed in its perfection only by Homer,
Cervantes, Shakespeare, and Goethe.　Nay, some of this new
school have even asserted that the three great " tendencies "
of the late century are the French Revolution, the Fichtian
Philosophy and " Wilhelm Meister's Lehrjahre."

This valuable addition to my acquaintance had been made
only a few days, when it was increased by that of the brother,
Clemens Brentano, — then known only by irregular ballads
and songs inserted in a very irregular novel, but a poet in
character, as that term is generally understood, and a man of
genius, though not an artist ; and after many years the author
of fairy tales which brought him *éclat*.　He was on terms of
intimacy with the Schlegels, Tieck, and others of the romantic
school ; but on account of peculiarities of temperament was

rather difficult to get on with.   As I shall have little to say of him hereafter, I may add that he married a poetess named Sophie Mereau, who however died after a short time.   Late in life he took a religious turn, and published a strange book, professedly relating from the lips of a diseased nun her visions of the sufferings of Christ; but the Bishop of Ratisbon, Seiler, would not allow the work to be printed without being accompanied by the declaration that the visions were given as the pious contemplations of a good woman, and not as preternatural revelations.

Personally I had more to do with a younger brother, whose education was unfinished, and who, learning that I was unsettled, proposed that I should accompany him on foot into Saxony, where I could go on with my study, while he completed his.   In my entirely isolated state an offer much less agreeable than this would have been acceptable.   I should visit a country which I longed to see.   Several months however elapsed before our plan was carried into effect.   In the mean while I pursued my studies with something like system; devoting myself steadily to German poetry and philosophy. All my vacant time was spent either with the Servieres or the Brentanos.   The manners of this little society were very free and easy; and my character as an Englishman contributed to my being treated as a pet.

Before my departure I made a short journey with Herr Mylius and his sister Mad. Kohl to Wetzlar, — a town of some importance because, under the old German constitution, it was the seat of a court of appeal from courts held in all the small states of Germany; in other respects an insignificant place. The noblesse of this old-fashioned "free city" were the bigwigs, the lawyers.   Our journey lay through a pleasing country, and this three days' excursion made me acquainted with the simple manners of a people who seemed to belong to a former age.   The tribunal has been abolished, and the town no doubt lost its privileges as a free city.

My tour with Christian Brentano began on the 14th of June. Our first object was to see his brother Clemens, who was then residing at Göttingen.   I will not stop to give particulars of any of the places through which we passed.   On our arrival I was received with kindness, and introduced to Clemens Brentano's friends.   Of these the principal was a young man of great promise, — a poet and scholar.   He lectured on poetry, and strengthened the interest I already felt in German philosophy and literature. His name was Winckelmann. He died a few years later, still a young man. It was he who first distinctly taught me that the new German philosophy — in connection with which Fichte was the most celebrated living teacher, and Schelling was rising into fame — was idealism. Winckelmann urged me to study Fichte's "Wissenschaftslehre," which he said was in its elements the philosophy of Plato, Spinoza, and Berkeley.

These two days, like the preceding weeks, served as a hot-bed to me. In my letter to my brother, I noticed what then was a novelty to me : "I must not forget a curious trait of the new school. They are all poetico-metaphysical religionists. Clemens Brentano declared religion to be ' philosophy taught through mystery.' And the heading of one of Winckelmann's lectures on poetry was, ' the Virgin Mary as the ideal of female beauty and perfection.' "

Christian Brentano and myself next proceeded to visit the celebrated mine mountains of the Harz, belonging to Hanover ; and some of our Göttingen friends accompanied us a day on the road. We stayed successively at Osterode and St. Andreasberg. At this place I gratified my curiosity by descending a mine, learning thereby that it is a fatiguing and particularly uninstructive and uninteresting spectacle. Generally speaking I know no sight which so ill repays the labor. Two things have fixed themselves on my mind : first, a number of men in narrow slanting passages knocking off bits of soil mixed with metal ; and, secondly, the motion of boxes up and down perpetually. I could hardly be angry with the vulgar inscription of an English "my lord" in the album : "Descended this d——d old hole."

We spent a night on the Brocken or Blocksberg, and I ought not to forget when mentioning this famous mountain that it has been from time immemorial the seat of witchcraft ; the witches of the Blocksberg till the present age being the most illustrious in Germany. The historians assign a reasonable cause. The region of the Harz was the very last converted to Christianity, and the heathen religious rites were for the last time performed on the Blocksberg. When the country was at last subdued, troops were stationed in the principal avenues up the mountain to prevent the natives exercising unlawful and ungodly ceremonies. Some of the more zealous, however, disguised themselves in various frightful forms, came at midnight, and frightened away the superstitious soldiery.

3*

Since that time the Brocken has been in ballads and old stories the seat of "monsters, hydras, and chimeras dire."

Passing over other local matters which afforded me much pleasure, I proceed to that part of my Diary in which I say : We had this day entered the Saxony which Goethe in his "Wilhelm Meister" so significantly terms *den gebildeten aber auch bildlosen Theil von Deutschland.* We lose the play of words when we render this "the cultivated but imageless part of Germany."*

While I was staying at Frankfort I seldom ventured to speak German when I was with those who spoke either English or French ; but during this journey I made as it were a spring, and found that I was very well able to make myself understood in the language of the country.

The place at which Christian Brentano was studying, and at which I was for a time to reside, was Grimma, a small town not very far from Leipzig and on the Mulde, — a very agreeable residence for a student. It had a large gymnasium or Prince's school, one of the feeders of the Leipzig University. The mathematical teacher at this school was one Töpfer, who received Brentano into his house. The family lived in a very plain way, and I was kindly received by them.

The chief person in the town was a Mr. Riese, a large manufacturer. I had seen him at Frankfort. He was very attentive to me, and offered me the use of his house ; but I thought lodgings would for the present be preferable. My prospect was a satisfactory one. I had access to Mr. Riese's very respectable library ; such society as the town afforded was open to me, and I should have Brentano as a frequent companion in my walks.†

* Goethe's meaning is not easily understood without the context. The whole sentence is: "Er kam in den gebildeten, aber auch bildlosen Theil von Deutschland, wo es zur Verehrung des Guten und Schönen zwar nicht an Wahrheit, aber oft an Geist gebricht." Carlyle has translated this as follows: "He came into the polished but also barren part of Germany, where, in worshipping the good and the beautiful there is indeed no want of truth, but frequently a grievous want of spirit." *Bildlos* is not much used in modern literature, in fact Grimm knows only this instance from Goethe besides those which he gives from writers of the 16th and 17th centuries. The meaning according to him is *imagine carens.* Gebildet corresponds with Wahrheit, and bildlos with want of Geist. If so, Goethe meant to say that the Saxons were indeed apt to acquire knowledge from others, but were wanting in original productiveness.

† Our tour seems to be insignificant on the map, but, with all our deviations, was not less than sixty German miles, at least 300 English miles. Our expenses together nine guineas; deducting therefore what I should have paid at Frankfort, my journey has cost me only two and a half guineas. And

Of the two months passed at Grimma at this time, and of
the short period I spent there later in the year, when I took
up my quarters at the house of Mr. Riese, I will say no more
than that I was very happy, and began to read Kant, at the
recommendation of Töpfer, who was a zealous Kantianer. I
looked also into the writings of Jacobi.

In a short tour which I made by myself in order to test my
power of finding interest in solitary travel, I availed myself
of the opportunity which offered itself of visiting a Moravian
establishment at Ebersdorf; and I had a great deal of pleasure, — the pleasure of sympathizing with a very benevolent
and truly Christian society. The day on which I was there
was Sunday, and I heard three sermons in one day with less
than usual ennui, and was introduced to the well-bred,
accomplished presidentess, Fräulein Gerstendorf. Without attempting to give a detailed account of the constitution of these
Moravian institutions, I may describe them as a kind of Protestant monasteries. They are distinguished from those of the
Roman Catholics by these two striking features : First, there
is no compulsion to stay, either openly enforced by the law,
or through a vow or secret understanding binding on the conscience. Any one may leave when he pleases. Secondly,
there are no idlers, — all are workers. The unmarried live
together, and sleep in two huge apartments. Going through
these two vast dormitories I was struck by their perfect cleanliness and sweetness. The married live in apartments by
themselves. They have private property, and have few or
many comforts according to their respective means. The sermons I heard were evangelical, perhaps Calvinistic; but in
one respect contrasted very advantageously with our English
orthodoxy. Little importance seemed to be attached to doctrine. I heard nothing about belief, but a great deal about
love. They had such set phrases as "the love of the Lord,"
"the faith of the heart." I would add that this is in perfect
correspondence with Goethe's confessions of a beautiful soul
in " Wilhelm Meister "; and, if the bringing together of things
so unlike may be permitted, my own dear mother's written
Experience when she was received into the Wattisfield church,
in which there is nothing about theological opinions, but

when it is considered that we included in our tour one of the most fashionable
and famous resident towns, and one of the celebrated districts of Germany, it
must be allowed that travelling is for me a cheap pleasure. Thanks to my
good health and sound limbs, I hope to see a great part of Germany and
France at a trifling expense. — H. C. R.'s *Journal.*

much about love, a consciousness of guilt, &c.   It occurred to
me that this institution seemed to come nearer to an apostolic
body than any I had ever seen, and that the Gospel age
seems to have had no presentiment of the legal and political
establishment of Christianity, but to have contemplated
rather a multiplication of brotherhoods resembling these of
the Herrnhuter. The founders named their first establishment in Moravia Herrnhut, i. e. the Lord's heed or guard.*

The churchyard, to which the kind-hearted attendant who
showed me about the place took me, was very prettily ornamented with shrubs and flowers, and I was much struck by
the unfeigned joy with which he talked of death, as, with a
childlike simplicity and almost gayety, he jumped on the grave
in which the remains of his wife had been recently laid.
Fräulein Gerstendorf was a woman of ability, exemplifying
the compatibility of practical wisdom with a devout spirit.

At Schneeberg I fell in with Anton Wall's "Amatonda," a
fairy tale which much delighted me.†

At Chemnitz I met with a Welshman, whose history interested me. He was by trade a watchmaker, living at Holy-
well, where he had great difficulty in supporting his wife and
three children ; but he was a mechanic and understood the
steam-engine. Graf —— was then travelling for the Elector
of Saxony, and made the man an offer of a fair stipend if he
would leave his country. " I know," said he, " that if I were
to attempt to go back to England, I should be hanged ; but I
do not want to go. I am at the head of a manufactory here,
and my employer gives me £ 200 per annum, besides perqui-
sites. My wife and children are here. Besides, the Elector
has given me a bond for £ 100 per annum during my life.
The only condition is that I remain in the country. I need do
nothing ; I may spend my time in a public-house if I like ;
I should still be entitled to my hundred a year." He told me
of several persons who were paid for living in the country,
with a perfect freedom of action.

On the day on which I expected to reach Grimma an agreeable incident detained me at Colditz. It was late in the
evening when I fell in with a parish clergyman, who having
found that I was what is here called an English Gelehrter,
and bound for Grimma, invited me to take a bed at his par-

---

* The Colony settled at the foot of the Hutberg, or pasture hill. The name
has a double meaning, — Hut signifying "guard" as well as "a place where
flocks are guarded."

† This tale was afterwards translated by Mr. Robinson.

sonage. He had a name singularly in contrast with his
character, — Hildebrand ; for he was very liberal in his opinions, and very anti-church in his tastes. We had many hours'
talk on subjects equally interesting to him and to me. He gave
me an account of the state of religious opinion among the
Saxon, i. e. Lutheran clergy. He professed himself to be a
believer in miracles, but evidently had no unfriendly feeling
towards the free-thinkers, whom he called *Naturalisten*, but
who are now better known under the name of Rationalists.
He declared that their ablest men were Socinians, if not
Naturalists. On my saying that Michaelis's "Introduction to
the New Testament" had been translated into English, he
said : "That work is already forgotten here ; we have a more
learned commentary in the work of Paulus." On my inquiring whether the clergy had no tests, "O yes," he replied,
"we affirm our belief in the symbolical books ; but we have
a very convenient saving-clause 'as far as they are not contradictory to the word of God.' The fact is, we pay very little attention to the old orthodox doctrines, but dare not
preach against them. We say nothing about them." This I
believe to be true. I recollect relating to my host the retort
which Wilkes is said to have made to a Roman Catholic, who
had asked, "Where was your religion before Luther ?" The
answer was, "Where were your hands before you washed
them ?" Hildebrand said that that very retort is to be found
in one of the pamphlets published in Germany at the time
of the Reformation.

During my tour I met with a young Saxon nobleman, Herr
von Carlowitz, a pupil of the Fürsten-Schule, who invited me
to accompany him to his mother's house. This plan left me
so little time at Grimma that I was barely able to write a few
letters and show myself to my friends.

Falkenstein, the seat of young Carlowitz's mother, was only
a walk of about four leagues. As we were not expected, we
found no one but the servants in the house. In the evening,
however, came my lady, with friends, who were staying with
her, and I had a specimen of the proverbial stiffness of the
Saxon nobility. She was a stately dame, and had but a short
time back been beautiful ; she was rich, and was addressed
with formal respect by all about her. At night on taking
leave every one kissed her hand, excepting myself; and I
omitted the ceremony through my ignorance, and gave offence. At supper grace was said in verse.

My intention was to proceed to Dresden and Prague, and I reached the former place after two more nights on the way. I was delighted with the *coup d'œil* from the bridge, including noble edifices, and the views up and down the river. There was also a stillness which soothed me. I will copy a remark or two I made at the time respecting the impression made on me by Dresden : " One sees more of elegance and the amusing formality of innocent aristocracy, than of the luxury of upstart wealth. One is neither oppressed by great. ness, nor confounded by bustle. Many an Excellency rides in a carriage which in London would be thought a shabby hackney-coach ; and the distinctions of rank are announced by formal appendages, — sword, big wig, &c., not costly attire.

" The most famous of the sights of Dresden is the Grüne Gewölbe, or Green Vaults, the most illustrious warehouse of jewelry and other toys in the world. Augustus, the lavish and the strong king of Poland, was the founder of this collection, consisting of all sorts of things wrought in ivory and gold, vessels of every form. I saw these in company with a French lady and her husband. Her raptures rose to something like hysterics.

" The picture gallery was the first of great excellence I had ever seen. It contains *the* picture, which now that I have seen all that Rome and Florence, Naples, Venice, and Paris have to exhibit, I still look back upon as the one which has afforded me the highest delight, — the Madonna di San Sisto, or Vierge aux Anges. When I first saw it, I exclaimed unintentionally, ' Looking at this, it is possible to believe the Immaculate Conception.' The Roman Catholic *custode* who was present looked offended, with no reason. I possess a fine copy of Müller's engraving. There are few pictures for which I would exchange it.*

" One other source of especial pleasure at Dresden was an almost daily visit to the Catholic chapel, for church music (though I am insensible to ordinary music) I can enjoy."

I did not omit to make an excursion, occupying a day, to Pillnitz, which has a castle of doubtful or disputed celebrity ;

* This copy of Müller's engraving was given by Mr. Robinson's will to E. W. Field.

This picture, unlike all Raphael's other altar-pieces, is painted on canvas, which gave rise to an opinion, strongly contested by Professor Hübner, Keeper of the Gallery at Dresden, that it was originally intended to serve as a Processional Banner. The picture was purchased by Augustus, King of Poland and Elector of Saxony, from the monks of the church of San Sisto, at Piacenza, in 1754, for about £ 10,000. — G. S.

it being still a question whether the treaty which bears the name of Pillnitz was ever entered into among the great powers in 1792 to partition France.

At the distance of a few miles from Dresden is a knot of little valleys, known by the name of the Saxon Switzerland. This district is about fifteen miles in length and two or three broad, and it affords in miniature every variety of mountain and valley scenery. The first place I came to, the little town of Pirna, detained me by its attractions. I had parted from my young companion, and was left here to myself in a country so beautiful, and in an inn so comfortable, that I stayed four days. One of the largest rocks in this neighborhood is the insulated and famous Königstein. It is said to have been rendered impregnable. Certainly it has never been taken. During the long French possession of Germany, Buonaparte could never obtain possession of this fortress from the otherwise obsequious King of Saxony, who retained it as a place of deposit for his green-vault and other treasures. It is too small to hold a large garrison, and therefore might be spared by Buonaparte. Amidst the recesses of a mountain forest is a vast mass of rocks, some eighty feet in height, with a natural cavity or hollow called the Kuhstall (Cowstall), and which, according to the legendary tales, was a place of refuge for the Saxon peasants from the imperial troops during the Seven Years' War. It might well be so now, for the brushwood and stunted trees would render the passage of troops impossible. This wild and desolate spot I crossed; and when I found myself again in the beautiful valley of the Elbe, I was in Bohemia.

The difference between a Roman Catholic country and that I had hitherto been in was apparent at once in the salutation of the peasantry. Every one who met me muttered, " Gelobt sei Jesus Christus " (Praised be Jesus Christ). To which I invariably answered, " In Ewigkeit " (To eternity). " Amen " was the rejoinder. Then the ordinary talk about weather or inquiry about roads followed. Had I not responded like a good Christian, I should have had no other greeting. The first night I slept at Teschen, in a small house with worthy people, and my first evening in Bohemia is worth recording. I have often told the story. In a large kitchen lay a bedridden old woman near the fire. She began questioning me : " Are you a Christian ? " — " Yes." — " A Catholic Christian ? " The landlord came up : " Don't trouble the gentleman with

questions ; you know he is an Englishman, and cannot be *such*
a Christian as we are." — " I know only one sort of Christian,"
muttered she. " Why, mother ! don't you know the priest
says it is the duty of everybody to remain of the religion they
are born in ? " This looked like indifference at least, and I got
into talk with him. I asked him about the Hussites. " O,
they are the most loyal and peaceable of all our people." —
" It did not use to be so." — " O no ! they were always
breeding disturbances, but the Emperor Joseph put an end to
that. Their priests were very poor and lived on the peasants ;
one man gave them a breakfast, another a dinner, another a
bed ; and so they went from house to house, beggars and pau-
pers. When the emperor came to Prague to be crowned,
among the decrees which he issued the first day was one that
the Hussite priests should be allowed the same pay as the
lowest order of the Catholic clergy. And since then we have
never had a disturbance in the country." I thought then,
and have often said, that had I ever been in the House of
Commons I would have related this as an instructive lesson
on the Irish priest question.

Next day I dined at Aussig. There I fell in with a traveller who, finding I was going to the watering-place Teplitz,
recommended me to a private lodging at the house of an
honest shoemaker. In the afternoon I was there.

Teplitz is a small but beautiful watering-place, in which is a
chateau, occupied at the time by the Prince de Ligne, who is
known as the friend of Madame de Staël. In this very agreeable little spot I took up my residence for six days. Here
I found a circulating library (prohibited in other Bohemian
towns), and in the beautiful country numberless walks. The
season for drinking the waters was over, so that I found myself quite in retirement ; but the residence of the Prince
afforded me an unexpected pleasure the day after my arrival.
I was told that there was an amateur theatre, at which the
Herrschaften, the noble inhabitants of the chateau, performed ;
and to which any one decently dressed might go, — the nobles
in the pit below, the citizens in the gallery above. I presented myself at the door of the pit. " Sind Sie adelig, mein
Herr ? " (Are you noble ?) said the doorkeeper. " I am English," I said, " and all English are noble." — " I know it, sir,"
he replied, and opened the door to me. This I said, not
meaning a joke, for everywhere in Germany English travellers
are treated as if they were noble, even at the small courts,

where there is no ambassador. No inquiry is made about birth, title, or place.

At the theatre a French comedy was acted, as it seemed to me with perfect good-breeding. The little I saw in this performance of the Princess and the rest of the family was in harmony with the character they possess as being among the most amiable and respectable of the higher French noblesse.

I lived a week of great enjoyment, — a sort of hermit's life. My breakfast consisted of grapes and cream, — and certainly I never lived at so little cost. I soon formed an acquaintance with a young man — a Herr von Schall — who, like myself, seemed to have nothing to do. With him I spent my days in walking. In the course of talk he used the expression " one of my subjects " (Unterthan). " Unterthan ? " I exclaimed ; " why, you are not a sovereign ? " — " Yes, I am," he said ; and then he explained that he was a knight. I thought he had been a Suabian knight, but my journal calls him a Silesian. According to the now-abolished old German constitution these knights were sovereigns, though they might be very poor. They had the power of appointing judges, in whom was the prerogative of life and death, — a jurisdiction the knights could not personally exercise. I did not stand in any awe of my new companion, nor did he claim any deference on account of his princely dignity. He was a light-hearted young man, as may be seen by an anecdote he told me of himself. A few weeks before I met him, he had the misfortune, on his way to Teplitz, to be robbed of his purse. He was forced to take his portmanteau on his back and bring it to Teplitz, selling a pair of stockings on the road, in order to get food. Arrived here, and not expecting a remittance for some time, he announced himself as a painter, being an amateur artist. He waited on Count Brühl with his papers and testimonials, and solicited employment. The Count gave him a miniature to copy ; this was finished in a day and a half, and three ducats paid for it. He went home, dressed, and in the evening went to a ball, where he met his employer the Count. Von Schall spent two ducats that evening, — worked two days longer, and earned four ducats more. He then received a remittance from home, shut up his portfolio, told his story to everybody, the ladies he danced with included, and figured away as one of the beaux of the season.

When I left Teplitz and my worthy host and hostess, Von Schall accompanied me over a mountain till we came within

E

sight of Lobositz and Leitmeritz, when I entered the plains of
Bohemia.   I slept the first night at Budin, a poor little town ;
but I met there with a sort of adventure which I have often
looked back upon with pleasure.

I was inquiring in the street for a circulating library, — an
idle inquiry, by the by, — when a very handsome young Jew
came up and offered me a book for the evening.   He accompanied me to the inn, and was my very agreeable companion,
but would not suffer me to treat him.   He had a fine manly
expression, and talked with great freedom, which I encouraged
by speaking of Moses Mendelssohn and Lessing, whom he
naturally held in reverence.   He seemed to have a taste for
free-thinking books ; and when I remarked that these books,
if they were successful against Christianity, must be still more
so against Judaism, he was embarrassed.   He professed to hold
Jesus Christ in the highest respect, but would not allow that
he had ever claimed to be the Messiah.   " Moses," he said,
" if his claim to inspiration be waived, must still be allowed to
be one of the greatest of men."   On my asking whether the
odium frequently cast on the Jews operated as a temptation
to embrace Christianity, he replied : " You forget that we are
brought up to that, and that we are trained to return contempt
with hatred.   All those I love are Jews.   Were I to go over
to your church, I should become an object of hatred and contempt to all I love.'   My father and mother would die of
shame ; and, after all, by the respectable Christians converted
Jews are more despised than those who remain firm.   Fortune
has made me what I am, and whatever difficulties my religion
may have I know of none better."   He said he did not believe
there was anything miraculous in the Israelites' passage of the
Red Sea.   This young man lent me the continuation of " Nathan der Weise."   The title of this continuation is " The
Monk of Lebanon," and its object to counteract the effect of
Lessing's work.

Next day eight hours' hard walking brought me to Prague,
— an imposing city, ancient and stately, containing 70,000 inhabitants.   I have seldom seen a spot so striking as the bridge
over the Moldau, with its thirty high statues.   The view from
this bridge of the cathedral on the hill is exceedingly fine.
But, on the whole, I found little to detain me at Prague.
Contrasting its churches with those at Dresden, I wrote to
my brother : " The nine paintings in the Chapel at Dresden
delight the eye, — the hundreds at Prague only oppress the

senses, — the more so, as there is no classification or harmony
in their arrangement.   Old paintings, curious perhaps for their
antiquity, are paired with flashy pieces glaring with varnish.
A colossal statue stands by the side of a rotten relic ; in one
place there was a complete skeleton, the skull covered with
satin, and the ribs adorned with crimson ribbon and tinsel.

<blockquote>' One would not sure look frightful when one's dead.'</blockquote>

Still more offensive were a long row of rotten teeth.   Not all
the objects, however, were of this class.   At the high altar in
St. Nicolai Church, I saw four colossal statues, not less than
fourteen feet high.   They impressed me solemnly, and I recollected the opinion expressed by Wieland, that size was probably the great charm which rendered so illustrious the Jupiter
of Phidias."

On my way back to Pirna I was amused by the slyness of an
inscription on a newly built wall.   It was in verse, and its import as follows : " This house is in the hand of God.   In the
year 1793 was the wall raised ; and if God will turn my
heart to it, and my father-in-law will advance the needful, I
will cover it with tiles."

I found I had still unseen beauties to explore in the Saxon
Switzerland.   Hohnstein I thought among the finest objects
of this very delightful country.

On the last day of my tour, when I was at Hubertsburg, I
met a party of show-folk and pedlers, and was treated both by
them and the landlord as if I were one of them.   A few
months before I had dined at the same inn, as a gentleman
visitor to the chateau.   Then my dinner cost me 1 s. 2 d. ;
now I paid for my afternoon luncheon, supper, bed, and breakfast, 1 s. 9 d., — a difference more agreeable to my pocket than
flattering to my vanity.   But travelling on foot, I found that
my journey, as a whole, cost me only a trifle more than I paid
for my ordinary board and lodging at Frankfort.

With respect to the society in this district — the cultivation
and manners of the higher classes — I have every reason to
speak favorably.   As far as I myself am concerned, I never
before experienced from strangers so much civility ; and my
external appearance was certainly not inviting, for I went as
usual in black.   My coat, which I brought with me from England, had necessarily lost much of its original brightness ; and
it was rather eclipsed than set off by velvet pantaloons and
gaiters, which I wore out of convenience, though they attracted

now and then a smile from the honest villagers. I met uniformly with civil treatment in the public-houses, where I was
always in high spirits, and by my gayety generally gained the
good-will of my host and his other guests.

T. R. TO H. C. R.

BURY, October 20, 1801.

. . . . The Peace is an event which has excited a tumult of
joy such as I never before saw equalled. The effect was the
stronger as the event was totally unexpected, — indeed, for two
or three days preceding, it was totally despaired of. The
Funds were falling, and the expectation of an invasion was
very general. All parties are therefore willing to give the
Ministry great credit for the secrecy with which they conducted the negotiation. The demonstrations of joy have risen
almost to madness. Illuminations have been general throughout the kingdom, and in London and some other places have
been repeated several times. Last Friday we illuminated at
Bury.

The papers will inform you of the reception which was given
by the London populace to the French general who brought
over the ratification of the preliminaries. It is said that " Long
live Buonaparte ! " was repeatedly cried in the streets ; and
among the transparencies exhibited in London his portrait was
shown with this inscription : " The Saviour of *the World.*"
Indeed it is curious to observe the change of style in the government newspapers. The " Corsican adventurer," " the atheistical usurper," is now " the august hero," " the restorer of
public order," &c. &c. ; in fact, everything that is great and
good. It reminds one of the transformation in a pantomime,
where a devil is suddenly converted into an angel. The blessings of peace begin already to be felt. An abundant harvest
promised a considerable reduction in the price of provisions,
but the fall in corn has been rapid beyond example. In the
course of about eight or ten weeks wheat has fallen in our
market from 92 *s.* to 30 *s.* the coomb, and it is expected to sink
lower. . . . .

On my return to Grimma, at the beginning of November, I
became an inmate in the house of Mr. Riese ; and there I remained during the winter. I spent my time pleasantly, partly
in reading, and partly with friends. The best society of the

place was freely open to me ; and at about this period I became acquainted with a very remarkable person, of whom there is an account in the " Conversations-Lexicon," and to whom I became indebted for a great pleasure. His name was Seume, the son of a poor woman who kept a public-house near Leipzig. She meant to make her boy a parson, as he was clever ; but he was wild, and after making some progress in his studies, left his books and took up a musket. He served in the American war as a private, and was afterwards a non-commissioned officer among the Hessians. He then went to the West Indies, and at length entered the Russian service, — was lieutenant under Suwarrow, and was present at the infamous storming and sacking of Praga, near Warsaw. Meanwhile he pursued his studies, and became occasionally a tutor to young noblemen. For some years he corrected the press at Leipzig. He also printed some volumes of poetry, and gave lessons in Greek, English, &c. He knew almost all the European languages. His countenance was very striking. Herder remarked to me that he had the physiognomy of a Greek philosopher. With Seume I was to pay a visit to Weimar and Jena. At Leipzig we were joined by Schnorr, whose son has since attained great eminence as a painter. The father was, I believe, the master of the government drawing-school at Weimar. We left Grimma on November 17th, and on the 19th I visited the most famous of the Fürsten-Schulen. The establishment had 150 scholars. The only particular I thought worthy of notice and imitation was a body of poor students called *collaborateurs,* and who assist the more wealthy but less advanced students, receiving for their trouble a salary of 200 dollars.

We arrived late the same day at the Eagle Hotel, Weimar ; and the two next days belong to the most interesting in all my life. They were devoted to visits to the most eminent men of their age and country.

. Our first call was at the house of the aged Wieland. The course of my late reading had not led me to form terrifying ideas of his mental greatness, though as a *littérateur* he is one of the first writers of his country. He is not less universally read and admired in Germany than Voltaire was in France. His works amount to more than fifty volumes, all written for the many. He resembles the French wit in the lightness of his philosophy, in the wantonness of his muse (though it is by no means so gross), and in the exquisite felicity of his style. But he surpasses Voltaire in learning, if not in philosophy ; for

Wieland is no school-philosopher, — he belongs to the sensual school of Locke. And his favorite opinions are those of the common-sense, sceptical school. He is a sworn foe to the Kantian metaphysics, and indeed to all others. In his writings, as in his person and manners, he is a perfect gentleman. He received us with the courteous dignity of a sage, who accepted without *hauteur* the homage of his admirers. I have already printed an account of this my first and subsequent interviews with him in a note to Mrs. Austin's "Characteristics of Goethe." * I shall in substance repeat what I have there said. He had already shrunk into the old man. His pale and delicate countenance was plain, and had something of the satyr in it. He wore a black skull-cap. The marble bust by Schadow, which I have the good fortune to possess, is an exact resemblance of him. I ventured to refer to his philosophical writings, and especially to his "Agathodämon," which gives but a sad view of Christianity and its influence on mankind. In this book he draws a parallel between Jesus Christ and Apollonius of Tyana, whom he considers as alike generous enthusiasts, willing to make use of superstition in order to teach a beneficent morality. I ventured to express my regret at the mournful conclusions at which he had arrived. He admitted that his hopes of any great improvement in mankind were faint.

To refer to another subject, the best if not the only advantage which in his judgment may be expected from the French Revolution is the promotion of the fine arts and the sciences ; for he holds the French nation absolutely incapable of forming a Republic. He vindicated the administration of Buonaparte, and did not censure the restoration of the Roman Catholic Church. What he said on this point is worth reporting : " We Protestants allow ourselves a great deal of injustice and habitual falsehood towards the Catholics. We forget that Roman Catholicism is, after all, real Christianity, and in my judgment preferable to the motley things produced by the *soi-disant* Reformation."

Speaking further of the Reformation, Wieland asserted that it had been an evil and not a good ; it had retarded the progress of philosophy for centuries. There were some wise men among the Italians who, if they had been permitted, would have effected a salutary reform. Luther ruined everything by making the people a party to what ought to have been left to the

* Vol. II. p. 227.

scholars. , Had he not come forward with his furious knock-down attacks on the Church, and excited a succession of horrible wars in Europe, liberty, science, and humanity would have slowly made their way. Melanchthon and Erasmus were on the right road, but the violence of the age was triumphant. It is needless to add that Wieland is a supporter of national religion.

He spoke with great feeling of his wife, who had died a few weeks before. " I help myself with illusions," he said ; " he whom I have once loved never dies to me. He is absent only from my outward senses; and that to be sure is painful. My wife was my good angel for thirty-five years. I am no longer young, — the recollection of her will never be weakened." He spoke in a faint half-whisper, as from the bottom of his throat.

My next call was on Böttiger, — a very laborious boot-maker and honest fagging scholar, noted for his courtesy to strangers, of which I both now and afterwards had the benefit. He had a florid complexion, and seemed to be in the possession of rustic health.

My companions then took me to Professor Meyer, who introduced us into the presence of Goethe, — the great man, the first sight of whom may well form an epoch in the life of any one who has devoted himself seriously to the pursuit of poetry or philosophy.

I had said to Seume that I wished to *speak* with Wieland, and *look* at Goethe, — and I literally and exactly had my desire. My sense of his greatness was such that, had the opportunity offered, I think I should have been incapable of entering into conversation with him ; but as it was, I was allowed to gaze on him in silence. Goethe lived in a large and handsome house, — that is, for Weimar. Before the door of his study was marked in mosaic, SALVE. On our entrance he rose, and with rather a cool and distant air beckoned to us to take seats. As he fixed his burning eye on Seume, who took the lead, I had his profile before me, and this was the case during the whole of our twenty minutes' stay. He was then about fifty-two years of age, and was beginning to be corpulent. He was, I think, one of the most oppressively handsome men I ever saw. My feeling of awe was heightened by an accident. The last play which I had seen in England was " Measure for Measure," in which one of the most remarkable moments was when Kemble (the Duke), disguised as a monk, had his hood pulled off by Lucio. On this, Kemble, with an expression of wonderful dignity, ascended the throne and delivered judgment on the wrongdoers.

Goethe sat in precisely the same attitude, and I had precisely the same view of his side-face. The conversation was quite insignificant. My companions talked about themselves, — Seume about his youth of adversity and strange adventures. Goethe smiled, with, as I thought, the benignity of condescension. When we were dismissed, and I was in the open air, I felt as if a weight were removed from my breast, and exclaimed, " Gott sei Dank ! " Before long I saw him under more favorable auspices ; but of that hereafter.

Goethe has been often reproached for his *hauteur,* and Bürger made an epigram which the enviers and revilers of the great man were fond of repeating. I believe, however, that this demeanor was necessary in self-defence. It was his only protection against the intrusion which would otherwise have robbed him and the world of a large portion of his life.

H. C. R. to T. R.

Goethe's " Iphigenia in Tauris " is perhaps the most perfect drama ever composed. I have read it three times within a month, and believe it has not a faulty line. W. Taylor has translated it. Do lay out half a crown on my judgment, — fancy Mrs. Siddons to be Iphigenia, — and you will feel that she is the most perfect ideal of the female character ever conceived, rivalling in that point of view even Milton's Eve. You will admire the solemn repose, the celestial tranquillity of her character, as well as of the events themselves ; and this is, in my mind, the characteristic of Goethe. His better and more perfect works are without disorder and tumult, — they resemble Claude Lorraine's landscapes and Raphael's historical pieces. Goethe's Songs and Ballads and Elegies all have the same character ; his Ballads in particular have a wildness of fancy which is fascinating, but without turbulence. No hurry-scurry, as in Bürger's " Leonora." Apropos, I believe you will find in Monk Lewis a translation of a ballad called the " Erl-King," — hunt for it and read it. Goethe knows his own worth. In the whole compass of his works I believe not a single preface, or an article in which he speaks of himself, is to be found, — it is enough that his works are there. . . . .

The same evening I had an introduction to one who in any place but Weimar would have held the first rank, and who in his person and bearing impressed every one with the feeling that he belonged to the highest class of men. This was Herder. The interview was, if possible, more insignificant than that with Goethe, — partly, perhaps, on account of my being introduced at the same time with a distinguished publicist, to use the German term, the eminent political writer and statesman Friedrich Gentz, the translator of Burke on the French Revolution, author of several Austrian state papers against France, and the great literary advocate of the Austrian cause. I naturally kept in the background, contenting myself with delivering a letter which Madame de la Roche had given me. But Herder sent for me next day. He had a fine clerical figure, and reminded me of Dr. Geddes. His expression was one of great earnestness. Though he filled the highest ecclesiastical office the little state of Weimar afforded, yet the greatness of Goethe seemed to throw him into the shade ; and this, perhaps, prevented him from appreciating Goethe's genius. For the present I shall content myself with saying that we had some controversial talk, — I not assenting to his contemptuous judgment of the English lyric poets, and he declaring the infinite superiority of Klopstock's Odes to all that Gray and Collins had ever written. We talked also about our English philosophers, and he gave me a shake of the hand for my praise of Hartley. Herder was a partisan of Locke.

Before I left Weimar I called on the one other great poet, Schiller, of whom unhappily I have as little to say as of the others. Indeed we were with him but a few minutes. I had just time to mention Coleridge's translation of Wallenstein, of which he seemed to have a high opinion. The translator was a man of genius, he said, but had made some ridiculous mistakes. Schiller had a wild expression and a sickly look ; and his manners were those of one who is not at his ease. There was in him a mixture of the wildness of genius and the awkwardness of the student. His features were large and irregular.

On Saturday night we went to the theatre, where I saw " Wallensteins Tod " performed in the presence of the author. Schlegel somewhere says : " Germany has two national theatres, — Vienna with a public of 50,000 spectators, Weimar with a public of 50." The theatre was at this time unique ; its managers were Goethe and Schiller, who exhibited there the works which were to become standards and models of dramatic literature. Schiller had his seat near the ducal box, Goethe an arm-chair in the centre of the first row of the pit. In general, theatres, whatever their size and beauty may be, are after all mere places where people, instead of sitting to enjoy themselves at their ease, are crowded together to see something at a distance, and it is considered a sort of infringement on the rights of others to take knee or elbow room. Here, on the contrary, I found myself in an elegant apartment, so lightly and classically adorned, and so free and easy in its aspect, that I almost forgot where I was. In the pit the seats are all numbered, each person has his own, and each seat has arms. The single row of boxes is supported by elegant pillars, under which the pit loungers stroll at pleasure. The boxes have no division except in front. They are adorned, too, by elegant pillars, and are open below ; instead of the boards commonly placed in front are elegant iron palisades. There are no fixed seats, only chairs, all of which, in front, are occupied by ladies. The gentlemen go into the pit when they do not, as courteous cavaliers, wait behind the chairs of their fair friends. The box in front is occupied by the Duke and Duchess with their suite, of course without the dull formality attending a Royal presence at Drury Lane. I beheld Schiller a great part of the evening leaning over the ducal box and chatting with the family. In the performance of this evening, I was pleased with Graff as the representative of the hero, and with Mademoiselle Jagermann as Thekla. She was a graceful and beautiful creature, the first actress of the company.

One other noted character we visited, — the one who, according to William Taylor of Norwich, was the greatest of all. This was August von Kotzebue, the very popular dramatist, whose singular fate it was to live at variance with the great poets of his country while he was the idol of the mob. He was at one time (about this time and a little later) a favorite in all Europe. One of his plays, " The Stranger," I have seen acted in German, English, Spanish, French, and I believe also Italian. He was the pensioner of Prussia, Austria, and Russia. The odium produced by this circumstance, and the imputation of being a spy, are assigned as the cause of his assassination by a student of Jena a few years after our visit. He was living, like Goethe, in a large house and in style. I drank tea with him, and found him a lively little man with small black eyes. He had the manners of a *petit maître*. He was a married man with a large family, and seemed to be not without the domestic feelings which he has so successfully painted in his works. We were ushered through a suite of rooms by a man-servant, and found Mr. President in state. Nor is it unworthy of remark that his house had thirty-seven windows in front. Indeed, the comfortable style in which all the poets I have mentioned lived would make me imagine the poet's fate must be singularly good in Germany, if I did not recollect that those I saw were the prime and elect of the German geniuses, — the favorites and idols of their nation. Wieland and Goethe both gained a fortune by their writings, and Schiller supported himself entirely by his pen.

Weimar * is an insignificant little town, without an object of beauty or taste but its park ; and even that among parks has no great excellence. It has been immortalized by many a passage in Goethe's poems. His house will no doubt be preserved for the sake of its associations, and so probably will be the residences of the other chief poets. These, alas, have all passed away ! †

On Sunday, amid snow and rain and wind, we left the seat of the Muses for the school of the philosophers, — Weimar for Jena. The University at the latter place has all the advantage of site, lying in a beautiful valley. The town itself, as approached from Weimar, looked interesting and promising as we descended the winding road called the Snake, but within it is a beggarly place. I at once made use of a strange letter of introduction given me at Göttingen by Winckelmann to a student here, — a character, — one Kölle, who, having passed through the ordinary years of study, continued to live here at the least possible expense, sauntering his time away, but by his conversation amusing and instructing others. He received me very cordially, though my introduction consisted only of my name with some verses from Goethe. Kölle took me to a concert-room, where I saw the students in genteeler trim than I had seen before. His enthusiastic talk about the poets and philosophers awakened in me the desire, which was afterwards gratified, of residing among them. We soon left Jena, and my companions, Seume and Schnorr, set out on that "Spaziergang nach Syrakus," an account of which was published. Seume in the first sentence says : " A few kind friends accompanied us a short distance." I was one of those friends.

---

* A very interesting and detailed description of Weimar as it appeared in the eighteenth century will be found in G. H. Lewes's " Life of Goethe," Vol. I. p. 311.

† Written in 1847.

CHAPTER VI.

GERMANY.—1802.

I FINALLY left Grimma on May 4, 1802. Brentano had finished his preparatory studies for the University, and wished me to accompany him to Frankfort. We intended to have gone thither by Carlsbad, but on my applying to Mr. Elliott for a certificate that I was an Englishman, he refused it very civilly on the ground that I had not a single letter or paper to corroborate my declaration. He said he had no doubt that I was what I declared myself to be, and he would speak in my behalf to the proper authorities. But Brentano objected to the delay, and we therefore changed our route, and took the opportunity of visiting some romantic scenes among the Fichtelgebirge, or Fir Mountains, the birthplace of Jean Paul Richter. Here are some very curious rocks, well known and celebrated by travellers in search of the picturesque. Houses of entertainment have been erected, and are adorned with arbors, which are furnished with inscriptions. On a lofty rock, under which there is a rich spring, there are two hexameters, which I thus translated : —

"Here from the rock's deep recesses, the nymph of the fount pours her
    treasures ;
  Learn, O man, so to give, and so to conceal, too, the giver."

On our arrival at Ansbach, which had recently been brought under the dominion of Prussia, we found in the peasantry an antipathy to the new government, on account of their becoming subject to military conscription, from which the subjects of the ecclesiastical states and of the small German princes were free. I could not but notice that the peasants under the ecclesiastical princes were unquestionably, in general, in a far better condition than those under the secular Protestant princes. The Calvinists and Lutherans had certainly the advantage in intelligence, but they had worse bread and less meat than their superstitious brethren, who doffed the hat at the wayside shrines and repeated the Pater Noster and Ave Maria three times a day. It was my observation on this and subsequent occasions that the peasantry in the bishoprics of Bamberg and Würzburg appeared to be in a state of more ease and comfort

than any I saw in Germany, excepting, perhaps, the Saxon
peasants in the Mine mountains.

In passing through the University town of Erlangen, I was
pleased with the gentlemanly appearance of the students,
though they had not the dashing impudence of the Cantabs or
Oxonians. We supped at the head inn, where there were
about fifty young men. Our polite host placed me by the side
of Professor Abicht, and I was again struck by the concurrence
of opinion among the German philosophers as to the transcendent genius of Shakespeare, Goethe, and Dante, — the triple
glory of modern poetry, and by the diversity of opinion as to
the great principles of metaphysics. Abicht was the first
German whom I had heard avow belief in Priestleyan necessity.

I also visited Nuremberg, famous for the manufactory of
toys ; and itself one of the most curious and national of cities.
On the morning after our arrival, I arose early and walked out
of the gates, and on my return was arrested by the guard ;
who ordered me to accompany him to the Governor. I observed that he carried some irons in his hand. The Governor
received me courteously, examined my pass, asked me a few
questions, and finding I was at the principal inn, dismissed me
with the assurance that he was satisfied that I was an Ehren-
mann (as we should say, a gentleman) ; "though," he added,
"the sentinel was not to blame." In the course of the day he
sent a powdered lackey to me with the message that he hoped
I should not think worse of the city for what had happened.
I asked the servant to explain the cause of my arrest, and he
showed me a hue and cry after a merchant who had become a
fraudulent bankrupt and fled. The *signalement* stated that
the fugitive had on pantaloons and cloth gaiters !

At Bischoffsheim, where Brentano had been at school, I was
amused by the cordial simplicity with which the old women
greeted him whom they had known as "little Christian" ; one
old woman exclaiming perpetually, "O thou holy Mother of
God ! O thou holy Antonius of Padua !" Another good
creature said she had never forgotten to pray for him, but now
that he had visited her, she would do it ten times oftener. I
could not but notice that Catholic piety seemed more lively as
well as more poetical than Calvinistic. I saw here in a poor
cottage an edifying book, which delighted me by the beautiful
simplicity of its style. It was entitled "Gnadenbilder"
(Grace-working Images), and was a collection of tales of mira-

cles wrought by images. The facts were briefly stated, with
no assertion of their truth, and no dogma or imprecation
against unbelievers ; and each tale had its prayer. The prayers
addressed to the Virgin were in a style of naïve and simple
affection, quite touching ; such as, " O thou chaste Dove,
who feddest with holy crumbs the heavenly Babe ! " — " O
thou pure Swan, who sailest on the lake of Divine Grace ! " —
" O thou Arch of triumph, through which alone the Lord of
Glory was permitted to pass ! " Brentano afterwards became a
zealous Romanist, and perhaps the circumstances of his early
education had something to do with this change.

In a certain sense, many of us mutilate the mind and render it impotent, for there is in the nature of man an irresistible tendency to religion ; it is founded in our wants and
passions, in the extent of our faculties, in the quality of mind
itself. Akenside's description of the *untired soul* darting
from world to world is a noble image of the restless longing
of the mind after God and immortality. The stronger his
sensibility, the more exalted his imagination, the more pious
will every man be. And in this inherent and essential quality
of our minds can we alone account for the various absurd and
demonstrably false dogmas believed so honestly and zealously
by some. Men run headlong into superstition in the same
way as young boys and girls run into matrimony.

On reaching Frankfort I took up my abode there for a short
time, and enjoyed the renewal of the society of the Servieres,
the Brentanos, and other former friends. The only incident I
have to mention is, that once or twice I was in the company
of Frau Rathinn Goethe,* who is almost an historic character
through the supreme eminence of her son. She had the mien
and deportment of a strong person. This impression of her is
confirmed by the anecdotes related of her in the " Briefwechsel
von Goethe mit einem Kinde," and indeed by every account
of her. She spoke of her son with satisfaction and pride. In
the course of her conversation she remarked, that Werter is
not in the beginning the Werter of the end, and that it is
only in the latter part of the work he may be said to represent Jerusalem, — a young man who really killed himself because he received an affront in public. She spoke also of the
origin of " Götz von Berlichingen." Her son came home one
evening in high spirits, saying, " O mother, I have found
such a book in the public library, and I will make a play of

* Known under the appellation of *Frau Rath* Goethe in German literature.

it ! What great eyes the Philistines will make at the Knight with the Iron-hand ! That's glorious, — the Iron-hand ! "

H. C. R. to T. R.

A few days since I had the pleasure of conversing with F. Schlegel, one of the first living poets, and a great Æsthetiker; he is the brother of the translator of Shakespeare. He seemed much pleased with one or two pieces by Wordsworth. We talked of our English poets. He holds Spenser to be the greatest in respect to the melody of verse. "When I read him," says he, "I can hardly think it is a Northern language, much less English." He holds his " Pastorals " to be his best work, and yet this is a book of which neither you nor I have read a word. I am resolved to leave my favorite authors and study those I have through mistaken notions or absurd prejudices neglected.

I met lately with a declaration by Wieland concerning Shaftesbury : " The author," says he, " to whom I owe more of my cultivation than to any other writer, and of whom I never think without humility when I reflect how far below him I now am." And yet I believe Shaftesbury is quite unknown to you. Mendelssohn calls him the English Plato for richness of style, and for the genial poetic character of his moral philosophy.

While I was at Frankfort I received an invitation from Christian Brentano to join him at Marburg and accompany him to Jena. One of the places I passed through was the University town of Giessen, which seemed to me a poverty-struck and remarkably uninteresting town. It belongs to Hesse, and has recently derived celebrity from its great chemical professor, Liebig. In five days I reached Marburg, also the seat of a University, and beautiful and romantic in situation. Delightful apartments had been taken for me in the house of Professor Tiedemann, the author of a learned History of Philosophy. But I saw nothing of him or his family. His house was nearly at the top of the town, and from my pillow I had towards the east a glorious view of a long valley. I lay on a sofa of metal rings, covered with hair, the most elastic of couches, and to me a novelty. Adjoining this apartment were the rooms of the then Doctor Docens, or perhaps Professor Extraordinarius, von Savigny, who was commencing the professional career which ended in his being placed in the highest position in Prussia, that of Minister of State for the Law Department, — a kind of Chancellor. He became the head of the historical school of law as opposed to the codifying school, of which in modern times Bentham was the most eminent advocate. Savigny's great work is a History of Roman Law. At the time of which I speak he was known by a learned work on Real Law, " Uber Besitz " (on Possession). A dinner for four was brought up to his apartments every day, for him, the two Brentanos, and myself; and we usually spent the rest of the day together. Savigny was altogether different in his manner from the Brentanos, — rather solemn in his tone. In the contests which constantly arose between them and me, I always found him on my side. He had a fine face, which strongly resembled the portraits of Raphael. At this very time he was paying his addresses to the eldest of the Miss Brentanos, Kunigunda by name. Several of her letters to him were sent under cover to me. I am ashamed to confess that, though I was fully sensible of the solidity of his attainments and the worth of his character, I had so little discernment as not in the least to foresee his great future eminence. Of his conversation I recollect only one thing that is characteristic. He said that an English lawyer might render great service to legal science by studying the Roman Law, and showing the obligations of English Law to it, which are more numerous than is generally supposed. One day I mentioned our fiction of a wager in order to try an issue, and he informed me that that was borrowed from the Roman Law.

After an agreeable residence of between five and six weeks at Marburg, I set out on foot with Christian Brentano for Jena. The only incident on the journey which I recollect, is a visit to the celebrated castle of Wartburg, where Luther underwent his friendly imprisonment, and made part of his famous translation of the Bible. On arriving at Jena I took up my residence in agreeable apartments,* and was at once introduced to a social circle which rendered my stay there, till the autumn of 1805, one of the happiest periods of my life.

Having resolved to become a student at the University, I matriculated on the 20th of October, the Prorector being Geheimerath (Privy Counsellor) Voigt.

It required only a few dollars to become enrolled among the

---

* My lodgings cost yearly somewhat less than seven pounds! — H. C. R.

Academischen Bürger. The fees amounted to little more than
half a guinea ; but for the honor of Old England I contrived
to spend nearly a guinea by increasing the gratuities to the
under officers. I received in return a large piece of printed
paper, with a huge seal, announcing in Latin that, on due
examination, I had been found worthy to study all the arts
and sciences. I had also acquired a variety of legal privileges,
and contracted certain obligations. I solemnly promised not
to knock anybody on the head, which I never felt any inclination to do: to enter into no clubs and societies, which nevertheless exist with the knowledge and connivance of the
authorities : to employ all the knowledge I should gain to the
advantage of religion and society, — a promise which might
be kept without, I fear, sensibly advancing either. And yet
I took pains enough to get wisdom, for I went to school four
times a day, and heard lectures on experimental physics, on
æsthetics, on speculative philosophy, and on physical anthropology. The shortest way of giving an account of my uniform
occupation during five days of the week will be by an extract
from a letter : —

"About six o'clock the man who brushes my clothes and
cleans my shoes will open my bedroom, or rather closet, door,
and light my candle. I shall instantly jump out of my
wretched straw hammock and go into my room, where in half
an hour our pretty chambermaid will bring my dried carrots,
called coffee, which I shall drink because I am thirsty, but
not without longing after tea and toast. This done, I shall
take up Schelling's 'Journal of Speculative Physics,' and, comparing the printed paragraphs with my notes taken last Friday, try to persuade myself that I have understood something.
Then I shall listen to another lecture by him on the same
subject. What my experience will then be, I can't say ; I
know what it has been."

I will interpose a sad but true commentary on the text.
I very lately read, in the *Prospective Review*, an article by
James Martineau, in which he says, "This is the age of metaphysical curiosity without metaphysical talent." In every
age, I believe, there have been students of whom this might
be said, and I do not repent of being one of them. I would
rather have failed in the attempt than not have made it.

"Precisely at ten I shall run to the Auditorium of his
'Magnificence,' the Prorector Voigt, and hear his lecture on
Experimental Physics, which we call Natural Philosophy. I

4 *   F

shall admire his instruments and smile at the egregious absurdity of his illustrations of the laws of nature, and at his attempts to draw a moral from his physical lessons. He may possibly repeat his favorite hypothesis of two sorts of fire, male and female ; or allude to his illustration of the Trinity, as shown in the creative or paternal, the preserving or filial, the combining or spiritual principles of nature. Or he may liken the operation of attraction and repulsion in the material world to the debit and credit of a merchant's cash-book. (N. B. These are all facts.) Wearied by the lecture, I shall perhaps hardly know what to do between eleven and twelve o'clock, when I shall reluctantly come home to a very bad dinner. Jena is famous for its bad eating and drinking. Then I shall prepare myself for a lecture at two from Geheimer-Hofrath Loder, on Physical Anthropology, by far the best delivered and most useful of the lectures I attend. I shall do my best to conquer my dislike of, and even disgust at, anatomical preparations, and my repugnance to inspect rotten carcasses and smoked skeletons. And I expect to learn the general laws and structure of the human frame, as developed with less minuteness for general students than he employs on his anatomical lectures for students of medicine."

I add here that the museum of Loder enjoyed as high a reputation in Germany as that of John Hunter in England, and that the museum and its professor were together invited soon after this time to the Russian University of Dorpat, — the malicious and envious affirming that the professor went as accessory.

"From Loder I shall proceed to Schelling, and hear him lecture for an hour on Æsthetics, or the Philosophy of Taste. In spite of the obscurity of a philosophy in which are combined profound abstraction and enthusiastic mysticism, I shall certainly be amused at particular remarks (however unable to comprehend the whole) in his development of Platonic ideas and explanation of the philosophy veiled in the Greek mythology. I may be, perhaps, a little touched now and then by his contemptuous treatment of our English writers, as last Wednesday I was by his abuse of Darwin and Locke. I may hear Johnson called thick-skinned, and Priestley shallow. I may hear it insinuated that science is not to be expected in a country where mathematics are valued only as they may help to make spinning-jennies and machines for weaving stockings. After a stroll by the riverside in Paradise, I shall at four attend Schelling's lecture on Speculative Philosophy, and I may be animated by the sight of more than 130 enthusiastic young men, eagerly listening to the exposition of a philosophy which in its pretensions is more aspiring than any publicly maintained since the days of Plato and his commentators, — a philosophy equally opposed to the empiricism of Locke, the scepticism of Hume, and the critical school of Kant, and which is now in the sphere of Metaphysics the Lord of the Ascendant. But if I chance to be in a prosaic mood, I may smile at the patience of so large an assembly, listening, because it is the fashion, to a detail which not one in twenty comprehends, and which only fills the head with dry formularies and rhapsodical phraseology. At six I shall come home exhausted with attention to novelties hard to understand ; and after, perhaps, an unsuccessful attempt to pen a few English iambics in a translation of Goethe's 'Tasso,' I shall read in bed some fairy tale, poem, or other light work."

This account of my first Semester studies may suffice for the present. Soon after writing the letter from which the above is taken, I was invited to a supper-party at Schelling's. The evening was a jovial one, and showed that philosophers can unbend as well as other folk ; and as it was only in a convivial way I could expect to be listened to by a great metaphysician, I ventured to spar with the Professor. Some strange and unintelligible remarks had been made on the mythology as well of the Orientalists as the Greeks, and the important part played by the Serpent. A gentleman present exhibited a ring, received from England, in the form of a serpent. "Is the serpent the symbol of English philosophy ?" said Schelling to me. "O no !" I answered, "the English take it to appertain to German philosophy, because it changes its coat every year." — "A proof," he replied, "that the English do not look deeper than the coat." Though I shall have occasion again to speak of Schelling, I will here. add that he had the countenance of a white negro, if the contradiction may be pardoned, — that is, the curly hair, flat nose, and thick lips, without the color of the African. After a time he was dethroned from his metaphysical rank by Hegel, who must have been his pupil.* Of him I have no recollection, though I find among my papers some memoranda of him. His philosophy was stigmatized as

* Hegel and Schelling were fellow-pupils at Tübingen. The former was five years the elder; nevertheless Schelling seems at first to have taken the lead in philosophy, and to have been of service to his friend.

Pantheistic ; Schelling managed to keep on better terms with Christianity. His learning is unquestionable, and he ranks among the first of German thinkers. Like his predecessors, he was fond of tracing a trinity in his scheme. The Absolute Being or All in All appears sometimes as the finite or nature, symbolized by the Son, who, according to the Christian revelation, is subject to the conditions of Time, like all natural and material things, and therefore dies ; sometimes as thought or the infinite, having no form, the Spirit ; and the union of the two, matter and spirit, is the Father. And thus who knows but that after all the Athanasian Creed will be resolved into high metaphysical truth ?

It may be thought that these metaphysical puzzles have no business in a paper of personal recollections ; but, in fact, these subjects occupied much of my time while in Jena, — and never more than now.

The old student Kölle, to whom I have already referred, introduced me to Professor Fries, the most distinguished Kantianer at that time, when the idealists of the Fichte and Schelling schools had nearly destroyed the Critical Philosophy. Fries was brought up among the Moravians, fond of talk, but of the simplest habits, — a shy man. Almost the only treat he allowed himself was a daily walk to Zwätzen, a village about two miles from Jena, in the charming valley of which Jena is the metropolis. Around Fries collected a number of young men ; and of his party I was considered an ordinary member. By him and by others I was well received, my chief merit being, I believe, there as elsewhere in Germany, that I was "der Englander." Nearly the whole of my time at Jena I was the only Englishman there. It was a passport everywhere. I could give information, at all events, about the language. With Fries I used to talk about the English philosophers, held very cheaply by him ; but he wanted historical knowledge about them, which I was able·to give. And he, in return, tried to inoculate me with Kantianism. The little I ever clearly understood I learned from him.

On passing through Schlangenbad I fell in with a Major K——, a gentlemanly man, who gave me a card to two students who were connected with him, — Frederick and Christian Schlosser. Christian, the younger, had a commanding intellect, and was a partisan of the new poetical school, as well as of the newest school of medical philosophy. His profession was that of medicine. He became a Roman Catholic, and his

elder brother followed him.   He died young.   At the time of
my writing this, Frederick is still living, and resides at Heidelberg, in a handsome house called the Stift, an ancient convent; he and his wife are both highly esteemed.   The Stift is
his own property; but he told me that as it had been Church
property, and was confiscated at the Reformation, he did not
purchase it until he had obtained the approbation and license
of the Pope.

Before the end of the year I left off dining at home, and
became an *abonné* at the Rose, the head inn, where my dinner
cost five shillings a week.   Here were the Schlossers and other
students of the higher class, and the conversation was in the
best University tone.   I was often applied to, to read passages
from Shakespeare.   Christian Schlosser remarked one day at
the Rose table-d'hôte, that in the "Midsummer Night's
Dream," the pervading idea is *mésalliance*, — among the super-
natural beings and on earth, matrimonial dissensions, — in the
comic characters also, when the mechanics presume to ally
themselves to fine art.   The Schlossers looked down upon the
Kantian school, and therefore upon Fries.   They and he, however, were united to a certain degree by a common love and
admiration of Goethe.   A third Schlosser, a cousin, was a
nephew of Goethe, and there was a friendly acquaintance between the Schlossers and Clemens Brentano.

I may here relate a curious phenomenon of which I myself
was a witness.   The house in which I lived was large, and a
number of students occupied apartments in it.   There was no
resident family, nor any female except a middle-aged woman,
Aufwärterinn (waitress), and a very pretty girl, Besen (broom),
in the cant language of the Burschen, — both respectable in
their situation.   It was the business of these women to let in
the students at all hours of the night, and by so doing a habit
was contracted of rising and opening the door without awaking.   It became possible to maintain a conversation with both
the woman and the girl without their being properly awake.
Their condition seems to have been very much like what is
now known as the mesmeric sleep.   The particulars which I
have to mention are still fresh in my memory, but I will copy
from an account written by me at the time : "Last night,
going into the kitchen for a candle, I saw the younger woman
of the house in this extraordinary state, and listened to a
dialogue between her and the elder : her answers were pertinent and even witty.   One question put to her was, 'What

sort of a man is Brentano?' She answered : ' The little fellow
in the front parlor? O, he 's a comical fellow, —like his brother
Clemens, — but *he* was artig' (polite). — ' And what of the
Englishman?' — ' O, he 's a guter Kerl (a good fellow), — he 's
so fond of talking.' So you see what she said in her sleep was
credible at all events. After several incidents, which I pass
over, I spoke in my own voice, and asked for a candle ; she
recognized me, and without awaking took the light and accompanied me to my room. A few days later I witnessed some
amusing but unwarrantable experiments on the elder woman,
when she was in the same state. The inquiry was made
whether she had any empty rooms. She replied, ' O yes !'
and then in an artificial tone praised the rooms and named the
price. Some of the questions were of a kind which I could not
approve, and when at length she awoke she was very reasonably angry at the tricks which had been played on her."

On seeking for an explanation of these facts, I found that
animal magnetism, so far from being considered in Jena as
mere quackery, was received by the most esteemed natural
philosophers as an admitted fact, and an important chapter in
the natural history of man.

H. C. R. TO T. R.

" On all points, natural philosophy, religion, metaphysics,
there seems to be a uniform opposition between German and
English opinion. You say with truth I am growing a mystic.
I rejoice to perceive it. Mystery is the poetry of philosophy.
It employs and delights the fancy at least, while your philosophy, and the cold rational quibbles of the French and English schools, furnish nothing but negatives to the understanding, and leave the fancy and the heart quite barren. After all,
what we want is strong persuasion, conviction, satisfaction ;
whether it be the demonstrated *knowledge* of the mathematician, the *faith* of the pietist, the *presentiment* of the mystic,
or the *inspiration* of the poet, is of less consequence to the
individual. And it seems that nature has sufficiently provided for this great blessing by that happy ductility of imagination which is called credulity."

So I wrote. But I should have thought more justly if I
had said that the best provision of nature or providence
(whichever name we give to the originating cause), for the fit
cultivation of the spheres of nature, physical and moral, lies

in the infinite varieties of human character. All the faculties which man has are found, generally speaking, in all men ; but with infinite degrees of strength and quantity, and with varieties in combination.

One of my employments during a part of 1802 – 3 was that of a contributor to a magazine entitled the *Monthly Register*, and edited by my friend Collier. The subjects on which I wrote were German literature, the philosophy of Kant, &c. I also gave many translations from Goethe, Schiller, and others, in order to exemplify the German theory of versification. As an apology for my being so much attracted to this subject, I quote on the epic hexameter : —

> " Giddy it bears thee away, on the waves ever restless and rolling;
> And thou, behind and before, seest but ocean and sky."

I sent one really wise paper, — a translation of an essay by Herr von Savigny on German Universities ; for the rest, I unaffectedly declare that they attracted no notice, and did not deserve any.

[This will be the best place for a letter from Savigny, though written somewhat later, on the subject of University teaching. — ED.]

SAVIGNY TO H. C. R. (TRANSLATED.)

MARBURG, January 9, 1803.

DEAR ROBINSON, — If you saw what a tremendous deal I have to do this winter, you would forgive me that I have not written to you before. Nevertheless I do not forgive myself, for I have all this time not heard from you, and that through my fault.

Moreover, in your letter you do me a wrong which I have to endure from many ; you imagine you see in me a teacher full of noble views with regard to you. God knows how I have incurred this suspicion, — I, who perhaps am too off-hand with myself and others, and act and speak almost entirely according to my mood, and consequently as I feel at the moment, without any generous thought about the future. If I were to keep silent at such an accusation, my relation to you would be really a mockery ; I should then put on a serious face, and could not help laughing at you in my heart.

About the oral lectures we are indeed of very different opinions, although I quite agree with you as to the method in which they are now given. If a rule is to be established

on the subject, it is necessary first to leave out of consideration those real geniuses who are great in practice, though even
these must find a place in the end.   Such a genius Schelling
is not, — Fichte may partially have been ; I have known only
one such, and that was Spittler.   To give one day full expression to my theory, and also to do something towards carrying
it out, is a matter which I have especially at heart.   Its principle is very simple : whatever man pursues, his own dignity,
as well as the interest of the work, and of the subject itself,
demands always that he should do it thoroughly.   Thoroughly
to do a thing means so to do it that the work shall penetrate
our innermost being and thus become a part of ourselves, and
then be spontaneously reproduced.   Thus arise master minds
who combine mastery of their subject with the maintenance
of their individuality.   But the only way in which we can
make a thing our own is by thoroughly working it out.
Therefore the whole art of a teacher consists in methodically
quickening the productive energy of the pupil, and making
him find out science for himself.   I am convinced, therefore,
that this is the one necessary method, and consequently that
it is possible.   Our lectures, as they are at present, have
little resemblance to it ; even in outward form almost everything must be changed.   I see clearly the possibility of carrying out a great part of this plan, — the greatest difficulty
being without doubt to teach philosophy in this way, although
it may be supposed to have been the method of the ancients.
Nothing can be more opposite than the diffuse way in which
Schelling authoritatively forces his ideas on crude understandings, and this method, according to which it ought to be the
highest glory of the teacher, if the pupils, with the greatest
love and veneration for him, should nevertheless stand to him,
the scientific individual, in no nearer relation than to any one
else.   The manner of lecturing should be in the highest degree unrestrained : teaching, talking, questioning, conversing,
just as the subject may require.   There is no calculating
what must result from this ; unquestionably the greatest difficulty would be to find a number of teachers adapted to it.
Yet nothing is impossible.   You see that this whole idea
might be expressed from another side, by the demand that the
free activity of the mind should be rendered possible by the
complete mastery of the whole subject-matter.   And, viewed
from this point, it stands in very decided connection with the
method of the excellent and enthusiastic Pestalozzi.

Last of all, because such is the custom, but in every other respect first of all, I beg the continuance of your friendly feeling.

                                                            SAVIGNY.

[Here also may be added two extracts respecting the fundamental principles of Kant's philosophy.]

H. C. R. TO T. R.

Kantianism professes to have detected the basis of metaphysical science, and to have established that science on a similar but not the same footing of sure evidence as the mathematical and natural sciences. It professes to annihilate *scepticism*, which is an eternal reproach to reason, (for what is scepticism but a confession of the impotence of reason?) by showing the precise limits of knowledge, and the extent and degree of belief which we are compelled to give to notions that are not susceptible of certain evidence. In the study of Kant, independently of his grand result, I have learnt to detect so many false reasonings in our school, and have acquired so many new views of intellect, that I rejoice in having undertaken the study of him, though it has caused me more pain than I scarcely ever felt, and produced that humiliating sense of myself, the free and unexaggerated expression of which you have been pleased to consider as chimerical. I have indeed conquered one vast difficulty, and have at length pierced the cloud which hung over his doctrine of liberty. I am converted from the dogmatical assertion of philosophical necessity, but on grounds of which the libertarians in England have no conception. I will still support necessity against all the world but Kant and the Devil. Don't ask me for these grounds, — they would be quite unintelligible till you had previously comprehended and adopted the Kantian theory of conceptions *a priori*, and of time and space. It was the fault of my last letter that I tried to say too much. I will confine myself at present to one single point, and I flatter myself that I shall make that one point intelligible. And I have hitherto found that to comprehend and to be a convert to Kant were the same. This point is the refutation of Locke's (or rather Aristotle's) famous principle, that there is nothing in intellect which was not before in sense, or that all our conceptions (ideas) are derived from sensation.

According to the empirical system, as stated in its utmost consistency by Horne Tooke, man has but one faculty, that of receiving sensation from external objects. But as it is certain we have innumerable notions and ideas which are not the copies of external object, the empirics, particularly Hartley, explain how these super-sensible notions and ideas yet arise (*mechanically* according to Hartley) from such sensations. But here is a clear defect in the system; every operation supposes a power working and a power worked upon. Mere *sensibility* can give us only sensations, but it is certain we have a thousand notions which are not material and sensible. External objects may be, and unquestionably are, necessary *conditions*, — the *sine qua non* of ideas, but there must be something more. There must be in us a capacity of being so affected, as well as in external objects a capacity of affecting. And this something is *a priori:* not that in the order of time the conceptions (general ideas) exist before experience, but that the source of such conceptions is independent of experience. You will therefore not accuse Kant of supporting innate ideas, of which he is the decided adversary.

What Kant asserts is, that in order to the arriving at knowledge there must be a *matter* and *form;* the former is furnished by the sensibility, the latter exists in the faculty of understanding. This word *form* is to you quite unintelligible. It was a long while ere I learnt its import. It is the Ass's Bridge of Kantianism. I will try to lift you over it. You have seen, I hope, a magic lantern. It is the best illustration I can find. In order to show off the figures, there must be a bright spot on the wall, upon which the colored figures are exhibited. This is an image of the human mind. Without figures, the luminous spot is an empty nothing, like the human mind till it has objects of sense. But without the spot the figures would be invisible, as without an *a priori* capacity to receive impressions we could have none. The matter, therefore, of the dancing spectacle on the wall is the ever-shifting figure; its form is the bright spot which is necessary to its being shown. According to Leibnitz, the figures are ready made in the spot. According to Locke, no spot is necessary. Kant is the first philosopher who explained the true mechanism of that wonderful magic lantern, the human mind. When, therefore, it is said we have the conceptions (general ideas) *a priori*, it is not meant that the actual conceptions lie in us, even in a sort of dormant state, — which would be a position with-

out meaning, and hence equally incapable of being proved or
disproved, — but that they are, or arise from *the pre-existent
capacity of the understanding*, and are determined by the
natural power of thinking which the mind possesses. In
other words, conceptions *a priori* are but the forms of conceptions *a posteriori*, i. e. conceptions whose matter is derived
from experience. Perceiving a ball on the edge of a table,
which lies still till pushed off and then falls to the ground, the
mind can observe this fact, remember it, and put it into words.
But how is the mind enabled by this observation to infer that
all bodies in a state of rest remain as they are till a foreign
substance operates on them, — or, in a more general form, that
all events *must* have a cause? The pushing of a ball is not *all
events*. And the fact that something *is*, is essentially different
from the knowledge that something *must be*. The latter
knowledge nature can never give, for nature gives only facts
and things, but we have the latter conception. Your Hartley
shows the circumstances under which these super-sensible conceptions are called forth. His facts are denied by no one, but
they do not prove the conceptions to be of sensible origin, any
more than the warmth necessary to hatch an egg proves that
the warmth is the principle of animal life. Conceptions themselves, which are essential to all knowledge, are *a priori*, — and
not only conceptions, even intuitions, — for instance *space*, which
is yet generally considered as a general or abstract idea (i. e. conception). Now it is the characteristic of conception (or general idea) that it includes under it many individuals, — as
" man " includes Jack, Tom, and Harry ; but when we think
of space it is always as *one whole*. And *different places* are not
like individual persons, — distinct beings having only common
qualities ; but different places are only *parts of space*. How,
then, did we come by the *a priori* intuition, space? You will
say by abstraction ; we unite all the places we have seen,
imagine an infinity of others, and call the whole *space*. But
on reflection, you will find this process requires that we should
set out with the notion of space, though your professed object
is to leave off with it ; for how could the mind have the consciousness, " I am in a place," or, " This is a place," if it had
not already a notion of space ? I will state the example in
another form. You have a conception of *body*. Most of its
requisites or component parts are empirical, and all that you
have acquired through experience you can imagine yourself not
to have ; for instance, you can dismiss at will color, hardness,

irresistibility, &c., but you cannot possibly think away space. In like manner you will find space to be included in all our intuitions of external objects, of which it is the form or condition *a priori*. In like manner, time is the formal condition, or *sine qua non*, of all appearances whatever, for we cannot think of any thought or event which does not take place in time.

As time and place — which, however general they seem, must nevertheless not be considered as general ideas (to use our scandalously incorrect phraseology) — are *a priori* intuitions grounding all *a posteriori* intuitions (i. e. sensations of experience), so all our conceptions (or general ideas) must be grounded by *a priori* conceptions, which conceptions are grounded on the nature of the human mind and its laws of thinking. The philosophy which shows how these *a priori* conceptions and intuitions are the basis of all knowledge is called the Transcendental (or, if you will, the high-flying) Philosophy.

H. C. R. to T. R.

1. Experience gives us the materials of knowledge, of which the form lies in the mind.

2. Consciousness is the ultimate source of all our notions, beyond which we cannot go, for we cannot step out of ourselves. This consciousness, when the subject of our thoughts, teaches us that we have a primitive productive faculty : *imagination*, whence everything is derived ; *sense*, which opens to us the external world ; *understanding*, which brings to rule the objects of sense ; and further, *reason*, which goes beyond all sense and all experience, — a faculty by which we attain ideas. (You know already the difference between idea and thought, &c.)

3. (And here I beg you to be very attentive, for I enter on a new topic, which I have hitherto not ventured to introduce.) There is in man a perpetual conflict between his reason and his understanding, whence all philosophical disputes arise, and which a critical investigation of the mind alone can solve. These disputes are of the following nature : The *reason postulates* a vast number of truths which the understanding in vain strives to comprehend. Hence the *antinomies* of pure reason. Hence it is easy to demonstrate the eternity and non-eternity of the world, — the being and no-being of God, — the existence and non-existence of a free principle. Kant has placed these

contradictory demonstrations in opposition, and gave, more
than twenty years ago, a public defiance to the whole philosophical world to detect a flaw in either side of these contradictory demonstrations : *and no one has yet accepted the challenge.*
And the solution of the riddle is, —

All these ideas, as ideas, have their foundation in the nature
of the mind, and as such we cannot shake them off. But
whether these ideas out of the mind have any reality whatever, the mind itself can never know ; and the result is,
not scepticism, which is uncertainty, but the certainty of our
necessary and inevitable ignorance. And here *speculative rea-*
son has performed its task. But now a second principle is
started by Kant. This is *practical reason.*

Kant proceeds on the same experimental basis of consciousness, and grounds all his moral philosophy on the *fact* that
we are conscious of a certain moral feeling *I ought.* Kant
will not reason with him who disputes this fact, and excludes
such a one from the rank of a rational and moral agent.

But the idea *I ought* includes in it *I can ;* and as speculative reason is quite neutral on all these ultimate points of
absolute knowledge, practical reason on this basis, weak as it
seems, raises the vast structure of moral philosophy and religion. *And the want of knowledge is supplied by faith,* but a
faith that is necessary, and, to an honest sound mind, irresistible. Its objects are God, immortality, and freedom, —
notions which all unsophisticated minds readily embrace,
which a certain degree of reason destroys, but which, according to Kant, reason in its consistent application shall restore
again to universal acceptance.

The seeming scepticism of the great results of speculative
reasoning is favorable to the interests of religion and morality
by keeping the coasts clear. I cannot, says Kant, demonstrate
the being of God, nor you his non-existence. But my moral
principle — the fact that I am conscious of a moral law — is a
something against which you have nothing. This, as respects
the first principle of morals and religion, and the reality and
foundation of human knowledge, is the essence of the Kantian
philosophy.

Of the numerous students with whom my University life
brought me into contact I shall not speak in detail ; but I
must say something about the student life, of which exag-

gerated accounts are current. In spite of the wildness and even coarseness of manners too generally prevalent, and though I was too advanced in age to be more than a looker-on at their amusements, yet I conceived quite an affection for the class. I thought I had never seen young men combining so many excellences of head and heart. Nearly all the under-graduates belonged to societies which were called Landsmann-schaften, — these Landsmannschaften being formed of the natives of separate countries or districts. Each held an oc-casional festival, called a Commerz, to which it was a great privilege for an outsider to be admitted. I was never present at more than two. The first was with the Rheinländer, — generally speaking, a warm-hearted, rough set. At these meetings only beer was drunk, but there was a great deal of smoking. There was, however, no excess to signify. Many Burschenlieder (student songs) were sung, some earnest, others jocular; but a gross song I never heard from a student, either here or elsewhere. Among the frequent practices was that of Schmollis trinken, which consisted in knocking glasses together, drinking healths, and kissing each other. After this the parties became Dutzbrüder, — that is, instead of greeting each other in the ordinary way by the third person plural, they made use of "thou"; and it was a legitimate cause of duel if, after Schmollis trinken, "Sie" was used instead of "Du." As I had drunk with scores of these Rheinländer, I used, in order to avoid all occasion of quarrel, when I met any one of them to say, "Wie gehts?" (How does it go?) instead of "How do you do?" which might be expressed in two ways. The only other grand Commerz which I attended was with the Curlän-der. A Curland nobleman, a very young man, brought with him to the chief inn of Jena, where he stayed two days, an English lady, whom he represented as his wife. He had among the students personal friends, whom he invited to his inn. He was said to be a lieutenant-colonel in the English service; at all events he was an Englishman in heart, had the Anglomania in the highest degree, and for this reason invited me to join his party. His companion was young and very pretty, and as wild as a colt; and as she knew no language but English, she constantly applied to me to interpret the cause of the merriment which was going on, — no slight task. In honor of this gentleman a grand Commerz was given, which made me intimate with the Curland body.

It is a remarkable circumstance that the two bodies of

students most opposed to each other in appearance and manners were both subjects of the Russian Empire, — the Liefländer* and the Curländer.

The former were the *petits maîtres*, — they dressed more smartly than any others, and were remarkably precise in their speech. Their German was said to be ultra-correct. The Curländer were the heartiest and most generous of youths, not superior in ability or scholarship, but among the most amiable. I find among my memoranda thirty-three Stammblätter (album-leaves) of engraved and ornamented paper signed by Curländer alone. It is the practice of students on leaving the University to exchange these tokens of remembrance. Those to which I have referred have revived tender feelings, but on looking over them I feel the truth and force of the words which fell from Madame de Staël on one occasion when I was with her. Goethe's son, a lad, called on her and presented to her his Stammbuch. When she had bowed him out of the room she threw the book on the sofa, and exclaimed, " Je n'aime pas ces tables mortuaires ! " Mortuary tables indeed they are. On one of those which I possess is written, " I shall never forget you, and I expect the same from you." But not even this memorial brings the writer to my mind.

An account of a German University would be very imperfect without some mention of duels, which, from the great exaggerations generally circulated, have brought more reproach than is deserved. Generally speaking, they are harmless. Very few indeed are the instances in which they are fatal, and not often is any serious injury inflicted. I knew of only one case of the kind ; it was that of a student who had received a wound in the breast, from which he said he should never cease to feel the effects.

Schelling said from the rostrum, " He that dares not boldly on occasion set his life at stake and play with it as with a top, is unquestionably one who is by nature unable to enjoy it, or even possess it in its highest vigor," — a hint which it is true was not wanted here, as in the course of the last six months near a hundred duels were fought.

At Jena the weapon used was the rapier, which with its three edges has certainly a murderous appearance ; but honor is satisfied if a triangle appears in the flesh ; a very slight wound is sufficient for that, and great care is taken that nothing more serious shall be inflicted. The combatants are made to stand

* From Liefland or Livland, Livonia.

at a distance from each other, and two seconds lie on the
ground with sticks to interpose the moment their principals

C

press too near. Thus A —|— B. A and B are the duellists,

D

and C D the seconds, who beat down the swords when a wound
is likely to be dangerous. In ninety-nine cases out of a hundred a flesh wound on the arm is all that is given. As the
issue is usually so unimportant, a very slight offence is considered a sufficient cause for fighting. There is a code of honor
among the students which might be derived from Touchstone's
famous code as to giving the lie. For instance, if A says of
anything that B says, " Das ist comisch " (that is comical) —
that is a *Touche* — an offence — which B must notice, or A
has the " advantage " (*Avantage*) of him. Or if A says, " It 's
a fine day, upon my honor," and B says, " Upon my honor it 's
a dull day," — that 's a *Touche*, for here the honor of one of
two Burschen is in imminent peril. But it is not to be supposed that a fight can take place *per saltum*. Wherever a
Touche has been received, the party sends his friend to the opponent's room with a Ziegenhainer (a stick cut from a neighboring wood),* who, without pulling off his hat, asks what was
meant. If the supposed offender says, " I meant nothing," or
" No offence was intended," the affair is over ; but a Bursch
who is jealous of his honor, though he actually did mean
nothing, is ashamed to say so, and then the usual answer is,
" He may take it as he likes." Thereupon the second says,
" A desires me to tell you that you are a dummer Junge, or a
dummer Kerl "; that is, " You are an ass or a fool," or, as we
should say in England, " You are no gentleman." This is the
offence which blood alone can redress. But then, as I said before, it is only arm blood, not heart's blood. During my stay
at Jena, it never happened but once that a man came to my
rooms with a Ziegenhainer. The student who came was a
sensible fellow, who volunteered in order to prevent a silly
young fellow sending as great a fool as himself. The messenger threw down his stick and his hat, and burst out laughing ;
but very gravely took back my answer that I meant nothing.
The sender was a young Hessian nobleman, and from that
time I refused to speak to him.

* This wood, Ziegenhain, was celebrated for the knotted sticks cut from a
kind of cherry-tree (Corneliuskirschen).

On one occasion I was myself present when, in a beautiful and romantic valley a few miles from Jena, some half-dozen duels were fought with due solemnity, including one intermediate duel, which arose in this way : A wound having been received, one of the seconds cried out, " A triangle, on my . honor." " No triangle, on my honor," answered the other. On this, the seconds, *sans phrase*, stripped and fought, and the result being in favor of him who said, " A triangle," his view of the matter was held to be established, and all four became as good friends as ever. It is to be understood that in these cases the parties still consider each other friends, though etiquette does not allow intercourse between them till the Ehrensache (affair of honor) is decided.

To connect great matters with small, as we constantly find them in human life, these duels in the Rauhthal had eventually a mighty effect on the fate of Europe. For in the famous campaign of 1806, Buonaparte having heard that there was a colonel in his army who had been a student at Jena, and foreseeing that Jena would be the seat of war, sent for him ; and he rendered most important service. Buonaparte held the town, and on the high ground between it and Weimar was the Prussian army. The colonel led the troops through the Rauhthal, which he probably became acquainted with from fighting or witnessing duels there. The Prussians were taken in the rear, and this movement contributed to a victory which for six years kept Germany in subjection to France.

During my stay at Jena I had the opportunity of seeing a man of science whose name I have never heard in England, but who is mentioned with honor in the " Conversations Lexicon," — Chladni, the inventor of a musical instrument called the Clavi-cylinder, and the author of a work on the theory of sound.* He travelled in Germany, Italy, and France in order to make known both his instrument and his theory. All I recollect is some curious experiments intended to show the relation between vibration and form. A plate of glass was thinly strewn with sand, the string of a fiddlestick was drawn across the side of the plate, and instantly the sand flew to certain parts, forming figures which had been previously described.

---

* His name is repeatedly mentioned in Professor Tyndall's work "On Sound," where this very experiment is referred to.

CHAPTER VII.

O N March 20, 1803, I attended the first performance of
Schiller's tragedy of "Die Braut von Messina." A visit
to the Weimar Theatre was the occasional treat of the Jena
students. The distance (from seven to ten miles) was such as
to allow those young men who had more strength in their
limbs than money in their purses, to walk to Weimar and
back on the same day. This I have done repeatedly, returning after the play was over. "The Bride of Messina" was an
experiment by the great dramatist, and it certainly did not
succeed, inasmuch as it led to no imitations, unless the representations of "Antigone" a few years since, both in Germany
and England, may be traced to it. In this tragedy Schiller
introduced choruses, after the fashion of the ancients. The
bride had two lovers, who were her brothers; the catastrophe is as frightful as the incidents are horrible. The double
chorus sometimes exchanged short epigrammatic speeches, and
sometimes uttered tragic declamations in lyric measure. I was
deeply impressed, and wrote to my brother that this tragedy
surpassed all Schiller's former works. But this feeling must
have been caught from my companions, for it did not remain.

It must, too, have been about this time that Goethe brought
out one of the most beautiful, though not the most popular,
of his dramas, "The Natural Daughter," — a play meant to be
the first of three in which he was to give a poetic view of his
own ideas on the great social questions of the day. Eugenia,
the well-born, is condemned to make an ignoble marriage for
reasons which are left unexplained; otherwise she is to be
consigned to a barren rock. The lawyer to whom she is to be
married is represented as a worthy man, whom she respects.
When she gives her consent, she exacts from him a promise
that he will leave her mistress of her actions, and not intrude
on her solitude. With her words, "To the altar," the curtain
drops. Herder professed a high admiration of the piece, but
it is utterly unfit for a large audience. The character of Eugenia was beautifully represented by Jagermann, who combined
dignity and grace. On my complimenting her on the per-

formance she said, " If I played the part well it was by chance, for I do not understand the character."

She would not have said this of another character in which I beheld her, though I do not precisely recollect at what time. I refer to Schiller's " Jungfrau von Orleans," which came out in 1801. A glorious work ! It was well remarked by Hofrath Jung of Mainz, that the characteristics of French and German literature were well exemplified by the name and the quality of the " Virgin of Orleans " by Schiller and " La Pucelle d'Orléans " by Voltaire. Jagermann recited with great effect the lyrical passages, both when the inspiration seizes Joan, and the heroic conclusion. I suppose it is because the English make such a bad figure in this tragedy that it has never been introduced on our own stage.

One other dramatic recollection I may mention. I saw at Weimar Lessing's " Nathan der Weise." The author pro-nounced a blessing on the town which should first dare to exhibit it to the world. He thought the lesson of tolerance would not be learned for generations. The play was adapted to the stage by Schiller, and the greatest actor of the day came to Weimar to perform the part of Nathan. Never probably, in any language, was the noble and benignant Jew more impressively represented than by Iffland. But the work has no dramatic worth. All one recollects of it is the tale of the rings, which was borrowed from Boccaccio.

I went to Weimar twice in the beginning of 1803, to visit Herder. What I had previously seen of him made me feel that in spite of his eminence there were many points of agree-ment in matters of taste and sentiment, and caused me to approach him with affection as well as fear. I lent him Wordsworth's " Lyrical Ballads," my love for which was in no respect diminished by my attachment to the German school of poetry. I found that Herder agreed with Wordsworth as to poetical language. Indeed Wordsworth's notions on that subject are quite German. There was also a general sympathy between the two in matters of morality and religion. Herder manifested a strong feeling of antipathy to the new anti-supernatural school of Paulus. With all his habitual toler-ance, he could hardly bear with the Jena professor, or with the government which permitted such latitudinarianism. Yet he was attached to Wieland personally, who was certainly no Christian. Herder was also tolerant towards anti-Christian writers of past generations. He was a warm admirer of

Shaftesbury, of whom the worst he had to say was that he
wrote like a lord.   His repugnance to some of Goethe's writings was perhaps still stronger than to those of Paulus ; and he
reprobated with especial warmth " Die Braut von Corinth,"
and " Der Gott und die Bajadere."   Though in some respects
the anti-supernatural professor was as opposite as possible to
the poetic and anti-metaphysical divine, yet they were in
sympathy in their hostility to the modern German philosophy
of the Kantian and post-Kantian schools.

Of Paulus I myself had some personal knowledge.   Notwithstanding his well-known opinions, he was one of the regular theological professors and members of the senate in the
University of Jena.   In the following year he was invited
by the Catholic King of Bavaria to the University of Würzburg.   No wonder, it may be thought, for that would be an
effectual mode of damaging the Protestant Church.   But he
did not long remain under a Roman Catholic government, for
he was soon called to occupy a high place in the University of
Heidelberg.   He was a laborious scholar and a very efficient
teacher, and always respected for his zeal and activity.   During the present session he lectured on the Epistles of St. Paul,
and on Dogmatic Theology, and held every Saturday a theological conversation.   I went one day as a visitor to hear his
lecture, and having already received some kindness from
him, ventured to call on him afterwards, when the following
conversation took place.   Referring to the lecture I had heard,
I said, " Herr Geheimer-Kirchen-Rath (Mr. Privy-Church-
Counsellor), will you oblige me by telling me whether I heard
you rightly in a remark I understood you to make ?   It was
this, that a man might altogether disbelieve in miracle, and
of course all prophecy and inspiration, and yet be a Christian."
His answer I distinctly recollect : " Don't imagine, Mr. Robinson, that I mean anything personally disrespectful when I say
that that seems to me a foolish question (eine dumme Frage)."
— " How ?   Is that possible ? " — " Why, it implies that Christianity may have something to do with inspiration, with prophecy, or with miracle ; but it has nothing to do with them.
(Es hat nichts damit zu thun.) "

Paulus, when a young man, visited England, and had cor-
responded with Geddes.   He also told me that he saw Dr.
Parr, and had received letters from several of the bishops ;
but he said : " Your English theologians did not much please
me.   I found but one man who really interested me, and him

I consider one of the most excellent men I ever saw. This was Robert Robinson of Cambridge ; with me he is the beau-ideal of a Christian minister.* I loved him even for his weaknesses. With all his peculiarities, he was thoroughly liberal. In his attachment to the Baptists there was a union of childlike simplicity and kind-heartedness that was quite charming." Paulus spoke of Priestley as superstitious.

Griesbach, the famous biblical scholar, was an older and soberer man ; I visited him in his garden-house, but have retained no particulars of his conversation.

Among those who held the office of Doctor docens at Jena was one Kilian, who wrote as well as lectured on a system of medicine. The proof-sheet of the preface was shown me, from which I extracted a sentence to this effect : " The science of medicine does not exist in order to cure diseases, but there are diseases in order that there should be a science of medicine." In the same book I was shown some verbal corrections made by himself. Wherever he had written " God " he struck it out and substituted " The Absolute."

Living at Jena, but neither as professor nor student, was Gries, who afterwards acquired reputation as the best translator in rhyme of the romantic poets. He was chiefly known by his versions of Ariosto and Tasso, but he also translated from the great Spanish dramatist Calderon.

On the 4th of April I closed my academical term by setting out student-fashion on a walking expedition, and had between three and four weeks of high enjoyment ; for which, indeed, nothing was requisite but health, spirits, and good-humor, all of which I possessed in abundance. I determined to take the opportunity of visiting Berlin, and on my way passed through the University towns of Halle and Wittenberg. The latter is known to every one as the place whence Luther promulgated the Reformation. The town, however, with its sunken University, was disappointing ; but I still retain a recollection of the portraits of Luther and Melanchthon. Both of them lived and preached and are buried here. Their monuments are very simple, — merely a brass plate on the ground with the common inscription of dates, and the two full-length portraits. The acute and sarcastic countenance of the one, and the bull-like head of the other, are strikingly contrasted. Mildness is the recorded virtue of Melanchthon ; but had subtlety and craft

* Robinsoniana, by H. C. R., will be referred to in a later part of this work.

been his qualities, I should have thought the portrait expressed
them.

Berlin, as a city, gave me little pleasure. A city in which
the sovereign prince applies the revenues of the state to the
erection of opera-houses and palaces has never been an agreeable object in my eyes. I hastened on my arrival to deliver a
letter of introduction to one of the Berlin notabilities, and indeed one of the remarkable men of the day. He is entitled to
a grateful notice from me for his generous hospitality ; and
what I have to say will not be altogether insignificant as illustrative of character. No one who has paid any attention to
the German literature of the eighteenth century can be ignorant of the name of Frederick Nicolai, the Berlin publisher.
And those who know of him merely as the object of the
satires of Goethe and Schiller, Tieck and the Schlegels, — that
is, of the most splendid writers in Germany, — may be excused
if they think of him as little better than an ass. But as he
would have greatly erred who took his notion of Colley Cibber
from Pope's "Dunciad," so would they who fancied Nicolai to
be the arch Philistine of the authors of the "Xenien." The
fact is, that Nicolai was really a meritorious and useful man
in his younger days ; but he lived too long. He was neither
more nor less than an active, clever fellow, — full of enterprise
in the pursuit of inferior objects which he attained, but destitute of all sense of the higher and nobler ends of science and
literature. When I visited him he was in his seventieth year.
He had been brought up by his father to the bookselling business, and had received a learned education. Early in life he
became the friend of Lessing—the most honored name of that
age — and of Moses Mendelssohn. In 1765 he established the
famous *Allgemeine Deutsche Bibliothek* (Universal German Library), a review which was as important in its day as, for so
many years, our *Monthly Review* was. But what that Review
now appears to be in comparison with the *Edinburgh*, the
Quarterly, and some others of a subsequent period, such is
the *Allgemeine Deutsche Bibliothek* compared with numerous
works of the modern German schools. When Lessing was
gone, Nicolai could not engage men of equal rank to supply
his place, and, unable to discern the signs of the times, became
the strenuous opponent of the moderns. When age and youth
commence a warfare, which is to last, every one knows which
will be the conqueror. "Denn der Lebende hat recht," says
Schiller ("For he who lives is in the right"). Now it unfortu-

nately happened that Nicolai ventured to oppose himself —
and that in the very offensive form of coarse satire — to the
two great schools of philosophy and poetry ; of philosophy in
the persons of Kant and Fichte, and of poetry in the person of
Goethe.　In a novel entitled " Leben und Meinungen Sem-
pronius Gundiberts," which he gave me, the hero is a sort of
metaphysical Quixote, who, on Kantian principles, acts like a
fool.　Nicolai's best book, " Sebaldus Nothanker," was translated into English by Dutton.　Nicolai also brought out a
squib against the " Sorrows of Werter," when at the height of
popularity, and called it " Werter's Joys."　Werter's pistol-
shot only wounds him, — he recovers, marries Charlotte, and
sustains the most disgraceful calamity that can befall a husband.　Many years afterwads Nicolai wrote a clever play, in
which Kotzebue's " Stranger " and the hero of Goethe's " Stella " are made to be the same, and the Stranger is represented
as compromising with his wife, and receiving her back on condition
of her living with him in partnership with Stella.　Such was
the Berlin publisher who attained a kind of literary notoriety.
I did not approach him with awe, but I found him a most
lively, active, and friendly man.　His conversation was without bitterness.　I told him of my fondness for some of the
objects of his satire, which did not seem to displease him.　He
was still editor of a periodical, a small insignificant monthly
magazine, entitled *Neue Berliner Monatschrift*.　A number,
which he placed in my hands contained a very foolish paper
on the opinions of the English respecting the Germans, — full
of absurd, vulgar falsehoods about the English, such as that
they can sell their wives according to law by taking them to
market with a rope round their necks, &c.　Nicolai said,
" Write me word what you think of it" ; and so I did.　It was
my amusement on my return to Jena ; and I own I was
pleased to find, on receiving a parcel from Berlin, that my answer was printed in full without corrections, and with a complimentary preface by the editor.

　While at Berlin I paid a visit to the Deaf and Dumb Institution.　Some of the pupils evinced so much perception, that
I might have supposed the deafness feigned if there had been
any motive for deception.　They are not all dumb, for many
of them, by imitating certain movements of the lips and tongue,
can produce sounds which they themselves do not hear, and
thus make themselves understood.　In the dark, the pupils
write on each other's backs and *feel* the words.　I observed

that one young man did not understand me so well as he did others. The preceptor said my foreign manner was puzzling.

Next day I met a pupil in the street, who smiled and took me by the hand, when this dialogue took place : I said, " Which is the way to St. ——'s Church ?" He made a flourish in the air with his hands, in imitation of a cupola with a spire above. It was the form of the church. I nodded assent. He pointed to a street, and stretching out his right arm, struck it twice, with his left hand ; then for the outstretched right arm substituted the left, and finished by one stroke on the left arm with the right hand. So that I at once understood that I had to take the second turning to the right, and the first to the left. Nothing could be clearer or more correct. I shook hands with him at parting, and he appeared delighted at his success in rendering me this little service.

I thought the Opera-house very splendid. I saw there " The Island of Spirits," founded on Shakespeare's " Tempest," with a skilful omission of everything beyond the story that could recall the great dramatist to the mind. Prospero's character was ruined by his appearing to be dependent on a spirit floating in the clouds, whose aid he implores ; and Caliban was a sort of clown, unmercifully thrashed as the clown is in our pantomimes. I saw also a comic *vaudeville*, with jokes of a bolder character than I should have expected. A dispute arises about geography, and an old map being brought, the remark that Germany and Poland are terribly torn was warmly applauded. I saw Iffland in a sentimental melodrama by Kotzebue, — " The Hussites before Naumburg." He charmed me by his tender and dignified representation of an old man.

The only occurrence on my way back to Jena worth noting took place at the little town of Altenburg, where I was asked at the inn whether I would not call on Anton Wall. Now Anton Wall was the *nom de guerre* of a writer of romances, in which he availed himself of Oriental imagery and machinery with humor and grace. Especially had his " Amatonda " pleased me.* It is considered not an intrusion, but a compliment, at all events by the minor writers, when a traveller calls on an author. The singular habits of Anton Wall might render such a visit peculiarly acceptable ; for, though he did not pretend to be ill, he had literally taken to his bed, and there

* Afterwards translated by H. C. R. Anton Wall is the *nom de guerre* of Christian Leberecht Heyne.

in a garret had lived for years. He had his books near, and
dreamed away his time, writing occasionally. I introduced
myself as an Englishman, and he was evidently flattered by
finding himself known to an Englishman. He inquired which
of his books I had read, and when I said "Amatonda," he told
me that the poetical brother was intended for Jean Paul. This
tale relates how a magician, dying, tells his three nephews
that the only way to secure happiness is by finding the fairy
Amatonda; but he dies without keeping his promise to any
one of the three, that he would tell them where she is to be
found. The two elder brothers set out in search of her. The
eldest fancies she must be glory, and becomes a warrior and
statesman; but adversity overtakes him, and in old age he
returns to his uncle's house a cripple and in poverty. On his
way back he falls in with the second brother, who had pursued
the fairy in literary fame, and was equally unsuccessful and
wretched. They find the third brother at home with a wife
and children, and in the enjoyment of the happiness of which
they had gone forth in search. He said to them, "I did not
think it worth while to go out of my way in pursuit of the
fairy; but she might come to me, if she liked, and she did
come. She made her appearance to announce that the true
Amatonda is a good wife." With Anton Wall I had a long
chat. He was remarkably clean in his person, and there was
an air of neatness and comfort in his apartment, which itself,
though a garret, was spacious. He himself was a compound
of kindliness and vanity. It was thought he was rather crazy,
but he was universally liked. He was fond of giving treats to
little children; and girls used to come to him to receive lessons. In announcing his "Bagatellen," Schlegel in his *Athenæum* says, "These are genuine 'Bagatellen,' and that is not a
trifle," — a compliment which Anton Wall heard from me with
satisfaction.

I commenced my second session at the University of Jena
much more auspiciously than the first. My position was very
much improved, and I was in excellent health and spirits. As
to my studies, I determined to endeavor to make up for my
want of an early grammar-school education. It is not without
a feeling of melancholy that I recollect the long list of Greek
and Latin authors whom I read during the next two years.*
That I never mastered the Greek language is certain; but I
am unwilling to suppose that I did not gain some insight into

---

* The list includes the principal authors in both languages.

5 *

the genius of Greek poetry, especially in its connection with philosophy.*

H. C. R. TO HIS BROTHER.

JENA, June 2, 1803.

DEAR THOMAS :—-

. . . . I have changed my lodgings, and have at present one of the best in the town. My sitting-room has four sash-windows opening into a beautiful walk of lime-trees, and affording a fine hilly prospect. Now, too, that spring is come, I find Jena one of the most beautiful spots I ever dwelt in. It stands in the centre of a valley of more than fifteen miles along the Saale, which in its course has many a picturesque winding, and passes through many pleasing villages. I have likewise remarked in myself two very happy changes. The one is that I can amuse myself without suffering ennui in mixed society, and that I have lost that eager thirst after new books which is rather a disease than a passion. I can now take a walk without a book in my pocket, and can be at ease if I do not find on my desk a new, unread publication.† . . . .

I have introduced among the students games at leap-frog and jumping over ditches ; and I attribute much of my well-being now to these bodily exercises. In short, I am without care and very lively, and withal by no means idle. I write or study attentively eight hours every day.

Notwithstanding my study of the ancient languages, I attended a course of lectures by Schelling on methodology ; and I fancied I had a glimpse of light every now and then. He pointed out the relation of the several sciences to one another, but dwelt chiefly on religion and jurisprudence, and said but little of the physical sciences. I will insert here a recollection, which seems to me important, and the accuracy of which was corroborated by one who ranks among those who have advanced the philosophy of science, and especially in connection with magnetism : I refer to Dr. Neeff. Schelling said : " We are accustomed to consider magnetism, electricity, and galvanism three distinct sciences ; and in a certain sense they are, inasmuch as the facts belonging to them are arranged in three classes. But in truth the magnetic, electric, and gal-

---

* Private lessons from an old student cost me three dollars six groschen for two months.

† At all events during the last forty years of his life, Mr. Robinson never took a walk without a book in his pocket.

vanic powers are only various forms of the same thing ; and before many years have elapsed some experimental naturalist will come forward and exhibit visible proofs of this fact." *

I kept up my acquaintance with Schelling by occasionally calling on him ; and, during one of my visits, I ventured to remonstrate with him on the contemptuous language he used respecting our great English authors, even Bacon and Newton. He gave the best turn he could to the subject by saying, "Because they are so dangerous. The English empiricists are more consistent than the French." (I doubt this, by the by, so far as Locke is concerned.) "There is Bacon, a man of vast talents, but a most mischievous philosopher. He and Newton may be regarded as the great enemies and destroyers of philosophy in modern times. But," he added, "it is no small matter to be able to do so much harm."

The name of Voss will have a lasting place in the history of German literature. He is known and prized as the greatest of German translators from the Greek. Especially is his "Homer" considered a masterpiece. To this he owes his fame. The one drawback on his good name is the acrimony of his polemical writings. He was an elderly man at the time I was introduced to him, — in his person tall and thin, with a sharp nose, and a sort of lanky figure, — a compound of subtlety and naïveté. He was living retired and quite domesticated. He was the son of a Mecklenburg peasant, and used to be called a "gelehrter Bauer" (a learned peasant). To this circumstance some ascribed the absence of good manners in controversy ; but I would rather ascribe a great portion of it to his intense conscientiousness. He was a rigidly virtuous man, and a Protestant ; and seemed hardly able to tolerate any departure from what he thought right and true. Roman Catholicism he called Jesuitism. When his noble friends, the Counts Stolberg, whom in his youth he must have deemed it a high honor to know, went over to the Roman Catholic Church, he treated the change as if it were hardly short of a crime. Nor was he much better able to bear difference of

* "In 1812 Oersted went to Germany, and whilst there he wrote his essay on the Identity of Chemical and Electrical Forces, thus laying the foundation for the subsequent identification of the forces of magnetism, electricity, and galvanism. In 1819 he made the announcement of his great discovery of the intimate relation existing between magnetism and electricity."— *Eng. Cyclop.*, Article " Oersted." " Faraday read his first paper on Magneto-electric Induction before the Royal Society on the 24th November, 1831 "; " his paper on Identity of Electricities on January 10th and 17th, 1833, also before the Royal Society." — *Faraday as a Discoverer*, by John Tyndall.

opinion on matters of taste.   Hence his furious disputes with
Heyne, the learned Göttinger, and (but that was later) with
Creuzer, the mythologist.   The latter explained the Greek
and Roman mythology, as Voss thought, mystically.   I was
quite unable to make him see the beauty of Dryden's exquisite translations from Horace, — such as the " Ode on Fortune."   Indeed, his love of English literature was nearly confined to Shakespeare and Milton, of both of whom he always
spoke in high admiration.   And he affirmed that Milton might,
had he pleased, have successfully introduced hexameters into
English poetry.

Voss's " Louisa " is the rival of " Hermann und Dorothea,"
and has perhaps more admirers.   He is delicate in his descriptions, and paints and describes nothing but the simple, the noble, the modest, and the good.   But this turn of mind, which
prevents his being a great poet, makes him one of the best
men imaginable.

It was understood that Voss's time for receiving callers was
after supper, and I frequently availed myself of the opportunity of seeing him.   For, with all his infirmities of temper
and his narrowness, there was in him an integrity, a simplicity, a purity, which placed him in the very first class of men
combining great mental power with the highest moral qualities; and it was no slight merit in my eyes, that he loved
Goethe and Wieland, notwithstanding the extreme difference
between his literary tastes and theirs.

I once saw at the house of Voss the accomplished scholar
Wolf, who had in Germany, in my time, as high a reputation
as at the same time Porson had in England.   Wolf's commanding person and figure of themselves attracted attention to
him.   His friendship with Voss was cemented by their united
opposition to Heyne.   Voss told me that he and Wolf used to
dispute which owed most to Heyne.   Both had been his pupils;
one had subscribed to two courses of lectures, and heard a
single lecture, — the other had subscribed to only one course,
and had heard three lectures.   Voss's attachment to Wolf may
be regarded as a great and rare act of liberality, seeing that
he altogether dissented from Wolf's theory concerning Homer.
Voss used to say, " It would be a greater miracle had there been
many Homers, than it is that there was one."   On the other
hand, Goethe has an epigram in which he gives the health of
him who freed the poets from the tyranny of the single-one,
with whom no one would dare to contend; " but to be *one of*

the Homeridæ is beautiful." This he said in allusion to his own "Achilleis," a continuation of the "Iliad."

Wolf frequently said good things. I heard Voss relate this *mot* of his against Meiners. He quoted some Latin book of Meiners,' "Minertis de," &c., and remarked it would have been better if the learned professor had written "Minertii de," but he always through life thought proper to decline himself according to *iners.*

When Madame de Staël came to Weimar, Voss was told that she wished to see him. He coolly replied that she might come. But she would have been sadly perplexed if she had taken him at his word; for he would not have spoken French to her. He was indignant at the homage paid to foreigners by speaking their language. "I should think it my duty," he said, "to learn French before I went to France. The French should do the same."

Out of his own peculiar line of philological and archæological study, he was not a man of great acuteness. When his poetical works were reviewed by Goethe in the Jena *Literarische Zeitung,* I was afraid he would take offence at what seemed to me some awkward compliments. For example, "While other poets raise to themselves the objects they describe, our amiable author descends to their level and becomes one of them." Goethe was speaking of the Idyllists, the class to whom Voss belonged. But my apprehension proved to be groundless. Goethe praised affectionately, picking out excellences and passing over defects, after his fashion, and Voss was well pleased. His "Louisa" is certainly a masterpiece, though I cannot but think Wordsworth greatly mistaken in prizing it more highly than "Hermann und Dorothea."

In the same house I once met the famous philosopher Frederick Jacobi, with whose personal dignity and beauty I was much struck. He was, take him for all in all, one of the handsomest men I ever saw. He was greatly respected. I should have said universally, but for the odium he incurred from the Romanist party.

He spoke with great respect of my friend Fries, and said, "If he be a Kantianer, so am I." Jacobi is at the head of a school of thought which has attracted men of feeling and imagination, but which men of a dry and logical turn have considered a corruption of philosophy. Yet opposed as he was to the critical philosophy on account of its dryness, and to the poets for their supposed want of religion, he was to no one's taste precisely. Some accused him of intolerance. But I believe it lay in his warm style, rather than in his heart. Goethe, however, seemed never to be quite reconciled to his way of showing religious zeal.

At the beginning of session 1803 – 4, the list of Jena professors showed a serious loss, no less than seven having left, including Schelling, Tennemann, Paulus, and Hufeland, a distinguished jurist. But another loss, which soon followed, affected me personally still more. It arose out of the New Year festivities.

It is a custom at Jena, as at other German Universities, to celebrate the New Year by a midnight frolic. The Burschen assemble in the market-place, and, when the town-clock strikes twelve, they shout a *pereat* to the Old Year, and a *vivat* to the New. Like base and disgraceful sycophants, they forget the good and exaggerate the evil the departed year may have brought, and dismiss it without ceremony to the shades. They then hail the new-comer with the complimentary salutation, " Das neue Jahr soll leben ! " — as we should say, " The New Year forever ! " Squibs and crackers frequently accompany this celebration. Now it is obvious that the darkness of night and the excitement arising from the Commerze which have probably taken place are not unlikely to lead to more or less rioting, especially if during the year offence have been given to influential Burschen. The previous year about thirty houses had their windows broken without resistance, or subsequent notice by the authorities. On the present occasion I did not anticipate any disturbance, and therefore, after supping with the Curländer, retired to my rooms before the stroke of the clock. Unluckily, however, a tradesman had given offence by sending a girl to Bridewell, and a body of students showed their displeasure by breaking a few panes of glass at his house. In an instant a number of hussars appeared, and a skirmish arose, in which the students, few in number, and these few more or less intoxicated, were driven out of the market-place. The cry resounded, " Bursch heraus ! " like the cry of " Gown against Town " at Cambridge, and the students came again into the field. The Prorector, who corresponds to the Cambridge Vice-Chancellor, was called up, and the demand was made that a wounded student who had been taken to the watch-house should be set free This was refused, and the hussars returned. The affair was already bad enough, but the students made it worse by a most indecorous memorial, which they called a petition, and in which they demanded an amnesty in behalf of the implicated students, compensation for what was considered an insult in the calling out of the military with fixed bayonets, and a pledge on the part of the government that on no occasion in future should troops not garrisoned at Jena be sent from Weimar. In case these demands were not complied with, two hundred and four students pledged themselves to leave the University at Easter. Among the subscribers were the Curländer, Rheinländer, and nearly all my personal friends. I, being a sort of privileged person, was not pressed for my name, though a blank was left for it. On the part of the academical senate, the negotiation was put into the hands of one who had no *savoir faire*. The result was that conference served rather to widen than to close the breach. Both parties secretly wished for a reconciliation, for the professors were unwilling to lose their pupils, and the students were aware that nowhere else could they enjoy so many advantages at so little expense; and yet neither were prepared to make the necessary concessions. Thinking myself perhaps a suitable person to interpose, I called on seven of the leading members of the senate. But meanwhile the matter had been laid before the Duke, whose pride was wounded by the insult offered to his soldiers; and he gave preparatory orders, which rendered all reconciliation impossible. I shall mention more in detail by and by an application made by me to Goethe in behalf of the students. It was of no avail.

CHAPTER VIII.

GERMANY. — 1804.

THE prospect of losing so many friends was to me a real sorrow, and I should have felt it still more deeply had not my interest in University studies been weakened by other pursuits, and especially by the very interesting acquaintance which I formed in the month of January (1804) with a lady who then enjoyed a European reputation, and who will have a lasting place in the history of French literature. I received a note from Böttiger, the curious beginning of which is worth

translating : " Madame de Staël, from whose lips flow spirit
and honeyed speech (Geist und Honigrede) wishes to make
your acquaintance, dearest Sir and Friend. She longs for a
philosophical conversation with you, and is now busied with
the Cahier (notes) on Schelling's ' Æsthetics,' which I possess
through your kindness. She has, indeed, translated some
portions of them with admirable skill." I was then requested
to fix a day for dining with her. I was delighted with this
invitation, and knew how to interpret Böttiger's flattering expressions in reference to myself. He further begged me to
draw up a sketch of Schelling's " All-philosophia," as he
termed it, adapted to the Verstandswelt, i. e. the world of the
ordinary understanding and common sense as opposed to the
philosophical reason. With this request I complied, not that
I imagined myself competent to write a sentence which would
satisfy a German philosopher, but I thought I might render
some service to a French lady, even though she were Madame
de Staël.

On the 28th of January I first waited on her. I was shown
into her bedroom, for which, not knowing Parisian customs,
I was unprepared. She was sitting, most decorously, *in* her
bed, and writing. She had her nightcap on, and her face was
not made up for the day. It was by no means a captivating
spectacle, but I had a very cordial reception, and two bright
black eyes smiled benignantly on me. After a warm expression of her pleasure at making my acquaintance, she dismissed
me till three o'clock. On my return then I found a very different person, — the accomplished Frenchwoman surrounded
by admirers, some of whom were themselves distinguished.
Among them was the aged Wieland. There was on this, and
I believe on almost every other occasion, but one lady among
the guests : in this instance Frau von Kalb. Madame de
Staël did not affect to conceal her preference for the society of
men to that of her own sex. If I mistake not, this dinner
was followed by five others during her short stay at Weimar ;
but my memoranda do not enable me to assign the exact
dates of the conversations to which I have now to refer.

She said, " Buonaparte sent his Marshal to me " — I think
it was Caulaincourt — " to say that he would not permit me
to receive company ; that he knew I was his enemy, — and
that my house was open to all his enemies. I might remain
at Paris, if I liked, but I must live alone. Now, you must be
sensible that is impossible, and therefore I set out on this

journey. I do not think it prudent to go to England at present. Buonaparte pretended, and it was asserted by *order* in the government newspapers, that his displeasure with me was not on account of himself, but because I was a partisan of foreign literature, and therefore a depreciator of the literary glory of France." This I may say, that she had a laudable anxiety to obtain a knowledge of the best German authors; and for this reason she sought my society, and I was not unwilling to be made use of by her. She said, and the general remark is true, "The English mind is in the middle between the German and the French, and is a medium of communication between them. I understand you better than I do any German with whom I have ever spoken." But this, it must be borne in mind, was at the beginning of her residence in Germany, and long before her acquaintance with August Wilhelm Schlegel.

One day after dinner the Duke came in. She introduced me to him, saying, "J'ai voulu connaître la philosophie allemande; j'ai frappé à la porte de tout le monde — Robinson seul l'a ouverte." The day after she said to me, "How like an Englishman you behaved yesterday! When the Duke came in you were in the middle of a story, and after a slight interruption you went on with it. No German would have dared to do this. With a sovereign, it is always understood that he is to begin every subject of conversation. The others answer questions and follow." I replied, "I see I was quite wrong, — I ought not to have gone on." — "Perhaps not; but I was delighted with you for doing it." This subject was introduced by her in connection with the remark that she could at once see whether or not a German was accustomed to good company, but not an Englishman. Then she abruptly said, "Are you rich?" I at once felt that this was not a complimentary question, especially so introduced, so I answered evasively, "As you please to take it; I am either a rich man of letters, or a poor gentleman," — and with that she was content. She expressed her pleasure at the manly and independent tone of my conversation with the Duke, and her contempt for the servile habits of some of the Germans.

When alone with her, it was my great aim to make her feel the transcendent excellence of Goethe. But I failed. She seemed utterly incapable of realizing wherein his excellence lay. But she caught by sympathy a portion of that admiration which every one felt for him. Among those excellences

H

which she was unable to perceive was that of naïveté. I read to her some half-dozen of Goethe's most subtle and exquisite epigrams. That, for instance, in which, after lamenting that his mistress having jilted him, and the Muses done the same, he, because he could not write, peered about for a halter or a knife. "But thou camest," he concludes, "to save me, Ennui! Hail, Mother of the Muses!" Enumerating the fine arts which he practised, "Bringing one only near to perfection," he says; "and so, miserable artist, I threw away my art on the worst of materials, writing German!" She could not comprehend these. She was precisely what Charles Lamb supposes all the Scotch to be, — incapable of _feeling_ a joke. Having tried her with a number of these ironical epigrams, I read a commonplace one against the German sovereigns for speaking French at their courts. "See what comes of it? Your subjects are only too fond of talking French," meaning French principles. This she thought admirable, and took down. Her success in spoiling a fine thing was strikingly shown in connection with a noble saying of Kant, which I repeated to her: "There are two things which, the more I contemplate them, the more they fill my mind with admiration, — the starry heavens above me, and the moral law within me." She sprang up, exclaiming, "Ah, que cela est beau! Il faut que je l'écrive," — and years after, in her "Allemagne," I found it Frenchified thus: "Car, comme un philosophe célèbre a très bien dit : Pour les cœurs sensibles, il y a deux choses." The grave philosopher of Königsberg turned into a "cœur sensible!"

It is very apparent from the correspondence of Goethe and Schiller that these two great poets regarded her visit to Weimar as an infliction. Schiller would not go near her, and Goethe made himself scarce. There was a report that she extorted from the latter, by some advice on his "Natürliche Tochter," this reply, "Madam, I am more than sixty years old!" But this is not after his fashion. I know, however, that she did speak irreverently of that masterly work, and provoked me to the utterance of a very rude observation. I said, "Madame, vous n'avez pas compris Goethe, et vous ne le comprendrez jamais." Her eye flashed, — she stretched out her fine arm, of which she was justly vain, and said in an emphatic tone, "Monsieur, je comprends tout ce qui mérite d'être compris ; ce que je ne comprends n'est rien." I bowed lowly. This was said at table. After dinner she gave me her hand very kindly. "I was angry for a moment," she said, "but it is all over now." I believe I owe the favor I experienced from her to my perfect frankness, and even freedom.

One day, in the presence of Böttiger and others, she read a translation of that "Scheussliches Gedicht" (according to Herder), the "Braut von Corinth." The most material point — indeed I might say the *peccant* point — she had not perceived, and therefore it was left out. When she ceased there was a burst of praise from every one but myself. "Et vous, Robinson, vous ne dites rien." — "Madame, je m'occupe en pensant si vous avez compris le véritable sens des mots." And then I read the words significantly. Böttiger began, "Madame a parfaitement rendu le vers." — "Taisez-vous!" she exclaimed, paused a moment, and then, giving me her hand, said, "Vous tous m'avez louée — Robinson seul m'a corrigée; Robinson, je vous remercie." Yet she had pleasure in being complimented, and took it as a sort of right, — like a quitrent, not requiring thanks, but a receipt. I must even quote one of the very few gallant speeches that I have ever made. Before her journey to Berlin, her court-dress for the King's birthday ball was produced at table after dinner. It was highly extolled by the guests. She noticed my silence. "Ah, vous, Robinson, vous ne dites rien?" — "Madame," I said, in a tone of assumed gravity, "vous êtes un peu exigéante. Je ne puis pas admirer vous et votre robe au même temps." — "Ah que vous êtes aimable!" she exclaimed, and gave me a smile, as if she had said, "I know this means nothing, but then these are the things we expect. You are really improving." For English frankness, abstaining from all compliment, had been my habit.

My irregular recollection takes me back to the day when the Duke joined our party. She was very eloquent in her declamation, and chose as her topic an image which she afterwards in her book quoted with applause, but which, when I first mentioned it to her, she could not comprehend. Schelling, in his "Methodology," calls Architecture "frozen music." This she vehemently abused as absurd, and challenged me to deny that she was right. Forced to say something, I made my escape by a compliment. "I can't deny that you have proved — que votre esprit n'est pas gelé." — "Fort bien dit," the Duke exclaimed; and certainly any way of getting out of such a challenge was better than accepting it. There has appeared since in English a treatise on Greek Architecture bearing the significant title, "The Music of the Eye."

I will conclude what I have to say of Madame de Staël personally, before I notice her companions. After some half-dozen dinners, and as many or more tête-à-têtes, she went to Berlin, from which place she wrote to me, proposing that I should remove to Berlin, take a lodging in her neighborhood, and be her constant guest at table. She would introduce me to the literary world at Berlin. This proposal was too advantageous to be declined. Such an introduction would have offered me probably more advantages than I could have profitably made use of. I made up my mind to remove in the summer. It was, therefore, with much sorrow that I heard, first, of the death of her father, the minister Necker, and then that she had arrived at Weimar, to stay a few days on her way to Switzerland. I of course waited on her. She was loud in her expression of grief at the loss which she had sustained. But her feeling was sincere. It would be judging uncandidly to infer that she did not feel because she had leisure to be eloquent. Among her declamatory bursts was this : " Oh ! il n'était pas mon père. Il était mon frère, mon fils, mon mari, mon Tout ! "

I will now refer to those with whom I became acquainted through her, or whom I saw in her company. Of these by far the most eminent was Benjamin Constant. The slanderous world, at least in France, has always affected to consider him her lover. In a society so generally profligate as that of the Parisian beau-monde, where the ascertained fact would be scarcely a subject of blame, and where any expressed doubt of the truth of the report would expose him who dared utter it to contempt, no wonder that this amour was taken for granted. It would never have occurred to me. She appeared to be the elder, and called him " Mon Benjamin," as she might have done a son or a younger brother. He, on the contrary, never spoke of her lightly, but always with respect as Madame de Staël. At her table he occupied the place of the master of the house; he was quite the *ami de la maison*. The worst thing about him was that he was separated from his wife, to whom it was said he had been a bad husband. He was a declared enemy to Buonaparte, and was a member of the Tribunat which Buonaparte abolished. After the Restoration he became a distinguished member of the Legislative Body. He was by birth a Swiss. As a man of letters he was highly esteemed, and had a first-rate reputation as a philosophical jurist. A zealous anti-Romanist, he wrote on Christianity. I should call him rather a sentimental than a Bible Christian ; but I should not be warranted in saying that he was an anti-supernaturalist. A novel of his, " Adolphe," was said to favor free opinions on marriage. I heard that he had translated Godwin's " Political Justice," and inquired whether he had really done so. He said he had made the translation, but had declined to publish it, because he thought it might injure the good cause in the then state of public opinion. Sooner or later, however, the work was to be published, for he regarded the original as one of the master-works of the age. In saying that his tone towards Madame de Staël was respectful rather than tender, I do not mean that it was deferential towards her opinions. On the contrary, his opposition was unsparing, and though he had not her colloquial eloquence, I thought he had always the advantage of her in argument. One remark on the French national character was made by him, which is worth quoting. I inquired whether Buonaparte really possessed the affections of the French people. He said, " Certainly not. But the French," he added, " are so vain, that they cannot bear the insignificance of neutrality, and will affect to belong to the triumphant party from an unwillingness to confess that they belong to the conquered." Hence Robespierre and Buonaparte have both, in their respective times, had the tacit support of a nation which in reality was not attached to either of them.

I have already said that Wieland was the most distinguished of Madame de Staël's German visitors. He was frequent in his attendance on her, and loud in his admiration. One day, when she was declaiming with her usual eloquence, he turned to me, and exclaimed, " Dass ich, in meinem hohen Alter, solche eine Frau sehen sollte ! " (That I, in my old age, should see such a woman !) I had remarked to her that of all the German great writers his mind was the most French. " I am aware of it," she said, " and therefore I do not think much of him. I like a German to be a German."

I, at the same time, told her that of all the then eminent writers, the two Schlegels were those who possessed in a high degree, and beyond all others, that peculiar mental quality which the French call esprit, as distinguished from genius, understanding, &c. ; and I advised her to cultivate the acquaintance of A. W. Schlegel, who was then at Berlin. She did what I advised, and more ; she engaged A. W. Schlegel to reside with her in the character of tutor to her children. And, in fact, the knowledge she would obtain from him was in every respect so superior to anything I could communicate to her, that I take very little credit for any part I may have had in supplying the materials of her book.   There are, indeed, many opinions in the book which Schlegel probably would have protested against being thought to have suggested.   Yet she said to me years after, " You know very well that I could never have written that book without the assistance of Schlegel." But all that is best in that work, the section on life and manners in Germany, came from herself alone.

Next to Wieland, the most eminent visitor whom I recollect seeing at her table, was the famous Swiss historian, Johannes von Müller of Schaffhausen.   I saw him frequently, and what I remarked in him deserves to be noticed as bearing on his life and conduct in middle age.   He is the most illustrious of literary turncoats on record,— if he deserve that degrading character, which possibly he does not.

When he first made himself known as a political writer, he was librarian to the Elector of Mayence ; and in that position he wrote, in 1782, a famous pamphlet on the celebrated visit of the Pope to Joseph II. at Vienna.   In this pamphlet, entitled " Reisen der Päbste," he represented the Papal power as exercised in favor of popular liberty against the great military governments.   His next and still more famous pamphlet was the " Fürstenbund " (League of Princes), written in 1787, and advocating the cause of the Princes of Germany against the House of Austria.   This was followed by his entering into the service of the Emperor.   In that service he remained many years.   During this time he continued the great work on which his fame chiefly rests, " The History of the Swiss League," which he commenced when young, and which was, in fact, the business of his life.   On the subject of his connection with the Austrian government, I heard him say : " The government passed a law which was aimed at me particularly.   It was a prohibition of all subjects printing any book out of the dominions of the Emperor.   The moment this law was passed I made my preparations for quitting Vienna.   I began by sending out of the country all my MSS. and my papers of every description.   I sent them in small parcels by many persons, and not one was lost."   When I saw him at Weimar he was, as I learn from the " Conversations-Lexicon," on his way to Berlin.   He at this time entered into the service of the King of Prussia.   Yet my impression was that the tone of his conversation was by no means favorable to the Prussian government.   And being, as he was, anti-French in his feelings, though perfectly liberal in his political opinions, and a sturdy Protestant, he might well be hostile to that fatal policy which for a time made Prussia the ally of France, and the tool of Buonaparte. After the fall of the Prussian government, Müller went into the service of the King of Westphalia, in which he died in 1809 ; and, as I heard, stayed by his death proceedings against him for writings in opposition to the Gallo-German government to which he belonged. Notwithstanding his having served so many rulers of an opposite character, my impression, from what I saw and heard of him, was, that he was an honest and conscientious man, and that, like many others who have incurred the reproach of inconsistency, he acted on the maxim of doing all the good he could in any station in which he might at the time be placed,—not hesitating to leave that station when he found himself no longer able to do good in it.

Müller's German pronunciation was extremely disagreeable. It was excessively Swiss, i. e. the guttural sounds were exaggerated in it. His French, on the contrary, was agreeable.

While he was at Weimar I witnessed the performance of "Wilhelm Tell," when the following incident took place. In the last act an occurrence is introduced for the sake of a great moral contrast, though at variance equally with history and dramatic unity. Parricida, the murderer of the Emperor, is coming on the stage, and the murder is spoken of. On the evening to which I refer, when Müller was present, there was introduced, as I understood for the first time, this passage : "How do you know it ? " — "It is certain ; a man worthy of credit, Johannes Müller, brought it from Schaffhausen." The name was pronounced aloud, and was followed by uproarious applause. It was talked of next day as a joke. But in my edition the passage stands in the text without any note.

At Madame de Staël's house I first became acquainted with several of the Weimar court, and so the way was prepared for that introduction which in the following winter became of some importance. My name was known pretty generally. A prominent court lady was Fräulein von Geckhausen, a shrewd lively little woman, who noticed me obligingly. Since her death the gossiping books speak of her as malignant and intriguing ; for myself, however, I have none but agreeable recollections of her. She read to me a short note to Madame de Staël, in which the compliments seemed to me to have an extravagance bordering on insincerity. I therefore ventured to

say, "Do me the favor, Fräulein, to read that in German."
She began, stammered, and stopped. "Das lässt sich nicht
Deutsch sagen." (You can't say that in German.) — "I know
you cannot; shall I tell you the reason why? The German is
an honest language, and your German habits are honest.
When, therefore, you have anything to say of mere compliment, which means nothing, you feel as you say, 'Das lässt
sich nicht Deutsch sagen.'"

In the present University session I saw a little of Schiller,
but not much. He had always the appearance of being unwell. His amiable wife, and her very clever sister, and indeed
all those who were about him, appeared to watch over him as
an object of solicitude. While the admiration excited by
Goethe was accompanied by awe, that which was felt towards
Schiller was mixed with love and pity. I may here mention
that at the end of a very early, if not the first, performance of
"Die Braut von Messina," a young doctor, son of the learned
Professor Schulz, the philologer, rose in the pit and exclaimed,
"Schiller der grosse Dichter soll leben" (Long live Schiller,
the great poet)! The numerous students in the pit all joined
in the cry, and there was a regular three times three of applause.
But this was regarded as a great impropriety and breach of
decorum in the presence of the Duke and Duchess, and we
heard that young Schulz received a severe reproof from the
government.

In March, 1804, I had a re-introduction, and not a mere
formal one, as the first was, to Goethe. It was at the theatre.
He was sitting in his arm-chair, in the front row of the pit.
I had repeatedly taken a seat near enough to him to have
an occasional glimpse of his countenance, but I never presented myself to his notice. On the evening of which I
write, I was sitting immediately behind him. Benjamin Constant came in with him, and after shaking hands with me,
whispered my name to Goethe, who immediately turned round,
and with a smile as ingratiating as his ordinary expression was
cold and forbidding, said, "Wissen Sie, Herr Robinson, dass
Sie mich beleidigt haben?" (Do you know, Mr. Robinson,
that you have affronted me?) — "How is that possible, Herr
Geheimerath?" — "Why, you have visited every one at Weimar excepting me." I felt that I blushed, as I said, "You
may imagine any cause, Herr Geheimerath, but want of reverence." He smiled and said, "I shall be happy to see you at
any time." I left my card, of course, the next morning, and

the next day there came an invitation to dinner ; and I dined
with him several times before I left the neighborhood of Weimar.

It was, I believe, on the very evening on which he spoke
to me in the theatre, that I asked him whether he was acquainted with our " Venice Preserved."   " O, very well, — the
comic scenes are particularly good."   I actually started at
so strange a judgment.   " Indeed ! in England those scenes
are considered so very bad that they are never acted." — " I
can understand that ; and yet, on reflection, you will perceive
that those scenes are quite essential to the piece.   It is they
alone which account for, and go near to justify, the conspiracy ; for we see in them how utterly unfit for government the
Senate had become."   I recognized at once the truth of the
criticism, and felt ashamed of myself for not having thought of
it before.   In all his conversation he spoke in the most simple
and unpretending manner, but there was in it remarkable
significance, — a quiet strength, a power without effort, remind-
ing me of what I read of a painting, in which a man was
wrestling with an angel.   An ignorant man abused the picture
on the ground that in the angel there was no sign of effort, —
no muscle was strained.   But this was designed to show the an-
gelic nature.   It is the same in the Greek sculpture of the gods.

When Madame de Staël returned from Berlin, and brought
A. W. Schlegel in her train, I dined at Goethe's with Schlegel,
Tieck the sculptor, and Riemer.   No one else but Madame
Goethe was present.   I was struck by the contrast between
Schlegel and Goethe.   Nothing could exceed the repose of
Goethe, whereas on Schlegel's part there was an evident striving after pun and point.   Of these I recollect nothing but
that Böttiger was his butt, whom he compared to Bardolph.
From Goethe I remember a word or two of deep significance.
He said to Schlegel : " I am glad to hear that your brother
means to translate the ' Sakontala.'   I shall rejoice to see that
poem as it is, instead of as it is represented by the moral Englishman."   And there was a sarcastic emphasis on the word
"moralischen."   He then went on, " Eigentlich aber hasse
ich alles Orientalische."   (But in truth, I hate everything Oriental.)   By which, probably, he meant rather that he infinitely
preferred the Greek to the Oriental mind.   He continued : " I
am glad there is something that I hate ; for, otherwise, one is
in danger of falling into the dull habit of literally finding all
things good in their place, — and that is destructive of all

true feeling." This casts some light on his sentiments respecting the two religions which had their origin in the East. And yet this might have been a transient feeling, for in less than ten years he withdrew himself from the contemplation of the miseries which then surrounded him, and took refuge in the study of Oriental literature. The result is given in his " West-Eastern Divan."

Were I a younger man, and did I fancy myself competent to the task, I would collect and translate all that Goethe has written on Judaism and Christianity. It should be published without note or comment, — for it is unlike anything I have ever met with from believer or unbeliever, and is absolutely unique. In one of his private letters to Lavater, he makes a distinction, for which our ordinary language has no equivalent. He says, " I am by no means *anti*-Christian, not even *un*-Christian, but I am indeed nicht-Christian." The difference between un-Christian and nicht-Christian may be conceived.

It was at no great distance from this time that I called on Goethe to see whether I could induce him to act as a mediator between the Duke and the students, in the quarrel that threatened an Auszug, or withdrawal, of the best young men of the University. Having listened to my representations, he coolly said : " So is it in these matters of police, in which both parties are right. The students, seeing the matter from their point of view, are perfectly in the right. But then the Duke is equally in the right; he has his own mode of looking at things from his point of view as sovereign."

During these occasional visits, I saw the companion of Goethe's table, the mother of his children. As is well known, she afterwards became his wife. She had an agreeable countenance, and a cordial tone. Her manners were unceremonious and free. Queer stories are told of her undignified ways and the freedom of her intercourse with him when she was young; but she had outgrown all such eccentricities when I saw her.

I have already referred to Goethe's son coming to Madame de Staël with his album. She allowed me to copy the two first verses of the little volume. I have never seen them in print.

In Goethe's hand were these distichs : —

> " Gönnern reiche das Buch, und reich' es Freund und Gespielen:
> Reich' es dem Eilenden hin, der sich vorüber bewegt —
> Wer des freundlichen Worts, des Namens Gabe dir spendet
> Häufet den edlen Schatz holden Erinnerns dir an."

That is : —

> " Hand to the Patron the book, and hand it to friend and companion;
> Hand to the traveller too, — rapidly passing away :
> He who with friendly gift of a word or a name thee enriches,"

[The last line is wanting in the translation.   The meaning
is : —

> " Stores up a noble treasure of tender remembrance for thee."]

In Schiller's hand were these lines : —

> " Holder Knab', dich liebt das Glück denn es gab dir der Güter,
> Erstes, Köstliches, dich rühmend des Vaters zu freuen
> Jetzo kennest du nur des Freundes liebende Seele.
> Wenn du zum Manne gereift, wirst du die Worte verstehen.
> Dann erst kehrst du zurück mit reiner Liebe Gefühle
> An des Trefflichen Brust der dir jetzt Vater nur ist;
> Lass ihn leben in dir, wie er lebt in den ewigen Werken,
> Die er, der Einzige, uns blühend unsterblich erschuf,
> Und das herzliche Band der wechselnden Neigung und Treue
> Das die Väter verknüpft, binde die Söhne nur fort."

" Cherished boy ! thou art the favorite of Fortune, for she gave thee the first
and most precious of gifts, to rejoice in the glory of thy father.   Now thou
knowest only the loving heart of the friend.   When thou art ripened into
manhood thou wilt understand the words.   Thou wilt then go back with
feelings of pure love to the bosom of the excellent who at present is merely
father to thee.   Let him live in thee, as he lives in the eternal works which he,
the only one, produced for us in everlasting bloom; and may the heartfelt bond
of reciprocal inclination and confidence, which united the fathers, continue to
unite the sons ! "

The son of Prorector Voigt was among the students with
whom I became most intimate.   Later in life he became Professor of Botany at Jena, and acquired reputation by his
writings.   Of the kindliness of his disposition I have a deep
sense ; our friendship has retained its original warmth for forty
years, and during that time there has been no interruption to
our correspondence.   At the time of which I am now writing
he had completed his studies, and settled at Gotha with the
object of practising as a physician ; and there I paid him a
visit.   An Englishman was then a phenomenon in the little
town, but I was cordially received in Voigt's circle of acquaintance ; and I recollect that when I had danced with a lady
and handed her to a seat, she somewhat surprised me by
saying, " And now, sir, I have to tell you that you are the last
gentleman I shall ever dance with in company." — " Indeed,
madam.   How is that ? " — " Why, sir, to-morrow my daughter
is to be confirmed, and I have always been of opinion that
when a lady is so far advanced in life as to have a daughter
confirmed, it is time to give up dancing."

But my object in referring to this visit to Gotha is to say something of a man whose name belongs to the history of the last century, though it was raised to undue importance by the malignant exaggerations of party spirit.

During the heat of the first Revolution in France, two works appeared, one in England, by Professor Robison of Edinburgh, and the other, the more voluminous, in France, by the Abbé Barruel, with the common object of showing that the Revolution and all the horrors consequent on it were the effect of a conspiracy deliberately planned and carried out on the Continent of Europe by an Order of Infidels, who, by means of secret societies, planned to destroy all thrones, overturn all altars, and completely upset the established order of things. The society to which this scheme was ascribed had the name of *The Illuminati*. They were supposed to have ramifications everywhere. The Kantian philosophy was one of the instruments. Indeed, more or less, every union of men, and every variety of thought, opposed to monarchy and popery had about it the suspicion of " Illumination." And of this tremendous evil the founder and archdeacon was Adam Weishaupt. When I found that this notorious man was leading a secluded life in Gotha, I determined to call on him. On entering his room, I remarked that he was both embarrassed and reserved, and it was not till I had introduced myself as one anxious to see him, though I knew of him only from his enemies, that he seemed willing to enter into conversation with me. On my taking leave, he even · invited me to repeat my visit, and I went to him three times. He frankly told me that I was let into his house through the stupidity of a servant-girl, whom he was on the point of turning away for it ; but he had forgiven her on account of the pleasure he had derived from our interviews. He said he held in abhorrence all travellers who made impertinent calls, and especially Englishmen. He would not gratify the curiosity of such men. But my candor and openness had rendered him willing to make an exception in my case. In saying this he was, perhaps, not departing from that character which his enemies ascribed to him. Indeed, as is usual in such instances, the statements made concerning him are founded in truth. The falsehood lies in the exaggeration of some parts of his history, and in the omission of others.

Weishaupt would not have denied that he was brought up among the Jesuits, or that in his opposition to them he availed himself of the resources which he acquired through his connection with them. And he did form a secret Order at a time when, especially in the South of Germany, an open expression of free opinions would have endangered liberty, and perhaps life. That the end was good according to his first intention, and that there was at all times, perhaps, a mixture of goodness in his motives, may reasonably be conceded. Many eminent men (Baron Knigge was one of the ablest) attached themselves to the Order. It has always been said that Maximilian, the first king of Bavaria, was favorable to it; nor does the history of his reign contradict the report. The Church, the courtiers, and the aristocracy were, however, too powerful for the conspirators. The society was broken up, a fierce persecution arose, and Weishaupt was happy in making his escape, and obtaining the protection of the learned Duke of Saxe-Gotha and the Duchess. When I saw him he was about fifty-six years of age, and his appearance was in no respect prepossessing; his features were coarse, his voice harsh, and his manners abrupt and awkward. But his conversation made a strong impression on my mind. He showed no great anxiety to vindicate himself against the prevailing opinion respecting him, or to dwell on those sentiments which would be most likely to gain popular favor; on the contrary, he uttered things which it requires boldness and indifference to evil report to express. Among his sayings, one was delivered with peculiar emphasis: "One of my tests of character is what a man says about *principle*. A weak man is always talking of acting on principle. An able man does always the right thing at the right moment, and therein he shows himself to be able." He even went so far as to say that there are occasions when it is foolish to be just. He took a desponding view of human life, and seemed to think human society unimprovable. No wonder! He had himself failed as a reformer; and therefore thought no one else could succeed. He said, "There is but one schoolmaster whose teaching is always effectual, — Necessity. Evil flourishes till it destroys itself. So it was with Popery; so it will be with monarchy." And he added, somewhat diffusely, that there is a constant interchange of progressive evil and partial reform. I said, I could not believe that his view was a correct one. He smiled and said, "You are quite right; if you can help it, don't believe it." I said, "You would not teach this to your children." — "If I attempted it," he answered, "I should not succeed. The young, with their good hearts, cannot believe it." — "But old men with cold heads?" I said in a voice of interrogation. "I am sorry for it," he said, "but it is true."

The practical writings of Weishaupt are of value; the speculative were never esteemed. He wrote against the Kantian philosophy, but his works were not read. His "Pythagoras," as he said, contains all the statistics of Secret Societies. But the vast extension of education since Weishaupt's time has rendered this learning of less importance than it was even then. He is said to have been an admirer of Buonaparte. This is natural with his peculiar habit of thought. For the French character he professed great contempt, and for the English high admiration. To poetry and the fine arts he was indifferent.

At the Easter recess of 1804, the students who had threatened to leave the University, unless the demands in their memorial were complied with, took their departure to pursue their studies elsewhere. Jena seemed deserted; I at least lost the greater number of my younger friends and companions. A large proportion of them repaired to the recently established University of Würzburg.

It happened, fortunately for myself, that, soon after this loss, I became intimate with one for whom, of all my German acquaintance, I have felt the warmest regard: this was Major von Knebel. He was at the time just sixty years of age. He had a fine military figure, and his temper and character were much better adapted to arms than to scholarship; yet his tastes were literary. A Franconian nobleman by birth, he entered early into the service of Prussia, and was brought up under the great Frederick. But the restraints and subordination of a military life were repugnant to him. He loved poetry intensely, and even wrote verses. On a journey which he accidentally made through Weimar, when under the government of the Duchess-Dowager Amelia, he had the good fortune to make himself acceptable to the Duchess Regent. She obtained from the King of Prussia his discharge from military duties, and he accepted office in the Court of Weimar as governor of the Prince Constantine, the second son, and became his travelling companion in France. This was just at that genial period when Goethe became, not precisely the governor, but the intimate companion of the heir and subsequent Duke of Saxe-Weimar who when I was at Weimar was the sovereign.

Knebel, therefore, was a participator in all those acts of extravagance of which public report was so full, and which have formed a subject for so much political and literary gossip. When his pupil died, which was in a few years, he had a pension allowed him, with the rank and emoluments of a Major ; and thus he was sufficiently provided for till the end of his days. He was without the early training of the scholar and the habits of the literary man ; but he had the tastes of a delicate organization, and all the feelings of a man of honor and refined sensibility, with a choleric temperament. His sense of honor rendered him very reserved on all matters connected with the Court, especially with the Duke and Goethe. That sense of honor at the same time also kept him aloof from the Court. While he shared the admiration which was universally felt towards Goethe, there was something which prevented the perfect feeling of cordiality which existed between Herder and himself. In that division of literary men at Weimar, which placed Goethe and Schiller at the head of one set, and Wieland and Herder at the head of the other, there could be no question as to which Knebel attached himself.

His own taste led him to occupy himself with translations. He published a German version of the " Elegies of Propertius," and devoted many years of his life to the production of a German Lucretius. In the course of his studies he had formed a high opinion of the critical taste of Gilbert Wakefield, whose text he adopted ; and it added not a little to my merit in his eyes, that I had known Wakefield. Elegiac tenderness and sententious wisdom were the directions which his faculty of verse-making took. He was a moral poet, and full of " natural piety," to borrow Bacon's expression.

From the moment of my being known to Knebel, I became intimate in his house. There was none into which I went with so much pleasure, and Knebel seemed to receive no one with so much satisfaction. He had a great deal to learn from me in English literature, and I from him in German. Though our opportunities of intercourse lasted but a short time, I yet attached greater value to his acquaintance than any other I formed in Germany. He had not the means of giving expensive entertainments, nor was it the custom in Jenâ to give them ; but he was by nature liberal and most gentlemanly in all his feelings. He was an object of universal love.

JENA, December 12, 1804.

I met Knebel first at the house of Frau von Wollzogen, and was immediately invited to visit him. I am now the most intimate *ami de la maison.* If for three days I omit calling, the servant comes with the Major's compliments to inquire after my health; and I find that I am never unwelcome. We sometimes read Shakespeare, but oftener reason about Lucretius. By what lucky mistake I know not, but the Major looks on me as a *Philolog,* lays scruples and difficulties before me, and listens to me with an attention that makes me internally blush. He is chatty, has seen much of life and literary men, and relates his anecdotes with pleasure. Nor is this all. A few years since he married a very pretty and amiable woman, just half as old as himself. She is lively and naïve in the highest degree, so that they often seem rather in the relation of parent and child than of husband and wife. He has besides a forward clever boy of ten, with whom I can very well entertain myself. Thus it needs no assurance of mine that in this house I am quite happy; indeed it is my prime enjoyment this winter, — a new tie to Jena. When persons of so excellent a character as Major Knebel attach themselves to me, I am always led to inquire into the cause, and that out of true modesty, for it seems a wonder to me. And in this case it lies more in the virtues of Knebel than in me. He loves the society of those to whom he can say everything. And my *betters* here are not of that description, — real scholars have not time, and have too much pretension. I am a man of leisure. I am frank, and as I take liberties myself, so others can take liberties with me. And then the main point is, *we ride one hobby-horse.* I know no source of friendship so productive as this. I should further say that Major Knebel is in other respects a most worthy man, — generous and sincere, — a courtier without falsity, — a soldier without frivolity. .The worst fault I know in him is that he admires Buonaparte. I lately dined with him in company with the venerable Griesbach, whom you know as a theologian; and the equally venerable Wieland.

I will here mention an interesting anecdote connected with

---

* This letter is given a little out of order as to time, but the reference in it to Knebel could come in nowhere else so well as here.

" Reynard the Fox," though it is already contained in my friend Naylor's translation of that work. One day, at Knebel's house, Herder said to Goethe, " Do you know that we have in the German language an epic poem with as much poetry in it as the ' Odyssey,' and more philosophy ? "

When " Reineke Fuchs " was named, Goethe said he had been deterred from looking into it, by its being published by Gottsched, a sort of evil spirit who presided over the infant genius of German literature in the eighteenth century. Goethe, however, took the book away with him on a visit to Carlsbad, where he frequently passed the summer ; and in a few weeks he wrote to Herder that his version of " Reineke " in hexameters was in the press.

To soften the painful effect of taking leave at once of a number of high-spirited and generous young men, I had promised to pay a visit to Würzburg. On two points, moreover, my curiosity was not a little excited : first, as to how the Deism of Paulus would amalgamate with the Romanism of the Bavarian aborigines ; and secondly, whether the peculiar character of a Jenaer-Bursche was fixed to the soil, or might be transplanted by so numerous a colony to the Maximilian school.

At the request of my new friend Knebel, I postponed my journey from the 8th to the 10th of September, in order to accompany his friend, Herr von Holzschuher. He was a patrician of the imperial city of Nuremberg, and I found him a most amiable and obliging man. His station and exterior figure did not seem promising for a long expedition on foot ; but, notwithstanding his shrivelled, swarthy face, slender limbs, and shuffling gait, he had an inborn nobility of legs that secured my esteem, and enabled him to accomplish from twelve to fourteen leagues a day during the short time we were together.

My reception at Würzburg was a very cordial one, and I found myself an object of interest to many former Jena students, who crowded round me to hear tidings of a place they loved more than their pride would allow them to confess. When I repaired to my inn, my companions, bent on fun, urged me to be the chief actor in playing off a trick on a a foolish landlord. Indeed, without preparing me for what they were going to do, they introduced me to him at once as the illustrious philosopher Fichte. The man was so egregious a simpleton, that the task on my part was an easy one. My companions gravely put to me questions of casuistry, which I answered sometimes with Delphic mysticism, i. e. sheer nonsense, at others with pompous triteness, — a still more successful method, perhaps, of befooling a fool. Our host was delighted to have his house honored by the presence of so great a man, and soon brought into the room a witness and sharer of his felicity, a young Catholic priest on his way to the Arch-chancellor, the Elector Dalberg. After my friends had left me, and when I was quite alone, this young priest came to me for the second time, and begged to have the honor of a few words in private with the great man. I thought I might innocently indemnify myself for my trouble by learning some of his sentiments. " Pray," said I, "now that the young people are away, let us talk openly. Men of *our* character understand each other. How is it that a person of your philosophic turn of mind can submit to the slavery of the Roman Catholic system? How do you dare to think philosophy?" He assumed a look that Hogarth might have borrowed, and said : " To tell you the truth, Herr Professor, there is not one of us who does not feel the yoke, and we envy you Protestants ; but we are poor, and submit for the sake of a maintenance. But I assure you we are more enlightened than you are aware of." And then he said with a smile of conceit : " Perhaps, after all, we do not believe so much even as you. In secret we are very enlightened." The style in which he went on prevented me from feeling any scruple at the joke to which I was a party. I have no doubt he was saying what he supposed would recommend him to my favorable opinion. I inquired about the disputes then going on between the King and the Bishop (of Würzburg), and found from his account, which now I could believe to be sincere, that he and his brethren were anxious to steer between the two powers ; for to the one they owed their subsistence, and to the other their clerical character. The next morning, Professor Fichte paid his bill, and took up his abode with one of his friends.

In the course of the day I beheld a strange sight, — a man beheaded for murder. He was of the lowest description of character, sunk in brutal stupidity and despair. The spectator could not but feel ashamed of such a degradation of human nature. The place of execution in Germany is usually a circular elevation, spacious enough to hold a chair and three or four persons, i. e. some fifteen or twenty feet in diameter.

In the present instance the criminal, having rapidly performed certain religious rites below, which I did not see, was blindfolded, and, with a crucifix in his hand, led by two men to the raised ground, and there placed in a chair. The executioner then stepped from behind, holding a broad sword under his cloak, and in an instant, with a back-handed blow, severed the head from the body. The headless trunk remained in the chair unmoved, as if nothing had happened. A Capuchin monk then came forward, and, lifting up a huge crucifix, exclaimed, " See, my friends, that thing which was a man sits there, and all because he neglected going to confession." A Protestant in like circumstances would have ascribed the catastrophe to the violation of the Sabbath. The address which followed was delivered with eloquence, and, though disgusting to me, was, I felt, well adapted to impress the sort of audience collected to hear it.

I spent two days visiting various acquaintances, and both days I had great pleasure in dining with Professor Paulus, an agreeable companion, very acute as well as clear-headed. Whatever opinion I may entertain of his Christianity, which is not so favorable now as it was then, I see no reason to withhold the acknowledgment of his perfect sincerity and integrity. He claimed the character of a Christian Professor, and this during his long academical life was not denied him by any official colleague, though refused to him by controversial adversaries. I learned from him that Schelling had already lost the favor of the government, and that a struggle of parties was going on which threatened (and soon produced its effect on) the infant University.*

The hope óf being able to render service to a friend caused me to extend my tour to Heidelberg and Carlsruhe. Of the former I need not speak ; the latter did not please me. The town is built in the shape of a fan, the palace forming the handle, and the streets radiating from it. Of the famous Bergstrasse I will only say, that I never felt more strongly the effect of scenery in giving strength and resolution. It is

---

* It should be not *infant*, but *rejuvenescent.* The University of Würzburg was originally established in 1403, but, having ceased to exist, was re-established in 1582; and an attempt was made at the beginning of the present century to widen its influence by the appointment of several very eminent professors; and it seems that a Protestant element was introduced in the theological staff of professors. At the present time Würzburg is a Roman Catholic university. The Protestant university of Bavaria is that of Erlangen, at which a large proportion of the students are theological.

said that a property of beauty is to enervate ; but this was not my experience in the present journey. The road was lined on both sides with fruit-trees of every description, especially walnuts, apples, and chestnuts. The principal harvest was over, but every variety of produce was left, including, besides more familiar objects, flax, tobacco, and Indian corn. I noticed one peach-tree standing by itself. The apples were not knocked down, but carefully gathered one by one by means of an instrument combining a rake and a basket.

While I was on this little tour Buonaparte paid a visit to Mayence, of which all the papers were full. I was amused at the prevailing timidity of the people in expressing their opinions. I never met with an individual who had a word to say in his favor, but no one ventured to speak against him. I alone talked freely, and I could see that people envied me my power of saying what I liked. One evening, at the table-d'hôte, I was rattling away as usual, when a well-looking man who sat next me asked where I was going? I said, " On foot to Frankfort." He took me by the hand, and in the tone of one about to ask a serious favor, begged me to take a seat between him and his wife in their carriage. " It will do my heart good," he said, " to talk with an Englishman about that vile people and their vile Emperor, who have thrust my nation into such misery. I am from Berne ; my name is Von Haller."—" Probably of the family of the great physiologist?" I said. " The same." The request was seconded by his very nice little wife, who had hardly ever before been out of her native place. I enjoyed my drive with my patriotic companions, and the first day after our arrival at Frankfort I devoted to them. I then spent four days in calling on my several acquaintance. But my visit was tantalizing rather than satisfying, and led to a reflection which on other occasions has forced itself on me, and which I think worth writing here. It is this, the sentiments we entertain for old friends are sometimes endangered by a *short* visit after a few years' absence. The recollection of the former intercourse with old friends has about it a charm, which is broken when they are seen for only a short time. If there be a second stay with them sufficiently lengthened to form a new image, then a double and strengthened attachment arises. Otherwise an illusion is destroyed, and no substitute is produced.

In my notes of the Brentano family, I find that *Bettina*

pleased me this time better than before. Now I may venture to mention Bettina, who has since gained a European notoriety at least. When I first came to Frankfort she was a short, stout, romping girl, the youngest and least agreeable of Madame de la Roche's grandchildren. She was always considered a wayward, unmanageable creature. I recollect seeing her climb apple-trees, and she was a great rattling talker. I recollect also hearing her speak in terms of extravagant admiration of the Mignon of Goethe's "Wilhelm Meister." Clasping her hands over her bosom, she said, " I always lie thus when in bed, in imitation of Mignon." I had heard nothing of her for many years, when there appeared "Goethes Briefwechsel mit einem Kinde" (Correspondence of Goethe with a Child). In this book Bettina wishes to have it thought that she was so much an object of interest to Goethe, that he framed sonnets out of her letters. My friend Fritz Schlosser says he is most certain that these letters were not written at the date they bear, but are mere inventions founded on the sonnets. My acquaintance at Frankfort are of the same opinion, and it is not opposed by the family.

On the way back to Jena I passed through Fulda, the residence of a prince bishop, and saw a play entitled "Uble Laune," by Kotzebue. I thought it did not justify the epigram made upon it by A. W. Schlegel : —

" Justly and wisely this piece by the author 's entitled ' Ill Humor " ;
Though *in* the play 't is not found, still *by* the play 't is engendered."

I visited one Salzmann, a famous practical pedagogue, who has established a large and distinguished seminary at Schnepfenthal.* This Salzmann has made himself generally known by the very elaborate and solicitous attention he pays to the gymnastical part of education, by the anti-disciplinarian principles, and by the universal tendency and direction of the studies. I saw that the boys were healthy, happy, and courageous. And Salzmann seemed to have succeeded in the difficult task (which the French have found impracticable) of giving liberty and repressing licentiousness. The boys are on no occasions struck, — this is a fundamental law. Another is to give them freedom in everything not obviously dangerous. They botanize and study natural history, and take long journeys with their preceptors on foot over the mountains. They climb trees, jump over hedges, swim, skate, &c., &c., and, as far

* A village near Waltershausen, in the Duchy of Saxe-Coburg-Gotha.

as general culture of the active powers is concerned, there is much to be applauded, but I fear solid learning is neglected, and the institution is not without affectation, and even what looks like quackery. A newspaper is printed here containing a history of all remarkable occurrences, prizes given, incidents in the house, exercises performed, visits of strangers, &c. With edifying improvements, Salzmann translated Mary Wollstonecraft's "Rights of Women," and he was in correspondence with her. One of her children's books is a translation of a work by him.

After my return, Knebel was anxious to take me to Weimar to see his sister, governess to the Hereditary Princess, and also Fraülein von Geckhausen, the Hofdame to the Duchess Dowager. We went on the 27th of October. I had the honor of sipping chocolate in the presence of the young Princess. I also visited Frau von Wollzogen, Schiller's wife's sister, afterwards his biographer, and I witnessed the performance of "Turandot." * This fairy tale, by Schiller, an imitation of Gozzi, is not considered one of his great works; but it proved versatility of talent, and afforded an opportunity of trying an experiment. It was played with *masks*, and certainly gave pleasure as soon as the spectators were reconciled to the novelty. At each performance, for some time, the interest was enhanced by the introduction of fresh riddles, by which the Chinese Princess tried the skill of her unwelcome lover.

On the 24th of November, an occurrence took place which at one time threatened me with serious consequences, but which eventually was of service to me by occasioning my introduction to the Duchess. Of all the Jena professors, the most unpopular was E——. He had the ear of the Grand Duke, but was disliked both by his colleagues and the students. He lectured this session on Homer and the Roman satirists. One of the students had put into my hands a commentary on Horace, from which we saw that the Professor read page after page. As soon as the lecture was over, and E—— had left the room, I called out to the students, " Gentlemen, I will read you the lecture over again," and began reading; I was a little too soon, E—— was within hearing, and rushed back to the room. An altercation ensued, and I was cited before the Prorector. It was reported that I should be sent away, that is, receive the *consilium abeundi.* My friend Knebel took up my

* Turandot, Prinzessin von China. Ein tragikomisches Mährchen nach Gozzi.

cause zealously. The Prorector interrogated me, and I related to him all that I could. In the Senate, my chief friend was the great jurist Thibaut, who, next to Savigny, was one of the great law authorities of the day in Germany. I soon learned that E—— had succeeded in misrepresenting the affair; and from Thibaut I received the advice to draw up a formal statement, and present it to the Prorector, with the request that he would lay it before the Senate. This I did; and I added a letter from a student corroborating every important fact, especially the fact that E—— had merely read from Haverkamp. The Senate requested the Professor to send in his answer. Thibaut said that for his own part he would never consent to my receiving the consilium, — for either I ought to be expelled with infamy as a liar, or I had told the truth, and then the less said about the matter the better. It was discovered that E—— was gone to Weimar, with the object it was believed of obtaining a Ducal order for my removal; therefore my friends resolved to introduce me to the Grand Duchess.

The Prorector affected to be my friend, and said the matter should be made up by the merely nominal punishment of a rustication for two days. I said I should submit to no punishment. If there were a sentence against me, I should appeal to the Duke; and if that did not avail, I should leave the University, and send a printed copy of my statement to all the other Universities. In my paper, I stated that if I were accused of making a false charge of plagiarism, I pledged myself to prove the charge. The Professor never answered my memorial; and so the matter ended.

In the mean while, however, it took me to Weimar. The Dowager Duchess Amelia, a niece of Frederick, King of Prussia, was a very superior woman; and German literature is under infinite obligations to her. She was the especial patroness of Wieland and Herder, but was honored by Goethe, Schiller, and indeed by every one. The first day I dined with her I felt as much at my ease as the last. Wieland was always at her table. On the present occasion she desired me to be at the theatre in Schiller's box. I called on him, and went with his party. The Duchess came and stood next me, and chatted with me. E—— was in the pit, and it was supposed the sight of me must have taken away his last hope of success. At all events, all apprehension on my account was removed early in the new year by my public appearance under the Duchess Dowager's protection.

H. C. R. TO HIS BROTHER.

March 2, 1805.

The Duchess is certainly one of the most estimable of the German princesses, and is not unworthy of being a niece of Frederick II. At the theatre I saw the wonder of the North, and the object of every one's idolatry here, — the hereditary Princess of Saxe-Weimar. As my residence here has given you an interest in everything that concerns our little court, I take for granted that you are not ignorant that a few months since our Hereditary Prince brought home his bride, — the sister of the Emperor of Russia, and a daughter of Paul. All tongues are lavish of her praise, and indeed she seems to be really an extraordinary person. She is young, and possesses a most cultivated mind and accomplished address. I stood by her some time, and smiled at myself at remarking the effect she had on me, — since, excellent as I doubt not she is, I am still sensible that the strange sensation I felt at hearing her say common things was principally occasioned by the magic of title and name.

CHAPTER IX.

GERMANY. — 1805.

IN 1805 Jena was to sustain a fresh loss in the departure of Voss, to whom a pension of 1,000 dollars a year was offered on the simple condition of his living at Heidelberg. On the other hand, there came to live at Weimar Mr. and Mrs. Hare Naylor, whom I found a very valuable addition to my circle of acquaintance. He was the son of the Whig Bishop Hare, and she the daughter of Bishop Shipley, brother of the patriotic Dean of St. Asaph, whom Erskine defended in the prosecution for publishing Sir W. Jones's famous Dialogue. The Hare Naylors had young children, of whom, at the time I am writing, the Archdeacon Julius is the only survivor. Miss Flaxman lived with them as governess.*

I have now to mention an event which cast its shadow far

---

* *Vide* Memoir of Julius Hare prefixed to the last edition of " Guesses at Truth." The property of Hurstmonceux came into the Naylor family in 1701, and was sold by Francis Hare Naylor in 1807. The name Naylor therefore was doubtless assumed by Francis Hare in order to inherit this property.

and wide, but especially over the neighborhood of Weimar, —
the death of Schiller.

It has frequently been to me a subject of regret that during
my residence at Jena I did not take more pains to be received
into the society of the great poets of Weimar. I saw Schiller
occasionally, as well as the others ; but I did not push myself
into their notice. This indeed I cannot regret. The only
conversation I recollect having had with Schiller arose from
my asking whether he did not know English, as I saw German
translations of Shakespeare among his books. He said : " I
have read Shakespeare in English, but on principle not much.
My business in life is to write German, and I am convinced
that a person cannot read much in foreign languages without
losing that delicate tact in the perception of the power of
words which is essential to good writing." I also asked him
whether he was acquainted with Lillo. He said he began a
play founded on the story of " George Barnwell." He thought
highly of Lillo's dramatic talent. I told him the story of
" Fatal Curiosity," which he thought a good subject. By the
by, Werner after this wrote a mystical play with the same
plot, and called it " The 24th of February," on which day,
for several generations, horrible events take place in a doomed
family.

During all the time I was at Jena, Schiller was in poor
health, though at this time his greatest works were produced.
He lived in a very retired way ; and his habit was to write at
midnight, taking a great deal of coffee as a stimulant. The
report of his being in a dangerous state had already been
spread abroad. Friday, the 10th of May, was Fries's last day
at Jena, and as usual I went with him and others to take
after-dinner coffee at Zwätzen. I left the party early, to keep
an engagement to drink tea with Knebel at Fahrenkrüger's.
While I was there some one came in with the news, — " Schiller ist todt." Knebel sprang up, and in a loud voice exclaimed, whilst he struck the table violently, " Der Tod ist der
einzige dumme Junge." It was ridiculous and pathetic. Dear
Knebel's passions were always an odd combination of fury and
tenderness. He loved Schiller, and gave to his feelings immediate and unconsidered expression. He had no other word for
them now than the comic student word of offence, the prelude
to a duel, " Death is the only fool." I had engaged to go to
a party in honor of Fries, and I went. We stayed up late,
student-songs were sung, but we could not be glad ; for there

was not one of us who did not grieve for the loss of Schiller, though perhaps no one was intimate with him.

I went next day to Weimar, where I remained till the 14th. I spent the Saturday in various company, for I had now many acquaintances. Schiller's death and character were the sole subjects of conversation. At a party at Fräulein Geckhausen's I was involved in a foolish squabble. I said unguardedly, "The glory of Weimar is rapidly passing away." One of the Kammerherrn (gentlemen of the chamber) was offended. "All the poets might die," he said angrily, "but the court of Weimar would still remain." The ladies took my part; they said, truly, that I was of course referring to no court glory. I was alluding to that in which Weimar threw into the shade Berlin, St. Petersburg, and Vienna.

The interment of Schiller took place by night. Voss came from Jena to be one of the bearers. It rained; I was depressed, and as there was to be no address or ceremony, I did not attend. This I have since regretted.

Next day I dined quietly with Mrs. Hare. No one was with her but Miss Flaxman. I found Mrs. Hare's conversation very interesting. She had known Priestley; and lent me the life of her brother-in-law, Sir W. Jones, of her connection with whom she was proud.

On the 13th I dined with the Duchess Dowager. Wieland was present, and spoke of Schiller's poetical character, remarking, with I believe perfect truth, that Schiller's excellence lay more in lyrical poetry than in dramatic. In reference to himself, Wieland said he was a precocious child. At four years of age he began Latin; at eight understood Cornelius Nepos as well as if he had written it; and at fourteen was well acquainted with Horace.

One little incident I must not forget. The Grand Duchess showed me a copy of Goethe's quarto volume, "Winckelmann und sein Jahrhundert," which she had just received from him. On taking it into my hand, there fell from it a slip of paper, on which was written a distich. I never felt so strong a temptation to commit a theft. But I brought away a copy of the lines, without stealing : —

"Freundlich empfange das Wort laut ausgesprochner Verehrung,
   Das die Parze mir fast schnitt von den Lippen hinweg."
[" Kindly receive the expression of loudly avowed veneration,
   Though from before my lips Fate nearly snatched it away."]

That Goethe's life was in danger when Schiller died is well

known; and this distich shows that about this time his
" Winckelmann " was written.

On the 8th of June I dined with the Duchess for the fourth
time, and found Wieland very communicative. He spoke of
French literature, and I asked him to recommend some French
novels. He said, of Count Hamilton *opera omnia*. He praised
even the tales of Crébillon, — " Le Sopha," " Ah, quelle Conte,"
and " Mémoires d'un Homme de Qualité," and some works by
Abbé Prévost. He spoke also of English literature, to which
he confessed great obligations. I had mentioned that the first
book I recollected having read was the " Pilgrim's Progress."
" That delights me," he said, " for in that book I learned to
read English. English literature had a great influence on me ;
and your Puritan writings particularly. The first book I attempted to write was an imitation of Mrs. Rowe's ' Letters
from the Dead to the Living.' " This was one of the favorite
books of my own dear mother. Wieland went on to say :
" The next work I read was a large didactic poem on Grace. I
said to myself, in future no one will speak of Lucretius. After
this I became acquainted with the lighter English poetry. I
made my ' Komische Erzählungen ' in imitation of Prior. I was
fond of Gay." Wieland thought English literature had declined since the age of Queen Anne.

On a later occasion I saw still more of Wieland. It was
when Knebel took me to Tieffurth, the country residence of
the Duchess. I rode with Wieland *tête-à-tête* to Tieffurth, from
his own house ; and he spoke of his own works with most interesting frankness. He considered his best work to be " Mu-
sarion." He had gone over it with Goethe line by line. He
was sensible that the characteristic of his prose style is what
the Greeks called στωμυλία, — not mere chatter, " Geschwätz,"
but an agreeable diffuseness.

At dinner I told him of the new publication of Gleim's
Letters, and quoted a passage written by Gleim in Switzerland
when Wieland, a mere lad, was staying at the house of Bod-
mer : " There is a clever young man here now named Wieland,
— a great talker, and a great writer. It is a pity that, as
one can see, he will very soon have exhausted himself." " Ich
erschöpft ! " (" I exhausted ") Wieland cried out, clasping his
hands. " Well, well ! I am now in my seventy-fourth year
(or seventy-third), and, by the blessing of God, I will still write
more than he ever did, and it shall last longer too." This he
said of the poet of Frederick the Great, whom the last gen-

eration used to regard as a Horace, and still more as a Tyr-
tæus.

After dinner I read aloud, among other things, a good translation by Schmidt of "Auld Robin Gray," which was much
admired.   Wieland told us to-day of his early attachment to
Madame de la Roche.   He said, "It was well it came to nothing, for we should have spoiled each other."

Humboldt, the great traveller, on his return from America,
was presented to the Emperor Napoleon.   Now, Humboldt
himself is a sort of Buonaparte among travellers, and expected
to be distinguished.   "Vous aimez la botanique," said the Emperor to him, "et ma femme aussi"; and passed on.   Is it
not admirable?   There are many occurrences of great and
little moment in life which can only be understood from their
relation to the character of the actor.   Was this address of
Buonaparte humor, or satire, or insolence, or impertinence?
Did he deserve a kick or a pat?   Ask his lord in waiting.

At the close of my residence in Jena I became rather intimate with a woman whose history is very remarkable, especially as given by herself in detail.   This was Frau von Einsiedel.
Compelled to marry against her will, she found her husband
so unfit for a woman to live with, that she feigned death, and,
making her escape, caused a log of wood to be buried in her
stead.   When the truth was discovered, a legal divorce took
place, and she became the wife of Herr von Einsiedel, who had
been the companion of her flight.   She gave me an account of
her strange adventures, that I might not despise her in the
distant country to which I was about to return.   All she said
was in language the most delicate, and was indicative of the
most refined sensibility.   She was held in high esteem by
Knebel and Wieland, and retained the regard of the Duchess
Dowager.   I saw her repeatedly with the Duchess when
she came to Jena, and took up her residence at the castle, in
order to attend a course of lectures on Craniology by Dr. Gall.

This science of Craniology, which keeps its place in the
world, though not among the universally received sciences,
was then quite new.   One or two pamphlets had appeared,
but the gloss of novelty was still upon it.   Goethe deemed it
worthy of investigation, and, when a satire upon it was put
into the form of a drama, would not allow it to be acted.   The
Duchess, who had a very active mind and a universal curiosity,
took a warm interest in the lectures, and was unremitting in
her attendance at them.

Gall, whom the Duchess invited me to meet at dinner, was a large man with a florid countenance, — of the same general complexion as Astley Cooper and Chantrey. He had not been brought up in cultivated society ; and so utterly wanting in tact was he, that on one occasion, having enumerated the different organs on a marked skull, he turned to the Duchess and regularly catechized her as if she had been an ordinary student. "What 's the name of that organ, your Highness ?" She gave me a very significant look, and smiled : there was a titter round the table, and the Professor looked abashed. Gall was attended by Spurzheim, as his famulus, who received our fee for the lectures.

It occurred to me that I might make this new science known in England, and accordingly I purchased of Spurzheim, for two Friedrichs d'or, a skull marked with the organs. I bought also two pamphlets, one by Hufeland, and the other by Bischof, explanatory of the system. And soon after my return to London I compiled on the subject a small volume, which was published by Longman.* The best part of the book was a happy motto from Sir Thomas Brown, for which I take credit : " The finger of God hath left an inscription upon all his works, not graphical or composed of letters, but of their several forms, constitutions, parts, and operations, which, aptly joined together, do make one word that doth express their nature." The work itself excited hardly any public interest ; but just at the time a new and enlarged edition of Rees's Cyclopædia was coming out, and the whole substance of the article on Craniology was copied from my work, the source being suitably acknowledged.

My student life was rapidly drawing to a close, — or perhaps I should say rather my life at Jena, — for I must confess I owe more to the society I enjoyed there than to what I learned in the lecture-rooms of the professors. My memoranda of my reading in Greek and Latin are to me a source of mingled shame and consolation, — consolation that I did not wholly neglect the great authors of antiquity, and shame that so little of what I read remains. To German literature and philosophy I continued also to devote a part of my time. But latterly I attended fewer lectures, and read more with friends and private tutors.

* Some Account of Dr. Gall's New Theory of Physiognomy, founded on the Anatomy and Physiology of the Brain, and the Form of the Skull. With the Critical Strictures of C. W. Hufeland, M. D. London: Longman & Co. 1807.

On the 8th of August, 1805, I went to Weimar to take leave. The Duchess was exceedingly kind, as also was Wieland. When I called on him he was writing, and I apologized for the interruption. " I am only copying," he said. On my expressing some surprise that he had not an amanuensis, he said : " I believe I have spent one sixth part of my life in copying, and I have no doubt it has had a salutary effect on me. Having devoted myself to the composition of works of imagination, copying has had a sedative and soothing influence, and tended to keep my mind in a healthy state." He was then copying one of the comedies of Aristophanes. He said he meant to translate all but two, which he deemed untranslatable. One was " Peace "; the title of the other I forget.

On the 15th of August I left Jena. It was my good fortune to come to Jena while the ancient spirit was still alive and active, and I saw the last not altogether insignificant remains of a knot of public teachers who have seldom been surpassed in any university. I have seen, too, a galaxy of literary talent and genius, which future ages will honor as the poetical ornament of the eighteenth century, and place above the more showy but less sterling beaux-esprits of France who flourished thirty or forty years before. Of my leave-taking at Jena I will only say that I parted with no one with so much regret as Knebel. My friend Voigt accompanied me three leagues. On the 21st I reached Brunswick, and on the 24th took my place in the Post-wagen to Hamburg. In this journey I had a narrow escape of being taken prisoner. I travelled with a passport, which I had procured as a Saxon. I was not without anxiety, for I had to pass through the French army, which was in possession of the north of Germany. Through the interposition of the King of Prussia, Hamburg had been declared neutral territory ; but I at that time spoke German fluently, and did not fear detection by Frenchmen. A more wearisome journey than the one I had now to make cannot be found, certainly in Germany. One of the passengers was a Frenchman, who rendered himself disagreeable to all the rest. I afterwards found that he was even then in the French service. On the way he and I had two or three rather angry discussions in German. But I was not fully aware till afterwards of the peril I encountered in his company. I read occasionally, and as often as I could walked forward, wishing there had been hills to give me more opportunity of walking. On one occasion I had gone on a considerable distance, when I came to a turnpike, the keeper of which had a countenance which struck me as remarkably like that of Erskine. Two soldiers were riding at a distance. I said to the man, " Who are they ? "

" Gens-d'armes."

" What are they about ? "

" Looking after suspicious characters."

" Do you mean people who have no passes ? "

" Ay, and those who have passes, — Englishmen who try to pass for Germans."

He laughed, and so did I. It was evident he had detected me, but I was in no danger from him. He said also : " Perhaps they are on the lookout for some one. They have their spies everywhere." This I own made me feel a little uncomfortable, and put me on my guard. In the evening, about six, the second day, we passed through Lüneburg, which was full of French soldiers. At length, about 1 A. M., we arrived at the Elbe, where the military were stationed whose duty it was to examine our passports. But it was too much trouble to rise from bed, and we were at once ferried over the river to the Hamburg side, where we were under Prussian protection. As soon as we were again in the carriage, and in motion, I felt unable to repress my feeling of triumph, and snapping my finger at the Frenchman, said, " Nun, Herr, ich bin ein Engländer " (" Now, sir, I am an Englishman"). He did not conceal his mortification, and said, " You ought to have been taken prisoner for your folly in running such a risk," — in which perhaps he was not far wrong. Had he discovered me a quarter of an hour before I should probably have been packed off to France, and kept prisoner till 1813. I was afterwards told by several of my fellow-passengers that they suspected me, and were apprehensive on my account.

At Hamburg I saw Iffland in the comedy entitled " Aussteuer," — one of the most perfect pieces of acting I ever saw. His character was that of a low-minded Amtmann, an incarnation of apathy. I still recollect his look and voice. They were not to be forgotten. It is the one character in which he appeared most perfect, though I saw him in others of greater celebrity.

I remained at Hamburg but a short time, returning to England by the ordinary way.

It was a critical moment. The very packet which took me over to England carried the news of the fatal battle of Austerlitz, which inflicted a deep wound on the already crippled power of Austria.   This victory encouraged Buonaparte to fresh insults on Prussia, which soon led to a Prussian war.   And as Prussia had looked on quietly, if not complacently, when the battle of Austerlitz was fought, so Austria beheld with a kind of resentful composure the victory gained by the French over the Prussians at Jena.

On our very disagreeable voyage we were not without fear of being attacked by a French privateer ; but, on the 17th of September, we arrived safely at Yarmouth, and on the 19th I proceeded to Bury.   I enjoyed the drive, the excellence of the roads, and the swiftness of the stage-coach ; and the revival of home feelings delighted me.   On the way I saw my father for a moment ; and on arriving at Bury, between twelve and one at night, I ran down to my brother's house to see whether by accident any one of the family was still up.   As this was not the case, I went back to the Greyhound to sleep.   In my walk I was uncomfortably impressed with the lowness and smallness of the Bury houses.   And now I will confess to having indulged myself in a little act of superstition.   I had not heard of my brother for some months ; and as a charm against any calamity to him or his family, I enumerated all possible misfortunes, with the feeling which I have had through life, that all calamities come unexpectedly ; and so I tried to insure a happy meeting by thinking of " all the ills that flesh is heir to."

CHAPTER X.

1805–1806.

AFTER my long absence in Germany, it was a great pleasure to see my English friends ; and for some weeks I spent most of my time with them.   To those who lived in the country I paid visits.

In December I formed a new acquaintance, of which I was reasonably proud, and in the recollection of which I still rejoice.   At Hackney I saw repeatedly Miss Wakefield,* a charming girl.   And one day at a party, when Mrs. Barbauld had been the subject of conversation, and I had spoken of her in enthusiastic terms, Miss Wakefield came to me and said,

* The daughter of Gilbert Wakefield.

"Would you like to know Mrs. Barbauld?" I exclaimed, "You might as well ask me whether I should like to know the angel Gabriel." — "Mrs. Barbauld is, however, much more accessible. I will introduce you to her nephew." She then called to Charles Aikin, whom she soon after married. And he said : "I dine every Sunday with my uncle and aunt at Stoke Newington, and I am expected always to bring a friend with me. Two knives and forks are laid for me. Will you go with me next Sunday?" Gladly acceding to the proposal, I had the good fortune to make myself agreeable, and soon became intimate in the house.

Mr. Barbauld had a slim figure, a weazen face, and a shrill voice. He talked a great deal, and was fond of dwelling on controversial points in religion. He was by no means destitute of ability, though the afflictive disease was lurking in him, which in a few years broke out, and, as is well known, caused a sad termination to his life.

Mrs. Barbauld bore the remains of great personal beauty. She had a brilliant complexion, light hair, blue eyes, a small elegant figure, and her manners were very agreeable, with something of the generation then departing. She received me very kindly, spoke very civilly of my aunt Zachary Crabb, and said she had herself once slept at my father's house. Mrs. Barbauld is so well known by her prose writings that it is needless for me to attempt to characterize her here. Her excellence lay in the soundness and acuteness of her understanding, and in the perfection of her taste. In the estimation of Wordsworth she was the first of our literary women, and he was not bribed to this judgment by any especial congeniality of feeling, or by concurrence in speculative opinions. I may here relate an anecdote connecting her and Wordsworth, though out of its proper time by many, many years; but it is so good that it ought to be preserved from oblivion. It was after her death that Lucy Aikin published Mrs. Barbauld's collected works, of which I gave a copy to Miss Wordsworth. Among the poems is a stanza on Life, written in extreme old age. It had delighted my sister, to whom I repeated it on her death-bed. It was long after I gave these works to Miss Wordsworth that her brother said, "Repeat me that stanza by Mrs. Barbauld." I did so. He made me repeat it again. And so he learned it by heart. He was at the time walking in his sitting-room at Rydal with his hands behind him; and I heard him mutter to himself, "I am not in

the habit of grudging people their good things, but I wish I
had written those lines."

> " Life! we 've been long together,
> Through pleasant and through cloudy weather:
> 'T is hard to part when friends are dear,
> Perhaps 't will cost a sigh, a tear:
> Then steal away, give little warning,
>   Choose thine own time;
> Say not good night, but in some brighter clime
> Bid me good morning."

My friend Collier had taken up his residence in a small
house in Little Smith Street, to the west of the Westminster
School. A bedroom was offered me, and here I was glad to
take refuge while I was equally without a home and without
employment. The most important of his engagements — important also to me eventually — was that of reporter to the
Times, under the management of John Walter, then the
junior.*

When the round of my acquaintance had been run through,
I set about finding some literary occupation, for I found myself unable to live with comfort on my small income, though
with my economical habits I needed only a small addition.

My first engagement was to translate a political work against
Buonaparte, for which a bookseller named Tipper, of Fen-
church Street, gave me a guinea and a half per sheet. My
friend King Fordham thought some diplomatic post abroad
would be suitable to me, and exerted himself in my behalf.
C. J. Fox wrote that he thought it probable he should soon
have occasion for the services of a person of my description.
I went so far as to offer myself to Mr. Fox, but nothing came
of it. And it is well, for I am not conscious of possessing
the kind of talent required for the position of a diplomatist.
Another thought was that I might be engaged as travelling
companion to some young man. And there was at one time
some prospect of my going to America in this capacity.
George Dyer suggested my name to a gentleman, whose sons
or nephews were desirous of visiting the New World ; and I
had several interviews with the celebrated American mechanist
Fulton, who invented the Catenarian and Torpedo, and offered to Buonaparte to destroy the whole English fleet by
means of explosives. Dining with him one day, I spoke of
the " Perpetual Peace " of Kant. Fulton said, " I believe in
the ' Perpetual Peace ' "; and on my expressing surprise, he

* The father of the recent M. P. for Berkshire.

added, " I have no doubt war will be put an end to by being rendered so murderous that by common consent it will be abandoned. I could myself make a machine by means of which I could in a few minutes destroy a hundred thousand men." After some time I was informed that the visit to America was postponed, and I heard no more of it.*

It was natural that, after having been away six years, I should be curious to see the old Forum where I had formed the valuable acquaintance of the Colliers. They too were desirous that I should go. The old place, the " old familiar faces," were there. I have forgotten the question, but I spoke, and was surprised at the start I had taken. I went a second time, and it was, I believe, this evening that an incident occurred which gave me more pleasure than any other praise I ever received. The subject was private theatricals, which Gale Jones defended, and I successfully attacked. I say successfully, for the success was proved by something more significant than applause. As I left the room with Mrs. Collier, when it was nearly empty, a little old man was waiting about at the door with a fine young girl under his arm, and on my coming up he stretched out his hand, and in an agitated voice said : " Will you allow me, sir, to take you by the hand, and thank you for your speech to-night ? You have made me a happy man, and I am under everlasting obligations to you." The poor girl colored exceedingly, and I felt for her. I therefore contented myself with saying that I rejoiced if anything that had fallen from me could be thought by him eventually useful ; and I believe I added, that I wished him to know I had spoken not for the sake of argument, but from my heart.

On the following week I went to the Forum once more. On my walking up the centre of the room there was general clapping, at which I felt so unaffectedly ashamed, that I turned back, and never entered the place again.

On November 4th I saw " Coriolanus." It was a glorious treat. I never saw Kemble so great. He played the aristocrat so admirably, and the democratic tribunes and the electors of Rome appeared so contemptible, that he drew down

---

* At this time Mr. Robinson had in contemplation a work on Kant's Philosophy. Friends advised him not to translate any of Kant's works, but under some original form to introduce a considerable portion of translated matter. He accordingly proceeded so far as to fix on the following title: " Locke and Kant: or, a Review of the Philosophy of the Eighteenth Century, as it respects the Origin and Extent of Human Knowledge, by H. C. R." But the work was never completed.

hisses on them. The house was crowded, and I was forced to stand.

In the month of December the Colliers removed from Little Smith Street to a good house in Hatton Garden, and I accompanied them.

By this time I had become acquainted with Charles Lamb and his sister; for I went with them to the first performance of " Mr. H." at Covent Garden, which took place in the month of December. The prologue was very well received. Indeed it could not fail, being one of the very best in our language. But on the disclosure of the name, the squeamishness of the vulgar taste in the pit showed itself by hisses ; and I recollect that Lamb joined, and was probably the loudest hisser in the house. The damning of this play belongs to the literary history of the day, as its author to the literary magnates of his age.*

I was introduced to the Lambs by Mrs. Clarkson. And I had heard of them also from W. Hazlitt, who was intimate with them. They were then living in a garret in Inner Temple Lane. In that humble apartment I spent many happy hours, and saw a greater number of excellent persons than I had ever seen collected together in one room. Talfourd, in his " Final Memorials," has happily characterized this circle.

CHAPTER XI.

ALTONA, SWEDEN, ETC. — 1807.

IN January, 1807, I received, through my friend J. D. Collier, a proposal from Mr. Walter that I should take up my residence at Altona, and become the *Times* correspondent. I was to receive from the editor of the *Hamburger Correspondenten* all the public documents at his disposal, and was to have the benefit also of a mass of information of which the restraints of the German press did not permit him to avail himself. The honorarium I was to receive was ample with my habits of life. I gladly accepted the offer, and never repented having done so.

---

* The farce of " Mr. H." was written by Lamb. Its absurdity turns on the hero being ashamed of his name, which is only revealed at the end as Hogs-flesh.

My acquaintance with Walter ripened into friendship, and lasted as long as he lived.

This engagement made me for the first time a man of business. How I executed my task may be seen by a file of the *Times*. My articles are from " the banks of the Elbe " ; the first is dated in March and the last in August, but there followed three letters from Stockholm and Gottenburg.*

Having defeated the Prussians at Jena, Napoleon had advanced into Poland, and the anxious attention of all Europe was directed to the campaign now going on there. Hamburg was in the possession of the French. Holstein, appertaining to the kingdom of Denmark, was a neutral frontier province ; and Altona, its capital, was to be my residence as long as it continued to be secure, and as the intelligence of the campaign had interest for English politicians.

I soon made my arrival known to my one only acquaintance, Dr. Ehlers, who, however, was sufficient for all purposes, as he forthwith initiated me into the best society of the place, and provided for my personal comforts by obtaining for me a lodging in a very agreeable family. I lived in the Königstrasse, in the house of Mr. Pauli, a mercantile agent, who had not been prosperous in business, but who was most happy in his wife, — a very sensible and interesting woman, the sister of Poel, the proprietor of the *Altona Mercury*, a political newspaper in which liberal principles were asserted with discretion and propriety. Poel's wife was also a woman of great personal worth, and even of personal attractions, a daughter of the celebrated Professor Busch of Hamburg. These ladies had a friend, Madame Sieveking, who formed with them a society which in few places is equalled. She was a widow, residing at Hamburg, and was a daughter of the well-known Reimarus. On the borders of the Elbe, Poel had a country-house, where, especially on Sundays, there used to be delightful dinner-parties. In this house my happiest hours were spent.

Among the most interesting of those, whose images still live in my memory, is the Count d'Angiviller. He had held in the court of Louis XVI. the office of Intendant of the Palaces, i. e. was a sort of Minister of Woods and Forests. His post

---

* This correspondence, from " the banks of the Elbe," has reference to the hopes and fears and reports, which ended in the fall of Dantzic, the Battle of Friedland, and the Treaty of Tilsit. The immediate cause of Mr. Robinson's leaving Altona was that naval coalition against England, which rendered it necessary for the British government to send Lord Cathcart to Copenhagen to secure the Danish fleet.

gave him extensive patronage among artists and men of letters, with all of whom he had lived on terms of intimacy. His tall person, very dignified manners, rank, and advanced age, combined to render him an object of universal interest. I was proud when I could get into conversation with him. One evening, at a party, I chanced to make use of the phrase, " Diderot et D'Alembert." He instantly put his hand on my shoulder, and said, " Je vous prie, monsieur, de ne prononcer jamais ces noms au même temps dans ma présence. Vous me blessez les oreilles." I will not answer precisely for the words, but in substance he continued, " Diderot was a monster, guilty of every vice, but D'Alembert was an angel."

At the hotel I first saw George Stansfeld,* a young man from Leeds, who came to learn German and to qualify himself for mercantile life. We became intimate and mutually serviceable ; and my friendship with him extended afterwards in England to all the members of his family.

I met one French man of letters, who has a name in connection with German philosophy. I thought his manners agreeable, but he did not appear to me likely to recommend the Kantian philosophy successfully to his countrymen. Yet his book, an account of Kant's philosophy, supplied for many years the sole information possessed by the French on that subject. His name was Charles Villers.

H. C. R. TO HIS BROTHER.

ALTONA, March 23, 1807.

DEAR THOMAS : —

. . . . My time has been spent very pleasurably indeed. I have seldom in so short a time made the acquaintance of so many excellent persons. My usual good fortune has brought me into the most intelligent circle in Altona ; so that my second residence in Germany yields as much enjoyment as my former. I have at the same time been able to renew my old acquaintances by letter. I have heard from Herr von Knebel and Dr. Voigt. Both of them have had the good fortune to suffer little or nothing personally by the war ; and Voigt seems rather to have enjoyed the scenes he has witnessed. Napoleon took up his lodgings in Voigt's father's house, and dwelt in a room where I have lounged many an hour. This at once secured the house from being plundered, and at the

* The uncle of the present M. P. for Halifax.

same time gave Voigt an opportunity of seeing most of the Marshals of France and the ruling men of the only ruling power in Europe. Knebel writes with more feeling, but with the resignation of a philosopher, who had foreseen all that has happened, and whose sensations are corrected by an admiration of Buonaparte, which was a source of contention between us, and a contempt of the German constitution and Princes, in which I joined with him. . . . .

H. C. R. TO HIS BROTHER.

ALTONA, June 7, 1807.

. . . . How do I spend my time ? I will give a sort of average journal. .I rise at seven, and carry into a summer-house in the garden my Italian books ; here I prepare my lesson till nine, when my master comes, and with him a fellow-scholar (a very amiable man who holds an office under government, and is also a man of letters). From nine to ten we receive our Italian lesson, — that is, four mornings of the week. On Sundays and the two post mornings (Wednesday and Saturday) my companion has letters of business to write, and therefore we cannot have lessons. The rest of the morning is spent either in reading Italian or at the Museum. This is a sort of London Institution in miniature, — here the newsmongers of the day associate, — every member brings his quota of falsehood or absurdity, reason or facts, as his good luck favors him. Unfortunately, the former are the ordinary commodities, and I have no little difficulty in understanding or appreciating the fables of the hour. There is more bonhomie than ill-will in this. Every one feels what *ought* to take place, and every one is apt to confound what ought to be, and what he wishes to be, with what *is*. Hence we are as often taken in by certain intelligence of Russian and Prussian victories as you can be. Here, too, the politics of the English cabinet are reviewed ; and I hear my old friends the Whig ministers derided and reproached for their scandalously weak, almost treacherous administration, while I am unable to say a word in their defence, and can only mutter between my teeth, " God grant that we do not jump out of the frying-pan into the fire ! " At half past one I dine in the house of a clergyman, who, having no wife, keeps a table for a number of bachelors like himself. Our dinner is not very good, but it is very cheap, and the company is better than the dishes. We have two Danish officers, two physicians (one a man of talent, but a political despairer, an ex-Jacobin), two jurists, two Englishmen. The *other* is a young man from Leeds (his name is Stansfeld), for whom I felt something like friendship when I found he is a Presbyterian. . . . . After dinner I either lounge with a book on the Elbe, or play chess with Mrs. Lütchens, a clever woman, the wife of Lütchens, whom I have before mentioned as an old acquaintance of Mr. Clarkson. In the evening I am engaged generally about three times a week in company. Otherwise I go to Aders (Jameson's partner), a very clever, agreeable man ; or he and one or two young men take tea with me. It is thus that day after day has slipt away insensibly, and I have been in danger of forgetting that the continuance of this most agreeable life is very precarious indeed. I am of opinion that it cannot possibly last long. In all probability we shall soon hear of a peace with Russia, or of a general engagement, which, it is ten to one, will end in the defeat of the Allies. In either event I have no doubt the French will take possession of Holstein. I am tolerably easy as to my personal security in this event, and should I even be caught napping and find a couple of gens-d'armes at the side of my bed when I awake some morning, the worst would be an imprisonment. I state the worst, hope the best, and expect neither the one nor the other. As long as Russia continues to bid defiance to Buonaparte, we shall be unmolested here. When this last protecting power is crushed or prevented from interfering in the concerns of the South, it is not difficult to foretell the measures the conqueror will take. Austria will again be partitioned, the northern maritime powers will be forced to shut up the Baltic, and perhaps arm their fleets against us. And the blockade will cease to be a mere bugbear. Then Napoleon will have to choose between an invasion, which will be a short but hazardous experiment ; or, being now (thanks to our Whig administration) so closely allied to Turkey, he will turn his arms into the East and destroy our Indian empire by an attack from the interior. This latter undertaking would suit the romantic valor and vanity of himself and his people. These things may be prevented by more military skill on the part of the Russians, more character and resolution on the part of the Austrians, and more disinterested zeal in the general cause of Europe on the part of the British administration, than I fear any of these bodies severally possess. The world might be saved if it did not still suffer under an infatuation which resembles that of the Egyptian monarch, — "And the Lord struck Pharaoh with blindness." How many Pharaohs have not sat as then twenty years on the thrones of Europe?

But I have omitted some particulars in the account of myself here, which I must insert. Of all my acquaintances, the most interesting is Mr. Poel. He is the brother of my landlady, proprietor of the *Altona Mercury*, a man of letters, affluent and hospitable. He keeps a good table, and gives dinners and suppers several times a week. He was an ardent friend of the French Revolution, but is now in all things an anti-Gallican. But he is one of the few who, like Mrs. Barbauld's lover, will still "hope though hope were lost." He is persuaded that in the end the good cause will conquer. . . . .

In my attention to the incidents of the day I was unremitting. I kept up a constant intercourse with England. On my first arrival I learned that, notwithstanding the affected neutrality of Denmark, the post from Altona to England was stopped, and, in consequence, all letters were sent by Mr. Thornton, the English minister there,* privately to Husum. I called on him early, informed him I should regularly send letters under cover to the Foreign Office, which he promised should be punctually delivered. And he kept his word.

The progress of the French arms in Poland was the object of overwhelming interest, and the incessant subject of conversation with all of us. As we had but one political feeling, — for I cannot call to mind having met with a single partisan of Napoleon, — our social intercourse was not enlivened by contest; but I perceived that as the events became more disastrous, our cordiality increased, and that calamity served to cement friendship.

I see from my notes that on the 20th of June the fatal news arrived of the great victory obtained over the Russians at Friedland, on the 14th. In ten days we were further informed of the armistice, which on the 7th of July was succeeded by the peace. But afflicting as these public events were to all of us, it was not till the middle of July that they began to affect me personally. On the 14th I learned that Mr. Thornton was gone. We had already heard reports that the English fleet was in the Sound, and the seizure of the Danish fleet by the English was the subject of speculation. Had I left Altona then, I could not have been reproached for cowardice; but I made up my mind to re-

* He was Minister Plenipotentiary to the Hanse Towns.

7 *

main where I was, until some act on the part of the government rendered my departure absolutely necessary.

Among the persons whose acquaintance I made at Poel's, was Major von Spät, the second in command in the town, under the chief magistrate, the Bürgermeister. With the Bürgermeister himself I used to play whist at the Museum. After the departure of Mr. Thornton, and other Englishmen, who had followed his example, I met the Major and said, " Do you not think, Major, that I am a very bold man in staying here, now that our minister is gone ? " — " Not at all," he answered. " The Danish government is much too honorable to resent on individuals, who are living in confidence in these dominions, the injustice of a foreign power." But, in the mean while, I took care to put my things in order, that, if necessary, I might decamp with the least possible encumbrance.

On Sunday, the 16th, however, two days before the actual bombardment of Copenhagen, an end was put to these uncertainties, and to my residence in Holstein. In the forenoon I had a call from Mr. Aldebert, my first German friend, with whom I went to Germany in 1800, and who had property to a considerable amount warehoused in this town.

He, his clerk (Pietsch), another German, and myself, dined at Rainville's beautiful hotel. It was a fine day, and, as usual on Sundays, the gardens of the hotel were full of company. And here the Major renewed his assurance of my safety, " even should a war break out." After dinner I had a stroll with Stansfeld, who had removed to Hamburg, but had come over to see me. About five o'clock I paid a visit to Madame Lütchens, whose husband was English, and in the service of the English government, in the commissariat department. A month before, as I knew in confidence, he had proceeded to Stralsund. After an hour's chat with her I was going home, when I saw the Bürgermeister in the street, talking with an acquaintance ; but, on my going up to them, he turned away abruptly, affecting not to see me. I thought this gross ill manners, and not warranted even by the reported demonstrations of hostility towards Denmark by England. By reference to the " Annual Register " I find it was on the 12th that Lord Cathcart, with a force of 20,000 men, joined the Admiral off Elsinore, and on the 16th (the day of which I am now speaking) that the army landed on the island of Zealand, eight miles from Copenhagen. But, of course, the public at Altona knew nothing correctly of these proceedings. On my way to Poel's in the evening I was met by William Sieveking, one of the sons of the lady whom I have mentioned. He had an air of anxiety about him, and told me I was wanted immediately at Mr. Poel's. I must go at once, — something was the matter, but he could not say what. A large party of ladies were in the garden, and as soon as Madame Poel saw me, she exclaimed, " Thank God, — there he is, — he at least is safe ! " I was then informed that Major von Spät had been there in great trouble. The Bürgermeister had received an order to arrest every Englishman, and at midnight there was to be a visitation of all the houses occupied by the English. The Major could not bear the thought of my being arrested, for perhaps I had remained there trusting to his assurance of my safety. I was therefore told that I must stay the night at Poel's country-house, and be smuggled next day into Hamburg. But to this I would not consent. I insisted on at least going back to my lodgings to put money in my purse ; and, disguising myself by borrowing a French hat, I immediately went back. Having arranged my own little matters, I resolved to give notice to all my fellow-countrymen with whose residences I was acquainted. And so effectual were my services in this respect, that no one, whom I knew, was arrested. Indeed the arrests were confined to a few journeymen, who were not considered worth keeping. Of course the Holsteiners had no wish to make prisoners, and therefore did their work very negligently.

I will relate a few anecdotes which have dwelt in my memory ever since. I need not say that the apparent rudeness of the Bürgermeister, which had so much annoyed me, was now accounted for.

There was one Ogilvy, a merchant, who resided with a lawyer, and to whom I sent the servant with a note. I was in a flurry, and wrote on a slip of paper, which was kept as a curiosity, and laughed at. It was shown to me afterwards at Hamburg. I had written on it these words : " They 'll catch us if they can to-night. I mean the Danes.. I 'm off. — H. C. R." It was shown to the master of the house. " That Robinson is an arrant coward. It is nothing ; you may depend on it." However, at midnight the police were at the door, and demanded admittance. When asked whether Mr. Ogilvy was at home, the servant, being forewarned, had a prompt answer : " I don't know. That 's his room. He often sleeps at Hamburg." The police went in, and said to the sleeper, " You are our prisoner." On which Ogilvy's " German servant " awoke. " Why, who are you ? " — " Mr. Ogilvy's servant. My master went to Hamburg last night, and as his bed is softer than mine, I sleep in his when he is away." — " O, that is it ? Well, it is lucky for him, for we should have taken him. We have nothing to say to you." — " The stupids ! " said Ogilvy ; " there was my watch on the table, and my clothes were about the room." Rather say, " Good-natured fellows."

I sent a note to Pietsch also. He had more than a thousand pounds' worth of Manchester goods in a warehouse. In haste he removed them into a coach-house, and covered them with loose straw. The police came, demanded the keys of the warehouse, sealed the door and windows with the government seal, and threatened Pietsch with imprisonment if he broke the seal, or entered the warehouse. He solemnly promised he would not, and most honorably kept his word. In the course of a few nights all the goods were transported over the Elbe. The empty warehouse was formally opened by the government officers, after the seals had been carefully examined, and it had been found that Pietsch had most conscientiously kept his promise.

There was then at Altona a Leeds merchant, named Bischoff, a connection of Stansfeld's. I did not know the name of the street in which he lived, and so was forced to go myself. He was in bed. Young Stansfeld accompanied me, and we went together into his room. After he had heard my story, he said to Stansfeld, " Ist das wahr was er sagt ? " (" Is what he says true ? ") I was half angry, and left him to give notice to one who would receive it more gratefully. There was, however, another Englishman in the house, and he thought it prudent to give heed to the warning ; they went out and begged a lodging in the stable of a garden-house in the suburb leading to Poel's. There they slept. At daybreak, the morning was so fine that they could not believe there was any evil going on. The sunshine made them discredit the story, and they resolved to re-enter the town. Fortunately they saw the servant of Pauli at the gate. " Is Mr. Robinson at home ? " — " No, sir, he went away last night, and it is well he did, for at midnight there came some soldiers to take him up." This was enough. Bischoff and Elwin took to their heels, and not daring to go into Hamburg by the Altona gate, made a circuit of many miles, and did not arrive at Hamburg till late in the day.

Having done all that patriotic good-nature required of me, and left everything in order, I went back to Neuemühle, where

a bed was provided for me.   Early in the morning Poel said :
"You cannot possibly remain here.   You must go immediately
after breakfast to Hamburg.   I have ordered a boat to be
here, and my children, and some of the Paulis and Sievekings,
shall go with you ; and if you are questioned you will be the
tutor."   Accordingly there was a boat well filled by the tutor
and his pupils.   We rowed towards the town, where I noticed
at the gate some soldiers sitting in a boat.   This was unusual,
and seemed to me suspicious.   So, as we were approaching, I
said to the boatman, "I never saw Altona from the Hanover
side of the river.   It must look very pretty from a distance."
— "Ay, sir, it does," said the man.   "I should like to see
it.   I'll give you a klein Thaler (about 2 s.) if you will row us
to that side."— "Thankee, sir," said the man ; and instantly
we crossed the Thalweg, that is, the centre of the river.   Now,
it would have been a breach of neutrality, — a crime, in any
police officers to make an arrest on the Hanoverian territory,
which included the left side of the river, — and I was there
safe.   To be perfectly secure, I would not land at the first Hamburg gate, but was rowed to the second.*   There the tutor
dismissed his pupils, and I went in search of Mr. Aldebert at
his lodgings.

I found a post-chaise at his door.   Pietsch had informed him
of what he had been doing on the notice I.had given him ;
and Mr. Aldebert was then going to Altona partly to look after
me.   After thanking me for the service I had rendered him, he
said : "I have provided for you here.   I occupy the first floor,
indeed all the apartments not occupied by the family ; but
there is a very small garret in which you can sleep, and you
can use my rooms as your own."   No arrangement could be
better ; and as on the same evening he left for several days, I
had the use of his handsome apartments.   The house was in
the Neue Wall, one of the most respectable streets : it was
among those burnt down in the late conflagration.†   But I
cannot pretend that my mind was quite at ease, or that I was
not sensible of the peril of my situation.

My clothes were brought piecemeal, and at last came my
empty trunk.   Among the German merchants I had several
acquaintances, and I occasionally met my English fellow-refu-
gees.   The French government at this moment cared nothing
about us ; nor the Danish, as it seemed, though, as I after-

* The French took possession of Hamburg after the battle of Jena, in 1806.
† This was written in 1853 ; the fire took place in 1842.

wards learned, I was an exception to this general indifference.

I have a very imperfect recollection of the incidents of the next few days, and I did not think it prudent to keep in my possession letters or memoranda which might compromise my friends.

H. C. R. to J. D. Collier, Esq.

Hamburg, August 22, 1807.

My dear Friend : —

. . . . You may think that a long letter of gossip would be very charming from a person in my situation; it would be absolutely romantic, and would be as far preferable to one from an ordinary correspondent, as an elopement in the eyes of Miss Lydia Languish to being asked at church. This is all very well for the reader, but not so for the writer. Give me leave to assure you that a man who is a prisoner, or, what is much the same thing, liable to become so every hour of his life, has little inclination to sit down and, as the phrase is, *open his heart* to his friends, because he is never sure that his enemies may not choose at the same time *to take a peep*. . . . . In the mean while I shall be forced to abstain from the enjoyment of almost all direct communication with my friends at home. . . . . Within the last three days nothing of importance has occurred.

25th August. . . . . Hitherto my good spirits have not often left me ; and I assure you it is the reflected concern of my different friends at home that most affects me. I must add, too, that I feel my own personal affairs to be infinitely insignificant compared with the dreadful calamity that overhangs us all. Never was England so nearly in the jaws of ruin. . . . . My late escape and that of my countrymen has occasioned me to observe many interesting and gratifying scenes. I, for my part, felt more flattered by being the object of concern to so many charming women, than alarmed by the personal danger. I have also made an observation curious to the psychologist, and that is the perfect repose which arises from the consciousness that nothing further is to be done by one's self. Formerly, when I came now and then to Hamburg to buy an old book or chat with a friend, it was done with great anxiety ; and I was not at ease till again within the Altona gates. Now I am quite comfortable, though the danger is ten times greater. I can do no more than I have done.

If I am taken, I shall bear as well as I can the positive evils of imprisonment ; but I shall suffer no reproaches from myself nor fear those of others. And it is this which I am most apprehensive of. If I had the means of escape, and was doubtful whether I should avail myself of them, I should be in constant alarm and perturbation ; but now I have nothing to do but to amuse myself as well as I can, and watch 'for opportunities of getting off, if any should offer. I am, generally speaking, comfortable. I am not without companions. My kind respects to all.

On the 19th I accompanied a merchant of the name of Kaufmann to his country-house at an adjacent village, Ham, and strolled about in an unsettled state ; and day by day I gained courage ; but on the 25th I again narrowly escaped capture.

My friend, the Major, called on me to warn me that I must be on my guard. The governor, or Bürgermeister, Mr. Levezow, had said to him that, *excepting* myself, he was very glad all the English had escaped. The suspicion had entered his mind that I was a secret agent of the government. I could not, he thought, be living at such a place at such a time without some especial purpose. " And I think " (added Von Spät), " that he has given a hint to the French authorities." I assured the Major that the suspicion was unfounded, and explained to him what might have given occasion to the mistake. " He was glad," he said, " to know this, and he would take care to inform Mr. Levezow of what I had told him."

It was, however, too late ; for a few hours afterwards, as I was returning home, after a short walk, my attention was excited by a sound — *St ! st !* But for the information I had just received, I should hardly have noticed it. I looked and saw a fellow, — the letter-carrier between Hamburg and Altona, who knew me well, beckoning to some persons at a little distance ; and at the same time, he looked back and pointed at me. At a glance I perceived that they were French gensd'armes. They were lolling by the side of a passage, and within sight of my door.

In an instant I was off. I ran into a market-place full of people, and was not pursued. If I had been, I have no doubt the populace would have aided my escape. I repaired to the house of one of Mr. Aldebert's friends, a Mr. Spalding, a senator. There I dined. I told my story, and it was agreed that

I should not sleep again at my lodgings. The next day but one Mr. Spalding was going to the Mecklenburg watering-place, Dobberan, with his family. He would take a passport for his clerk, and in that capacity I might accompany him.

The intermediate day was spent in removing my clothes and taking leave of my friends. Yet in that day I twice thought I saw a suspicious person lurking in the vicinity of my last asylum; and next day, when I had left the town several hours, my lodging was beset by the military. Some gens-d'armes, without asking any questions, went to my garret, burst open the door, and expressed great disappointment at finding the room empty. They used violent threats towards the women of the house, who told the truth with equal safety to themselves and me. Through a friend I had obtained from the French authorities a *visa* to my old Jena pass; and I had a passport from Netzel, the Swedish consul at Altona, with a letter from him, which might, and in fact did, prove useful. Dobberan was then a small village, with a few large houses to accommodate the bathing guests; but the sea was nearly three miles off. Travelling all night, we arrived on the following day, in time to dine at a table with one hundred and fifty covers, at which the sovereign Duke, though absent this day, was accustomed to take a seat.

I had now to ascertain what vessels were about to set sail for Sweden. In the afternoon I took a solitary walk to the seaside. There I found none of the "airy forces" which, according to Dr. Watts's bad sapphic, "roll down the Baltic with a foaming fury," but a naked sea-coast with a smooth sea, enlivened by a distant view of several English men-of-war, part of a blockading squadron.

Next day I took a walk of about ten miles to the little town of Rostock, a university town, and also a seaport. But no vessel was there; nor had I any prospect of being able to make my escape. In ordinary circumstances, indeed, *escape* would be an unmeaning term, for I was known to the sovereign, who had occasionally chatted with me at Altona. I took an early opportunity of calling upon one of his household, and begged I might be excused for not waiting on His Serene Highness, as I was aware of his position, and was anxious not to embarrass him. This message was very courteously received. I was assured of every protection in the Duke's power; but was requested not to call myself an Englishman, and excuse his affecting not to know me.

The good Duke, however, could not act on his own sage counsel, for, as I was one day not far from him at the table-d'hôte, but carefully avoiding speaking to him or catching his eye, I was surprised by hearing behind me in a loud whisper, "Prosit Herr Engländer." His Serene Highness had filled a bumper, and leaning back behind the guests, drank to me as an Englishman, though he had pretended to consider me an American.   And one morning, having walked to the seaside, and jumped into the water from a long board built into the sea (the humble accommodation provided in those days), I was stártled by a loud cry, which proceeded from the Duke at the end of the board, — "Herr Engländer, Herr Engländer, steigen Sie gleich aus — 10,000 Franzosen sind gleich ange-kommen, und wenn Sie nicht aussteigen und weglaüfen, wird man Sie arretiren." ("Make haste out, Englishman, — 10,000 Frenchmen are just come, and unless you come out and run for it, you will be made a prisoner.")

More good-nature than dignity in this certainly.   But the Duke of Mecklenburg-Schwerin was one of that class of petty sovereigns in Germany, who, if they conferred no honor on their rank and power, did not abuse them to the injury of their subjects.   I had a formal offer from him to send me on board the fleet, which was in the offing, if I would guarantee the safety of his men.   This offer I declined.   I could be more sure of being taken in than set down again.   And mean-while I relied on the friendly interest which every one took in me ; for, though the Mecklenburg flag had been declared hos-tile, I was satisfied that every one whom I saw was well dis-posed towards me.

On the evening of the first of September, I received a letter informing me that a ship was on the point of sailing from Wismar to Stockholm.   Next day I proceeded to Wismar, where I remained till the 8th.   The only circumstance which made me remember these few days was the intercourse which I had with the guests at the inn, and which I recall with pleasure as evidence of the kindness of disposition generally found among those who are free to be actuated by their natural feelings.

On the evening of my arrival the waiter laid me a cover near the head of the table.   Above me sat a colonel of Napo-leon's Italian Guard, who was resting here for a few weeks after the fatigues of the campaign ended by the recent peace. At the head of the table was a Dutch general, then on his

K

way to join Napoleon in Prussia.   Other officers were present ;
and there were also civilians, chiefly merchants.

I passed myself for a German, talking bad French to the
Italians, with whom I soon became well acquainted, and remained on the best terms till my departure.   They were glad
to read a few very common Italian books, which I was able to
lend them.   Without any hypocrisy, I could praise Italian
literature ; and I found I could with perfect safety abuse the
French.   " Is it not to be lamented " (I said in one of our
walks after dinner) " that Italy, which in former ages has been
the mistress of the world in different ways, should be over-
powered by a nation that never produced a great man ? "   This
was strong, but not too strong: The eyes of my companions
glistened with pleasure.   One of them exclaimed, " Don't suppose it is the Italians who are conquered by the French.   It
is the French who are governed by an Italian.   As long as
Napoleon lives he will be master of Europe.   As soon as he
goes, Italy will be independent ! " — " I hope to God it will be
so ! "   Sometimes I ventured to touch on Buonaparte himself ;
but that was tender ground.   They looked grave, and I
stopped.   On general politics they talked freely.   They had
liberal opinions, but little information, — were a sort of republican followers of Buonaparte, — good-natured men, with
little intelligence, and no fixed principles of any kind, especially on religion.

One evening a Dutch merchant came.   He looked me full
in the face and said : " Napoleon is all but omnipotent ; but
there is one thing he cannot do, — make a Dutchman hate an
Englishman."   I asked him to drink with me.

Among the stray visitors was a German who had formerly
studied at Jena.   We became good friends at once.   I had
told him at table that I was Jenenser (true in one sense).
After dinner, when we had gone aside, I said, " I am — "
" You are," he said, interrupting me, " an Englishman."
— " Who told you so ? " — " Everybody.   Were you not at
Rostock a few days ago ? " — " Yes." — " And did you not sit
next a gentleman in green, a Forester ? " — " I did." — " I
thought you must be the same from the description.   My
father said you talked with admirable fluency, — quite well
enough to deceive a Frenchman, — but he had no doubt you
had escaped from Altona.   I was here a few days ago, and
after you had left the room I said to the colonel, ' Who is that
gentleman ? '   He said, ' C'est un Anglais qui veut bien

jouer l'Allemand, mais c'est un bon enfant, — nous le laissons passer.'"

This information rather assured than alarmed me. From my companions here I had no apprehension; but I had letters from Stansfeld telling me on no account to return to Hamburg.

At length, on the 8th of September, after various disappointments, the master of the little vessel in which I had taken my passage came to me with the news that he should weigh anchor in an hour.

I went to my landlady and paid my bill, my portmanteau being already gone. I said to her, "Do you know what countryman I am?"—"Lord love you!" she cried out, "every one knows you. When you walk in the streets, the children say, 'Da geht der Engländer.'"—"And the Italian officers, do they know who I am?"—"To be sure they do. I have heard them speak about you when they did not suppose I understood them. It is useful in our situation to know more than people are aware of. They like you. I have heard them say they had no doubt you had run away from the Danes. And I am very sure that if they were ordered to take you up, they would give you an opportunity of escape." This I believe. I sent a friendly message to them, with an apology for not taking formal leave.

I made my voyage in a poor little vessel with a cargo of salt fish on board. The voyage lasted five long days. There was no passenger but myself; and the crew consisted of only four or five, including boys. One night we had a storm, and I was shut up alone in the cabin. I never before felt such entire wretchedness.

On the other hand, the pleasure was intense when the master came to me in my cabin, and said I should have something good for breakfast if I would get up. I had just begun to have an appetite. On my rising he poured part of a bowl of cream into my cup. I was quite astonished, and, hastening on deck, found myself surrounded by picturesque and romantic masses of rock on every side. We were on the coast of Sweden, not far from Dalarö, the port of Stockholm. On these barren and naked rocks I saw some huts, and a momentary feeling of envy towards the happy residents on those quiet solid spots of earth caused me to laugh at myself.

Dalarö is a miserable little village in a wild position at the mouth of the winding river on which Stockholm is built. Here passengers are accustomed to alight, as the windings of the river render the voyage long.   My intention, however, was to remain in the vessel ; but I was led to change my plan.   My portmanteau was brought to me quite wet.   It had fallen into the water ; and this accident afforded me another opportunity of witnessing the kindness of strangers.   The collector of the customs could speak Swedish only, but, through a person present who knew English, he invited me to spend the evening at his house.   Calling his servants, and asking me for my key, he opened my box, and all my clothes and linen were at once seized and carried off by the women.   My books and papers were carefully collected, and laid on a stove to dry.   In a few minutes I was told that my host was going to fetch his wife, who was on a visit to a friend, and I was invited to accompany him.   We entered a stately boat, and were rowed by six men, through — what shall I say ? — streets and valleys of stone, a labyrinth of rocks and water.   We alighted at steps which led to a neat house, surrounded by fir-trees, the only trees of the place. There Madame had been, but she was gone.   The master of the house, a sea-captain, named Blum, spoke a little bad English, and regaled me with dried beef, biscuit, and brandy.   It was a scene, and my companions were fit for the characters of a romance.   On our return by another water-way we found the lady and her sister had arrived.   They were pretty women, and spoke a little French.   My supper was nice, and consisted chiefly of novelties ; dried goose (cured as we cure hams, and as red), salt fish, oaten cakes, and hot custard.

After supper, seeing that I was fatigued, the lady of the house took a candle, and said she would accompany me to my room.   Those who were present rose ; I was shown into a neat room with a bed in an alcove, and they sat with me five minutes, as if they were paying me a visit in my own apartment.   When I got up next morning, after a long and sound night's sleep, I found in an antechamber all my clothes dry and clean, the linen washed and ironed.

The next day, the 15th of September, I proceeded to Stockholm.   The drive in a little wagon or open chaise, not broader at the wheels than a sedan chair, was very amusing.   I passed a succession of rocky and wooded scenes, with many pieces of water, — I could not tell whether sea or lake.   In addition to the fir, I noticed the birch, and a few oaks ; but the latter seemed to languish.   Few houses were to be seen, — all of wood bedaubed with red ochre, which at a distance gives the appearance of a brick building.   The road was most excellent, and the horses, though small, were capital goers. We kept on in one trot without intermission, and made the journey in less than five hours.

"The entrance into Stockholm, through the southern suburb" (I wrote at the time), "disappoints the expectation raised by the brilliant view in the distance; for the greater number of the houses are low and poor, some even roofed with earth, and the larger houses have an uncomfortable air of nakedness and coldness from the absence of architectural decorations, — the windows without sills, the fronts without cornice, pediment, &c. But its position is singularly striking. In England — but then it would be no longer Stockholm — it would be one of the most remarkable cities in the world. In other words, were English capital and English enterprise applied to it, it would be unrivalled. It stands on seven islands, but is cut into three great divisions by large basins of water, two salt and one fresh, which are not crowded with vessels, but are beautiful streets of still water, exhibiting shores at various distances and of diversified character. The island on which stand the royal palace and the state buildings presents a remarkable mass of picturesque and romantic objects."

More than thirty years ago I wrote this description in a letter. I have since seen Edinburgh, Rome, Venice, Naples, and Palermo; and I now think, if I am not deceived by imperfect recollection, that Stockholm would, for beauty of situation, bear comparison with any of these.

Having fixed myself in the best hotel in the city, I delivered a letter which had been given to me at Dalarö. It was addressed to a young man, named Tode, a merchant's clerk, who I was assured knew English, was intelligent and obliging, and would be proud to be my cicerone. I found him all this, and even more. He was my companion to churches, palaces, and public buildings, and was most kind and assiduous in his attentions.

I also went in search of a lady not unknown in the literary world, and who as a poetess is still recollected with respect under the name of Amelia von Imhoff. She had been Maid of Honor to one of the Duchesses of Saxe-Weimar, which office she held when I visited Weimar in 1803 – 4. Her reputation she owed chiefly to an Idyllic tale, "Die Schwester von Lesbos." She had married a Swedish general, Von Helwig. I was received by her with great cordiality. During my stay at Stockholm, Herr von Helwig was from home. I was almost the first Weimar acquaintance she had seen since her marriage, and I had interesting facts to relate concerning her native country. She was engaged to dine that day with a Polish countess, wife of Herr von Engerström, an historic character ; and she instantly wrote a note intimating that she should bring with her an English gentleman, a personal friend, just arrived. There came an answer, in which the Countess expressed her regret that her dinner was not such as she could with propriety set before a foreign gentleman. She would receive me some other day. Frau von Helwig laughed at this, and with reason. I went, and certainly never was present at a more copious banquet, or one at which the company seemed more distinguished, judging by title and appearance. I cannot specify foreign dishes after thirty-six years, but I did make a memorandum that I used eleven plates at the meal. One national custom I recollect. The company being assembled in the drawing-room before dinner, two large silver waiters were brought in, one full of liqueur glasses of brandy, the other of little pieces of bread and cheese. Whilst these were being carried round to the gentlemen, the ladies went by themselves into the dining-room ; and when we followed we found them seated at table, every alternate chair being left vacant. This was an interesting day, and I regret that I am not better able to remember the conversation, which was indicative of the state of opinion among the Swedish gentry and nobility at a most critical period.

This was the 16th of September, and it should be borne in mind that Copenhagen capitulated to the English on the 7th, and that before very long (March, 1809) the King of Sweden was driven from the throne. Partly by my own observation at the dinner-party, and partly by the information given me by Frau von Helwig, I became fully aware of the unpopularity of the King. I was struck by the coldness with which every remark I made in his praise was received ; but I was in some measure prepared for this by what I had heard from the minister at Altona. On my reading to him Wordsworth's sonnet, his only comment was that the poet had happily and truly described the King as " above all consequences " ; and on my eulogizing the King to Herr von Engerström for his heroic refusal to negotiate with Buonaparte, the reply was, " Personne ne doute que le roi soit un homme d'honneur."

Among the company were two military men of great personal dignity, and having the most glorious titles imaginable.

One was a knight of the " Northern Star " ; the other a knight of the " Great Bear," the constellation.   I had been intro-duced as a German, and was talking with these Chevaliers when Frau von Helwig joined us, and said something that be-trayed my being an Englishman.   Immediately one of them turned away.   The cause was so obvious that my friend was a little piqued, and remonstrated with him.   He made an awkward apology, and unsuccessfully denied her imputation. This anti-English feeling was so general in Sweden at this time that I was advised to travel as a German through the country, and in fact did so.

On the 18th I dined with Frau von Helwig.   She had in-vited to meet me a man whom I was happy to see, and whose name will survive among the memorable names of the last age. I refer to the patriotic Arndt.   He had fled from the pro-scription of Buonaparte.   His life was threatened, for he was accused, whether with truth I do not know, of being the au-thor of the book for the publication of which Salm had been shot.   My falling in with him now caused me to read his works, and occasioned my translating entire his prophecy in the year 1805 of the insurrection of the Spaniards, which actually took place within less than a year of our *rencontre* in Sweden.   This I inserted in a review* of Wordsworth's pamphlet on the convention of Cintra.   I was delighted by this lively little man, very spirited ánd luminous in his con-versation, and with none of those mystifying abstractions of which his writings are full.   He spoke with great admiration of our " Percy's Reliques."

On the 21st I set out on my journey to Gottenburg, having bought a conveyance, with whip and other accompaniments, which altogether cost me about £ 4.   The peasants are obliged to supply horses, and I paid 9 d. per horse for each stage of about seven miles.   My driver was sometimes a man or boy, but sometimes also a woman or girl.   I am not accustomed to make economical statements, but it is worth mentioning that, including the loss on the resale of my carriage, the whole ex-pense of my journey, over 350 miles, during seven days, was less than £ 6 !   I had been furnished with a card, not bigger than my hand, and yet containing all the Swedish words I should want.   With this I managed to pass through the coun-try, without meeting with any incivility or inconvenience ; and, after what I have said as to expense, I need not add,

---

* In Cumberland's " London Review."

without being imposed upon.   How many Swedes will say the same of a journey in England?   The only occasion on which I thought I had reason to complain, was when a peasant provided for my driver a child who could not hold the reins.

With the name of Sweden I had associated no other idea than that of barren rocks; but during the first four days of my journey, in which I left behind me two hundred and fifty miles, there was an uninterrupted succession of beautiful forest scenery.   The roads were admirable, needing no repair, for the substance was granite.   There was no turnpike from beginning to end.   The scenery was diversified by a number of lakes, every now and then a small neat town, or a pretty village, and a very few country-houses.   The fir, or pine, and beech were almost the only trees.

I reached Gottenburg on the 27th.   The environs of the town consist of masses of rock with very scanty interstices of meagre vegetation, — a scene of dreary barrenness; yet commerce has enriched this spot, and the Gottenburg merchants, as I witnessed, partake of the luxuries which wealth can transport anywhere.

On the 30th I commenced my voyage homewards; the age of steam was not come, but after a comfortable passage of eight days, I sighted the coast of my native country.   We landed at Harwich on the afternoon of the 7th of October.

H. C. R. to T. R.

Harwich, 7th October, 1807.

Thank God I once more touch English land.   To-night I mean to sleep at Witham.   To-morrow I shall be in town. And I suppose before long shall come to Bury.   I shall in the mean while expect your letter of congratulation.

Kind love to father, sister, little Tom, and everybody.

CHAPTER XII.

VERY soon after my return from Holstein, Mr. Walter proposed that I should remain in the service of the *Times* as a sort of foreign editor; that is, I was to translate from the foreign papers, and write on foreign politics.   This engagement began at the close of the year; and I entered on my duties in high spirits.   I could not easily find in my life a six months in

which I was more happy in every respect. I began to feel that
I had something to do, and could do it.   In looking back on
my work, I see nothing to be proud of in it; but it connected
me with public life, and that at least was agreeable.   And
though I did not form a portion of the literary society of
London, I was brought into its presence.

It was my practice to go to Printing House Square at five,
and to remain there as long as there was anything to be done.

After a time I had the name of editor, and as such opened
all letters.   It was my office to cut out odd articles and paragraphs from other papers, decide on the admission of correspondence, &c.; but there was always a higher power behind.
While I was in my room, Mr. Walter was in his, and there the
great leader, the article that was talked about, was written.
Nor did I ever write an article on party politics during my
continuance in that post.   I may, however, add, that in February I inserted a letter with my initials, which was, I believe,
of real use to the government.   It is to be found in the paper
printed on February 13th.   It is a justification of the English
government for the seizure of the Danish ships.   The Ministry
defended themselves very ill in the House of Commons.   In my
letter, I stated the fact that the Holstein post-office refused to
take in my letters to England, and alleged as a reason that
Buonaparte had obliged the government to stop the communication with England.   The same evening, in the House of
Lords, this fact was relied upon by the Marquis of Wellesley
as conclusive.   Indeed, it was more to the purpose than any
fact alleged by the government speakers.

In the month of March I was invited to dine with Southey
at Dr. Aikin's.   I was charmed with his person and manners,
and heartily concurred with him in his opinions on the war.   I
copy from a letter to my brother : " Southey said that he and
Coleridge were directly opposed in politics.   He himself thought
the last administration (Whig) so impotent that he could conceive of none worse except the present ; while Coleridge maintained the present Ministry to be so corrupt that he thought it
impossible there could be a worse except the late." On poetry
we talked likewise : I *bolted* my critical philosophy, and was defended by Southey throughout.   I praised Wordsworth's " Sonnets" and preface.   In this, too, Southey joined ; he said that
the sonnets contain the profoundest political wisdom, and the
preface he declared to be " the quintessence of the philosophy
of poetry."

A few days after this (viz. on March 15th) I was introduced to Wordsworth. I breakfasted with him at Lamb's and accompanied him to Mr. Hardcastle's, at Haleham, Deptford, with whom Mrs. Clarkson was on a visit. Wordsworth received me very cordially, owing, I have no doubt, to a favorable introduction by Mrs. Clarkson, aided, of course, by my perfect agreement with him in politics ; and my enthusiastic and unconcealed admiration of his poetry gave me speedy admission to his confidence. At this first meeting he criticised unfavorably Mrs. Barbauld's poetry, which I am the less unwilling to mention as I have already recorded a later estimate of a different kind. He remarked that there is no genuine feeling in the line,

> In what brown hamlet dost thou joy ? *

He said, " Why *brown ?* " He also objected to Mrs. Barbauld's line,

> " The lowliest children of the ground, moss-rose and violet," &c.

" Now," said he, " moss-rose is a shrub." The last remark is just, but I dissent from the first ; for evening harmonizes with content, and the brown hamlet is the evening hamlet. Collins has with exquisite beauty described the coming on of evening : —

> . " And hamlets brown, and dim discovered spires."

Wordsworth, in my first *tête-à-tête* with him, spoke freely and praisingly of his own poems, which I never felt to be unbecoming, but the contrary. He said he thought of writing an essay on " Why bad Poetry pleases." He never wrote it, — a loss to our literature. He spoke at length on the connection of poetry with moral principles as well as with a knowledge of the principles of human nature. He said he could not respect the mother who could read without emotion his poem,

> " Once in a lonely hamlet I sojourned."

He said he wrote his " Beggars " to exhibit the power of physical beauty and health and vigor in childhood, even in a state of moral depravity. He desired popularity for his

> " Two voices are there, one is of the sea,"

as a test of elevation and moral purity.

I have a distinct recollection of reading in the *Monthly Review* a notice of the first volume of Coleridge's poems before I

* Ode to Content.

went abroad in 1800, and of the delight the extracts gave me; and my friend Mrs. Clarkson having become intimate with him, he was an object of interest with me on my return from Germany in 1805. And when he delivered lectures in the year 1808, she wished me to interest myself in them. I needed, however, no persuasion. It was out of my power to be a regular attendant, but I wrote to her two letters, which have been printed, for want of fuller materials, in the "Notes and Lectures on Shakespeare," edited by Mrs. Henry Coleridge.* At the time of my attending these lectures I had no personal acquaintance with Coleridge. I have a letter from him, written in May, 1808, sending me an order for admission. He says : "Nothing but endless interruptions, and the necessity of dining out far oftener than is either good for me, or pleasant to me, joined with reluctance to move (partly from exhaustion by company I cannot keep out, for one cannot, dare not always be 'not at home,' or 'very particularly engaged,' — and the last very often will not serve my turn) these, added to my bread-and-cheese employments, + my lectures, which are — bread and cheese, i. e. a very losing bargain in a pecuniary view, have prevented me day after day from returning your kind call. I will as soon as I can. In the mean time I have left your name with the old woman and the attendants in the office, as one to whom I am always 'at home' when I am at home. For Wordsworth has taught me to desire your acquaintance, and to esteem you; and need I add that any one so much regarded by my friend Mrs. Clarkson can never be indifferent, &c., &c., to S. T. Coleridge." †

* Pickering, 1849.
† I find among my papers two pages of notes of Coleridge's lecture, February 5, 1808:—
Feb. 5th, 1808. Lecture 2d on Poetry (Shakespeare), &c.
Detached Minutes.
The Grecian Mythology exhibits the symbols of the powers of nature and Hero-worship blended together. Jupiter both a King of Crete and the personified Sky.
Bacchus expressed the organic energies of the Universe which work by passion, — a joy without consciousness; while Minerva, &c., imported the pre-ordaining intellect. Bacchus expressed the physical origin of heroic character, a felicity beyond prudence.
In the devotional hymns to Bacchus the germ of the first Tragedy. Men like to imagine themselves to be the characters they treat of, — hence dramatic representations. The exhibition of action separated from the devotional feeling. The Dialogue became distinct from the Chorus.
The Greek tragedies were the Biblical instruction for the people.
Comedy arose from the natural sense of ridicule which expresses itself naturally in mimicry.
Mr. Coleridge, in Italy, heard a quack in the street, who was accosted by

In a visit to Bury, my friend Hare Naylor being a guest at the house of Sir Charles Bunbury, my brother and I were invited to dinner by this beau-ideal of an English sportsman, who was also well known as a Whig politician and a man of honor. A few months afterwards I met him in London, when I was walking with Lamb. Sir Charles shook hands with me, and asked where my regiment was. I evaded the question. Lamb was all astonishment — " I had no idea that you knew Sheridan." — " Nor do I. That is Sir Charles Bunbury." — " That 's impossible. I have known him to be Sheridan all my life. That *shall* be Sheridan. You thief! you have stolen my Sheridan ! "

That I did not quite neglect my German studies is shown by my having translated for the *Monthly Repository* Lessing's " Education of the Race." *

Though I had not the remotest intention now of studying the law, yet during this spring I luckily entered myself a member of the Middle Temple ; and I at the same time exer-

his servant-boy smartly ; a dialogue ensued which pleased the mob ; the next day the quack, having perceived the good effect of an adjunct, hired a boy to talk with him. In this way a play might have originated.

The modern Drama, like the ancient, originated in religion. The priests exhibited the miracles and splendid scenes of religion.

Tragi-Comedy arose from the necessity of amusing and instructing at the same time.

The entire ignorance of the ancient Drama occasioned the reproduction of it on the restoration of literature.

Harlequin and the Clown are the legitimate descendants from the Vice and Devil of the ancient Comedy. In the early ages, very ludicrous images were mixed with the most serious ideas, not without a separate attention being paid to the solemn truths ; the people had no sense of impiety ; they enjoyed the comic scenes, and were yet edified by the instruction of the serious parts. Mr. Coleridge met with an ancient MS. at Helmstädt, in which God was represented visiting Noah's family. The descendants of Cain did not pull off their hats to the great visitor, and received boxes of the ear for their rudeness ; while the progeny of Abel answered their catechism well. The Devil prompted the bad children to repeat the Lord's Prayer backwards.

The Christian polytheism withdrew the mind from attending to the whisperings of conscience ; yet Christianity in its worst state was not separated from humanity (except where zeal for Dogmata interfered). Mahometanism is an anomalous corruption of Christianity.

In the production of the English Drama, the popular and the learned writers by their opposite tendencies contributed to rectify each other. The learned would have reduced Tragedy to oratorical declamation, while the vulgar wanted a direct appeal to their feelings. The many feel what is beautiful, but they also deem a great deal to be beautiful which is not in fact so : they cannot distinguish the counterfeit from the genuine. The vulgar love the Bible and also Hervey's " Meditations."

The essence of poetry *universality*. The character of Hamlet, &c. affects all men : addresses to personal feeling ; the sympathy arising from a reference to individual sensibility spurious. [N. B. This applies to Kotzebue.]

* *Monthly Repository*, Vol. I., 1806, pp. 412, 467.

cised myself in business speaking by attending at the Surrey Institution.

During some weeks my mind was kept in a state of agitation in my editorial capacity. The Spanish revolution had broken out, and as soon as it was likely to acquire so much consistency as to become a national concern, the *Times*, of course, must have its correspondent in Spain ; and it was said, who so fit to write from the shores of the Bay of Biscay, as he who had successfully written from the banks of the Elbe ? I did not feel at liberty to reject the proposal of Mr. Walter that I should go, but I accepted the offer reluctantly. I had not the qualifications to be desired, but then I had experience. I had some advantage also in the friendship of Amyot, who gave me letters which were eventually of service ; and I was zealous in the cause of Spanish independence.

I left London by the Falmouth mail on the night of July 19th, reached Falmouth on the 21st, and on the 23d embarked in a lugger belonging to government, — the *Black Joke*, Captain Alt. The voyage was very rough, and as I afterwards learnt, even dangerous. We were for some time on a lee shore, and obliged to sail with more than half the vessel under water ; a slight change in the wind would have overset us ; but of all this I was happily ignorant.

I landed at Corunna on the evening of Sunday, July 31st, and was at once busily employed. I found the town in a state of great disorder ; but the excitement was a joyous one, the news having just arrived of the surrender of a French army in the south under Marshal Dupont. This little town, lying in an out-of-the-way corner of Spain, was at this period of importance, because, being the nearest to England, it became the point of communication between the Spanish and English governments. The state of enthusiastic feeling in Galicia, as well as in every other province of Spain where the French were not, rendered the English objects of universal interest. I took with me several letters of introduction, both to merchants and to men in office, but they were hardly necessary. As soon as I could make myself intelligible in bad Spanish, and even before, with those who understood a little French, I was acceptable everywhere, and I at once felt that I should be in no want of society. I put myself in immediate connection with the editor of the miserable little daily newspaper, and from him I obtained Madrid papers and pamphlets. There were also a number of Englishmen in the place, — some engaged in commerce, others attracted by curiosity. And there was already in the harbor the *Defiance*, a 74-gun ship, Captain Hotham, with whom and his officers I soon formed an interesting acquaintance. Of the town itself I shall merely say this : it lies at the extremity of one horn of a bay, and is very picturesque in its position. The rocks which run along the tongue of land are exceedingly beautiful ; on that tongue, between the city and the sea, are numerous low windmills, which, as I first saw them in the dusk of evening, made me think that Don Quixote needed not to have been so very mad to mistake them for giants. As I looked on the narrow streets of the town, and the low and small houses with shoots throwing the rain-water into the middle of the street, the thought more than once occurred to me, that probably in the times of good Queen Bess the streets of London presented a somewhat similar appearance. The windows are also doors, and every house has its balcony, on which, when it is in the shade, the occupants spend much time. The intrigues of which the Spanish plays and romances are full are facilitated by the architecture, — it being equally easy to get access by the windows and escape from the roof. The beggars are charmingly picturesque, and have in their rags a virtuosity worthy a nation whose most characteristic literature consists of beggar-romances.

H. C. R. TO T. R.

In the evening about seven all is life and activity. The streets are crowded, especially those towards the bay, and it is at this time that if everybody had a wishing-cap all the world would fly to Spain for two or three hours. The beauty of the evenings is indescribable. There is a voluptuous feeling in the atmosphere, which diffuses joy, so that a man need not think to be happy. There is a physical felicity, which renders it superfluous to seek any other. And when we add the languor produced by the heat in the middle of the day (which, however, I have not felt so much as I expected), we can account for the indolence of the Spanish character.

My business was to collect news and forward it by every vessel that left the port,* and I spent the time between the

---

* My letters to the *Times* are dated " Shores of the Bay of Biscay " and " Corunna." The first appeared on August 9, 1808; the last on January 26, 1809.

An extract from Mr. Robinson's first communication, dated August 2, will

reception and transmission of intelligence in translating the public documents and in writing comments. I was anxious to conceal the nature of my occupation, but I found it necessary from time to time to take some friends into my confidence.

Among the earliest and latest of my Corunna acquaintance were the officers of the *Defiance*. I became especially intimate with Lieutenants Stiles and Banks, and Midshipman Drake. They seemed to have more than a brother's love for each other. This perhaps is the natural consequence where, as in this instance, each felt that in the hour of danger he might owe his life to his companions. I at length imagined I could be happy on shipboard. These young men and I rendered each other mutual service. My lodgings were frequently their home, and they assisted me in the transmission of letters. I introduced them to partners at balls, and gained credit with the ladies for so doing.

There were several houses at which I used to visit; occasionally I was invited to a formal Tertulia. At these Tertulias the ladies sit with their backs against the wall on an elevated floor, such as we see in old halls. The gentlemen sit before them, each cavalier on a very small straw-bottomed chair before his *dama*, and often with his guitar, on which he klimpers, and by aid of which, if report say truly, he can make love without being detected. The company being seated, a large silver plate is given to each guest, and first a cup of rich and most delicious chocolate is taken, — then, to correct it, a pint tumbler of cold water. Preserved fruits and

---

show the high spirits and the favorable prospects which animated the Spanish people at the time of his arrival. " When we consider, as is officially stated, that *not a Frenchman exists in all Andalusia, save in bonds;* that in Portugal, Junot remains in a state of siege; that all the South of Spain is free; and that in the North the late victories of the patriots in Arragon have broken the communication between the French forces in Biscay and Catalonia, we need not fear the speedy emancipation of the capital, and the compression of the French force within the provinces adjoining Bayonne. When this arrives it will be seen whether the long-suffering of the powers of the North, as well as of the whole French people, may not find an end, and whether thus at length a period may not be put to that tyranny which seemed so firmly established."

The next communication (August 4) announced the surrender of Dupont's army; and the third (on August 8) the flight of Joseph Napoleon from Madrid.

On September 26, Mr. Robinson writes: " The glorious and astonishing exertions of the Spanish Patriots, of which it is more correct to say that the Spaniards became soldiers in performing them, than that they performed them because they were soldiers, ended in the capture or destruction of the greater part of the numerous forces which had penetrated the interior of the country, while the few that could effect their escape were driven to the Northern provinces."

other sweetmeats follow in abundance, and these in their turn are corrected by a second pint of water. Nothing can exceed the dulness of these parties, but I found them useful as lessons in Spanish. It was not till October that I had admission to the tables of the Spanish gentry. I dined usually at the Fontana d'Oro, the chief hotel, where the dinners were the worst I was ever condemned to sit down to, — the meat bad, and rendered intolerable by garlic. The only excellent meat was the Spanish ham, cured with sugar; and the only dish for an epicure was the *olla podrida*, a medley to be compared with, though differing from, a Yorkshire pie.

Among my earliest English acquaintance was a Captain Kennedy, who filled the office of Minister to the Galician Junta. We became well acquainted, and were of use to each other. He sang charmingly, and was a very handsome man; his mother was the famous Mrs. Kennedy, the actress.

On the 13th of October the first of a series of events took place, which mark one of the most memorable periods of my life. On that day there arrived a detachment of English troops under the command of Sir David Baird. Luckily for myself, I had a few days before become acquainted with General Brodrick, and he had introduced me to Admiral de Courcy, who was stationed in the *Tonnant*, a ship of the line. Captain Hancock and I had received an invitation to dine with the Admiral this day. In the morning, when I was over my books, I was startled by the report of cannon, and, running to the ramparts, beheld more than 150 vessels, transports, sailing in a double row before a gentle breeze. It was a striking spectacle, and I felt proud of it. But I remarked that the sight was rather mortifying than gratifying to the pride of some of the Spanish gentry, who were looking on, and who might feel humiliated that their country needed such aid.* We had dined, when, on a sudden, the Admiral rose and cried out, "Gentlemen! open your quarters"; on our doing which an officer placed himself between each two of us. Among the arrivals were Sir David Baird, General Crawford, &c. We had half an hour's formal chat and drank success to the expedition.

---

* Mr. Robinson says in his letter of the 22d of October: " In one respect I was almost pleased to remark the indifference of our reception, — they do not want us, thought I, *tant mieux!* and God grant they may not find themselves mistaken! There is great confidence on the part of the people; they have no idea, apparently, that it is possible for them to be beaten; their rage is unbounded when the name of Buonaparte is mentioned; but their hatred of the French is mixed with contempt."

After remaining a few days in Corunna the troops proceeded to the interior, to join the army under Sir John Moore. The expedition, I have understood, was ill planned ; the result belongs to the history of the war.

On the 20th there was an arrival which, more than that of the English, ought to have gratified the Spaniards. I witnessed a procession from the coast to the Town Hall, of which the two leading figures were the Spanish General Romana and the English Minister, Mr. Frere. Few incidents in the great war against Napoleon can be referred to as rivalling in romantic interest the escape of the Spanish soldiers under General Romana from the North of Germany ; but, on beholding the hero, my enthusiasm subsided. Romana looked, in my eyes, like a Spanish barber. I was therefore less surprised and vexed than others were when, in the course of events, he showed himself to be an ordinary character, having no just sense of what the times and the situation required from the Spanish nation. On the other hand, I received a favorable impression from the person and address of Mr. Frere. And when, in a few months, the public voice in England was raised against him as the injudicious counsellor who imperilled the English army by advising their advance on Madrid, my own feeling was that he was unjustly treated.

On November 3d there was an arrival from England, which was to me a source of some amusement. Early in the morning a servant from my friend Madame Mosquera* came in great haste to request that I would go to her immediately. I found her full of bustle and anxiety. "There is just arrived," said she, "an English *grandeza*, — a lord and lady of high rank. They will dine on board their ship, and come here in the evening. All the arrangements are made : I am to attend them in a carriage on shore, and the Duke of Veraguas is to accompany me ; and there must be a second gentleman, and we hope you will go with us. They are to take a *refresco* here, and to-morrow they are to dine with the Countess Bianci. You are to be invited to be at the dinner ; and what I want of you now is that you instruct me how I am to receive my lord and lady." My first inquiry was who these great persons were. No other than my Lord and Lady Holland. My determination was at once taken. I told Madame that it was impossible for me to attend her on shore ; I was not of noble birth, nor a fit companion for the descendant and representative of Co-

* Mr. Robinson sometimes spells this name Moschera.

lumbus. Colonel Kennedy, by birth no better than myself, was, in virtue of his diplomatic position, the first Englishman at Corunna, and must therefore be invited. (Poor Kennedy received his invitation, and when he heard that he owed to me the honor, he declared he would never forgive me, for he and the Duke and the Baroness were made to sit in the carriage between three and four hours waiting for the mistress of Holland House.) As to the reception, I said, you have only to do for them what you would do for the Spanish grandees of the first rank, — and besides the usual chocolate and sweetmeats, send up tea and bread-and-butter. That there might be no mistake I requested a loaf to be brought, and I actually cut a couple of slices as thin as wafers, directing that a plate should be filled with such. The tea equipage I was assured was excellent, — procured in London. I said there would be no impropriety in my meeting my lord and lady at the house, and therefore promised to attend. After a wearisome waiting on our part, the noble visitors and their escort arrived. Lady Holland, with her stately figure and grand demeanor; my lord, with his countenance of bonhomie and intelligence; a lad, said to be the second son of the Duke of Bedford, a Lord Something Russell, — perhaps the present Prime Minister * of England; and a gentleman whom I have heard called satirically Lady Holland's atheist, a Mr. Allen, but better known as an elegant scholar and Edinburgh reviewer, who in that character fell into a scrape by abusing some Greek that was by Pindar. The party was a small one. In a few minutes after the arrival of the guests the *refresco* was brought in. All the servants were in gala dresses, and a table being set out in the large reception-room, a portly man brought in a huge silver salver, resembling in size the charger on which in Italian pictures the head of John the Baptist is usually brought by Herod's step-daughter. This huge silver dish was piled up with great pieces of bread-and-butter an inch thick, sufficient to feed Westminster School. This was set down with great solemnity. Next came a large tea-tray of green and red tin, such as might have been picked up at Wapping. This was covered with all sorts of indescribable earthenware. The teapot, which was of tin, had probably not been in use for years, and therefore the moment Madame Mosquera took hold of it to pour out the tea, the lid fell in and filled the room with steam. She managed to pour out a cup, which she ran with to my lady,

* This was written in 1848.

who good-naturedly accepted it.   This done, she ran with
another cup to Lord Holland.   She was full of zeal, and her
little round figure perspired with joy and gladness.   Mosquera
saw the ridicule of the exhibition and tried to keep her back,
twitching her gown and whispering audibly, "Molly, you are
mad!"   She, however, ran to me full of glee, "Have not I
done well?"   The gentlemen were glad to inquire of us, the
residents, the news of the day.   Lord Holland was known to
be among the warmest friends of the Spanish cause; in that
respect differing from the policy of his Whig friends, who by
nothing so much estranged me from their party as by their
endeavor to force the English government to abandon the
Spanish patriots.

Before the events occurred which precipitated the departure
of us all, I had made the acquaintance of one highly interesting and remarkable woman.   This was Madame Lavaggi.   Her
husband was the Treasurer of the kingdom, that is of Galicia.
He owed his place, and indeed everything, to her, — he was
younger than she, and a well-looking man.   She was one of the
plainest women I ever saw, — I should say the very plainest.
The fortune was hers, and she took the lead in all things.   She
had character and energy, and I felt more interest in her conversation than in that of any other person.   But she was altogether uneducated.   She spoke French very ill, and could hardly
write, — for instance, in a short note she spelt *quand, cant,* —
but her zeal against the French rendered her eloquent, almost
poetical.   She was very religious, and loyal without being insensible to the abuses of the government.   Her father had been
Prime Minister under Charles VI., and she was fond of relating
that at one time six portfolios or seals of office were held by him.
At her house I was a frequent and favored guest, and I was able
to return these civilities by substantial services.

The time was approaching when these services would be
wanted.   Before this occurred, however, I determined on
taking a holiday, and having made the acquaintance of Mur-
phy, the architect who wrote a book on "The Gothic Architecture of Portugal," proposed that we should go together to Madrid; he agreed to this, and went to buy a carriage for our journey, but returned with the information, which was a great secret, that it was not advisable to advance, for the English army
was on its retreat!   This was on November 22d.*

* In his letter of November 12th, Mr. Robinson says: "My last letter, which
was of the 9th, imparted to you the anxious feelings with which I was impressed

As the intelligence became daily worse in December, others were led to consider how their personal safety might be secured, and left the place. This was the means of increasing my intimacy with the Lavaggis and the English officers in authority ; I became known also to some of the Spaniards in office, including members of the Junta, — that is, the Galician government, which collectively had the quality of *Majesty* in formal addresses.

I was repeatedly in the company of Arguelles, the famous statesman and orator, whose person and manners inspired me with greater respect that those of any other Spaniard.

In the midst of these troubles I was learning the language rapidly, and was able to read Spanish books ; and before the close of the year I found myself able to take interest in general society. But, excepting Madame Lavaggi, there was not a woman who appeared to have any intelligence or strength of mind, though all were warm patriots. There were several agreeable women, but only one to be conversed with except on balls and operas. When I received from England the famous pamphlet of Cevallos, which first exposed to Europe the infamous treatment of the Spanish princes by Buonaparte, I carried it to a Spanish lady who spoke French ; she looked at the title gravely, and returned it saying, " I never look into any book that is not given me by my confessor." The ordinary conversation of the ladies was frivolous and undignified, but innocent, and their in-

when I wrote it. You learned from it that the campaign was opened by an attack on several parts of the Spanish line by the French; and you were informed that those attacks had been successful."

" *November 25th.* — The intelligence brought by the *Lady Pellew* packet from Corunna is of an unfavorable complexion, yet such as we might perhaps have expected from the first appearance of Buonaparte upon the theatre of war. General Blake's army, after sustaining repeated attacks, is said at last to have been completely defeated, while the advanced body of the French have even reached Valladolid.

" The news from the English army on its way from Portugal is no less distressing. It is said that 3,000 of the men under Sir John Moore are sick."

" Corunna, *December 8th.* — A serious responsibility is incurred, by that government, whichever it was, to which the lamentable delay is to be imputed, which followed the arrival of those troops in the harbor of Corunna. The utter want of all preparations for promoting the march of that army was seen with deep affliction by both British and Spaniards. No man pretends to fix the culpability upon any one; they can only judge of those who are privy to the negotiations which preceded the expedition. The sad effect, however, is very obvious: for but for this delay the united British army would not have been compelled to retreat before the foe, leaving him a vast reach of territory at his command."

" *December 10th.* — A tale is current which, if not true, has been invented by an Arragonese, that Buonaparte has sworn that on the 1st of January his brother shall be at Madrid, Marshal Bessieres at Lisbon, and himself at Saragossa."

delicacies were quite unconscious. Every Spanish woman is christened Mary, and to this there is some addition by which they are generally known. I was puzzled at hearing a very lively laughing girl called "Dolores," but was told she was christened Maria de los Dolores, — the Mother of Sorrows. One other was always called "Conche"; that I found to be an abridgment of Conception, — Maria de la Concepçion being her proper name.

I had till the very last leisure to amuse myself occasionally both with books and society, but as the year drew to a close the general anxiety and trouble augmented; and before it was at an end I confidently anticipated the result, though I felt bound in honor to remain at my post till the last; and from the number of my acquaintance among the English officers and diplomatists, I felt no apprehension of being abandoned.[*]

1809.

My notes are too few to enable me to give a precise date to some of the more interesting and notable occurrences of this year. Several of these have a bearing on the *morale* of public men, but I would not insert them here if I were not perfectly sure of the substantial correctness of what I relate.

This I must state as the general impression and result, that in the economical department of our campaign in Spain there was great waste and mismanagement, amounting to dishonesty. One day —— came to me full of glee, and said : " I have done a good day's work : I have put £ 50 in my pocket. C—— [who was one of the Commissariat] wanted to buy some [I am not sure of the commodity]. He is bound not to make the purchase himself, so he told me where I could get it and what I was to give, and I have £ 50 for my commission." On my expressing surprise, he said, " O, it is always done in all purchases."

Another occurrence, not dishonorable in this way, but still greatly to be regretted, must be imputed, I fear, to a very honorable man. Only a very few days before the actual embarkation of the troops, there arrived from England a cargo of clothing, — a gift from English philanthropists (probably a large proportion of them Quakers) to the Spanish soldiers. The Supercargo spoke to me on his arrival, and I told him he must on no account unload, — that every hour brought fugi-

[*] On December 23d, Mr. Robinson says: "A letter from Salamanca announced that Joseph, the Usurper, is at Madrid, and issues his mandates as if Spain were already conquered, though no one obeys him."

tives, — that the transports were collected for the troops, which were in full retreat, — and that if these articles were landed they would become, of course, the prey of the French. He said he would consult General Brodrick. I saw the Supercargo next day, and he told me that the General had said that the safest thing for him to do was to carry out his instructions literally, — land the clothes, get a receipt, and then whatever happened he was not to blame. And he acted accordingly.*

Some weeks before the actual embarkation Lavaggi applied to me for assistance in placing in security the papers and accounts belonging to Galicia, and held by him as Treasurer. He could not let it be known that he was about to run away, and therefore requested me to purchase the charter-party of one of the merchant vessels lying in the harbor. This I effected. There was a vessel laden with a sort of beans called caravanzes, the property of a well-known character, one Captain Ashe, who held the charter-party. He became afterwards notorious as author of "The Book" about the Queen of George IV., which was the subject of so many rumors, and ultimately suppressed. In the transaction with Captain Ashe I took care to have all the legal documents. When the cargo was dis-

* In a letter to the *Times*, January 6th, Mr. Robinson writes: "Within a single day everything has changed its appearance in this place; and both English and Spanish seem to be seriously alarmed, not for the fate of the country alone, or even the province, but of the town and themselves.

" On whichever side we look, we see cause for distress; the enemy advancing in the front, Portugal abandoned to the right, the Asturias defenceless to the left; and in the distance, uncertainty and obscurity."

"*January 8th.* — The peril is drawing nigh, and the apprehensions and fears of the unmilitary are therefore increased; but the danger is now unequivocally perceived, and people begin to meet it manfully. As a public expression of the sense of our situation, the theatre is this evening shut for the first time."

" There is a strong sentiment in favor of the English troops, notwithstanding their retreat. This has relieved our minds from a great embarrassment. A Spanish populace, especially the female half of it, is no despicable power; and it was apprehended by some, that in case the English were unsuccessful, the people might rise in favor of the French. Hitherto, the contrary is apparent. I have once or twice heard exclamations from the women which seem to tend to a disturbance, exclaiming against the traitors, who had sent for the English to be massacred, and then abandoned them."

" During the day there has been a number of arrivals. Our streets swarm, as a few weeks since, with English officers; but the gayety and splendor which graced their first entrance into Spain have given way to a mien and air certainly more congenial with the horrid business of war. I do not mean that they manifest any unworthy or dishonorable sentiment; on the contrary, as far as I can judge from the flying testimony of those I converse with, the army has throughout endured with patience its privations and long suffering; and, since its arduous and difficult retreat, displayed an honorable constancy and valor. They speak with little satisfaction of all that they have seen in Spain, and I fear are hardly just towards the people whom they came to protect and rescue."

charged at Plymouth, caravanzes were so high in price that all the expense of the voyage to England, which was not contemplated, was defrayed. The ship was chartered to Cadiz, to which place we were bound. I was the legal owner, and as such passed to and fro.

On January 11th a number of troops arrived, and it was announced that the French were near. During this time the Spaniards did not conceal their indignation at the retreat. It was affirmed, with what truth I had not the means of judging, that there were many passes capable of defence, and that the enemy might have been easily stopped. Why this easy task was not undertaken by General Romana was never explained to me. But I certainly heard from the retreating officers themselves that the retreat was more properly a flight, and that it was conducted very blunderingly and with precipitation. I was assured that cannon were brought away, while barrels of dollars were thrown down precipices; and I witnessed the ragged and deplorable condition of officers. One day, going over to *my* ship, there was a common sailor, as he seemed, most indecently ragged, who was going to a transport vessel near mine. I began joking with " my lad," when he turned round, and I at once perceived in the elegance of his figure and the dignity of his countenance that I was addressing one of the young aristocracy. He received my apologies very good-humoredly ; told me that he had been subject to every privation, and that he had on his flight been thankful for a crust of bread and a pair of old shoes. On board a transport he had a wardrobe awaiting him.*

As the time of departure approached, the interest of Lavaggi in the ship became known, and on the 11th, one

* In the letter to the *Times* dated January 11th, Mr. Robinson says: " In the course of this day the whole English army has either entered within, or planted itself before, the walls of this town. The French army will not fail to be quick in the pursuit; and as the transports which were so anxiously expected from Vigo are still out of sight, and, according to the state of the wind, not likely soon to make their appearance, this spot will most probably become the scene of a furious and bloody contest.

" The late arrivals have, of course, made us far better acquainted than we possibly could be before with the circumstances of this laborious and dishonorable campaign, which has had all the suffering, without any of the honors of war. Without a single general engagement, — having to fight an enemy who always shunned the contest, — it is supposed that our army has lost upwards of 3,000 men, a larger number of whom perished by the usual causes, as well as labors of a retreating soldiery."

" *January* 12th. — An alarming symptom is the extreme scarcity of every kind of provisions. The shops are shut, the markets are abandoned. Perhaps the imperious wants of future importunate visitors are especially recollected. If the transports arrive, there will be abundance of every necessity: if not, famine stares us in the face."

of the Junta, Don Padre Gil, came to me in great distress, imploring me to take him on board. He would die, he said, rather than submit to the French. I let him come to me a second time, having obtained permission to take him on board. By way of trial, I asked him if he knew what it was to become an exile. " O yes ; I have a brother in America and friends at Cadiz." — " But have you supplied yourself with the means of living abroad and supporting yourself on the voyage ? " — " O yes ; I have plenty of chocolate." The man at last actually went down upon his knees to me. This was irresistible, — I took him, but did not scruple to try his feelings ; for I made him in the evening put on a sailor's jacket, and take a portmanteau on his head. I could command the sentinels to open the gates of the town, which he could not. He went on board, but next day he was fetched away by another member of the Junta, a priest named Garcia, a subtle if not an able man. A few weeks afterwards I read in the French papers a flaming address from the inhabitants of Corunna, gratefully thanking the French General for having emancipated them from their oppressors and tyrants the English, and the very first name among the list of subscribers was that of Padre Gil.

It was on the 13th that I took on board Madame Lavaggi and a handsome and amiable young officer, a native of America, named T——, a relation of the Duke of Veraguas. There were on board Lavaggi, Pyecroft, a gentleman named Pipiela, with his wife, servants, of course, and, as I afterwards learned, others of whom I had no knowledge. Madame Lavaggi I heard was very ill during the night, and next day her husband gave orders that we should return, in order that she might be taken on shore. It was not until afterwards that I discovered the real cause of our going back was that Madame had found out that their young friend T—— had smuggled on board some one who had no right to be there ; she therefore determined on quitting the vessel. I accompanied her to her house, and as we approached the door a rich perfume of cedar-wood was apparent, — it proceeded from the burning of a costly cabinet which she much prized. The destruction of this and other valuable articles of furniture had not been prevented by the officers who were left in the house, and the poor lady burst into tears as she told me that these gentlemen had been most hospitably treated at her table.*

* Letter to the *Times*, January 15th. " The last two days have materially changed the appearance of things. Yesterday evening, the fleet of transports,

I slept in my old lodging, and the morning of the 16th I spent in making calls and in writing the last letter to the *Times*. The whole town was in commotion, — the English hurrying away, at least those of them who were not engaged in protecting the embarkation of the others, — the Spaniards looking on in a sort of gloomy anger, neither aiding nor opposing them. On going to dine at the hotel, I found the table-d'hôte filled with English officers. After a time, on looking round I saw that the room was nearly empty, — not a red-coat to be seen. On inquiry of the waiters, one said : " Have you not heard ? The French are come : they are fighting." * Having finished my dinner, I walked out of the town. Townspeople, stragglers, were walking and loitering on the high road and in the fields. We could hear firing at a distance. Several carts came in with wounded soldiers. I noticed several French prisoners, whose countenances expressed rather rage and menaces than fear. They knew very well what would take place. I walked with some acquaintances a mile or more out of the town, and remained there till dark, —long enough to know that the enemy was driven back ; for the firing evidently came from a greater distance. Having taken leave of Madame Lavaggi, whom I sincerely esteemed, and of my few acquaintances in the town, I went on board, and our vessel was judiciously stationed by the Captain out of the harbor, but immediately on the outside. There were numerous ships like ours sailing about the bay. The Captain said to me overnight : " You may be sure the French will be here in the morning ; I will take care to place the vessel so that we may have no difficulty in making our escape." The morning was fine and the wind favorable, or our position might have been perilous. Early in the forenoon my attention was drawn to the sound of musketry, and by a glance it could be ascertained that the soldiers were shooting such of their fine horses as could not be taken on board. This was done, of course, to prevent their strength-

which had been dispersed in their passage from Vigo, began to enter the harbor, and the hearts of thousands were relieved by the prospect of deliverance. I beheld this evening the beautiful bay covered with our vessels, both armed and mercantile, and I should have thought the noble three-deckers, which stood on the outside of the harbor, a proud spectacle, if I could have forgotten the inglorious service they were called to perform."

* This was the celebrated battle of Corunna, at which Sir John Moore was killed. In Mr. Robinson's memoranda, written at the time, he says that the cannonading seemed to be on the hills about three miles from the town. At five o'clock he embarked, and though the vessel remained not far off till the 18th, he does not appear to have heard of the death of the English commander, or any particulars of the battle.

ening the French cavalry. One very loud explosion brought us all on deck. There was on the shore a large powder magazine, which had been often the boundary of my walk. When the cloud of smoke which had been raised was blown away, there was empty space where there had been a solid building a few moments before ; but this was a less exciting noise than when, about one o'clock, we heard a cannonading from the shore at the inland extremity of the bay. It was the French army. They were firing on ships which were quietly waiting for orders. I remarked the sudden movement in the bay, — the ships before lying at anchor were instantly in motion. I myself noticed three vessels which had lost their bowsprits. The Captain told me that twelve had cut their cables. We were not anxious to quit the spot, and therefore sailed about in the vicinity all night. Two vessels were on fire, and next day I was shocked at beholding the remains of a wreck, and the glee with which our sailors tried to fish them up as we passed. Lavaggi was very desirous to go to Cadiz, but the Captain solemnly declared that the ship was not sea-worthy for that course, the wind being direct for England ; he would not risk our lives by attempting it. Of course, as we could not disprove his assertion, we submitted, and proceeded straight to Falmouth, which we reached on the 23d.

On my return to London I resumed my occupation at the *Times* office. But a change had taken place there ; Collier had transferred his services to the *Chronicle*. In the mean while I had less given me to do, but I did it with cheerfulness, and soon renewed my old habits and old acquaintance.

At this time, too, I was frequent in my calls on the Spanish political agents. The names of Durango, Lobo, and Abeilla appear in my pocket-book. I rendered a service to Southey by making him acquainted with the last-named, who supplied him with important documents for his history of the Spanish war.

On the 13th of July I was invited to a small party at Mrs. Buller's. There were not above half a dozen gentlemen. Mrs. Buller told me, before the arrival of Horace Twiss, that some of her friends had heard of his imitations of the great orators, and that he was to *exhibit*. The company being assembled, he was requested to make a speech in the style of Mr. Pitt or Mr. Fox, as he had done at Lady Cork's. Twiss was modest, not to say bashful, — he could not do such a thing unless excited ; but if Mr. Mallett or Mr. Robinson would make a speech on any subject, he would immediately reply.   Unfortunately, both Mr. Mallett and Mr. Robinson were modest too, and their modesty was inflexible.   At length a table being set in the doorway between the two drawing-rooms, the orator was so placed that a profile or oblique view was had of his face in both rooms, and he began : " Mr. Speaker ! " and we had two speeches in succession, in imitation of Fox and Pitt, — I think on the subject of Irish union, or it might be Catholic emancipation.   I have forgotten all but the fact that the lady who sat next to me said, " O, the advantages you gentlemen have ! — I never before knew the power of *human oratory.*"   Human oratory I will swear to.

On the 12th of August I received a letter from Mr. Walter, informing me that he had no longer need of my services, and on the 29th of September I formally laid down my office of Foreign Editor of the *Times.*   I left Mr. Walter on very good terms ; he had a kindly feeling towards me, and his conduct had been uniformly friendly and respectful.   He had never treated me as one who received his wages, and at his table no one could have guessed our relation to each other.   On two occasions he wished me to undertake duties which are only confided to trustworthy friends.   Let me here bear my testimony to his character.   He may not have fixed his standard at the highest point, but he endeavored to conform to it.

This is the proper place for me to mention two persons connected with the *Times* while I wrote for it.   The writer of the great leaders — the flash articles which made a noise — was Peter Fraser, then a Fellow of Corpus Christi, Cambridge, afterwards Rector of Kegworth, in Leicestershire.   He used to sit in Walter's parlor and write his articles after dinner. He was never made known as editor or writer, and would probably have thought it a degradation ; but he was prime adviser and friend, and continued to write long after I had ceased to do so.   He was a man of general ability, and when engaged for the *Times* was a powerful writer.   The only man who in a certain vehemence of declamation equalled or perhaps surpassed him, was the author of the papers signed " Vetus," — that is Sterling, the father of the younger Sterling, the free-thinking clergyman, whose remains Julius Hare has published.

There is another person belonging to this period, who is a character certainly worth writing about ; indeed I have known few to be compared with him.   It was on my first acquaintance with Walter that I used to notice in his parlor a remarkably fine old gentleman. He was tall, with a stately figure and handsome face. He did not appear to work much with the pen, but was chiefly a consulting man. When Walter was away he used to be more at the office, and to decide in the *dernier ressort*. His name was W. Combe. It was not till after I had left the office that I learned what I shall now relate. At this time and until the end of his life he was an inhabitant of the King's Bench Prison, and when he came to Printing House Square it was only by virtue of a day rule. I believe that Walter offered to release him from prison by paying his debts. This he would not permit, as he did not acknowledge the equity of the claim for which he suffered imprisonment. He preferred living on an allowance from Walter, and was, he said, perfectly happy. He used to be attended by a young man who was a sort of half-servant, half-companion. Combe had been for many years of his life a man of letters, and wrote books anonymously. Some of these acquired a great temporary popularity. One at least, utterly worthless, was for a time, by the aid of prints as worthless as the text, to be seen everywhere, — now only in old circulating libraries. This is "The Travels of Dr. Syntax in search of the Picturesque." It is a long poem in eight-line verse; in external form something between Prior and Hudibras, but in merit with no real affinity to either. Combe wrote novels; one I recollect reading with amusement, — the "German Gil Blas." He was also the author of the famous "Letters of a Nobleman to his Son," generally ascribed to Lord Lyttelton. Amyot told me that he heard Windham speak of him. "I shall always have a kindness for old Combe," said Windham, "for he was the first man that ever praised me, and when praise was therefore worth having." That was in "Lord Lyttelton's Letters." Combe had, as I have said, the exterior of a gentleman. I understand that he was a man of fortune when young, and travelled in Europe, and even made a journey with Sterne; that he ran through his fortune, and took to literature, when "house and land were gone and spent," and when his high connections ceased to be of service. Of these connections, and of the adventures of his youth, he was very fond of talking, and I used to enjoy the anecdotes he told after dinner, until one day, when he had been very communicative, and I had sucked in all he related with greedy ear, Fraser said, laughing, to Walter: "Robinson, you see, is quite a flat; he believes all old Combe says." — " I believe whatever a gentleman says till I have some reason to the contrary."— "Well, then," said Fraser, "you must believe nothing he says that is about himself. What he relates is often true, except that he makes himself the doer. He gives us well-known anecdotes, and only transfers the action to himself." This, of course, was a sad interruption to my pleasure. I might otherwise have enriched these reminiscences with valuable facts about Sterne, Johnson, Garrick, Mrs. Siddons, and other worthies of the last generation.

This infirmity of old Combe was quite notorious. Amyot related to me a curious story which he heard from Dr. Parr. The Doctor was at a large dinner-party when Combe gave a very pleasant and interesting account of his building a well-known house on Keswick Lake ; he went very much into details, till at last the patience of one of the party was exhausted, and he cried out : " Why, what an impudent fellow you are ! You have given a very true and capital account of the house, and I wonder how you learned it ; but that house was built by my father ; it was never out of the family, and is in my own possession at this moment." Combe was not in the least abashed, but answered, with the greatest *nonchalance :* " I am obliged to you for doing justice to the fidelity of my description ; I have no doubt it is your property, and I hope you will live long to enjoy it."

The first occasion of my appearing in my own name as an author was about this time. Tipper, who estimated my talents as a writer by my reputation as a speaker, solicited me to become a *collaborateur*, under Cumberland, the well-known dramatist, in getting up a new Review, called the *London Review,* of which the distinguishing feature was to be that each writer should put his name to the article. I was flattered by the application, and readily consented. Four half-crown quarterly numbers were published. I dined once at Tipper's with Cumberland, and thought him a gentlemanly amiable man, but did not form a high opinion of his abilities ; and I thought the less of him because he professed so much admiration of my single article as to direct it to be placed first in the number. This was a review of the great pamphlet on the " Convention of Cintra," by Wordsworth. The only valuable portion of the article was a translation of Arndt's " Geist der Zeit," which treated of the Spanish character, and predicted that the Spaniards would be the first to resist the tyranny of Buonaparte.

In November I began keeping my terms at Middle Temple Hall, but was unable to make up my mind to study the law seriously, as I ought at once to have done. One of my severest self-reproaches is that I did not, without delay, immediately become the pupil of some pleader. It needed a special inducement for that; and all I did was merely to keep a term. On November 18th I ate my first dinner, having deposited my £ 100 with the Treasurer. I entered the beautiful hall with an oppressive sense of shame, and wished to hide myself as if I were an intruder. I was conscious of being too old to commence the study of law with any probability of success. My feelings, however, were much relieved by seeing William Quayle in the hall. He very good-naturedly found a place for me at his mess. But this dining at mess was so unpleasant that, in keeping the twelve terms required, I doubt whether I took a single superfluous dinner, although these would only have cost 6 d. each.

On the 23d of December Mr. Rutt, his nephew George Wedd, and myself walked to Royston. There was a remarkable gradation of age among us. We were on a visit to Mr. Nash, who was fifteen years older than Mr. Rutt, who was fifteen years older than myself, and I was in my thirty-fourth year, and fifteen years older than George Wedd. Mr. Rutt and I were proud of our feat, — a walk of thirty-eight miles! But old Mr. Wedd, the father of George, was displeased with his son. He was a country gentleman, proud of his horses, and conscious of being a good rider. I was told that he disliked me, and would not invite me to his house. I offered a wager that I would gain his good-will. After dinner we talked of books; Mr. Wedd detested books and the quoters of books; but I persisted, and praised Lord Herbert of Cherbury, and illustrated the beauty of his writing by citing that *wise and fine saying of his*, "A fine man upon a fine horse is the noblest object on earth for God to look down upon." Mr. Wedd declared that he never thought Mr. Robinson could make himself so agreeable, and I was invited to his house.

CHAPTER XIII.

1810.

I REMAINED all the spring and summer in London, with the exception of making short journeys; and spent my time at Collier's, keeping up all my old visiting acquaintance and making new. I became more intimate with Godwin, who was keeping a bookseller's shop in his wife's name. I now and then saw interesting persons at his house ; indeed, I saw none but remarkable persons there. Among the most remarkable was the great Irish orator, Curran. His talk was rich in idiom and imagery, and in warmth of feeling. He was all passion, — fierce in his dislikes, and not sparing in the freedom of his language even of those with whom he was on familiar terms. One evening, walking from Godwin's house, he said of a friend, " She is a pustule of vanity." He was not so violent in his politics. The short ministry of the Whigs had had the good effect of softening the political prejudices of most of us, though not of all the old Jacobins, as is shown by a speech made by Anne Plumptre, the translator of Kotzebue, whom I met at a dinner-party at Gamaliel Lloyd's. She said : " People are talking about an invasion, — I am not afraid of an invasion ; I believe the country would be all the happier if Buonaparte were to effect a landing and overturn the government. He would destroy the Church and the aristocracy, and his government would be better than the one we have."

I amused myself this spring by writing an account of the insane poet, painter, and engraver, Blake. Perthes of Hamburg had written to me asking me to send him an article for a new German magazine, entitled " Vaterländische Annalen," which he was about to set up. Dr. Malkin having in the memoirs of his son given an account of Blake's extraordinary genius, with specimens of his poems, I resolved out of these materials to compile a paper. This I did, and it was translated into German by Dr. Julius, who many years afterwards introduced himself to me as my translator. The article appears in the single number of the second volume of the " Vaterländische Annalen." For it was at this time that Buonaparte united Hamburg to the French empire, on which Perthes manfully gave up the magazine, saying, as he had no longer a "Vaterland," there could be no "Vaterländische Annalen." But before I drew up this paper I went to see a gallery of Blake's paintings, which were exhibited by his brother, a hosier in Carnaby Market. The entrance fee was 2 s. 6 d., catalogue included. I was deeply interested by the catalogue as well as the pictures. I took four copies, telling the brother I hoped he would let me come again. He said, "O, as often as you please."* I afterwards became acquainted with Blake, but will postpone what I have to relate of this extraordinary character.

In the June of this year I made the acquaintance of Ayrton, with whom I was intimate for many years; and soon afterwards the name of his friend Captain Burney occurs in my notes. They lived near each other, in Little James Street, Pimlico. I used to be invited to the Captain's whist parties, of which dear Lamb was the chief ornament. The Captain was himself a character, a fine, noble creature, — gentle, with a rough exterior, as became the associate of Captain Cook in his voyages round the world, and the literary historian of all these acts of circumnavigation. Here used to be Hazlitt, till he affronted the Captain by severe criticisms on the works of his sister, Madame D'Arblay. Another frequenter of these delightful whist parties was Rickman, the Speaker's secretary, and who then invited me to his house. Rickman's clerk Phillips and others used also to be present.

It was in the course of this summer that my friend Mrs. Charles Aikin invited me to meet Sergeant Rough at dinner. We became intimate at once. I ought to have made his acquaintance before, for when I was at Weimar in 1805 Miss Flaxman, then a governess in the family of Mr. Hare Naylor, gave me a letter of introduction to him. His wife, a daughter of John Wilkes, was a woman of some talents and taste, who could make herself attractive.

During a visit I made to Bury about this time, Miss Wordsworth was staying with the Clarksons; I brought her up to London, and left her at the Lambs'.

MISS WORDSWORTH TO H. C. R.

GRASMERE, November 6, 1810.

MY DEAR SIR, — I am very proud of a commission which my brother has given me, as it affords me an opportunity of express-

* This visit is referred to in Gilchrist's "Life of Blake," Vol. I. p. 226.

ing the pleasure with which I think of you, and of our long journey side by side in the pleasant sunshine, our splendid entrance
into the great city, and our rambles together in the crowded
streets. I assure you I am not ungrateful for even the least
of your kind attentions, and shall be happy in return to be
your guide amongst these mountains, where, if you bring a
mind free from care, I can promise you a rich store of noble
enjoyments. My brother and sister too will be exceedingly
happy to see you ; and, if you tell him stories from Spain of
enthusiasm, patriotism, and destestation of the usurper, my
brother will be a ready listener ; and in presence of these
grand works of nature you may feed each other's lofty hopes.
We are waiting with the utmost anxiety for the issue of that
battle which you arranged so nicely by Charles Lamb's fireside.
My brother goes to seek the newspapers whenever it is possible
to get a sight of one, and he is almost out of patience that the
tidings are delaying so long.

Pray, as you most likely see *Charles* at least from time to
time, tell me how they are going on. There is nobody in the
world out of our own house for whom I am more deeply interested. You will, I know, be happy that our little ones are all
going on well. The little delicate Catherine, the only one for
whom we had any serious alarm, gains ground daily. Yet it
will be long before she can be, or have the appearance of being,
a stout child. There was great joy in the house at my return, which each showed in a different way. They are sweet
wild creatures, and I think you would love them all. John is
thoughtful with his wildness ; Dora alive, active, and quick ;
Thomas innocent and simple as a new-born babe. John had
no feeling but of bursting joy when he saw me. Dorothy's
first question was, " Where is my doll ? " We had delightful
weather when I first got home ; but on the first morning
Dorothy roused me from my sleep with, " It is time to get up,
aunt, it is a *blasty* morning, — it does blast so." And the
next morning, not more encouraging, she said, " It is a *hailing*
morning, — it hails so hard." You must know that our house
stands on a hill, exposed to all hails and blasts. . . . .

D. WORDSWORTH.

CHARLES LAMB TO H. C. R.

1810.

DEAR R———— : My brother, whom you have met at my
rooms (a plump, good-looking man of seven-and-forty), has

written a book about humanity, which I transmit to you herewith. Wilson the publisher has put it into his head that you can get it reviewed for him. I dare say it is not in the scope of your Review; but if you could put it in any likely train he would rejoice. For, alas! our boasted humanity partakes of vanity. As it is, he teases me to death with choosing to suppose that I could get it into all the Reviews at a moment's notice. I !! who have been set up as a mark for them to throw at, and would willingly consign them all to Megæra's snaky locks.

But here's the book, and don't show it to Mrs. Collier, for I remember she makes excellent *eel* soup, and the leading points of the book are directed against that very process.

Yours truly,
C. LAMB.

Miss Wordsworth left London just at the time of the arrival of Madame Lavaggi, the Spanish lady of whom I have already spoken. She came to England because the presence of the French rendered her own country intolerable to her. She was a high-spirited patriot and also a good Catholic, but thoroughly liberal as far as her narrow information permitted. The only occasion on which she showed any bigoted or ungenerous feeling was on my showing her at the Tower of London the axe with which Anne Boleyn was beheaded. "Ah! que j'adore cet instrument!" she exclaimed. On my remonstrating with her, she told me she had been brought up to consider Anne Boleyn as one possessed by a devil; that naughty children were frightened by the threat of being sent to her; and that she was held to be the great cause of the Reformation, as the seducer of the King, &c., &c. No wonder that Romanists should so think, when Protestants have extensively circulated that very foolish line ascribed to Gray, —

"When Gospel truth first beamed from Anna's eyes."

Madame Lavaggi received my correction of her notions in the very best spirit. She is the one Spaniard of whom I think with especial respect and kindness. We of colder temperament and more sober minds feel ourselves oppressed by the stronger feelings of more passionate characters, — at least this is the case with me. At the same time I fully recognize the dignity of passion, and am able to admire what I have not, and am not.

At the end of this year I wrote a few pages entirely devoted to Coleridge. The following is the substance of them : —

November 14th. — Saw Coleridge for the first time in private, at Charles Lamb's. A short interview, which allowed of little opportunity for the display of his peculiar powers.

He related to us that Jeffrey, the editor of the *Edinburgh Review,* had lately called on him, and assured him that he was a great admirer of Wordsworth's poetry, that the Lyrical Ballads were always on his table, and that Wordsworth had been attacked in the *Review* simply because the errors of men of genius ought to be exposed. Towards me, Coleridge added, Jeffrey was even flattering. He was like a school-boy, who, having tried his man and been thrashed, becomes contentedly a fag.

November 15th. — A very delightful evening at Charles Lamb's ; Coleridge, Morgan, Mr. Burney, &c., there. Coleridge very eloquent on German metaphysics and poetry, Wordsworth, and Spanish politics.

Of Wordsworth he spoke with great warmth of praise, but objected to some of his poems. Wishing to avoid an undue regard to the high and genteel in society, Wordsworth had unreasonably attached himself to the low, so that he himself erred at last. He should have recollected that verse being the language of passion, and passion dictating energetic expressions, it became him to make his subjects and style accord. One asks why tales so simple were not in prose. With " malice prepense " he fixes on objects of reflection, which do not naturally excite it. Coleridge censured the disproportion in the machinery of the poem on the Gypsies. Had the whole world been standing idle, more powerful arguments to expose the evil could not have been brought forward. Of Kant he spoke in terms of high admiration. In his " Himmel's System " he appeared to unite the genius of Burnet and Newton. He praised also the " Träume eines Geistersehers," and intimated that he should one day translate the work on the Sublime and Beautiful. The " Kritik der Urtheilskraft " he considered the most astonishing of Kant's works. Both Fichte and Schelling he thought would be found at last to have erred where they deviated from Kant ; but he considered Fichte a great logician, and Schelling perhaps a still greater man. In both he thought the want of gratitude towards their master a sign of the absence of the highest excellence. Schelling's system resolves itself into fanaticism, not better than that of Jacob Boehme. Coleridge

had known Tieck at Rome, but was not aware of his eminence
as a poet.   He conceded to Goethe universal talent, but felt a
want of moral life to be the defect of his poetry.   Schiller he
spoke more kindly of.   He quoted " Nimmer, das glaubt mir,
erscheinen die Götter, nimmer allein." *   (He has since translated it.)   Of Jean Paul he said that his wit consisted not in
pointing out analogies in themselves striking, but in finding
unexpected analogies.   You admire, not the things combined,
but the act of combination.   He applied this also to Windham.
But is not this the character of all wit ?   That which he contrasted with it as a different kind of wit is in reality not wit,
but acuteness.   He made an elaborate distinction between
fancy and imagination.   The excess of fancy is delirium, of
imagination mania.   Fancy is the arbitrarily bringing together
of things that lie remote, and forming them into a unity.   The
materials lie ready for the fancy, which acts by a sort of jux-
taposition.   On the other hand, the imagination under excitement generates and produces a form of its own.   The " seas of
milk and ships of amber " he quoted as fanciful delirium.   He
related, as a sort of disease of imagination, what occurred to
himself.   He had been watching intently the motions of a
kite among the mountains of Westmoreland, when on a sudden he saw two kites in an opposite direction.   This delusion
lasted some time.   At last he discovered that the two kites
were the fluttering branches of a tree beyond a wall.

November 18th. — At Godwin's with Northcote, Coleridge,
&c. Coleridge made himself very merry at the expense of Fuseli,
whom he always called Fuzzle or Fuzly.   He told a story of Fuseli's being on a visit at Liverpool at a time when unfortunately he had to divide the attention of the public with a Prussian
soldier, who had excited a great deal of notice by his enormous
powers of eating.   And the annoyance was aggravated by persons persisting in considering the soldier as Fuseli's countryman.   He spent his last evening at Dr. Crompton's,† when
Roscoe (whose visitor Fuseli was) took an opportunity of giving a hint to the party that no one should mention the
glutton.   The admonition unfortunately was not heard by a
lady, who, turning to the great Academician and lecturer, said :
" Well, sir, your countryman has been surpassing himself ! " —
" Madame," growled the irritated painter, " the fellow is no

---

* " Never alone, believe me, do the Gods appear."   This poem is entitled
" Dithyrambe " in the twelve-volume edition of Schiller's works, 1838. Vol. I
p. 240.
    † The father of Judge Crompton.

countryman of mine." —" He is a foreigner ! Have you not heard what he has been doing ? He has eaten a live cat ! " — " A live cat ! " every one exclaimed, except Fuseli, whose rage was excited by the suggestion of a lady famous for her blunders, " Dear me, Mr. Fuseli, that would be a fine subject for your pencil." — " My pencil, madam ? " — " To be sure, sir, as the horrible is your forte."— " You mean the *terrible*, madam," he replied, with an assumed composure, muttering at the same time between his teeth, " if a silly woman can mean anything."

December 20th. — Met Coleridge by accident with Charles and Mary Lamb. As I entered he was apparently speaking of Christianity. He went on to say that miracles are not an essential in the Christian system. He insisted that they were not brought forward *as* proofs ; that they were acknowledged to have been performed by others as well as the true believers. Pharaoh's magicians wrought miracles, though those of Moses were more powerful. In the New Testament, the appeal is made to the knowledge which the believer has of the truths of his religion, not to the wonders wrought to make him believe. Of Jesus Christ he asserted that he was a Platonic philosopher. And when Christ spoke of his identity with the Father, he spoke in a Spinozistic or Pantheistic sense, according to which he could truly say that his transcendental sense was *one* with God, while his empirical sense retained its finite nature. On my making the remark that in a certain sense every one who utters a truth may be said to be inspired, Coleridge assented, and afterwards named Fox and others among the Quakers, Madame Guyon, St. Theresa, &c., as being also inspired.

On my suggesting, in the form of a question, that an eternal absolute truth, like those of religion, could not be *proved* by an accidental fact in history, he at once assented, and declared it to be not advisable to ground the belief in Christianity on historical evidence. He went so far as to affirm that religious belief is an act, not of the understanding, but of the will. To become a believer, one must love the doctrine, and feel in harmony with it, and not sit down coolly to inquire whether he should believe it or not.

Notwithstanding the sceptical tendency of such opinions, Coleridge added, that accepting Christianity as he did in its spirit in conformity with his own philosophy, he was content for the sake of its divine truths to receive as articles of faith, or, perhaps I ought to say, leave undisputed, the miracles of the New Testament, taken in their literal sense.

In writing this I am reminded of one of the famous sayings of Pascal, which Jacobi quotes repeatedly : " The things that belong to men must be understood in order that they may be loved ; the things that belong to God must be loved in order to be understood."

Coleridge warmly praised Spinoza, Jacobi on Spinoza, and Schiller " Ueber die Sendung Moses," &c. And he concurred with me in thinking the main fault of Spinoza to be his attempting to reduce to demonstration that which must be an object of faith. He did not agree with Charles Lamb in his admiration of those playful and delightful plays of Shakespeare, " Love's Labor's Lost " and the " Midsummer Night's Dream " ; but both affirmed that not a line of " Titus Andronicus " could have been from Shakespeare's pen.

December 23d. — Coleridge dined with the Colliers, talked a vast deal, and delighted every one. Politics, Kantian philosophy, and Shakespeare successively, — and at last a playful exposure of some bad poets. His remarks on Shakespeare were singularly ingenious. Shakespeare, he said, delighted in portraying characters in which the intellectual powers are found in a pre-eminent degree, while the moral faculties are wanting, at the same time that he taught the superiority of moral greatness. Such is the contrast exhibited in Iago and Othello. Iago's most marked feature is his delight in governing by fraud and superior understanding the noble-minded and generous Moor. In Richard III. cruelty is less the prominent trait than pride, to which a sense of personal deformity gave a deadly venom. Coleridge, however, asserted his belief that Shakespeare wrote hardly anything of this play except the character of Richard : he found the piece a stock play and re-wrote the parts which developed the hero's character : he certainly did not write the scenes in which Lady Anne yielded to the usurper's solicitations. He considered " Pericles " as illustrating the way in which Shakespeare handled a piece he had to refit for representation. At first he proceeded with indifference, only now and then troubling himself to put in a thought or an image, but as he advanced he interested himself in his employment, and the last two acts are almost entirely by him.

Hamlet he considered in a point of view which seems to agree very well with the representation given in " Wilhelm Meister." Hamlet is a man whose ideal and internal images are so vivid that all real objects are faint and dead to him.

This we see in his soliloquies, on the nature of man and his disregard of life : hence also his vacillation, and the purely convulsive energies he displayed.   He acts only by fits and snatches.   He manifests a strong inclination to suicide.   On my observing that it appeared strange Shakespeare did not make suicide the termination of his piece, Coleridge replied that Shakespeare wished to show how even such a character is at last obliged to be the sport of chance, — a salutary moral doctrine.

But I thought this the suggestion of the moment only, and not a happy one, to obviate a seeming objection.   Hamlet remains at last the helpless, unpractical being, though every inducement to activity is given which the very appearance of the spirit of his murdered father could bring with it.

Coleridge also considered Falstaff as an instance of the predominance of intellectual power.   He is content to be thought both a liar and a coward in order to obtain influence over the minds of his associates.   His aggravated lies about the robbery are conscious and purposed, not inadvertent untruths.   On my observing that this account seemed to justify Cooke's representation, according to which a foreigner imperfectly understanding the character would fancy Falstaff the designing knave who does actually outwit the Prince, Coleridge answered that, in his *own* estimation, Falstaff is the superior, who cannot easily be convinced that the Prince has escaped him ; but that, as in other instances, Shakespeare has shown us the defeat of mere intellect by a noble feeling ; the Prince being the superior moral character, who rises above his insidious companion.

On my noticing Hume's obvious preference of the French tragedians to Shakespeare, Coleridge exclaimed : " Hume comprehended as much of Shakespeare as an apothecary's phial would, placed under the falls of Niagara."

We spoke of Milton.   He was, said Coleridge, a most determined aristocrat, an enemy to popular elections, and he would have been most decidedly hostile to the Jacobins of the present day.   He would have thought our popular freedom excessive.   He was of opinion that the government belonged to the wise, and he thought the people fools.   In all his works there is but *one* exceptionable passage, — that in which he vindicates the expulsion of the members from the House of Commons by Cromwell.   Coleridge on this took occasion to express his approbation of the death of Charles.

Of Milton's " Paradise Regained," he observed that however inferior its kind is to " Paradise Lost," its execution is superior.

This was all Milton meant in the preference he is said to have given to his later poem. It is a didactic poem, and formed on the model of Job.

Coleridge remarked on the lesson of tolerance taught us by the opposite opinions entertained concerning the death of Charles by such great men as Milton and Jeremy Taylor.

Jeremy Taylor's "Holy Dying," he affirmed, is a perfect poem, and in all its particulars, even the rhythm, may be compared with Young's "Night Thoughts." In the course of his metaphysical conversation, Coleridge remarked on Hartley's theory of association. This doctrine is as old as Aristotle, and Hartley himself, after publishing his system, when he wrote his second volume on religion, built his proofs, not on the maxims of his first volume, which he had already learnt to appreciate better, but on the principles of other schools. Coleridge quoted (I forget from whom) a description of association as the "law of our imagination." Thought, he observed, is a laborious breaking through the law of association ; the natural train of fancy is violently repressed ; the free yielding to its power produces dreaming or delirium. The great absurdity committed by those who would build everything on association is that they forget the things associated : these are left out of the account.

Of Locke he spoke, as usual, with great contempt, that is, in reference to his metaphysical work. He considered him as having led to the destruction of metaphysical science, by encouraging the unlearned public to think that with mere common sense they might dispense with disciplined study. He praised Stillingfleet as Locke's opponent ; and he ascribed Locke's popularity to his political character, being the advocate of the new against the old dynasty, to his religious character as a Christian, — though but an Arian, — for both parties, the Christians against the sceptics, and the liberally minded against the orthodox, were glad to raise his reputation ; and to the nationality of the people, who considered him and Newton as the adversaries of the German Leibnitz. Voltaire, to depress Leibnitz, raised Locke.

H. C. R. to T. R.

" Coleridge kept me on the stretch of attention and admiration from half past three till twelve o'clock. On politics, metaphysics, and poetry, more especially on the Regency, Kant, and Shakespeare, he was astonishingly eloquent. But I cannot help remarking that, although he practises all sorts of delightful tricks, and shows admirable skill in riding his hobby, yet he may be easily unsaddled. I was surprised to find how one may obtain from him concessions which lead to gross inconsistencies. Though an incomparable declaimer and speechmaker, he has neither the readiness nor the acuteness required by a colloquial disputant ; so that, with a sense of inferiority which makes me feel humble in his presence, I do not feel in the least afraid of him. Rough said yesterday, that he is sure Coleridge would never have succeeded at the bar even as a speaker."

This I wrote when I knew little of him ; I used afterwards to compare him as a disputant to a serpent ? — easy to kill, if you assume the offensive, but if you let him attack, his bite is mortal. Some years after this, when I saw Madame de Staël in London, I asked her what she thought of him : she replied, " He is very great in monologue, but he has no idea of dialogue." This I repeated, and it appeared in the *Quarterly Review.*

It was at the very close of the year that I made an acquaintance which afforded me unqualified satisfaction, except as all enjoyments that are transient are followed by sorrow when they are terminated. This new acquaintance was the great sculptor, John Flaxman.

Having learned from Rough that my German acquaintance, Miss Flaxman, had returned, and was living with her brother, I called on her to make my apologies for neglecting to deliver my letter to Rough. She received them, not with undignified indifference, but with great good-nature. On this occasion I was introduced to Mrs. Flaxman, a shrewd lively talkative woman, and received an invitation to spend the last night of the year with them. The whole day was interesting. I find from my pocket-book that I translated in the forenoon a portion of Goethe's " Sammler und die Seinigen," which I never ended, because I could not invent English comic words to express the abuses arising from one-sidedness in the several schools of painting. In the afternoon I sat with Mrs. Barbauld, still in all the beauty of her fine taste, correct understanding, as well as pure integrity ; and, in the evening, I was one of a merry party at Flaxman's. But this evening I saw merely the good-humored, even frolicsome, kind-hearted man.   Every sportive word and action of Flaxman's was enhanced by his grotesque figure.   He had an intelligent and benignant countenance, but he was short and humpbacked, so that in his laughter it often seemed as if he were mocking himself. There were the Roughs and a few others, enough to fill two very small rooms (No. 7 Buckingham Street, which Flaxman bought when he settled in London on his return from Italy, and in which he died).   He introduced to me a lively, rather short, and stout girl, whom he called his " daughter Ellen."   I took him literally, and said I thought he had no child.   " Only in one way she is my daughter.   Her other father, there, is Mr. Porden, the architect."   This same Ellen Porden became ultimately the wife of Captain Franklin, the North Pole voyager.

It was also in this year that I became acquainted with Manning,* then a special pleader, now, perhaps, the most learned man at the bar, sergeant or barrister.   He was the son of a well-known Arian divine at Exeter, and he has had the manliness and integrity never to be ashamed of Dissent.

I ought not to omit the circumstance that I kept four terms this year.

H. C. R. to Miss Wordsworth.

56 Hatton Garden, December 23, 1810.

My dear Madam : —

.... I have postponed answering your acceptable letter till I could speak to you concerning our common friends, the Lambs.

Mary, I am glad to say, is just now very comfortable.   But I hear she has been in a feeble and tottering condition.   She has put herself under Dr. Tuthill, who has prescribed water. Charles, in consequence, resolved to accommodate himself to her, and since lord-mayor's day has abstained from all other liquor, as well as from smoking.   We shall all rejoice, indeed, if this experiment succeeds.

Who knows but that this promising resolution may have been strengthened by the presence of Coleridge ?   I have spent several evenings with your friend.   I say a great deal when I

---

* The Queen's Ancient Sergeant, who died in 1866.
In early life Manning devoted himself for a year and a half to agriculture. Afterwards he went to Germany for a year, to learn the language, in order to fit himself for mercantile pursuits.   Finally he fixed on the law as a profession.

declare that he has not sunk below my expectations, for they were never raised so before by the fame of any man. He appears to be quite well, and if the admiration he excites in me be mingled with any sentiments of compassion, this latter feeling proceeds rather from what I have heard, than from what I have seen. He has more eloquence than any man I ever saw, except perhaps Curran, the Irish orator, who possesses in a very high degree the only excellence which Coleridge wants to be a perfect parlor orator, viz. short sentences. Coleridge cannot *con*verse. He addresses himself *to* his hearers. At the same time, he is a much better listener than I expected.

Your kind invitation to the Lakes is most welcome. If I do not embrace the offer, be assured it is not from want of a strong desire to do so. I wish for no journey so much, except, indeed, another voyage to Spain. My admiration, my love, and anxious care continue to be fixed on that country; and I have no doubt that if my hopes are not so lofty as those your brother cherishes, it is only because I am myself not so lofty.

.   .   .   .   .

Coleridge spent an afternoon with us on Sunday. He was delightful. Charles Lamb was unwell, and could not join us. His change of habit, though it on the whole improves his health, yet when he is low-spirited leaves him without a remedy or relief.

.   .   .   .   .

To Mr. Wordsworth my best remembrances. We want unprofaned and unprostituted words to express the kind of feeling I entertain towards him.

Believe me, &c., &c.,

H. C. R.

P. S. — I was interested in your account of the children, and their reception of you ; but it is not only mountain children that *make* verbs. I heard an Essex child of seven say lately, in delight at a fierce torrent of rain, " How it is storming ! " The same boy had just before said, " I love to see it roaring and pouring." I have more than once remarked the elements of poetic sense in him.

CHAPTER XIV.

1811.

THIS year I began to keep a Diary. This relieves me from one difficulty, but raises another. Hitherto I have had some trouble in bringing back to my memory the most material incidents in the proper order. It was a labor of *collection*. Now I have to *select*. When looking at a diary, there seems to be too little distinction between the insignificant and the important, and one is reminded of the proverb, " The wood cannot be seen for the trees." *

January 8th.— Spent part of the evening with Charles Lamb (unwell) and his sister. He had just read the " Curse of Kehama," which he said he liked better than any of Southey's long poems. The descriptions he thought beautiful, particularly the finding of Kailyal by Ereenia. He liked the opening, and part of the description of hell ; but, after all, he was not made happier by reading the poem. There is too much trick in it. The three statues and the vacant space for Kehama resemble a pantomime scene ; and the love is ill managed. On the whole, however, Charles Lamb thinks the poem infinitely superior to " Thalaba."

We spoke of Wordsworth and Coleridge. To my surprise, Lamb asserted the latter to be the greater man. He preferred the " Ancient Mariner " to anything Wordsworth had written. He thought the latter too apt to force his own individual feelings on the reader, instead of, like Shakespeare, entering fully into the feelings of others. This, I observed, is very much owing to the lyrical character of Wordsworth's poems. And Lamb concluded by expressing high admiration of Wordsworth, and especially of the Sonnets. He also spoke of " Hart-leap Well " as exquisite.

Some one, speaking of Shakespeare, mentioned his anachronism in which Hector speaks of Aristotle. " That's what Johnson referred to," said Lamb, " when he wrote, —

'And panting Time toils after him in vain!' "

---

* Henceforward selections will be given from the Diary, with additions from the Reminiscences. These additions will be marked [*Rem.*], and the year in which they were written will be stated at the foot of the page.

January 17th. — In the evening a call at Flaxman's. Read to Mrs. Flaxman a part of Schlegel's "Critique on the Designs for Dante," which of course gratified her. She told me they were done in Italy for Mr. Hope, on very moderate terms, merely to give Flaxman employment for the evening. Fuseli, when he saw them, said, "I used to think myself the best composer, but now I own Flaxman to be the greater man." Some years ago, when I met Flaxman at Mrs. Iremonger's, I mentioned Schlegel's praise of him for his preference of Dante to Milton. It was, said Schlegel, a proof that he surpassed his countrymen in taste. Flaxman said he could not accept the compliment on the ground of preference. He thought Milton the very greatest of poets, and he could not forgive Charles James Fox for not liking him. He had three reasons for choosing Dante. First, he was unwilling to interfere with Fuseli, who had made choice of Milton for his designs. Second, Milton supplies few figures, while Dante abounds in them. And, third, he had heard that Michael Angelo had made a number of designs in the margin of a copy of Dante.

Mrs. Flaxman said, this evening, that the common cloak of the lower classes in Italy suggested the drapery for Virgil and Dante. While we were talking on this subject Flaxman came in. He spoke with great modesty of his designs; he could do better now, and wished the Germans had something better on which to exercise their critical talents.

January 19th. — With Collier, &c., at Covent Garden. "Twelfth Night," — Liston's Malvolio excellent. I never saw him to greater advantage. It is a character in all respects adapted to him. His inimitable gravity till he receives the letter, and his incomparable smiles in the cross-gartered scene, are the perfection of nature and art united.

January 29th. — I walked with Coleridge to Rickman's, where we dined. He talked on Shakespeare, particularly his Fools. These he regarded as supplying the place of the ancient chorus. The ancient drama, he observed, is distinguished from the Shakespearian in this, that it exhibits a sort of abstraction, not of character, but of idea. A certain sentiment or passion is exhibited in all its purity, unmixed with anything that could interfere with its effect. Shakespeare, on the other hand, imitates life, mingled as we find it with joy and sorrow. We meet constantly in life with persons who are, as it were, unfeeling spectators of the most passionate situations. The Fool serves to supply the place of some such uninterested person, where all the other characters are interested.   The most genuine and real of Shakespeare's Fools is in " Lear."   In " Hamlet " the fool is, as it were, divided into several parts, dispersed through the play.

On our walk back Coleridge spoke warmly and eloquently on the effect of laws in the formation of moral character and feeling in a people.   He differed from Bentham's censure of the laws of usury, Coleridge contending that those laws, by exciting a general contempt towards usurers, had a deterring effect on many.   Genoa fell by becoming a people of money-lenders instead of merchants.   In money loans one party is in sorrow ; in the traffic of merchandise, both parties gain and rejoice.   This led to talk on the nature of criminal law in general.   Some acts, viz. murder, rape, unnatural offences, are to be punished for the sake of the effect on the public mind, that a *just sentiment* may be taught, and not merely for the sake of prevention.   The acts ought in themselves to be punished.   He dwelt on the influence of law in forming the public mind, and giving direction to moral feeling.

February 1st. — A visit to a most accomplished lady of the old school, Mrs. Buller.*   The poems of Southey and Scott she has put into her Index Expurgatorius.   She cannot bear the irregularity of their versification.   Mr. Jerningham was present, and she called him to his face " the last of the old school."   He is already forgotten, more completely than those will be whom his friend and contemporary treated so contemptuously.

February 18th. — At the Royal Academy.   Heard Flaxman's introductory Lecture on Sculpture.   It was for the most part, or entirely, historical.   He endeavored to show that in all times English sculptors have excelled when not prevented by extraneous circumstances.   This gave great pleasure to a British audience.   In one or two instances the lecture was applauded in a way that he would be ashamed of.   He spoke of some cathedral sculpture of the time of Henry VIII., and, contrasting the remains of different artists, said, " Here, too, we find that the British artists were superior to their rivals on the Continent."   This was received with loud clapping.   The John-Bullism displayed was truly ridiculous.   Flaxman, however, pleased me in every respect in which I had a right to be pleased.   He spoke like an artist who loved and honored his art, but without any personal feeling.   He had all the unpre-

* See page 252.

tending simplicity of a truly great man.   His unimposing
figure received consequence from the animation of his countenance ; and his voice, though feeble, was so judiciously managed
and so clear, and his enunciation was so distinct, that he was
audible to a large number of people.

March 12th. — Tea and chess with Mrs. Barbauld.   Read on
my way to her house Chapters VIII. to XIV. of Southey's
" Madoc."   Exceedingly pleased with the touching painting in
this poem.   It has not the splendid glare of " Kehama," but
there is a uniform glow of pure and beautiful morality and
interesting description, which renders the work very pleasing.
Surely none but a pedant can affect or be seduced to think
slightingly of this poem.   At all events, the sensibility which
feels such beauties is more desirable than the acuteness which
could suggest severe criticism.

March 13th. — A talk with Coleridge, who called on me.
Speaking of Southey, he said S. was not able to appreciate
Spanish poetry.   He wanted modifying power : he was a
jewel-setter, — whatever he found to his taste, he formed it
into, or made it into, the ornament of a story.

March 24th. — A call on Coleridge, who expatiated beautifully on the beneficial influence of brotherly and sisterly love
in the formation of character.   He attributed, he said, certain
peculiarities in persons whom he named to the circumstance
that they had no brother.*

March 29th. — Spent the evening with W. Hazlitt.   Smith,
his wife and son, Hume, Coleridge, and afterwards Lamb there.
Coleridge philosophized as usual.   He said that all systems of
philosophy might be reduced to two, the dynamical and the
mechanical ; the one converting all quantity into quality, the
other *vice versa.*   He and Hazlitt joined in an obscure statement about abstract ideas.   Hazlitt said he had learnt from
painting that it is difficult to form an idea of an individual
object, — that we first have only a *general idea ;* that is, a
vague, broken, imperfect recollection of the individual object.
This I observed was what the multitude meant by a general
idea, and Hazlitt said he had no other.   Coleridge spoke of
the impossibility of referring the individual to the class without
having a previous notion of the class.   This is Kantian logic.

We talked of politics.   It was amusing to observe how

* On some other occasion I recollect his saying that he envied Wordsworth
for having had a sister, and that his own character had suffered from the want
of a sister. — H. C. R.

Coleridge blundered against Scotchmen and Frenchmen. He represented the *Edinburgh Review* as a concentration of all the smartness of all Scotland. Edinburgh is a talking town, and whenever, in the Conversaziones, a single spark is elicited, it is instantly caught, preserved, and brought to the *Review*. He denied humor to the nation. Smith appealed in behalf of Smollett. Coleridge endeavored to make a distinction, i. e. to maintain his point, and yet allow the claim of Smith.

Before Lamb came, Coleridge had spoken with warmth of his excellent and serious conversation. Hazlitt imputed his puns to humility.

March 30th. — At C. Lamb's. Found Coleridge and Hazlitt there, and had a half-hour's chat. Coleridge spoke feelingly of Godwin and the unjust treatment he had met with. In apology for Southey's review of Godwin's " Life of Chaucer," Coleridge ingeniously observed that persons who are themselves very pure are sometimes on that account *blunt* in their moral feelings. This I believe to be a very true remark indeed. Something like this I have expressed respecting ——. She is perfectly just herself, and expects everybody to be equally so. She is consequently severe, and occasionally even harsh in her judgments.

> " For right too rigid hardens into wrong."

Coleridge used strong language against those who were once the extravagant admirers of Godwin, and afterwards became his most bitter opponents. I noticed the infinite superiority of Godwin over the French writers in moral feeling and tendency. I had learned to hate Helvetius and Mirabeau, and yet retained my love for Godwin. This was agreed to as a just sentiment. Coleridge said there was more in Godwin, after all, than he was once willing to admit, though not so much as his enthusiastic admirers fancied. He had openly opposed him, but nevertheless visited him. Southey's severity he attributed to the habit of reviewing. Southey had said of Coleridge's poetry that he was a Dutch imitator of the Germans. Coleridge quoted this, not to express any displeasure at it, but to show in what way Southey could speak of him.

Went with C. Lamb to the Lyceum. " The Siege of Belgrade " afforded me considerable amusement. The comic scenes are droll, though commonplace enough, and Miss Kelly and Mathews gave due effect to them. But Braham's singing delighted me. His trills, shakes, and quavers are, like those of all other great singers, tiresome to me; but his pure melody, the simple song clearly articulated, is equal to anything I ever heard. His song was *acted* as well as sung delightfully. Indeed I think Braham a fine actor while singing; he throws his soul into his throat, but his whole frame is awakened, and his gestures and looks are equally impassioned.

When Dignum and Mrs. Bland came on the stage together, Charles Lamb exclaimed,

" And lo, two puddings smoked upon the board! "

April 2d. — A walk to Clapton, reading, " Colonel Jack," the latter half of which is but dull and commonplace. The moment he ceases to be a thief, he loses everything interesting. Yet there runs through the work a spirit of humanity which does honor to De Foe. He powerfully pleaded for a humane treatment of the slaves of America, at a time when no man thought of abolishing slavery itself.

April 4th. — At Pope's benefit, at the Opera House. "The Earl of Warwick." Mrs. Siddons most nobly played her part as Margaret of Anjou. The character is one to which she can still render justice. She looked ill, and I thought her articulation indistinct, and her voice drawling and funereal during the first act; but as she advanced in the play, her genius triumphed over natural impediments. She was all that could be wished. The scene in which she wrought upon the mind of Warwick was perfect. And in the last act, her triumphant joy at the entrance of Warwick, whom she had stabbed, was incomparable. She laughed convulsively, and staggered off the stage as if drunk with delight; and in every limb showed the tumult of passion with an accuracy and a force equally impressive to the critic and the man of feeling.

Her advancing age is a real pain to me. As an actor, she has left with me the conviction that there never was, and never will be, her equal.

Elliston played Edward. He is a fine bustling comedian; but he bustles also in tragedy.

Braham sang delightfully "Said a Smile to a Tear." He is incomparably the most delightful male singer I ever heard.

Liston, in the "Waterman," gave a burlesque song with admirable humor. I believe he will soon be acknowledged to be our first comedian. He raises more universal laughs than any one, excepting perhaps Mathews, who is only a first-rate

N

mimic. Liston burlesqued Braham, and there arose a contest between the lovers of burlesque and the jealous admirers of exquisite music; but the reasonable party prevailed, and Liston's encored song was received with great applause, though the burlesque was not less apparent than before.

Incledon sang " The Storm." It was said to be fine. Mathews sang his " Mail Coach," — a most excellent thing in its way.

I have seldom had so much pleasure at the theatre.

April 28th. — Anthony Robinson related an anecdote of Horne Tooke, showing the good-humor and composure of which he was capable. Holcroft was with him at a third person's table. They had a violent quarrel. At length Holcroft said, as he rose to leave the room : " Mr. Tooke, I tell you, you are a —— scoundrel, and I always thought you so." Tooke detained him, and said : " Mr. Holcroft, some time ago you asked me to come and dine with you ; do tell me what day it shall be." Holcroft stayed.

May 7th. — In the afternoon a pleasant chat with Flaxman alone. He spoke of artists and art with his unaffected modesty and kindness. I asked him why the Germans, who appreciated him, would not acknowledge the merit of our painters, even Reynolds. " My art," Flaxman answered, " led me to make use of classical fable, of which the Germans are fond. Reynolds was only a gentlemanly scholar." Sir Joshua judged ill of sculpture ; on that subject he wrote not so well as Rafael Mengs, of whom Flaxman spoke slightingly, just as I recollect hearing Fernow at Jena speak.

May 9th. — Dined with Thelwall. A large party. The man whom we went to see, and, if we could, admire, was Dr. Wolcott, better known as Peter Pindar. He talked about the artists, said that West could paint neither ideal beauty nor from nature, called Opie the Michael Angelo of old age, complained of the ingratitude of certain artists who owed everything to himself, spoke contemptuously of Walter Scott, who, he said, owed his popularity to hard names. He also declaimed against rhyme in general, which he said was fit only for burlesque. Not even Butler would live. At the same time he praised exceedingly the " Heroic Epistle to Sir W. Chambers." Congreve he considered the greatest miracle of genius, and that such a man should early abandon literature was to him unaccountable. As Peter Pindar was blind, I was requested to help him to his wine, which was in a separate pint bottle, and was not wine at all, but brandy.* After dinner he eulogized brandy, calling it τὸ πᾶν, and said, "He who drinks it heartily must make interest to die."

He said he had made a rhyme that morning, of which But-ler might not have been ashamed : —

> Say, would you long the shafts of death defy,
> Pray keep your inside wet, your outside dry.

I referred to his own writings. He said he recollected them with no pleasure. " Satire is a bad trade."

May 15th. — A very pleasant call on Charles and Mary Lamb. Read his version of the story of Prince Dorus, the long-nosed king.† Gossiped about writing. Urged him to try his hand at a metrical *Umarbeitung* (working up) of "Reynard the Fox." He believed, he said, in the excellence of the work, but he was sure such a version as I suggested would not suc-ceed now. The sense of humor, he maintained, is utterly ex-tinct. No satire that is not personal will succeed.‡

24th. — Devoted the day to a speech to be delivered at the Academical Society. § The question, " Which among the Arts of Oratory, History, and Poetry is most capable of being ren-dered serviceable to Mankind ? " I spoke for somewhat more than an hour.

The three arts are alike liberal arts, since they are carried on with knowledge and freedom, and not slavishly. They constitute the great body of elegant learning, — Humanity.

Oratory is the art of persuasion as opposed to logic, — the art of reasoning. It is mischievous by withdrawing attention from the substance to the show, from the matter of discourse to its ornaments. I. Deliberative or senatorial oratory. The evil of accustoming a people to the stimulus of eloquence. This I illustrated by the French Revolution. For some years the people were kept in a frenzy by the orators. The result was not the acquirement of any habits favorable either to knowledge or liberty. The mind was left as barren and as unsusceptible of good influence as the earth from which the salt sea has receded. In the English Senate, Burke was not

---

* In telling this story Mr. Robinson would humorously relate how, by pour-ing some into a second glass, he contrived to ascertain the fact for himself.

† This is not in his collected works, and, as well as two volumes of Poems for Children, is likely to be lost. — H. C. R.

‡ An English version of " Reineke der Fuchs " was afterwards prepared by Samuel Naylor, Jun., and dedicated to his friend H. C. R. Published by Longman, 1844.

§ As Mr. Robinson was a frequent attendant and speaker at Debating Societies, the notes of his speech on one of these occasions are given as a specimen.

listened to.   Fox has left no memorial of any good he has wrought by eloquence ; his Libel Bill being the only good law he ever introduced.   Neither the Habeas Corpus Act, nor the Bill of Rights, nor Magna Charta, originated in eloquence.   A senate of orators is a symptom of national decay.   II. Judicial eloquence.   I expatiated on the glorious spectacle of an English court of justice, and affirmed that its dignity would be lost if the people went into it as into a theatre, to admire the graces of the orators.   But, in fact, there is little eloquence at present at the English bar.   Erskine the only prominent man in our time.   I contrasted the state of popular feeling in Greece and Britain.   I noticed the assertion of Demosthenes, that action is the first, second, and third part of an orator, and the fact that he was taught to speak by an actor.   I admitted, however, that eloquence might occasionally be useful (though its resources were at the service alike of the tyrant and the free man, the oppressor and the oppressed), but it is only a sort of convulsive effect that can be produced.   The storm which drives from a populous city the pestilential vapor hanging over it may accidentally save it for once from the plague ; but it is the sun, which rises day by day, and the dew, which falls night by night, that give fertility to the valleys, though the silent operation of these causes does not so forcibly strike the senses.

History, I observed, could instruct only by enabling us to anticipate future events from the past.   But this it cannot do.   The great events of political life are too unique to admit of a parallel.   The Crusades, Reformation, &c.   The emancipation of Switzerland, Holland, Portugal, Sweden, each took place on grounds of its own ; and no inference could be drawn from one to another.   No Irishman, for instance, wishing to deliver his country from English rule, could draw an argument from the success of any other rebellion.   The great outline of historical occurrences is beyond the sphere of human agency ; it belongs to the economy of Divine Providence, and is illustrated in the gradual civilization of mankind.   All the rest is pure uncertainty.   Horace Walpole's historical doubts.   Character of the Queen of Scots.   The death of Charles XII. of Sweden.

History may be thought to improve the affections.   This is so far from being true, that history shows the triumph of fraud, violence, and guilt ; and if there were no resource elsewhere, the mind, by mere history, would be driven to despair.

[I omitted to show how little private persons can be, improved by that which treats merely of public events, and also that statesmen have been guided by sagacity in the just comprehension of the actual state of things, and that learned men have seldom had any marked influence in public affairs.]

Poetry I described as having its origin in a principle of our nature, by which we are enabled to conceive of things as better than any actually known. The mind is cheered by its own images of excellence, and is thus enabled to bear up against the 'evils of life. Besides, we are more instructed by poetic than historic truth ; for the one is but a series of insignificant accidents, while the other contains the essential truth of things. Homer's Achilles is a fine picture of a warrior whose breast is full of all the irascible, and yet all the affectionate, feelings. The baseness of a grovelling ambition of regal dominion is better exemplified in Shakespeare's " Richard III.," the tremendous consequence of yielding to the suggestions of evil in " Macbeth," the necessity of having the sensible and reflective qualities balanced by active energy in " Hamlet," the nature of jealousy in " Othello," than in any mere historic narratives.

What can the historian do ? He can give us plausible speculations. What the orator ? Stir our feelings, but for a time only. Whereas the poet enriches our imaginations with images of every virtue.

I was followed by Twiss, Dumoulin, and Temple. At the close of the discussion, the few persons who had remained held up their hands, — five for history, and one each for poetry and eloquence.

May 26th. — As Robert Hall was to preach in the Borough, I went to hear him. The discourse was certainly a very beautiful one. He began by a florid but eloquent and impressive description of John the Baptist, and deduced from his history, not with the severity of argument which a logician requires, but with a facility of illustration which oratory delights in, and which was perfectly allowable, the practical importance of discharging the duty which belongs to our actual condition.

June 6th. — Met Coleridge at the Exhibition. He drew my attention to the " vigorous impotence " of Fuseli, especially in his " Macbeth." * " The prominent witch," said Coleridge,

* No. 12 of the Royal Academy Catalogue, where it is entered " Macbeth consulting the Vision of the Armed Head." — SHAKESPEARE. *Macbeth.* Act IV., Scene 1.

" is smelling a stink." He spoke of painting as one of the lost arts.

June 11th. — Called on Coleridge. He made some striking observations on the character of an excellent man. " I have long," he said, " considered him an abstraction, rather than a person to be beloved. He is incapable of loving any excepting those whom he has benefited. He has been so in the habit of being useful, that he seems to lose his interest in those to whom he can be of no further use."

June 13th. — After tea a call on C. Lamb. His brother with him. A chat on puns. Evanson, in his " Dissonance of the Gospels," thinks Luke most worthy of credence. P—— said that Evanson was a *luke*warm Christian. I related this to C. Lamb. But, to him, a mere play of words was nothing without a spice of the ridiculous. He was reading with a friend a book of Eastern travels, and the friend observed of the *Mantschu* Tartars, that they must be cannibals. This Lamb thought better. The large room in the accountant's office at the East India House is divided into boxes or compartments, in each of which sit six clerks, Charles Lamb himself in one. They are called Compounds. The meaning of the word was asked one day, and Lamb said it was " a collection of simples."

June 16th. — Dined at Sergeant Rough's, and met the once celebrated Mrs. Abington.* From her present appearance one can hardly suppose she could ever have been otherwise than plain. She herself laughed at her snub nose. But she is erect, has a large blue expressive eye, and an agreeable voice. She spoke of her retirement from the stage as occasioned by the vexations of a theatrical life. She said she should have gone mad if she had not quitted her profession. She has lost all her professional feelings, and when she goes to the theatre can laugh and cry like a child ; but the trouble is too great, and she does not often go. It is so much a thing of course that a retired actor should be a *laudator temporis acti*, that I felt unwilling to draw from her any opinion of her successors. Mrs. Siddons, however, she praised, though not with the warmth of a genuine admirer. She said : " Early in life Mrs. Siddons was anxious to succeed in comedy, and played Rosalind before I retired." In speaking of the modern declamation, and the too elaborate emphasis given to insignificant words,

---

* Mrs. Abington first appeared at the Haymarket as Miranda, in the " Busy Body." Her last public appearance was April 12, 1799. She died in her house in Pall Mall, March, 1815.

she said, "That was brought in by them" (the Kembles). She spoke with admiration of the Covent Garden horses, and I have no doubt that her praise was meant to have the effect of satire. Of all the present actors, Murray most resembles Garrick. She spoke of Barry with great warmth. He was a nightingale. Such a voice was never heard. He confined himself to characters of great tenderness and sweetness, such as Romeo. She admitted the infinite superiority of Garrick in genius. His excellence lay in the bursts and quick transitions of passion, and in the variety and universality of his genius. Mrs. Abington would not have led me to suppose she had been on the stage by either her manner or the substance of her conversation. She speaks with the ease of a person used to good society, rather than with the assurance of one whose business it was to imitate that ease.

Mr. and Mrs. Flaxman called in the evening. An argumentative conversation, which is not Flaxman's forte. He is delightful in the great purity of his moral sense, and the consequent delicacy of his taste on all subjects of ethics: but his understanding is not cast in a logical mould ; and when he has a fixed idea, there is no possibility of changing it. He said Linnæus had made a great blunder in classing the whale with man, merely because it belongs to the *mammalia*. And it was impossible to make him acknowledge, or apparently to comprehend, the difference between an artificial and a natural classification. As a proof that Hume wished to apologize for Charles II., he quoted the sentence, "Charles was a polite husband and a generous lover" ; and he did not perceive that this was a mere statement of fact, and by no means implied a wish to defend or vindicate. Hume could not have imagined that politeness is the appropriate virtue of a husband, or that the profusion of a king towards his mistresses is laudable. But it is not necessary, even for the purposes of edification, to ring the changes of moral censure.

June 18th. — Accompanied Mrs. Pattisson and her son William to Lawrence the painter. On entering the room, he fixed his eyes on William with evident admiration, not noticing the mother, who *had been* handsome. On my asking him whether he could find time to paint the boy, he said in a half-whisper, "To be sure, he must be painted." The picture was to include his brother Jacob. It was arranged that the two boys should wait on Mr. Lawrence on Wednesday, the 26th inst.

I may here mention an occurrence which took place in 1809,

while I was at Witham on a visit to the Pattissons. There was a grand jubilee to celebrate the termination of the fiftieth year of the reign of George III. At morning prayers, William, aged eight, said, "Mamma, ought I not to pray for the King?" — "To be sure, if you feel the desire." On which he folded his hands, and said, "O God, grant that the King may continue to reign with justice and victory." The words were scarcely out of his mouth, when Jacob, then six years and a half, said "May n't I pray too?" The mother could not refuse. "O God, be so' good as to let the King live another fifty years."

June 21st. — A pleasant party at Collier's. Lamb in high spirits. One pun from him at least successful. Punsters being abused, and the old joke repeated that he who puns will pick a pocket, some one said, "Punsters themselves have no pockets." — "No," said Lamb, "they carry only a *ridicule.*"

June 26th. — Went with the Pattissons to Lawrence's. He consented to paint the two boys for 160 guineas. They had their first sitting to-day. I took an opportunity of telling him an anecdote respecting himself, which did not seem to displease him, though eminent men are in many instances well pleased to forget the day of little things. His father was the master of the Bear Inn at Devizes, and he himself was for a short time at Mr. Fenner's school. Some time between 1786 and 1789 a stranger, calling at Mr. Fenner's, remarked, "They say, Mr. Fenner, that your old pupil, Tommy Lawrence, is turning out a very pretty painter."

July 9th. — Evening at Lady Broughton's. W. Maltby, in our walk home, related an anecdote which he himself had from the Bishop of Llandaff. The Bishop was standing in the House of Lords, in company with Lords Thurlow and Loughborough, when Lord Southampton accosted him : "I want your advice, my Lord ; how am I to bring up my son so as to make him get forwards in the world?" — "I know of but one way," replied the Bishop ; "give him parts and poverty." — "Well, then," replied Lord S., "if God has given him parts, I will manage as to the poverty."

July 11th. — Called on Mrs. Barbauld, Mr. and Miss Belsham, and Mr. and Mrs. Tooke, Sen. Tooke told a good story. Lord Bolingbroke dined one day with Bishop Burnet. There was a sumptuous entertainment, and Lord Bolingbroke asked the Bishop whether the Apostles fared so well. "O no, my lord." — " And how do you account for the difference between the clergy of the present day and those of the primitive Church ? " — " It is so," replied Burnet, " on all occasions ; we always see that inventors and speculators are ruined, while others reap the gain." But surely the repartee is applied to the wrong person. Burnet would not have so compromised himself to Bolingbroke.

July 24th. — Late at C. Lamb's. Found a large party there. Southey had been with Blake, and admired both his designs and his poetic talents. At the same time he held him to be a decided madman. Blake, he said, spoke of his visions with the diffidence which is usual with such people, and did not seem to expect that he should be believed. He showed Southey a perfectly mad poem, called " Jerusalem." Oxford Street is in Jerusalem.

July 26th. — At the Lyceum Theatre with Amyot. " The Quadrupeds," otherwise the Tailors, revived under a new name. The prelude represents a poor manager in distress. He is assailed by a bailiff, and, leading him to a trap-door, forces him down. Sheridan looked on, and clapped. The burlesque scene between the master-tailor (Lovegrove) and his wife (Miss Kelly), who is alarmed by a dream, was excellent.

July 28th. — After dinner walked to Morgan's, beyond Kensington, to see Coleridge, and found Southey there. Coleridge, talking of German poetry, represented Klopstock as compounded of everything bad in Young, Harvey, and Richardson. He praised warmly an essay on Hogarth by C. Lamb, and spoke of *wrongers* of subjects as well as *writers* on them. He was in spirits, and was apparently pleased with a letter I brought him from Mrs. Clarkson.

Coleridge and Southey spoke of Thelwall, calling him merely " John." Southey said : " He is a good-hearted man ; besides, we ought never to forget that he was once as near as possible being hanged, and there is some merit in that."

Enjoyed exceedingly my walk back with Southey. Speaking of forms of government, he said, there is no doubt a republic is the best form of government in itself, — as a sun-dial is in itself the most certain and perfect instrument for ascertaining the hour. And if the sun shone always, men would never have been at the trouble of making clocks. But, as it is, these instruments are in most frequent use. If mankind were illuminated by the pure sun of reason, they would dispense with complicated forms of government. He talked largely about Spain. A Jacobin revolution must purify the country before any good can be done. Catholicism is absolutely incompatible with great improvements. In the Cortes, he says, nine tenths of the members are bigoted papists, and one tenth Jacobin atheists. Barcelona might have been purchased, had our government been on the alert. Southey spoke highly of Blanco White.

July 29th. — Read four books of "Thalaba," and one book of the "Castle of Indolence." Thomson's poem most delightful. Surely, in the *finish* of such a work, there is a charm which surpasses the effect produced by the fitful and irregular beauties of a work like Southey's.

August 3d. — Bathed for the first time in Peerless Pool, originally *perilous* pool; but it deserves neither title. In the evening at Charles Lamb's. He was serious, and therefore very interesting. I accidentally made use of the expression " poor Coleridge ! " Lamb corrected me, not angrily, but as if really pained. " He is," he said, " a fine fellow, in spite of all his faults and weaknesses. Call him Coleridge ; I hate *poor*, as applied to such a man. I can't bear to hear such a man pitied." He then quoted an expression to the same effect by (I think) Ben Jonson of Bacon.

*Reminiscences.** — I frequently saw Coleridge about this time, and was made privy to an incident which need no longer be kept a secret. Coleridge was then a contributor to the *Courier*, and wrote an article on the Duke of York, which was printed on Friday, the 5th of July. But the government got scent of it, and therefore, by the interference of Mr. Arbuthnot of the Treasury, after about 2,000 copies had been printed, it was suppressed. This offended Coleridge, who would gladly have transferred his services to the *Times*. I spoke about him to Walter, but Fraser was then firmly established, and no other hand was required for the highest department. I have found a paper in Coleridge's hand in reference to this affair. It states what service he was willing to render, — such as attending six hours a day, and writing so many articles per week. One paragraph only has any significance, because it shows the state of his mind : " The above, always supposing the paper to be truly independent, first, of the Administration, secondly, of Palace Yard, and that its fundamental principle is, the due proportion of political power to property, joined with the removal of all obstacles to the free circulation and transfer of

* Written in 1849.

property, and all artificial facilitations of its natural tendency
to accumulate in large and growing masses."

August 8th. — At C. Lamb's. Coleridge there. A short but
interesting conversation on German metaphysics. He related
some curious anecdotes of his son Hartley, whom he represented as a most remarkable child. A deep thinker in his
infancy, — one who tormented himself in his attempts to solve
the problems which would equally torment the full-grown man,
if the world and its cares and its pleasures did not abstract his
attention. When about five years old, Hartley was asked a
question concerning himself by some one who called him
" Hartley." — " Which Hartley ?" asked the boy. " Why, is
there more than one Hartley ?" — " Yes, there 's a deal of
Hartleys." — " How so ? " — " There 's Picture Hartley (Hazlitt had painted a portrait of him), and Shadow Hartley, and
there 's Echo Hartley, and there 's Catch-me-fast Hartley," —
at the same time seizing his own arm with the other hand very
eagerly, an action which shows that his mind must have been
led to reflect on what Kant calls the great and inexplicable
mystery that man should be both his own subject and object,
and that these should yet be one. " At the same early age,"
said Coleridge, " he used to be in an agony of thought about
the reality of existence. Some one said to him, ' It is not now,
but it is to be.' — ' But,' said he, ' if it is to be, it *is.*' Perhaps
this confusion of thought lay not merely in the imperfection
of language. Hartley, when a boy, had no pleasure in *things ;*
they made no impression on him till they had undergone a sort
of process in his mind, and become thoughts or feelings." With
a few abatements for fatherly affection, I have no doubt Hartley is a remarkable child. But of his subsequent progress
Coleridge said little.

August 17th. — Tea at Dr. Aikin's. Found the Dr., Miss
Aikin, &c., very agreeable. Indeed there has seemed to me
of late less to dislike in the political and religious opinions of
this circle than I thought formerly. A successful game of
chess with Miss Aikin, which I proposed as a sort of ordeal to
test whether I was right in recommending " Benvenuto Cellini "
for its interest and beauty, or she in sending it home with disgust. Early at home. Read Scott's note on Fairies in the
" Minstrelsy." A shallow and unsatisfactory essay. The subject is so interesting, that nothing can be altogether unattrac-
tive that treats of it. A work at once critical and philosophical, on the popular superstitions of mankind in different ages,

would be most curious. It would embrace a vast mass of important matter, closely connected with philosophy and religion. Scott's collection, Vol. II., contains much that is valuable and beautiful. " Tamlane " is one of the best poems. It has the levity and grace of a genuine fairy fiction, and at the same time there is about it a tone of earnestness which suits a legend of popular belief. In " Thomas the Rhymer," the enigmatic lines which speak of our national and distinctive character and glory ought to become popular : —

> " The waters worship shall his race;
> Likewise the waves of the farthest sea;
> For they shall ride over ocean wide
> With hempen bridles, and horse of tree."

August 23d. — A run up to Lawrence's. He has made a most delightful picture of William and Jacob Pattisson. The heads only are finished. William's is a side-face, — very beautiful, but certainly not more so than the original. Jacob is a smiling, open-faced boy, with an admirably sweet expression. William has had justice done him. More was not to be expected of any mortal colors. Jacob has had more than justice done him, but not in a way that can fairly be a matter of reproach. If the artist has idealized somewhat, and given an expression which is not on the boy's face every day, still, he has not given a grace or a charm which lies not in his moral frame. He has no more said in his picture the thing that is not, than the magnifying glass, which never invents, or gives more or other objects than there really are, but merely assists the infirm optics of the beholder. William is painted without any momentary expression, i. e. he does not appear, like Jacob, to be under an immediate inspiring influence, which occasions an arch smile not likely to be permanent even on the cheeks of Robin Goodfellow himself. *

October 15th. — Journey to London. Incledon the singer was in the coach, and I found him just the man I should have expected. Seven rings on his fingers, five seals on his watch-ribbon, and a gold snuff-box, at once betrayed the old beau. I spoke in terms of rapture of Mrs. Siddons. He replied, " Ah ! Sally's a fine creature. She has a charming place on the Edgeware Road. I dined with her last year, and she paid me one of the finest compliments I ever received. I sang ' The Storm '

---

* After a long interval the picture was finished, and exhibited at the Royal Academy in 1817, No. 44 of the Catalogue, as " Portraits of the Sons of W. Pattisson, Esq. Sir T. Lawrence, R. A." It was subsequently engraved by John Bromley, in mezzotint, under the title of " Rural Amusement."

after dinner. She cried and sobbed like a child. Taking both of my hands, she said, 'All that I and my brother ever did is nothing compared with the effect you produce!'". Incledon spoke with warmth and apparent knowledge on church music, praising Purcell especially, and mentioning Luther's simple hymns. I was forced to confess that I had no ear for music, and he, in order to try me, sang in a sort of song-whisper some melodies which I certainly enjoyed, — more, I thought, than anything I had heard from him on the stage. He related two anecdotes that had no reference to himself. Garrick had a brother living in the country, who was an idolatrous admirer of his genius. A rich neighbor, a grocer, being about to visit London, this brother insisted on his taking a letter of introduction to the actor. Not being able to make up his mind to visit the great man the first day, the grocer went to the play in the evening, and saw Garrick in Abel Drugger. On his return to the country, the brother eagerly inquired respecting the visit he had been so anxious to bring about. "Why, Mr. Garrick," said the good man, "I am sorry to hurt your feelings, but there's your letter. I did not choose to deliver it." — "Not deliver it!" exclaimed the other, in astonishment. — "I happened to see him when he did not know me, and I saw that he was such a dirty, low-lived fellow, that I did not like to have anything to do with him." Foote went to Ireland, and took off F——, the celebrated Dublin printer. F—— stood the jest for some time, but found at last that Foote's imitations became so popular, and drew such attention to himself, that he could not walk the streets without being pointed at. He bethought himself of a remedy. Collecting a number of boys, he gave them a hearty meal, and a shilling each for a place in the gallery, and promised them another meal on the morrow if they would hiss off the scoundrel who turned him into ridicule. The injured man learnt from his friends that Foote was received that night better than ever. Nevertheless, in the morning, the ragged troop of boys appeared to demand their recompense, and when the printer reproached them for their treachery, their spokesman said, "Plase yer honor, we did all we could, for the actor-man had heard of us, and did not come at all at all. And so we had nobody to hiss. But when we saw yer honor's own dear self come on, we did clap, indeed we did, and showed you all the respect and honor in our power. And so yer honor won't forget us because yer honor's enemy was afraid to come, and left yer honor to yer own dear self."

October 22d. — Called on Godwin. Curran, the Master of the Rolls in Ireland, was with him. Curran told an anecdote of an Irish Parliament-man who was boasting in the House of Commons of his attachment to the trial by jury. " Mr. Speaker, with the trial by jury I have lived, and, by the blessing of God, with the trial by jury will I die! " Curran sat near him, and whispered audibly, " What, Jack, do you mean to be hanged ? "

November 4th. — Hab.* told me that Clarkson had lately been to see the Bishop of Norwich, Bathurst. He found him very liberal indeed. He told Clarkson that one of his clergymen had written to him to complain that a Mr. Dewhurst had opened a meeting in his parish and was preaching against him. " I wrote him word," said the Bishop, " that he must preach against Mr. Dewhurst. I could not help him."

November 13th. — Fraser related a humorous story of his meeting in a stage-coach with a little fellow who was not only very smart and buckish in his dress, but also a pretender to science and philosophy. He spoke of having been at Paris, and of having read Helvetius, Voltaire, &c., and was very fluent in his declamation on the origin of ideas, self-love, and the other favorite doctrines of the new school. He said, " I have no objection to confess myself a *materialist.*" On this an old man, who had listened for a long time to the discourse, and had more than once betrayed symptoms of dissatisfaction and scorn towards the philosopher, could not contain himself any longer. " D—— it, that 's too bad ! You have the impudence to say you are a *materialist,* when I know you are a *dancing-master.*" The voluble orator was dumfoundered, and Fraser could not restrain the most violent laughter, which mortally offended the cutter of capers. " It is too bad," muttered the old man, who did not comprehend the cause of Fraser's merriment, — " it is too bad for a man to say he is of one trade when he is of another."

December 5th. — Accompanied Mrs. Rutt to Coleridge's lecture.† In this he surpassed himself in the art of talking in a

---

* H. C. R.'s brother, Habakkuk.

† This course of lectures was delivered at the room of the London Philosophical Society, Scots Corporation Hall, Crane Court, Fleet Street. The first lecture was delivered on the 18th of November. Mr. Robinson attended the greater part of the course, but, through absence from London, was not present at the whole. The subject announced was: " Shakespeare and Milton, in Illustration of the Principles of Poetry, and their Application as Grounds of Criticism to the most Popular Works of later English Poets, those of the Living included." Of these lectures, fifteen in number, Mr. J. P. Collier took notes

very interesting way, without speaking at all on the subject announced. According to advertisement, he was to lecture on "Romeo and Juliet," and Shakespeare's female characters. Instead of this he began with a defence of school-flogging, in preference at least to Lancaster's mode of punishing, without pretending to find the least connection between that topic and poetry. Afterwards he remarked on the character of the age of Elizabeth and James I., as compared with that of Charles I.; distinguished not very clearly between wit and fancy; referred to the different languages of Europe; attacked the fashionable notion concerning poetic diction; ridiculed the tautology of Johnson's line, "If observation, with extensive view," &c.; and warmly defended Shakespeare against the charge of impurity. While Coleridge was commenting on Lancaster's mode of punishing boys, Lamb whispered: "It is a pity he did not leave this till he got to 'Henry VI.,' for then he might say he could not help taking part against the Lancastrians." Afterwards, when Coleridge was running from topic to topic, Lamb said: "This is not much amiss. He promised a lecture on the Nurse in 'Romeo and Juliet,' and in its place he has given us one in the *manner* of the Nurse."

Mrs. Clarkson to H. C. R.

December 5, 1811.

Do give me some account of Coleridge. I guess you drew up the account in the *Times* of the first lecture. I do hope he will have steadiness to go on with the lectures to the end. It would be so great a point gained, if he could but pursue one object without interruption. . . . . I remember a beautiful expression of Patty Smith's, after describing a visit at Mr. Wilberforce's. "To know him," she said, "all he is, and to see him with such lively childish spirits, one need not say, 'God bless him!'—he seems already in the fulness of every earthly gift." . . . . Of all men, there seems most need to say, "God bless poor Coleridge!" One could almost believe that an enchanter's spell was upon him, forcing him to be what he is, and yet leaving him the power of showing what he might be.

in short-hand, but the notes of all excepting the first, second, sixth, seventh, eighth, ninth, and twelfth were lost. Those notes which were preserved were published in 1856: "Seven Lectures on Shakespeare and Milton. By the late S. T. Coleridge." By J. P. Collier, Esq.

December 9th. — Accompanied Mrs. Rough to Coleridge's seventh and incomparably best lecture. He declaimed with great eloquence about love, without wandering from his subject, " Romeo and Juliet." He was spirited, methodical, and, for the greater part, intelligible, though profound. Drew up for the *Morning Chronicle* a hasty report, which was inserted.

10th. — Miss Lamb dined with us. In the evening Charles Lamb, Manning, and Mrs. Fenwick. A pleasant evening. Lamb spoke well about Shakespeare. I had objected to Coleridge's assertion, that Shakespeare, as it were, identified himself with everything except the vicious ; and I observed that if Shakespeare's *becoming* a character is to be determined by the truth and vivacity of his delineation, he had *become* some of the vicious characters as well as the virtuous. Lamb justified Coleridge's remark, by saying that Shakespeare never gives characters wholly odious and detestable. I adduced the King in " Hamlet " as altogether mean ; and he allowed this to be the worst of Shakespeare's characters. He has not another like it. I cited Lady Macbeth. " I think this one of Shakespeare's worst characters," said Lamb. " It is also inconsistent with itself. Her sleep-walking does not suit so hardened a being." It occurs to me, however, that this very sleep-walking is, perhaps, the vindication of Shakespeare's portraiture of the character, as thereby the honor of human nature, if I may use the expression, is saved. The *voluntary* actions and sentiments of Lady Macbeth are all inhuman, but her *involuntary* nature rises up against her habitual feelings, which sprang out of depraved passions. Hence, though while awake she is a monster, she is a woman in her sleep. I then referred to the Bastard in " Lear," but Lamb considered his character as the result of provocation on account of his illegitimacy. Lamb mentioned Iago and Richard III. as admirable illustrations of the skill with which Shakespeare could make his worst characters interesting. I noticed King John and Lewis, as if Shakespeare meant, like a Jacobin, to show how base kings are. Lamb did not remark on this, but said, " ' King John ' is one of the plays I like least." He praised " Richard II."

December 11th. — In the evening with Lamb at tea. An hour's call on Parkin. I was sorry to find that he was hurt by my mode of replying to him last Friday at the Academical Society. He thought that, though I spoke of him in words very handsomely, there was yet in my manner something which implied a want of moral esteem. I believe I satisfied him of

his mistake ; but I know my easily besetting sin, of unconsciously assuming an offensive tone on such occasions, and I
will, if possible, be on my guard that my manner may not
give pain when what I say is substantially innocent. Parkin
mentioned that, in a letter to the editor of the *Eclectic Review*,
Coleridge had declared his adherence to the principles of Bull
and Waterland. There are, I know, some persons who deem
Coleridge hardly sincere ; I believe him to be only inconsistent.
I certainly am altogether unable to reconcile his metaphysical
and empirico-religious opinions.

December 12th. — Tea with Mrs. Flaxman, who accompanied
me to Coleridge's lecture. He unhappily relapsed into his
desultory habit, and delivered, I think, his worst lecture. He
began with identifying religion with love, delivered a rhapsody
on brotherly and sisterly love, which seduced him into a dissertation on incest. I at last lost all power of attending to
him.

H. C. R. to Mrs. Clarkson.

56 Hatton Garden, November 29, 1811.

My dear Friend, — Of course you have already heard of
the lectures on poetry which Coleridge is now delivering, and
I fear have begun to think me inattentive in not sending you
some account of them. Yesterday he delivered the fourth, and
I could not before form anything like an opinion of the probable result. Indeed, it is hardly otherwise now with me, but
were I to wait till I could form a judgment, the very subject
itself might escape from observation. He has about one hundred and fifty hearers on an average. The lectures have been
brilliant, that is, in passages ; but I doubt much his capacity
to render them popular. Or rather, I should say, I doubt any
man's power to render a system of philosophy popular which
supposes so much unusual attention and rare faculties of thinking even in the hearer. The majority of what are called sensible and thinking men have, to borrow a phrase from Coleridge, "the passion of clear ideas" ; and as all poets have a
very opposite passion, — that of warm feelings and delight in
musing over conceptions and imaginings beyond the reach of
the analytic faculty, — no wonder there is a sort of natural
hostility between these classes of minds. This will ever be a
bar to Coleridge's extensive popularity. Besides which, he has
certain unfortunate habits, which he will not (perhaps *cannot*)
correct, very detrimental to his interests, — I mean the vices

10 *   o

of apologizing, anticipating, and repeating. We have had four lectures, and are still in the Prolegomena to the Shake-spearian drama. When we are to begin Milton, I have no idea. With all these defects, there will always be a small circle who will listen with delight to his eloquent effusions (for that is the appropriate expression). I have not missed a lecture, and have each time left the room with the satisfaction which the heark-ening to the display of truth in a beautiful form always gives. I have a German friend who attends also, and who is delighted to find the logic and the rhetoric of his country delivered in a foreign language. There is no doubt that Coleridge's mind is much more German than English. My friend has pointed out striking analogies between Coleridge and German authors whom Coleridge has never seen. . . . .

H. C. R. TO MRS. CLARKSON.

56 HATTON GARDEN, December 13, 1811.

MY DEAR FRIEND : —

. . . . Yesterday I should have been able to send you a far more pleasant letter than I can possibly furnish you with now ; for I should then have had to speak of one of the most grati-fying and delightful exertions of Coleridge's mind on Monday last ; and now I am both pained and provoked by as unworthy a sequel to his preceding lecture. And you know it is a law of our nature,

> "As high as we have mounted in delight,
> In our dejection do we sink as low."

You have so beautifully and exactly expressed the senti-ment that every considerate and kind observer of your friend must entertain, that it is quite needless to give you any ac-count of his lectures with a view to direct any judgment you might wish to form, or any feeling you might be disposed to encourage. You will, I am sure, anticipate the way in which he will execute his lectures. As evidences of splendid talent, original thought, and rare powers of expression and fancy, they are all his *admirers* can wish ; but as a discharge of his under-taking, a fulfilment of his promise to the public, they give his *friends* great uneasiness. As you express it, "an enchanter's spell seems to be upon him," which takes from him the power of treating upon the only subject his hearers are anxious he should consider, while it leaves him infinite ability to riot and run wild on a variety of moral and religious themes. In his sixth lecture he was, by advertisement, to speak of " Romeo

and Juliet" and Shakespeare's females ; unhappily, some de-
mon whispered the name of Lancaster in his ear : and we had,
in one evening, an attack on the poor Quaker, a defence of
boarding-school flogging, a parallel between the ages of Elizabeth and Charles, a defence of what is untruly called unpoetic
language, an account of the different languages of Europe, and
a vindication of Shakespeare against the imputation of gross-
ness ! ! ! I suspect he did discover that offence was taken at
this, for his succeeding lecture on Monday was all we could
wish. He confined himself to " Romeo and Juliet " for a time,
treated of the inferior characters, and delivered a most eloquent discourse on love, with a promise to point out how
Shakespeare had shown the same truths in the persons of the
lovers. Yesterday we were to have a continuation of the
theme. Alas ! Coleridge began with a parallel between religion and love, which, though one of his favorite themes, he
did not manage successfully. Romeo and Juliet were forgotten. And in the next lecture we are really to hear something
of these lovers. Now this will be the fourth time that his hearers have been invited expressly to hear of this play. There
are to be only fifteen lectures altogether (half have been delivered), and the course is to include Shakespeare and Milton, the modern poets, &c. ! ! ! Instead of a lecture on a
definite subject, we have an immethodical rhapsody, very delightful to you and me, and only offensive from the certainty
that it may and ought to offend those who come with other
expectations. Yet, with all this, I cannot but be charmed
with these *splendida vitia*, and my chief displeasure is occasioned by my being forced to hear the strictures of persons
infinitely below Coleridge, without any power of refuting or
contradicting them. Yet it is lucky he has hitherto omitted
no lecture. Living with the Morgans, they force him to come
with them to the lecture-room, and this is a great point
gained. . . . .

December 15th. — Called on Godwin, who thinks Coleridge's
lectures far below his conversation. So far from agreeing with
Coleridge, that Shakespeare's plays ought only to be read and
not acted, Godwin said : " No plays but Shakespeare's deserve
to be represented, so admirably fitted are his for performance."

16th. — Took Miss Flaxman to Coleridge's lecture. Very
desultory again at first, but when about half-way through, he
bethought himself of Shakespeare ; and though he forgot at

last what we had been four times in succession to hear, viz.. of Romeo and Juliet as lovers, yet he treated beautifully of the " Tempest," and especially Prospero, Miranda, Ariel, and Caliban. This part most excellent.

Christmas day (at Royston). — A very agreeable *tête-à-tête* walk with Mr. Nash, Sen., round his farm. I enjoyed his society with more relish, probably, than I ever shall again. He is getting old, though, excepting in the decline of his memory, there are no traces yet of bodily infirmity. Sometimes, however, the effects of old age throw a tender grace over men of his amiable and excellent character. In his youth he was a Methodist, and he was industrious, patient, abstinent, capable of continuous labor, mental and bodily. His education was not of a superior kind, but he had the advantage of great personal beauty, as well as ability in business. He was brought up to the law, and had offers of a partnership in London ; but these he declined, because he saw practices of which his conscience disapproved. Marrying early, he settled down as a country practitioner. In religious opinions he became a Unitarian, and Robert Robinson * was the object of his admiration. His single publication, in which he called himself " A Country Attorney," was one of the hundred and one answers to Burke on the French Revolution. His life was prosperous, and alike honorable to himself and, within his limited sphere, useful to others. The latter days of a good man are not a melancholy object, even when one thinks that his moral and intellectual qualities might have been more advantageously employed in a wider field. This alone renders departing excellence a subject of melancholy observation.†

December 28th. — A gossip with E. till late. He related a curious Quaker anecdote, which suggests a law question. One friend, a merchant, proposes to another, an underwriter, to insure his ship, lost or not lost, which ought soon to arrive. The underwriter hesitates, takes the policy home, and says, " I will return it to-morrow, signed or unsigned." Early in the morning the merchant receives intelligence of the loss of his vessel. He knows his religious brother, and sends a clerk (who is ignorant of the loss) to say, " Neighbor A. informs

* An eminent Dissenting Minister of Cambridge. Born 1735. Died 1790. His immediate successor was the Rev. Robert Hall.
Memoirs of the Life and Writings of Robert Robinson were written by George Dyer. This biography was pronounced by Wordsworth to be one of the best in the English language. See also p. 101.
† See *ante*, pp. 23, 188.

thee that if thou hast not underwritten, thou needest not do it." The underwriter draws the inference that the vessel is safe. He has not actually signed, but, pretending to look for the policy, contrives to sign it by stealth, and says to the clerk, "Tell thy master I *had* signed." E. assured me that this was a real occurrence.

December 30th. — Attended Coleridge's lecture, in which he kept to his subject. He intimated to me his intention to deliver two lectures on Milton. As he had written to me about his dilemma, having so much to do in so little time, I gently hinted in my reply at his frequent digressions, — those *splendida peccata* which his friends best apologized for by laying the emphasis on the adjective.

December 31st. — In the evening at a very pleasant party at Flaxman's. A Mrs. Wilkinson there with her son, a most interesting young man, with one of those expressive countenances which imply intellect and heart alike. Flaxman ad-. mires him much, and says he would prefer him as a son to all the young men he ever saw.

*Rem.** — Closed the year most agreeably, in the act, I believe, of repeating to Mr. Flaxman Charles Lamb's prologue to " Mr. H." The society I beheld at the dawn of the New Year consisted of people possessing as high moral and intellectual excellences combined as are to be found in this great city.

I had now made up my mind to study for the bar. This resolution was formed through an apparently insignificant occurrence. It was on the 1st of March, when my sister (who with my brother had been on a visit to London) was about to leave, that Mr. Collier received an application from York to send down a reporter for the State Trials there. He requested me to go, but I declined on the ground of the objection taken to reporters being called to the bar. Speaking of this to my sister,† she said : " For a man who has the repute of having sense, you act very like a fool. You decline reporting because that might be an obstacle to your being called to the bar, and yet you take no steps towards being called to the bar. Now, do one or the other. Either take to newspaper employment, or study the law at once, and lose no more time." There was no reply to such a remonstrance. On the Sunday following, I went to Amyot to consult with him. There was then visiting him a Norwich attorney, Mr. Adam Taylor, who strongly ad-

---

* Written in 1849.   † Mrs. Thomas Robinson.

vised me to go the bar, adding, " There is an opening on the
Norfolk circuit. I am sure you would succeed. You shall
have such business as I have, and as I can obtain." It was
this that more than anything determined me. My old acquaintance, Walter Wright, my new acquaintance, Sergeant
Rough, and my friend Anthony Robinson,* all supported me
in the resolution ; but perhaps they all feel as Benvenuto Cellini felt on a similar occasion : " Have you, my lord, really
bought the picture, or do you only think of buying it ? " —
" What has that to do with your opinion, Cellini ? " — " A
great deal. If you have really bought the picture, then I have
only to make such remarks as will render you satisfied with
your bargain ; but if you are only thinking of buying it, then
it is my duty to tell you my real opinion."

H. C. R. TO HIS BROTHER.

56 HATTON GARDEN, 14th March, 1811.

DEAR THOMAS, — I have at length (after hesitating only
from twelve to thirteen years) made up my mind to abandon
all my hobby-horsical and vain, idle, and empty literary pursuits, and devote myself to the law. It is now ten days since
I have given words and form to this determination, which an
accident after all has occasioned me to make. My sister, perhaps, told you of a proposal Mr. Collier made me, that I should
go to York to transact a business which certainly would not
agree with the professional character. But my sister did not
tell you, because she was not herself aware of the fact, that it
was a simple sentence which dropped from her, which made me
sensible (more strongly than I had ever been before) of the extreme folly of my conduct. As we were walking down to the
Inn on Saturday morning she said : " There is something very
inconsistent in your behavior. You refuse a profitable job,

---

* Anthony Robinson (born in 1762) was originally brought up in connection
with the Established Church; but, changing his opinions, was educated at
Bristol for the Dissenting ministry. Robert Hall was one of his fellow-students.
He did not long remain in the ministry, but entered into business as a sugar-
refiner, in which he continued till his death. Though, however, he professed
to be merely a tradesman, he yet retained a lively interest in social and religious
questions, and was a steady and active supporter of civil and religious liberty.
He published several pamphlets and articles in reviews. Among the former
was an able examination of Robert Hall's celebrated " Sermon on Modern
Infidelity." H. C. R. said of him: " As I scarcely ever knew Anthony Robinson's equal in colloquial eloquence, in acuteness and skill, and promptitude in
debate, so I never knew his superior in candor and sincerity." Between H. C. R.
and his friend there was no relationship, though they have the same surname.

because it is incompatible with the character of a barrister, and yet you cannot be made to open a law-book. Now, you ought to do one or the other. Make up your mind at least."

.   .   .   .   .

Your affectionate brother,

H. C. R.

In the spring, and just before I was induced seriously to prepare for being called to the bar, I translated "Amatonda," a fairy tale by Anton Wall.* I have already given some account of the work itself.† My translation was published by Longman, but I believe fell dead from the press. None but friends ever praised it. I have a letter of praise from Coleridge. And Lamb at least liked the translations from Jean Paul (at the end), which were, I believe, the first translations from Jean Paul into English. He said they were the finest things he ever saw from the German language. The book, so far as I know, was never reviewed, and I obtained no credit for my work. Perhaps *happily*, for it was the failure of my attempt to gain distinction by writing that made me willing to devote myself honestly to the law, and so saved me from the mortification that follows a *little* literary success, by which many men of inferior faculties, like myself, have been betrayed into an unwise adoption of literature as a profession, which after this year I never once thought of.

COLERIDGE TO H. C. R.

I have to thank you, my dear Robinson, for the pleasure I have enjoyed in the perusal of Anton Wall's delightful tale. I read it first with my eyes only, and only to myself; but the second time aloud to two amiable women. Both times I felt myself in the embrace of the fairy Amatonda. The German critic has noticed as a defect and an oversight what I regard as one of the capital beauties of the work, and thus convinced me that for reviewers the world over, and for readers whose intellects are commensurate with theirs, an author must write *under* his best conceptions. . . . . I recollect no fairy tale with so just and fine a moral as this of Anton Wall's. Virtue itself, though joined with outward competence, cannot give that happiness which *contents* the human heart, without love ;

* "Amatonda." A Tale from the German of Anton Wall. London: Printed for Longman, Hurst, Rees, Orme, and Brown. 1811.

† See *ante*, pp. 104, 105.

but *love* is impossible without virtue, — love, true human love, — i. e. two hearts, like two correspondent concave mirrors having a common focus, while each reflects and magnifies the other, and in the other itself is an endless reduplication by sweet thoughts and sympathies.

Hassan's love for Amina is beautifully described as having had a foundation from early childhood. And this I many years ago planned as the subject-matter of a poem, viz. long and deep affections suddenly, in one moment, flash-transmuted into *love*. In short, I believe that *love* (as distinguished both from lust and that habitual attachment which may include many objects diversifying itself by *degrees* only), that that *feeling* (or whatever it may be more aptly called), that specific mode of being, which one object only can possess, and possess totally, is always the abrupt creation of a moment, though years of *dawning* may have preceded. I said *dawning*, for often as I have watched the sun rising from the thinning, diluting blue to the whitening, to the fawn-colored, the pink, the crimson, the glory, yet still the sun itself has always *started* up out of the horizon ! Between the brightest hues of the dawning, and the first rim of the sun itself, there is a *chasm*, — all before were differences of degrees, passing and dissolving into each other, — but this is a difference of *kind*, — a chasm of kind in a continuity of time ; and as no man who had never watched for the rise of the sun could understand what I mean, so can no man who has not been in love understand what love is, though he will be sure to imagine and believe that he does. Thus, —— is by nature incapable of being in love, though no man more tenderly attached ; hence he ridicules the existence of any other passion than a compound of lust with esteem and friendship, confined to one object, first by accidents of association, and permanently by the force of habit and a sense of duty. Now this will do very well, — it will suffice to make a good husband ; it may be even desirable (if the largest sum of easy and pleasurable sensations in this life be the right aim and end of human wisdom) that we should have this, and no more, — but still it is not *love*, — and there is such a passion as love, — which is no more a compound than oxygen, though like oxygen it has an almost universal affinity, and a long and finely graduated scale of elective attractions. It combines with lust, — but how ? Does lust call forth or occasion love ? Just as much as the reek of the marsh calls up the sun. The sun calls up the vapor, — attenuates, lifts it, — it becomes a cloud, — and now it is the veil of the divinity; the divinity, transpiercing it at once, hides and declares his presence. We *see*, we are conscious of *light* alone; but it is light embodied in the earthly nature, which that light itself awoke and sublimated. What is the body but the fixture of the mind, — the stereotype impression? Arbitrary are the symbols, — yet symbols they are. Is terror in my soul? — my heart beats against my side. Is grief? — *tears* pour in my eyes. In her homely way, the body tries to interpret all the movements of the soul. Shall it not, then, imitate and symbolize that divinest movement of a finite spirit, — the yearning to complete itself by union? Is there not a sex in souls? We have all eyes, cheeks, lips, — but in a lovely woman are not the eyes womanly, — yea, every form, in every motion of her whole frame, *womanly?* Were there not an identity in the substance, man and woman might *join*, but they could never *unify;* were there not throughout, in body and in soul, a corresponding and adapted difference, there might be addition, but there could be no combination. 1 and $1 = 2$; but 1 cannot be multiplied into 1: $1 \times 1 = 1$. At best, it would be an idle echo, the same thing needlessly repeated, as the idiot told the clock, — one, one, one, one, &c.

It has just come into my head that this scrawl is very much in the style of Jean Paul. I have not, however, as yet looked into the books you were so kind as to leave with me, further than to see the title-page. If you do not want them for some time, I should be glad to keep them by me, while I read the original works themselves. I pray you procure them for me week by week, and I will promise you most carefully to return them, you allowing me three days for two volumes. I am very anxious to have them, and shall fill one volume of the " Omniana " with the extracts, quoting your criticism as my introduction : only, instead of the shelves or steps, I must put the ladder of a library, or whatever name those movable steps are called which one meets with in all well-furnished libraries.

I have been extremely unwell, though rather better. George Burnet's * death told too abruptly, and, in truth, exaggerated,

---

* George Burnet was a very early friend of Coleridge; he joined with him, Southey, and Lovell in the scheme for emigrating to America, and there forming a colony, to be called a Pantisocracy, the main principle of which was a community of goods, and where selfishness was to be proscribed.

overset my dear, most dear, and most excellent friend and heart's sister, Mary Lamb,—and her illness has almost overset me. Troubles, God knows! have thronged upon me, — alas! alas! all my dearest friends I have of late either suffered *from*, or suffered *for*. 'T is a cruel sort of world we live in. God bless you

And yours, with affectionate esteem,

S. T. COLERIDGE.

Southampton Buildings.

P. S. I began with the scrap of paper, meaning only to write half a score lines, and now I have written enough for half a dozen letters * unnecessarily, when to have written to half a dozen claimants is a moral (would it were a physical) necessity. But moral obligation is to me so very strong a stimulant, that in nine cases out of ten it acts as a narcotic. The blow that should rouse *stuns* me.

[Though Mr. Robinson was never married, some of his friends occasionally volunteered their advice to him on the subject of matrimony. A letter containing such advice belongs to this year, and may be inserted here. — ED.]

CAPEL LOFFT TO H. C. R.

October 3, 1811.

DEAR SIR, — Perhaps one man ought never to advise another, unasked; especially when that other is probably better able to advise himself. I do, however, advise you, if ever you marry, never (as a man of feeling, and who loves literature, and liberty, and science) to marry a woman of what is called a strong mind. The love of dominion and the whirlwind of instability are, I fear, inseparable from a female mind of that character. All women and all beings love power; but a woman of a mild and compliant mind seeks and maintains power by correspondent means. These are not called strong minds. No matter, if they are mild, and modest, and delicate, and sympathizing minds, such as the Julie of Rousseau, the Alcestis of Euripides, the Antigone of Sophocles, and the Eve of Milton. Hence every woman should be a lover of music, — and of feminine music; and particularly of the vocal. And in that she should cultivate the soft, the low, and the sweet. "Her voice

---

* The beginning of the letter is on a scrap, after filling which the writer took a sheet of foolscap.

was ever low, gentle, and sweet ; an excellent thing in woman," says that great depicter of character, and particularly of women, who has so exquisitely imagined and delineated Miranda, Viola, Ophelia, Desdemona, Cordelia, Helena.

I am,

Yours, &c.

CAPEL LOFFT.

CHAPTER XV.

1812.

H. C. R. TO MRS. CLARKSON.

56 HATTON GARDEN, 3d January, 1812.

MY DEAR FRIEND, — I received your letter last night, and will write the answer immediately, though I cannot forward it till I have seen your brother for your address. I have a better, much better, account to give of Coleridge's lectures than formerly. His last three lectures have, for the greater part, been all that his friends could wish, — his admirers expect. Your sister heard the two last, and from her you will learn much more than I could put into a letter, had I all the leisure I now want, or the memory I never had. His disquisitions on the characters of Richard III., Iago, Falstaff, were full of paradox, but very ingenious, and in the main true. His remarks on Richard II. and Hamlet very excellent. Last night he concluded his fine development of the Prince of Denmark by an eloquent statement of the moral of the play. " Action," he said, " is the great end of all ; no intellect, however grand, is valuable, if it draw us from action and lead us to think and think till the time of action is passed by, and we can do nothing." Somebody said to me, " This is a satire on himself." — " No," said I, " it is an elegy." A great many of his remarks on Hamlet were capable of a like application. I should add that he means to deliver several lectures beyond the promised number. This will gain him *credit* in the City sense of the word ; and for the sake of his future success in lecturing, I am very glad he is thus prudent.

You see I am looking at the subject from a very low point of view ; at the same time I am able to place myself on higher ground, and then I lament equally with the Wordsworths and yourself that such a man should be compelled to have recourse to such means ; but, after all, what is there in this lamentation more than a particular instance of the general complaint of all ages, that highmindedness should stoop to vulgarity, that the low wants of man should drag down the elevated to low pursuits, and that the noblest powers of intellect should not be accompanied with meaner but indispensable capacities ? *

January 8th. — Called on Mrs. B., who was in much better spirits than I expected to find her. She spoke of her father with much tenderness and love, but without violent emotion. I referred to my own mother, and the treasure her memory is to me. Thinking of her and talking of her are a great delight, and I said I knew it would be so also with Mrs. B. The joy is great of *having had* an excellent parent. This she admitted, and seemed to feel, as if I had touched the true key.

January 9th. — Evening at Coleridge's lecture on Johnson's "Preface." Though sometimes obscure, his many palpable hits must have given general satisfaction.

January 13th. — Accompanied Mrs. C. Aikin to Coleridge's lecture. A continuation of remarks on Johnson's "Preface," but feeble and unmeaning compared with the last. The latter part of the lecture very excellent. It was on "Lear," in which he vindicated the melancholy catastrophe, and on "Othello," in which he expressed the opinion that Othello is not a jealous character.

January 14th. — Heard Hazlitt's first lecture on the "History of English Philosophy." † He seems to have no conception of the difference between a lecture and a book. What he said was sensible and excellent, but he delivered himself in a low monotonous voice, with his eyes fixed on his MS., not once daring to look at his audience ; and he read so rapidly that no one could possibly give to the matter the attention it required. ‡

* Coleridge was sadly annoyed at the necessity of appealing to the kindness of friends. He repeated to me an epigram, of which I recollect only the point: "I fell asleep, and fancied I was surrounded by my friends, who made me marvellous fine promises. I awoke and found these promises as much a dream as if they had actually been made." — H. C. R.

† These lectures were delivered at the Russell Institution.

‡ Hazlitt had in vain striven to become a painter. He had obtained the patronage of Clarkson, who said he had heard Hazlitt was more able to paint like Titian than any living painter. Some one had said that his portrait of Lamb had a Titianesque air about it. And certainly this is the only painting by Hazlitt I ever saw with pleasure. He made a portrait of my brother, which he knew to be bad, and it was destroyed. — H. C. R.

January 15th. — Tea with the Lambs. An evening at cards. Hazlitt there, much depressed. He seemed disposed to give up the lectures altogether. The cause of his reading so rapidly was, that he was told to limit himself to an hour, and what he had prepared would have taken three hours if it had been read slowly.

January 16th. — At Coleridge's lecture. He reviewed Johnson's "Preface," and vindicated warmly Milton's moral and political character, but I think with less than his usual ability. He excited a hiss once by calling Johnson a *fellow*, for which he happily apologized by observing that it is in the nature of evil to beget evil, and that we are thus apt to fall into the fault we censure. He remarked on Milton's minor poems, and the nature of blank verse. The latter half of the lecture was very good.

January 17th. — Dinner at J. Buck's.* Mr. and Mrs. Buck, Coleridge, the Gores, Jameson, and Aders.† Coleridge was less profound than usual, but exceedingly agreeable. He related anecdotes of himself. Once he was arrested as a spy at Fort St. George. The Governor, as soon as he saw him, muttered, "An ill-looking fellow." At first everything that Coleridge could say for himself was ingeniously perverted and applied against him; but at length a card he accidentally had by him, from a person of quality, convinced the Governor that he was a gentleman, and procured for him an invitation to breakfast next morning. Coleridge then took an opportunity of asking the Governor what it was in his appearance that induced him to say, "An ill-looking fellow." "My dear sir," said the Governor, squeezing him by the hand, "I nearly lost my sight in the West Indies, and cannot see a yard before me." At Bristol, Coleridge delivered lectures in conjunction with Southey. A fellow who was present hissed him, and an altercation ensued. The man sneered at him for professing public principle, and asked, "Why, if you have so much public spirit, do you take money at the door?" — "For a reason," answered Coleridge, "which I am sorry in the present instance has not been quite successful, — to keep out blackguards." In reference to the schools of Lancaster and Bell, — a delicate subject in such a society, — Coleridge contented himself with urging that it is unsafe to leave religion untaught while *anything* is taught.

---

* See *ante*, p. 19.

† Jameson and Aders were for some time in partnership as merchants. Mr. Aders had a valuable collection of pictures, which are frequently referred to in the diary, and which were eventually sold by auction.

Reading and writing must not be supposed to be in themselves education.

At ten went to Barron Field's.* Charles Lamb and Leigh Hunt there. I found they had had a discussion about Coleridge, whom Hunt had spoken of as a bad writer, while Lamb thought him the first man he ever knew. Lamb, in his droll and extravagant way, abused every one who denied the transcendent merits of Coleridge's writings.

January 20th. — A day of some importance, perhaps, in its consequences. Sergeant Rough introduced me to Mr. Littledale,† whose pupil I became by presenting him with the usual fee of 100 guineas, and by entering at once on my employment.

In the evening at Coleridge's lecture. Conclusion of Milton. Not one of the happiest of Coleridge's efforts. Rogers was there, and with him was Lord Byron. He was wrapped up, but I recognized his club foot, and, indeed, his countenance and general appearance.

January 21st. — Hazlitt's second lecture. His delivery vastly improved, and I hope he will now get on. He read at Basil Montagu's last night half his first lecture. He was to read the whole, but abruptly broke off, and could not be persuaded to read the remainder. Lamb and other friends were there.

February 21st. — In the evening at the Academical Society. Mr. Sheil spoke, who was blackballed lately after a violent and pompous speech. His present speech was sensible and temperate. Blake, his countryman, watched over him to keep him in order. He spoke as if he had been fed for three weeks on bread and water in order to be tamed.

Rem.‡ — He was blackballed again on a later occasion. What alone makes this worth mentioning is that he who was twice rejected by an insignificant society of young men is now one of the most popular and admired speakers in the House of Commons, the Right Honorable Richard Lalor Sheil.

February 26th. — A dinner-party. Coleridge, Godwin, &c., &c. The company rather too numerous. Coleridge by no means the eloquent man he usually is. It was not till ten minutes before he went away that he fell into a declaiming mood; "having," as Godwin said, "got upon the indefinites and the infinites," viz. the nature of religious conviction. He

* Afterwards a Judge in New South Wales, and subsequently at Gibraltar. Some of Lamb's most amusing letters were written to him.
† Afterwards Judge of the Queen's Bench.
‡ Written in 1849.

contended that the external evidence of Christianity would be
weak but for the internal evidence arising out of the necessity
of our nature, — our *want* of religion. He made use of one
very happy allusion. Speaking of the mingling of subordinate
evils with great good, he said, " Though the serpent does twine
himself round the staff of the god of healing." *

H. C. R. TO MRS. CLARKSON.

GRAY'S INN,† 28th January, 1812.

You will be interested to hear how Coleridge's lectures
closed : they ended with *éclat*. The room was crowded, and
the lecture had several passages more than brilliant, — they
were luminous, and the light gave conscious pleasure to every
person who knew that he could both see the glory and the objects around it at once, while (you know) mere splendor, like
the patent lamps, presents a flame that only puts out the eyes.
Coleridge's explanation of the character of Satan, and his vindication of Milton against the charge of falling below his
subject, where he introduces the Supreme Being, and his
illustration of the difference between poetic and abstract truth,
and of the *diversity in identity* between the philosopher and the
poet, were equally wise and beautiful. He concluded with a
few strokes of satire ; but I cannot forgive him for selecting
alone (except an attack on Pope's " Homer," qualified by in-
sincere eulogy) Mrs. Barbauld. She is a living writer, a woman,
and a person who, however discordant with himself in character and taste, has still always shown him civilities and attentions. It was surely ungenerous. . . . .

February 27th. — Coleridge's concluding lecture. A dinner
at John Thelwall's. The American poet Northmore there ;
also the Rev. W. Frend ; ‡ George Dyer, § whose gentle man-

---

* Godwin and Rough met at this party for the first time. The very next
day Godwin called on me to say how much he liked Rough, adding: " By the
by, do you think he would lend me £ 50 just now, as I am in want of a little
money ? " He had not left me an hour before Rough came with a like question. He wanted a bill discounted, and asked whether I thought Godwin
would do it for him. The habit of both was so well known that some persons
were afraid to invite them, lest it should lead to an application for a loan from
some friend who chanced to be present. — H. C. R.

† Mr. Littledale's chambers were in Gray's Inn.

‡ The eminent mathematician, and former Fellow and Tutor of Jesus College, Cambridge. For a pamphlet published by him in 1793, and containing
expressions of dislike to the doctrines and discipline of the Established
Church, he was, after a trial of eight days by the University authorities, sentenced to *banishment* from the University. His *fellowship* he retained till his
marriage.

§ See *ante*, pp. 39, 40.

ners were a contrast to the slovenliness of his dress ; North-cote the painter ; and a very interesting man named Nicholson, who has raised himself out of the lowest condition, though not out of poverty, by literary and scientific labors. What he has written (not printed) would fill three hundred moderate-sized volumes. For an introduction to Natural Philosophy he re-ceived £ 150. He has the air of a robust man, both in body and in mind.

March 10th. — Mrs. Collier and I went to Covent Garden Theatre. " Julius Cæsar." We were forced to stand all the time. Young as Cassius surpassed Kemble as Brutus. Indeed the whole performance of the latter was cold, stiff, and pedan-tic. In the quarrel scene only, his fine figure gave him an advantage over Young. He was once warmly applauded ; but, on the whole, Young seemed to be the favorite, and where he instigated Brutus to concur in the plot, he drew down peals of applause. The two orations from the rostrum produced no effect whatever. The architectural scenery was very grand.

March 15th. — A pleasant walk to Hampstead. Had much conversation with Hamond. Some years ago he called on Jeremy Bentham without any introduction, merely to obtain the acquaintance of the great man. Bentham at first declined to receive him, but on seeing Hamond's card altered his mind, and an intimacy arose. Bentham himself, when a young man, was so enthusiastic an admirer of Helvetius, that he actually thought of offering himself as a servant to him. " You," said he to Hamond, in reference to his desire, " took a better way." When Hamond told me this, I did not confess that, sixteen years ago, the idea of doing a similar thing floated before my own mind ; but I was pleased to find that the same extrava-gancy of sentiment had affected so superior a man as Ben-tham.

March 16th. — Flaxman's lecture. The short characteristics of the most famous pieces of sculpture of antiquity very inter-esting. There was not in this, any more than in preceding lec-tures I have heard from him, great power of discrimination, or much of what in a lower sense is called understanding, though Flaxman's beautiful *sense* and refined taste are far superior to any understanding the mere critic can possess. The artist needs a different and higher quality, — *Kunstsinn* (feeling for art), and that Flaxman possesses in a greater degree than any other man I know. Returned to Charles Lamb, with whom

were Barron Field, Leigh Hunt, and Barnes.* The latter, with
a somewhat *feist* appearance, has a good countenance, and is a
man who, I dare say, will make his way in the world. He has
talents and activity, and inducements to activity. He has obtained high honors at Cambridge, and is now a candidate for a
fellowship. He reports for Walter. Charles Lamb was at his
best, — very good-humored, but at the same time solid. I
never heard him talk to greater advantage. He wrote last
week in the *Examiner* some capital lines, " The Triumph of
the Whale," † and this occasioned the conversation to take
more of a political turn than is usual with Lamb. Leigh
Hunt is an enthusiast, very well intentioned, and I believe
prepared for the worst. He said, pleasantly enough: " No one
can accuse me of not writing a libel. Everything is a libel, as
the law is now declared, and our security lies only in their
shame." He talked on the theatre, and showed on such points
great superiority over the others.

March 18th. — Evening at Porden's, the Society of the Attic
Chest. This is a small society, the members of which send
verses, which are put into a box, and afford an evening's
amusement at certain intervals. The box was actually made at
Athens. Some verses, I suspect by Miss Flaxman, on music,
pleased me best. The company was numerous, — the Rogets,‡
Phillips § the painter, and his wife. Old General Franklin,

---

* For a long time editor of the *Times.*

† H. C. R. says that in *Galignani* this poem was incorrectly ascribed to
Lord Byron. A few lines will serve as a specimen of the kind of wit it contains: —

> . . . . " Next declare,
> Muse, who his companions are.
> Every fish of generous kind
> Scuds aside, or slinks behind.
>
> .   .   .
>
> For his solace and relief,
> Flat-fish are his courtiers chief.
> Last and lowest in his train,
> Ink-fish, libellers of the main,
> Their black venom, shed in spite;
> Such on earth *the things that write.*
>
> In his stomach, some do say,
> No good thing can ever stay.
> Had it been the fortune of it
> To have swallowed that old prophet,
> Three days there he 'd not have dwelled,
> But in one had been expelled."

‡ Dr. Roget was the author of " Animal and Vegetable Physiology," one of
the Bridgewater Treatises, published in 1834.

§ Afterwards R. A., and father of the recent R. A. of that name.

son of the celebrated Benjamin, was of the party. He is eighty-four years of age, has a courtier-like mien, and must have been a very fine man. He is now very animated and interesting, but does not at all answer to the idea one would naturally form of the son of the great Franklin.

*Rem.** — At these meetings Ellen Porden was generally the reader, and she was herself a writer of poetry. She even ventured to write an epic poem, called " Richard the Second." When she presented a copy to Flaxman, who loved her for her amiable qualities (and more than amiable, for she was a good domestic character, an excellent sister and daughter), he thanked her and said : " Why, Ellen, my love, you 've written a poem longer than Homer." She married Captain, afterwards Sir John Franklin. The marriage took place with an express consent on her part to his making a second voyage of discovery towards the North Pole, if the government should give its permission. Before he went a daughter was born ; but her own health had become so bad that her life was despaired of. I was one of the few friends invited to the last dinner at his house before his departure. Flaxman was of the party, and deeply depressed in spirits. Captain F. took an opportunity in the course of the evening to say to me : " My wife will be left alone with the infant. You will do me a great favor, if you will call on her as often as your engagements permit." I promised. In a few days I went to the Quarter Sessions, and before I returned Mrs. Franklin was dead.

March 23d. — With Lawrence, who showed me a painting of Kemble as Cato, in the last scene, about to inflict on himself the *nobile letum*. It is a very strong likeness, as well as a very beautiful picture.†

March 26th. — Dined with Messrs. Longman and Co. at one of their literary parties. These parties were famous in their day. Longman himself is a quiet gentlemanly man. There were present Dr. Abraham Rees,‡ a very good-humored, agreeable companion, who would in no respect disgrace a mitre ; " Russia " Tooke, as he was called ; Sharon Turner,§ a chatty man, and pleasant in his talk ; Abernethy, who did not say a word ; and Dr. Holland,‖ the Iceland traveller. The only one

---

* Written in 1849.
† This picture was exhibited the same year at Somerset House, No. 57 of the Royal Academy Catalogue.
‡ His brother was a partner in Longman's house.
§ The historian.
‖ Afterwards Sir Henry Holland, the Court Physician.

who said anything worth reporting was Dr. Rees, the well-known Arian, " Encyclopædic Rees."   He related that when, in 1788, Beaufoy made his famous attempt to obtain the repeal of the Corporation and Test Act, a deputation waited on the Lord Chancellor Thurlow to obtain his support.   The deputies were Drs. Kippis, Palmer (of Hackney), and Rees.   The Chancellor heard them very civilly, and then said : " Gentlemen, I 'm against you, by G—.   I am for the Established Church, d—mme !   Not that I have any more regard for the Established Church than for any other church, but because *it is* established.   And if you can get your d——d religion established, I 'll be for that too ! "   Rees told this story with great glee.

April 12th. — A call on the Aikins.   The whole family full of their praises of Charles Lamb.   The Doctor termed him a brilliant writer.   The union of so much eloquence with so much wit shows great powers of mind.   Miss Aikin was not less warm in her praise.   She asked why he did not write more.   I mentioned, as one cause, the bad character given him by the reviewers.   She exclaimed against the reviewers. I then spoke of the *Annual Review* (Arthur Aikin, the editor, was present), as having hurt him much by its notice of " John Woodvil."*   She exclaimed, " O that Tommy ; that such a fellow should criticise such a man as Lamb."   I then mentioned that some persons had attributed the article to Mrs. Barbauld. I was impressed with the sincerity and liberality of the Aikins, in acknowledging a merit so unlike their own.   They evinced a universality of taste which I had not supposed them to possess.

April 13th. — Met a Mr. Anderson, a north-country divine, a hard-headed, shrewd man, of blunt manners, who ought to have been chaplain to the Parliamentary army at the commencement of the civil wars in the time of Charles I.   He is a *laudator temporis præsentis*, rather than *acti*.   He laughed heartily at old Jameson's advertisement, that persons taking apartments in his house " might be accommodated with family prayer."

April 20th. — Called on the Godwins.†   They very much admire Miss Flaxman's designs for " Robin Goodfellow " ; but do not think they would sell.   Parents are now so set against all stories of ghosts, that fifty copies of such designs would not be sold in a year.

---

* Lamb's Works, 1855, Vol. IV. p. 299.
† Godwin was at this time largely engaged in publishing books for children. He published Lamb's " Tales from Shakespeare," and Miss Lamb's " Mrs. Leicester's School."

April 21st. — Accompanied Cargill * to Covent Garden. Mrs. Siddons in Mrs. Beverley. Her voice appeared to have lost its brilliancy (like a beautiful face through a veil) ; in other respects, however, her acting is as good as ever. Her " O that my eyes were basilisks ! " was her great moment in the play. Her smile was enchantingly beautiful ; and her transitions of countenance had all the ease and freedom of youth. If she persist in not playing Mrs. Beverley again, that character will, I am confident, never be played with anything like equal attractions. And without some great attraction in the performers, such a play ought not to be represented. It is a dull sermon ; the interest kept up by commonplace incidents, and persons who are absolutely no characters at all. Young did not *look* the part of Beverley well. As Amyot says, he is a bad waistcoat-and-breeches actor.

April 27th. — At Hazlitt's last lecture. Very well delivered, and full of shrewd observation. At the close, he remarked on the utility of metaphysics. He quoted and half assented to Hume's sceptical remark, that perhaps they are not worth the study, but that there are persons who can find no better mode of amusing themselves. He then related an Indian legend of a Brahmin, who was so devoted to abstract meditation, that in the pursuit of philosophy he quite forgot his moral duties, and neglected ablution. For this he was degraded from the rank of humanity, and transformed into a monkey. But, even when a monkey, he retained his original propensities, for he kept apart from other monkeys, and had no other delight than that of eating cocoanuts and studying metaphysics. " I, too," said Hazlitt, " should be very well contented to pass my life like this monkey, did I but know how to provide myself with a substitute for cocoanuts."

May 3d. — Left a card at Sir George Beaumont's for Wordsworth. On my return a call on Coleridge. He said that from Fichte and Schelling he has not gained any one great idea. To Kant his obligations are infinite, not so much from what Kant has taught him in the form of doctrine, as from the discipline gained in studying the great German philosopher. Coleridge is indignant at the low estimation in which the post-Kantianers affect to hold their master.

Rem.† — *May 5th.* — This day I saw at the exhibition a

---

* A native of Jamaica, and a pupil of Thelwall. He studied the law under Sergeant Rough, by H. C. R.'s advice, but afterwards became a clergyman.
† Written in 1849.

picture by Turner, the impression of which still remains. It seemed to me the most marvellous landscape I had ever seen, — Hannibal crossing the Alps in a storm. I can never forget it.*

May 6th. — R. says Johnson, the bookseller, made at least £ 10,000 by Cowper's poems. The circumstances show the hazard of bookselling speculations. Cowper's first volume of poems was published by Johnson, and fell dead from the press. Author and publisher were to incur equal loss. Cowper begged Johnson to forgive him his debt, and this was done. In return, Cowper sent Johnson his " Task," saying : " You behaved generously to me on a former occasion ; if you think it safe to publish this new work, I make you a present of it." Johnson published it. It became popular. The former volume was then sold with it. When Cowper's friends proposed his translating " Homer," Johnson said : " I owe Cowper much for his last book, and will therefore assist in the publication of ' Homer ' without any compensation. The work shall be published by subscription. I will take all the trouble and risk, and Cowper shall have all the profit." Johnson soon had occasion to inform the poet that a thousand pounds were at his disposal.

May 8th. — A visit from Wordsworth, who stayed with me from between twelve and one till past three. I then walked with him to Newman Street. His conversation was long and interesting. He spoke of his own poems with the just feeling of confidence which a sense of his own excellence gives him. He is now convinced that he never can derive emolument from them ; but, being independent, he willingly gives up all idea of doing so. He is persuaded that if men are to become better and wiser, the poems will sooner or later make their way. But if we are to perish, and society is not to advance in civilization, " it would be," said he, " wretched selfishness to deplore the want of any personal reputation." The approbation he has met with from some superior persons compensates for the loss of popularity, though no man has completely understood him, not excepting Coleridge, who is not happy enough to enter into his feelings. " I am myself," said Wordsworth, " one of the happiest of men ; and no man who does not partake of that happiness, who lives a life of constant bustle, and whose felicity depends on the opinions of others, can possibly comprehend

---

* The picture is now in the National Gallery, Turner Collection. It was No. 258 of the Somerset House Catalogue, and entitled " Snow-Storm: Hannibal and his Army crossing the Alps. — J. M. W. TURNER, R. A."

the best of my poems." I urged an excuse for those who can really enjoy the better pieces, and who yet are offended by a language they have by early instruction been taught to consider unpoetical; and Wordsworth seemed to tolerate this class, and to allow that his admirers should undergo a sort of education to his works.

May 11th. — Called at Coleridge's, where I found the Lambs. I had just heard of the assassination of Mr. Perceval, which had taken place about an hour and a half before. The news shocked Coleridge exceedingly, and he was at once ready to connect the murder with political fanaticism, Burdett's speeches, &c. Charles Lamb was apparently affected, but could not help mingling humor with his real concern at the event.*

Spent the evening at Miss Benger's.† Miss Jane Porter ‡ there. Her stately figure and graceful manners made an impression on me. Few ladies have been so gifted with personal attractions, and at the same time been so respectable as authors.

May 13th. — Wordsworth accompanied me to Charles Aikin's.§ Mrs. Barbauld, the Aikins, Miss Jane Porter, Montgomery the poet, Roscoe, ‖ son of the Liverpool Roscoe, &c. The most agreeable circumstance of the evening was the homage involuntarily paid to the poet. Everybody was anxious to get near him. One lady was ludicrously fidgety till she was within hearing. A political dispute rather disturbed us for a time. Wordsworth, speaking of the late assassination, and of Sir Francis Burdett's speech ten days ago, said that probably the murderer heard that speech, and that this, operating on his mind in its diseased and inflamed state, *might be* the determining motive to his act. This was taken up as a reflection on Sir Francis Burdett, and resented warmly by young Roscoe, who maintained that the speech was a constitutional one, and

---

* About this time there was an attack on Charles Lamb in the *Quarterly Review*, in an article on Weber's edition of "Ford's Works." Lamb was called a "poor maniac." It was this attack which occasioned and justified Lamb's sonnet, "St. Crispin to Mr. Gifford," a happy *jeu d'esprit.* That Charles Lamb had, for ever so short a time, been in confinement was not known to me till the recent disclosure in Talfourd's "Final Memorials." — H. C. R.

† Miss Benger obtained considerable literary celebrity as a writer of historical biographies. She was much esteemed in the circle of friends to which she was introduced on first coming to London. Among those friends were Mrs. Barbauld, Miss Aikin, Mrs. Joanna Baillie, Mrs. Elizabeth Hamilton, Dr. Aikin, and Dr. Gregory.

‡ The authoress of "Thaddeus of Warsaw," and other popular novels.

§ Mr. Charles Aikin was then in practice as a medical man in Broad Street, City.

‖ Probably William Stanley Roscoe.

asked what the starving were to do? " Not murder people," said Wordsworth, " unless they mean to eat their hearts." *

May 15th. — A call on Flaxman in the evening. He spoke of Turner's landscape with great admiration, as the best painting in the Exhibition. He praised parts of Hilton's " Christ Healing the Blind," especially the hands of the principal figures, and the contrasted expression of the one expecting the operation of the miracle, and the one on whom it has already taken place. Miss Flaxman pointed out Allingham's " Grief and Pity," and a landscape, " Sadac Seeking the Waters of Oblivion."

May 19th. — Went to Covent Garden Theatre. Mrs. Siddons played Queen Catherine to perfection, and Kemble as Wolsey, in the scene of his disgrace, was greatly applauded. I think I never saw Mrs. Siddons's pantomime in higher excellence. The dying scene was represented with such truthfulness, as almost to go beyond the bounds of beautiful imitation, viz. by shifting her pillow with the restlessness of a person in pain, and the suspended breath in moving, which usually denotes suffering. It was, however, a most delightful performance.

In an earlier part of the day heard part of Coleridge's first lecture in Willis's Rooms.† As I was present only about a quarter of an hour, I could not enter much into his subject. I perceived that he was in a digressing mood. He spoke of religion, the spirit of chivalry, the Gothic reverence for the female sex, and a classification of poetry into the ancient and the romantic.

May 23d. — Coleridge's second lecture. A beautiful dissertation on the Greek drama. His analysis of the trilogy of Æschylus, the " Agamemnon," &c. was interesting ; and his account of the " Prometheus," and his remarks on the " Antigone," were more connected than when I heard him speak on the same subjects on a former occasion.

May 24th. — A very interesting day. At half past ten joined Wordsworth in Oxford Road ; we then got into the fields, and walked to Hampstead. I read to him a number of Blake's poems, with some of which he was pleased. He regard-

* In a note to Mr. Robinson, dated two days after this visit Wordsworth says: " I have never been well since I met your city politicians; yet I am content to pay this price for the knowledge of so pleasing a person as Mrs. Charles Aikin, being quite an enthusiast when I find a woman whose countenance and manners are what a woman's ought to be."

† A course on Shakespeare, with introductory matter on poetry, the drama, and the stage.

ed Blake as having in him the elements of poetry much more than either Byron or Scott. We met Miss Joanna Baillie, and accompanied her home. She is small in figure, and her gait is mean and shuffling, but her manners are those of a well-bred woman. She has none of the unpleasant airs too common to literary ladies. Her conversation is sensible. She possesses apparently considerable information, is prompt without being forward, and has a fixed judgment of her own, without any disposition to force it on others. Wordsworth said of her with warmth : " If I had to present any one to a foreigner as a model of an English gentlewoman, it would be Joanna Baillie."

May 26th. — Walked to the Old Bailey to see D. I. Eaton in the pillory.* As I expected, his punishment of shame was his glory. The mob was not numerous, but decidedly friendly to him. His having published Paine's " Age of Reason " was not an intelligible offence to them. I heard such exclamations as the following : " Pillory a man for publishing a book, — shame ! " — " I wish old Sir Wicary was there, my pockets should not be empty." — " Religious liberty ! " — " Liberty of conscience ! " Some avowed their willingness to stand in the pillory for a dollar. " This a punishment ? this is no disgrace ! " As his position changed, and fresh partisans were blessed by a sight of his round, grinning face, shouts of " Bravo ! " arose from a new quarter. His trial was sold on the spot. The whole affair was an additional proof of the folly of the Ministers, who ought to have known that such an exhibition would be a triumph to the cause they meant to render infamous.

Heard Coleridge's third lecture. It was wholly on the Greek drama, though he had promised that he would to-day proceed to the modern drama. The lecture itself excellent and very German.

May 27th. — Went to Miss Benger's in the evening, where I found a large party. Had some conversation with Miss Porter. She won upon me greatly. I was introduced to a character, — Miss Wesley, a niece of the celebrated John, and daughter of Samuel Wesley. She is said to be a devout and most actively benevolent woman. Eccentric in her habits, but most estimable in all the great points of character. A very

---

* Daniel Isaac Eaton, the publisher of free theological works (Paine's " Age of Reason," " Ecce Homo," &c.). He underwent not less than eight prosecutions by government for his publications. For publishing the third part of the " Age of Reason " he suffered eighteen months' imprisonment. He died in 1814. (D. I. Eaton is not to be confounded with David Eaton, a bookseller, and the friend of Theophilus Lindsey.)

lively little body, with a round short person, in a constant fidget of good-nature and harmless vanity. She has written novels, which do not sell; and is reported to have said, when she was introduced to Miss Edgeworth, "We sisters of the quill ought to know each other." She said she had friends of all sects in religion, and was glad she had, as she could not possibly become uncharitable. She had been in Italy, and loved the Italians for their warmth in friendship. Some one remarked, "They are equally warm in their enmities." She replied, "Of course they are." When I said I loved the people of every country I had been in, she said, in a tone which expressed much more than the words, "How glad I am to hear you say so!"

May 29th. — Coleridge's fourth lecture. It was on the nature of comedy, — about Aristophanes, &c. The mode of treating the subject very German, and of course much too abstract for his audience, which was thin. Scarcely any ladies there. With such powers of original thought and real genius, both philosophical and poetical, as few men in any age have possessed, Coleridge wants certain minor qualities, which would greatly add to his efficiency and influence with the public. Spent the evening at Morgan's. Both Coleridge and Wordsworth there. Coleridge very metaphysical. He adheres to Kant, notwithstanding all Schelling has written, and maintains that from the latter he has gained no new ideas. All Schelling has said, Coleridge has either thought himself, or found in Jacob Boehme.* Wordsworth talked very finely on poetry. He praised Burns for his introduction to "Tam O'Shanter." Burns had given an apology for drunkenness, by bringing together all the circumstances which can serve to render excusable what is in itself disgusting; thus interesting our feelings, and making us tolerant of what would otherwise be not endurable.

Wordsworth praised also the conclusion of "Death and Dr. Hornbook." He compared this with the abrupt prevention of the expected battle between Satan and the archangel in "Paradise Lost"; but the remark did not bring its own evidence with it. I took occasion to apply to Goëthe the praise given to Burns for the passage † quoted, and this led to my warm

---

* The German Visionary and Theosophist (1575–1624).
† The passage from Burns's "Vision" which H. C. R. afterwards quoted to Goethe as resembling the Zueignung (dedication) to his own works. "Each poet confesses his infirmities, — each is consoled by the muse; the holly-leaf of the Scotch poet being the 'veil of dew and sunbeams' of the German."

11 *

praise of the German. Coleridge denied merit to " Torquato Tasso," and talked of the impossibility of being a good poet without being a good man, adducing at the same time the immoral tendency of Goethe's works. To this I demurred.

May 31st. — A day of great enjoyment. Walked to Hampstead. Found Wordsworth demonstrating to Hamond some of the points of his philosophical theory. Speaking of his own poems, he said he valued them principally as being *a new power* in the literary world. Hamond's friend Miller * esteemed them for their pure morality. Wordsworth said he himself looked to the powers of mind they call forth, and the energies they presuppose and excite as the standard by which they should be tried. He expatiated also on his fears lest a social war should arise between the poor and the rich, the danger of which is aggravated by the vast extension of the manufacturing system.†

Wordsworth defended earnestly the Church Establishment. He even said he would shed his blood for it. Nor was he disconcerted by a laugh raised against him on account of his having before confessed that he knew not when he had been in a church in his own country. " All our ministers are so vile," said he. The mischief of allowing the clergy to depend on the caprice of the multitude he thought more than outweighed all the evils of an Establishment. And in this I agreed with him.

Dined with Wordsworth at Mr. Carr's.‡ Sir Humphry and Lady Davy there. She and Sir H. seem to have hardly finished their honeymoon. Miss Joanna Baillie said to Wordsworth the other day, " We have witnessed a picturesque happiness." Mrs. Walter Scott was spoken of rather disparagingly, and Miss Baillie gave her this good word : " When I visited her I thought I saw a great deal to like. She seemed to admire and look up to her husband. She was very kind to

---

* A clergyman with whom H. C. R. afterwards became intimate.

† This was a topic which at this time haunted alike Wordsworth and Southey. Now that thirty-six years have elapsed, not only has the danger increased, but the war has actually broken out ; and as evidence that men distinctly perceive the fact, in France a word has been applied, not invented, which by implication recognizes the fact. Society is divided into *propriétaires* and *prolétaires*. And here we have an incessant controversy carried on by our political economists, as to the respective claims of labor and capital. — H. C. R., 1848.

‡ Carr was Solicitor to the Excise, — a clever man, whom I visited occasionally at Hampstead. His eldest daughter married Dr. Lushington. His youngest married Rolfe (Lord Cranworth), after the latter became one of the best of judges. — H. C. R., 1849.

her guests. Her children were well-bred, and the house was in excellent order. And she had some smart roses in her cap, and I did not like her the less for that."

June 3d. — Wordsworth told me that, before his ballads were published, Tobin implored him to leave out "We are Seven," as a poem that would damn the book. It became, however, one of the most popular. Wordsworth related this in answer to a remark that, by only leaving out certain poems at the suggestion of some one who knew the public taste, he might avoid giving offence.

June 5th. — At Covent Garden. For the first time in my life I saw Mrs. Siddons without any pleasure. It was in the part of the Lady in "Comus." She was dressed most unbecomingly, and had a low gypsy hat with feathers hanging down the side. She looked old, and I had almost said ugly. Her fine features were lost in the distance. Even her declamation did not please me. She spoke in too tragic a tone for the situation and character.

June 6th. — Lent "Peter Bell" to Charles Lamb. To my surprise, he does not like it. He complains of the slowness of the narrative, as if that were not the *art* of the poet. He says Wordsworth has great thoughts, but has left them out here. In the perplexity arising from the diverse judgments of those to whom I am accustomed to look up, I have no resource but in the determination to disregard all opinions, and trust to the simple impression made on my own mind. When Lady Mackintosh was once stating to Coleridge her disregard of the beauties of nature, which men commonly affect to admire, he said his friend Wordsworth had described her feeling, and quoted three lines from "Peter Bell" : —

> "A primrose by a river's brim
> A yellow primrose was to him,
> And it was nothing more."

"Yes," said Lady Mackintosh, "that is precisely my case."

June 17th. — At four o'clock dined in the Hall * with De Quincey, who was very civil to me, and cordially invited me to visit his cottage in Cumberland. Like myself, he is an enthusiast for Wordsworth. His person is small, his complexion fair, and his air and manner are those of a sickly and enfeebled man. From this circumstance his sensibility, which I have no doubt is genuine, is in danger of being mistaken for

* That is Middle Temple Hall.

effeminateness. At least coarser and more robustly healthful persons may fall into this mistake.

June 29th. — This evening Mrs. Siddons took her leave of the stage.

*Rem.** —About this time, July 2, 1812, my Diary refers to the death of Mrs. Buller,† — of those who never in any way came before the public one of the most remarkable women whom I have ever known. She was a lady of family, belonging to the Bullers of Devonshire, and had lived always at Court. She said once, incidentally : " The Prince Regent has, I believe, as high a regard for me as for any one, — that is, none at all. He is incapable of friendship." On politics and on the affairs of life she spoke with singular correctness and propriety. On matters of taste she was altogether antiquated. She was the friend of Mrs. Montague and Mrs. Carter. She showed me in her bookcase some bound quarto volumes, which she assured me consisted of a translation of Plato by herself, in her own hand. She was far advanced in years, and her death did not come upon her unexpectedly. Not many days before she died I called to make inquiries, and the servant, looking in a book and finding my name there, told me I was to be admitted. I found her pale as ashes, bolstered up in an arm-chair. She received me with a smile, and allowed me to touch her hand. " What are you reading, Mr. Robinson ? " she said. " The wickedest cleverest book in the English language, if you chance to know it." — " I have known the ' Fable of the Bees ' ‡ more than fifty years." She was right in her guess.

July 26th. — Finished Goethe's " Aus meinem Leben ; Dichtung und Wahrheit." The book has given me great delight. The detailed account of the ceremonies on electing Joseph II. has great interest. Goethe unites the grace and perfect art of the most accomplished writer, with a retention of all the childlike zeal and earnestness which he felt when the impressions were first conveyed to him. I know of no writer who can, like Goethe, blend the feeling of youth with the skill and power of age. Here a perfect masterpiece is produced by the exercise of this rare talent. The account of the election of Joseph derives a pathetic interest from the subsequent destruction of the German Empire. His own innocent boyish amour with Gretchen is related with peculiar grace. The characteristic

---

* Written in 1849.　　　† For Mrs. Buller, see *ante*, p. 206.
‡ The " Fable of the Bees ; or, Private Vices Public Benefits." By Bernard Mandeville, 1723. A work of great celebrity, or rather notoriety, in the last century.

sketches of the friends of his father are felt by the reader to be portraits of old acquaintances. How familiar the features of the old Hebrew master seem to me, as he encourages the free-thinking questions of his pupil about the Jews by laughing, though nothing is to be got by way of answer excepting, " 'Ei! närrischer Junge?" (" Eh! foolish boy?") The florist, the admirer of Klopstock, the father and grandfather, are all delightfully portrayed. And the remark Wordsworth made on Burns is here also applicable, " The poet writes humanely." There is not a single character who is *hated*, certainly not the lying French player-boy, arrant knave though he is. Perhaps Gretchen's kinsfolk are the least agreeable of the minor characters.

August 4th. — After tea called at Morgan's. The ladies were at home alone. I took a walk with them round the squares. They stated some particulars of Coleridge's family and early life, which were new and interesting to me. His father was a clergyman at Ottery, in Devonshire. Judge Buller, when a young man, lived many years in his family. Indeed he was educated by him. On the death of Mr. Coleridge, Buller went down to offer his services to the widow. She said all her family were provided for, except the tenth, a little boy. Buller promised to provide for him, said he would send him to the Charterhouse, and put him into some profession. Coleridge went to town, and Buller placed him in the Blue-Coat School. The family, being proud, thought themselves disgraced by this. His brothers would not let him visit them in the school dress, and he would not go in any other. The Judge (whether he was judge then I cannot tell) invited him to his house to dine every Sunday. One day, however, there was company, and the blue-coat boy was sent to a second table. He was then only nine years old, but he would never go to the house again. Thus he lost his only friend in London; and having no one to care for him or show him kindness, he passed away his childhood wretchedly. But he says he was thus led to become a good scholar, for, that he might forget his misery, he had his book always in his hand.

Coleridge and Morgan came back to supper. Coleridge was in good spirits. He is about to turn again to Jean Paul.

August 12th. — Paid a visit to Flaxman in his lodgings at Blackheath, and spent the night there. On the following morning I returned with him to town and accompanied him to Burlington House to see Lord Elgin's Marbles. The new cargo was not yet unpacked. I have neither the learning nor the taste of an artist, but it was interesting even to me to behold fragments of architectural ornaments from cities celebrated by Homer. Flaxman affirmed with confidence that some of the fragments before us were in existence before Homer's time. A stranger came in, whom I afterwards understood to be Chantrey. Flaxman said to him, laying his hand on a piece of stone, " The hand of Phidias was on that ! " The stranger remarked that there was one leg which could not have been by Phidias. The stranger conjectured that some ornaments on a sarcophagus were meant to represent the lotus. Two sorts of lotus and the egg, he said, were three of the most sacred objects of antiquity, and were found carved on urns. The lotus, he thought, was the origin of the cornucopia.

At six I went by appointment to Coleridge, with whom I spent several hours alone, and most agreeably. I read to him a number of scenes out of the new " Faust." He had before read the earlier edition. He now acknowledged the genius of Goethe as he has never before acknowledged it. At the same time, the want of religion and enthusiasm in Goethe is in Coleridge's estimation an irreparable defect. The beginning of " Faust " did not please Coleridge. Nor does he think Mephistopheles a *character*. He had, however, nothing satisfactory to oppose to my remark that Mephistopheles ought to be a mere abstraction, and no character. I read to Coleridge the Zueignung, and he seemed to admire it greatly. He had been reading Stolberg lately, of whom he seems to have a sufficiently high opinion. He considers Goethe's " Mahomets Gesang " an imitation of Stolberg's " Felsenstrom "; but the " Felsenstrom " is simply a piece of animated description, without any higher import, while Goethe's poem is a profound and significant allegory, exhibiting the nature of religious enthusiasm. The prologue in heaven to " Faust " did not offend Coleridge as I thought it would, from its being a parody on Job. Coleridge said of Job, this incomparable poem has been most absurdly interpreted. Far from being the most patient of men, Job was the most impatient. And he was rewarded for his impatience. His integrity and sincerity had their recompense because he was superior to the hypocrisy of his friends. Coleridge praised " Wallenstein," but censured Schiller for a sort of ventriloquism in poetry. By the by, a happy term to express that common fault of throwing the sentiments and feelings of the writer into the bodies of other persons, the characters of the poem.

August 20th. — More talk with Coleridge about " Faust." The additions in the last edition he thinks the finest parts. He objects that the character of Faust is not *motivirt.* He would have it explained how he is thrown into a state of mind which led to the catastrophe. The last stage of the process is given. Faust is wretched. He has reached the utmost that finite powers can attain, and he yearns for infinity. Rather than be finitely good, he would be infinitely miserable. This is indeed reducing the wisdom and genius of Goethe's incomparable poem to a dull, commonplace, moral idea; but I do not give it as the thing, only the abstract form. All final results and most general abstractions are, when thus reduced, seemingly trite. Coleridge talks of writing a new Faust! He would never get out of vague conceptions, — he would lose himself in dreams! In the spirited sketch he gave of Goethe's work, I admired his power of giving interest to a prose statement.

September 6th. — A delightful walk with my friend Amyot.* He told some anecdotes of Dr. Parr, whom he knew. The Doctor was asked his opinion on some subject of politics ; with an affectation of mystery and importance he replied : " I am not fond of speaking on the subject. *If I were in my place in the House of Lords, I should, &c., &c."*

13th. — A delightful day. The pleasantest walk by far I have had this summer. The very rising from one's bed at Hamond's house is an enjoyment worth going to Hampstead overnight to partake of. The morning scene from his back room is exceedingly beautiful. We breakfasted at seven. He and his sisters accompanied me beyond The Spaniards, and down some fields opposite Kenwood. The wet grass sent them back, and I went on (rather out of my way) till I entered the Barnet road just before the west end of Finchley Common. I crossed the common obliquely, and, missing the shortest way, came to a good turnpike road at Colney Hatch. On the heath I was amused by the novel sight of gypsies. The road from Colney Hatch to Southgate very pleasing indeed. Southgate a delightful village. No distant prospect from the green, but there are fine trees admirably grouped, and neat and happy houses scattered in picturesque corners and lanes. The great houses, Duchess of Chandos's, &c., have, I suppose, a distant view. I then followed a path to Winchmore Hill, and another to Enfield : the last through

* See page 16.

some of the richest verdure I ever saw. The hills exquisitely undulating. Very fine clumps of oak-trees. Enfield town, the large white church, the serpentine New River, Mr. Mellish's house, with its woody appendages, form a singularly beautiful picture. I reached Enfield at about half past ten, and found Anthony Robinson happy with his family. As usual, I had a very pleasant day with him. Our chat interesting and uninterrupted. Before dinner we lounged round the green, and saw the Cedar of Lebanon which once belonged to Queen Elizabeth's palace, of which only a chimney now remains. A little after five I set out on my walk homeward, through Hornsey and Islington. Till I came to Hornsey Church, where I was no longer able to see, I was occupied during my walk in reading Schlegel's " Vorlesungen " ; his account of Æschylus and Sophocles, and their plays, very excellent. I was especially interested in his account of the Trilogy. How glad I should be to have leisure to translate such a work as this of Schlegel's ! I reached my chambers about nine. Rather fatigued, though my walk was not a long one, — only eighteen or twenty miles.

September 19th. — After an early dinner walked to Blackheath, reading a very amusing article in the *Edinburgh Review* about ants. I cannot, however, enter into the high enjoyment which some persons have in such subjects. What, after all, is there that is delightful or soul-elevating in contemplating countless myriads of animals, endowed with marvellous powers, which lead to nothing beyond the preservation of individual existence, or rather the preservation of a race ? The effect is rather sad than animating ; for the more wonderful their powers are, the more elaborately complex and more curiously fitted to their end, and the more they resemble those of human beings, the less apparent absurdity is there in the supposition that our powers should cease with their present manifestation. For my part, I am convinced that the truths and postulates of religion have their sole origin and confirmation in *conscience and the moral sense.*

September 21st. — Took tea at C. Aikin's. A chat about Miss Edgeworth. Mrs. Aikin willing to find in her every excellence, whilst I disputed her power of interesting in a long connected tale, and her possession of poetical imagination. In her numerous works she has certainly conceived and executed a number of forms, which, though not representatives of ideas, are excellent characters. Her sketches and her con-

ceptions of ordinary life are full of good sense ; but the tendency of her writings to check enthusiasm of every kind is of
very problematical value.

October 3d. — Coleridge walked with me to A. Robinson's
for my Spinoza, which I lent him. While standing in the
room he kissed Spinoza's face in the title-page, and said :
" This book is a gospel to me." *   But in less than a minute

---

* Mr. H. C. Robinson's copy of the works of Spinoza is now in the library
of Manchester New College, London, with *marginalia* from the hand of Coleridge.
They are limited to the first part of the Ethica, " De Deo "; and to some letters in his correspondence, especially with Oldenburg, one of the earliest sec-
retaries of the Royal Society in London. It appears from these marginal notes,
that Coleridge heartily embraced Spinoza's fundamental position of the Divine
Immanence in all things, as distinguished from the ordinary anthropomorphic
conceptions of God, but was anxious to guard it from the pantheistic conclusions which might be supposed to result from it, and to clear it from the ne-
cessarian and materialistic assumptions with which he thought Spinoza himself
had gratuitously encumbered it. Everywhere Coleridge distinctly asserts the
Divine Intelligence and the Divine Will against the vague, negative generality
in which Spinoza's overpowering sense of the incommensurability of the Divine
and the Human had left them ; and strenuously contends for the freedom of
human actions as the indispensable basis of a true theory of morals. " It is
most necessary," he says, in a note on Propos. XXVIII. (of the first part of the
Ethics), " to distinguish Spinozism from Spinoza, — i. e. the necessary consequences of the immanence in God as the one only necessary Being whose essence
involves existence, with the deductions, — from Spinoza's own mechanic *real-
istic* view of the world."   " Even in the latter," he continues, " I cannot accord
with Jacobi's assertion, that Spinozism as taught by Spinoza is atheism; for
though he will not consent to call things essentially disparate by the same
name, and therefore denies human intelligence to Deity, yet he adores his wisdom, and expressly declares the identity of Love, i. e. perfect virtue or concen-
tric will in the human being, and that with which the Supreme loves himself,
as all in all."   " Never," he concludes, " has a great man been so hardly and
inequitably treated by posterity as Spinoza: no allowances made for the prev-
alence, nay universality, of dogmatism and the mechanic system in his age;
no trial, except in Germany, to adopt the glorious truths into the family of
Life and Power. What if we treated Bacon with the same harshness! "
    One other note on the same subject (appended to Epist. XXXVI.) is so char-
acteristic, and in so beautiful a spirit, that it ought to be transcribed: —
    " The truth is, Spinoza, in common with all the metaphysicians before him
(Böhme perhaps excepted), began at the wrong end, commencing with God as
an object. Had he, though still dogmatizing *objectively*, begun with the *natura
naturans* in its simplest terms, he must have proceeded on ' per intelligentiam '
to the subjective, and having reached the other pole = idealism, or the ' I,' he
would have reprogressed to the equatorial point, or the identity of subject
and object, and would thus have arrived finally not only at the clear idea of
God, as absolute Being, the ground of all existents (for so far he did reach, and
to charge him with atheism is a gross calumny), but likewise at the faith in
the living God, who hath the ground of his own existence in himself.   That
this would have been the result, had he lived a few years longer, I think his
Epist. LXXII. authorizes us to believe; and of so pure a soul, so righteous a
spirit as Spinoza, I dare not doubt that this *potential* fact is received by the
Eternal as actual.
    In the epistle here referred to, Spinoza expresses his intention, should his
life be spared, of defining more clearly his ideas concerning " the eternal and
infinite Essence in relation to extension," which he thought Des Cartes had
wrongly taken as the definition of Matter.   J. J. T.

Q

he added : "His philosophy is nevertheless false. Spinoza's system has been demonstrated to be false, but only by that philosophy which has demonstrated the falsehood of all other philosophies. Did philosophy commence with an *it is*, instead of an *I am*, Spinoza would be altogether true." And without allowing a breathing-time, Coleridge parenthetically asserted : "I, however, believe in all the doctrines of Christianity, even the Trinity." A. Robinson afterwards observed, "Coleridge has a comprehensive faith and love." Contrary to my expectation, however, he was pleased with these outbursts, rather than offended by them. They impressed him with the poet's sincerity. Coleridge informs me that his tragedy is accepted at Drury Lane. Whitbread * admires it exceedingly, and Arnold, the manager, is confident of its success. Coleridge says he is now about to compose lectures, which are to be the produce of all his talent and power, on education. Each lecture is to be delivered in a state in which it may be sent to the press.

October 10th. — Dined at the Hall. A chatty party. It is said that Lady —— invited H. Twiss to dinner, and requested him to introduce an amusing friend or two. He thought of the authors of the "Rejected Addresses," and invited James Smith and his brother to come in the evening of a day on which he himself was to dine with her ladyship. Smith wrote, in answer, that he was flattered by the polite invitation, but it happened unluckily that both he and his brother had a prior engagement at Bartholomew Fair, — he to eat fire, and his brother to swallow two hundred yards of ribbon.

October 22d. — Heard W. Huntington preach, the man who puts S. S. (sinner saved) after his name.† He has an admirable exterior ; his voice is clear and melodious ; his manner singularly easy, and even graceful. There was no violence, no bluster, yet there was no want of earnestness or strength. His language was very figurative, the images being taken from the ordinary business of life, and especially from the army and navy. He is very colloquial, and has a wonderful biblical memory ; indeed, he is said to know the whole Bible by heart.

---

* Mr. S. Whitbread, M. P., was a proprietor of shares in Drury Lane Theatre, and through friendship for Sheridan took an active part in its affairs.
† He thus explained his adoption of these mysterious letters. "M. A. is out of my reach for want of learning, D. D. I cannot attain for want of cash, but S. S. I adopt, by which I mean sinner saved." His portrait is in the National Portrait Gallery. He commenced his own epitaph thus: "Here lies the coal-heaver, beloved of God, but abhorred of men." He died at Tunbridge Wells in 1813. His published works extend to twenty volumes.

I noticed that, though he was frequent in his citations, and always added chapter and verse, he never opened the little book he had in his hand. He is said to resemble Robert Robinson of Cambridge. There was nothing shrewd or original in the sermon to-day, but there was hardly any impropriety. I detected but a single one : Huntington said : " Take my word for it, my friends, they who act in this way will not be beloved by God, or by *anybody else.*"

December 15th. — Hamond mentioned that recently, when he was on the Grand Jury, and they visited Newgate Prison, he proposed inquiring of Cobbett whether he had anything to complain of.* Cobbett answered, " Nothing but the being here." Hamond said, the reverent bows his fellow-jurymen made to Cobbett were quite ludicrous.

December 20th, Sunday. — A large family party at the Bischoff's, of which not the least agreeable circumstance was, that there was a family religious service. There is something most interesting and amiable in family devotional exercise, when, as in this instance, there is nothing austere or ostentatious. Indeed everything almost that is done by a family, as such, is good. Religion assumes a forbidding aspect only when it is mingled with impure feelings, as party animosity, malignant intolerance, and contempt.

December 23d. — Saw " Bombastes Furioso " and " Midas." In both Liston was less funny than usual. Is it that he has grown fatter ? Droll persons should be very fat or very thin. Mathews is not good as the king in " Bombastes." He is excellent chiefly as a mimic, or where rapidity of transition or volubility is required.

Rem.† — It was in the early part of this year that dear Mrs. Barbauld incurred great reproach by writing a poem entitled " 1811." It is in heroic rhyme, and prophesies that on some future day a traveller from the antipodes will from a broken arch of Blackfriars Bridge contemplate the ruins of St. Paul's ! ! This was written more in sorrow than in anger ; but there was a disheartening and even gloomy tone, which even I with all my love for her could not quite excuse. It provoked a very coarse review in the *Quarterly*, which many years afterwards Murray told me he was more ashamed of than any other article in the *Review.*

---

* In 1810 Cobbett was tried for publishing certain observations on the flogging of some militiamen at Ely. He was sentenced to pay a fine of £1,000, or be imprisoned for two years; he chose the latter.

† Written in 1849.

[During this year a misunderstanding arose between Coleridge and Wordsworth, to which as " all 's well that ends well," it is not improper to allude. The cause of the misunderstanding was the repetition to Coleridge, with exaggerations, of what, with a kindly intent, had been said respecting him by Wordsworth to a third person. C. Lamb thought a breach would inevitably take place, but Mr. Robinson determined to do all he could to prevent such a misfortune. Accordingly he set about the work of mediation, and he certainly did his part most thoroughly. Going repeatedly from one friend to the other, he was able to offer such explanations and to give such assurances that the ground of complaint was entirely removed, and the old cordiality was restored between two friends who, as he knew, loved and honored each other sincerely. In these interviews he was struck alike with the feeling and eloquence of the one, and the integrity, purity, and delicacy shown by the other. On the 11th of May he went to Coleridge's, and found Lamb with him. The assassination of Mr. Perceval had just taken place.* The news deeply affected them, and they could hardly talk of anything else ; but the Diary has this entry : " Coleridge said to me in a half-whisper, that Wordsworth's letter had been perfectly satisfactory, and that he had answered it immediately. I flatter myself, therefore, that my pains will not have been lost, and that through the interchange of statement, which but for me would probably never have been made, a reconciliation will have taken place most desirable and salutary." † — ED.]

CHAPTER XVI.

1813.

JANUARY 23d. — In the evening at Drury Lane, to see the first performance of Coleridge's tragedy, " Remorse." ‡

* See *ante*, p. 246.

† The Diary contains many details on this subject; but it has not been thought necessary to give them a place in these selections.

‡ Coleridge had complained to me of the way in which Sheridan spoke in company of his tragedy. He told me that Sheridan had said that in the original copy there was in the famous cave scene this line : —

" Drip! drip! drip! There 's nothing here but dripping."

However, there was every disposition to do justice to it on the stage, nor were the public unfavorably disposed towards it.

I sat with Amyot, the Hamonds, Godwins, &c. My interest *for* the play was greater than *in* the play, and my anxiety for its success took from me the feeling of a mere spectator. I have no hesitation in saying that its poetical is far greater than its dramatic merit, that it owes its success rather to its faults than to its beauties, and that it will have for its less meritorious qualities applause which is really due to its excellences. Coleridge's great fault is that he indulges before the public in those metaphysical and philosophical speculations which are becoming only in solitude or with select minds. His two principal characters are philosophers of Coleridge's own school ; the one a sentimental moralist, the other a sophisticated villain, — both are dreamers. Two experiments made by Alvez on his return, the one on his mistress by relating a dream, and the other when he tries to kindle remorse in the breast of Ordonio, are too fine-spun to be intelligible. However, in spite of these faults, of the improbability of the action, of the clumsy contrivance with the picture, and the too ornate and poetic diction throughout, the tragedy was received with great and almost unmixed applause, and was announced for repetition without any opposition.

January 26th. — Heard Coleridge's concluding lecture. He was received with three rounds of applause on entering the room, and very loudly applauded during the lecture and at its close. That Coleridge should ever become a popular man would at one time have been thought a very vain hope. It depends on himself ; and if he would make a sacrifice of some peculiarities of taste (his enemies assert that he has made many on essential points of religion and politics), he has talents to command success. His political opinions will suit a large portion of the public ; and, though not yet a favorite with the million, the appreciation of his genius is spreading.

February 2d. — I went with Aders to see Coleridge, who spoke to my German friend of Goethe with more warmth than usual. He said that if he seemed to depreciate Goethe it was because he compared him with the greatest of poets. He thought Goethe had, from a sort of caprice, underrated the talent which in his youth he had so eminently displayed in his "Werter," — that of exhibiting man in a state of exalted sensibility. In after life he delighted in representing objects of pure beauty, not objects of desire and passion, — rather as statues or paintings, — therefore he called Goethe *picturesque.* Coleridge accused Schlegel of one-sidedness in his excessive admiration of Shakespeare.

February 23d. — I underwent a sort of examination from Mr. Hollist, the Treasurer of the Middle Temple. He inquired at what University I had been educated, and this caused me to state that I was a Dissenter, and had studied at Jena. This form being ended, all impediments to my being called to the bar next term are cleared away.

This day a Mr. Talfourd called with a letter from Mr. Rutt ; he is going to study the law, and wants information from me concerning economical arrangements ; he has been for some time Dr. Valpy's head boy, and wishes, for a few years, to occupy himself by giving instruction or otherwise, so as to be no encumbrance to his father, who has a large family. He is a very promising young man indeed, has great powers of conversation and public speaking, not without the faults of his age, but with so much apparent vigor of mind, that I am greatly mistaken if he do not become a distinguished man.

February 24th. — Attended a conference in the vestry of the Gravel Pit Meeting, Mr. Aspland presiding. The subject was " Infant Baptism." Young Talfourd spoke in a very spirited manner, but in too oratorical a tone.* We walked from Hackney together ; his youthful animation and eagerness excited my envy. It fell from him accidentally, that a volume of poems, written by him when at school, had been printed, but that he was ashamed of them.

Rem.† — Talfourd combined great industry with great vivacity of intellect. He had a marvellous flow of florid language both in conversation and speech-making. His father being unable to maintain him in his profession, he had to support himself, which he did most honorably. He went into the chambers of Chitty, the great special pleader, as a pupil ; but he submitted, for a consideration, to drudgery which would be thought hardly compatible with such lively faculties, and at variance with his dramatic and poetic taste. These, too, he made to a certain extent matters of business. He connected himself with magazines, and became the theatrical critic for several of them. He thereby contracted a style of flashy writing, which offended severe judges, who drew in consequence unfavorable conclusions which have not been realized. He wrote pamphlets, which were printed in the *Pamphleteer,* published by his friend Valpy. Among these was a very

---

* In his early life Mr. Talfourd was a Dissenter, and occasionally took part in the conferences held in the vestry at the Gravel Pit Meeting, Hackney, to discuss religious subjects.

† Written in 1847.

vehement eulogy of Wordsworth. He became intimate with Lamb, who introduced him to Wordsworth. It was in these words: "Mr. Wordsworth, I introduce to you Mr. Talfourd, *my only admirer.*" That he became in after life the executor of Lamb and his biographer is well known. Among his early intimacies was that with the family of Mr. Rutt, to whose eldest daughter, Rachel, he became attached. After a time Talfourd came to me with the request that I would procure for him employment as a reporter for the *Times*, that he might be enabled to marry. This I did, and no one could fill the office more honorably, as was acknowledged by his associates on the Oxford Circuit. He made known at once at the bar mess what he was invited to do. Others had done the same thing on other circuits secretly and most dishonorably. Consent was given by the bar of his circuit; and in this way, as a writer for papers and magazines, and by his regular professional emoluments, he honorably brought up a numerous family. As his practice increased he gradually gave up writing for the critical press, and also his office of reporting. But when he renounced literature for emolument, he carried it on for fame, and became a dramatic writer. His first tragedy, " Ion," earned general applause, and in defiance of the advice of prudent or timid friends he produced two other tragedies.* He did not acquire equal reputation for these; probably a fortunate circumstance, as literary fame is no recommendation either to an Attorney or to a Minister who seeks for a laborious Solicitor-General. It was after he was known as a dramatist that Talfourd † obtained a seat in Parliament, where he distinguished himself by introducing a bill in favor of a copyright for authors, to which he was urged mainly by Wordsworth, who had become his friend. *His* bill, however, did not pass, and the work was taken out of his hands. The act ‡ which at length passed the legislature did not grant as much as Talfourd asked for. The one act which ought to be known by his name was one conferring on unhappy wives, separated from their husbands, a right to have a sight of their children.

---

* " Ion " was produced at Covent Garden Theatre in May, 1836. The principal character, first performed by Macready, was afterwards undertaken by Miss Ellen Tree. Talfourd's second tragedy, " The Athenian Captive," in which Macready played Thoas, was produced at the Haymarket, 1838. The third and least successful was " Glencoe," first represented at the Haymarket, May 23, 1840. Macready again played the hero. — G. S.

† Talfourd was Member for Reading, where he had been a pupil at the Grammar School, under Dr. Valpy.

‡ This is always, however, spoken of as Talfourd's Act.

Talfourd soon acquired popularity at the bar, from the mere faculty of speaking, as many have done who were after all not qualified for heavy work. I might have doubted of the Sergeant's qualifications in this respect, but some years ago I heard the late Lord Chief Justice Tindal praise him highly for judgment and skill in the management of business. He said he was altogether a successful advocate. No man got more verdicts, and no man more deserved to get them. Talfourd is a generous and kind-hearted man. To men of letters and artists in distress, such as Leigh Hunt, Haydon, &c., he was always very liberal. He did not forget his early friends, and at the large parties he has hitherto delighted to give, poets, players, authors of every kind, were to be seen, together with barristers, and now and then judges.

February 26th. — Went to the Royal Academy and heard Sir John Soane deliver his third lecture on Architecture; it was not very interesting, but the conclusion was diverting. " As the grammarian has his positive, comparative, and superlative, and as we say, ' My King, my Country, and my God,' so ought the lover of fine art to say, Painting, Sculpture, Architecture ! ! ! "

March 18th. — Went to Covent Garden. Saw "Love for Love." * Mathews, by admirable acting, gave to Foresight a significance and truth strikingly contrasted with the unmeaning insipidity of most of the other characters. Mrs. Jordan played Miss Prue, and certainly with great spirit. She looked well, but her voice has lost much of its sweetness and melody; yet she is still the most fascinating creature on the stage. She also took the part of Nell in "The Devil to Pay"; in this her acting was truly admirable. Her age and bulk do not interfere with any requisite in the character.

April 5th. — With Walter, who introduced me to Croly, his dramatic critic, who is about to go to Hamburg to discharge the duty I performed six years before. Croly is a fierce-looking Irishman, very lively in conversation, and certainly has considerable talent as a writer; his eloquence, like his person, is rather energetic than elegant, and though he has great power and concentration of thought, he wants the delicacy and dis-

---

* Congreve's animated comedy of " Love for Love " was produced under Betterton at Lincoln's Inn Fields in 1695. The part of Ben was written for Doggett. Mrs. Abington was celebrated for her performance of Miss Prue, and the excellence of the play was especially manifest when performed by a powerful company under Mr. Macready's management at Drury Lane Theatre, in 1843. — G. S.

crimination of judgment which are the finest qualities in a critic.*

April 9th. — Accompanied Andrews † to the House of Lords, to hear Lord Wellesley's speech on East Indian affairs. I was very much disappointed, for I discerned in the speech (evidently a prepared and elaborate one) not one of the great qualities of an orator or statesman. His person is small, and his animation has in it nothing of dignity and weighty energy. He put himself into a sort of artificial passion, and was in a state of cold inflammation. He began with a parade of first principles, and made a fuss about general ideas, which were, I thought, after all very commonplace. Yet the speech had excited curiosity, and brought a great number of members of the House of Commons behind the Throne. But after listening for an hour and a half my patience was exhausted, and I came home.

April 15th. — A useful morning at the King's Bench, Guildhall. My friend John Buck ‡ was examined as a witness in a special jury insurance cause. Garrow rose to cross-examine him. "You have been many years at Lloyd's, Mr. Buck?" — "Seventeen years." Garrow sat down, but cross-examined at great length another witness. Lord Ellenborough, in his summing up, said: "You will have remarked that Mr. Attorney did not think it advisable to ask Mr. Buck a single question. Now on that gentleman's testimony everything turns, for if you think that his statement is correct —" Before he could complete the sentence the foreman said: "For the plaintiff, my Lord." — "I thought as much," said the Chief Justice.

May 8th. — In the evening went to the Temple, where I learned that I had been called to the bar. The assurance of the fact, though I had no reason to doubt it, gave me pleasure.

Rem. § — I have frequently asserted, since my retirement, that the two wisest acts of my life were my going to the bar when, according to the usual age at which men begin practice, I was already an old man, being thirty-eight, and my retiring from the bar when, according to the same ordinary usage, I was still a young man, viz. fifty-three.

---

* Croly's career has been a singular one. He tried his hand as a contributor to the daily press in various ways. He wrote tragedies, comedies, and novels, — at least one of each; and at last settled down as a preacher, with the rank of Doctor, but of what faculty I do not know. — H. C. R., 1847.

† Afterwards Sergeant Andrews.

‡ See *ante*, p. 19.   § Written in 1847

H. C. R. to T. R.

MY DEAR THOMAS : —

.... Before I notice the more interesting subject of your letter, I will dismiss the history of yesterday in a few words, just to satisfy your curiosity. At four o'clock precisely I entered the Middle Temple Hall *in pontificalibus,* where the oaths of allegiance and abjuration were administered to me. I then dined, dressed as I was, at a table apart. I had five friends with me. After dinner we ascended the elevation at the end of the Hall. My friends and acquaintance gradually joined our party. We were just a score in number. I believe you are acquainted with none of them but the Colliers, Amyot, Andrews, and Quayle. The rest were professional men. After drinking about six bottles of humble port, claret was brought in, and we broke up at ten. What we had been doing in the mean while I shall be better able to tell when I have received the butler's bill. I cannot say that it was a day of much enjoyment to me. I am told, and indeed I felt, that I was quite nervous when I took the oaths. And I had moments of very serious reflection even while the bottle was circulating, and I was affecting the boon companion. One incident, however, did serve to raise my spirits. On my coming home, just before dinner, I found with your letter the copy of an Act of Parliament which Wedd Nash had left. He had nominated me Auditor in a private Inclosure Act, and the fee, he informed Mrs. Collier, would be ten guineas. The timing of this my first professional emolument does credit to Nash's friendliness and delicacy.

June 13th. — Went to Mrs. Barbauld's. Had a pleasant chat with her about Madame de Staël, the Edgeworths, &c. The latter are staying in London, and the daughter gains the good-will of every one; not so the father. They dined at Sotheby's. After dinner Mr. Edgeworth was sitting next Mrs. Siddons, Sam Rogers being on the other side of her. " Madam," said he, " I think I saw you perform Millamont thirty-five years ago." — " Pardon me, sir." — " O, then it was forty years ago ; I distinctly recollect it." — " You will excuse me, sir, I never played Millamont." — O, yes, ma'am, I recollect." — " I think," she said, turning to Mr. Rogers, " it is time for me to change my place "; and she rose with her own peculiar dignity.*

June 24th. — A *Dies non*, and therefore a holiday. Called on Madame de Staël at Brunet's. She received me very civilly, and I promise myself much pleasure from her society during the year she intends remaining in England. I intimated to her that I was become a man of business, and she will be satisfied with my attending her evening parties after nine o'clock. Her son is a very genteel young man, almost handsome, but with something of a sleepy air in his eye, and the tone of his conversation a whisper which may be courtly, but gives an appearance of apathy. The daughter I scarcely saw, but she seems to be plain.

July 6th. — Went to a supper-party at Rough's, given in honor of the new Sergeant, Copley. Burrell, the Pordens, Flaxmans, Tooke, &c. there.

Rem.† — This was the first step in that career of success which distinguished the ex-chancellor, now called the *venerable* Lord Lyndhurst.

July 11th. — Called this morning on Madame de Staël at 3 George Street, Hanover Square. It is singular that, having in Germany assisted her as a student of philosophy, I should now render her service as a lawyer. Murray the bookseller was with her, and I assisted in drawing up the agreement for her forthcoming work on Germany, for which she is to receive 1,500 guineas.

July 14th. — Going into the country for the summer, I quitted the house and family of the Colliers, in which I had lived as an inmate for years with great pleasure. I am to return, though only as a visitor, in the autumn, after my first experience of law practice on the circuit and at the sessions.

July 18th. — My first dinner with the bar mess, at the Angel Inn at Bury, where I took my seat as junior on the Sessions Circuit. Our party consisted of Hunt, Hart, Storks,‡ Whitbread, and Twiss. I enjoyed the afternoon. Hunt is a gentlemanly man, Hart an excellent companion. Storks was agreeable, and Whitbread has a pleasing countenance.

Rem.§ — Hart was in every way the most remarkable man

---

* This anecdote is given with a difference in the Reminiscences and the Diary. In the latter, the dinner-party is said to have been at Lord Lonsdale's, and the person to whom Mrs. Siddons turned on leaving her seat, Tom Moore.
† Written in 1847.
‡ Afterwards Sergeant Storks.
§ Written in 1847.

of our circuit. He was originally a preacher among the Calvinistic Baptists, among whom he had the reputation of being at the same time so good a preacher and so bad a liver that it was said to him once, " Mr. Hart, when I hear' you in the pulpit, I wish you were never out of it ; when I see you out of it, I wish you were never in it." He married a lady, the heir in tail after the death of her father, Sir John Thorold, to a large estate.

At the death of Sir John, Hart left his profession. When I saw him a couple of years after, he had taken the name of Thorold ; and then he told me that he never knew what were the miseries of poverty until he came into the possession of an entailed estate, — all his creditors came upon him at once, and he was involved in perpetual quarrels with his family. His wretchedness led to a complete change in his habits, and he became in his old age again a preacher. He built a chapel on his estate at his own expense, and preached voluntarily to those who partook of his enthusiasm, and could relish popular declamations of ultra-Calvinism.

August 20th. — (At Norwich.) I defended a man for the murder of his wife and her sister by poison. It was a case of circumstantial evidence. There was a moral certainty that the man had put corrosive sublimate into a tea-kettle, though no evidence so satisfactory as his Tyburn countenance. I believe the acquittal in this case was owing to this circumstance. The wife, expecting to die, said, " No one but my husband *could* have done it." As this produced an effect, I cross-examined minutely as to the proximity of other cottages, — there being children about, — the door being on the latch, &c. ; and then concluded with an earnest question : " On your solemn oath, were there not twelve persons at least who *could* have done it ? " — " Yes, there were." And then an assenting nod from a juryman. I went home, not triumphant. But the accident of being the successful defender of a man accused of murder brought me forward, and though my fees at two assize towns did not amount to £ 50, yet my spirits were raised.

Rem.* — Sergeant Blosset (formerly Peckwell) was, taking him for all in all, the individual whose memory I respect the most of my departed associates on the circuit. He was a quiet unpretending man, with gentlemanly, even graceful manners, and though neither an orator nor a man of eminent

* Written in 1847.

learning or remarkable acuteness, yet far beyond every other man on our circuit. He had the skill to advocate a bad cause well, without advocating that which was bad in the cause,— which greater men than he were sometimes unable to do. Hence he was a universal favorite.

My immediate senior on the circuit was Henry Cooper. He was very far my superior in talent for business, — indeed in some respects he was an extraordinary man. His memory, his cleverness, were striking ; but so was his want of judgment, and it often happened that his clever and amusing hits told as much against as for his client. One day he was entertaining the whole court, when Rolfe (now the Baron, then almost the junior) * whispered to me : " How clever that is ! How I thank God I am not so clever ! "

I once saw Cooper extort a laugh from Lord Ellenborough in spite of himself. " But it is said my client got drunk. Why, everybody gets drunk." Then, changing his voice from a shrill tone to a half-whisper, and with a low bow, he added : " Always excepting your Lordships and the Bishops."

October 18th. — Dined with Madame de Staël, — a party of liberals at her house, viz. : Lady Mackintosh, Robert Adair the diplomatist, Godwin, Curran, and Murray, &c.

Our hostess spoke freely of Buonaparte. She was introduced to him when a victorious general in Italy ; even then he affected princely airs, and spoke as if it mattered not what he said, — he conferred honor by saying anything. He had a pleasure in being rude. He said to her, after her writings were known, that he did not think women ought to write books. She answered : " It is not every woman who can gain distinction by an alliance with a General Buonaparte." Buonaparte said to Madame de Condorcet, the widow of the philosopher, who was a great female politician, and really a woman of talent : " I do not like women who meddle with politics." Madame de Condorcet instantly replied : " Ah, mon Général, as long as you men take a fancy to cut off our heads now and then, we are interested in knowing why you do it."

On one occasion Buonaparte said to a party of ladies : " Faites moi des conscrits."

Our hostess asserted that every political topic could be exhausted in one hour's speech ; but, when pressed, it was evident that by exhausting a subject she understood uttering all the possible generalities and commonplaces it involves. She

---

* Afterwards Lord Chancellor Cranworth.

praised Erskine's speeches. Curran, who listened, held his tongue; he said but one thing on the subject of oratory, and that was in praise of Fox, who he said was the most honest and candid of speakers, and spoke only to convince fairly. "It seemed to me," said Curran, "as if he were addressing himself to me personally." Adair praised Sheridan highly in the *past* tense, but said he injured himself by an injudicious imitation of Burke in his speech before the lords on the impeachment of Hastings. Sheridan was praised for his faculty of abstracting his mind from all other things and working up a subject.

Curran, who is in his best moments a delightful companion, told some merry stories, at which our hostess exclaimed, "Ah, que cela est charmant!" He was, however, also melancholy, and said he never went to bed in Ireland without wishing not to rise again. He spoke of the other world and those he should wish to see there. Madame de Staël said that after she had seen those she loved (this with a sentimental sigh), she should inquire for Adam and Eve, and ask how they were born. During a light conversation about the living and the dead, Lady Mackintosh exclaimed: "After all, the truth of it seems to be that the sinners have the best of it in this world, and the saints in the next." Curran declared "Paradise Lost" to be the worst poem in the language. Milton was incapable of a delicate or tender sentiment towards woman. Curran did not render these heresies palatable by either originality or pleasantry. Godwin defended Milton with zeal, and even for his submission to Cromwell, who, he said, though a usurper, was not a tyrant, nor cruel. This was said in opposition to Madame de Staël, who was not pleased with the philosopher. She said to Lady Mackintosh, after he was gone: "I am glad I have seen this man, — it is curious to see how naturally Jacobins become the advocates of tyrants; so it is in France now." Lady Mackintosh apologized for him in a gentle tone; "he had been harshly treated, and almost driven out of society; he was living in retirement." The others spoke kindly of him.

November 1st. — After a short visit to Anthony Robinson, came to chambers and slept for the first time in my own bed. I felt a little uncomfortable at the reflection of my solitude, but also some satisfaction at the thought that I was at least independent and at home. I have not yet collected around me all that even I deem comforts, but I shall find my wants

very few, I believe, if I except those arising from the desire
to appear respectable, not to say wealthy, in the eyes of the
world.

November 12th. — In the evening a party at Anthony Robinson's. The Lambs were there, and Charles seemed to enjoy
himself. We played cards, and at the close of the evening he
dryly said to Mrs. Robinson: "I have enjoyed the evening
much, which I do not often do at people's houses."

November 15th. — Called on Madame de Staël, to whom I
had some civil things to say about her book, which she received
with less than an author's usual self-complacence; but she
manifested no readiness to correct some palpable omissions and
mistakes I began pointing out to her. And when I suggested
that, in her account of Goethe's "Triumph" (der Empfind-
samkeit), she had mistaken the plot, she said: "Perhaps I
thought it better as I stated it!"

She confessed that in her selection of books to notice she
was guided by A. W. Schlegel; otherwise, she added, a whole
life would not have been sufficient to collect such information.
This confession was not necessary for me. She says she is
about to write a book on the French Revolution and on the
state of England, in which she means to show that all the
calamities which have arisen in France proceeded from not
following the English constitution. She says she has a number of questions to put to me concerning the English law, and
which she is to reduce to writing. We talked on politics. She
still thinks that unless Buonaparte fall he will find means to
retrieve his fortune. Perhaps she is still influenced by *French*
sentiments in conceiving that Buonaparte must be victorious
at last if he persist in the war. But she is nevertheless a
bigoted admirer of our government, which she considers to be
perfect!

COLERIDGE TO H. C. R.

Monday Morning, December 7, 1812.

Excuse me for again repeating my request to you, to use
your best means *as speedily as possible* to procure for me (if
possible) the perusal of Goethe's work on Light and Color.*
In a thing I have now on hand it would be of *very important
service to me;* at the same time do not forget Jacobi to Fichte,†

---

* "Goethe's Theory of Colors. Translated from the German; with Notes
by Charles Lock Eastlake, R. A., F. R. S." London, 1840.
† Jacobi's "Sendschreiben an Fichte."

and whatever other work may have bearings on the Neuere, neueste, und allerneueste Filosofie. It is my hope and purpose to devote a certain portion of my time for the next twelve months to theatrical attempts, and chiefly to the melodrama, or *comic opera* kind ; and from Goethe (from what I read of his little Singspiele in the volume which you lent me) I expect no trifling assistance, especially in the songs, airs, &c., and the happy mode of introducing them. In my frequent conversations with W. (a composer and music-seller), I could not find that he or the music-sellers in general had any knowledge of those compositions, which are so deservedly dear to the German public. As soon as I can disembarrass myself, I shall make one sturdy effort to understand music myself, so far at least of the *science* as goes to the composition of a simple air. For I seem frequently to form such in my own mind, to my inner ear. When you write to Bury, do not forget to assure Mrs. Clarkson of my never altered and unalterable esteem and affection.

S. T. COLERIDGE.

December 30th. — After dinner a rubber at Lamb's ; then went with Lamb and Burney to Rickman's. Hazlitt there. Cards, as usual, were our amusement. Lamb was in a pleasant mood. Rickman produced one of Chatterton's forgeries. In one manuscript there were seventeen different kinds of e's. " O," said Lamb, " that must have been written by one of the

Mob of gentlemen who write with ease."

December 31st. — Spent the evening at Flaxman's. A New Year's party. It consisted only of the Pordens, some of Mrs. Flaxman's family, and one or two others. We were comfortable enough without being outrageously merry. Flaxman, of all the great men I ever knew, plays the child with the most grace. He is infinitely amiable, without losing any of his respectability. It is obvious that his is the relaxation of a superior mind, without, however, any of the ostentation of condescension. We stayed late, and the New Year found us enjoying ourselves.

CHAPTER XVII.

1814.

JANUARY 2d. — Read lately the first volume of "John
Buncle."* It contains but little that is readable, but that
little is very pleasing. The preachments are to be skipped
over, but the hearty descriptions of character are very interesting from the *love* with which they are penned. Lamb says,
with his usual felicity, that the book is written *in better spirits*
than any book he knows.† Amory's descriptions are in a
high style ; his scene-painting is of the first order ; and it is
the whimsical mixture of romantic scenery, millennium-hall
society, and dry disputation in a quaint style, which gives this
book so strange and amusing a character. For instance, John
Buncle meets a lady in a sort of Rosamond's bower studying
Hebrew. He is smitten with her charms, declares his love to
"glorious Miss Noel," and when, on account of so slight an acquaintance, — that of an hour, — she repels him (for his love
had been kindled only by a desperately learned speech of hers
on the paradisiacal language), and threatens to leave him, he exclaims, " O, I should die were you to leave me ; therefore, if
you please, we will discourse of the miracle of Babel." And
then follows a long dialogue on the confusion of tongues, in
which "illustrious Miss Noel" bears a distinguished part.

March 7th. — At Drury Lane, and saw Kean for the first
time. He played Richard, I believe, better than any man I
ever saw ; yet my expectations were pitched too high, and I
had not the pleasure I expected. The expression of malignant
joy is the one in which he surpasses all men I have ever seen.
And his most flagrant defect is want of dignity. His face is
finely expressive, though his mouth is not handsome, and he
projects his lower lip ungracefully ; yet it is finely suited to

* The "Life of John Buncle, Esq.; containing various Observations and
Reflections made in several Parts of the World, and many extraordinary Relations." By Thomas Amory. Hollis, 1766. Two vols.
  † " John (says Leigh Hunt) is a kind of innocent Henry the Eighth of private life, without the other's fat, fury, and solemnity. He is a prodigous hand
at matrimony, at divinity, at a song, at a loud ' hem,' and at a turkey and
chine."
  In No. 10 of Leigh Hunt's *London Journal* (June 4, 1834), there is an abstract
of " John Buncle."

Richard. He gratified my eye more than my ear. His action very often was that of Kemble, and this was not the worst of his performance ; but it detracts from his boasted originality. His declamation is very unpleasant, but my ear may in time be reconciled to it, as the palate is to new cheese and tea. It often reminds me of Blanchard's. His speech is not fluent, and his words and syllables are too distinctly separated. His finest scene was with Lady Anne, and his mode of lifting up her veil to watch her countenance was exquisite. The concluding scene was unequal to my expectation, though the fencing was elegant, and his sudden death-fall was shockingly real. But he should have lain still. Why does he rise, or awake rather, to repeat the spurious lines? He did not often excite a strong persuasion of the truth of his acting, and the applause he received was not very great. Mrs. Glover had infinitely more in the pathetic scene in which she, as Queen Elizabeth, parts from her children. To recur to Kean, I do not think he will retain all his popularity, but he may learn to deserve it better, though I think he will never be qualified for heroic parts. He wants a commanding figure and a powerful voice. His greatest excellences are a fine pantomimic face and remarkable agility.

March 26th. — I read Stephens's " Life of Horne Tooke." All the anecdotes respecting him, as well as his letters, are excellent. They raise a favorable impression of his integrity, and yet this stubborn integrity was blended with so impassioned a hatred, that it is difficult to apportion the praise and reproach which his admirers and enemies, with perhaps equal injustice, heap upon him.

April 10th. — Went early to the coffee-room. To-day it was fully confirmed that Buonaparte had voluntarily abdicated the thrones of France and Italy, and thus at once, as by the stroke of an enchanter's wand, the revolutionary government of France, after tormenting the world for nearly twenty-five years, has quietly yielded up its breath.

April 12th. — Again at the coffee-room in the morning, though now the public papers must of necessity decline in interest. There must follow the winding up of accounts, and there may arise disputes in the appropriation of territory and in the fixing of constitutions ; but no serious obstacle in the way of peace is to be apprehended. My wish is that means could be found, without violating the honor of the allies, to break the treaty so imprudently made with that arch-knave

Murat. Bernadotte ought to retain his crown, but I should be glad to see Norway succeed in emancipating herself from his dominion, so unworthily obtained. Saxony ought to revert to the house which lost it during the wars produced by the Reformation, and the Duke of Weimar deserves to succeed to his ancestors. Poland has no chance of regaining her independence, and perhaps would not be able to make use of it. Russia will descend deeper into Europe than I can contemplate without anxiety, notwithstanding the actual merits of her Emperor. Prussia I wish to see mistress of all Protestant Germany; and it would give me joy to see the rest of Germany swallowed up by Austria; but this will not be. The Empire will, I fear, be restored, and with it the foundation laid for future wars of intrigue. France will resume her influence over Europe; and this is the one evil I apprehend from the restoration of the Bourbons, — that the jealousy which ought to survive against France, as France, will sleep in the ashes of the Napoleon dynasty. Such are my wishes, hopes, fears, and expectations.

The counter-revolution in France has not gratified our vanity. It comes like a blessing of Providence or a gift of nature, and these are received with quiet gratitude. Hence the want of enthusiasm in the public mind, although the general sentiment is joy. Cobbett and Sir Richard Phillips* alone express sorrow, and the *Morning Chronicle* betrays an unpatriotic spirit. Of my own personal acquaintance, only Will Hazlitt and poor Capel Lofft are among the malecontents.

May 7th. — Took tea at Flaxman's. He spoke highly of the great variety of talents possessed by Lawrence. On occasion of the contest for the professorship of painting between Opie and Fuseli, Flaxman says, Lawrence made an extempore speech in support of Fuseli better than any speech he (Flaxman) ever heard. " But," said Flaxman, " Lawrence's powers are almost his ruin. He is ever in company. One person admires his singing, another his reading, another his conversational talents, and he is overwhelmed with engagements. I have heard Hazlitt say, " No good talker will ever labor enough to become a good painter."

May 15th. — Called on the Colliers. I am glad to feel that there is a return of cordiality which had been on the decline between me and these old friends. There is so much positive pleasure in every kindly feeling, that certainly it is not wisdom

* The author and bookseller. He was editor and proprietor of the *Monthly Magazine*, and was the compiler of many popular volumes.

to criticise whether it is justified. Friendship, more assuredly than virtue, is its own reward. Lamb and his sister were there, and expressed great kindness towards me, which gave me much pleasure. They are, indeed, among the very best of persons. Their moral qualities are as distinguished as their intellectual.

May 19th. — I accompanied Anthony and Mrs. Robinson to Drury Lane to see Kean play Othello. The long trial of waiting before the door having been endured, the gratification was very great. Of all the characters in which I have yet seen Kean, Othello is the one for which by nature he is the least qualified; yet it is the one in which he has most delighted me. Kean has little grace or beauty in mere oratorical declamation, but in the bursts of passion he surpasses any male actor I ever saw. His delivery of the speech in which he says, " Othello's occupation 's gone," was as pathetic as a lover's farewell to his mistress. I could hardly keep from crying; it was pure feeling. In the same scene the expression of rage is inimitable.

May 26th. — Dined with Mr. George Young.* A large party. Present were Dr. Spurzheim, now the lion of the day, as the apostle of craniology, — ten years ago he was the famulus of the discoverer Gall; Mason Good, poet, lecturer, and surgeon; Drs. Gooch and Parke; my friend Hamond; Charles Young, the rival of Kean at Covent Garden, and another brother of our host; Ayton, an attorney; and Westall, the R. A. Spurzheim appeared to advantage as the opponent of Mason Good, who was wordy, and I thought opposed close intellectual reasoning by a profusion of technicalities. Spurzheim preached from the skulls of several of us, and was tolerably successful in his guesses, though not with me, for he gave me theosophy, and tried to make a philosopher of me. To Hamond he gave the organs of circumspection and the love of children. To Charles Young that of representation, but he probably knew he was an actor.

May 27th. — The forenoon at the Old Bailey Sessions. Walked back with Stephen.† He related that Romilly thinks Lord Eldon one of the profoundest and most learned lawyers who ever lived; yet he considers his infirmity as a practical doubter so fatal, that he infinitely prefers Erskine as a Chan-

---

* An eminent surgeon, of whom more hereafter.

† The emancipationist. He was brother-in-law to Wilberforce, and the father of the late Sir James Stephen, the Professor of History.

cellor. Though his mind and legal habits are of so different a class, his good sense and power of prompt decision enable him to administer justice usefully.

June 18th. — This was a high festival in the City, the corporation giving a superb entertainment to the Prince Regent and his visitors, the Emperor of Russia, King of Prussia, &c. Took a hasty dinner at Collier's, and then witnessed the procession from Fleet Street. It was not a gratifying spectacle, for there was no continuity in the scene ; but some of the distinct objects were interesting. The Royal carriages were splendid, but my ignorance of the individuals who filled them prevented my having much pleasure. My friend Mrs. W. Pattisson brought her boys to see the sight, and she did wisely, for she has enriched their memories with recollections which time will exalt to great value. It will in their old age be a subject of great pleasure that at the ages of eleven and ten they beheld the persons of the greatest sovereigns of the time, and witnessed the festivities consequent on the peace which *fixed* (may it prove so !) the independence and repose of Europe.

June 21st. — Again in the King's Bench. The sentence of the pillory was passed against Lord Cochrane and others for a fraud to raise the price of stock by spreading false news. The severity of the sentence has turned public opinion in favor of his Lordship, and they who first commiserated him began afterwards to think him innocent. His appearance to-day was certainly pitiable. When the sentence was passed he stood without color in his face, his eye staring and without expression ; and when he left the court it was with difficulty, as if he were stupefied.*

June 29th. — Called on Lamb in the evening. Found him as delighted as a child with a garret he had appropriated and adorned with all the copper-plate engravings he could collect, having rifled every book he possesses for the purpose. It was pleasant to observe his innocent delight. Schiller says all great men have a childlikeness in their nature.

---

* Lord Dundonald, in a note to an extract from Campbell's " Lives of the Chief Justices," where it is mentioned that he was sentenced to stand in the pillory, says : —

" This vindictive sentence the government did not dare carry out. My high-minded colleague, Sir Francis Burdett, told the government that, if the sentence was carried into effect, he would stand in the pillory beside me, when they must look to the consequences. What these might have been, in the then excited state of the public mind, as regarded my treatment, the reader may guess." — *The Autobiography of a Seaman.* By Thomas, Tenth Earl of Dundonald, G. C. B. Second edition. London, 1861. Vol. II. p. 322, note.

July 3d. — A day of great pleasure. Charles Lamb and I walked to Enfield by Southgate, after an early breakfast in his chambers. We were most hospitably received by Anthony Robinson and his wife. After tea, Lamb and I returned. The whole day most delightfully fine, and the scenery very agreeable. Lamb cared for the walk more than the scenery, for the enjoyment of which he seems to have no great susceptibility. His great delight, even in preference to a country walk, is a stroll in London. The shops and the busy streets, such as Thames Street, Bankside, &c., are his great favorites. He, for the same reason, has no great relish for landscape painting. But his relish for historic painting is exquisite. Lamb's peculiarities are very interesting. We had not much conversation, — he hummed tunes, I repeated Wordsworth's "Daffodils," of which I am become very fond. Lamb praised T. Warton's "Sonnet in Dugdale" as of first-rate excellence.* It is a good thought, but I find nothing exquisite in it. He praised Prior's courtly poems, — his "Down Hall," — his fine application of the names of Marlborough, so as to be offensive in the ears of Boileau.

July 4th. — Took early tea with Flaxman, to whom I read an admirable criticism by Hazlitt on West's picture of the "Rejection of Christ." A bitter and severe but most excellent performance. Flaxman was constrained to admit the high talent of the criticism, though he was unaffectedly pained by its severity ; but he was himself offended by West's attempt to represent this sacred subject.

July 6th. — Dr. Tiarks † breakfasted with me, and we spent an hour and a half very pleasantly. Tiarks says that he understands Buonaparte said to the Austrian commissioner, "The King of Saxony is the honestest king in Europe. If the allies dethrone him, they will do a more tyrannical act than I ever did. I have dethroned many kings in my time, but I was a parvenu, and it was necessary for my safety. The old legitimate sovereigns should act on other principles."

July 29th. — Mr. Wakefield called on me with Jeremy Bentham's "Panopticon," and he occupied me till one o'clock.

---

* This Sonnet was "Written in a Blank Leaf of Dugdale's ' Monasticon.' "

† A Frieslander by birth, he became a candidate in theology at Göttingen, but had notice that he had been drawn as a conscript, and would be seized as such. Flying from the army, he begged his way to England, where he maintained himself first as a private librarian to Sir Joseph Banks, and afterwards, with considerable success, as a teacher of German, Greek, and mathematics. — H. C. R.

Wakefield belongs to Jeremy Bentham's select society. He is voted *nobody*, i. e. free of the house. He gives an interesting account of the philosopher's abode, where a Panopticon school is to be erected. Bentham's constant inmates are Koe, whom I have seen, and Mill, whom I dined with at Hamond's, and whom Wakefield represents as one of the greatest men of the present day. He is writing a history of India. Wakefield says that Bentham has considerable respect for Hamond's understanding.

July 31st. — Read Bentham's "Panopticon" and first Appendix. All that respected the moral economy of his plan interested me greatly, but for want of plates I could not comprehend the mechanical structure. The book is (as all Bentham's are) full of original and very valuable matter. But it would possibly have had more effect if it had contained fewer novelties in substance and in language. Men are prepared to oppose when novelty is ostentatiously announced.

August 13th. — (At Norwich.) Accompanied some friends to the theatre. The actors did not edify me. Stole out to call on Madge, at whose apartments I found the great new poem of Wordsworth, "The Excursion." I could only look into the preface and read a few extracts with Madge. It is a poem of formidable size, and I fear too mystical to be popular. It will, however, put an end to the sneers of those who consider, or affect to consider, him puerile. But it will possibly draw on him the imputation of dulness. Still, I trust it will strengthen the zeal of his few friends. My anxiety is great to read it.

August 18th. — Tiarks brought Kastner to me. Kastner is an enthusiast, but his enthusiasm impels to action, and it is accompanied by talent of very high rank and great variety. Having distinguished himself as a chemist, he became Volksredner (orator for the people) ; and he is now striving to interest the government in favor of freemasonry, in order to oppose priestcraft, which he thinks is reviving. He also conducted a newspaper, and assisted in raising the Prussian Landwehr. Having fought with this body in France, he came to England to solicit a grant out of the contributions for the Germans in favor of the Landwehr. Though every one thought his attempts vain, he has succeeded in obtaining £ 1,000, and hopes for much more, out of the Parliamentary grant.

H. C. R. TO MRS. PATTISSON.

BURY ST. EDMUNDS, July 27, 1814.

MY DEAR FRIEND, — Though my own plans were in some measure disarranged by it, I was sincerely glad to hear that you had resolved to undertake the northern journey. I trust it has proved to you a source of other pleasures than those for the sake of which you made it. The reward which Solomon received for a wise choice of the blessings of life I have very frequently seen conferred on a small scale. . . . . I should be very glad if some accident were to bring you acquainted with any of the Stansfelds. That is so highly estimable a family, that I could almost consider myself the *friend* of every member of it, meaning only to express my very peculiar esteem for them. . . . .

I have just risen from the perusal of the most admirable discourse on friendship which I believe was ever penned. It is a sort of sermon without a text by Jeremy Taylor ; so delightful that, if I had no other means of conveying it to you, I think I could almost walk to Witham from Bury with the folio volume containing it in my hand, in order to have the delight of reading it to you. Though it is arrant pedantry to fill a letter with quotations, I cannot resist the temptation of quoting two or three golden sayings.

Soame Jenyns, you may recollect, vindicates Christianity for excluding from its system those *false virtues*, patriotism, valor, and friendship ! ! ! This very insidious paradox — in effect, not intention, I mean — is as to friendship, with equal truth and beauty, thus exhibited by Jeremy Taylor : " By friendship you mean the greatest love, the greatest usefulness, and the most open communication, and the noblest sufferings, and the severest truth, and the heartiest counsel, and the greatest union of minds, of which brave men and women are capable. But then I must tell you that Christianity hath new christened it, and called it charity. . . . . Christian charity is friendship to all the world. And when friendships were the noblest things in the world " (referring, I suspect, to Cicero, &c.), " charity was little like the sun drawn in at a chink, or his beams drawn into the centre of a burning-glass ; but Christian charity is friendship expanded, like the face of the sun when it mounts the eastern hills." Still, the individual appropriation of love was to be explained ; he therefore goes on : " There is enough in every man that is willing to make him become our friend, but where men contract friendships they enclose the commons, and what nature intended should be every man's, we make proper to two or three." In these lines are contained all the ideas necessary to a development of friendship speculatively. The following sentences are gems : " He that does a base thing in zeal for his friend burns the golden thread that ties their hearts together." " Secrecy is the chastity of friendship." " Friendship is charity in society."

If I can, I will take a *bait* at Witham on my way from Norwich to London ; but I do not know that I can stay even a day with you. One circumstance may call me to town earlier than I might otherwise have thought necessary. I have received some letters from a most amiable and worthy man, a Jena acquaintance, who has made a journey to London, in order to solicit relief for a particular class of sufferers, — the Prussian Landwehr. He seems to expect great assistance from me, and it will be a painful task to me to show him that I can do nothing. He is a benevolent Quixote. He has written me an account of his life, and his sufferings and pathetic tale will interest you. He is made up of love of every kind, — to his wife and children, to his country, for which he fought, and to religion, to which he seems devotedly attached. I wrote to Aders to offer Kastner my chambers during my absence ; but Aders has procured him a lodging at six shillings a week. Kastner has luckily met with my friends in town.

You will expect to hear of the success of my Sessions Circuit. It was not so productive as I expected, from the retirement of Twiss, but this was more from the want of business than from the preference of others before me. At Norwich and Bury, I had more than my reasonable share of business. At Bury, not even Alderson held a brief, or had a motion ; the very little was divided between Storks and myself, I taking a third. However, my individual success is great, though the decline of professional business in general is enough to alarm a man now entering into it. Lawyers have had their day !

Your affectionate Friend,
H. C. ROBINSON.

*Rem.** — During my fifteen years at the bar, I relieved myself from the dulness of a London professional life by annual excursions, of all of which I kept Journals. In collecting reminiscences from them, I shall for the most part omit de-

* Written in 1850.

scriptions of places, and confine myself to the persons I saw. The present journey in France immediately followed that great event, the restoration of the French monarchy, after twenty-five years of revolution.

August 26th. — Arrived at Rouen in the evening, and heard that Mademoiselle Duchesnois was to perform. Tired and even hungry as I was, I instantly set out for the theatre, and went into the pit, which had no seats, and where the audience was very low. The play was the "Hamlet," not of Shakespeare but of Ducis, and therefore the first impression was a very mixed one. On my entrance Duchesnois, as Queen, was relating to her confidante the history of her two marriages. So much I could understand, and that was all; and this annoyed me. Then the actress herself was really ugly. But, in spite of all this, such is the power of real talent, that in a very short time I caught myself violently applauding. Of the actress's declamation I was no judge, but of course it was good, as the French are inexorable on this point. I could, however, feel the truthfulness of her expression of passion. Her tones were pathetic. Yet there must be something conventional in such things. Of the other actors I have nothing to say; nor of the play, but that it is truly French. The unities are preserved, and Hamlet is victorious. No more need be said. But what was more remarkable than the play was the display of national feeling. At Dieppe, indeed, the children had shouted after us in the street, "Allez vous en"; and in the scene in which Shakespeare has but a poor joke about the English being mad, Ducis has substituted a line of grave reproach, —

> "L'Angleterre fut toujours dans les crimes féconde."

On this the fellows who were next me all turned their faces towards me and clapped lustily. I may mention that, after dinner, as I was walking, I stopped to talk with a peasant, who laid down his tool and jumped over a ditch to chat with me. He was a strong anti-revolutionist. The good king, he said, must take care to disband his army, or he would never be safe. The army are friendly to the Emperor, their opinions about him having a great deal of a *professional* character.

August 29th. — I went by the lower road to Paris in a diligence through St. Germains, &c., and arrived at Paris the next day; and an accident led me at once to a decent hotel in the

Rue Montmartre. Fortunately for me, Mr. Clarkson is here, hoping by personal intercourse with the Emperor of Russia, Duke of Wellington, &c., to obtain some stringent measures to enforce the abolition of the slave-trade. Mrs. Clarkson is with him.

September 1st. — I walked with John Thelwall and his party to the famous Château or prison of Vincennes, being introduced to the governor by the curate. We afterwards dined at a restaurant and walked back. As we reached the *barrière*, Thelwall discovered that he had lost his purse, containing about twenty napoleons. He recollected taking it out of his pocket to pay for the dinner. We all returned with him to the hotel ; the house was shut. On knocking, a chamber window was opened, and we heard a female voice exclaim, " Ah ! ce sont Messieurs les Anglais, pour la bourse ! " The maid and her mistress came down together ; the former, who had found the purse on the table, had it in her hand, with an expression of great joy at being able to restore it ; and she received Thelwall's present very becomingly.

September 2d. — I accompanied Mr. and Mrs. Clarkson to the library of the institution at the Quatre Nations, where I was introduced to the celebrated ex-Bishop of Blois, Grégoire, leader of the society of the *Amis des Noirs*, which made him the close ally of Clarkson.

*Rem.** — I acquired the privilege of calling on Grégoire on my future visits to Paris, and generally availed myself of it. The impression he made on me to-day was not removed by the disgrace cast on him afterwards. He seemed to me to be a kind-hearted, benevolent man, with no great strength of understanding, and somewhat of a *petit-maître* in his habits.

September 4th. — I accompanied the Thelwall party to the Louvre, and thence to the house of David, who was there the exhibitor of his own paintings. Whether it was because I knew him to have been the friend of Robespierre, and a member of the Revolutionary tribunal, or not, I cannot say, but his countenance seemed to me to express ferocity. It was deformed by a harelip.

September 7th. — The consecration of the colors of the National Guard, at which attended the King and all the authorities of Paris, was of course not to be neglected. The applause given to the King was faint. From a few there were loud cries. One voice was remarkable, and I recognized it on several days.

* Written in 1850.

September 8th. — I had the satisfaction of recognizing Talleyrand from his resemblance to the engravings of him. The expression of his countenance as he passed was, I thought, that of a voluptuary and a courtier, rather than that of a politician and man of business. He spoke to his coachman in an arrogant tone. His thin legs and sorry figure below the waist hardly justify the term *cripple;* but I looked for and perceived the club-foot, to remove all doubt as to his identity. I fancy I can judge better of Talleyrand's character from having had a glimpse of his person.

September 9th. — My brother was with me at the Théâtre Français, and I was amused by being asked twice whether he was not " le grand tragique Kemble, — celui qui joue les premières rôles à Londres." The inquirers seemed to disbelieve my denial.

September 10th and 11th. — These days were distinguished by my being in the company of one of the most remarkable men of the French Revolution, General La Fayette. By no means one of the ablest or greatest, but I believe, in intention at least, one of the best ; and one who has been placed in positions both of danger and of show at critical moments beyond every other individual. Of all the revolutionary leaders, he is the one of whom I think most favorably ; and my favorable impression was enhanced by what I heard from him. I was with Mr. Clarkson when La Fayette called on him, and I was greatly surprised at his appearance. I expected to see an infirm old man, on whose countenance I should trace the marks of suffering from long imprisonment and cruel treatment. I saw a hale man with a florid complexion, and no signs of age about him. In fact, he is fifty-seven years old, his reddish complexion clear, his body inclining to be stout. His tone of conversation is staid, and he has not the vivacity commonly ascribed to Frenchmen. There is apparently nothing enthusiastic about him.

The slave-trade was the subject which brought the General and Clarkson together, and it engrossed, I thought, too much of the conversation. La Fayette confirmed Clarkson's opinion, that the Emperor of Russia was perfectly sincere and even zealous in the wish which he expressed at Madame de Staël's, in opposition to the Portuguese Minister, to secure the abolition of the slave-trade. He also gave credit to Talleyrand for his sincerity in the same wish ; " But certainly," said La Fayette, " he is not an *enthusiast* in anything." Among the subjects of reproach against Buonaparte was his restoration of slavery; and La Fayette imputed to him an artifice by which he had made it appear that La Fayette had sold slaves.   He had purchased an estate in order to assist the abolition, and when slavery was abolished by law, he sold the estate, and the notary put the word *slaves* into the contract.   La Fayette refused to sign unless the word was erased.   " But," said the notary, " if there are none, the word has no effect, and no one can tell what may happen."   La Fayette inferred from this that the scheme to restore slavery was formed, which did soon take place.   And though he had done all he could by law to declare these slaves free, they were made slaves at last.

I was particularly desirous of hearing from La Fayette himself some account of the relation in which he stood towards Buonaparte, and of knowing his opinion of the Emperor.   In this I was gratified.   He related that, after enduring a severe imprisonment of three years in an Austrian dungeon,* on which he seemed unwilling to enlarge, he was at last set at liberty because the French Directory refused to discuss the terms of the treaty at Leoben until he and his friends were released.   Buonaparte was one of the commissioners in making that treaty, and he executed his orders with firmness.   La Fayette went at first to Hamburg, and would not proceed at once to Paris, because a declaration was required of him which he could not make.   At the time of the negotiations about him the revolution of Fructidor took place, when two of the Directory were sent to Cayenne.   " Now," said La Fayette, " I was called upon to make such an acknowledgment as would give all the credit of my release to those remaining in power. This I refused."   This would have given the men then in power all the *éclat* of his deliverance.   But on the revolution which made Buonaparte First Consul, he went to Paris without a passport.   He had scarcely arrived when he was waited upon by — I doubt whether Duroc or Caulaincourt, who said that the First Consul wished him to return to Hamburg secretly, in order that he might show his high esteem for him by calling him back in a formal manner.   " I saw through the trick," said La Fayette, " and would not be a party to it.   I therefore said that I had come back because I had a right, being a Frenchman who had committed no crime ; that if the chief magistrate commanded me to go I would obey.   I was told that the First Consul meant only to do me honor.   Though

* In the fortress of Olmutz in Moravia.

I had defeated his scheme of doing an act of ostentatious display, he received me with politeness ; and for a time I was deceived, but not long, and I never concealed my opinion of him. I saw him eight or ten times on business, and at a fête given by Joseph Buonaparte on the peace between France and America (for the Directory had made a war as foolish as your present war with America) we had some conversation. He assured me that his designs were all in favor of liberty, and that whatever might appear to be otherwise would be only temporary expedients. I answered that it was the *direction* (tendency) of some of his actions that I disapproved of more than of the actions themselves. On another occasion Buonaparte said to me, ' You see the French are tired of liberty.' I answered, ' They are tired of licentiousness, and what they have suffered from the abuse of liberty makes them more anxious to have real liberty, and more fit to enjoy it ; and this, Citizen First Consul, the French expect from you.' Buonaparte turned away, but in a few minutes came back and talked on indifferent subjects. After this I retired into the country, and took no share in public business. Buonaparte afterwards tried to involve me in some sham plot, but my entire seclusion rendered that impossible. When Buonaparte returned from Russia he made a speech, in which he spoke of the antimonarchical principles of the first authors of the Revolution, which made them impede the measures of the government, alluding to, but not naming, me."

I have pleasure in writing down these recollections of La Fayette's words, because they are distinct, and because they disprove what has been falsely asserted by the partisans of Buonaparte, that La Fayette was reconciled to him.

Of the future, La Fayette spoke with a hope which it gratified me to hear, and he spoke respectfully of the royal family then restored. On general subjects I have a few notes worth abridging. He asserted that the manners of the French, especially the lower classes, had been improved by the Revolution ; that the mob of France were less violent than an English mob ; and the common people he thought more honest. This he ascribed to the Revolution.

La Fayette is a strong partisan of America, as opposed to England. He is strongly opposed to our maritime claims, and thinks we might concede these in return for the renunciation of the slave-trade by other powers.

On my relating that, at the distribution of the colors, I

heard some exclamations of "Vive l'Empereur," La Fayette said : "You are not to suppose that this proceeded from love to Buonaparte. It was only a mode of showing dissatisfaction with the present state of things, and because it would not do to cry 'A bas le roi,' or 'A bas les ministères.'"

Of Spanish America he said that Jefferson was of opinion that those states would ultimately become independent, but that this would rather retard than advance civilization.

*Rem.** — I visited the residence of Josephine at Malmaison, which has left a more distinct impression on my mind than the other regal palaces of the capital. One picture there impressed me so strongly that I have never forgotten it. Of the artistic merits I know nothing. It was a prison scene. A man in chains has drawn with chalk a figure of the Virgin and Child, which the other prisoners are worshipping; that is, they are kneeling, — all except one wretch who is in despair, the officers of justice having come to take him to the gallows.†

I read also in my Journal a name which brings to my recollection a fact omitted in the Journal itself. The name is Count St. Maurice, an elegant cavalier, an emigrant and high-toned royalist, also a warm abolitionist. One day, when I was present, Clarkson saying that he was going to see La Fayette and Grégoire, the Count, in a plaintive rather than reproachful tone, said, "My dear sir, I wish you did not see so much of those people." Clarkson replied, very gravely : "Monsieur le Comte, you forget that, now that I am at Paris, I know but two classes of persons, — the friends and the enemies of Africa. All the friends of Africa are my friends, whatever they may be besides. You and Monsieur La Fayette are the same in my eyes." St. Maurice smiled and said, "I believe you are in the right."

September 22d. — I was in the grand gallery at the Louvre when I heard some one say, "Mrs. Siddons is below." I instantly left the Raphaels and Titians, and went in search of her, and my Journal says : "I am almost ashamed to confess that the sight of her gave me a delight beyond almost any I have received in Paris." I had never seen her so near. She was

---

* Written in 1850.

† "Stella drawing a Picture of the Virgin and Child on his Prison Wall." Painted by Granet, at Rome, in 1810. The picture was purchased by the Empress, and was afterwards transported to Munich. It now forms part of the Leuchtenberg Collection, No. 245, and has been engraved by Muxel. Stella, on his arrival in Rome, was arrested, but soon after found innocent and liberated. So late as the end of the eighteenth century, this sketch of the Madonna was shown to travellers in Rome. — G. S.

walking with Horace Twiss's mother. I kept as near her as I could with decorum, and without appearing to be watching her; yet there was something about her that disturbed me. So glorious a head ought not to have been covered with a small chip hat. She knit her brows, too, on looking at the pictures, as if to assist a failing sight. But I recognized her fascinating smile with delight, though there was a line or two about her mouth which I thought coarse.

September 23d. — At the Jardin des Plantes with E. Hamond's friend, R——, and we spent great part of the day together. I believe it was not on this, but some other day, when R—— said, "I will call for you to-morrow," I answered, "I will thank you not to call. I would rather not see anything else with you, and I will tell you frankly why. I am come to Paris to enjoy myself, and that enjoyment needs the accompaniment of sympathy with others. Now, you dislike everything, and find fault with everything. You see nothing which you do not find inferior to what you have seen before. This may be all very true, but it makes me very uncomfortable. I believe, if I were forced to live with you, I should kill myself. So I shall be glad to see you in London, but no more in Paris."

*Rem.** — I several times attended French Courts of Justice, and heard both arguments before judges and trials in criminal cases before juries. I have no remark to make on the arguments, for I never understood them sufficiently; and, indeed, I very imperfectly understood the examination of witnesses; but I did understand enough to enable me to come to this conclusion, that if I were guilty, I should wish to be tried in England, — if innocent, in France. Making this remark once to Southey, he changed the expression, and said: "The English system seems to have for its object that no innocent person should be unjustly found guilty, — the French system, that no criminal should escape." Now, if it be the fact that of the accused by far the greater number are guilty, it will follow that injustice is more frequent in the English than in the French courts.

It is customary for the admirer of English law to boast of that feature of it which prohibits all attempts to make the prisoner convict himself, as if the state represented in the court had not a right to the truth, and as if a man who had violated the law were privileged through the violation. This

* Written in 1850.

surely betrays want of discrimination. It is right that no violence should be used to compel an answer, because that may as often produce falsehood as truth, — nor is any used in the French courts ; but the prisoner is interrogated as well as the prosecutor and witnesses, and the same means are used to detect falsehood in all. If he refuse to answer, he is made to understand the unfavorable inferences that will be drawn. And this interrogation taking place before the public, no great injustice can be done. On this point I entirely approve of the French practice.

In another material respect, the practice of the English and the French courts is different. In the French courts, the facts being already known by preliminary proceedings, the prisoners are heard, and then the witnesses are called. Their hearing begins with " Contez à la cour les faits," — relate the facts to the court, — and then questions follow. This is done in presence of the prisoner, who, if he interrupts, is not silenced or reproved, as he would be in England. I once heard a French prisoner exclaim, " You lie ! " An English judge would be in danger of falling into fits at such an outrage. The French President very quietly and even courteously said, " In what does the lie consist ? " And the answer being given, he went on, " But you yourself said so and so." And afterwards he said, " But if this is a lie, was that a lie too " (stating something else the witness had said) " which you did not contradict ? " In a few minutes the prisoner had involved himself in contradictions which proved his guilt. Who can blame this ? Publicity is unquestionably necessary to secure this practice from abuse, and there may be parts of the preliminary proceedings which, if I were acquainted with them, I might disapprove of. I write only of what I witnessed.

There is always an advocate (Procureur du Roi) who represents the Crown, and who gives his judgment as between the prosecutor and the accused ; and he retires with the judges.*

Rem.† — One other particular struck me at once, and I have urged on English lawyers the propriety of its adoption in our courts, — but never with effect, I fear. The prisoner does not *stand*, but has a little box to himself, with a desk and papers. A soldier, as guard, sits with him. And this box is so placed that he can communicate with his counsel. Our law says

* My impression respecting the French courts, as compared with the English, has been confirmed by later visits to them. — H. C. R.

† Written in 1850.

the accused are to be presumed to be innocent until they are proved guilty; and yet on their trial they are degraded by being forced to stand, unless they consent to urge a falsehood, as that they are ill. On application, they are always allowed to sit.

On September 28th I went to the Théâtre Français, to see the greatest of the French comedians. I abstain from writing of the French theatre, as I do of the public buildings, the galleries of paintings, &c., but I may make exceptions. One is in favor of a great theatrical name, Fleury, whom I have seen several times. He was already aged and near the end of his career, yet he appeared to me to be perfect in a certain class of comic characters. Genteel comedy and aged characters were his department. One *rôle* made a lasting impression. In the "Ecole des Bourgeois," he played a Marquis who is driven to project a *mésalliance* to recruit his finances; but a blunder of his servant defeats his plan. He delivers to the vulgar family a letter which is written to the Marquis's friend, the Duke. It begins, "Enfin, ce soir je m'encanaille." The opening of this letter, and the repetition of the words by every one of the party was excellent, especially the spelling of the word *encanaille* by the servant. In the midst of a family of *enragés*, the Marquis makes his appearance. The gay impudence with which he met their rage reminded me of a similar character by Iffland. Though I could not relish French tragedy, I thought the comedy perfection, — and I still think so. Our best comedians are gross caricaturists in comparison. The harmonious keeping and uniformly respectable acting at the Théâtre Français, even in the absence of their *stars*, are what give the French stage its superiority over the English. Yet the Français had ceased to be popular. The little Boulevard theatres were crowded, while the Français was empty. Two admirable low comedians I enjoyed this year at the Porte St. Martin, — Brunet and Pothier. But I did not this time see the two greatest French performers, Talma and Mademoiselle Mars.

September 29th. — A call on Madame de Staël. She expressed herself strongly in favor of the abolition of the slave-trade, though she was not sanguine of success. She was in Geneva when I arrived in Paris, and regretted that the Clarksons left before her return. From her house, the Château de Clichy, I walked to St. Denis, and on the way met with an adventure. I overtook a French soldier: he had a sunburnt face and a

somewhat ruffianly appearance. As I came up to him, he
startled me by running up and putting his hands on my
shoulders : he said in a loud voice, but with a smiling face
which at once removed all fear of violence : " Ah ! vous êtes
Anglais : que je vous aime ! si je n'avais que deux sous, vous
en auriez un. Mais si vous étiez Espagnol, je vous égorgerois."
And then he shook me as if to show me that he would execute
his threat. Before he had explained himself I guessed the
fact, and having disengaged myself from his unwelcome embrace, I had a regular conversation with him, and in vain tried
to reason with him. He told me that, when in Spain, he was
taken prisoner and *beaten* by the Spaniards. They would have
killed him, he said, but the "*braves*" English rescued him out
of their hands. This was the burden of his song. He exhibited his wounds, — they were shocking, — and he seemed
to be capable of no feelings but gratitude and revenge. I said :
" You call me a good man ; if I had by chance been born in
Spain, I should have been what I am now ; I could not help
it." — " Tant pis pour vous — I would kill you." — " But why ?
you meet with good people and bad people everywhere."—" Non,
pas en Espagne." — " What, kill me, when I have done nothing
to you." — " Si ce n'était pas vous, c'était votre frère ; si ce
n'était pas votre frère, c'était votre cousin — c'est la même
chose. On ne peut pas trouver l'individu — c'est impossible."
To strengthen my moral arguments, I treated him with a
bottle of wine at an inn on the road.

October 4th. — A dinner at Madame de Staël's, where I had
an opportunity of renewing my slight acquaintance with Benjamin Constant and William Schlegel. Constant praised
highly the " Dichtung und Wahrheit," which our hostess does
not like, — how should she ? The *naïveté* of the confessions and
sacrifice of dignity to truth were opposed to all the convention-
alities to which she was accustomed. Asking Schlegel for an
explanation of the title " Dichtung und Wahrheit," he said :
" I suppose it is used merely as an apology, if taxed with anything." This was the poorest thing he said. Schlegel asserted
that Tieck was sincere in his profession of Catholicism. Fichte,
he said, was aware before his death that he had survived his
fame. Schlegel spoke of Rogers as the only poet of the *old*
school ; the modern English poets having taken a direction
like that of the Germans, though without any connection between them. In answer to my inquiries, he said that a
national spirit was rising in Germany ; but he talked with

reserve on politics.   Of Arndt, he said that he had not a clear head, but that he had been of use by exciting a sentiment of nationality.

October 5th. — At the Louvre for the last time.   There I met Miss Curran, Dawe, and Chantrey.   A remark by the latter struck me, and I made a note of it.   " The ancients," he said, " worked with a knowledge of the place where the statue was to be, and anticipated the light to which it would be exposed. If it were to be in the open air, they often introduced folds in the drapery, for the sake of producing a shade."   He pointed out to us the bad effect of light from two windows falling on a column.

October 8th. — After a five weeks' residence, without a moment's ennui, I left Paris without a moment's regret.   D—— was my companion.   He was famous for his meanness and love of money, which I turned to account.   We went the first day in the cabriolet of a diligence to Amiens, where we spent the night.   The next day we proceeded towards the coast.   I found that there was only one seat in the cabriolet on this occasion, price 32 *fr.*, 40 *fr.* being charged for the interior ; on which I said to D—— : " Now, we must travel on fair terms.   The best place, in fact, is the cheapest, and I don't think it fair that one man should have both advantages ; therefore I propose that whoever has the cabriolet shall pay 40 *fr.*"   He consented ; I gave him his choice, and it was amusing to see the eagerness with which he chose the interior.

My arrangement turned out well, for I had the company of a very sensible, well-informed clergyman, Dr. Coplestone, and we ran a round of literary and political topics.   We travelled all night, and breakfasted at Boulogne.   It was in the morning that we all walked up a hill to relieve our limbs, when I saw the Doctor talking to a stranger ; and referring to him, I said afterwards, " Your friend." — " He is no friend of mine," said Coplestone, angrily ; " he is a vulgar, ignorant man ; I do not know what he is ; I thought he was an auctioneer at first ; then I took him for a tailor : he may be anything."   I heard afterwards from D—— that this stranger had been very annoying in the coach, by talking on every subject very ill. When we came to breakfast he addressed his conversation to me, and having used the word *peccadillo*, he asked me whether I had ever been in Spain, to which I made no answer.   He went on : " Peccadillo is a Spanish word ; it means a little sin ; it is a compound of two words, — pecca, little, and dillo, sin."

I happened to catch Coplestone's eye, and, encouraging each other, we both laid down our knives and forks and roared out-right.*

My first Continental trip, after my call to the bar, has afforded me great pleasure, without at all indisposing me to go on with my trial of the bar, as a profession. I left my friends in Germany, but in France I have not formed a single acquaintance which is likely to ripen into friendship. A singular fact, because I believe the character of my own mind has much more of the French than of the German in it.

October 14th. — Received a call from Tiarks, for whom I had purchased some books. Kastner, I learned, is still in London. His endeavors to obtain money for the Prussians have been successful, and he is in good spirits about his own affairs. He hopes to have an appointment on the Rhine ; and he believes a University will be formed at Bonn.

October 23d. — Walked from Cambridge to Bury. During the greater part of the time I was reading Schlegel " Ueber die Sprache und Weisheit der Indier." The book on language I could not follow or relish, but the second book on Indian philosophy I found very interesting, and far more intelligible than the other philosophical writings of the author. He treats of the leading doctrines of the Indian philosophers, and represents them as forming epochs in Indian history. The notions concerning the *Emanation* from the divine mind are connected with the doctrine of the pre-existence and transmigration of the soul. These ideas were followed by the worship of nature and its power, out of which sprung the tasteful and various mythology of the Greeks. The doctrine of *two principles* is treated by Schlegel with more respect than I expected, and that which followed it, and came out of it, — *Pantheism*, — with far less. He asserts of Pantheism what I have long felt to be equally true of Schelling's *Absolute*, that it is destructive of all moral impressions, and productive merely of indifference to good and evil. This little book is an admirable hortative to

* Coplestone published a collection of letters, &c., with a Memoir of Lord Dudley, my slight acquaintance at Corunna. On the appearance of this work an epigram was circulated, ascribed to Croker : —

> " Than the first martyr's, Dudley's fate
> Still harder must be owned,
> Stephen was only stoned to death,
> Ward has been Coplestoned."

Samuel Rogers has the credit of having written

> " Ward has no heart, they say, but I deny it,
> He has a heart, and gets his speeches by it." — H. C. R.

the study of Oriental literature. Schlegel regards the study of Indian philosophy as a powerful stimulus to the mind, to preserve it from the fatal consequences of modern scepticism and infidelity. It also, he thinks, facilitates the comprehension of the Bible.

October 27th. — In the forenoon I went for a few minutes into the fair. It made me melancholy. The sight of Bury Fair affects me like conversation about a deceased friend. Perhaps it would be more correct to say about a friend with whom all acquaintance has ceased. I have no pleasure whatever now in a scene which formerly gave me delight, and I am half grieved, half ashamed, to find myself or things so much altered. This is foolish, for why should the man retain the attachments of the boy? But every loss of youthful taste or pleasure is a partial death.

October 31st. — In the afternoon went to Flaxman's. Found Miss Flaxman alone. From her I learnt that, about six weeks ago, Mrs. Flaxman was seized with a paralytic stroke, which had deprived her of the use of her limbs on one side for a time, but from which she had since in a great measure recovered. She is now in Paris with Miss Denman, where she is able to walk. This seizure, though she may survive it many years, will sensibly affect her during her life. I should, indeed, have thought such a blow a sentence of death, with execution respited. But Anthony Robinson informs me that he had a paralytic stroke many years ago, from which he has suffered no evil consequences since. I observed, both to Miss Flaxman this day, and to Anthony Robinson the day after, that I had a presentiment I should myself at some time be attacked with paralysis or apoplexy. They treated this idea as a whim, but I have still the feeling ; for I frequently suffer from dizziness, and sometimes feel a tightness over my eyes and in my brain, which, if increased, would, I fancy, produce a paralytic affection. These apprehensions are, however, by no means painful. I am not acquainted with any mode of death which is less fearful in imagination.*

November 13th. — Dined with Mr. Porden, having invited myself thither. A Captain Stavely and Miss Flaxman were there, and afterwards Mr. Flaxman and a Mr. Gunn came. The evening was very pleasantly spent. We talked about Gothic architecture. Mr. Flaxman said he considered it but a

---

* This anticipation proved wholly groundless, though Mr. Robinson complained of occasional dizziness till his death.

degeneracy from the Roman. I observed that it was not enough to say that generally, it should be shown *how ;* that as the architects of the Middle Ages could not but have some knowledge of the ancient Roman works, of course this knowledge must have influenced their taste, but they might still have views of their own ; and certainly the later and purer Gothic did not pretend to the same objects. Flaxman did not object to this. He observed that Gothic, like other architecture, sprang out of the wants of the age, and was to be explained from the customs of the time. The narrow lancet windows were used when glass was little or not at all known, and when a cloth was put up. At this time there were no buttresses, for they were not rendered necessary. But when, glass being introduced, large windows followed, and thin walls were used, buttresses became necessary. It was casually observed this evening, that the Greeks had little acquaintance with the arch. Mr. Gunn observed that the first deviation from the Greek canon was the placing the arch *upon* instead of *between* the pillars.* The Greek architecture was adapted to wooden buildings : all the architectural ornaments consist of parts familiar to builders in wood. The arch was easier than the stone architraves, &c., for it might consist of small stones. Speaking of the Lombard columns, Mr. Flaxman said the old architects in the Middle Ages frequently cut up the ancient pillars. The circular corners to the pillars in our churches are frequently subsequent additions to the pillars to give them grace. Mr. Porden is of opinion that Gothic architecture has its origin in the East, and Mr. Flaxman seems also to favor this idea. Porden says the historic evidence is great, and the Spanish churches furnish the chain of communication. Flaxman derived the Norman zigzag from the incapacity of the workmen to produce the flower which was used by the Greeks and Romans. Speaking of ornaments, he said they were all significant among the Greeks : the pattern called the Grecian Key, for instance, was meant to represent the Labyrinth at Crete ; and so of a number of decorations which we use without discernment, but which had not lost their symbolic sense among the ancients. Mr. Gunn † I found almost

---

* In *Grecian* architecture the arch, as a principle of construction, is not to be found. It was known in the East, and has been met with in the foundations of the Egyptian Pyramids.

† I afterwards heard that Mr. Gunn, of Norfolk, a man of taste and a traveller, was the clergyman who married the Duke of Sussex to Lady Augusta Murray. This involved him in embarrassments, and was a bar to his future promotion. — H. C. R.

an intolerant enemy to the Gothic. He spoke of "extravagant deviation from good taste," &c., yet I made him confess that the Gothic, though further from the Greek than the Saxon, was far more beautiful, because it had acquired a consistency and character of its own.

November 14th. — Spent the forenoon in court. We were all much pleased by a manly and spirited reply of Brougham to Lord Ellenborough. A man convicted of a libel against Jesus Christ offered an affidavit in mitigation, which Lord Ellenborough at first refused to receive, on the ground that if the defendant were the author of the book, there was nothing by which he could swear. When Brougham rose to remark on this, Ellenborough said : " Mr. Brougham, if you are acquainted with this person's faith, you had better suggest some other sanction; you had better confer with him." Brougham said in reply : " It is very unpleasant to be thus mixed up with my client, of whom I know nothing but that I am his retained advocate. As a lawyer and a gentleman, I protest against such insinuations." This he repeated in a tone very impressive. Lord Ellenborough was evidently mortified, and said in a faint voice that no insinuation was intended.

November 17th. — After nine I went to Charles Lamb's, whose parties are now only once a month. I played a couple of rubbers pleasantly, and afterwards chatted with Hazlitt till one o'clock. He is become an Edinburgh Reviewer through the recommendation of Lady Mackintosh, who had sent to the *Champion* office to know the author of the articles on Institutions. Hazlitt sent those and other writings to Jeffrey, and has been in a very flattering manner enrolled in the corps. This has put him in good spirits, and he now again hopes that his talents will be appreciated and become a subsistence to him.

November 21st. — In the evening I stepped over to Lamb, and sat with him from ten to eleven. He was very chatty and pleasant. Pictures and poetry were the subjects of our talk. He thinks no description in " The Excursion " so good as the history of the country parson who had been a courtier. In this I agree with him. But he dislikes " The Magdalen," which he says would be as good in prose ; in which I do *not* agree with him.

November 23d. — This week I finished Wordsworth's poem. It has afforded me less intense pleasure on the whole, perhaps, than I had expected, but it will be a source of frequent gratification. The wisdom and high moral character of the work are beyond anything of the same kind with which I am acquainted, and the spirit of the poetry flags much less frequently than might be expected. There are passages which run heavily, tales which are prolix, and reasonings which are spun out, but in general the narratives are exquisitely tender. That of the courtier parson, who retains in solitude the feelings of high society, whose vigor of mind is unconquerable, and who, even after the death of his wife, appears able for a short time to bear up against desolation and wretchedness, by the powers of his native temperament, is most delightful. Among the discussions, that on Manufactories, in the eighth book, is admirably managed, and forms, in due subordination to the incomparable fourth book, one of the chief excellences of the poem. Wordsworth has succeeded better in light and elegant painting in this poem than in any other. His Hanoverian and Jacobite are very sweet pictures.

December 1st. — Went to Drury Lane Theatre, where my pleasure was less than I had expected. Kean is not an excellent Macbeth. Nature has denied him a heroic figure and a powerful voice. A mere faculty of exhibiting the stronger malignant passions is not enough for such a character. There is no commanding dignity in Kean, and without this one does not see how he could so easily overawe the Scottish nobility. His dagger scene pleased me less than Kemble's. He saw the dagger too soon, and without any preparatory pause. Kemble was admirable in the effect he gave to this very bold conception. In his eye you could see when he lost sight of the dagger. But in the scene in which he returns from the murder, Kean looks admirably. His death is also very grand. After receiving his death-wound he staggers and gives a feeble blow. After falling he crawls on the floor to reach again his sword, and dies as he touches it. This is no less excellent than his dying in Richard, but varied from it ; so that what is said of Cawdor in the play may be said of Kean, " Nothing in his life became him like the leaving it." In no other respect did he impress me beyond an ordinary actor.

December 7th. — Met Thomas Barnes at a party at Collier's, and chatted with him till late. He related that at Cambridge, having had lessons from a boxer, he gave himself airs, and meeting with a fellow sitting on a stile in a field, who did not make way for him as he expected, and as he thought due to a gownsman, he asked what he meant, and said he had a great mind to thrash him. "The man smiled," said Barnes, " put

13 *

his hand on my shoulder, and said, " Young man, I 'm Cribb."
I was delighted ; gave him my hand ; took him to my room,
where I had a wine-party, and he was the lion." Cribb was
at that time the Champion of England.

December 11th. — After reading at home from eight to ten I
called on Miss Lamb, and chatted with her. She was not unwell, but she had undergone great fatigue from writing an
article about needle-work, for the new *Ladies' British Magazine.*
She spoke of writing as a most painful occupation, which only
necessity could make her attempt. She has been learning
Latin merely to assist her in acquiring a correct style. Yet,
while she speaks of inability to write, what grace and talent
has she not manifested in " Mrs. Leicester's School," &c.

December 18th. — Finished Milner on " Ecclesiastical Architecture in England." He opposes Whittington's opinion that
Gothic architecture originated in the East, and that it attained
perfection in France before it did in England. Neither question interests me greatly ; what is truly curious and worthy of
remark is the progress of the mind in the cultivation of art.
All the arts of life are originally the produce of necessity ; and
it is not till the grosser wants of our nature are supplied that
we have leisure to detect a beauty in what was at first only a
relief. How each necessary part of a building became an
architectural ornament is shown by the theoretical writers on
ancient architecture. The same has not yet been done for
Gothic architecture ; and in this alone the study of modern art
is less interesting than that of the ancient. But still it
would be highly interesting to inquire how the architecture of
the moderns sprang out of the art of the ancients, and how
different climates, possibly, and certainly different countries,
supplied various elements in the delightful works of the Middle Ages. As to the books I have read, and the different the-
ories in each, I cannot appreciate them, because they appeal to
facts with which I am unacquainted, and each disputes the existence of what the others confidently maintain. For instance,
the writers are still at variance about what is surely capable
of being ascertained, viz. whether there be any real specimen
of the Gothic in Asia.

December 19th. — Took tea with the Flaxmans, and read to
them and Miss Vardel Coleridge's " Christabel," with which
they were all delighted, Flaxman more than I expected. I
also read some passages out of " The Excursion." Flaxman
took umbrage at some mystical expressions in the fragment in

the Preface, in which Wordsworth talks of *seeing Jehovah unalarmed.** "If my brother had written that," said Flaxman, "I should say, 'Burn it.'" But he admitted that Wordsworth could not mean anything impious in it. Indeed I was unable, and am still, to explain the passage. And Lamb's explanation is unsatisfactory, viz. that there are deeper sufferings in the mind of man than in any imagined hell. If Wordsworth means that all notions about the personality of God, as well as the locality of hell, are but attempts to individualize notions concerning Mind, he will be much more of a metaphysical philosopher *nach deutscher Art*, than I had any conception of. And yet this otherwise glorious and magnificent fragment tends thitherwards, as far as I can discern any tendency in it.

December 20th. — Late in the evening Lamb called, to sit with me while he smoked his pipe. I had called on him late last night, and he seemed absurdly grateful for the visit. He wanted society, being alone. I abstained from inquiring after his sister, and trust he will appreciate the motive.

December 23d. — Saw Miss O'Neil in Isabella. She was, as Amyot well said, "a hugging actress." Sensibility shown in grief and fondness was her forte, — her only talent. She is praised for her death scenes, but they are the very opposite of Kean's, of which I have spoken. In Kean, you see the ruling passion strong in death, — that is, the passion of the individual. Miss O'Neil exhibits the sufferings that are common to all who are in pain. To imitate death closely is disgusting.

December 25th. — I called on George Brentano, and was greatly interested by his account of his family, and especially of my former friend, his brother Christian. During the last ten years Christian has been managing the estates of his family in Bohemia, where, says his brother, he has been practising a number of whimsical absurdities. Among other economical projects, he conceived the plan of driving a number of sheep into a barn and forcing them, by flogging, &c., to tread the grain, instead of using a flail. To show that animals might be made to sustain the remedies which art has discovered for human miseries, he broke the legs of some cocks and hens, in order to make them walk with wooden legs.

· * "All strength — all terror, single or in bands,
That ever was put forth in personal form —
Jehovah — with his thunder, and the choir
Of shouting angels, and the empyreal thrones —
I pass them unalarmed."
(Preface to "The Excursion.")

Of politics George Brentano spoke freely. He is not so warmly anti-Buonapartist as I could have wished, but he is still patriotic. He wishes for a concentration of German power.

December 27th. — Rode to Witham on the outside of the Colchester coach, and amused myself by reading Middleton's "Letter from Rome," a very amusing as well as interesting work. His proof that a great number of the rites and ceremonies of the Romish Church are derived from the Pagan religion is very complete and satisfactory. And he urges his argument against the abuses of the Roman Church with no feelings unfavorable to Christianity. That the earliest Christians voluntarily assimilated the new faith and its rites to the ancient superstition, in order to win souls, and with that accommodating spirit which St. Paul seems to have sanctioned, cannot be doubted. It admits of a doubt how far such a practice is so entirely bad as rigid believers now assert. Certainly these peculiarities are not the most mischievous excrescences which have gradually formed themselves on the surface of the noble and sublimely simple of Jesus Christ. The worst of these adscititious appendages may be looked upon as bad poetry; but the ineradicable and intolerable vice of Romanism is the infallibility of the Church, and the consequent intolerance of its priests. It is a religion of slavery.

CHAPTER XVIII.

1815.

*J*ANUARY *3d*. — My visit to Witham was made partly that I might have the pleasure of reading "The Excursion" to Mrs. W. Pattisson. The second perusal of this poem has gratified me still more than the first, and my own impressions were not removed by the various criticisms I became acquainted with. I also read to Mrs. Pattisson the *Eclectic Review.* It is a highly encomiastic article, rendering ample justice to the poetical talents of the author, but raising a doubt as to the religious character of the poem. It is insinuated that Nature is a sort of God throughout, and consistently with the Calvinistic orthodoxy of the reviewer, the lamentable error of representing a love of Nature as a sort of purifying state of mind, and the study of Nature as a sanctifying process, is emphatically pointed out.

Mrs. Pattisson further objected that, in Wordsworth, there is a want of sensibility, or rather passion ; and she even maintained that one of the reasons why I admire him so much is that I never was in love. We disputed on this head, and it was at last agreed between us that Wordsworth has no power because he has no inclination to describe the passion of an unsuccessful lover, but that he is eminently happy in his description of connubial felicity. We read also the *Edinburgh* review of the poem. It is a very severe and contemptuous article. Wordsworth is treated as incurable, and the changes are rung on the old keys with great vivacity, — affectation, bad taste, mysticism, &c. He is reproached with having written more feebly than before. A ludicrous statement of the story is given, which will not impose on many, for Homer or the Bible might be so represented. But though the attack on Wordsworth will do little mischief among those who are already acquainted with *Edinburgh Review* articles, it will close up the eyes of many who might otherwise have recovered their sight.

Perhaps, after all, " The Excursion " will leave Mr. Wordsworth's admirers and contemners where they were. Each will be furnished with instances to strengthen his own persuasions. Certainly I could wish for a somewhat clearer development of the author's opinions, for the retrenchment of some of the uninteresting interlocutory matter, for the exclusion of the tale of the angry, avaricious, and unkind woman, and curtailments in some of the other narratives. But, with these deductions from the worth of the poem, I do not hesitate to place it among the noblest works of the human intellect, and to me it is one of the most delightful. What is good is of the best kind of goodness, and the passages are not few which place the author on a level with Milton. It is true Wordsworth is not an epic poet ; but it is also true that what lives in the hearts of readers from the works of Milton is not the epic poem. Milton's story has merit unquestionably ; but it is rather a lyric than an epic narrative. Wordsworth is purely and exclusively a lyric poet, in the extended use of that term.

January 8th. — Called on Mrs. Clarkson (at Bury), and talked with her about " The Excursion." She had received a letter from Wordsworth himself, in which he mentioned the favorable as well as unfavorable opinions he had already heard.

January 21st. — On my ride to London outside the Bury coach I read part of Goethe's Autobiography (3d vol.) with great pleasure. It is a delightful work, but must be studied, not read as a mere personal history. His account of the " Système de la Nature " and of his theological opinions is peculiarly interesting. All that respects his own life and feelings is delightfully told. It is a book to make a man wish to live, if life were a thing he had not already experienced. There is in Goethe such a zest in living. The pleasures of sense and thought, of imagination and the affections, appear to have been all possessed by him in a more exuberant degree than in any man who has ever renewed his life by writing it. He appears in his youth to have had something even of religious enthusiasm. It would be interesting to know how he lost it, but we shall hardly be gratified by a much longer continuance of this incomparable memoir.

January 23d. — Called on Amyot. He informs me that Lord Erskine is writing a life of C. J. Fox. This work will determine what is at present doubtful, — whether Erskine has any literary talent. I shall be gratified if the book does the author and subject credit ; for it is lamentable to witness the premature waste of a mind so active as that of the greatest jury-orator. And it has been supposed that since his retreat from the Chancellorship he has devoted himself merely to amusement." *

January 26th. — Dined at Mr. Gurney's.† He appeared to advantage surrounded by his family. The conversation consisted chiefly of legal anecdote. Of Graham it was related, that in one case which respected some parish rights, and in which the parish of A. B. was frequently adverted to, he said in his charge : " Gentlemen, there is one circumstance very remarkable in this case, that both the plaintiff's and defendant's counsel have talked a great deal about one A. B., and that neither of them has thought proper to call him as a witness ! ! " It was Graham who, one day, at the Old Bailey, having omitted to pass sentence of death on a prisoner, and being told that he had forgotten it, exclaimed, very gravely, " Dear me, I beg his pardon, I am sure ! " The late Justice Willes was spoken of as having had a habit of interrupting the counsel ; and on such an occasion, —— said to him : " Your Lordship is even a greater man than your father. The Chief Baron used

---

* In 1825 Fox's collected speeches were published, with a short biographical and critical introduction by Erskine, six vols.
† Afterwards one of the Barons of the Exchequer.

to understand me after I had done, but your Lordship understands me before I begin."

January 30th. — Dined at the Hall. After dinner went to Flaxman's. He was very chatty and pleasant, and related some curious anecdotes of Sharp the engraver, who seems the ready dupe of any and every religious fanatic. I have already referred to his notion, that he was about to accompany the Jews under the guidance of Brothers to the Promised Land.* Sharp became a warm partisan of Joanna Southcott, and endeavored to make a convert of Blake ; but, as Flaxman judiciously observed, such men as Blake are not fond of playing second fiddle. Blake lately told Flaxman that he had had a violent dispute with the angels on some subject, and had driven them away. Barry had delusions of another kind. He informed Flaxman that he could not go out of his house on account of the danger he incurred of assassination. And in the lecture-room of the Academy he spoke of his house being broken into and robbed, and fixing his eyes on Smirke and other head Academicians, said, " These were *not common* robbers."

February 3d. — Dined with Walter ; Combe and Fraser were there. Combe related an anecdote of Sergeant Davy. The sergeant was no lawyer, but an excellent Nisi Prius advocate, having great shrewdness and promptitude. On one occasion Lord Mansfield said he should sit on Good Friday, there being a great press of business. It was said no barrister would attend, and in fact no one did ; but the Chief Justice tried the causes with the attorneys alone. When the proposal was made to the bar, Sergeant Davy said to Lord Mansfield, " There has been no precedent since the time of Pontius Pilate."

I heard the other day of Jekyll the following pun. He said : " Erskine used to hesitate very much, and could not speak well after dinner. I dined with him once at the Fishmongers' Company. He made such sad work of speechifying, that I asked him whether it was in honor of the Company that he *floundered* so."

February 12th. — Called on Thelwall, whom I had not seen for a long time. Mrs. Thelwall looked ill ; he, bating a little hard riding on his hobby, was not unpleasant. He is nearly at the close of his epic poem, which he talked about in 1799, when I visited him in Wales. At least there is no precipitation here. He talked of " The Excursion " as containing finer

* See *ante*, p. 35.

verses than there are in Milton, and as being in versification most admirable ; but then Wordsworth borrows without acknowledgment from Thelwall himself ! !

March 4th. — Dined at Collier's. After dinner took a hasty cup of tea with Anthony Robinson, Jr., and Miss Lamb, and went with them to Covent Garden Theatre to see Miss O'Neil. We sat in the first row, and thus had a near view of her. She did not appear to me a great actress, but still I was much pleased with her. She is very graceful without being very pretty. There is an interesting tenderness and gentleness, the impression of which is, however, disturbed by a voice which I still find harsh. In her unimpassioned acting she pleases from her appearance merely, but in moments of great excitement she wants power. Her sobs in the last act of "The Stranger" were very pathetic, but her general acting in the first scenes was not that of a person habitually melancholy. Young is a mere copy of Kemble throughout in "The Stranger," but certainly a very respectable copy.

After accompanying Miss Lamb to the Temple I returned to see "The Sleep-Walker." Mathews's imitations of the actors in his sleep were exceedingly droll ; and his burlesque acting as laughable as anything I ever saw or heard in my life, but of course mere farce and buffoonery.

February 5th. — Dined with the Colliers. After dinner, Mrs. Collier having lent me "Waverley," I returned to my chambers, and having shut myself within a double door, I took my tea alone and read a great part of the first volume.

The writer has united to the ordinary qualities of works of prose fiction excellences of an unusual kind. The portraits of Baron Bradwardine, a pedantic Highland laird, and of Fergus, a chivalrous rebel, in whom generosity and selfishness, self-devotion and ambition, are so dexterously blended and entangled that we feel, as in real life, unable to disentangle the skein, are very finely executed. The robber, Donald Bean, the assassin, Callum Beg, the Lieutenant, and all the subordinate appendages to a Highland sovereignty, are given in such a manner as to carry with them internal evidence of their genuineness. And the book has passages of great descriptive excellence. The author's sense of the romantic and picturesque in nature is not so delicate, or his execution so powerful, as Mrs. Radcliffe's, but his paintings of men and manners are more valuable. The incidents are not so dexterously contrived, and the author has not produced a very interesting

personage in his hero, Waverley, who, as his name was probably intended to indicate, is ever hesitating between two kings
and two mistresses.   I know not that he meant to symbolize
the two princes and the two ladies.   Flora, whom Waverley at
last leaves, certainly bears with her more of our reverence and
admiration than Rose ; but we are persuaded that the latter
will make her husband happier than he could be with so sublime a personage as her romantic rival.   There is more than
the usual portion of good sense in this book, which may enjoy,
though not immortality, at least a long life.

March 14th. — (At Royston.)   The news of the day was
alarming.   Before I left town the intelligence reached us
that Buonaparte had entered France, but it was not till to-
day that I feared seriously that he might at last succeed in
displacing the present government.   Now (I write on the 15th)
it appears that he is at Lyons, and one cannot but fear that he
has the army with him.   If so, the case is dreadful indeed.
I fear the French are so imitative a people, that if any one
marshal or considerable corps espouse his cause, all the others
will follow.

On the first blow, perhaps, everything depends ; for what
the French have hitherto most anxiously avoided is civil war.
There have not yet been in France two parties sufficiently strong
to secure to their partisans the treatment of prisoners of war.
The insurgents of La Vendée have always been considered as
rebels, and so will be, I think it probable, the adherents of
Louis or Buonaparte.   If the parties were at all balanced, the
interference of the Foreign Powers would at once decide the
contest.   But, if that interference take place too soon, will it
not determine the neutral party to embrace the cause of the
ex-Emperor ?   And yet if there be no interference, will not the
army be decidedly on the side of the military chieftain ?

April 8th. — Went to Bury by the coach.   Finding Hart
was alone inside, I joined him, and never had a more pleasant
ride.   Hart was very chatty and very agreeable.   Of Mr. ——
Hart seems when young to have thought very rightly.   Mr.
—— passed then for a great man among good people.   Hart
said : " When I was a little boy he shocked me by saying to a
man who was lamenting his backslidings to him, ' Ah ! sir, you
must not take these things too much to heart ; you must
recollect you were predestined to do them ?' "   A use of the
doctrine of Necessity which shocked a sensible child of ten
years old.

                                                              T

April 15th. — I called at the Colliers', and finding that Miss Lamb was gone to Alsager's, from whom I had an invitation, I also went.   There was a rather large party, and I stayed till near two o'clock, playing whist ill, for which I was scolded by Captain Burney, and debating with Hazlitt, in which I was also unsuccessful, as far as the talent of the disputation was involved, though Hazlitt was wrong, as well as offensive, in almost all he said.   When pressed, he does not deny what is bad in the character of Buonaparte.   And yet he triumphs and rejoices in the late events.   Hazlitt and myself once felt alike on politics.   And now our hopes and fears are directly opposed.   He retains all his hatred of kings and bad governments, and believing them to be incorrigible, he, from a principle of revenge, rejoices that they are punished.   I am indignant to find the man who might have been their punisher become their imitator, and even surpassing them all in guilt.   Hazlitt is angry with the friends of liberty for weakening their strength by joining with the common foe against Buonaparte, by which the old governments are so much assisted, even in their attempts against the general liberty.   I am not shaken by this consequence, because I think, after all, that, should the governments succeed in the worst projects imputed to them, still the evil will be infinitely less than that which would arise from Buonaparte's success.   I say : " Destroy him, at any rate, and take the consequences."   Hazlitt says : " Let the enemy of the old tyrannical governments triumph, and I am glad, and do not much care how the new government turns out."   Not that I am indifferent to the government which the successful kings of Europe may establish, or that Hazlitt has lost all love for liberty, but that his *hatred* and my *fears* predominate and absorb all weaker impressions.   This I believe to be the great difference between us.

April 16th. — In the evening, in my chambers, enjoyed looking over Wordsworth's new edition of his poems.   The supplement to his preface I wish he had left unwritten.   His reproaches of the bad taste of the times will be ascribed to merely personal feelings, and to disappointment.   But his manly avowal of his sense of his own poetic merit I by no means censure.   His preface contains subtle remarks on poetry, but they are not clear ; and I wish he could incorporate all his critical ideas into a work of taste, in either the dialogue or novel form ; otherwise his valuable suggestions are in danger of being lost.   His classification of his poems displeases me from an obvious fault, that it is partly subjective and partly objective.

April 17th. — Spent the forenoon in the Hall, without interest. The court rose early, and I walked homewards with Burrell. He is a zealous anti-Buonapartist, and on high principles. It is a pleasure to talk with so noble-minded a man. He observed that Buonaparte, if sincere, could not possibly remain a friend to peace. Like Satan, when peace was restored, ease would lead him to recant " vows made in pain, as violent and void." It is contrary to human nature that such a mind could ever rest in tranquillity.

April 18th. — Called on Anthony Robinson. He was vehemently abusive of the allies, and angrily strenuous for peace. I had a difficulty in keeping my temper, but when he was spent he listened to me. It seems in fact that, after all, if the question were peace or war with Buonaparte, we must conclude in favor of peace ; but the question is, war by us now in France, or by him two years hence in Germany, — and then surely the answer must be for war with him now. At the same time the prospect is tremendous, if we are to have war ; for how are our resources to endure, which seem now nearly exhausted ?

April 22d. — Mr. Quayle breakfasted with me in the expectation of meeting Tiarks, who called for a moment, but could not stay. Mr. Quayle proposed to me the writing for a new Review, but I gave an indecisive answer. He informs me that Valpy has engaged Tiarks for the Lexicon in consequence of my letter to him. Accompanied Mr. Quayle to Greek Street, and on my return found a letter from my sister announcing that my father had been attacked by apoplexy, and was lying in a state which rendered it unlikely that he would survive many hours. This intelligence could not surprise me, nor, in the state of my father's health, could it grieve me. His faculties were rapidly wasting away, his body enfeebled by disease and age, — he was nearly eighty-eight. He retained his appetite alone of all his sources of pleasure. I rejoiced to hear that his state was that of torpidity, almost of insensibility.

April 23d. — I spent the forenoon at home. Mr. Green brought me a letter announcing the expected event; my poor father died between twelve and one o'clock yesterday morning.

He has lived among men a blameless life ; and, perhaps,

that he has never excited in his children the best and most delightful emotions has been his misfortune rather than his fault. O, how difficult, not to say impossible, to assign the boundaries between natural and moral evil, between the defects of character which proceed from natural imbecility, which no man considers a reproach, and those errors of the will, about which metaphysicians may dispute forever! Only this I know, that I sincerely wish I was other than I am ; and that I acknowledge among those I see around me individuals whom I believe to be of a nobler and better nature than myself. The want of sensibility in myself I consider as a radical defect in my nature ; but on what does sensibility depend? On constitution, or habits, or what? I cannot tell. I know only that I was not my own maker. I know also that I respect others more than I do myself; though I have hitherto been preserved from doing any act grossly violating the rights of others, and I am *yet* incapable of a deliberate act of injustice or hardheartedness. But how long may I be able to say this? How wise and admirable the prayer, " Lead me not into temptation ! " I cannot understand the mysteries of religion, but this I am sensible of, that there is a consciousness of good and evil in myself, of strength and weakness, of a goodness out of me which is not in me, and of a something which *I* can neither attain nor think unattainable. And on this consciousness, common to all men, rests the doctrine of grace and prayer, which I wish to comprehend and duly to feel. I wish to be religious, as an excellence and grace of character, at the least.

April 24th. — Spent the greater part of the forenoon at home. Read Hazlitt's article on the great novelists in the *Edinburgh Review.* A very intelligent article. His discrimination between Fielding and Le Sage is particularly excellent. His characters of Cervantes, Richardson, and Smollett are also admirable ; but his strictures on Sterne are less pointed ; and his obtrusive abuse of the politics of the king, as occasioning the decline of novel-writing during the present reign, is very far-fetched indeed. He is also severe and almost contemptuous towards Miss Burney, whose " Wanderer " was the pretence of the article.

May 7th. — On returning from a walk to Shooter's Hill, I found a card from Wordsworth, and, running to Lamb's, I found Mr. and Mrs. Wordsworth there. After sitting half an hour with them, I accompanied them to their lodgings, near Cavendish Square. Mrs. Wordsworth appears to be a mild and amiable woman, not so lively or animated as Miss Wordsworth, but, like her, devoted to the poet.

May 8th. — I dined with the Colliers, and after dinner called on the Flaxmans. Mrs. Flaxman admitted me to her room. She had about a fortnight before broken her leg, and sprained it besides, by falling down stairs. This misfortune, however, instead of occasioning a repetition of the paralytic stroke, which she had a year ago, seemed to have improved her health. She had actually recovered the use of her hand in some degree, and her friends expect that she will be benefited by the accident. Poor Flaxman, however, had a relapse of his erysipelas, and he is still so weak and nervous that he sees no one. His situation is the worse of the two.

May 9th. — Took tea with the Lambs. Mr. and Mrs. Wordsworth were there. We had a long chat, of which, however, I can relate but little. Wordsworth, in answer to the common reproach that his sensibility is excited by objects which produce no effect on others, admits the fact, and is proud of it. He says that he cannot be accused of being insensible to the real concerns of life. He does not waste his feelings on unworthy objects, for he is alive to the actual interests of society. I think the justification is complete. If Wordsworth expected immediate popularity, he would betray an ignorance of public taste impossible in a man of observation.

He spoke of the changes in his new poems. He has substituted *ebullient* for *fiery*, speaking of the nightingale, and *jocund* for *laughing*, applied to the daffodils ; but he will probably restore the original epithets. We agreed in preferring the original reading. But on my alluding to the lines,

"Three feet long and two feet wide,"

and confessing that I dared not read them aloud in company, he said, "They ought to be liked."

Wordsworth particularly recommended to me, among his Poems of Imagination, "Yew-Trees," and a description of Night. These he says are among the best for the imaginative power displayed in them. I have since read them. They are fine, but I believe I do not understand in what their excellence consists. The poet himself, as Hazlitt has well observed, has a pride in deriving no aid from his subject. It is the mere power which he is conscious of exerting in which he delights, not the production of a work in which men rejoice on account of the sympathies and sensibilities it excites in them. Hence he does not much esteem his " Laodamia," as it belongs to the inferior class of poems founded on the affections. In this, as in other peculiarities of Wordsworth, there is a German bent in his mind.

May 20th. — Went to Covent Garden to see " Venice Preserved." Miss O'Neil's Belvidera was our only attraction, and it proved our gratification. In spite of her untragical face, she strongly affected us by mere sweetness and grace. Her scenes of tenderness are very pleasing, and, contrary to my expectation, she produced a great effect in the last scenes of strong passion. She threw her whole feeling into her acting, and by this *abandon*, as it were, she wrought wonders, — that is, for her, — considering that nature has denied her powers for the higher characters.

May 23d. — Between five and six I was at Islington during a long shower. I waited till I despaired of better weather, and then returned to town. Just as I reached the Temple, wetted to the skin, the rain subsided, and the evening became very fine. However, I could hardly repent of my impatience, for I went to Lamb's, and took tea with Wordsworth there. Alsager,* Barron Field, Talfourd, the Colliers, &c. stepped in late. Wordsworth was very chatty on poetry. I had some business to attend to, which rendered me restless, so I left at eleven. Miss Hutchinson was of the party; she improves greatly on acquaintance. She is a lively, sensible little woman.

May 25th. — After dining with the Colliers, I accompanied Miss Lamb to the theatre, where we were joined by the Wordsworths. We had front places at Drury Lane and saw " Richard II." It is a heavy and uninteresting play; principally because the process by which Richard is deposed is hardly perceived. Kean's acting in the first three acts has in it nothing worth notice; but in the fourth and fifth acts he certainly exhibits the weak, passionate, and eloquent monarch to great advantage. In the scene in which he gives up the crown, the conflict of passion is finely kept up; and the blending of opposite emotions is so curious as to resemble incipient insanity. Several admirable artifices of the actor gave great

---

* Alsager had, at one time, a manufactory and a bleaching-ground near the King's Bench Prison; but ne gave this up, and, being a great lover of music, recommended himself to the *Times* as an amateur reporter on musical matters. He became City Correspondent, and wrote the " State of the Money Market" for many years. He was also a shareholder in the paper till he had a serious misunderstanding with Walter.

satisfaction, — one in particular, in which he derides Bolingbroke for affecting to kneel, and intimates by a sign with his
hand that Bolingbroke aims at the level of his crown.

May 28th. — I dined at Collier's with a party assembled to
see Wordsworth. There were Young, Barnes, Alsager, &c.
The afternoon passed off pleasantly, but the conversation was
not highly interesting. Wordsworth was led to give an opinion of Lord Byron which flattered me by its resemblance to
my own. He reproached the author with the contradiction
in the character of the Corsair, &c. He also blamed Crabbe
for his unpoetical mode of considering human nature and
society.

I left the party to inquire concerning the Anthony Robinsons, and on my return found the Wordsworths gone; but I
went to Lamb's, where they came, and I enjoyed their company till very late. I began to feel quite cordial with Mrs.
Wordsworth. She is an amiable woman.

June 4th. — Mr. Nash, Sen., and my brother Thomas,
breakfasted with me. I conducted Mr. Nash to Mr. Belsham's
meeting, and came home to read "The White Doe of Rylstone,"
by Wordsworth. This legendary tale will be less popular than
Walter Scott's, from the want of that vulgar intelligibility, and
that freshness and vivacity of description, which please even
those who are not of the vulgar. Still, the poem will be better liked than better pieces of Wordsworth's writing. There
are a delicate sensibility and exquisite moral running through
the whole; but it is not the happiest of his narrative poems.

June 5th. — Dined at Mr. Porden's. Sir James Smith of
Norwich, the botanical professor, there, also Phillips* the
painter, and Taylor, the editor or proprietor of the *Sun.*† I
spent a pleasant afternoon. Sir James is a very well-bred
man, and though his conversation was not piquant, amenity
supplied an equal charm; though that word is not applicable
to the correct propriety and rather dry courtesy of the Unitarian professor. Phillips was very agreeable, but the hero of

---

* Thomas Phillips, R. A., painted all the leading characters of the day. He
was a peculiarly refined artist, but scarcely ever exceeded the sphere of portrait painting. Coleridge, Southey, Byron, Crabbe, Chantrey, Blake, Sir
Joseph Banks, Lord Brougham, Faraday, and Walter Scott sat to him. His
lectures on Painting and contributions to Rees's *Cyclopædia* show extensive
learning and originality of thought. He was born at Dudley, in Warwick-
shire, 1770, and died in George Street, Hanover Square, 1845.

† John Taylor, son of a celebrated oculist in Hatton Garden, born 1752.
Was oculist to George III. and William IV. He published "The Records of
my Life," various Poems, and "Monsieur Tonson." Died 1832.

the day was Taylor, — "everybody's Taylor," as he is sometimes designated. He has lively parts, puns, jokes, and is very good-natured. The Flaxmans were not there. Mrs. Flaxman is gone to Blackheath. Miss Porden, in a feeling manner, spoke of her apprehension that the Flaxman family is broken up as a happy and social circle. Mrs. Flaxman's health is very precarious, and her husband is dependent on her, and suffers himself through her complaint. This, I fear, is a fact; and it is a melancholy subject. These breakings-up of society are mournful at all times, and peculiarly so when they befall the very best of persons.

June 6th. — I dined with Amyot. A small party were there, consisting of Sharon Turner, the historian and antiquarian; Charles Marsh,* ex-barrister and M. P.; William Taylor of Norwich; and Penn, a clerk in one of the public offices, a descendant of William Penn. Charles Marsh stayed with us but a short time; he was sent for to the House of Commons. His manners are easy and gentlemanly; he said little, but he spoke with great vivacity. Sharon Turner is a good converser, but with a little pedantry. He spoke of Martin Burney handsomely, but oddly. He said : "I always thought he would flower, though it might be late. He is a man of great honor and integrity. He never told me a lie in his life ! "

William Taylor was amusing, as usual. He gravely assured me that he believes the allies will succeed in penetrating into France; that the French will then offer the crown to the Emperor Alexander, who will accept it; and then the allies will fight against Alexander, to prevent the union of the two crowns. William Taylor enjoys nothing so much as an extravagant speculation, — the odder the better. He spoke of Wordsworth, — praised his conversation, which he likes better than his poetry, — says he is solid, dignified, eloquent, and simple. "But he looked surprised," said Taylor, "when I told him that I considered Southey the greatest poet and the greatest historian living." — " No great matter of surprise," I answered, "that Wordsworth should think himself a greater poet than Southey."

June 15th. — I allowed myself a holiday to-day. Mord Andrews breakfasted with me. Afterwards I called on Wordsworth at his lodgings. He was luckily at home, and I spent the forenoon with him, walking. We talked about Hazlitt, in consequence of a malignant attack on Wordsworth by him in

* See *ante,* p. 15.

Sunday's *Examiner*.* Wordsworth that very day called on Hunt, who in a manly way asked him whether he had seen the paper of the morning; saying, if he had, he should consider his call as a higher honor. He disclaimed the article. The attack by Hazlitt was a note, in which, after honoring Milton for being a consistent patriot, he sneered at Wordsworth as the author of " paltry sonnets upon the Royal fortitude," &c., and insinuated that he had left out the " Female Vagrant," a poem describing the miseries of war sustained by the poor.

June 17th. — I went late to Lamb's. His party were there, and a numerous and odd set they were, — for the greater part interesting and amusing people, — George Dyer, Captain and Martin Burney, Ayrton, Phillips, Hazlitt and wife, Alsager, Barron Field, Coulson, John Collier, Talfourd, White, Lloyd, and Basil Montagu. The latter I had never before been in company with; his feeling face and gentle tones are very interesting. Wordsworth says of him that he is a " philanthropized courtier." He gave me an account of his first going the Norfolk Circuit. He walked the circuit generally, and kept aloof from the bar; in this way he contrived to pay his expenses. He began at Huntingdon, where he had a half-guinea motion; and as he was then staying at his brother's house, he walked to Bury with that money in his pocket, picked up a fee there, and so went on. Mackintosh was the immediate senior of Montagu, and assisted in bringing him forward. Mackintosh had business immediately as a leader, and after a short time the two travelled together. But during some time Montagu lived on bread and cheese. He is a strenuous advocate for all reforms in the law, and believes that in time they will all take place.

June 18th. — Breakfasted at Wordsworth's. Wordsworth was not at home, but I stayed chatting with the ladies till he returned; and several persons dropping in, I was kept there till two o'clock, and was much amused.

* The attack referred to is contained in the following remarks on Milton, in the *Examiner*, for 11th June, 1815: " Whether he was a *true* patriot we shall not inquire; he was at least a *consistent* one. He did not retract his defence of the people of England; he did not say that his sonnets to Vane or Cromwell were meant ironically; he was not appointed Poet Laureate to a Court he had reviled and insulted; he accepted neither place nor pension; nor did he write paltry sonnets upon the ' Royal fortitude ' of the House of Stuart, by which, however, they really lost something." To these words a foot-note is appended, referring to a sonnet to the King, " in the Last Edition of the Works of a Modern Poet."

Scott, editor of the *Champion*,* and Haydon the painter,†
stayed a considerable time. Scott is a little swarthy man.
He talked fluently on French politics, and informed me that
he has learnt from good authority that La Fayette was applied to by the King on Buonaparte's reappearance in France;
that La Fayette said he wished the King success, and would
serve under him on conditions which he gave in writing; that
the King refused to accede to them, and La Fayette retired to
his estate. On Buonaparte's arrival he, too, sent for La
Fayette, who refused to serve under him or accept a place
among the peers, but said that, if elected, he would become a
member of the legislative body.

Haydon has an animated countenance, but did not say
much. Both he and Scott seemed to entertain a high reverence
for the poet.

June 22d. — I spent the evening by appointment with Godwin. The Taylors were there. We talked politics, and not
very comfortably. Godwin and I all but quarrelled; both
were a little angry, and equally offensive to each other. Godwin was quite impassioned in asserting his hope that Buonaparte may be successful in the war. He declares his wish that
all the allies that enter France now may perish, and affirmed
that no man who did not abandon all moral principles and
love of liberty could wish otherwise. I admitted that, in
general, foreigners have no right to interfere in the government of a country, but, in this case, I consider the foreign
armies as coming to the relief of the people against the oppres-
sions of domestic soldiers; and in this lies the justice of the
war. Richard Taylor ‡ maintained that nothing could justify
the invasion of a country. I treated it as mere formalism and
pedantry to ask *where* is the battle fought. In the spirit of

* John Scott, editor of the *Champion*, and afterwards of the *London
Magazine*, an intimate friend of Haydon the artist. He was killed in a duel
with Mr. Christie, in 1821, which arose from a misunderstanding with Mr.
Lockhart.—See the "Annual Register" for 1823.

† This powerful, but seldom judicious, artist obtained considerable distinction as a young man, by his independence of spirit and by determined opposition to the weak and blind imitation of academic traditions of painting. He
viewed the Elgin Marbles with rapture, and contributed much to secure a proper estimation of the works of Phidias, and the great Athenian sculptors in this
country. His own performances were not equally successful. His "Raising
of Lazarus," the best example of his merits and defects, has been recently purchased for the National Gallery. He was born at Plymouth, 1786, and died by
his own hand in Burwood Place, London, 1846. His lectures are learned and
practical. His eloquence is vehement. His autobiography, edited by Tom
Taylor, was published in three volumes, 1853.

‡ The printer.

the idea the invaders may be, as is now the fact, carrying on a purely defensive war. And the moral certainty that Buonaparte would have made war as soon as it became convenient, justifies the allies in beginning. Godwin considered the acting on such a surmise unjustifiable. I asserted that all the actions of life proceed on surmises. We, however, agreed in apprehending that Buonaparte may destroy the rising liberties of the French, and that the allies may attempt to force the old Bourbon despotism on the French. But Godwin thinks the latter, and I the former, to be the greater calamity. I also consider the future despotism of Buonaparte a certain consequence of his success in the campaign ; and, besides, I believe that even if the French be so far beaten as to be obliged to take back Louis on terms, yet they will still remain so formidable that the allies will not dare to impose humiliating conditions ; so that the French may at last be led to offer the Crown again on terms of their own imposing. Richard Taylor would be satisfied with this, but Godwin would on no account have the allies successful.

I am no longer very anxious for the liberties of the French. It is infinitely more important for Europe that their national spirit of foreign conquest should be crushed, than that their civil liberties should be preserved. Like the Romans, they may be the conquerors of all other nations, even while they are maintaining their own liberties. And I no longer imagine, as I once did, that it is only monarchs and governments which can be unjust and love war.

June 23d. — I went to the Surrey Institution to read the detailed account of the glorious victory at Waterloo. This is indeed most glorious ; but still I fear it will not so affect the French people as to occasion a material defalcation from Buonaparte. And if he be, after all, supported by the French, numerous and bloody must be the victories which are to overthrow him.

After nine o'clock I walked to Ayrton's. The illuminations were but dull, and there were scarcely any marks of public zeal or sympathy. I stayed at Ayrton's till half past one. Lamb, Alsager, &c. were there, but it was merely a card-party.

June 30th. — Called on Thelwall. He was in unaffected low spirits. Godwin, Lofft, and Thelwall are the only three persons I know (except Hazlitt) who grieve at the late events. Their intentions and motives are respectable, and their sorrow proceeds from mistaken theory, and an inveterate hatred of old names. They anticipate a revival of ancient despotism in France ; and they will not acknowledge the radical vices of the French people, by which the peace of Europe is more endangered than the liberties of the French are by the restoration of the Bourbons.

July 2d. — I spent the forenoon at home, except that Long * and I lounged with Wordsworth's poems in the Temple Gardens. Long had taken the sacrament at Belsham's, for which I felt additional respect towards him. Though I am not religious myself, I have great respect for a conduct which proceeds from a sense of duty, and is under the influence of religious feelings. I greatly esteem Long in all respects, both for his understanding and his moral feelings, which together comprise nearly all that is valuable in man.

July 4th. — At half past four I went to Thelwall's, to witness a singular display. Thelwall exhibited several of his young people, and also himself, in the presence of the Abbé Sicard, and several of his deaf and dumb pupils. Thelwall delivered a lecture to about sixty or seventy persons. He gave an account of his plan of curing impediments in the speech. He makes his pupils read verse — beating time. And I have no doubt that the effect is produced by the facility of repeating a movement once begun, and partly by the effect of imagination. The attention is fixed and directed by the movement and time-beating. This simple fact, or phenomenon, Thelwall has not distinctly perceived or comprehended. His boys read, or rather recited, verse very pleasantly, and without stammering, so as to produce an effect far more favorable to his system than his own explanation of it. After this two hours' display we dined, and in the evening Sicard's pupils afforded amusement in the drawing-room by the correspondence they carried on with the ladies. One of them wrote notes to Mrs. Rough, and gave a gallant turn to all he wrote, for even the deaf and dumb retain their national character. I wrote some ridiculous question in Mrs. Rough's name. She wrote to him that I was an advocate, and therefore not to be believed. He answered, " I am glad to hear it, as he can defend me if I have the misfortune to offend you."

July 7th. — I called on Amyot early, and found on going out that Paris had been again taken by the allies. But the public did not rejoice, for Paris had capitulated on honorable terms, and Buonaparte had escaped. During the day Mr.

* George Long, the barrister, and afterwards police magistrate.

Whitbread's death was more a subject of interest than the possession of Paris. The death of so watchful a member of Parliament is really a national loss. He belonged to the noblest class of mankind.

In the evening joined Amyot and his family, in the front dress-boxes of Covent Garden. Miss O'Neil's Jane Shore, I think, delighted me more than any character I have seen her play. Her expression of disgust and horror when she meets with her husband, as well as her general acting in that scene, are as fine as can be conceived, coming from so uninteresting a face. What a treasure were Mrs. Siddons now as young as Miss O'Neil!

July 29th. — (At Norwich, on circuit.) This day was devoted to amusement, and accordingly passed away heavily. I called after breakfast on Millard, and then went to Amyot, with whom I spent the remainder of the day. He introduced me to Dr. Bathurst, Bishop of Norwich. The bishop's manners are very pleasing. His attentions to me would have been flattering, could I have thought them distinguishing, but probably they proceed from a habit of courtesy. I had scarcely exchanged ten words with him when, speaking of ancient times in reference to the former splendor of the buildings attached to the Palace, he said : "Ah! Mr. Robinson, bishops had then more power than you or I wish them to have," as if he knew I was born a Nonconformist. I afterwards met him in the gardens, where a balloon was to ascend ; he was arm-in-arm with a Roman Catholic, and on my going up to him he took hold of me also, and remained with us a considerable time walking about. On my uttering some jest about bishops *in partibus,* he eulogized the Roman Catholic bishops in Ireland as eminently apostolic. The bishop's manners are gentle, and his air is very benignant. He is more gentlemanly than Grégoire, and more sincere than Hohenfels.

TOUR IN BELGIUM AND HOLLAND.

*Rem.** — The Battle of Waterloo having taken place in June, I was determined to make a tour in Belgium, to which I was also urged by my friend Thomas Naylor,† who was my

* Written in 1850.
† Father of Samuel Naylor, the translator of "Reineke Fuchs," and son of Samuel Naylor, of Great Newport Street, agent to Mr. Francis, in whose office Mr. Robinson was an articled clerk. H. C. R. says: "S. Naylor, Sen , took me to the first play I ever saw in London; it was 'Peeping Tom of Coventry.' I have forgotten all about it, excepting that I was troubled by the number of people on the stage, and that I saw and admired Jack Banister."

travelling companion from Sunday, August 6th, to Saturday, September 2d.

I kept a journal of this tour, and have just finished a hasty perusal of it. It contains merely an account of what occurred to myself, and the incidents were so unimpressive that the narrative has brought to my recollection very few persons and very few places. I shall, therefore, not be tempted to dwell upon the events.

Naylor and I went to Margate on the 6th, and next day, after visiting Ramsgate, embarked in a small and unpromising vessel, which brought us to Ostend early on the following morning. There were on board four young men, who, like ourselves, were bound for Waterloo. We agreed to travel together, and I, being the only one who understood any language but English, was elected governor; most of us remained together till the end of the journey. I have lost sight of them all, but I will give their names. There was a young Scotch M. D., named Stewart, whom I afterwards met in London, when he told me the history of his good fortune. It was when travelling in France, after our *rencontre*, that he by accident came to a country inn, where he found a family in great alarm. An English lady was taken in premature labor. The case was perilous. No medical man was there. He offered his services, and continued to attend her until her husband, a General, and personal friend of the Commander-in-Chief, Lord Wellington, arrived. The General acknowledged him to be the savior of his wife's life, and in return obtained for him a profitable place on the medical staff of the English army.

The other young men were Barnes, a surgeon, and two merchants or merchants' clerks, Watkins and Williams.

Our journey lay through Bruges, Ghent, Brussels, Antwerp, Breda, Utrecht, Amsterdam, Haarlem, Leyden, the Hague, Delft, Rotterdam, and the Briel, to Helvoetsluys, and from thence to Harwich.

No small part of the tour was in barges. One in particular I enjoyed. It was the voyage from Bruges to Ghent, during which I certainly had more pleasure than I had ever before had on board a vessel, and with no alloy whatever. This canal voyage is considered one of the best in the Netherlands, and our boat, though not superbly furnished, possessed every convenience. We took our passage in the state-cabin, over which was an elegant awning. I found I could write on board with perfect ease; but from time to time I looked out of the cabin window on a prospect pleasingly diversified by neat and comfortable houses on the banks. The barge proceeded so slowly that we could hardly perceive when it stopped. A man was walking on the side of the canal for a great part of the way, and I therefore suppose our pace was not much more than four miles an hour.

We embarked at half past ten, and at two o'clock an excellent dinner was served up, consisting of fish, flesh, and fowl, with rich pastry, and plenty of fruit. For this dinner, and the voyage of between thirty and forty miles, we paid each 5 fr.

The main object of the tour was to visit the field of the recent great Battle of Waterloo. It was on the 14th of August when we inspected the several points famous in the history of this battle. Not all the vestiges of the conflict were removed. There were arms of trees hanging down, shattered by cannon-balls, and not yet cut off. And there were ruined and burnt cottages in many places, and marks of bullets and balls on both houses and trees ; but I saw nothing in particular to impress me, except that in an inn near the field I had a glimpse of a lady in weeds, who was come on a vain search after the body of her husband, slain there. A more uninteresting country, or one more fit for " a glorious victory," being flat and almost without trees, than that round Waterloo cannot be imagined. I saw it some years afterwards, when ugly monuments were erected there, and I can bear witness to the fact of the great resemblance which the aspect of the neighborhood of Waterloo bears to a village a mile from Cambridge, on the Bury road.

On the field and at other places the peasants brought us relics of the fight. Dr. Stewart purchased a brass cuirass for a napoleon, and pistols, &c. were sold to others. For my own part, with no great portion of sentimental feeling, I could have wished myself to pick up some memorial ; but a mere purchase was not sufficient to satisfy me.

We dined at Waterloo. Our host was honest, for on my ordering a dinner at 2 fr. a head, he said he never made two prices, and should charge only 1½ fr. In the village, which is naked and wretched, a festival was being held in honor of the patron saint; but we were told that, in consequence of the battle, and out of respect to brave men who lay there, there was to be no dancing this year.

In the circular brick church of Waterloo we saw two plain marble monuments, bearing simply the names of the officers of the 1st Foot Guards and 15th King's Hussars who had fallen there. Even the reward of being so named is given but to one in a thousand. Sixty thousand men are said to have been killed or wounded at Waterloo. Will sixty be named hereafter?

In general I admired the towns of Belgium, but Ghent was my favorite. The fine architecture of the Catholic churches of the Netherlands gratified me, while I was disgusted with the nakedness and meanness of the Protestant churches of Holland.

Among the few objects which have left any traces in my memory, the one which impressed me most was the secluded village of Broek, near Amsterdam. My journal for the 21st of August contains the account of our visit to this village and that of Saardam. The people of Broek live in a state of proud seclusion from the rest of mankind, and, being industrious, are able to banish the appearance of poverty, at least from their cottages. We walked for about an hour through the narrow streets, which are moated on a small scale. There were a great number of inferior houses, but not a single *poor* one, — all were adorned more or less. Most of them are painted white and green, — some entirely green. In general the blinds were closed, so that we could scarcely get a peep into any of them. When we did look in we observed great neatness and simplicity, with marks of affluence at the same time. The shops had a few goods in the windows as a sort of symbol, but were as secluded as the private houses.

Scarcely an individual did we see in the streets. We met one woman with a flat piece of gold or gilt metal on the forehead, and a similar piece behind : she wore also long gold ear-rings. This, however, is not an unusual costume for the affluent peasantry elsewhere. We pulled off our hats to the Broek belle, but had no salutation in return. The general seclusion of the village, from which nothing could be seen but meadows with ditches, the silence of the streets, the perfect stillness and neatness of the objects, every dwelling resembling a summer-house rather than an ordinary residence, the cheerful and unusual colors, and the absence of all the objects which denote a hard-working race of men, gave to the whole place an air absolutely Arcadian. The only objects which disturbed this impression were several houses of a better description, with large windows, gilded shutters, carved frontispieces, and the other ornaments of a fashionable house. One in particular had a porch with Corinthian pillars, and a large garden with high, clipped trees.

One surgeon's house had an announcement that wine and strong liquors were to be had, — as if these were still, in this Dutch Arcadia, articles of medicine only. It is said that there is no public-house in Broek. We saw one, but did not go in. It did not look like the rest of the houses.

We were next driven to Saardam, where we visited the hut which alone brings many an idle traveller to the place, and in which Peter of Russia resided while he learnt the trade of ship-building, performing the work of a common shipwright. It is certainly right to perpetuate the memory of an act in which an admirable sentiment prevailed, whatever want of good sense and judgment there might be in it. The hut has nothing particular about it, except that it is worse than the other huts, it being of course a principle to keep it in its original condition. While in this singular village we saw a school in which the children were singing to the tune of " God save the King." This is become the general tune throughout Europe for the partisans of legal and restored monarchs, though originally written in honor of an elected sovereign house.

This belongs to the agreeable days of my tour. I had seen life in a new shape,—one of the varieties of human existence with which it is, or rather *may be*, useful to become acquainted. Yet I ought to add that I saw little of these North-Hollanders, and cannot tell what their manners and morals may be. There is certainly no virtue in selfish seclusion from the world. The neighborhood of such a city as Amsterdam must supply opportunities for the vices which will spring up in any soil. Yet, certainly, in the insulated and clannish spirit which prevails in these villages there is generated a benevolence, or extension of selfishness beyond the individual, which may protect the members of the clan and inhabitants of the island from the severest evils of life. So that, though perhaps these peasants are not especial objects of love or admiration, yet they may be envied by those who have witnessed, if not experienced, the heavier calamities so frequently arising in the more polished and more highly civilized circles of life elsewhere.

At Haarlem I heard the celebrated organ in the great church. I am half afraid to say in writing how much I was gratified. I have been in the habit of saying and believing that I have no ear for music, and certainly I have suffered ennui at listening to some which others thought very fine, but to this I listened with delight, and was quite sorry when it ceased.

14 *   U

I was amused with the gorgeous show in the Greek church at Amsterdam. I was pleased with the Hague, and with the Royal Palace called the House in the Wood. I was struck also with the Bies Bosch, the melancholy memorial of a frightful inundation near Dort, which took place in the fifteenth century.

On the church tower of Utrecht I fell in with the Masqueriers, with whom was Walton, an attorney. With him I afterwards became acquainted. I returned to England on the 2d of September.

September 22d. — At the end of a visit to my friends Mr. and Mrs. W. Pattisson, at Witham, I went to take leave of Mrs. Pattisson, Sen. She began interrogating me about my religious opinions. This she did in a way so kind and benevolent that I could not be displeased, or consider her impertinent. I was unable to answer her as I could wish. However, I did not scruple to declare to her that such orthodoxy as Mr. N——'s would deter me from Christianity. I cannot wish to have a belief which excludes from salvation such persons as my own dear mother, my uncle Crabb, and a large portion of the best people I have ever known.

October 4th. — (On a visit to my brother Habakkuk at Bagshot.) After dining *tête-à-tête* with my niece Elizabeth, and playing backgammon with her, we called on Mrs. Kitchener and took tea with her. Mrs. Cooper (the widow of the former clergyman at Bagshot), who was there, related to me some singular circumstances about the state of her husband's mind in his last illness. He was then more than eighty years of age. He imagined himself to be dead, and gave directions as for the burial of a dead man ; and he remained in this persuasion for several weeks. At one time he desired a note to be sent to the Duke of Gloucester announcing his death. At another time he desired that the mourners might be well provided for, and inquired about the preparations made. In particular on one occasion when a clean shirt was being put on, he reminded the servants that, being a corpse, they must put on nothing but woollen, or they would incur a penalty. When told that, if dead, he could not talk about it, he for a moment perceived the absurdity of his notion, but soon relapsed.

October 26th. — At work in my chambers in the forenoon.

After dining at Collier's I went to Flaxman's. I had not seen him for many months, and was glad to find all the family well, Mrs. Flaxman in particular recovered. We chatted about my journey to Holland. Flaxman speaks with contempt of Dutch statuary. He rejoices in the restoration of the works of art tò Italy.*

November 5th. — (At Royston on a visit to Mr. Wedd.) We dined late. W. Nash and T. Nash of Whittlesford with us. The afternoon spent agreeably. In the evening Mr. Nash came to us. He was in good spirits. The cheerful benignity of the old gentleman renders him delightful, but age is advancing rapidly on him, and his faculties are growing blind with years. He is, however, with all his infirmities, the model of a venerable old man. It is a felicity to live within the influence of such a character, who creates a society by his personal virtues.

November 11th. — Went to see the play of " Percy," by Hannah More. It is much like " Gabrielle de Vergy." The situation is highly interesting. A chaste and noble-minded woman having been forced to marry a man she hates, the rival, whom she loves, suddenly returns, ignorant of her marriage. The husband furiously jealous and cruel, &c., &c. Of course they all die as in " Gabrielle." Miss O'Neil gave great interest to the play during the first three acts. Her tenderness is exquisite, and her expression of disgust and horror, while she averts her countenance and hides it with her hands, is peculiarly masterly. This single expression she has elaborately studied. Young played the jealous husband with spirit, but Charles Kemble was a mere ranting lover as Percy. *He* ought not to have given the name to the play.

November 12th. — Continued reading Wraxall. A repartee of Burke's pleased me. David Hartley, Member for Hull, was the dullest of speakers in the House of Commons. Having spoken so long as to drive away the greater number of the members (more than three hundred having dwindled down to eighty), he moved that the Riot Act should be read at the table, on which Burke, who sat next him, exclaimed : " My

---

* When, in 1815, the allied sovereigns arrived in Paris, they insisted upon the restoration of the objects of art which had been pillaged from various places by the orders of Napoleon. " A memorial from all the artists of Europe at Rome claimed for the Eternal City the entire restoration of the immortal works of art which had once adorned it. The allied sovereigns acceded to the just demand; and Canova, impassioned for the arts, and the city of his choice, hastened to Paris to superintend the removal. It was most effectually done." — Alison's *Europe*, Vol. XII., 286, 9th edition.

dear friend ! why, in God's name, read the Riot Act ? Do not you see that the mob are dispersed already ? " *

November 14th. — Dined at the Hall. After nine I called on Charles Lamb. He was much better in health and spirits than when I saw him last. Though *tête-à-tête*, he was able to pun. I was speaking of my first brief, when he asked, " Did you not exclaim, —

Thou great first cause, least understood ? "

November 22d. — Accompanied Miss Nash to the theatre, and saw " Tamerlane," a very dull play. It is more stuffed with trite declamation, and that of an inferior kind, than any piece I recollect. It is a compendium of political common-places. And the piece is not the more valuable because the doctrines are very wholesome and satisfactory. Tamerlane is a sort of regal Sir Charles Grandison, — a perfect king, very wise and insipid. He was not unfitly represented by Pope, if the character be intended merely as a foil to that of the ferocious Bajazet. Kean performed that character throughout under the idea of his being a two-legged *beast*. He rushed on the stage at his first appearance as a wild beast may be supposed to enter a new den to which his keepers have transferred him. His tartan whiskers improved the natural excellence of his face ; his projecting under-lip and admirably expressive eye gave to his countenance all desirable vigor ; and his exhibition of rage and hatred was very excellent. But there was no relief as there would have been had the bursts of feeling been only occasional. In the happy representation of one passion Kean afforded me great pleasure ; but this was all I enjoyed.

November 24th. — I called on Lamb, and chatted an hour with him. Talfourd stepped in, and we had a pleasant conversation. Lamb has a very exclusive taste, and spoke with equal contempt of Voltaire's Tales and " Gil Blas." He may be right in thinking the latter belongs to a low class of compositions, but he ought not to deny that it has excellence of its kind.

November 27th. — I dined at Collier's, and somewhat late went to Mrs. Joddrel's. There was an illumination to-night for the Peace, but it did not occur to me to look at a single public building, and I believe no one cared about it. A duller re-

* " Historical Memoirs of my Own Time," by Sir N. W. Wraxall. Vol. II. p. 377.

joicing could not be conceived. There was hardly a crowd in the streets.

December 5th. — Went to the Surrey Institution in the evening, and heard a lecture on the Philosophy of Art, by Landseer.* He is animated in his style, but his animation is produced by indulgence in sarcasms, and in emphatic diction. He pronounces his words in *italics;* and by coloring strongly he produces an effect easily.

December 7th. — I spent several hours at the Clerkenwell Sessions. A case came before the court ludicrous from the minuteness required in the examination. Was the pauper settled in parish A or B? The house he occupied was in both parishes, and models both of the house and the bed in which the pauper slept were laid before the court, that it might ascertain how much of his body lay in each parish. The court held the pauper to be settled where his head (being the nobler part) lay, though one of his legs at least, and great part of his body, lay out of that parish. Quod notandum est !

December 9th. — I read term reports in the forenoon, and after dining with the Colliers returned to my chambers till seven, when I went to Alsager's. There I met the Lambs, Hazlitt, Burrell, Ayrton, Coulson, Sleigh, &c. I enjoyed the evening, though I lost at cards, as I have uniformly done. Hazlitt was sober, argumentative, acute, and interesting. I did not converse with him, but enjoyed his conversation with others. Lamb was good-humored and droll, with great originality, as usual. Coulson was a new man almost to me. He is said to be a prodigy of knowledge, — a young *élève* of Jeremy Bentham, — a reporter for *The Chronicle.*

December 19th. — Spent the morning at Guildhall agreeably. After dining at the Colliers', I took a hasty cup of tea with Naylor, and was followed by him to Drury Lane Theatre. We saw Beaumont and Fletcher's play of " The Beggar's Bush." For the first time I saw Kean without any pleasure whatever. He has no personal dignity to supply the want of dress. No one suspects the Prince in the Merchant, and even as the Mer-

---

* John Landseer, an engraver of considerable talent, and father of the present Sir Edwin Landseer. He was born at Lincoln, 1769. In his later years the pen superseded the burin. He delivered a course of lectures on engraving at the Royal Institution in 1806; his best known literary works are " Sabæan Researches " and a " Descriptive Catalogue of Pictures in the National Gallery." His best engraving is from his son's well-known picture, " The Dogs of St. Bernard." He died in February, 1852.

chant he has not an air of munificence. He inspires no respect whatever; and he has no opportunity for the display
of his peculiar excellence, — bursts of passion. The beggar-
scenes and the loyal burgomaster of Bruges are very pleasant.
"Who's Who?" a farce by Poole, has an amusing scene or
two. Munden as a knavish Apothecary's shopman, and Harley as the Apothecary, are very comic. By the by, Harley is
a young and promising actor.

December 23d. — I read several chapters of Paley's "Evidences of Christianity," having resolved to read attentively
and seriously that and other works on a subject transcendently
important, and which I am ashamed thus long to have delayed
studying. I dined with the Colliers and spent some time at
home, taking tea alone. I called on Long, and had a short
chat with him. The lively pleasure he expressed at my informing him of the books I intended to study quite gratified me.
He is a most excellent creature. I look up to him with admiration the more I see of him.

December 27th. — Spent the morning at home reading industriously law reports. I dined with Collier, and having read
again in my room, I went after six o'clock to Thelwall's, and
was present at an exhibition which was more amusing than I
expected. "Comus" was performed by Thelwall's family and
his pupils. The idea of causing Milton's divine verse to be
theatrically recited by a troop of stutterers is comic enough,
but Thelwall has so far succeeded in his exertions, that he can
enable persons who originally had strong impediments in their
speech to recite verse very agreeably. Thelwall inserted some
appropriate short verses, to be delivered by the younger children as Bacchanals in an interlude, which had a pleasing effect.
He teaches his boys to read with a *cantilena ;* and the accent
at the close of their lines is very agreeable. It is only when
such words as dĕcīsiŏn are pronounced as four syllables, that we
are reminded of the master uncomfortably.

December 31st. — I spent this morning at my chambers,
but Thomas breakfasted with me, and Habakkuk came afterwards.

At half past five I went with the Amyots to Mr. Hallet's,
and dined there. It was a family party, and the evening
passed away comfortably. I was in good spirits, and the rest
of the party agreeable. The year was dismissed not festively
but cheerfully.

It has been, like most of the years of my life, a year of un-

interrupted health and prosperity. Besides, it is a year in
• which I have been so successful in my profession, that I have
a prospect of affluence if the success continues, which I dare
not expect, and about which I am far less anxious than I used
to be. I do not now fear poverty. I am not, nor ever was,
desirous of riches, but my wants do not, perhaps, increase in
proportion to my means. My brother Thomas makes it a reproach to me that I do not indulge myself more. This I do
not think a duty, and shall probably not make a practice. I
hope I shall not contract habits of parsimony.*

CHAPTER XIX.

1816.

JANUARY 9th. — (At Norwich.) This morning I went immediately after breakfast to a Jew dentist, C——, who put
in a natural tooth in the place of one I swallowed yesterday.
He assured me it came from Waterloo, and promised me it
should outlast twelve artificial teeth.

January 17th. — (At Bury.) I called with sister on Mrs.
Clarkson, to take leave of her. The Clarksons leave Bury to-
day, and are about to settle on a farm (Playford) near Ipswich.
No one deserves of the present race more than Clarkson to have
what Socrates proudly claimed of his judges, — a lodging in
the Prytaneion at the public expense. This ought to exclude
painful anxiety on his account, if the farm should not succeed.
They were in good spirits.

February 6th. — I attended the Common Pleas this morning, expecting that a demurrer on which we had a consultation
last night would come on, but it did not. I heard, however,
an argument worthy of the golden age of the English law, *scil.*
the age of the civil wars between the Houses of York and Lancaster, when the subtleties and refinements of the law were in
high flourishing condition, — or the silver age, that of the
Stuarts. An almshouse corporation, the warden and poor of
Croydon, in Surrey, on the foundation of Archbishop Whitgift,
brought an action for rent against their tenant. He pleaded

---

* These remarks were occasioned by the rise in H. C. R.'s fees from £ 219
in 1814, to £ 321 15 *s.* in the present year!

that, for a good and valuable consideration, they had sold him the land, as authorized by the statute, for redeeming land-tax. They replied that, in their conveyance, in setting out their title, they had omitted the words, " of the foundation of Arch- bishop Whitgift," and therefore they contended the deed was void, and that they might still recover their rent, as before. Good sense and honesty prevailed over technical sense.

February 11th. — I walked to Newington, and dined with Mrs. Barbauld and Miss Finch. Miss Hamond and Charles Aikin were there. As usual, we were very comfortable. Mrs. Barbauld can keep up a lively argumentative conversation as well as any one I know; and at her advanced age (she is turned of seventy), she is certainly the best specimen of female Presbyterian society in the country. N. B. — Anthony Robinson requested me to inquire whether she thought the doctrine of Universal Restoration scriptural. She said she thought we must bring to the interpretation of the Scriptures a very liberal notion of the beneficence of the Deity to find the doctrine there.

February 12th. — I dined with the Colliers, and in the even- ing went to Drury Lane with Jane Collier and Miss Lamb, to see " A New Way to pay Old Debts," a very spirited comedy by Massinger. Kean's Sir Giles Overreach is a very fine piece of acting indeed. His rage at the discovery of the fraud in the marriage of his daughter is wrought up to a wonderful height, and becomes almost too tragical. On the contrary, Munden, who also plays admirably the part of a knavish confidant, is infinitely comical, and in one or two instances he played too well, for he disturbed the impression which Kean was to raise by the equally strong effect of his own acting. Oxberry played Greedy, the hungry magistrate, pleasantly, and Harley was thought to perform Wellborn well; but he displeases me in this, that he seems to have no keeping. Sometimes he re- minds one of Banister, sometimes Lewis; so that at last he is neither a character nor himself. Mrs. Glover was agreeable in playing Lady Allworth.

February 15th. — A curious argument on the law of Primo- geniture. It was used by my friend Pattisson, and is a scrip- tural one. In the parable of the Prodigal Son, the father says to his dissatisfied elder son, " Son, all that I have is thine," which is a recognition of the right in the first-born.

February 25th. — At eight I went to Rough's, where I met Kean, — I should say to *see* him, not to hear him; for he scarcely spoke. I should hardly have known him. He has certainly a fine eye, but his features were relaxed, as if he had undergone great fatigue. When he smiles, his look is rather constrained than natural. He is but a small man, and from the gentleness of his manners no one would anticipate the actor who excels in bursts of passion.

March 10th. — (On Circuit at Bedford.) I was a little scandalized by the observation of the clerk of a prosecutor's solicitor, in a case in which I was engaged for the prosecution, that there was little evidence against one of the defendants, — that, in fact, he had not been very active in the riots, — but he was a sarcastic fellow, and they wished to punish him by putting him to the expense of a defence without any expectation of convicting him!

April 6th. — I rode to London by the old Cambridge coach, from ten to four.

Soon after I arrived I met Miss Lamb by accident, and in consequence took tea with her and Charles. I found Coleridge and Morgan at their house. Coleridge had been ill, but he was then, as before, loquacious, and in his loquacity mystically eloquent. He is endeavoring to bring a tragedy on the stage, in which he is not likely, I fear, to succeed ; and he is printing two volumes of Miscellanies, including a republication of his poems. But he is printing without a publisher ! He read me some metaphysical passages, which will be laughed at by nine out of ten readers ; but I am told he has written popularly, and about himself. Morgan is looking very pale, — rather unhappy than ill. He attends Coleridge with his unexampled assiduity and kindness.

April 21st. — After dining I rode to Wattisfield by the day-coach. I reached my uncle Crabb's by tea-time, and had an agreeable evening with him and Mrs. Crabb. I was pleased to revive some impressions which years have rendered interesting.

April 22d. — This was an indolent day, but far from an unpleasant one. I sat with Mr. and Mrs. Crabb a great part of the morning, and afterwards walked with Mr. Crabb, who was on horseback, through the street to Hill Green Farm. On the road family anecdotes and village narratives, suggested by the objects in view, rendered the walk agreeable to us both. Mr. Crabb is arrived at an age when it is a prime pleasure to relate the history of his early years ; and I am always an interested listener on such occasions. I am never tired by personal talk.* \The half-literary conversation of half-learned people, the commonplaces of politics and religious dispute, are to me intolerable ; but the passions of men excited by their genuine and immediate personal interest always gain my sympathy, or sympathy is supplied by the observations they suggest.   And in such conversations there is more truth and originality and variety than in the others, in which, particularly in religious conversations, there is a mixture of either Pharisaical imposture or imperfect self-deception.   Men on such occasions talk to convince themselves, not because they have feelings they must give vent to.

April 27th. — (At Cambridge.)   I walked to the coffee-room and read there the beginning of the trial of Wilson, Bruce, and Hutchinson, for concealing Lavalette.   In the examination of Sir R. Wilson, previous to the trial, he gave one answer which equals anything ever said by an accused person so examined. He was asked, " Were you applied to, to assist in concealing Lavalette ? " — " I was." — " Who applied to you ? " — " I was born and educated in a country in which the social virtues are considered as public virtues, and I have not trained my memory to a breach of friendship and confidence."

I dined in the Hall.   Each mess of four was allowed an extra bottle of wine and a goose, in honor of the marriage of the Princess Charlotte of Wales and the Prince of Saxe-Coburg, which took place this evening.

May 4th. — I rode to Bury on the outside of the " Day " coach from six to three. . . . . Between nine and ten we were alarmed by the intelligence that a fire had broken out.   I ran out, fearing it was at one of the Mr. Bucks ; but it was at a great distance.   Many people were on the road, most of whom were laughing, and seemingly enjoying the fire.   This was the fifth or sixth fire that had taken place within a week or two, and there could be no doubt it was an act of arson.   These very alarming outrages began some time since, and the pretence was the existence of threshing-machines.   The farmers in the neighborhood have surrendered them up, and exposed them broken on the high-road.   Besides, the want of work by the poor, and the diminished price of labor, have roused a dangerous spirit in the common people, — when roused, the most formidable of enemies.

* It was otherwise with his friend Wordsworth : —

> " I am not one who much or oft delight
> To season my fireside with personal talk."

Sonnets entitled " Personal Talk."   Vol. IV. p. 200.

May 28th. — Called on Godwin.   He was lately with
Wordsworth, and, after spending a night at his house, seems
to have left him with feelings of strong political difference ;
and it was this alone, I believe, which kept them aloof from
each other.   I have learned to bear with the intolerance of
others when I understand it.   While Buonaparte threatened
Europe with his all-embracing military despotism, I felt that all
other causes of anxiety and fear were insignificant, and I was
content to forget the natural tendencies of the regular governments to absolute power, of the people in those states to corruption, and of Roman Catholicism to a stupid and degrading
religious bigotry.   In spite of these tendencies, Europe was
rising morally and intellectually, when the French Revolution,
after promising to advance the world rapidly in its progress
towards perfection, suddenly, by the woful turn it took, threw
the age back in its expectations, almost in its wishes, till at
last, from alarm and anxiety, even zealous reformers were glad
to compromise the cause of liberty, and purchase national independence and political liberty at the expense of civil liberty
in France, Italy, &c.   Most intensely did I rejoice at the
counter-Revolution.   I had also rejoiced, when a boy, at the
Revolution, and I am ashamed of neither sentiment.   And I
shall not be ashamed, though the Bourbon government should
be as vile as any which France was cursed with under the ancestors of Louis XVIII., and though the promises of liberty given
to the Germans by their sovereigns should all be broken, and
though Italy and Spain should relapse into the deepest horrors
of Papal superstition.   To rejoice in *immediate* good is permitted to us.   The immediate alone is within our scope of
action and observation.   But now that the old system is restored, with it the old cares and apprehensions revive also.
And I am sorry that Wordsworth cannot change with the
times.   He ought, I think, now to exhort our government to
economy, and to represent the dangers of a thoughtless return
to all that was in existence twenty-five years ago.   Of the integrity of Wordsworth I have no doubt, and of his genius I
have an unbounded admiration ; but I doubt the discretion
and wisdom of his latest political writings.

June 12th. — Flaxman spoke about West.   I related the anecdote in his Life * of his first seeing the Apollo, and comparing

* The Life and Studies of Benjamin West, Esq., President of the Royal
Academy of London, prior to his Arrival in England, compiled from Materials
furnished by Himself." By John Galt. London, 1816. This book was pub-

it to a Mohawk warrior. Flaxman laughed, and said it was
the criticism of one almost as great a savage ; for though there
might be a coarse similarity in the attitude, Apollo having
shot an arrow, yet the figure of the Mohawk must have been
altogether unlike that of the god. This anecdote Flaxman
says he heard West relate more than twenty years ago, in a
discourse delivered as President of the Academy. The anecdotes of West's first drawing before he had seen a picture
Flaxman considers as fabulous.

June 14th. — Manning, after breakfasting with me, accompanied me to the Italian pictures.* The gratification was not
less than before. The admirable " Ecce Homo " of Guido in
particular delighted me, and also Murillo's " Marriage at
Cana." Amyot joined me there. Also I met Flaxman, and
with him was Martin Shee, whom I chatted with. Shee was
strong in his censure of allegory, and incidentally adverted to
a lady who reproached him with being unable to relish a certain poet because he wanted piety. The lady and poet, it appeared, were Lady Beaumont and Wordsworth. Both Flaxman
and Shee defended the conceit in the picture of the " Holy
Family in the Stable," in which the light issues from the
child ; and Flaxman quoted in its justification the expression
of the Scriptures, that Christ came as a light, &c.

June 23d. — I dined at Mr. Rutt's. I had intended to sleep
there ; but as Mr. Rutt goes early to bed, I preferred a late
walk home, from half past ten to twelve. And I enjoyed the
walk, though the evening was not very fine. I met a tipsy
man, whom I chatted with, and as he was a laborer of the lowest class, but seemingly of a quiet mind, I was glad to meet
with so fair a specimen of mob feeling. He praised Sir Francis

---

lished during the painter's life. A Second Part, relating to his life and studies
after his arrival in England, appeared just after his death in 1820, most of it
having been printed during his last illness. The anecdote referred to will be
found in the First Part, p. 105.

* At the British Institution, previously Boydell's Shakespeare Gallery, in
Pall Mall, and within the last few months destroyed. This Exhibition, opened
in May, 1816, was the first collection which the directors had formed of Italian
and Spanish paintings. The " Ecce Homo " by Guido, mentioned in the text,
was probably the one (No. 33 of the Catalogue) from Stratton, belonging to Sir
T. Baring. A second " Ecce Homo." No. 55, then belonging to Mr. West, and
afterwards bequeathed by the poet Rogers to the National Gallery, would have
been too painful in treatment to have elicited the expression used above. Murillo's " Marriage at Cana," No. 10 of the Catalogue, then belonged to Mr. G.
Hibbert. It had formerly been in the Julienne, Presle, and Robit Collections.
It is now at Tottenham Park, Wilts, the property of the Marquis of Ailesbury.
The " Holy Family in the Stable " was the " Adoration of the Magi." either
No. 22, the fine Paul Veronese, from the Crozat Collection, or 115, the Carlo
Dolci, belonging respectively to the Earl of Aberdeen and to Earl Cowper.

Burdett as the people's friend and only good man in the kingdom ; yet he did not seem to think flogging either sailors or
soldiers a very bad thing.   He had been assisting in building
the new Tothill Fields Prison, and said he would rather be .
hanged than imprisoned there seven years. He was somewhat
mysterious on this head. He said he would never sing, " Britons never shall be Slaves," for Britons are all slaves. Yet he
wished for war, because there would be work for the poor. If
this be the general feeling of the lower classes, the public peace
can only be preserved by a vigilant police and severe laws.

July 4th. — I dined with Walter. A small party. Dr.
Stoddart, Sterling, Sydenham, &c. The dinner was small but
of the first quality, — turbot, turtle, and venison, fowls and
ham ; wines, champagne, and claret. Sydenham was once reputed to be " Vetus," but his conversation is only intelligent
and anecdotic and gentlemanly ; he is neither logical, nor sarcastic, nor pointedly acute. He is therefore certainly not
" Vetus." He is a partisan of the Wellesleys, having been
with the Duke in India. Sterling is a sensible man. They
were all unfavorable to the actual ministry, and their fall
within six months was very confidently announced.

July 6th. — I took tea with Mrs. Barbauld, and played chess
with her till late. Miss H—— was there, and delighted at the
expectation of hearing a song composed by her sung at Covent
Garden.   When, however, I mentioned this to her brother, in
a jocular manner, he made no answer, and seemed almost offended. Sometimes I regret a want of sensibility in my nature,
but when such cases of perverted intensity of feeling are brought
to my observation, I rejoice at my neutral apathetic character,
as better than the more sanguine and choleric temperament,
which is so dangerous at the same time that it is so popular
and respectable. The older I grow, the more I am satisfied,
on prudential grounds, with the constitution of my sensitive
nature. I am persuaded that there are very few persons who
suffer so little pain of all kinds as I do ; and if the absence of
vice be the beginning of virtue, so the absence of suffering is
the beginning of enjoyment. I must confess, however, that I
think my own nature an object of felicitation rather than applause.

July 13th. — An unsettled morning. My print of Leonardo
da Vinci's " Vierge aux Rochers " was brought home framed. I
took it to Miss Lamb as a present. She was much pleased with
it, and so was Lamb, and I lost much of the morning in chat-

ting with Miss Lamb. I dined at the Colliers'. After dinner
I went to Lamb's and took tea with him. White of the India
House was there. We played three rubbers of whist. Lamb
was in great good-humor, delighted like a child with his present; but I am to change the frame for him, as all his other
frames are black. How Lamb confirms the remark of the childlikeness of genius!

Sunday, 14th. — I walked to Becher, and he accompanied
me to Gilman's, an apothecary at Highgate, with whom Coleridge is now staying. And he seems to have profited already
by the abstinence from opium, &c., for I never saw him look
so well. He talked very sensibly, but less eloquently and vehemently than usual. He asked me to lend him some books,
&c., and related a history of the great injustice done him in
the reports circulated about his losing books. And certainly I
ought not to join in the reproach, for he gave me to-day Kant's
works, three vols., miscellaneous. Coleridge talked about
Goethe's work on the theory of colors, and said he had some
years back discovered the same theory, and would certainly
have reduced it to form, and published it, had not Southey
diverted his attention from such studies to poetry. On my
mentioning that I had heard that an English work had been
published lately, developing the same system, Coleridge answered, with great *naïveté*, that he was very free in communi-
cating his thoughts on the subject wherever he went, and
among literary people.

July 18th. — The day was showery, but not very unpleasant.
I read and finished Goethe's first No. "Ueber Kunst," &c.,
giving an account of the works of art to be met with on the
Rhine. It is principally remarkable as evincing the great
poet's generous and disinterested zeal for the arts. He seems
to rejoice as cordially in whatever can promote the intellectual
prosperity of his country as in the success of his own great
masterpieces of art. His account of the early painting discovered at Cologne, and of the discovered design of the
Cathedral, is very interesting indeed. I also read "Des
Epimenides Erwachen," a kind of mask. It is an allegory, and
of course has no great pretensions; but there are fine moral
and didactic lines in very beautiful diction.

July 23d. — (At Bury.) This day was spent in court from
ten to half past five. It was occupied in the trial of several
sets of rioters, the defence of whom Leach brought me. I was
better pleased with myself than yesterday, and I succeeded in

getting off some individuals who would otherwise have been convicted. In the trial of fifteen Stoke rioters, who broke a threshing-machine, I made rather a long speech, but with little effect. All were convicted but two, against whom no evidence was brought. I urged that the evidence of mere presence against four others was not sufficient to convict them ; and had not the jury been very stupid, and the foreman quite incompetent, there would have been an acquittal.

On the trial of five rioters at Clare, I submitted to the conviction of four. One was acquitted.

On the trial of six rioters at Hunden, three were convicted, for they were proved to have taken an active share in destroying the threshing-machine. Alderson, who conducted all the prosecutions, consented to acquit one, and two others were acquitted because the one witness who swore to more than mere presence was contradicted by two witnesses I called, though the contradiction was not of the most pleasing kind.

We adjourned at half past five. One trial for a conspiracy took place, in which I had no concern, and it was the only contested matter in which I was not employed, — a very gratifying and promising circumstance.

July 24th. — I was in court from ten o'clock to three. The Rattlesden rioters, thirty in number, were tried. All were convicted except four, whom Alderson consented to discharge, and one who proved that he was compelled to join the rioters. Morgan, a fine, high-spirited old man of near seventy, who alone ventured among the mob, defying them without receiving any injury and by his courage gaining universal respect, deposed with such particularity to every one of the rioters, that it was in vain to make any defence. I made some general observations in behalf of the prisoners, and the Bench, having sentenced one to two years' imprisonment, and others to one year and six months' imprisonment, dismissed the greater number on their finding security for their good behavior.

August 3d. — (Bedford.) An agreeable day, being relieved from the burdensome society of the circuit. I breakfasted with Mr. Green, and about ten, Swabey and Jameson accompanied me to the village of Cardington. Here we looked over the parish church, in which is erected a beautiful monument by Bacon in memory of the elder Whitbread. Two female figures in alto and basso relief are supporting a dying figure.

The church has other monuments of less elaborate workmanship, and is throughout an interesting village church, very neat
and handsome without finery.

Jameson and I then looked into the garden of Captain
Waldegrave, remarkable as having been planted by the celebrated John Howard, who lived here before he undertook the
voyages which rendered his life and his death memorable. An
old man, Howard's gardener, aged eighty-six, showed us the
grotto left in the condition in which it was when Howard lived
there. The garden is chiefly interesting from the recollections
which it introduces of the very excellent man who resided
on the spot, and in which should be placed, as the most significant and desirable memorial, some representation of his
person. The village is very pretty. Howard's family are
buried in the church, and there is a small tablet to his memory : " John Howard, died at Cherson, in Russian Tartary.
January 20, 1790."

July 19th. — (Ipswich.) I rose at six, and enjoyed a leis-
urely walk to Playford, at four miles' distance, over a very
agreeable country, well cultivated and diversified by gentle
hills. Playford Hall stands in a valley. It consists of one
half of an ancient hall of considerable antiquity, which had
originally consisted of a regular three-sided edifice, a row of
columns having filled the fourth side of the square. There is
a moated ditch round the building, and by stopping the issue
of water, which enters by a never-failing, though small stream,
the ditch may be filled at any time. The mansion is of
brick, and the walls are very thick indeed. Some ancient
chimneys, and some large windows with stone frames of good
thickness, show the former splendor of the residence. Lord
Bristol is the owner of the estate, to which belongs four or five
hundred acres, and which Mr. Clarkson now has on a twenty-
one years' lease. Mr. Clarkson, on my arrival, showed me
about the garden ; and after I had breakfasted, Mrs. Clarkson
came down, and I spent a long morning very agreeably with
her. We walked to the parish church, up and down the
valley, round the fields, &c., and I readily sympathized with
Mrs. Clarkson in the pleasure with which she expatiated on the
comforts of the situation, and in the hope of their continued
residence there.

*Rem.** — To this place Mr. Clarkson retired after the great
work — the only work he projected, viz. the abolition of the

* Written in 1851.

slave-trade — was effected ; not anticipating that slavery itself would be abolished by our government in his day. This, however, would hardly have taken place had it not been for his exertions to accomplish the first step.

When the present extent of the evil is adverted to, as it frequently is, ungenerously, in order to lessen the merit of the abolitionists, it is always forgotten that if, on the revival of commerce after the peace of 1813, and the revival of the spirit of colonization by the European powers, the slave-trade had still been the practice of Europe, it would have increased tenfold. All Australia, New Zealand, and every part of the New World, would have been peopled by Africans, purchased or stolen by English, Dutch, and French traders.

August 29th. — At half past eight I mounted the Oxford stage, at the corner of Chancery Lane, on a tour, intended to embrace the lakes of Cumberland and Westmoreland.

Next day I met with two gentlemen, with whose appearance and manner I was at once struck and pleased, and with whom I became almost immediately acquainted. The name of one is Torlonia, a young Italian (about twenty), and of the other Mr. Walter, his tutor, about twenty-eight.

September 1st. — Strolling into the old church * at Manchester, I heard a strange noise, which I should elsewhere have mistaken for the bleating of lambs. Going to the spot, a distant aisle, I found two rows of women standing in files, each with a babe in her arms. The minister went down the line, sprinkling each infant as he went. I suppose the efficiency of the sprinkling — I mean the fact that the water did touch — was evidenced by a distinct squeal from each. Words were muttered by the priest on his course, but one prayer served for all. This I thought to be a christening by wholesale ; and I could not repress the irreverent thought that, being in the metropolis of manufactures, the aid of steam or machinery might be called in. I was told that on Sunday evenings the ceremony is repeated. Necessity is the only apology for so irreverent a performance of a religious rite. How the essence of religion is sacrificed to these formalities of the Establishment !

September 2d. — (At Preston.) My companions were glad to look into the Catholic chapel, which is spacious and neat. Mr. Walter purchased here a pamphlet, which afforded me some amusement. It is a narrative extracted from Luther's

* Then, I believe, the only parochial church of the town, and now raised to the rank of a cathedral. — H. C. R.

writings, of the dialogue related by Luther himself to have been carried on between him and the Devil, who, Luther declares, was the first who pointed out to him the absurdity and evil of private mass. Of course, it is strongly pressed upon the pious reader that even Luther himself confesses that the Father of Lies was the author of the Reformation ; and a pretty good story is made out for the Catholic.

September 5th. — (Ambleside.) This was one of the most delightful days of my journey ; but it is not easy to describe the gratification arising partly from the society of most excellent persons, and partly from beautiful scenery. Mr. Walter expressed so strong a desire to see Wordsworth, that I resolved to take him with me on a call. After breakfast we walked to Rydal, every turn presenting new beauty. The constantly changing position of the screen of hill produced a great variety of fine objects, of which the high and narrow pass into Rydal Water is the grandest. In this valley, to the right, stands a spacious house, the seat of the Flemings, and near it, in a finer situation, the house of Wordsworth. We met him in the road before the house. His salutation was most cordial. Mr. Walter's plans were very soon overthrown by the conversation of the poet in such a spot. He at once agreed to protract his stay among the lakes, and to spend the day at Grasmere. Torlonia was placed on a pony, which was a wild mountaineer, and, though it could not unhorse him, ran away with him twice. From a hillock Wordsworth pointed out several houses in Grasmere in which he had lived.*

During the day I took an opportunity of calling on De Quincey, my Temple Hall acquaintance. He has been very much an invalid, and his appearance bespoke ill health.

Our evening was spent at Wordsworth's. Mr. Tillbrook of Cambridge, formerly Thomas Clarkson's tutor,† was there. The conversation was general, but highly interesting. The evening was very fine, and we for the first time perceived all the beauties (glories they might be called) of Rydal Mount. It is so situated as to afford from the windows of both sitting-rooms a direct view of the valley, with the head of Windermere at its extremity, and from a terrace in the garden a view on to Rydal Water, and the winding of the valley in that direction. These views are of a very different character, and may be regarded as supplementing each other.

---

* The cottage at Townend, Allan Bank, and the Parsonage.
‡ Son of the abolitionist.

The house, too, is convenient and large enough for a family man.   And it was a serious gratification to behold so great and so good a man as Wordsworth in the bosom of his family enjoying those comforts which are apparent to the eye.   He has two sons and a daughter surviving.   They appear to be amiable children.   And, adding to these external blessings the *mind* of the man, he may justly be considered as one of the most enviable of mankind.   The injustice of the public towards him, in regard to the appreciation of his works, he is sensible of. But he is aware that, though the great body of readers — the admirers of Lord Byron, for instance — cannot and ought not. to be his admirers too, still he is not without his fame.   And he has that expectation of posthumous renown which has cheered many a poet, who has had less legitimate claims to it, and whose expectations have not been disappointed.

Mr. Walter sang some Scotch airs to Mr. Tillbrook's flute, and we did not leave Rydal Mount till late.   My companions declare it will be to them a memorable evening.

Just as we were going to bed De Quincey called on me.   He was in much better spirits than when I saw him in the morning and expressed a wish to walk with me about the neighborhood.

September 8th. —I returned to Kendal, partly to accommodate my friends, who were pledged to omit no opportunity of hearing Sunday mass.   I went to the Catholic chapel ; and as I stood up while others were kneeling, I found my coat tugged at violently.   This was occasioned by a combination of Roman Catholic and Italian zeal.   The tug of recognition came from an Italian boy, a Piedmontese image-seller, whom we had met with before on the road, — a spirited lad, who refused a shilling Torlonia offered him, and said he had saved enough by selling images and other Italian articles to buy himself land in Savoy.   I understood him to say £ 80 ; but that is probably a mistake.   He had, however, been several years in England.

September 9th. — (Keswick.)   We were gratified by receiving an invitation to take tea with the Poet Laureate.   This was given to our whole party, and our dinner was, in consequence, shortened.   I had a small room on a second floor, from the windows of which I had a glimpse only of the fine mountain scenery, and could see a single house only amid gardens out of the town.   The mountain was Skiddaw.   The house was Southey's.

The laureate lives in a large house in a nurseryman's

grounds. It enjoys a panoramic view of the mountains; and as Southey spends so much of his time within doors, this lovely and extensive view supplies the place of travelling beyond his own premises.

We spent a highly agreeable evening with Southey. Mr. Nash, Mr. Westall, Jun., several ladies, Miss Barker, Mrs. Southey, Mrs. Coleridge, and Mrs. Lovell, were of the party. The conversation was on various subjects. Southey's library is richly stored with Spanish and Portuguese books. These he showed to my Catholic friends, withholding some which he thought might give them uneasiness. Looking at his books, he said, with great feeling, that he sometimes regarded them with pain, thinking what might hereafter become of them, — a pathetic allusion to the loss of his son.

On Spanish politics he spoke freely. At the same time that he reproached Ferdinand with a want of generosity, he stated his conviction that he acted *defensively*. The liberals would have dethroned him at once, had they been permitted to carry into effect the new constitution.

I found his opinions concerning the state and prospects of this country most gloomy. He considers the government seriously endangered by the writings of Cobbett, and still more by the *Examiner*. Jacobinism he deems more an object of terror than at the commencement of the French Revolution, from the difficulties arising out of the financial embarrassments. He says that he thinks there will be a convulsion in three years !

I was more scandalized by his opinions concerning the press than by any other doctrine. He would have transportation the punishment for a seditious libel ! ! ! I ought to add, however, that I am convinced Southey is an honest alarmist. I did not dispute any point with him.

Hartley Coleridge is one of the strangest boys I ever saw.* He has the features of a foreign Jew, with starch and affected manners. He is a boy pedant, exceedingly formal, and, I should suppose, clever.

Coleridge's daughter has a face of great sweetness.†

Derwent Coleridge I saw at Wordsworth's. He is a hearty boy, with a good-natured expression. Of literature not much was said. Literature is now Southey's trade ; he is a manu-

---

* Hartley Coleridge is the author of "Northern Worthies," and numerous beautiful poems. His life was written by his brother Derwent.

† Afterwards Mrs. Henry Nelson Coleridge, the editor of many of her father's works.

facturer, and his workshop is his study, — a very beautiful one certainly, but its beauty and the delightful environs, as well as his own celebrity, subject him to interruptions. His time is his wealth, and I shall therefore scrupulously abstain from stealing any portion of it.

September 11th. — I left Torlonia and his tutor with feelings almost of friendship, certainly of respect and regard, and I look forward with pleasure to the continuance of our acquaintance.

*Rem.** — The tutor was gentlemanly in his manners, and as liberal as a sincere Roman Catholic could be. The young man was reserved and well-bred, but already an artificial character, so that I was prepared for what I afterwards experienced from him.†

September 10th. — After I had taken a cold dinner, Mr. Wordsworth came to me, and between three and four we set out for Cockermouth ; he on horseback, I on foot. We started in a heavy shower, which thoroughly wetted me. The rain continued with but little intermission during a great part of the afternoon, and therefore the fine scenery in the immediate neighborhood of Keswick was entirely lost. The road, too, was so very bad, that all my attention was requisite to keep my shoes on my feet. I have no recollection of any village or of any scenery, except some pleasing views of the lake of Bassenthwaite, and of Skiddaw, from which we seemed to recede so little, that even when we were near Cockermouth the mountain looked near to us. In the close and interesting conversation we kept up, Mr. Wordsworth was not quite attentive to the road, and we lost our way. A boy, however, who guided us through some terribly dirty lanes, put us right. By this time it was become dark, and it was late before we reached the Globe at Cockermouth.

If this were the place, and if my memory were good, I could enrich my journal by retailing Wordsworth's conversation. He is an eloquent speaker, and he talked upon his own art, and his own works, very feelingly and very profoundly ; but I cannot venture to state more than a few intelligible results, for I own that much of what he said was above my comprehension.

He stated, what I had before taken for granted, that most of his lyrical ballads were founded on some incident he had

---

* Written in 1851.
† See a future chapter in reference to H. C. R.'s residence in Rome.

witnessed or heard of. He mentioned the origin of several poems.

"Lucy Gray," * that tender and pathetic narrative of a child mysteriously lost on a common, was occasioned by the death of a child who fell into the lock of a canal. His object was to exhibit poetically entire *solitude,* and he represents the child as observing the day-moon, which no town or village girl would even notice.

The "Leech-Gatherer" † he did actually meet near Grasmere, except that he gave to his poetic character powers of mind which his original did not possess.

The fable of "The Oak and the Broom" ‡ proceeded from his beholding a rose in just such a situation as he described the broom to be in. Perhaps, however, all poets have had their works suggested in like manner. What I wish I could venture to state after Wordsworth is his conception of the manner in which the mere fact is converted into poetry by the power of imagination.

He represented, however, much as, unknown to him the German philosophers have done, that by the imagination the mere fact is exhibited as connected with that infinity without which there is no poetry.

He spoke of his tale of the dog, called "Fidelity." § He says he purposely made the narrative as prosaic as possible, in order that no discredit might be thrown on the truth of the incident. In the description at the beginning, and in the moral at the end, he has alone indulged in a poetic vein ; and these parts, he thinks, he has peculiarly succeeded in.

He quoted some of the latter poem, and also from " The Kitten and the Falling Leaves," ‖ to show he had connected even the kitten with the great, awful, and mysterious powers of nature. But neither now, nor in reading the Preface to Wordsworth's new edition of his poems, have I been able to comprehend his ideas concerning poetic imagination. I have not been able to raise my mind to the subject, further than this, that imagination is the faculty by which the poet conceives and produces — that is, images — individual forms, in which are embodied universal ideas or abstractions. This I do comprehend, and I find the most beautiful and striking illustrations of this faculty in the works of Wordsworth himself.

---

* Wordsworth's " Poetical Works." Vol. I. p. 156.
† " Resolution and Independence." Vol. II. p. 124.
‡ Vol. II. p. 20.   § Vol. IV. p. 207.
‖ Vol. II. p. 61.

The incomparable twelve lines, "She dwelt among the un-trodden ways," * ending, "The difference to me!" are finely imagined. They exhibit the powerful effect of the loss of a very obscure object upon one tenderly attached to it. The opposition between the apparent strength of the passion and the insignificance of the object is delightfully conceived, and the object itself well portrayed.

September 12th. — This was a day of rest, but of enjoyment also, though the amusement of the day was rather social than arising from the beauties of nature.

I wrote some of my journal in bed. After my breakfast I accompanied Mr. Wordsworth, Mr. Hutton, and a Mr. Smith to look at some fields belonging to the late Mr. Wordsworth,† and which were to be sold by auction this evening. I may here mention a singular illustration of the maxim, "A prophet is not without honor save in his own country." Mr. Hutton, a very gentlemanly and seemingly intelligent man, asked me, "Is it true, — as I have heard reported, — that Mr. Wordsworth ever wrote verses?"

September 13th. — This morning I rose anxious to find the change of weather of which yesterday had afforded us a reason-able hope. For a time I was flattered by the expectation that summer would come at last, though out of season; but the clouds soon collected, and the day, to my great regret, though still not to the loss of my spirits or temper, proved one of the worst of my journey.

I wrote in my journal till I was called to accompany Words-worth and Mr. Hutton. They were on horseback. The first part of our road, in which one lofty and precipitous rock is a noble object, lay to the right of the mountains in Lorton Vale, which we skirted at a distance. As we advanced the weather grew worse. We passed Lampleugh Cross, and when we came near the vale of Ennerdale, and were at the spot where the vale is specially beautiful and interesting, the mist was so thick as to obscure every object. Nothing was distinguishable. We crossed the bridge at Ennerdale, and there the road led us over Cold Fell. Cold and fell certainly were the day and the scene. It rained violently, so that it was with difficulty I could keep up my umbrella. The scene must be wild at any time. The only object I could discern was a sort of naked glen on our

---

* "Resolution and Independence." Vol. I. p. 215.
† Wordsworth's eldest brother, Richard, who was Solicitor to the Commis-sioners of his Majesty's Woods and Forests.

right ; a secluded spot, rendered lively, however, by a few farm-houses. As we descended the fell the weather cleared up, and I could discern an extensive line of the Irish Sea. And as we approached Calder Bridge we beheld the woods of Ponsonby, in which Calder Abbey stands, together with an interesting champaign scene of considerable extent. I ought not to omit that it was on this very Cold Fell that Mr. Wordsworth's father lost his way, and spent a whole night. He was instantly taken ill, and never rose again from the attack. He died in a few weeks.

The dreary walk had been relieved by long and interesting conversations, sometimes on subjects connected with the business arising out of the late Mr. Wordsworth's will, and sometimes on poetry.

We had, too, at the close of the walk, a very great pleasure. We turned out of the road to look at the ruins of Calder Abbey. These ruins are of small extent, but they are very elegant indeed. The remains of the centre arches of the Abbey are very perfect. The four grand arches, over which was the lanthorn of the church, are entire. There are also some pillars, those of the north side of the nave, and one or two low Norman doors, of great beauty. We inserted our names in a book left in a small apartment, where are preserved some remains of sculpture and some Roman inscriptions.

At half a mile distance is the inn at Calder Bridge, where we dined and took tea. Wordsworth was fatigued, and therefore, after an hour's chat, he took the *Quarterly Review*, and I took to my journal, which I completed at twelve o'clock.

I omitted to notice that I read yesterday Southey's article on the Poor, in the last *Quarterly Review*, a very benevolently conceived and well-written article, abounding in excellent ideas, and proving that, though he may have changed his opinions concerning governments and demagogues, he retains all his original love of mankind, and the same zeal to promote the best interests of humanity.

September 14th. — (Ravenglass.) We left our very comfortable inn, the Fleece at Calder Bridge, after breakfast. The day appeared to be decidedly bad, and I began to despair of enjoying any fine weather during my stay in the country. As I left the village, I doubly regretted going from a spot which I could through mist and rain discern to be a delicious retreat, more resembling the lovely secluded retirements I have often seen in Wales, than anything I have met with on the present journey. We had but seven miles to walk. We were now near the sea, with mountains on our left hand. We, however, went to see the grounds of an Admiral Lutwidge, at Holm Rook; and, sending in a message to the master of the house, he came out, and dryly gave the gardener permission to accompany us over the garden. He eyed us closely, and his manner seemed that of a person who doubted whether we were entitled to the favor we asked. The grounds are pleasingly laid out. The Irt — to-day at least a rapid river — runs winding in a valley which has been planted on each side. From the heights of the grounds fine views may be seen on fine days. We went into a hot-house, and after admiring the rich clusters of grapes, were treated with a bunch of them.

Having ascertained that we could cross the estuary of the Mite River, we came to Ravenglass by the road next the sea, and found Mr. Hutton in attendance.

I was both wet and dirty, and was glad, as yesterday, to throw myself between the blankets of a bed and read the *Quarterly Review*. A stranger joined us at the dinner-table, and after dinner we took a stroll beyond the village. Near Ravenglass, the Esk, the Irt, and the Mite flow into the sea; but the village itself lies more dismally than any place I ever saw on a sea-shore; though I could hear the murmur of the sea, I could barely see it from a distance. Sand-hills are visible on each side in abundance.

The place consists of a wretched street, and it has scarcely a decent house, so that it has not a single attraction or comfort in bad weather. On a clear day, I understand, there are fine views from the adjacent hills.

The auction — of some pieces of land — did not begin till we had taken tea. This is the custom in this country. Punch is sent about while the bidding is going on, and it is usual for a man to go from one room to another, and report the bidding which is made in the rooms where the auctioneer is not. While I have been writing this page, I have continually heard the voice of this man.

I have also been once down stairs, but the passage is crowded by low people, to whom an auction must be an extraordinary and remarkable occurrence in a place so secluded and remote as this, and who, besides, contrive to get access to the punch-bowl. I have been reading the article in the *Quarterly Review* about Madame la Roche Jacquelein, by Southey. It is very interesting, like the *Edinburgh* review of the same work, — a

15*

good epitome of the narrative. But though I am removed sufficiently from the bustle of the auction not to be disturbed by it, yet the circumstances are not favorable to my being absorbed by my book.

I slept in a double-bedded room with Wordsworth. I went early to bed and read till he came up stairs.

September 15th. — On Hardknot Wordsworth and I parted, he to return to Rydal, and I to Keswick.

Rem.* — Making Keswick my head-quarters, I made excursions to Borrowdale, which surpasses any vale I have seen in the North, to Wastdale, to Crummock Water, and to Buttermere; during a part of the time the weather was favorable. At the last-named place, the landlady of the little inn, the successor to Mary of Buttermere, is a very sweet woman, — even genteel in person and manners. The Southeys and Wordsworths all say that she is far superior to the celebrated Mary.

September 22d. — (Keswick.) Though I felt unwilling to quit this magnificent centre of attractions, yet my calculations last night convinced me that I ought to return. Half of my time, and even more, is spent, and almost half my money. Everything combines to render this the solstice of my excursion.

Having breakfasted, I carried a book to Southey and took leave of the ladies. He insisted on accompanying me, at least to the point where the Thirlmere Road, round the western side of the lake, turns off. I enjoyed the walk. He was both frank and cordial. We spoke freely on politics. I have no doubt of the perfect purity and integrity of his mind. I think that he is an alarmist, though what he fears is a reasonable cause of alarm, viz. a *bellum servile*, stimulated by the press. Of all calamities in a civilized state, none is so horrid as a conflict between the force of the poor, combining together with foresight and deliberation, and that of the rich, the masters, the repositaries of whatever intellectual stores the country possesses. The people, Southey thinks, have just education and knowledge enough to perceive that they are not placed in such a condition as they ought to be in, without the faculty of discovering the remedy for the disease, or even its cause. In such a state, with the habit of combination formed through the agency of benefit societies, as the system of the Luddites †

---

* Written in 1851.

† Serious riots were caused in 1812, 1814, 1816, and subsequently, by large parties of men under this title. They broke frames and machinery in factories, besides committing other excesses.

shows, judgments are perverted, and passions roused, by such writers as Cobbett and Hunt, and the war is in secret preparing. This seems to be the idea uppermost in Southey's mind, and which has carried him very honestly further than perhaps he ought to be carried in support of government. But he is still, and warmly, a friend to national education, and to the lower classes, and as humane as ever he was. He has convinced me of the perfect exemption of his mind from all dishonorable motives, in the change which has taken place in his practical politics and philosophy.

We conversed also on literature, — on Wordsworth and his own works. He appreciates Wordsworth as he ought. Of his own works he thinks " Don Roderick " by far the best, though Wordsworth prefers, as I do, his " Kehama." Neither of us spoke of his political poems.

September 24th. — (Ambleside.) I called on Wordsworth, who offered to accompany me up Nab Scar, the lofty rocky fell immediately behind and hanging over his house. The ascent was laborious, but the view from the summit was more interesting than any I had before enjoyed from a mountain on this journey. I beheld Rydal Water from the brow of the mountain, and afterwards, under a favorable sun, though the air was far from clear, I saw Windemere, with little interruption, from the foot to the head, Esthwaite Lake, Blelham Tarn, a part of Coniston Lake, a very extensive coast with the estuary near Lancaster, &c., &c. These pleasing objects compensated for the loss of the nobler views from Helvellyn, which I might have had, had I not engaged to dine with De Quincey to-day.

Wordsworth conducted me over the fell, and left me, near De Quincey's house, a little after one. He was in bed, but rose on my arrival. I was gratified by the sight of a large collection of books, which I lounged over. De Quincey, about two, set out on a short excursion with me, which I did not so much enjoy as he seemed to expect. We crossed the sweet vale of Grasmere, and ascended the fell on the opposite corner of the valley to Easdale Tarn. The charm of this spot is the solemnity of the seclusion in which it lies. There is a semicircle of lofty and gray rocks, which are wild and rugged, but promote the repose suggested by the motionless water.

We returned to dinner at half past four, and in an hour De Quincey accompanied me on the mountain road to Rydal Mount, and left me at the gate of Wordsworth's garden-terrace.

I took tea with Mr. and Mrs. Wordsworth, and Miss Hutchinson, and had four hours of conversation as varied and delightful as I ever enjoyed; but the detail ought not to be introduced into a narrative like this.

Wordsworth accompanied me on the road, and I parted from him under the impressions of thankfulness for personal attentions, in addition to the high reverence I felt before for his character. I found De Quincey up, and chatted with him till past twelve.

September 25th. — This was a day of unexpected enjoyment. I lounged over books till past ten, when De Quincey came down to breakfast. It was not till past twelve we commenced our walk, which had been marked out by Wordsworth. We first passed Grasmere Church, and then, going along the opposite side of the lake, crossed by a mountain road into the vale of Great Langdale. The characteristic repose of Grasmere was fully enjoyed by me.

My return from the Lakes comprehended a visit to my friend George Stansfeld,* then settled at Bradford. With him I made an excursion to Halifax, where was then living Dr. Thompson, who, after being an esteemed Unitarian preacher, became a physician. An early death deprived the world of a very valuable member of society, and my friend Mrs. William Pattisson of a cousin, of whom she and her husband had reason to be proud.

At Leeds, I took a bed at Mr. Stansfeld's, Sen. I always feel myself benefited by being with the Stansfeld family. There is something most gratifying in the sight of domestic happiness united with moral worth.

At Norwich, where I joined the Sessions, I heard the city member, William Smith, address his constituents on a petition for parliamentary reform, which he promised to present. I admired the tact with which he gave the people to understand that little good could be expected from their doings, and yet gave no offence.

October 14th. — To-day my journey ends, — a journey of great pleasure; for I had good health, good spirits, and a will determined to be pleased. I had also the advantage of enjoying occasionally the very best society. Otherwise my tour would have been a sad one, having been undertaken in a season the worst which any man recollects, and peculiarly unfavorable to the enjoyment of picturesque scenery.

* See *ante*, p. 150.

H. C. R. TO WORDSWORTH.

[No date.]

MY DEAR SIR, — I fear I must have appeared very ungrateful to you, and yet I do not reproach myself for my silence so much as I perhaps ought, for I am conscious how much you and your family, and everything connected with you, have dwelt on my mind since last September, and that I have not lost, and do not fear to lose, the most lively and gratifying recollection of your kindness and attentions. It is these alone that prevent my regretting the selection of such an unpropitious summer for my tour. Did I once see a bright sun in Cumberland or Westmoreland? I very much doubt it.

At last, however, the sun, as if to show how much he could do without any accompaniment whatever, made his appearance in the middle of a Lincolnshire wash, and I actually walked several days with perfect contentment, though I had no other object to amuse me. I was supported by that internal hilarity which I have more than once found an adequate cause of happiness. At some moments, I own, I thought that there was an insulting spirit in the joyous vivacity and freshness with which some flat blotches of water, without even a shore, were curled by the breeze, and made alive and gaudy by moorfowl, small birds, and insects, while floating clouds scattered their shadows over the dullest of heaths. Or was all this to admonish and comfort a humble Suffolk-man, and show him how high the meanest of countries may be raised by sunshine, and how low the most glorious may be depressed by the absence of it, or the interference of a mere vapor?

November 2d. — At ten o'clock I called on the Lambs. Burney was there, and we played a rubber, and afterwards Talfourd stepped in. We had a long chat together.

We talked of puns, wit, &c. Lamb has no respect for any wit which turns on a serious thought. He positively declared that he thought his joke about my "great first cause, least understood," a bad one. On the other hand, he said : "If you will quote any of my jokes, quote this, which is really a good one. Hume and his wife and several of their children were with me. Hume repeated the old saying, 'One fool makes many.' 'Ay, Mr. Hume,' said I, pointing to the company, 'you have a fine family.'" Neither Talfourd nor I could see the excellence of this. However, he related a piece of wit by Coleridge which we all held to be capital. Lamb had written to Coleridge about one of their old Christ's Hospital masters, who had been a severe disciplinarian, intimating that he hoped Coleridge had forgiven all injuries. Coleridge replied that he certainly had ; he hoped his soul was in heaven, and that when he went there he was borne by a host of cherubs, all face and wing, and without anything to excite his whipping propensities !

We talked of Hazlitt's late ferocious attack on Coleridge, which Lamb thought fair enough, between the parties ; but he was half angry with Martin Burney for asserting that the praise was greater than the abuse. " Nobody," said Lamb, " will care about or understand the 'taking up the deep pauses of conversation between seraphs and cardinals,' but the satire will be universally felt. Such an article is like saluting a man, 'Sir, you are the greatest man I ever saw,' and then pulling him by the nose."

Sunday, 24th. — I breakfasted with Basil Montagu. Arriving before he was ready to receive me, he put into my hands a sermon by South, on Man as the Image of God, perfect before the Fall, — a most eloquent and profound display of the glories of man in an idealized condition, with all his faculties clarified, as it were, and free from the infirmities of sense. It is absurd to suppose this as the actual condition of Adam, for how could such a being err ? But as a philosophical and ideal picture it is of superlative excellence. In treating of the intellect, I observed a wonderful similarity between South and Kant. I must and will read more of this very great and by me hitherto unknown writer.

I read at Montagu's Coleridge's beautiful " Fire, Famine, and Slaughter," written in his Jacobinical days, and now reprinted, to his annoyance, by Hunt in the *Examiner.* Also an article on commonplace critics by Hazlitt. His definition of good company excellent, — " Those who live on their own estates and other people's ideas."

December 1st. — This was a pleasantly though idly spent day. I breakfasted with Walter and Torlonia, and then accompanied them to the Portuguese Minister's chapel, where the restoration of the Braganza family to the throne of Portugal was celebrated by a grand performance of mass. I had the advantage of knowing the words, and they assisted my dull sense in properly feeling the import of the music, which I unaffectedly enjoyed. Strutt was there, and declared it was most excellent. " I was like the unbeliever," said he, " and ready to cry out, 'Almost thou persuadest me.'" I was myself particularly pleased with the finale of the creed, — a triumphant flourish, as if the believer, having declared his faith, went away rejoicing. The transition and the pathetic movements in the *Te Deum* are, from the contrast, very impressive.

Cargill was telling me the other day that in a letter written by Lord Byron to Hogg, the Ettrick Shepherd, in his rattling way he wrote : " Wordsworth, stupendous genius ! D——d fool ! These poets run about their ponds though they cannot fish. I am told there is not one who can angle. D——d fools."

December 2d. — I dined at the Colliers', and afterwards went to Drury Lane with Naylor, who had procured orders and a box for us. We saw " The Iron Chest "; a play of little merit, I think. The psychological interest is all the work of Godwin. Colman has added nothing that is excellent to " Caleb Williams." The underplot is very insipid, and is hardly connected with the main incident. But the acting of Kean was very fine indeed. He has risen again in my esteem. His impassioned disclosure of the secret to Wilford, and his suppressed feelings during the examination of Wilford before the magistrates, were most excellent ; though it is to be observed that the acting of affected sensations, such as constrained passion under the mask of indifference, is an easy task. If the poet has well conceived the situation, the imagination of the spectator wonderfully helps the actor. I was at a distance, and yet enjoyed the performance.

December 21st. — Called on Coleridge, and enjoyed his conversation for an hour and a half. He looked ill, and, indeed, Mr. Gilman says he has been very ill. Coleridge has been able to work a great deal of late, and with success. The second and third Lay Sermons and his Poems, and Memoirs of his Life, &c., in two volumes, are to appear. These exertions have been too great, Mr. Gilman says.

Coleridge talked easily and well, with less than his usual declamation. He explained, at our request, his idea of fancy, styling it memory without judgment, and of course not filling that place in a chart of the mind which imagination holds, and which in his Lay Sermon he has admirably described.* Wordsworth's obscure discrimination between fancy and imagination, in his last preface, is greatly illustrated by what Coleridge has here written. He read us some extracts from his new poems,

* H. C. R. had probably in his mind " Biographia Literaria," V. I. pp. 81, 82.

&c., and spoke of his German reading. He praises Steffens and complains of the Catholicism of Schlegel and Tieck, &c.

He mentioned Hazlitt's attack upon him with greater moderation than I expected.

*Rem.** — It was the day after this conversation with Coleridge, that I broke altogether with Hazlitt, in consequence of an article in the *Examiner*,† manifestly written by him, in which he abused Wordsworth for his writings in favor of the King.

After I had cut Hazlitt, Mary Lamb said to me : " You are rich in friends. We cannot afford to cast off our friends because they are not all we wish." And I have heard Lamb say : " Hazlitt does bad actions without being a bad man."

Rem.‡ — My fees during the year had risen from £ 321 15s. to £ 355 19 s.

At the Spring Assizes we had Baron Wood, a judge who was remarkable for his popular feelings. He was praised by some of our Radicals for being always *against* the Church and King. In one case he exhibited a very strong *moral* feeling, which perhaps betrayed him to an excess. He had a very honorable dislike to prosecutions or actions on the game laws, and this led him to make use of a strong expedient to defeat two actions. A and B had gone out sporting together. The plaintiff brought two actions, and in the action against B called A to prove the sporting by B, and meant to call B to prove the case against A. This was apparent, indeed avowed. But the Baron interposed, when the witness objected to answer a question that *tended* to convict himself. A squabble arising between the counsel, the Baron said to the witness : " I do not ask you whether you ever went out sporting with the defendant, because, if I did, you would very properly refuse to answer. But I ask you this : Except at a time when you might have been sporting with the defendant, did you ever see him sport ? "

" Certainly not, my lord."

" Of course you did not."

Then the Baron laughed heartily, and nonsuited the plaintiff. No motion was made to set this nonsuit aside.

It was at the Summer Circuit that Rolfe made his first appearance. He had been at the preceding Sessions. I have a

---

* Written in 1851.

† The *Examiner* of December **24, 1815,** contains some contemptuous remarks on Wordsworth's poetry, signed **W.**

‡ Written in 1850.

pleasure in recollecting that I at once foresaw that he would become a distinguished man. In my Diary I wrote : " Our new junior, Mr. Rolfe, made his appearance. His manners are genteel ; his conversation easy and sensible. He is a very acceptable companion, but I fear a dangerous rival." And my brother asking me who the new man was, I said : " I will venture to predict that you will live to see that young man attain a higher rank than any one you ever saw upon the circuit." It is true he is not higher than Leblanc, who was also a puisne judge, but Leblanc was never Solicitor-General ; nor, probably, is Rolfe yet at the end of his career. One day, when some one remarked, " Christianity is part and parcel of the law of the land," Rolfe said to me, " Were you ever employed to draw an indictment against a man for not loving his neighbor as himself ? "

Rolfe is, by universal repute, if not the very best, at least one of the best judges on the Bench. He is one of the few with whom I have kept up an acquaintance.*

I was advised to attend the Old Bailey Sessions, which I did several times this year ; whether beyond this time or not I cannot tell, but I know that it never produced me a fee. And I should say I am glad it did not, except that my not being employed shows that I wanted both a certain kind of talent and a certain kind of reputation. I was once invited by the Sheriffs to dine with the Lord Mayor and the Judges. It was the practice to ask by turns two or three men, both at three and five o'clock. I know not whether this is still done.†

In the autumn of this year died Mrs. Thelwall, for whom I felt a very sincere respect. She was her husband's good angel. Before she died he had become acquainted with a Miss Boyle, who came to him as a pupil to be qualified for the stage. She failed in that scheme, and ultimately became Thelwall's wife, without any imputation on her character. She is still living with her son, and is a Roman Catholic.

* Since writing the above, Baron Rolfe has verified my prediction more strikingly by being created a peer, by the title of Lord Cranworth, and appointed a Vice-Chancellor. Soon after his appointment, he called on me, and I dined with him. I related to Lady Cranworth the anecdote given above, of my conversation with my brother, with which she was evidently pleased. Lady Cranworth was the daughter of Mr. Carr, Solicitor to the Excise, whom I formerly used to visit, and ought soon to find some mention of in my journals. Lord Cranworth continues to enjoy universal respect. — H. C. R., 1851.

Lord and Lady Cranworth continued their friendship for H. C. R. until his death. Lord Cranworth was twice Lord Chancellor.

† It is.

w

During this year my acquaintance with Hamond continued. I now became acquainted with his cousin Miller, the clergyman, and I for the first time visited his friend Pollock, now Lord Chief Baron. Hamond went to France, having declined an offer by Sergeant Rough, who would have taken him as his private secretary to Demerara. He assigned as a reason that he should be forced to live in the daily practice of insincerity, by subscribing himself the humble servant of those towards whom he felt no humility.

CHAPTER XX.

1817.

FEBRUARY 5th. — I had to-day the pleasure of being reminded of old times, and of having old enjoyments brought back to my mind. I saw for the first time Mrs. Alsop, Mrs. Jordan's daughter, the plainest woman, I should think, who ever ventured on the stage. She, nevertheless, delighted me by the sweet tones of her voice, which frequently startled me by their resemblance to her mother's. Mrs. Alsop has the same, or nearly the same, hearty laugh as Mrs. Jordan, and similar frolicsome antics. The play was a lively Spanish comedy. How I should have enjoyed her acting, if I had not recollected her mother, I cannot tell.

February 8th. — On stepping to my chambers I was surprised by finding there, handsomely framed and glazed, prints of Domenichino's " St. John the Evangelist," * and of the " Madonna di S. Sisto," by Müller. The latter engraving delighted me beyond expression. As I considered the original painting the finest I had ever seen, twelve years ago, so I deem the print the very finest I ever saw.

February 11th. — I called late on Aders. He informed me that the fine engravings I found at my chambers on Saturday are a present from Mr. Aldebert. The Madonna diffuses a

---

* The original picture of the inspired Evangelist about to write, and the eagle bringing him the pen, from which Christian Frederich Müller took his engraving, was formerly at Stuttgart, in the Frommann Collection, and is now the property of Prince Narischkin, in St. Petersburg. There is an excellent repetition of this picture (formerly in the Orleans Gallery) at Castle Howard, belonging to the Earl of Carlisle.

serenity and delight beyond any work of art I am acquainted with. I hope it will be my companion through life.* What a companion for a man in prison ! I read at night a very ill-written German book about Raphael by one Braun,† but which will nevertheless assist me in acquiring the knowledge about Raphael's works in general which I am anxious to possess.

March 11th. — (On Circuit at Aylesbury.) We dined with Baron Graham, and the dinner was more agreeable than any I ever had with any judge. The Baron was very courteous and chatty. He seemed to enjoy talking about old times when he attended the Circuit as counsel. It was, he said, forty years this spring since he first attended the Circuit. " At that time," he said, " there were three old Sergeants, Foster, Whitaker, and Sayer. They did business very ill, so that Leblanc and I soon got into business, almost on our first coming." Whitaker, in particular, he spoke of as a man who knew nothing of law, — merely loved his joke. Foster did know law, but could not speak. He spoke of Leblanc in terms of great praise. He had the most business-like mind of any man he ever knew. He was exceedingly attentive and laborious. He regularly analyzed every brief in the margin. He had pursued the habit through life. He talked a good deal about the late George Harding. He said he came into life under auspices so favorable, and he possessed so great talent, that with ordinary discretion and industry he might have attained the highest honors of the profession. He was an eloquent speaker and a fine scholar, but a child in legal knowledge. He would cram himself to make a set speech, and he would succeed, but in a week's time be unable to state even the principles on which the case turned. He was nephew to Lord Camden, then very popular, and his uncle expected everything from his nephew. He had therefore great business at once ; but the best clients soon left him. " And," said the Baron, " we must draw a veil over his latter years."

Friday, 14th. — (At Bedford.) Only one case was interesting. It was a *Qui tam* action by Dr. Free, rector of Sutton, against Sir Montague Burgoyne, Bart., the squire of the parish, to recover £ 20 a month for Sir Montague's not going to church. This was founded on one of the ancient and forgotten statutes,

---

* These engravings hung on Mr. Robinson's walls till his death, and were left a legacy to a friend greatly attached to art.

† George Christian Braun. Raphael's " Leben und Wirken." Wiesbaden, 8vo. 1815.

unrepealed in fact, but rendered inoperative by the improved spirit of the age. Jameson prosecuted, and he was not sufficiently master of himself to give any effect or spirit to his case. In a hurried manner he stated the law and the facts. He proved the defendant's non-attendance at church. Blosset made for Sir Montague a good and impressive speech. Unluckily he had a good case on the facts, so that the most interesting question as to the existence of the act itself was evaded. He proved that during many of the months there was no service in the church, it being shut up, and that the defendant was ill during the rest of the time ; so that on the merits he had a verdict.

*Rem.** — Baron Graham was fidgety, and asked Sergeant Blosset whether the act was not repealed by the Toleration Act. "My client," said the Sergeant, "would rather be convicted than thought to be a Dissenter."† It appeared that, to make assurance doubly sure, the Bishop's chaplain was in court, with the Bishop's written declaration that the defendant, if he had offended, was reconciled to the church. If this declaration were presented, after verdict and before judgment, no judgment could be entered up. A few years ago, Sir Edward Ryan being one of a commission to report on the penal laws in matters of religion, I mentioned this case to him, and it is noticed in the report. Parson Free was, after much litigation, and a great expense to the Bishop of London, deprived of his living for immorality. His case illustrated the fact that, while bishops have, perhaps, too much power over curates, they have certainly too little over the holders of livings.

April 5th. — (At Bury.) A Mr. P——, a Methodist preacher, called to consult with me on account of an interruption which took place while preaching at Woolpit. After this business subject had been discussed, we talked on religious matters, and I questioned Mr. P—— concerning the Arminian notion about Grace. I could not quite comprehend Pascal's letters on the doctrine of *Grace suffisante* and *Grace efficace.* Nor did Mr. P—— relieve me from the difficulties entertained on the subject. The Wesleyan Methodists, it seems, maintained that a *measure of Grace* is given to all men ; but since all men do not

---

* Written in 1851.
† The Toleration Act, 1 William and Mary, Chap. XVIII. Sec. 16, continued the old penalties for non-attendance at Divine Service on the Lord's Day, unless for the sake of attending some place of worship to which that Act gives toleration.

avail themselves of this, I inquired why not. Mr. P—— answered they were not disposed. On my asking what gave the disposition, he replied : "God's influence." — "That, then," said I, "must be Grace." — "Certainly." — "Then it seems God gives a measure of grace to all men, and to some an additional portion, without which the common measure is of no use ! " He could not parry the blow. This common measure is a subterfuge, to escape the obvious objections to the Calvinistic notion of election and reprobation, but nothing is gained by it. The difficulty is shoved off, not removed.

April 10th. — (Witham.) I spent the forenoon with Mrs. Pattisson, reading to her Pope's "Ethical Epistles," which were new to her, and which she enjoyed exceedingly. We had much to talk about besides. Sir Thomas Lawrence had given great delight to Mr. and Mrs. Pattisson, by informing them that the picture of the boys was at length gone, after a delay of six years, to the exhibition.*

May 2d. — I went in the forenoon into B. R.,† Westminster. After my return I had a call from Robert Southey, the Laureate. I had a pleasant chat and a short walk with him. He spoke gayly of his "Wat Tyler." He understood thirty-six thousand copies had been printed. ‡ He was not aware how popular he was when he came to town. He did not appear to feel any shame or regret at having written the piece at so early an age as twenty. He wrote the drama in three mornings, anno 1794. We spoke of his letter to W. Smith, § of which I thought and spoke favorably. I did not blame Southey, but commended him, for asserting the right of all men, who are wiser at forty than at twenty years of age, to act on such superiority of wisdom. "I only wish," I added, "that you had not appeared to have forgotten some political truths you had been early impressed with. Had you said : 'It is the people who want reform *as well as* the government,' instead of '*not* the government,' I should have been content." Southey answered : "I spoke of the present time only. I am still a friend to Reform."

* See *ante*, p. 220.   † King's Bench.
‡ The original edition was published in 1794. The edition referred to is doubtless the one published by Sherwood, in 1817, " with a preface suitable to recent circumstances." Against this edition Southey applied for an injunction, but Lord Eldon refused to grant it. the tendency of the work being mischievous. — Lowndes's "Bibliographer's Manual."
§ This letter was a reply to remarks by W. Smith, in the House of Commons, on "Wat Tyler," and is intended as a vindication of the author's right to change his opinions.

May 8th. — I went into the King's Bench. There I heard the news which had set all Westminster Hall in motion. Gifford has been appointed Solicitor-General.* Gifford's father was a Presbyterian grocer at Exeter. He was himself articled to an attorney, and was never at a university. He was formerly a warm Burdettite! On the other hand, I believe he has long abandoned the conventicle, and has been quiet on political subjects, if he has not changed his opinions. He is patronized by Gibbs. Both are natives of Exeter.

My only concern is that a man hitherto universally beloved should thus early in life be in danger of making bankrupt of his conscience, which Lord Bacon says has been the fate of so many who have accepted the offices of Attorney-General and Solicitor-General.

May 17th. — Another uncomfortable forenoon. It was rendered interesting by the arraignment of Watson and three other men brought up to plead to a charge of high treason for the Spa Fields Riots.† Watson has a face much resembling Sergeant Copley's in profile. The other three men, Preston, Hooper, and Thistlethwaite, had countenances of an ordinary stamp. All of them, on being arraigned, spoke like men of firmness and with the air of public orators, — a sort of *forumizing* tone and manner. I was made melancholy by the sight of so many persons doomed probably to a violent death within a few weeks. They did not require counsel to be assigned them in court. Watson inquired whether they might speak for themselves if they had counsel. Lord Ellenborough answered: "You are not deprived of the power of addressing the court by having counsel assigned you," — rather an ambiguous answer. On entering the court, the prisoners, who had been separated for some time, shook hands with each other in an affecting manner, their hands being below the bar, and they seemed to do it as by stealth. All but Preston seemed unconcerned.

There was a comic scene also exhibited. One Hone,‡ of Fleet Street, was brought up at his own suggestion. He

---

* Afterwards Lord Gifford, and Master of the Rolls.

† In 1816 meetings were held in Spa Fields to petition the Prince in behalf of the distressed manufacturing classes. The first meeting was held on the 15th November: thirty thousand persons were said to be present. After the second meeting, held December 2d, what was called the Spa Fields riot took place; gunsmiths' shops were broken into to procure arms. In one of the shops, a Mr. Platt was seriously wounded. The riot was quelled by the military, but not before considerable damage had been done.

‡ The bookseller, whose trial by Lord Ellenborough will be referred to hereafter.

moved to be discharged on the ground of ill-treatment on his arrest. One ground of his motion was, that on the commitment it was said he had prayed an imparlance to next Term to plead. He put in an affidavit that he had done no such thing. Lord Ellenborough said that his refusal to plead was a constructive demand of time. . He was again asked whether he would plead, and refused. He was remanded. Shepherd appeared for the first time as Attorney-General on this occasion.

May 19th. — I devoted the forenoon to the Nashes. It being the last day of Term, I felt no obligation to attend in court. I went into the British Museum. For the first time I saw there the Elgin Marbles. Mr. Nash, with his characteristic simplicity, exclaimed, " I would as soon go into a church pit!" Indeed, how few are, there who ought not to say so, if men ought on such subjects to avow their want of feeling! It requires science and a habit of attention to subdue the first impression produced by the battered and mutilated condition in which most of these celebrated fragments remain. Of the workmanship I can understand nothing. The sentiment produced by the sight of such *posthumous* discoveries is, however, very gratifying.

May 26th. — After dining at the Colliers' I walked to Newington, and took tea with Mrs. Barbauld. I found that Dr. Aikin had been very seriously ill. Mrs. Barbauld herself retains her health and faculties, and is an interesting instance of a respected and happy old age. I played chess with her, and then went to Becher late.

Tuesday, 27th. — I spent the forenoon at home, and I made one or two calls. On Thelwall; for, though I could not cordially congratulate him on a marriage to a girl scarcely twenty (he being perhaps sixty), yet I thought I might, without impropriety, do an act of courtesy. I found him well, his bride but poorly. She looked more interesting as an invalid ; and as her manners were retiring she pleased me better than when I saw her as Miss Boyle, — a candidate for the stage.

June 9th. — The high-treason trials of Watson and others, for the Spa Fields transactions, began to-day.

11th. — To-day Castle, the government informer, was examined seven and a half hours by Gurney.

12th. — This day I was again in court from past eight till near seven, excepting dinner-time. The principal interest to-day arose from the cross-examination of Castle by Wetherell,[*] from which it resulted that he had been guilty of uttering

* Afterwards Sir Charles Wetherell, Attorney-General.

forged notes, and had, as King's evidence, hanged one accomplice and transported another, though the latter pleaded guilty. He had been concerned in setting at liberty some French officers, to which business he was recommended by a person he had visited in Tothill Fields Prison, and who has since been hanged. There were other things against him. 'So absolutely infamous a witness I never heard of. It appeared, too, from his own statement, that he was the principal actor in this business throughout. He was the plotter and contriver of most of the overt acts, and the whole conspiracy was his. It also appeared that he was furnished with pocket-money by Mr. Stafford, the Bow Street office clerk ; and Mr. Stafford also gave him money to send away his wife, who might have been a witness to confirm his testimony. This latter disgraceful fact, I have no doubt, weighed greatly with the jury.

June 13th. — This day, like the preceding, I passed in court, from a little after eight till near six ; and I could get no dinner, as Wetherell was speaking for the prisoner Watson. Wetherell's speech was vehement and irregular, and very unequal, with occasional bursts of eloquence that produced a great effect. But the reasoning was very loose ; he rambled sadly, and his boldness wanted discretion and propriety. He kept on his legs five hours and a half ; but my attention could not follow him throughout, and the latter half-hour I was away, for an interesting engagement forced me to leave the court before six o'clock.

I dined at Mr. Green's, No. 22 Lincoln's Inn Fields.* Coleridge and Ludwig Tieck were of the party. It was an afternoon and evening of very high pleasure indeed.

Ludwig Tieck has not a prepossessing exterior. He has a shrewd clever face, but I should rather have thought him an able man of the world than a romantic poet. He was not the greatest talker to-day ; indeed, the course of the conversation led others to give him information, but what he did say was sensible and judicious. Coleridge was not in his

---

* Joseph Henry Green, the eminent surgeon. He was the intimate friend of Coleridge. In 1818 he became associated with Sir Astley Cooper as Lecturer at St. Thomas's Hospital, and was for many years Professor and Lecturer on Anatomy at the Royal Academy of Arts, both at Somerset House and in Trafalgar Square. In 1840 and 1847 he delivered the Hunterian oration. His portrait hung over the chimney-piece in Coleridge's bedroom at Highgate, and I remember seeing it there when I went with my father to see the room after Coleridge's death. My father made an elaborate drawing of the room, which was afterwards lithographed. J. H. Green died 1863, December 13, aged 71, at Hadley, near Barnet. — G. S.

element. His German was not good, and his English was not free. He feared he should not be understood if he talked his best. His eloquence was, therefore, constrained.

Tieck's journey to England is undertaken with a view to the study of our old English dramatists, contemporaries of Shakespeare.* He incidentally gave opinions of our elder poets more favorable than I expected. He estimates them highly, as it seems.

June 14th. — After a fortnight's delay, I shall be able to say but little of these days, though they were in part highly interesting. To-day I spent almost entirely in court. It was the most interesting day of Watson's trial. I heard Copley's and Gifford's speeches. Copley spoke with great effect, but with very little eloquence. He spoke for about two and a half hours, and sat down with universal approbation. He said nothing that was not to the purpose. There were no idle or superfluous passages in his speech. He dwelt little on the law, and that was not very good; but his analysis of the evidence of Castle against Watson was quite masterly.

The young Solicitor-General followed him. Opinions were divided about him. I believe envy at his recent appointment contributed to the unfavorable judgments of some men. He certainly began too verbosely, and dwelt injudiciously on unimportant points, but I thought him very acute and able in the latter part of his speech. Yet both Gifford and Copley had less eloquence than Wetherell in the better parts of his speech.

June 16th. — I allowed myself some relief from the trial this morning. I attended, at the auction mart, the sale of chambers No. 5 King's Bench Walk, first floor, for a life and assignment. They sold for 1,355 guineas, and it would have cost me, to substitute my life for that of the present *cestui que vie*, more than £ 100 more ; so that I declined bidding, though the chambers are so good, and mine are so bad, that I felt great reluctance at the inability to purchase.

When I went down to Westminster Hall, the jury were out

---

* Before this visit to England, Tieck had written " Briefen über Shakespeare " (Letters about Shakespeare), in the " Poetisches Journal," 1800, and various articles about him in the " Altenglisches Theatre," 1811 (Old-English Theatre). After the visit he published the following works : " Shakespeare's Vorschule " (Shakespeare's Predecessors), 1823 – 29; notices of Shakespeare, in his " Dramatische Blätter " (Dramatic Leaves), 1828; a novel called " Dichterleben " (The Life of a Poet), in which Shakespeare is introduced; a treatise on Shakespeare's sonnets, 1826; and, in company with A. W. Schlegel, the famous German translation of Shakespeare, 1825 – 29.

of court deliberating on their verdict. The second time I went with the Naylors. We met many people in St. Martin's Lane. Their silence led me to augur ill till a drunken fellow shouted out, " England's glory forever ! " We soon ascertained the fact that an acquittal had taken place. There were crowds in the street, but quite peaceable. At Westminster Hall, I saw old Combe, Barnes, &c. Every one was pleased, apparently. I afterwards met the mob round a hackney-coach in which Watson was. I called on Walter and on Collier, and I played chess late.

June 18th. — I went to the King's Bench. The three other indicted men were brought up and acquitted, no evidence being given against them. I came away early, and then went into the Middle Temple Garden to see the Waterloo Bridge procession.* The sight was interesting. Vast crowds were visible on the bridge and near it, on the Surrey shore. Flags were hoisted over very pier, and guns discharged on the approach of the royal barges. Several of these barges, with a number of boats forming no part of the ceremony, and yet giving it interest, were on the Thames. These royal barges were rowed round a frigate's boat, on which were flags and music. The great personages present, the Prince, Duke of Wellington, &c., ascended the bridge on the Surrey side, and crossed over ; but this we could not see.

I spent the evening in writing a dull review of Coleridge's second Lay Sermon for the *Critical Review.*†

COLERIDGE TO H. C. R.

June, 1817.

MY DEAR ROBINSON, — I shall never forgive you if you do not try to make some arrangement to bring Mr. L. Tieck and yourself up to Highgate very soon. The day, the dinner-hour, you may appoint yourself; but what I most wish would be, either that Mr. Tieck would come in the first stage, so as either to walk or to be driven in Mr. Gilman's gig to Caen Wood, and its delicious groves and alleys (the finest in England, a grand cathedral aisle of *giant* lime-trees, POPE's favorite composition walk when with the old Earl, a brother rogue of yours in the law line), or else to come up to dinner, sleep here, and return (if then return he must) in the afternoon four-o'clock stage the day after. I should be most happy to make him and that

---

* Constable chose this subject for a picture, which was engraved.
† The *Critical Review*, June, 1817, p. 581.

admirable man, Mr. Frere, acquainted, their pursuits have been so similar ; and to convince Mr. Tieck that he is *the* man among us in whom Taste at its maximum has vitalized itself into productive power, — Genius, you need only show him the incomparable translation annexed to Southey's " Cid " (which, by the by, would perhaps give Mr. Tieck the most favorable impression of Southey's own power) ; and I would finish the work off by Mr. Frere's " Aristophanes." In *such* GOODNESS, too, as both *my* Mr. Frere (the Right Hon. J. H. Frere), and his brother George (the lawyer in Brunswick Square), live, move, and have their being in, there is *Genius.* . . . .

I have read two pages of " Lalla Rookh," or whatever it is called. Merciful Heaven ! I dare read no more, that I may be able to answer at once to any questions, " I have but just looked at the work." O Robinson ! if I could, or if I dared, act and feel as Moore and his set do, what havoc could I not make amongst their crockery-ware ! Why, there are not three lines together without some adulteration of common English, and the ever-recurring blunder of using the possessive case, " *compassion's* tears," &c., for the preposition " of," — a blunder of which I have found no instances earlier than Dryden's slovenly verses written for the trade. The rule is, that the case *'s* is always *personal ;* either it marks a person, or a personification, or the relique of some proverbial personification, as, " Who for their belly's sake," in " Lycidas." But for A to weep the tears of B puts me in mind of the exquisite passage in " Rabelais " where Pantagruel gives the page his cup, and begs him to go down into the court-yard, and curse and swear for him about half an hour or so.

God bless you !
S. T. COLERIDGE.

Sunday Morning, HIGHGATE.

June 22d. — I sat at home all the forenoon, in the expectation of a call from Tieck. He did not come, so that between one and two I walked to Dalston. The day was not so oppressively hot as it was yesterday, though still the heat was very unusual. After dinner I read Lord Byron's " Manfred " to Mrs. Becher and Miss Lewis. I had occupied myself during the forenoon in writing a critique on this painful poem, which nevertheless has passages of great beauty. The ladies would have been greatly delighted with it, I dare say, if I had encouraged their admiration.

June 24th. — This was a highly interesting day, of which, however, I have not recollected enough to render this note of any interest. I accompanied Ludwig Tieck and Mr. Green in the stage to Kentish Town, whence we walked to Highgate, where we found Coleridge expecting us. Mr. Gilman joined our party, and the forenoon till four was spent very agreeably indeed. We chatted miscellaneously. Coleridge read some of his own poems, and he and Tieck philosophized. Coleridge talked most. Tieck is a good listener, and is an unobtrusive man. He cannot but know his own worth and excellence, but he has no anxiety to make himself and his own works the subject of conversation. He is by no means a zealous Roman Catholic. On the contrary, he says, " With intolerant persons of either party, I take the opposite side." I ventured to suggest the incompatibility of the Catholic religion with any great improvement. He said it was difficult to decide on questions of national character. Without the Catholic religion the people in Catholic countries would be worse. He thought the Spaniards owed their deliverance from the French to their religion. At the same time he admitted that England owes all her greatness and excellence to the Reformation ; and the existence of the Catholic system as such requires the existence of Protestantism. This is a very harmless Catholicism.

He spoke with great love of Goethe, yet censured the impious Prologue to " Faust," and wishes an English translation might be made from the earlier edition written in Goethe's youth. He does not speak kindly of Voss. Of the Schlegels he did not say much. He does not like Flaxman's Lord Mansfield, but appears to entertain a high opinion of him still. (By the by, sitting near Sam Rogers on Talma's night at the Opera House, and mentioning Flaxman, Rogers said that Canova seemed not very willing to praise Flaxman, saying his designs were " pretty inventions." " Invention," said Rogers, " is precisely what Canova wants.")

Coleridge related anecdotes of himself in Germany very pleasantly indeed.

June 26th. — This was another idle day. I called on Tieck, and chatted with him about his tour in England, and went to the Westminster Library for books to assist him in travelling. I also conversed with Baron Burgsdorf, a sensible man, who is anxious to obtain information about our English courts of justice. I dined in the Hall, and after dinner Talfourd chatted with me. I took a hasty cup of tea at the Colliers', and at nine I went to the Opera House Concert Room, and heard Talma and Mdlle. Georges recite. I grudged a guinea for payment, but I do not regret having gone.

Talma performed a scene out of La Harpe's "Philoctète," and out of "Iphigenia in Tauris." His first appearance disappointed me. He has little gray eyes, too near each other, and, though a regular and good face, not a very striking one. His voice is good, but not peculiarly sweet. His excellence lies in the imitation of intense suffering. He filled me with horror, certainly, as Philoctète, but it was mingled with disgust. Bodily pain is no fit or legitimate subject for the drama; and too often he was merely a man suffering from a sore leg. Of his declamation I do not presume to judge. The character of Orestes affords finer opportunities of display. The terror he feels when pursued by the Furies was powerfully communicated, and his tenderness towards Pylades on parting was also exquisite. Mdlle. Georges had more to do, but she gave me far less pleasure. Her acting I thought radically bad. Instead of copying nature in the expression of passion, according to which the master feeling predominates over all the others, she merely minces the words. If in the same line the words *crainte* and *joie* occur, she apes fear and joy by outrageous pantomime; and in the suddenness of the transition forces applause from those who are glad to understand something, and gratefully applaud what has enabled them to understand. Her acting appeared to me utterly without feeling. She pleased me best in "Athalie," — the scene where she recounts the dream and first appearance of Joad. Her imprecations against Horace for slaying her lover were, I thought, violent without being sincere; and her performance of the sleep-walking scene in "Macbeth" was very poor. In the French play, Macbeth keeps in confinement a son of Duncan, and Lady Macbeth is contemplating his murder as well as the former murders she had committed, by which the fine moral taught by Shakespeare is quite lost. But the French author could not conceive, I dare say, why a successful murder of former days should excite any remorse or anxiety.

I chatted with Rogers the poet. He informs me that Madame de Staël is considered in great danger.

June 28th. — At six I dined with Pollock.* A genteel dinner-party. Coleridge and Mr. and Mrs. John Ray, &c. The afternoon went off exceedingly well. An anecdote was told of

* Afterwards Chief Baron.

Horne Tooke, very characteristic and probable. At school, he was asked *why* he put a word in some case or mood, and answered, " I do not know," for which he was instantly flogged. Another boy was then asked, who repeated the grammatical rule, and took his place in the class. On this Tooke cried. His master asked him what he meant, and Tooke said : " I knew the rule as well as he did, but you did not ask for the rule, but the reason. You asked *why* it is so, and I do not know that now." The master is said to have taken him aside and given him a Virgil in memory of the injustice done him, of which Virgil Tooke was very proud.

I went late to Tieck, and chatted some time about the books, &c. he had still to buy.

June 29th. — I had more conversation with Tieck this evening than before on general literary subjects. He is well read in the English dramatic literature, having read all the English plays which were accessible in Germany ; and he has a decision of opinion which one wonders at in a foreigner. He has no high opinion of Coleridge's critique, but he says he has learned a great deal from Coleridge, who has glorious conceptions about Shakespeare (*herrliche Ideen*). Coleridge's conversation he very much admires, and thinks it superior to any of his writings. But he says there is much high poetry in " Christabel." He thinks well of the remarks on language in Lord Chedworth's book about Shakespeare,* and that Strutt's remarks are acute. Of Ben Jonson he thinks highly. The pieces he distinguished were " Bartholomew Fair" (perhaps his best piece), " The Devil is an Ass," " The Alchymist," " The Fox," " The Silent Woman," &c. He says his work on Shakespeare will be minute as to the language, which, he thinks, underwent changes. Of German literature he does not speak promisingly. The popular writers (such as Fouqué) he despises, and he says that unhappily there have sprung up a number of imitators of himself. He praises Solger's work † very much, and he is the only recent writer whom I mentioned. Of Goethe he spoke with less enthusiasm than I expected, but with as much as he ought, perhaps. The want of religion in Goethe is a great scandal to Tieck, I have no doubt. His later writings, Tieck thinks, are somewhat loquacious.

* " Notes upon some of the Obscure Passages in Shakespeare's Plays." By the late Right Hon. John Lord Chedworth. London, 1805. Privately printed.
† " Erwin, vier Gespräche über das Schöne und die Kunst " (Four Conversations on the Beautiful and Art). 1815. A more systematic work by him entitled " Vorlesungen über die Æsthetik " (Lectures on Æsthetics), 1829, was published after his death.

*Rem.** — This summer I made my second visit to Paris. Of places I shall write nothing, but a few personal incidents may be mentioned.

I undertook to escort my sister, who had a companion in Esther Nash. And my nephew was the fourth to fill the carriage which we hired at Calais. My brothers crossed the water with us. We slept at Dover on the 15th of August, and reached Paris on the 21st, — six days on the road. Last year I left Paris after a comfortable breakfast, and slept at Dover; my travelling companion, however, reached London the same night, and would have gone to a ball, if he had not unexpectedly found his family at home.

At Paris were then dwelling, under the care of the celebrated Madame Campan, the two Miss Hutchisons, who accompanied us repeatedly in our sight-seeings. To the youngest my nephew was then betrothed. We were at the Hôtel Valois, Rue Richelieu, from whence we issued daily to see the well-known sights of Paris. Our acquaintances were not numerous. The ladies knew Miss Benger, with whom was Miss Clarke, and were glad to be introduced to Helen Maria Williams.† Her nephews were then become young men, — at least the elder, Coquerel, now the eloquent and popular preacher, and a distinguished member of the House of Representatives. He has managed to retain his post of preacher at the Oratoire. His theology was then sufficiently pronounced, and indicated what has been since made public. There was a manifest disinclination to enter on matters of controversy, and he had the authority of his own church to justify him. He informed me of the commands issued by the ecclesiastical council of the once too orthodox church of Geneva, and addressed to the clergy, to abstain from preaching on the Trinity, Eternity of Hell, Corruption of Human Nature, and Original Sin, between which last two doctrines French theologians make a distinction.

Professor Froriep of Weimar was then at Paris. He introduced me to a remarkable man, — Count Schlaberndorf, about seventy years of age, a Prussian subject, a cynic in his habits,

---

* Written in 1851.

† Mr. Robinson had been introduced to Miss Williams by Mrs. Clarkson in 1814. Miss Williams wrote several works in connection with the political state of France, as a Republic and as an Empire. She also wrote a novel called "Julia," "A Tour in Switzerland," "Miscellaneous Poems," and "Poems on various Occasions." During her residence in Paris, which extended over many years, she was, by Robespierre, confined for some time in the Temple.

though stately in figure and gentlemanly in his air. He was residing in a very dirty apartment in the third floor of the Hôtel des Siciles, Rue Richelieu. His hands and face were clean, but his dress, consisting of a bedgown of shot satin of a dark color, was very dirty. He had a gray beard, with bushy hair, mild eyes, handsome nose, and lips hid by whiskers. He came to France at the beginning of the Revolution ; was in prison during the Reign of Terror, and escaped. That he might not be talked about, he lived on almost nothing. On my answering his French in German, he replied with pleasure, and talked very freely. His vivacity was very agreeable, and without any introduction he burst at once upon the great social questions of the age. In my journal I wrote : " He comes nearer my idea of Socrates than any man I ever saw, except that I think Socrates would not have dressed himself otherwise than his fellow-citizens did." He spoke of his first arrival in France. " I used to say," he said, " I was a republican, and then there were no republics. The Revolution came, and then I said : ' There are republics, and no republicans.' " I asked him how he came to be arrested. He said : " On the denunciation of a political fanatic, a kind-hearted and very benevolent man. He probably reasoned thus : ' Why is this stranger and nobleman here ? What has he done for which the Allies would hang him ? He is therefore a suspicious character. If he is guilty, he ought to be secured ; if he is a republican and innocent, he will be reconciled to a fate which the public interest requires.' That was the logic of the day. When I was arrested I had but 300 francs. It was not safe to attempt getting any supply by means of writing, so I lived on bread and boiled plums." Froriep inquired why he did not return to Germany. He said : "I should be made a centre of intrigues. I am a reformer, but an enemy to revolutions." He metaphysicized obscurely. Yet he distinguished fairly enough between patriotism and nationality. He denied the one, but allowed the other to the English aristocracy, who would sell the liberties of the people to the crown, but not the crown to a foreign power.

During my stay at Paris I renewed my acquaintance with Grégoire.* He had been unjustly expelled from the Legislative Body, on the ground that he had voted for the death of Louis XVI. In fact, he voted him guilty, but voted against the punishment of death in any case, and that he should be

---

* Vide 1814, ante, p. 283.

the first spared under the new law. No wonder that Louis
XVIII. ordered his name to be struck out of the list of members of the Institute, and that he should be otherwise disgraced.
Without being one of the *great* men of the Revolution, he was
among the best of the popular party. He was certainly a
pious man, as all the Jansenists were, — the Methodists of the
Catholic Church, — with the inevitable inconsistencies attached
to all who try to reconcile private judgment with obedience.
He affirmed, as indeed many Catholics do, that the use of
actual water was not indispensable to a saving baptism.

One of the most interesting circumstances of my visit to
Paris was that I fell in with Hundleby,* who became one of
my most intimate friends. With him and two other solicitors,
Walton (a friend of Masquérier) and Andros, I made an excursion to Ermenonville, where Rousseau died, — a wild forest
scene precisely suited to that unhappy but most splendid
writer.

[Mr. Robinson returned from France on the 20th of September, but visited Brighton, Arundel, and the Isle of Wight after
his return, and did not settle down in London till the 4th of
October.]

November 6th. — I went to Godwin's. Mr. Shelley was there.
I had never seen him before. His youth, and a resemblance to
Southey, particularly in his voice, raised a pleasing impression,
which was not altogether destroyed by his conversation, though
it is vehement and arrogant and intolerant. He was very
abusive towards Southey, whom he spoke of as having sold
himself to the Court. And this he maintained with the usual
party slang. His pension and his Laureateship, his early zeal
and his recent virulence, are the proofs of gross corruption. On
every topic but that of violent party feeling, the friends of
Southey are under no difficulty in defending him. Shelley
spoke of Wordsworth with less bitterness, but with an insinuation of his insincerity, &c.

November 9th. — I dined with Mr. and Mrs. Flaxman, making
a fourth with Miss Denman. I enjoyed the afternoon. Flaxman is a delightful man in the purity and simplicity of his
feelings and understanding, though an uncomfortable opponent
in disputation. I so much fear to offend him, that I have a
difficulty in being sincere. I read extracts from Coleridge's

---

* He has been dead many years. His widow, a daughter of a wealthy man,
named Curtis, is now the wife of Mr. Tite, the architect of the Exchange. —
H. C. R., 1851. Mr. Tite is M. P. for Bath.

16 *   x

poems. The verses to the Duchess of Devonshire, in particular, pleased him. Certainly Coleridge has shown that he could be courteous and courtly without servility.

November 16th. — The death of the Princess Charlotte has excited more general sorrow than I ever witnessed raised by the death of a royal personage.

November 17th. — I witnessed to-day a scene which would have been a reproach to Turkey, or the Emperor of Dahomey, — a wager of battle in Westminster Hall. Thornton was brought up for trial on an appeal after acquittal for murder.* No one seemed to have any doubt of the prisoner's guilt ; but he escaped, owing to the unfitness of a profound real-property lawyer to manage a criminal trial. For this reason the public sense was not offended by recourse being had to an obsolete proceeding. The court was crowded to excess. Lord Ellenborough asked Reader whether he had anything to move, and he having moved that Thornton should be permitted to plead, he was brought to the bar. The declaration or count being read to him, he said : " Not Guilty. And this I am ready to defend ·with my body." And at the same time he threw a large glove or gauntlet on to the floor of the court. Though we all expected this plea, yet we all felt astonishment — at least I did — at beholding before our eyes a scene acted which we had read of as one of the disgraceful institutions of our half-civilized ancestors. No one smiled. The judges looked embarrassed. Clarke on this began a very weak speech. He ·was surprised, " at this time of day," at so obsolete a proceeding ; as if the appeal itself were not as much so. He pointed out the person of Ashford, the appellant, and thought the court would not award battle between men of such disproportionate strength. But being asked whether he had any authority for such a position, he had no better reply than that it was shocking, because the defendant had murdered the sister, that he should then murder the brother. For which Lord Ellenborough justly reproved him, by observing that what the law sanctioned could not be murder. Time was, however, given him to counter-plead, and Reader judiciously said in a single sentence, that he had taken on himself to advise the wager of battle, on account of the prejudices against Thornton, by which a fair trial was rendered impossible.

---

* An appeal of murder was a criminal prosecution at the suit of the next of kin to the person killed, independently of any prosecution by the Crown, and might take place, as in this case, after an acquittal. The word " appeal," however, has in this usage no reference to former proceedings.

*Rem.** — The appellant, in the following Term, set out all
the evidence in replication, it being the ancient law that, when
that leaves no doubt, the wager may be declined.   Hence a
very long succession of pleading, during which Thornton remained in prison.   The court ought probably, according to
the old law, to have ordered battle, and if the appellant refused, awarded that he should be hanged.   To relieve the
court and country from such monstrosities, the judgment was
postponed, and an Act of Parliament passed to abolish both
the wager of battle and the appeal ; which some of my
Radical city friends thought a wrong proceeding, by depriving
the people of one of their means of protection against a bad
government ; for the King cannot pardon in appeal of murder,
and the Ministry may contrive the murder of a friend to
liberty.

Tindal and Chitty argued the case very learnedly, and much
recondite and worthless black-letter and French lore were lav-
ished for the last time.   This recourse to an obsolete proceeding terminated in Thornton's acquittal.

November 19th. — This being the day of the funeral of the
Princess Charlotte, all the shops were shut, and the churches
everywhere filled with auditors.

November 23d. — I walked to Newington, which I reached
in time to dine with Mrs. Barbauld.   Mr. and Mrs. Charles
Aikin were there.   The afternoon passed off without any dulness or drowsiness.   We had matter for conversation in Mrs.
Plumptre, — a subject on which I talk *con amore*, in the wager -
of battle, and in the Princess's death.

November 25th. — This was to me an anxious day.   I had
received from Naylor a brief to speak in mitigation of punishment for one Williams, at Portsea, who had sold in his shop
two of the famous Parodies, one of the Litany, in which the
three estates, Kings, Lords, and Commons, are addressed with
some spirit and point on the sufferings of the nation, and the
other of the Creed of St. Athanasius, in which the Lord Chancellor, Lord Castlereagh, and Lord Sidmouth are, with vulgar
buffoonery, addressed as Old Bags, Derry-Down Triangle, and
the Doctor, and the triple Ministerial character spoken of under
the well-known form of words.

These parodies had been long overlooked by the late Attorney-General, and he had been reproached for his negligence by
both Ministerialists and Oppositionists.   At length prosecu-

* Written in 1851.

tions were begun, and the subject was talked of in Parliament. Hone and Carlile had both been prosecuted, and by their outrageous conduct had roused a strong sense of indignation against them. Unhappily this poor Portsea printer was the first brought up for judgment. Applications in his behalf had been made to the Attorney-General, who did not conduct the case with any apparent bitterness. In his opening speech on the Litany, he with considerable feeling, though in a commonplace way, eulogized the Litany, but he admitted to a certain extent the circumstances of mitigation in defendant's affidavit, viz. that he had destroyed all the copies he could, after he had heard of the prosecution.

I then addressed the court, saying that the Attorney-General's speech was calculated to depress a man more accustomed to address the court than I was ; but that I thought it appeared, even from the Attorney-General's own words, that there were no circumstances of aggravation arising out of the manner in which the crime was committed. I then dwelt, and I believe impressively, on the hardship of the case for the defendant, who, though the least guilty, was the first brought up for punishment, and deprecated the infliction of an exemplary punishment on him. This was the best part of my speech. I then repeated and enforced the ordinary topics of mitigation.

The Attorney-General then brought on the Creed information, and was rather more bitter than at first, and he was followed by Topping.

I replied, and spoke not so well as at first, and was led by an interruption from Bayley, to observe on the Athanasian Creed, that many believed in the doctrine who did not approve of the commentary. At least my remarks on the Creed were sanctioned by the judgment, which sentenced the defendant, for the Litany, to eight months' imprisonment in Winchester Jail, and a fine of £100, and for the Creed to four months' imprisonment.

I stayed in court the rest of the afternoon, and at half past four dined with Gurney. No one but Godfrey Sykes, the pleader, was there. He is an open-hearted, frank fellow in his manner, and I felt kindly towards him on account of the warm praise which he gave to my friend Manning, and of the enthusiasm with which he spoke of Gifford.

December 3d. — Hamond called and chatted on law with me. I walked home with him. He lent me the last *Examiner.* In the account of my law case, there is a piece of malice. They have put in italics, " Mr. Robinson was ready to agree with his Lordship to the fullest extent " ; and certainly this is the part of my speech which I most regret, for I ought to have observed to the court, that the libel is not charged with being against the doctrines of Christianity. I lost the opportunity of saying much to the purpose, when Bayley observed that the libel was inconsistent with the doctrines of Christianity.

December 4th. — I breakfasted early, and soon after nine walked to Dr. Wordsworth's, at Lambeth. I crossed for the first time Waterloo Bridge. The view of Somerset House is very fine indeed, and the bridge itself is highly beautiful ; but the day was so bad that I could see neither of the other bridges, and of course scarcely any objects.

I found Mr. and Mrs. Wordsworth and the Doctor at breakfast, and I spent a couple of hours with them very agreeably. We talked about poetry. Wordsworth has brought MSS. with him, and is inclined to print one or two poems, as it is the fashion to publish small volumes now. He means then to add them to the " Thanksgiving Ode," &c., and form a third volume. He read to me some very beautiful passages.

December 6th. — I dined with the Colliers, and in the evening Hundleby called on me, and we went together to Covent Garden. I have not been so well pleased for a long time. In " Guy Mannering " there were four interesting performances. First, Braham's singing, the most delicious I ever heard, though I fear his voice is not so perfect as it was ; but in this piece I was particularly delighted, as he sang in a style of unstudied simplicity. Second, Liston's Dominie Sampson, an absolutely perfect exhibition. His terror when accosted by Meg Merrilies was the most amusing and correctly natural representation I ever witnessed. Emery's representation of Dandie Dinmont also most excellent ; and, though not equal to the other attractions of the piece, Mrs. Egerton gave great effect to Meg Merrilies. But the piece itself is worth nothing.

December 18th. — I spent the greater part of the morning at the King's Bench sittings, Guildhall. Hone's first trial took place to-day. It was for publishing a parody on the Church Catechism, attacking the government. Abbott * sat for Lord Ellenborough. Hone defended himself by a very long and rambling speech of many hours, in which he uttered a thou-

---

* Afterwards Lord Tenterden, Lord Chief Justice of King's Bench.

sand absurdities, but with a courage and promptitude which completely effected his purpose. · Abbott was by no means a match for him, and in vain attempted to check his severe reproaches against Lord Ellenborough for not letting him sit down in the King's Bench, when he was too ill to stand without great pain. Hone also inveighed against the system of special juries, and rattled over a wide field of abuses before he began his defence, which consisted in showing how many similar parodies had been written in all ages. He quoted from Martin Luther, from a Dean of Canterbury, and a profusion of writers, ancient and modern, dwelling principally on Mr. Reeves and Mr. Canning.*

Hone had not knowledge enough to give his argument a technical shape. It was otherwise a very good argument. He might have urged, in a way that no judge could object to, that *new* crimes cannot be created without Act of Parliament, and that he ought not to be charged by the present Attorney-General with a crime, in doing what no other Attorney-General had considered to be a crime. Least of all would a jury convict *him* of a crime, who was a known adversary of the government, when others, of an opposite political character, had not been prosecuted. This last point he did indeed urge correctly and powerfully enough.

I left him speaking to go to dinner at Collier's. The trial was not over till late in the evening, when he was acquitted.

I spent the evening at Drury Lane, and saw Kean as Luke in "Riches."† It was an admirable performance. His servile air as the oppressed dependant was almost a caricature. But the energy of his acting when he appeared as the upstart tyrant of the family of his brother was very fine indeed. Though he looked ill in health, and had a very bad voice throughout, still his performance was a high treat. I could not sit out a poor farce called "The Man in the Moon," and came home to a late tea in chambers.

---

* Hone's defence was that the practice of parodying religious works, even parts of the Holy Scriptures and the Book of Common Prayer, had been adopted by men whose religious character was above suspicion. Examples were adduced from Martin Luther, Dr. John Boys, Dean of Canterbury in the reign of James I., Robert Harley, Earl of Oxford, Lord Somers, Mr. Canning, and Mr. Reeves. Of Mr. Reeves Hone said: "His name stood in the title-page of the Book of Common Prayer, in most general use, as patentee," "he was a barrister, and had been a commissioner of bankrupts." Having shown from these instances, that parodies were not necessarily disrespectful to the work parodied, and that they had been hitherto allowed, Hone declared that his ought not to be regarded as an exception, and that on this ground, and this alone, he asked for a verdict of "Not Guilty."

† Altered from Massinger's play of "The City Madam."

December 19th. — I went again to the King's Bench, Guild-hall. Lord Ellenborough sat to-day. I was curious to see how he would succeed where Abbott had failed, and whether he could gain a verdict on Hone's second trial after a former ac-quittal. Hone was evidently less master of himself before Ellenborough than before Abbott, and perhaps would have sunk in the conflict, but for the aid he received from the former acquittal. He pursued exactly the same course as before. This charge was for publishing a parody on the Litany, and it was charged both as an anti-religious and a political libel; but the Attorney-General did not press the political count. After a couple of hours' flourishing on irrele-vant matter, Hone renewed his perusal of old parodies. On this Lord Ellenborough said he should not suffer the giving them in evidence. This was said in such a way that it at first appeared he would not suffer them to be read. However, Hone said, if he could not proceed in his own way he would sit down, and Lord Ellenborough might send him to prison. He then went on as before. Several times he was stopped by the Chief Jus-tice, but never to any purpose. Hone returned to the offensive topic, and did not quit it till he had effected his purpose, and the judge, baffled and worn out, yielded to the prisoner : —

> " An eagle, towering in the pride of place,
> Was by a moping owl hawked at and killed."

I came away to dinner and returned to the Hall to hear the conclusion of the trial. Shepherd was feeble in his reply. But Lord Ellenborough was eloquent. In a grave and solemn style becoming a judge he declared his judgment that the parody was a profane libel. The jury retired, and were away so long that I left the court, but I anticipated the result.

December 20th. — Having breakfasted early, I went again to the court at Guildhall. The government had, with incon-ceivable folly, persisted in bringing Hone to a third trial after a second acquittal ; and that, too, for an offence of far less magnitude, the publishing a parody on the Athanasian Creed, which the court punished Williams for by a four months' imprisonment, while the parody on the Litany, of which Hone was yesterday acquitted, was punished by eight months' imprisonment and a fine of £ 100. The consequence was to be foreseen. He was again acquitted, after having carried his boldness to insolence. He reproached Lord El-lenborough for his yesterday's charge, and assumed almost a menacing tone. He was, as before, very digressive, and the greater part of his seven hours' speech consisted of very irrelevant matter. He did not fail to attack the bar, declaring there was not a man who dared to contradict Lord Ellenborough, for fear of losing the ear of the court, — a most indecent, because a most true, assertion. I expected he would fall foul of me, for my speech on behalf of Williams, but I escaped. He drew a pathetic picture of his poverty, and gained the good-will of the jury by showing how much he had already suffered. He declared that, if convicted, his life would be lost, and at the same time he scorned to ask any favor. He was very ill when the trial began, but he would not have it put off, &c.

Before he got into his defence I left the court, and called on Mrs. Meyer. I dined and took tea with the Colliers, and afterwards went to Amyot. I found him liberally disposed on the subject of the late trials. Though he considered the parodies political libels, he thought the Ministry justly taken in for their canting pretence of punishing irreligion and profanity, about which they did not care at all.

To recur to the singular scene of this morning, without a parallel in the history of the country, I cannot but think the victory gained over the government and Lord Ellenborough a subject of alarm, though at the same time a matter of triumph. Lord Ellenborough is justly punished for his inhumanity to Hone on a former occasion, and this illiterate man has avenged all our injuries. Lord Ellenborough reigned over submissive subjects like a despot. Now he feels, and even the bar may learn, that the fault is in them, and not in their stars, if they are underlings.* Lord Ellenborough has sustained the severest shock he ever endured, and I really should not wonder if it shortened his life.†

H. C. R. to T. R.

December, 1817.

I am quite ashamed of myself. After the notice so attentively sent by my sister about the turkeys, I ought not to have forgotten to write yesterday; but the infirmities of old age

---

* Mr. Robinson says elsewhere that he never felt able to do his best before Lord Ellenborough.

† Lord Ellenborough resigned his office as Lord Chief Justice on account of ill health in the month of October, 1818, and died on December 13th, in the same year. As to the effect of Hone's trial upon Lord Ellenborough's health, there has always been a difference of opinion.

are growing fast upon me, and loss of memory is the chief.[*]
Of course I do not wish my sister to trouble herself to-morrow,
but as soon as she can, I will thank her to send as usual to
the Colliers and to Charles Lamb. But the latter, you are to
know, is removed to lodgings, and I will thank you to let his
turkey be directed minutely to Mr. Lamb, at Mr. Owen's, Nos.
20 and 21 Great Russell Street, Drury Lane.

You have, of course, been greatly interested by the late un-
paralleled trials. I attended every day, though not during
the whole days, and listened with very *mixed* emotions. . . . .

Lord Ellenborough is, after all, one of the greatest men of
our age. And though his impatience is a sad vice in a judge,
he yet becomes the seat of justice nobly; and in the display
of powerful qualities adds to our sense of the dignity of which
man is capable. And that a man of an heroic nature should
be reduced to very silence, like an imbecile child, is indeed a
sad spectacle. And the Attorney-General too, — a mild, gentlemanly, honorable nature. But he suffered little in comparison with the chief, and he conducted himself with great propriety. Hone said, very happily : " It is a pity Mr. Attorney
was not instructed to give up this third prosecution. I am
sure he would have done it with great pleasure. Had the
Ministry given him a hint, — a mere hint, — I am sure he
would have taken it."

December 21st. — I breakfasted with Ed. Littledale, and met
Burrell and Bright (also at the bar) there. We talked, of
course, about the late trials, and Burrell was warm, even to
anger, at hearing me express my pleasure at the result. He
went so far as to declare I was a mischievous character; but
this was said with so much honest feeling, that it did not make
me in the least angry, and I succeeded in bringing him to
moderation at last. He feels, as Southey does, the danger
arising from the popular feeling against the government; and
he considers the indisposition of the London juries to convict
in cases of libel as a great evil. Bright, who came after the
heat of the battle was over, took the liberal side, and Ed.
Littledale inclined to Burrell. The beauty of Littledale's
chambers,[†] and his capital library, excited my envy.

December 27th. — I called on Lamb, and met Wordsworth
with him; I afterwards returned to Lamb's. Dined at Monk-

---

[*] In 1864. Mr. Robinson notes on this: " What did I mean by old age forty-
seven years ago? "
[†] These looked into Gray's Inn Gardens.

house's.* The party was small, — Mr. and Mrs. Wordsworth and Miss Hutchison, Coleridge and his son Hartley, and Mr. Tillbrook. After dinner Charles Lamb joined the party.

I was glad to hear Coleridge take the right side on Hone's trial. He eloquently expatiated on the necessity of saving Hone, in order to save English law, and he derided the legal definition of a libel, — whatever tends to produce certain consequences, without any regard to the intention of the publisher.†

Among the light conversation at dinner, Tillbrook related that Southey had received a letter from a person requesting him to make an acrostic on the name of a young lady in Essex. The writer was paying his addresses to this young lady, but had a rival who beat him in writing verses. Southey did not send the verses, and distributed the money in buying blankets for some poor women of Keswick.

December 30th. — I dined with the Colliers, and spent the evening at Lamb's. I found a large party collected round the two poets, but Coleridge had the larger number. There was, however, scarcely any conversation beyond a whisper. Coleridge was philosophizing in his rambling way to Monkhouse, who listened attentively, — to Manning, who sometimes smiled, as if he thought Coleridge had no right to metaphysicize on chemistry without any knowledge of the subject, — to Martin Burney, who was eager to interpose, — and Alsager, who was content to be a listener ; while Wordsworth was for a great part of the time engaged *tête-à-tête* with Talfourd. I could catch scarcely anything of the conversation. I chatted with the ladies. Miss Lamb had gone through the fatigue of a dinner-party very well, and Charles was in good spirits.

December 31st. — The last day of the year was one of the darkest days I remember in any year. A thick fog came over London between eight and nine, and remained all the day. Late at night it cleared up.

The increase of my fees from £355 19 *s.* to £415 5 *s.* 6 *d.* is too paltry to be worth notice. Yet my journal shows that I had not relaxed in that attention which the Germans call Sitzfleiss, — *sitting industry,* — which is compatible with sluggishness of mind.

---

* Mr. Monkhouse was a London merchant and a connection of Mrs. Wordsworth. He married a daughter of Mr. Horrocks, who for a long time represented Preston in Parliament.

† Compare with this Coleridge's letter to Lord Liverpool, written in July this year. Yonge's " Life of Lord Liverpool," Vol. II. p. 300.

*Rem.** — During this year, my intimacy with Walter not declining, and his anxieties increasing, he authorized me to inquire of Southey whether he would undertake the editorship on liberal terms. Southey declined the offer, without inquiring what the emolument might be; and yet the *Times* was then supporting the principles which Southey himself advocated.†

SOUTHEY TO H. C. R.

March 13, 1817.

MY DEAR SIR, — Your letter may be answered without deliberation. No emolument, however great, would induce me to give up a country life and those pursuits in literature to which the studies of so many years have been directed. Indeed, I should consider that portion of my time which is given up to temporary politics grievously misspent, if the interests at stake were less important. We are in danger of an insurrection of the Yahoos : it is the fault of government that such a caste should exist in the midst of civilized society ; but till the breed can be mended it must be curbed, and that too with a strong hand.

I shall be in town during the last week in April, on my way to Switzerland and the Rhine. You wrong our country by taking its general character from a season which was equally ungenial over the whole continent.

Believe me, my dear sir,
Yours very truly,
ROBERT SOUTHEY.

CHAPTER XXI.

1818.

JANUARY 6th. — I dined at the Colliers', and at seven Walton and Andros came to me. We spent several hours very agreeably in looking over between thirty and forty new engravings, chiefly sacred subjects. I find the appetite for these things grows by what it feeds on. I enjoyed many of them, and rejoiced at the prospect of seeing a print of Guido's

---

* Written in 1851.
† The fact is stated in the "Life of Southey," Vol. IV. p. 261.

" Hours "* over my chimney-piece. Walton is a man of taste, and feels the beauty of such things.

January 12th. — I read in a volume of Voltaire's Miscellanies to-day his life of Molière, — amusing enough : and his " critique of Hamlet," a very instructive as well as entertaining performance ; for it shows how a work of unequalled genius and excellence may be laughably exposed. I forgive Frenchmen for their disesteem of Shakespeare. And Voltaire has taken no unfair liberties with our idol. He has brought together all the *disconvenances*, according to the laws of the French drama, as well as the national peculiarities. To a Frenchman, " Hamlet " must appear absurd and ridiculous to an extreme. And this by fair means, the Frenchman not perceiving how much the absurdity, in fact, lies in his own narrow views and feelings.

January 16th. — (At Cambridge.) After nine Mr. Chase accompanied me to Randall's, where I stayed till half past eleven. We debated on the principles of the Ascetics. I contended that the Deity must be thought to take pleasure in the improvement of civilization, in which is to be included the fine arts; but I was set down by the text about " the lust of the flesh, the lust of the eyes, and the pride of life," which are said not to proceed from the Father. Thus, I fear, every pleasing or bright conception of the Supreme Being and of the system of the universe may be met by a text !

January 27th. — I went to the Surrey Institution, where I heard Hazlitt lecture on Shakespeare and Milton. He delighted me much by the talent he displayed ; but his bitterness of spirit broke out in a passage in which he reproached modern poets for their vanity and incapacity of admiring and loving anything but themselves. He was applauded at this part of his lecture, but I know not whether he was generally understood.

From hence I called at Collier's, and, taking Mrs. Collier with me, I went to a lecture by Coleridge in Fleur-de-lis Court, Fleet Street.† I was gratified unexpectedly by finding a large

---

* The well-known engraving by Raphael Morghen to which Rogers alludes, as hanging on his wall, in his " Epistle to a Friend," —

> " O mark ! again the coursers of the Sun,
> At Guido's call, their round of glory run."

† The syllabus of this course, which included fourteen lectures, is given at length in Vol. II. of Coleridge's " Lectures upon Shakespeare and other Dramatists." The subjects are very comprehensive, — Language, Literature, and Social and Moral Questions.

and respectable audience, generally of superior-looking persons, in physiognomy rather than dress. Coleridge treated of the origin of poetry and of Oriental works ; but he had little animation, and an exceedingly bad cold rendered his voice scarcely audible.

February 4th. — I called on Godwin, and at his house met with a party of originals. One man struck me by his resemblance to Curran, — his name Booth. Godwin called him, on introduction, a master of the English language, and I understand him to be a learned etymologist. His conversation was singular, and even original, so that I relished the short time I stayed. A rawboned Scotchman, ———, was there also, less remarkable, but a hard-headed man. A son of a performer, R—— by name, patronized by Mr. Place,* talked very well too. All three Jacobins, and Booth and R—— debaters. I was thrown back some ten years in my feelings. The party would have suited me very well about that time, and I have not grown altogether out of taste for it. I accepted an invitation to meet the same party a week hence.

February 10th. — I dined with Walter. A small and very agreeable party. Sydenham, Commissioner of Excise, suspected to be " Vetus," a great partisan of the Wellesleys; Sterling, more likely to be the real " Vetus," — a sensible man ; Dr. Baird, a gentlemanly physician, and Fraser. The conversation was beginning to be very interesting, when I was obliged to leave the party to attend Coleridge's lecture on Shakespeare. Coleridge was apparently ill.

February 15th. — At two, I took a ride with Preston in his gig, into the Regent's Park, which I had never seen before. When the trees are grown this will be really an ornament to the capital ; and not a mere ornament, but a healthful appendage. The Highgate and Hampstead Hill is a beautiful object, and within the Park, the artificial water, the circular belt or coppice, the bridges, the few scattered villas, &c., are objects of taste. I really think this enclosure, with the new street † leading to it from Carlton House, will give a sort of glory to the Regent's government, which will be more felt by remote posterity than the victories of Trafalgar and Waterloo, glorious as these are.

---

* Mr. Place was a tailor at Charing Cross, — a great Westminster Radical, an accomplished metaphysician, a frequent writer on political affairs, a man of inflexible integrity and firmness, and a friend and *protégé* of Jeremy Bentham.

† Regent Street.

February 17th. — I stayed at home a great part of the fore-noon. Wirgmann, the Kantianer, called on me. His disinter-ested proselyte-making zeal for the critical philosophy, though I no longer share his love for that philosophy, is a curious and amusing phenomenon. He worships his idol with pure affec-tion, without sacrificing his domestic duties. He attends to his goldsmith's shop as well as to the works of Kant, and is a. careful and kind educator of his children, though he inflicts the categories on them.

I took tea at home, and, Hamond calling, I accompanied him to Hazlitt's lecture. He spoke of the writers in the reign of Queen Anne, and was bitter, sprightly, and full of political and personal allusions. In treating of Prior, he quoted his un-seemly verses against Blackmore to a congregation of saints. He drew an ingenious but not very intelligible parallel between Swift, Rabelais, and Voltaire, and even eulogized the modern infidel. So indiscreet and reckless is the man !

February 20th. — I dined at Collier's, and went to Cole-ridge. It was agreed that I should invite Mrs. Pattisson to go with me to the lecture, and I also took Mira May and Rachel Rutt. We found the lecture-room fuller than I had ever seen it, and were forced to take back seats ; but it was a pleasure to Mrs. Pattisson to sit behind Sir James Mackintosh. He was with Sergeant Bosanquet and some fashionable lady. The party were, however, in a satirical mood, as it seemed, through-out the lecture. Indeed, Coleridge was not in one of his happiest moods to-night. His subject was Cervantes, but he was more than usually prosy, and his tone peculiarly drawl-ing. His digressions on the nature of insanity were carried too far, and his remarks on the book but old, and by him often repeated.

February 23d. — Heard a lecture by Flaxman at the Royal Academy. He was not quite well, and did not deliver it with so much animation and effect as I have known him on former occasions throw into his lectures.

February 24th. — I dined and took tea at Collier's, and then heard part of a lecture by Hazlitt at the Surrey Institution. He was so contemptuous towards Wordsworth, speaking of his letter about Burns, that I lost my temper. He imputed to Wordsworth the desire of representing himself as a superior man.

February 27th. — I took tea with Gurney, and invited Mrs. Gurney to accompany me to Coleridge's lecture. It was on

Dante and Milton, — one of his very best.   He digressed less than usual, and really gave information and ideas about the poets he professed to criticise.   I returned to Gurney's and heard Mr. Gurney read Mrs. Fry's examination before the committee of the House of Commons about Newgate, — a very curious examination, and very promising as to the future improvements in prison discipline.

March 19th. — I had six crown briefs at Thetford.   One was flattering to me, though it was an unwelcome one to hold.   It was on behalf of Johnson, whose trial for the murder of Mr. Baker, of Wells, lasted the whole of the day.   I received, a day or two before, a letter from Dekker, the chaplain to the Norwich Jail, saying that some gentlemen (the Gurneys principally) had subscribed, to furnish the prisoner with the means of defence.   The evidence against him was merely circumstantial, and he had told so consistent a tale, stating where he had been, that many believed him innocent.   He, Dekker, had witnessed my " admirable and successful defence of Massey, for the murder of his wife," (such were his words), and had recommended me for the present case.

April 18th. — (At C. Lamb's.)   There was a large party, — the greater part of those who are usually there, but also Leigh Hunt and his wife.   He has improved in manliness and healthfulness since I saw him last, some years ago.   There was a glee about him which evinced high spirits, if not perfect health, and I envied his vivacity.   He imitated Hazlitt capitally ; Wordsworth not so well.   Talfourd was there.   He does not appreciate Wordsworth's fine lines on " Scorners."   Hunt did not sympathize with Talfourd, but opposed him playfully, and that I liked him for.

April 23d. — I had a note from Hundleby, proposing to go with me to hear Mathews's Imitations, at eight.   He came to me accordingly, and I accompanied him into the pit of the Lyceum.

The entertainment consisted of a narrative (for the greater part) of a journey in a mail-coach, which gave occasion to songs, imitations, &c.   The most pleasant representation was of a Frenchman.   His broken English was very happy.   And Mathews had caught the mind as well as the words of Monsieur.   His imitation of French tragedians was also very happy.   Talma was admirably exhibited.

A digression on lawyers was flat.   I did not feel the ridicule, and I could not recognize either judge or barrister.

Mathews was not without humor in his representation of a French valet, attending his invalid master in bed ; and his occasional bursts as master, and as the invisible cook and butler, were pleasant.   He took a child, i. e. a doll, out of a box, and held a droll dialogue.

The best dramatic exhibition was a narrative as an old Scotchwoman.   He put on a hood and tippet, screwed his mouth into a womanly shape, and, as if by magic, became another creature.   It was really a treat.   He concluded by reciting part of Hamlet's speech to the players, as Kemble, Kean, Cooke, Young, Banister, Fawcett, and Munden, with great success.

April 24th. — I went to Westminster Hall as usual, but had a very unusual pleasure.   I heard one of the very best forensic speeches ever delivered by Sir Samuel Romilly.   He had to oppose, certainly, very moderate speeches from Gifford and Piggott, and a better one from Horne.   It was in support of an application by Mrs. M. A. Taylor, that the Countess of Antrim should abstain from influencing her daughter, Lady Frances Vane Tempest, in favor of Lord Stewart, who had applied for a reference to the Master to fix the marriage settlements, which application Romilly resisted.   His speech was eloquent without vehemence or seeming passion, and of Ulyssean subtlety.   He had to address the Chancellor against the Regent's friend, the Ambassador at Vienna, and Lord Castlereagh's brother, and he continued to suggest, with as little offence as possible, whatever could serve his purpose as to the fortune, age, morals, &c. of his Lordship.   He exposed with much humor and sarcasm the precipitation with which the marriage was urged, after a few weeks' acquaintance, two or three interviews, and a consent obtained at the first solicitation.

April 30th. — I called on Lamb and accompanied him to Mr. Monkhouse, St. Anne Street East.   Haydon and Allston,* painters, were there, and two other gentlemen whose names I

---

* Washington Allston, distinguished as an historical painter of a very high class, was born in South Carolina, 1779.   In England, 1803, he enjoyed the friendship of B. West and Fuseli.   At Rome, he was known by the resident German artists as " *The American Titian.*"   He there formed a lasting friendship with Coleridge and Washington Irving.   He said of Coleridge, " To no other man whom I have ever known do I owe so much *intellectually.*"   Allston's portrait of Coleridge, painted at Bristol in 1814 for Joshua Wade, is now in the National Portrait Gallery.   His two best-known pictures in this country are " Jacob's Dream," at Petworth, painted in 1817, and " Uriel in the Sun," at Trentham.   He married a sister of the celebrated Dr. Channing.   He died at Cambridge Port, near Boston, in America, 1843.

did not collect. The conversation was very lively and agreeable. Allston has a mild manner, a soft voice, and a sentimental air with him, — not at all Yankeeish ; but his conversation does not indicate the talent displayed in his paintings. There is a warmth and vigor about Haydon, indicating youthful confidence, often the concomitant of talents and genius, which he is said to possess. His conversation is certainly interesting. Monkhouse himself is a gentlemanly sensible man. Lamb, without talking much, talked his best. I enjoyed the evening.

May 4th. — At six I dined with Masquérier,* and met a singular party. The principal guest was the once famous Major Scott Waring,† he who, when censured by the Speaker, on Burke's saying that he hoped it would not occasion feelings too painful, started up and said he need not fear that : he had already forgotten it.

The Major now exhibits rather the remains of a military courtier and gentleman of the old school than of a statesman, the political adversary of Burke. But good breeding is very marked in him.

COLERIDGE TO H. C. R.

May 3, 1818.

MY DEAR SIR, — Ecce iterum Crispinus ! Another mendicant letter from S. T. C. ! But no, it is from the poor little children

* John James Masquérier, a portrait-painter by profession. Without aspiring to academical rank, he attained an independence by his professional life of twenty-eight years. He was descended on both the father's and the mother's side from French Protestant refugees. Being sent to school in Paris, he witnessed some of the most thrilling scenes of the Revolution. Being again at Paris in 1800, he obtained permission to make a likeness of the First Consul without his being aware of what was going on. With this and other sketches he returned to England, and composed a picture of "Napoleon reviewing the Consular Guards in the Court of the Tuileries." It was the first genuine likeness of the famous man; and being exhibited in Piccadilly in 1801, produced to the young artist a profit of a thousand pounds. Beattie, in his Life of Thomas Campbell (Vol. I. p. 429), quotes a description of Masquérier by the poet as "a pleasant little fellow with French vivacity." In 1812 he married a Scotch lady, the widow of Scott, the Professor of Moral Philosophy at Aberdeen. This lady was by birth a Forbes, and related to the Frasers and Erskines. After Mr. Masquérier retired from his profession, he went to live at Brighton, where he was the respected associate of Copley Fielding, Horace Smith, and other artists and literary men. H. C. R. was his frequent guest, and on several occasions travelled with him. Mr. Masquérier died March 13, 1855, in his 77th year.
  Abridged from an obituary notice by H. C. R. in the *Gentleman's Magazine*, May, 1855.
  † The friend and zealous supporter of Warren Hastings in his trial. — H. C. R. *Vide* Macaulay's "Essays," Vol. III. pp. 436, 442, &c.

employed in the Cotton Factories, who would fain have you in the list of their friends and helpers; and entreat you to let *me* know for and in behalf of them, whether there is not some law prohibiting, or limiting, or regulating the employment either of children or adults, or of both, in the White Lead Manufactory. In the minutes of evidence before the Select Committee of the House of Commons on the state of children in the Cotton Factories, in 1816, the question is put to Mr. Astley Cooper, who replies, "I believe there is such a law." Now, can you help us to a more positive answer? Can you furnish us with any other instances in which the Legislature has directly, or by immediate consequence, interfered with what is ironically called "Free Labor"? (i. e. DARED to prohibit soul-murder and infanticide on the part of the rich, and self-slaughter on that of the poor!) or any dictum of our grave law authorities from Fortescue to Bacon, and from Bacon to Kenyon and Eldon: for from the borough in Hell I wish to have no representative, though on second thoughts I should have no objection to a good word in God's cause, though it should have slipped from the Devil's mouth. In short, my dear sir, the only objection likely to produce any hesitation in the House of Lords respecting Sir Robert Peel's Bill, which has just passed the House of Commons, will come from that Scottish ("der Teufel *scotch* man all for snakes!") plebeian earl, Lord L——, the dangerous precedent of legislative interference with free labor, of course implying that this bill will provide the first precedent. Though Heaven knows that I am seriously hurting myself by devoting my days daily in this my best harvest-tide as a lecture-monger, and that I am most *disinterestedly* interested in the fate of the measure, yet interested I am. Good Mr. Clarkson could scarcely be more so! I should have bid farewell to all ease of conscience if I had returned an excuse to the request made for my humble assistance. But a little legal information from you would do more than twenty S. T. C.s, if there exists any law in point in that pithy little manual yclept the Statutes of Great Britain. I send herewith two of the circulars that I have written as the most to the point in respect of what I now solicit from you.* Be so good (if you have time to write at all, and see aught that can be of service) as to direct to me, care of Nathaniel Gould, Esq., Spring Garden Coffee-House. I need not add, that in the

* This Bill was by the *father* of the late Sir Robert Peel. (See an interesting reference in Yonge's "Life of Lord Liverpool," Vol. II. p. 367.) The Ten Hours Bill, restricting the hours of labor in factories for children and persons of tender years to ten hours, passed in 1844.

present case, Bis dat qui cito dat. For procrastination is a
monopoly (in which you have no partnership) of your sincere,
and with respectful esteem, affectionate friend,

S. T. COLERIDGE.

May 7th. — I lounged at the Surrey Institution till it was
time to go to Covent Garden Theatre, where I went by appointment with Thomas Stansfeld. We heard " The Slave,"
and saw " The Sorrows of Werther." "The Slave" is a sentimental musical drama, which exhibits Macready to great advantage. He is an heroic, supergenerous, and noble African,
who exercises every sort of virtue and self-denial, with no
regard to propriety, but considerable stage effect. Miss
Stephens's singing is as unlike an African as her fair complexion. She is very sweet in this character. Braham's voice
was husky, and he hardly got as much applause as Sinclair.
Liston as a booby cockney, come to see an old maiden aunt;
Emery as his Yorkshire friend, who is to help him out of difficulties, are decently funny.

"The Sorrows of Werther" is a pleasant burlesque, and Liston infinitely comic. I cannot account for the caprice which
made this piece so unpopular, in spite of Liston's capital acting. The great objection is that the satire is not felt. Werther's sentimentality is ridiculous enough, but who cares in
England for foreign literature? Had we a party here who
were bent on supporting, and another resolved to ruin, the
German poet, there would be an interest. Besides, I am not
sure that the sapient public knew what was meant for burlesque. Is it certain that the author knew?

May 11th. — I lounged away this day entirely. I went first
to the Exhibition. There I saw a number of gaudy portraits,
— and a few pictures, which at the end of a week I recollect
with pleasure. A splendid landscape by Turner, " The Dort
Packet Boat," has a richness of coloring unusual in water
scenes, and perhaps not quite true to nature; but this picture
delights me, notwithstanding. On the contrary, Turner's
" Field of Waterloo " is a strange incomprehensible jumble.
Lawrence's " Duke of Wellington " is a fine painting.

I called on Miss Lamb, and so passed away the forenoon. I
dined with the Colliers and took tea with the Flaxmans. Mr.
Flaxman has more than sixty engravings by Piranesi, not better
than mine, and only seventeen the same, though part of the
same series. Fraser says the collection amounts to 120.

May 24th. — This was an agreeable day. I rose early, and walked to Norwood. The weather as fit for walking as possible, and the book I lounged with very interesting. From half past six to nine on the road. It was near ten before Hamond came down. I did not suffer him to be called. I found him in pleasantly situated small apartments, where he contrives to pass away his time with no other society than a little child, whom he teaches its letters, and a mouse, that feeds out of his hands. I was the first friend who called on him there. He writes for his amusement on whatever subject chances to engage his attention, but with no purpose, I fear, literary or mercantile. Yet he says he suffers no ennui.

May 31st. — I wrote an opinion in the forenoon, on which I spoke with Manning. I walked then to Clapton, reading Lord Byron, but finding the Kents from home, I went to Mrs. Barbauld's, with whom I dined. Several people were there, and young Mr. Roscoe called. Mrs. Barbauld speaks contemptuously of Lord Byron's new poem,* as being without poetry, and in horrible versification. It may be so.

June 9th. — I took tea with the Miss Nashes, and accompanied them to Covent Garden, where we were very much amused by "She Stoops to Conquer." Liston's Tony Lumpkin is a delightful performance. The joyous folly, the booby imbecility, of Tony are given with exquisite humor and truth. And I was charmed by the beauty of Miss Brunton, though her acting is not very excellent. Charles Kemble overacted the sheepishness of the bashful rake, and underacted the rakishness, — in both particulars wanting a just perception of the character. And Fawcett but poorly performed old Hardcastle. But the scenes are so comic that, in spite of moderate acting, I was gratified throughout.

June 18th. — During the general election, nothing has hitherto much gratified me but the prospect of Sir Samuel Romilly's triumphant election for Westminster, and the contempt into which Hunt seems to have fallen, even with the mob he courts. His absence from the poll, the folly of his committee in joining with Kinnaird, — and even the secession of the few who have split their votes for Cartwright and Hunt, will, I expect, in concurrence with the decided hostility of the Court, and the semi-opposition of the Whigs, fix Captain Maxwell as second to Romilly.

July 3d. — I dined at the Colliers', and then walked to the

---

* "Beppo," published in May, 1818.

hustings. The crowd was great. Burdett and Romilly are again higher on the poll than Captain Maxwell. I consider the election as decided.

July 4th. — I spent the forenoon at Guildhall, and took a cold dinner at the Colliers' early, being desirous to see something of the election at Covent Garden. I was too late, however, to get near the hustings, and suffered more annoyance from the crowd than sympathy with or observation of their feelings could compensate. The crowd was very great, and extended through the adjacent streets. There was not much tumult. The mob could not quite relish Sir Samuel Romilly being placed at the head of the poll, though, their hero being elected, they could not complain. All the Burdettites, therefore, acceded to the triumph of to-day, though, a few deep-blue ribbons were mingled with the light blue and buff of the Whigs. Sir Samuel sat in a barouche with W. Smith, &c. Streamers, flags, and a sort of palanquin were prepared, to give this riding the air of a chairing. He looked rather pale, and as he passed through the Strand, and it appeared as if the mob would take off the horses, he manifested anxiety and apprehension.*

Rem.† — Thirteen years had elapsed since I left Jena. I had kept up a correspondence, though not a close one, with two of my friends, and though I had ceased to devote myself to German literature, I felt a desire to renew my German acquaintance. I wished also to become better acquainted with the Rhine scenery, and with portions of the Netherlands yet unknown. I shall not dwell on places, but confine my reminiscences to persons.

At Frankfort I saw my old friends, at least those of them who were not from home. I found that my Jena fellow-student, Frederick Schlosser, had been frightened into Romanism by ill health and low spirits. These led, first to the fear of hell, and then to the Romish Church as an asylum. His brother was converted at Rome, and then made a proselyte of him. They were wrought on, too, by Werner, Frederick Schlegel, and the romantic school of poets and artists. Of Goethe, Schlosser said : " What a tragical old age his is ! He is left alone. He opposes himself to the religious spirit that prevails among the young ; therefore justice is not done him. But he

---

* A few weeks after this, in a fit of despair on the death of his wife, he destroyed himself, — an event which excited universal sorrow. — H. C. R.

† Written in 1851.

is still our greatest man." He ought, perhaps, to have said also, " He is opposed to the democratic tendencies of the age."

On August 23d I parted from Naylor, and accompanied a Mr. Passavant in his carriage to Weimar, which, after travelling all night, we reached the second evening, passing through Eisenach, Erfurth, &c.

At Jena I found my friend Knebel * in a garden-house. I was not expected, but was soon recognized, and met with a reception which justified the long and fatiguing journey. My old friend was the same as ever, — a little feebler, of course ; but in character and habits the same affectionate, generous, high-minded, animated old man I knew years ago. With the same quick sensibility to everything good and beautiful, the same comical irritability without anger, and the same rough, passionate tone, which could not for a moment conceal the tenderness of his disposition. Mrs. Von Knebel I found the same hospitable and friendly person, — attentive to her husband's guests, and most anxious to make me comfortable. There was a new member of the family, — a boy, Bernard, — a sweet child, delicately framed, who died young. The first affectionate greetings were scarcely over, and we were in the very act of projecting how I could be brought to see Charles, the Major's eldest son, who is a lieutenant in the Prussian service, when he suddenly entered the room. The parents were overjoyed at seeing him, and I was glad too. Thirteen years ago he was a boy, now he had become a fine young man, with as fierce an appearance as a uniform, whiskers, and mustache can give ; but, in spite of these, a gentle creature, and full of affection towards his parents.

My visit to the Knebels was interrupted by an excursion of two days to Weimar, of which *dignitatis causa* I must give an account. While at Knebel's, the Crown Prince of Weimar called on him, and was courteous to me, so that it was incumbent on me to call on him and accept an invitation to dine at Court, which I did twice. On the first occasion, I was recognized by the chamberlain, Count Einsiedel, who introduced me to the Grand Duchess. Einsiedel was an elegant courtier-poet, author of some comedies from Terence, acted in masks after the Roman fashion. Prince Paul, the second son of the King of Bavaria, was also a visitor. There might have been thirty at table, including Goethe's son. On our return to the drawing-room, I was introduced to the Crown Princess, and

* See *ante*, pp. 126 – 128.

had rather a long conversation with her. She was somewhat deaf, and I took pains to be understood by her in German and English. I mentioned the familiarities of the English lower classes towards her brother, the Emperor Alexander, and expressed a fear lest such things should deter her from a visit to England. She said the Emperor was perfectly satisfied, and that, as to herself, she wished to see England : " *Es gehört zu den frommen Wünschen* " (It belongs to the pious wishes). We talked of languages. I said I hoped to see the dominion of the French language destroyed, as that of their arms had been. She smiled and said, " *Das wäre viel* " (That would be much).

I was called out of the circle by the Grand Duchess, and chatted a considerable time with her. I referred to the well-known interview between herself and Napoleon, after the battle of Jena, of which I said England was well informed (not adding, " through myself " *). She received my compliment

---

* The account alluded to was communicated by H. C. R. to the *Times,* December 26, 1807, and republished in Mrs. Austin's " Characteristics of Goethe," Vol. III. p. 203. The following extracts will give the substance and result of this interesting interview : —

" When the fortunes of the day began to be decided (and that took place early in the morning), the Prussians retreating through the town were pursued by the French, and slaughtered in the streets. Some of the inhabitants were murdered, and a general plunder began. In the evening, the conqueror approached and entered the palace of the Duke, now become his own by the *right* of conquest. It was then that the Duchess left her apartment, and seizing the moment of his entering the hall, placed herself on the top of the staircase, to greet him with the formality of a courtly reception. Napoleon started when he beheld her. ' Qui êtes vous ? ' he exclaimed, with his characteristic abruptness. ' Je suis la Duchesse de Weimar.' — ' Je vous plains,' he retorted fiercely; ' j'écraserai votre mari.' He then added, ' I shall dine in my apartment,' and rushed by her.

" On his entrance next morning, he began instantly with an interrogative (his favorite figure). ' How could your husband, Madame, be so mad as to make war against me ? ' ' Your Majesty would have despised him if he had not,' was the dignified answer he received. ' How so ? ' he hastily rejoined. The Duchess slowly and deliberately rejoined: ' My husband has been in the service of the King of Prussia upwards of thirty years, and surely it was not at the moment that the King had so mighty an enemy as your Majesty to contend against that the Duke could abandon him.' A reply so admirable, which asserted so powerfully the honor of the speaker, and yet conciliated the vanity of the adversary, was irresistible. Buonaparte became at once more mild, and, without noticing the answer already received, continued his interrogatories. ' But how came the Duke to attach himself to the King of Prussia ? ' — ' Your Majesty will, on inquiry, find that the Dukes of Saxony, the younger branches of the family, have always followed the example of the Electoral House; and your Majesty knows what motives of prudence and policy have led the Court of Dresden to attach itself to Prussia rather than Austria.' This was followed by further inquiries and further answers, so impressive, that in a few minutes Napoleon exclaimed with warmth: ' Madame, vous êtes la femme la plus respectable que j'ai jamais connue: vous avez sauvé votre mari.' Yet he could not confer favor unaccompanied with insult; for reiterat-

favorably, — said, as some one must stay in the house, she was the proper person; that, after the plundering was over, Buonaparte behaved civilly enough in his fashion.

The Grand Princess inquired whether I had heard the Russian service performed, and on my saying " No," she said she would give orders that I should be admitted the next day (Sunday). I accordingly went. The Russian language I thought very soft, and like Italian. But I was guilty of an oversight in not staying long, which the Princess noticed next day after dinner. She said she had ordered some music to be played on purpose for me. She seemed an intelligent woman, — indeed, as all her children have been, she was *crammed* with knowledge.

To terminate at once my mention of the court, I dined here a second time on Sunday, and was introduced to the Grand Duke. He talked freely and bluntly. He expressed his disapprobation of the English system of jurisprudence, which allowed lawyers to travel for months at a time. " We do not permit that." I said, " When the doctor is absent, the patient recovers." A bad joke was better than contradiction; besides, he was right.

The intimacy in which the Grand Duke had lived all his life with Goethe, and the great poet's testimony to his character, — not ordinary eulogy, — satisfy me that he must have been an extraordinary man. On the whole, this visit to Weimar did not add to my prepossessions in its favor. The absence of Goethe was a loss nothing could supply.

I went to the theatre, — no longer what it was under the management of Goethe and Schiller. Jagermann, then the favorite of the Grand Duke, was at this time become fat; her face had lost all proportion, and was destitute of expression. She performed, without effect, the part of Sappho, in Grillparzer's disagreeable tragedy of that name. Mademoiselle Beck played the slave, and the scene in which she bewailed her forlorn state, and gained the love of Phaon, was the only one that affected me. I sat part of the evening with Mesdames Wolzogen and Schiller.

---

ing his assurances of esteem, he added : ' Je le pardonne, mais c'est à cause de vous seulement; car, pour lui, c'est un mauvais sujet.' The Duchess to this made no reply; but, seizing the happy moment, interceded successfully for her suffering people. Napoleon gave orders that the plundering should cease.

" When the treaty which secured the nominal independence of Weimar, and declared its territory to be a part of the Rhenish League, was brought from Buonaparte to the Duke by a French general, and presented to him, he refused to take it into his own hands, saying, with more than gallantry, ' Give it to my wife; the Emperor intended it for her.' "

I went to Tiefurth, the former residence of the Dowager Duchess Amelia, where Sturm * has his establishment, and among the characters I called on was Herr von Einsiedel, the morose and cynical husband of my old acquaintance, Madame von Einsiedel.

August 29th. — I accompanied Knebel to Madame Griesbach's garden, the most delightful spot in the neighborhood of Jena. This has been bought for £ 1,000 by the Grand Duchess. Her children were there, and I was introduced to the Princesses, — mere children yet ; but it is surprising how soon they have acquired a sense of their dignity. These children are over-crammed ; they learn all the sciences and languages, and are in danger of losing all personal character and power of thought in the profusion of knowledge they possess. This is now the fashion among the princes of Germany.

I saw Griesbach's widow. The old lady knew me in a moment, and instantly began joking, — said she supposed I was come to pay a visit to E——'s † lecture-room.

My last few days at Jena were spent almost alone with Knebel. He told me of Wieland's death, which was, he said, delightful. Wieland never lost his cheerfulness or good-humor ; and, but a few hours before his death, having insisted on seeing his doctor's prescription, " I see," said he, " it is much the same with my life and the doctor's Latin, they are both at an end." He was ill but a week, and died of an indigestion.

My last day at Jena was spent not without pleasure. It was one of uninterrupted rain ; I could not, therefore, take a walk with Fries, as I had intended, so I remained the whole day within doors, chatting with my friend Knebel. We looked over books and papers. Knebel sought for MSS. of the great poets, Goethe, Wieland, and Herder for me, and talked much about his early life, his opinions, &c. As *Andenken* (for remembrance) he gave me a ring with Raphael's head on it, given him by the Duchess Amelia, and four portraits in porcelain and iron of the four great German poets. In return, I gave him Wordsworth's poems, which had occupied so much of our attention.

---

* Professor Sturm taught at this establishment the economical sciences, i. e. all that pertains to agriculture and the useful arts. — H. C. R.

† The Professor with whom H. C. R. had a misunderstanding. — See *ante*, p. 134.

17 *

On the 9th of September, I left my friend Knebel with sorrow, for I could not expect to see him again, and I loved him above every German. His memory is dear to me. I sauntered, not in high spirits, to Weimar, where I slept, and on the 10th set out in a diligence towards Frankfort. I spent a little time with Knebel's son at Erfurth, where he is stationed. I had to spend three nights on the road, reaching Frankfort at 4 A. M., on the 13th. A more wearisome journey I never made.

I spent my time at Frankfort almost entirely with my friends of the Aldebert connection, and the Brentano family and their friends.

September 13th. — When I met Christian Brentano he embarrassed me by kissing me, with all outward marks of friendship. After being an *économe* for some years in Bohemia, after dabbling in philosophy and mathematics, and rejecting medicine and law, he is now about to become a priest. In a few words, he said that he had been, by God's providence, brought to see that religion alone can give comfort to man. " I was," said he, " first led to this by seeing what faith can do in making men good. I was led to know my own worthlessness. Nature opened to me somewhat of her relation to God. I saw wonderful phenomena — miracles ! " — " Do you mean," said I, " such miracles as the Scriptures speak of ? " — " Yes," said he, " of the same kind." I had not the assurance to ask him of what kind they were, but merely said, I had often wished in my youth to see a miracle, in order to put an end to all further doubt and speculation. Brentano then talked mystically. That he is a deceiver, or playing a part, I am far from suspecting. That he has a wrong head with great powers of intellect, I have long known. But I was not prepared for such a change. In society he is, however, improved ; he is now quiet, and rather solicitous to please than to shine ; but his wild Italian face, with all its caricature ferocity, remains.

Rem.* — The Brentano circle was extended by the presence of Savigny and his wife. He was already a great man, though not arrived at the rank he afterwards attained. It is a remarkable circumstance, that when I lately introduced myself to him in Berlin, — he being now an ex-Minister of Justice, fallen back on his literary pursuits, and retired from official life, which is not his especial province, — both he and I had forgotten our few interviews in this year (1818), and had thought

* Written in 1851.

that we had not seen each other since I left Germany at the beginning of the century, that is, in 1805.

My course led me to Baden-Baden. It is enough for me to say that I walked through the admirable Murg-Thal with great delight, and had for my book during the walk " Scenes out of the World of Spirits," by Henry Stilling (or Jung). The theory of the spiritual world entertained by this pious enthusiast is founded on the assumption that every witch and ghost story is to be taken as indubitably true. He has many believers in England as elsewhere. Having been reproached as a fanatic, he desires all *unbelievers* to consider his tales as mere visions, — these tales being narratives of sentences passed in heaven on great criminals, &c., by an eye-witness and auditor. In Goethe's Life is an interesting account of him.* Goethe protected him from persecution when a student at Strasburg, but became at last tired of him. Goethe corrected the first volume of his Autobiography by striking out all the trash. This I learned from Knebel. That volume, therefore, should be read by those who might find the subsequent volumes intolerable. Stilling was the *nom de guerre* of Jung.

I spent six days at Paris, where were Miss Nash, M. Andrews, &c. The only object of great interest was Mademoiselle Mars. " She a little resembles Miss Mellon † when she was young, — i. e. Miss Mellon when she stood still, neither giggling nor fidgety." I did not foresee that I was writing of a future duchess.

November 30th. — Thelwall called. His visit gave me pain. He has purchased *The Champion*, and is about to take up the profession of politician, after so many years' pause. An old age of poverty will be his portion.

December 3d. — I bought at Dove Court, St. Martin's Lane, a marble bust of Wieland by Schadow, for ten guineas. Flaxman informed me of this bust being there. He says it is an excellent head, which he would have bought himself, had he had a room to put it in. I am delighted with my purchase. It is a very strong likeness, and in a style of great simplicity. The head is covered with a cap, which is only distinguished from the skull by two lines crossing the head ; the hair curls round below the cap, and the head stoops a very little, with

* *Vide* " Dichtung und Wahrheit," Books IX. and X.
† Afterwards Mrs. Coutts, and then Duchess of St. Albans.

the sight rather downwards. The forehead and temples are exquisitely wrought, and the drapery is pleasingly folded. It is unwrought at the sides, in each of which is a square opening. Having this fine object constantly before me will generate a love for sculpture.*

December 4th. — I dined with John Collier, and in the evening, after taking tea with Miss Lamb, accompanied her to Covent Garden. We saw "The Rivals," and Farren for the first time, the last theatrical tyro that has appeared. His Sir Anthony Absolute appeared to me delightful. He is a young man, I am told, yet he was so disguised by painted wrinkles, and a face and figure made up by art, that I could hardly credit the report. The consequence of a manufactured countenance and constrained unnatural attitudes is, that the actor has a hard and inflexible manner. Liston's Acres, however, gave me the greatest pleasure. It was infinitely comic and laughable, and none the worse for being even burlesque and farcical.

Rem.† — My journal mentions Farren as an admirable comic actor, only twenty-five or twenty-six years old. This must be a mistake. He is now worn out, and apparently a very old man.

December 19th. — I dined with Sergeant Blossett. No one with him but Miss Peckwell and a nephew of the Sergeant's, a Mr. Grote, a merchant, who reads German, and appears to be an intelligent, sensible man, having a curiosity for German philosophy as well as German poetry. I read a number of things by Goethe and others to the Sergeant, who has already made great advances in the language, and can relish the best poetry. Grote has borrowed books of me.

Rem.‡ — This year I became a "barrister of five years' standing," an expression that has become almost ridiculous, being the qualification required for many offices by acts of Parliament, while it is notorious that many such barristers are ill qualified for any office. I was no exception, certainly, at any time of my life, being never a learned lawyer or a skilful advocate, and yet in this my fifth year I attained some reputation; and of this year I have some anecdotes to relate of myself and others not uninteresting to those who may care for me or for the profession.

There was but an insignificant increase of fees, from £ 415

---

* There will be further reference to this bust in the year 1829. It is a magnificent work of art. A cast of it is or was to be seen at the Crystal Palace.
† Written in 1851.   ‡ Written in 1851.

in 1817 to £ 488 during this year; but this little practice brought me into connection with superior men, and into superior courts.

For instance, I had an appeal in the Council Chambers from Gibraltar with Sir Samuel Romilly. It was a case of mercantile guaranty. I have forgotten the facts, and I refer to the case merely because it shows Sir Samuel's practice. He read from the printed statement, in the most unimpressive manner, the simple facts, adding scarcely an observation of his own. I followed at some length, not comprehending the course taken by my excellent leader, and Hundleby,* my client, was satisfied with my argument. I pleaded before Sir W. Grant, Sir William Scott, &c. Hart, afterwards Chancellor of Ireland, and Lovett were for the respondents. Then Sir Samuel Romilly replied in a most masterly manner. I never heard a more luminous and powerful argument. He went over the ground I had trod, but I scarcely knew my own arguments, so improved were they. Judgment was ultimately given in our favor. I have since understood that it was Sir Samuel's practice, when he had the reply, to open the case in this way, and not even to read the brief before he went to court, knowing that his junior and adversaries would give him time enough to become master of the facts and settle his argument.

At the Spring Assizes, at Thetford, I made a speech which gained me more credit than any I ever made, either before or after, and established my character as a speaker : luckily it required no law. I thought of it afterwards with satisfaction, and I will give an account of the case here (it will be the only one in these Reminiscences), partly because it will involve some questions of speculative morality. It was a defence in a *Qui tam* action for penalties for usury to the amount of £ 2,640.† My attorney was a stranger. He had offered the brief to Jameson, who declined it from a consciousness of inability to speak, and recommended me. The plaintiff's witness had requested my client to lend him money, which, it is stated by the single witness, he consented to do on the payment of £ 20. A mortgage also was put in ; and on this the case rested. The

---

* Hundleby was a solicitor, the partner of Alliston, who still lives. He married the daughter of Curtis, a wealthy man. He has been dead many years, and his widow is now the wife of Tite, the architect of the Royal Exchange. — H. C. R., 1851.

† A *Qui tam* action is an action brought by an informer for penalties of which a half-share is give to the informer by the statute. The suit would be by Moses, plaintiff, who sues " as well for himself " (*Qui tam*) as for our Lord the King.

defence was a simple one. It could lie only in showing that the witness could not safely be relied on ; and this I did in a way that produced applause from the audience, a compliment from the judge, and a verdict in my favor. Now, what I look back upon with pleasure is, that I gained this verdict very fairly and by no misstatement.   I will put down some of the salient points of my speech, of which I have a distinct recollection.

I began : " Gentlemen, I have often thought that juries, as conscientious men, anxious to do justice, must be distressed by perceiving that they are called upon to decide a case on most imperfect evidence, where, from the nature of the case, they can only guess what the truth may be, hearing only one side. This is one of those cases.   There can be no doubt that my client lent a sum of money to that man, his own attorney, whom you have seen in that box ; and that man has thought proper to tell you that, in order to obtain that loan, he was forced to give £ 20. Now, this was a transaction between these persons, and I cannot possibly contradict him. For, were I to read you my brief, or tell you what my client says, of course denying all this, I should be reproved by his Lordship, and incur the ridicule of my learned friends around me ; because, what the party in the cause says is not evidence.*   This is a hardship, but it is the law ; and I refer to it now, not to censure the law, which would be indecorous, but to draw your attention to this most important consequence, that since you are compelled to hear the witness, — one party alone, — and are not at liberty to hear the other party, in a transaction between them and none other, you have the duty imposed on you closely to examine what that witness has said, and ask yourselves this question, whether such a statement as he has thought proper to make, knowing that he may swear falsely with safety (for he can never be contradicted), *must* be credited by you.

" Gentlemen, at the same time that I am not in a condition to deny what that man has said, I add, with the most entire confidence, that it is impossible for you, acting under those rules which good sense and conscience alike dictate, to do other than by your verdict declare that you cannot, in this essentially criminal case, convict the defendant on the uncorroborated testimony of that single witness."

I then pointedly stated that, though in form an action, this was in substance a criminal case, and to be tried by the rules

---

* This law is now altered.

observed in a criminal court; and that, unless they had a perfect conviction, they would not consign this old retired tradesman to a jail or a workhouse for the rest of his days in order to enrich Mr. Moses (the common informer, who had luckily a Jew name) and the Treasury. And I pledged myself to show that in this case were combined all imaginable reasons for distrust, so as to render it morally impossible, whatever the fact might be, to give a verdict for the *Qui tam* plaintiff.

I then successively expatiated on the several topics which the case supplied, — on the facts that the single witness was the plaintiff's own attorney, — an uncertificated bankrupt who was within the rules of the King's Bench Prison; that he came down that morning from London in the custody of a sheriff's officer, though, when asked where he came from, he at first said from home, having before said he was an attorney at Lynn. And I had laid a trap for him, and led him to say he expected no part of the penalty. This I represented to be incredible; and I urged with earnestness the danger to society if such a man were of necessity to be believed because he dared to take an oath for which he could not be called to account here. And I alluded to recent cases in which other King's Bench prisoners had been transported for perjury, and to the known cases of perjury for blood-money. As I have already said, I sat down with applause, which was renewed when the verdict for the defendant was pronounced. The man I had so exposed gave me something to do afterwards on his own account; and, more than once, attorneys, new clients, in bringing me a brief, alluded to this case. But the power of making such a speech does not require the talents most essential to the barrister, — none of which did I, in fact, possess.

In the spring Term of this year, Gurney,* the King's Counsel's clerk, brought me a bag, for which I presented him with a guinea. This custom is now obsolete, and therefore I mention it. It was formerly the etiquette of the bar that none but Sergeants and King's Counsel could carry a bag in Westminster Hall. Till some King's Counsel presented him with one, however large the junior (that is, stuff-gowned) barrister's business might be, he was forced to carry his papers in his hand. It was considered that he who carried a bag was a rising man.

At the following Bury Assizes I was concerned in a case no otherwise worth noticing than as it gave occasion to good-natured joking. I defended Ridley, the tallow-chandler, in an

* Afterwards Baron Gurney.

action against him for a nuisance in building a chimney in Still Lane. The chief witness for plaintiff was Blomfield (father of the present Bishop of London).* He had said that he was a schoolmaster, and the plaintiff and defendant and defendant's counsel had all been his pupils. When I rose to cross-examine him, C. J. Dallas leaned over, and in an audible whisper said, " Now, Mr. Robinson, you may take your revenge." Good-natured sparring took place between Blomfield and myself, and I got a verdict in a very doubtful case, — insisting that, if a nuisance, it must be a general one, and so the subject of an indictment. Afterwards, on an indictment, I contended that the remedy was by action, if it were a grievance, and in this I failed.

Before the summer Assizes I dined with C. J. Gibbs. Others of the circuit were with me. Some parts of his conversation I thought worth putting down, though not very agreeable at the time, as it was manifestly didactic, and very like that of a tutor with his pupils. He spoke with great earnestness against the " Term Reports," † which he considered as ruinous to the profession in the publication of hasty decisions, especially those at Nisi Prius, and urged the necessity of arguing every case on principle. On my remarking on the great fame acquired by men who were eminently deficient, he was malicious enough to ask for an instance. I named Erskine. He was not sorry to have an opportunity of expressing his opinion of Erskine, which could not be high. He remarked on Erskine's sudden fall in legal reputation, " Had he been well-grounded, he could not have fallen."

This same day, on my speaking of the talents required in an opening and reply, he said that the Lord Chancellor (Eldon) reproached Sir James Mansfield with the practice I have noticed in Sir Samuel Romilly, of leaving his argument for the reply, which was ascribed to laziness. Gibbs praised Bell, the Chancery practitioner, as a man who was always in the right. " He always gave the most satisfactory answer to a question in the fewest words."

In the winter of this year I heard from Gurney some interesting facts about fees, which within about eleven or twelve years had risen much above what was formerly known. Kaye,‡ the solicitor, told Gurney once that he had that day carried the

* See *ante*, p. 3.
† One of the earliest series of periodical law reports.
‡ Solicitor to the Bank of England, &c.

Attorney-General (Gibbs) 100 general retainers, that is 500 guineas. These were on the Baltic captures and insurance cases. Gibbs did not think that Erskine ever made more than 7,000 guineas, and Mingay confessed that he only once made 5,000 guineas. He observed that the great fortunes made in ancient times by lawyers must have been indirectly as the stewards of great men. Otherwise they were unaccountable.

I must here add that all this is little compared with the enormous gains of my old fellow-circuiteer, Charles Austin, who is said to have made 40,000 guineas by pleading before Parliament in one session.

This year there were great changes in the law courts. Of the judicial promotions Jekyll said, being the professional wag, that they came by titles very different, viz. : C. J. Abbott by *descent*, J. Best by *intrusion*, and Richardson by the *operation of law*. The wit of the two first is pungent; the last, a deserved compliment. It was expected, said Jekyll, that Vaughan would come in by *prescription*. This was not so good. Sir Henry Halford,* the King's physician, was his brother.

I must not forget that, on Aldebert's death, his books were taken by a bookseller, but I was allowed to have what I liked at the bookseller's price. I laid out £ 40 in purchasing Piranesi's prints and other works of art, and had many calls from men of taste to see them.

The Colliers, with whom I used to dine, left London this year. Their place was to some extent supplied by John Payne Collier,† who took a house in Bouverie Street. It was not then foreseen that he would become a great Shakespearian critic, though he had already begun to be a writer.

---

* Sir Henry Halford was the son of Dr. Vaughan of Leicester, but changed his name in 1809, when he inherited a fortune from his mother's cousin, Sir Charles Halford.

† J. P. Collier wrote " History of English Dramatic Poetry to the Time of Shakespeare," 1831 ; " New Facts regarding the Life of Shakespeare," 1835; " Shakespeare Library ; a Collection of the Romances, Novels, Poems, and Histories used by Shakespeare as the Foundation of his Dramas," 1843 ; and various other works.

CHAPTER XXII.

1819.

J ANUARY 4th. — (At Bury.) I walked early up town and left with Mr. Clarkson his MS. account of his interview with the Emperor of Russia, at Aix-la-Chapelle, on the subject of the slave-trade. This interview must receive its explanation from future events. The Emperor talked of the Quakers and Bible Societies, of the Society against War, of which he considered himself a member, and of the slave-trade, as one might have expected a religious clergyman would have done. Mr. Clarkson is a sincere believer in the Emperor's sincerity.

THOMAS R. TO HABAKKUK R.

BURY ST. EDMUNDS, January 6, 1819.

. . . . The Buck party were at my house last Friday, when we were entertained, and most highly interested, by Mr. Clarkson's account of his interview with the Emperor of Russia, at Aix-la-Chapelle. His reception by the most powerful potentate in the world was extremely gracious. The Emperor took him most cordially by both his hands, drew a chair for him and another for himself, when they sat down, in Mr. Clarkson's language, "knee to knee, and face to face." The principal subject of their conversation was, of course, the abolition of the slave-trade, in which the Emperor takes an extraordinary interest, and seems to be most earnestly anxious to use his powerful interest to induce the other powers of Europe to concur in this measure. . . . .

The Emperor, at this meeting, professed likewise the most pacific sentiments, and spoke with great energy of the evil and sin of war, admitting that it was altogether contrary to the spirit of Christianity, and said that he desired to inculcate this sentiment in the minds of the different powers, and should therefore propose frequent congresses to adjust disputes, without having recourse to the too common arbitration of the sword. You know, perhaps, that, for the purpose of eradicating the warlike spirit, *Peace Societies* have been formed both in this country and in America. (We have a small one in this town.) The Emperor assured Mr. Clarkson that he highly approved of them, and wished to be considered as belonging to them. And no longer ago than yesterday, Mr. Clarkson received a copy of a letter, written in English by the Emperor with his own hand, and addressed to Mr. Marsden, the Chairman of the London Peace Society, in which he repeats the same sentiments in favor of the principles of the society. It is at any rate a curious phenomenon to find an advocate of such principles in such a person. There are those who doubt his sincerity, but where can be the motive to induce the *Autocrat of all the Russias* to flatter even such an individual, however excellent, as Mr. Clarkson, or Mr. Marsden, a stock-broker in London ?

January 14th. — I spent the day partly in reading some very good political writings by Benjamin Constant, — the first part of his first volume. His principles appear excellent, and there is to me originality in them. His treating the monarchical power as distinct from the executive pleases me much. He considers the essence of the monarch's office to lie in the superintending everything and doing nothing. He controls the legislature by convoking and dismissing their assemblies ; and he even creates and annihilates the ministers. Being thus separated from the executive body, — *that* may be attacked, and even destroyed (as is constantly done in England), without any detriment to the state.

*Rem.** — Had Louis Philippe felt this, he might have retained his throne, but he would be an autocrat, which did not suit the French people.†

January 26th. — We saw "Brutus." This play has had great success, and with reason, for it exhibits Kean advantageously ; but it seems utterly without literary merit, though the subject admitted of a great deal of passionate poetry. Kean's exhibition of the Idiot in the first act was more able than pleasing ; when he assumed the hero, he strutted and swelled, to give himself an air he never can assume with grace. It was not till the close of the piece, when he had to pass sentence on his own son, that he really found his way to my heart through my imagination. His expression of feeling was deep and true, and the conflict of affection and principle well carried out. An

---

* Written in 1851.
† Added in the margin of the MS.: "Palpable ignorance, this ! At this hour a bold usurper and autocrat has succeeded because he knew how to go to work. An accident may, indeed, any day destroy his power. April 17, 1852. The date is material."

awkward effect was produced by the attempt to blend too much in one play. The act by which Brutus overturned the Tarquins was not that of a man who had a son capable of treason against his country.

February 2d. — Naylor took tea with me ; and soon after, Charles and Mary Lamb came to look at my prints. And the looking them over afforded us pleasure. Lamb has great taste and feeling ; his criticisms are instructive, and I find that enjoyment from works of art is heightened by sympathy. Talfourd came while we were thus engaged. He stayed with us, and afterwards joined us in a rubber, which occupied us till late. Talfourd stayed till near one, talking on personal matters.

February 18th. — I lounged for half an hour before the Covent Garden hustings, — a scene only ridiculous and disgusting. The vulgar abuse of the candidates from the vilest rabble ever beheld is not rendered endurable by either wit or good temper, or the belief of there being any integrity at the bottom. I just saw Hobhouse. His person did not please me ; but Sir Richard Phillips, whom I met there, tells me I am like him, which I do not think to be the fact. Lamb * I could scarcely see, but his countenance is better. Orator Hunt was on the hustings, but he could not obtain a hearing from the mob ; and this fact was the most consolatory part of the spectacle.

February 28th. — After dining at Collier's I went to Godwin, with whom I drank tea. Curran was there, and I had a very agreeable chat with him ; he is come to print his father's life, written by himself ; and he projects an edition of his speeches. He related an affecting anecdote of Grattan in the House of Commons. He was speaking in a style that betrayed the decline of the faculties of a once great man ; he was rambling and feeble, and being assailed by coughing, he stopped, paused, and said in an altered voice, "I believe they are right, sir !" and sat down.

April 3d. — By coach to Ipswich ; then on foot in the dark to Playford (four miles). Mrs. Clarkson was in high health and spirits ; Tom and Mr. Clarkson also well. I met with some visitors there, who rendered the visit peculiarly agreeable. Mr., Mrs., and Miss Grahame, from Glasgow. He is a Writer to the Signet, a brother to the late James Grahame the

---

* The Honorable George Lamb, son of the first Lord Melbourne, and brother of William, who afterwards became Prime Minister.

poet ; a most interesting man, having a fine handsome face and figure, resembling Wordsworth in his gait and general air, though not in his features, and being a first-rate talker, as far as sense and high moral feeling can render conversation delightful. We talked, during the few days of my stay, about English and Scotch law. He complained that the *Comitas gentium* was not allowed to Scotchmen ; that is, a lunatic having money in the funds must be brought to England to have a commission issued here (though he is already found a lunatic in Scotland) before dividends can be paid, &c. ; and bank powers of attorney must be executed according to English forms, even in Scotland. The first case is certainly a great abuse. Mr. Grahame pleased me much, and I have already nearly decided on going to Scotland this summer. In politics he is very liberal, inclining to ultra principles. He was severe against Southey and Wordsworth for their supposed apostasy. He speaks highly of the Scotch law, and considers the administration of justice there much superior to ours.

April 28th. — My ride to-day was very agreeable ; the weather was mild and fine, and I had no ennui. I travelled with the Rev. Mr. Godfrey, with whom I chatted occasionally, and I read three books of the " Odyssey," and several of Burke's speeches. Burke's quarrel with Fox does not do honor to Burke. I fear he was glad of an opportunity to break with his old friend ; yet he appears to have been provoked. In the fourth volume of Burke's Speeches, there is the same wonderful difference between the reports of the newspapers and the publications of Burke himself.

His own notes of his speech on the *Unitarian Petition* are full of profundity and wisdom ; his attack on the *Rights of Man* as an abstract principle is justified on his own representation. How true his axiom, " Crude and unconnected truths are in practice what falsehoods are in theory ! " Strange that he should have undergone so great obloquy because this wise remark has not been comprehended !

May 3d. — I dined with Walter, Fraser, and Barnes. Fraser I attacked on a trimming article in yesterday's *Times* about Catholic Emancipation. And Barnes attacked me about " Peter Bell " ; but this is a storm I must yield to. Wordsworth has set himself back ten years by the publication of this work. I read also Tom Cribb's Memorial to the Congress, — an amusing volume ; but I would rather read than have written it. It is really surprising that a gentleman (for so

Moore is in station and connections) should so descend as to exhibit the Prince Regent and the Emperor of Russia at a boxing-match, under the names of Porpus and Long Sandy. The boxing cant language does not amuse me, even in Moore's gravely burlesque lines.

May 23d. — I spent several hours at home, looking over reports, &c., and then walked to Clapton. I had a fine walk home over Bethnal Green. Passing Bonner's Fields, a nice boy, who was my gossiping companion, pointed out to me the site of Bishop Bonner's house, where the Bishop sat and saw the *Papists* burnt : such is the accuracy of traditional tales. He further showed me some spots in which the ground is low : here the poor burnt creatures were buried, it seems ; and though the ground has been filled up hundreds of times, it always sinks in again. " I do not suppose it is true," said the boy, " but I was afraid once to walk on the spot, and so are the little boys now." The feeling that Nature sympathizes with man in horror of great crimes, and bears testimony to the commission of them, is a very frequent superstition, — perhaps the most universal.

June 4th. — My sister consulted Astley Cooper. She was delighted to find him far from unkind or harsh. He treated her with great gentleness, and very kindly warned her as much as possible to correct her irritability, — not of temper, but of nerves.

June 10th. — Clemens Brentano is turned monk !

June 14th. — Coming home, I found Hamond in town, and went with him to the Exhibition. I stayed a couple of hours, but had no great pleasure there. Scarcely a picture much pleased me. Turner has fewer attractions than he used to have, and Callcott's " Rotterdam " is gaudier than he used to be ; he is aiming at a richer cast of color, but is less beautiful as he deviates from the delicate grays of Cuyp. Cooper's " Marston Moor " did not interest me, though what I have heard since of the artist does. I am told he was lately a groom to Meux, the brewer, who, detecting him in the act of making portraits of his horses, would not keep him as a groom, but got him employment as a horse-painter. He was before a rider at Astley's, it is said. He went into the Academy to learn to draw with the boys. Flaxman says he knew nothing of the mechanism of his art, — he could not draw at all, — but by dint of genius, without instruction (except, as he says, what he learned from a shilling book he bought in the Strand), he could paint very finely. He is already, says Flaxman, a great painter, and will probably become very eminent indeed. He is about thirty-five years of age, and is already an Associate. He paints horses and low life, but his " Marston Moor" is regarded as a fine composition. His appearance does not bespeak his origin. " I introduced him to Lord Grey," said Flaxman, " and as they stood talking together, I could not discern any difference between the peer and the painter."

June 16th. — I was much occupied by a scrape John Collier had got into. A few nights ago he reported that Mr. Hume had said in the House of Commons that Canning had risen above the sufferings of others by laughing at them. Bell * being last night summoned before the House, John Collier gave himself as the author, and was in consequence committed to the custody of the Sergeant-at-Arms. Mr. Wynn moved that he should be committed to Newgate, but this was withdrawn in consequence of Collier's manly and becoming conduct. I was exceedingly alarmed lest this might hurt Collier with Walter, but, to my satisfaction, I found that Collier had raised himself in Walter's opinion; for, by his gentlemanly behavior, he raised the character of the reporters, and he completely relieved Walter from the imputation of having altered the article. I called on Collier in the House of Commons Prison ; he was in good spirits. Mrs. Collier was there, and Walter came too, with Barnes. I chatted with Walter about the propriety of petitioning. He wished Collier to lie in custody till the end of the session, but I differed in opinion, and corrected the petition, which was ultimately adopted. After a hasty dinner in Hall, I ran down to the House. Barnes procured me a place, and I stayed in the gallery till quite late. There was no opposition to Mr. W. Smith's motion for Collier's discharge. He was reprimanded by the Speaker in strong unmeaning words. W. Smith moved for the bill to relieve the Unitarians against the Marriage Act.† The speech had the merit of raising a feeling favorable to the speaker, and it was not so intelligible as to excite opposition. Lord Castlereagh did not pretend to understand it, and Mr. Wilberforce spoke guardedly and with favor of the projected measure. The rest of the speaking this evening was

---

* The publisher of the *Times.*

† Mr. W. Smith's object was to obtain for Unitarians at their marriage the omission of all reference to the Trinity. He did not venture to propose the more rational and complete relief, — which was after a time obtained, — the marriage of Dissenters in their own places of worship. *Vide* May's Constitutional History, Vol. II. p. 384.

very poor indeed, — much below my expectation. I was heartily tired before eleven o'clock. I then came home, and read a little of Homer in bed.

June 23d. — I called late on Mrs. John Collier. She informs me that Walter has been doing a very handsome thing by John Collier. He gave him a bank-note for £50, saying he need not return the surplus after paying the fees, and hoped that it would be some compensation for the inconvenience he had suffered by his imprisonment. Now, the fees amounted to not more than £14 or £15. This is very generous certainly.

July 6th. — I dined with Collier, and had a game of chess for an hour. I then looked over papers, &c. in chambers; and between seven and eight went to Godwin's by invitation. Charles and Mary Lamb were there, also Mr. Booth, — a singular character, not unlike Curran in person; a clever man, says Godwin, and in his exterior very like the Grub Street poet of the last century. I had several rubbers of whist. Charles Lamb's good-humor and playfulness made the evening agreeable, which would otherwise have been made uncomfortable by the painful anxiety visible in Mrs. Godwin, and suspected in Godwin. I came home late.

July 7th. — I dined by invitation with Mr. Belsham. T. Stansfeld had written to me by Mr. Kenrick (a nephew of Mr. Belsham),[*] requesting me to give Mr. Kenrick letters of introduction to Germany. Kenrick left me the letter with an invitation from Belsham. I had an agreeable visit: a small party, — Mr. and Miss Belsham, Spurrell, Senr., Martineau, Jardine,[†] a Mr. Reid, and Mr. Kenrick. We kept up a conversation with very little disputation. Belsham (and I joined him) defended Church Establishments, which he thought better than leaving religion to make its way alone.[‡] He said, I think *my* Church ought to be established; but as that cannot be, I would rather the Anglican Church should be maintained, with all its errors and superstitions, than that the unlearned should be left at large, each man spreading abroad his own follies and absurdities.[§] Kenrick opposed him, and had on some points the best of the argument. Jardine, and indeed all the party, were

---

* There was no actual relationship between Mr. Kenrick and Mr. Belsham; Mr. Kenrick's father married, as his second wife, the sister of Mr. Belsham.
† The Barrister, afterwards a Police Magistrate.
‡ Written in 1851.
§ Mr. Belsham's views on this subject were published in three sermons, entitled " Christianity pleading for the Patronage of the Civil Power, but protesting against the Aid of Penal Laws." Hunter, St. Paul's Churchyard, 1820.

against Mr. Belsham and myself. We talked of animal magnetism, and told ghost stories, and ghosts seemed on the whole to be in credit.

July 8th. — Mr. Kenrick breakfasted with me. I was much pleased with him; he has been, and indeed still is, tutor at the Manchester New College, York, and is going for a trip to Germany to improve in philological studies. He is a stanch Unitarian, with a deal of zeal, but is mild in his manners, a tenacious disputant, but courteous, — a very promising young man.*

July 12th. — (At Bury.) I had an agreeable walk with Mrs. Kent over the skirts of Hardwick Heath, — rather, enclosure, — and home by the West Gate Street. Mrs. Kent was gradually brought to recollect scenes familiar to her in childhood, but I could recall few. How little do I recollect of my past life! and the idea often recurs to me that it seems difficult to reconcile responsibility with utter oblivion. Coleridge has the striking thought that possibly the punishment of a future life may consist in bringing back the consciousness of the past.

July 21st. — Mrs. Kent had left us in the morning. I therefore thought it right to dine with the magistrates; and I am glad I did so, as I had a pleasing day. We discussed the question, how far a barrister may lawfully try to persuade the Bench to a decision which he himself knows to be wrong. I endeavored to establish this distinction, that an advocate may practise sophistry, though he may not misstate a case or a fact.

July 25th. — I breakfasted with Basil Montagu, and had an hour's pleasant chat with him. He related that Dr. Scott informed him that he waited on Oliver Goldsmith, with another gentleman, to make a proposal, on the part of Lord North, that Goldsmith should write on behalf of the Ministry. They found him in chambers in the Temple. He was offered any compensation he might desire. He said he could earn from the booksellers as much as his necessities required, and he would rather live without being obliged to any one. Scott told this story as a proof of Goldsmith's ignorance of the world.

August 7th. — This was a morning of disappointment. I

---

* He is now the most learned of the English Unitarians, and has taken the lead in the free investigation of the Old Testament, presuming to apply to it, notwithstanding its sacred character, the rules of profane criticism. He has lately retired from presiding over the Manchester College. — H. C. R., 1851. H. C. R. had especially in view Mr. Kenrick's work on Primeval History.

had intended to do my best in defending some Lavenham riot-ers for bull-baiting, but Burr cut the matter short by asserting that, though bull-baiting is a lawful sport, in an enclosure of private property, it could not be tolerated in the market-place of a town, over which there is a right of way. I endeavored to contend that, if the bull-baiting had lasted from time im-memorial, that fact must modify the right of way. I consent-ed that a verdict of Guilty should be entered, on an engage-ment that no one should be brought up for judgment, even if the riot should be renewed next 5th November.

August 10th. — On the evening of my arrival at Norwich I was even alarmed at the quantity of business there. It ex-ceeded, in fact, anything I ever had before. I had during these assizes seventeen briefs, of which *thirteen* were in *causes.**
The produce, seventy-five guineas, including retainers, exclu-sive of the fee of an arbitration. This raises my fees on the circuit to *one hundred and thirty-four* guineas, a sum exceeding by twenty-nine guineas the utmost I ever before received. Of these causes I shall mention three or four afterwards. I had one consultation this evening at Sergeant Blossett's, and I was engaged the rest of the time till late reading briefs.

August 29th, Rem.† — This day commenced a valuable ac-quaintance with Mr. Benecke, of whom I think very highly, as among the most remarkable Germans I have ever known. I had received a letter from Poel of Altona, introducing to me a Miss Reinhardt, who wished to establish herself in England as a teacher of music. She was on a visit at the Beneckes'. I called on her, and was invited to dine with them soon after, and my acquaintance ripened into intimacy. Benecke was a man of great ability in various departments; he was a chem-ist, and in that science he had a manufactory, by which he lived. He had been engaged as the conductor of an insurance office at Hamburg, and wrote an elaborate work on the law of insurance in German, which in Germany is the great au-thority on the subject. This induced him, after our acquaint-ance, to write a small volume on the law of insurance in English, which I saw through the press. There was absolute-ly nothing to correct in the language. The book did not sell, but Lord Tenterden spoke well of it as a work of principle, and allowed it to be dedicated to him. But these were merely works and pursuits of necessity. He was a philosopher, and of the most religious character : he professed orthodoxy, but

* That is, not criminal cases.   † Written in 1851.

he would not have been tolerated by our high-and-dry orthodox. He had a scheme of his own, of which the foundation
was — the belief in the pre-existence of every human being.
His speculation was, that every one had taken part in the
great rebellion in a former state, and that we were all ultimately to be restored to the Divine favor. This doctrine of
final restoration was the redeeming article of his creed. He
professed to believe in the divinity of Christ, and when I put
the question to him, he said, that he considered that doctrine
as the most essential truth of religion ; that God alone without Christ would be nothing to us ; Christ is the *copula* by
means of whom man is brought to God. Otherwise, the idea
of God would be what the Epicureans deem it, — a mere idle
and empty notion. I believe Benecke was first led to think
well of me by hearing me observe, what I said without any
notion of his opinions, that an immortality *à parte post* supposed a like immortality *à parte ante;* and that I could not
conceive of the creation in time of an imperishable immortal
being.

September 13th. — I rode to London. During the ride I
was strikingly reminded of the great improvement of the
country within thirty or forty years. An old man, on the box,
pointed out to me a spot near a bridge on the road, where
about forty years ago the stage was turned over and seven
people drowned ; and he assured me that, when he was a boy,
the road beyond Hounslow was literally lined with gibbets, on
which were, in irons, the carcasses of malefactors blackening in
the sun. I found London all full of people, collected to receive Hunt * in triumph, and accompany him to the Crown
and Anchor to a dinner, — a mere rabble, certainly, but it is a
great and alarming evil that the rabble should be the leaders
in anything. I hear that when, in the evening, Hunt came,
the crowds were immense, and flags were waved over him with
" *Liberty or Death* " inscribed.

September 22d. — I called on Talfourd for a short time. I
dined with Collier and then hastened to Flaxman's. I had a
very pleasant chat with him and Miss Denman.† He related
an interesting anecdote of Canova. He had breakfasted with
Canova at, I believe, Mr. Hope's, and then examined with him
the marbles and antiques. Among them was a beautiful bust

* " Orator " Hunt, the Radical, afterwards M. P. for Preston.
† Miss Denman was Mrs. Flaxman's sister, and Flaxman's adopted daughter,
by whom the Flaxman Gallery at University College was founded.

of Antoninus Pius. Flaxman pointed it out to Canova, on which Canova, without answering him, muttered to himself, with gestulations of impatience : " I told him so, — I told him so, — but he would never take counsel." This was repeated several times in a fit of absence. At length Flaxman tapped him on the shoulder and said : " Whom did you tell so ? " Of course, the conversation was in Italian. Receiving no reply, Flaxman pressed the question. " Why, Buonaparte," said he. " I observed to him repeatedly, that the busts of Antoninus Pius were to be seen everywhere ; they were to be found in every part of Italy in great abundance, he had made himself so beloved. But he would take no advice."—"And did you expect him to take any ? " said Flaxman. Canova could not say that he did, but stated that the courtiers of Buonaparte were often astonished at the freedoms he took.

Rem.* — Flaxman always spoke of Canova as a man of great moral qualities, of which I believe he thought more highly than of his character as an artist.

October 2d. — Colonel D'Arcy was at Masquérier's this evening, — a very agreeable man, who has been some years in Persia. He explained to us the meaning of the signets so often mentioned in the Bible and Oriental writings. In Persia every man has three seals : a large one, with which he testifies his messages to an inferior ; a small one, sent to a superior ; and a middle-sized, for an equal. Every man has about him an Indian-ink preparation, and, instead of signing his name, he sends an impression of his seal, as a proof that the messenger comes from him. Colonel D'Arcy speaks Persian fluently. He says it is a simple and easy language, as spoken, but the written language is blended with the Arabic, and is make complex and difficult.

October 12th. — I took an early breakfast, and a little after nine was in the King's Bench, Guildhall. There was a vast crowd already assembled to hear the trial of Carlile for blasphemy, which had attracted my curiosity also. The prosecution was for republishing Paine's " Age of Reason." The Attorney-General opened the case in an ordinary way. His pathos did not seem to flow from him, and his remarks were neither striking nor original. Carlile is a pale-faced, flat-nosed man, not unlike Schelling, but having no intellectual resemblance ; though he has shown astonishing powers of voice, and a faculty of enduring fatigue that is far more wonderful than

* Written in 1851.

enviable. He does not appear in any respect a man of mind or originality. His exordium was an hour long, and was a mere rhapsodical defence. His chief argument was derived from the late Trinity Bill,* which, said he, authorizes any one to attack the Trinity ; and there being no statute law to declare what may *not* be attacked, anything may. He attacked the Attorney-General † as an ex-Unitarian, and was both pert and insolent in the matter, though not in the manner. He then set about reading the "Age of Reason" through, and therefore I left him.

October 13th. — I lounged for half an hour into Guildhall. I found Carlile on his legs; he had been speaking without interruption from half past nine, and I heard him at half past six, with no apparent diminution of force ; but he merely read from paper, and what he said seemed very little to the purpose. He attempted a parallel between his case and Luther's, and asserted the right to preach Deism. I see no reason why he should not go on for a month in the same style.

October 14th. — I would have walked with H—— to hear some part of Carlile's trial, but it was just over. The man had been speaking for near three days, and this will be regarded by many people, I have no doubt, as a proof of great talent. He was, however, convicted, to my great satisfaction.

October 24th. — (At Bury.) I heard Mr. Fenner preach in the forenoon to about twenty persons. How our sensations influence our thoughts? The meeting-house striking my eye, and the voice of my old preceptor striking my ear, I was made serious, and almost melancholy.

November 10th. — I went early to Sergeant Frere's chambers, 3 King's Bench Walk, and agreed for a fourteen years' lease of them from next midsummer, at seventy-five guineas per annum. These chambers consist of one tolerably sized room; a second, which by pulling down a partition may be made into a very comfortable room ; and a third small room, which may be used by a clerk ; three fireplaces. Between the two larger rooms is a small room, large enough to place a bed in, and convenient for that purpose ; there is also a dark place, in which a bed has been placed for Frere's clerk and his wife, besides one or two lock-up places. The chambers, without being excellent, are yet good for their price, and I am pleased at the

---

* "An Act to relieve Persons who impugn the Doctrine of the Holy Trinity from certain Penalties." This was commonly called Mr. William Smith's Act.
† Gifford. See *ante*, p. 358.

idea of occupying them.   They are quite light, and look into a garden, and the staircase is handsome, compared with my present one.

December 7th. — I dined at the Colliers', and then took tea with Flaxman *tête-à-tête.*   He makes religion most amiable and respectable at the same time.   A childlike faith is delightful in a man of distinguished genius.   He spoke of his fortune, and without ostentation he said he had by God's providence prospered ; but he must add (what he would say to few but me), that no man who had worked for him had been in want, when sick or dying.

Rem.* — When Flaxman died, his effects were sworn to be worth under £ 4,000 ; and I have been in the habit of citing his comparative poverty as a disgrace to the country ; for while he died worth £ 4,000, Chantrey died worth above £ 150,000.   Such is the different reward for genius and useful talent !

December 9th. — The bills now passing through Parliament will be, I fear, sad monuments of the intemperance of the government and people.   Reformers and Ministry alike exaggerate the alarm justly to be feared from the excesses of their adversary, and in so doing furnish a reasonable ground for a moderated apprehension.   There are a few seditious spirits in the country who would raise a rebellion if they could, but they cannot ; and there are some among the Ministry, perhaps, who would not scruple to give the Crown powers fatal to the liberties of the people.   But neither the courts of law nor the people (who as jurymen concur in the administration of the law) would assist in a project destructive of liberty ; nor would the Ministry themselves dare make a violent attempt.   At the same time, the " Six Acts " are objectionable.†

---

* Written in 1851.

† " Papers were laid before Parliament containing evidence of the state of the country, which were immediately followed by the introduction of further measures of repression, — then designated, and since familiarly known as, the ' Six Acts.'   The first deprived defendants, in cases of misdemeanor, of the right of traversing: to which Lord Holland induced the Chancellor to add a clause, obliging the Attorney-General to bring defendants to trial within twelve months. By a second it was proposed to enable the court, on the conviction of a publisher of a seditious libel, to order the seizure of all copies of the libel in his possession; and to punish him, on a second conviction, with fine, imprisonment, banishment, or transportation.   By a third, the newspaper stamp duty was imposed upon pamphlets and other papers containing news, or observations on public affairs; and recognizances were required from the publishers of newspapers and pamphlets for the payment of any penalty.   By a fourth, no meeting of more than fifty persons was permitted to be held without six days' notice being given by seven householders to a resident justice of the peace;

December 15th. — I spent this forenoon, like too many of the preceding, loungingly. I called on Walter after being at the Book Auction. He informed me of what I never knew before, that the *Times* was prosecuted once for a libel of my writing; but the prosecution was dropped. He did not inform me of the circumstance at the time, thinking, probably, the intelligence would pain mè. I do not know whether I am to consider this an honor or not, as I am ignorant whether the libel was an observation on, or the misstatement of, a fact.

December 18th. — I dined at Collier's, and then went to Covent Garden. I had rather more pleasure than usual. The " Comedy of Errors " is better to see than read : besides, a number of good songs by Miss Stephens * and others are introduced. The two Dromios, Liston and Farren, though not sufficiently alike (nor did they strive to be so, for neither would adopt the other's peculiarities), afforded amusement, and the incidents, barring the improbability, pass off pleasantly enough. Some fine scenery is introduced, though out of character and costume. The scene is in Ephesus, and yet one of the paintings is the Piazza of Venice, &c.

December 25th. — Christmas day. I spent this festival not in feasting, but very agreeably, for, like a child, I was delighted in contemplating my new toy. I was the whole forenoon occupied, after writing some of the preceding Mems., in collecting books, &c., in my old, and in arranging them in my new, chambers. The putting in order is a delightful occupation, and is at least analogous to a virtue. Virtue is the love of moral order; and taste, and cleanliness, and method are all connected with the satisfaction we have in seeing and putting things where they ought to be.

---

and all but freeholders or inhabitants of the county, parish, or township were prohibited from attending, under penalty of fine and imprisonment. The justice could change the proposed time and place of meeting: but no meeting was permitted to adjourn itself. Every meeting tending to incite the people to hatred and contempt of the King's person or the government and constitution of the realm was declared an unlawful assembly; and extraordinary powers were given to justices for the dispersion of such meetings and the capture of persons addressing them. If any person should be killed or injured in the dispersion of an unlawful meeting, the justice was indemnified. Attending a meeting with arms, or with flags, banners, or other ensigns or emblems, was an offence punishable with two years' imprisonment. Lecture and debating rooms were to be licensed, and open to inspection. By a fifth, the training of persons in the use of arms was prohibited; and by a sixth, the magistrates in the disturbed counties were empowered to search for and seize arms." — May's *Constitutional History*, Vol. II. pp. 199, 200.

* Afterwards Countess of Essex.

December 26th. — I read the trial of Sir Thomas More. It is quite astonishing that the understanding and the courage of men could be so debased as they appear to have been in the reign of Henry VIII. I doubt whether the legislation of any other country has an instance of an enormity so gross and absurd as that of rendering it a capital offence to refuse answering a question : yet for this offence the Lord Chancellor was put to death, — a man of incorruptible integrity, a martyr. Yet he was himself a persecutor, having superintended the infliction of torture.

I am at length settled in my new chambers, and though my books are not yet put in order, I have a comfortable fire, and a far more pleasing scene from my window and within my room than I had in my former apartments.

December 28th. — The satisfaction I have in changing my residence is accompanied by the serious reflection that I cannot reasonably expect so much enjoyment, and such uninterrupted ease, as I enjoyed in Essex Court. During my six years' residence there I have not once been kept awake at night by pain of mind or body, nor have I ever sat down to a meal without an appetite. My income is now much larger than it was when I entered those chambers, and my health is apparently as firm. I have lost no one source of felicity. I have made accessions to my stock of agreeable companions, if not friends. I have risen in respectability, by having succeeded to a certain extent in my profession, though perhaps not so greatly as some of my friends expected. But then I have grown six years older, and human life is so short that this is a large portion. This reflection, I say, is a serious one, but it does not sadden me.

Rem.* — Let me add merely this, — that I believe I could have written the same in 1829.† We shall see, if I go so far in these Reminiscences. This year I took no journey.

---

* Written in 1851.
† The first year after H. C. R.'s retirement from the bar.

CHAPTER XXIII.

ON ELTON HAMOND [WITH NOTE].

1820.

JANUARY 1st. — No New Year ever opened to me with an
event so tragical as that which occurred this morning. Nor
indeed has my journal contained any incident so melancholy.

I had scarcely begun my breakfast, when two men, plain in
dress but respectable in appearance, called on me, and one of
them said, in a very solemn tone, " Pray, sir, do you know a
Mr. Elton Hamond ? " — " Yes, very well." — " Was he a particular friend of yours ? " My answer was, " He has destroyed
himself."

Rem.* — I have heretofore omitted to write of Hamond,
postponing till this awful catastrophe all I have to say of him.
He was born in 1786, and was the eldest of two sons of a tea-
dealer who lived in the city. He had also sisters. His father died
in 1807, leaving him sole executor ; and being the eldest, — at
least of the sons, — and a man of imposing and ingratiating
manners, he was looked up to by his family. I became acquainted with him through the Aikins, — I cannot say precisely *when,* but soon after my return from Germany. His
elder sister lived many years with Mrs. Barbauld. When I
first visited him he lived in Milk Street, where his father had
carried on the business. Some time afterwards Hamond told
me that in order to set an example to the world of how a business should be carried on, and that he might not be interfered with in his plans, he turned off the clerks and every
servant in the establishment, including the porter, and I rather think the cook. There could be but one result. The business soon had to be given up. His perfect integrity no one
doubted. Indeed, his character may be regarded as almost
faultless, with the exception of those extravagances which may
not unreasonably be set down to the account of insanity.
When he was satisfied that he was right, he had such an overweening sense of his own judgment, that he expected every
one to submit to his decision ; and when this did not take

* Written in 1851.

18 *   A A

place, he was apt to consider the disobedience as criminal. On this account he broke off acquaintance with his family and nearly all his friends.

I have only to relate some illustrations, which will be found curious, of this unhappy state of mind. When he was about eleven years old, he said to his sister, "Sister Harriet, who is the greatest man that ever lived?" She said, "Jesus Christ." He replied, "No bad answer, — but I shall be greater than Jesus Christ." His after-misery lay in this, that while he had a conviction that he was to have been, and ought to have been, the greatest of men, he was conscious that in fact he was not. And the reason assigned by him for putting an end to his life was, that he could not condescend to live without fulfilling his proper vocation.

His malady lay in a diseased endeavor to obey the injunction, "Nosce teipsum." He was forever writing about himself. Hundreds of quarto pages do I possess, all full of himself and of his judgment respecting his friends. And he felt it to be his duty to make his unfavorable opinion known to the friends themselves, in a way which, save for the knowledge of his infirmity, would have been very offensive.*

In the anxious pursuit of self-improvement, he sought the acquaintance of eminent men, among whom were Jeremy Bentham and his brother, General Bentham, James Mill, the historian of India, and Sir Stamford Raffles, governor of Java. On Sir Stamford he made a demand of the most ridiculous kind, maintaining that as Sir Stamford owed everything to his father, he, Sir Stamford was morally bound to give Hamond one half of what he acquired in his office as governor. Sir Stamford gave him an order on his banker for £1,000, which Hamond disdained to take. He went to Scotland and made the acquaintance of Dugald Stewart. The eminent philosopher and professor wisely advised him to think nothing

* As an instance of the sort of authority he assumed over his friends, I may mention that, when the reduction of the 5 per cent stock to 4½ was in contemplation, I had entertained an opinion in favor of the reduction, on which we had some discussion. In a few days he wrote me a letter, saying that he deemed my opinion so mischievous, that, if I gave any publicity to it, he should be obliged to renounce my further acquaintance. I replied that I honored the firmness with which on all occasions he did what he deemed right, regardless of all consequences to himself, but that he must allow me to follow his example, and act on *my own* sense of right, — not his; and that, in consequence, I had that morning sent a letter to the *Times* in support of my opinion. Whether the letter appeared I do not know; but, at all events, what I wrote to Hamond had its just weight. He took no offence at my resistance. Nor was he offended at the course I took on account of my suspicion of his intention to destroy himself.

about himself, which poor Elton most characteristically misinterpreted. He wrote in his diary : " I do think nothing of myself, — I know that I am nothing." That this was his sincere opinion is shown in a letter, in which, recommending his own papers to Southey's careful perusal, with a view to publication, he says : " You will see in them the writings of a man who was in fact nothing, but who was near becoming the greatest that ever lived." This was the mad thought that haunted him. After he left Milk Street, he took a house at Hampstead, where his younger sister lived with him.

At the time of my first acquaintance, or growing intimacy with Hamond, Frederick Pollock, now the Lord Chief Baron, was his friend. There was no jealousy in Hamond's nature, and he loved Pollock the more as he rose in reputation. He wrote in his journal : " How my heart burned when I read of the high degree taken by Pollock at Cambridge ! " [*]

In 1818 I visited him at Norwood, where I found him lodging in a cottage, and with no other occupation than the dangerous one of meditation on himself. He journalized his food, his sleep, his dreams. His society consisted of little children, whom he was fond of talking to. From a suspicion that had forced itself on my mind, I gave him notice that if he destroyed himself, I should consider myself released from my undertaking to act as his trustee. I think it probable that this caused him to live longer than he would otherwise have done. It also occasioned his application to Southey to take charge of his papers. One of Southey's letters to him was printed in the poet's life; unfortunately, I cannot find the other.[†] To Anthony Robinson, to whom I had introduced him, Hamond said that he was on the point of making a discovery, which would put an end to physical and moral evil in the world.

In justice to his memory, and that no one who reads this may misapprehend his character, I ought not to omit adding, that his overweening sense of his own powers had not the effect which might have been expected on his demeanor to the world at large. He was habitually humble and shy, towards inferiors especially. He quarrelled once with a friend (Pollock)[‡] for not

[*] He was Senior Wrangler.
[†] The other has been found among H. C. R.'s papers; and both are contained in the Note to this chapter.
[‡] The name has been given by Sir Frederick Pollock himself, who has kindly looked through this chapter in proof, and stated some details. The woman's burden was a large tray to be carried from Blackfriars' Bridge to the Obelisk.

being willing to join him in carrying a heavy box through the streets of London for a poor woman. His generous offer of an annuity to W. Taylor,* when he was reduced in circumstances, has been made known in the Life of Taylor. Reference has already been made (p. 354) to his refusal of a private secretaryship to a colonial chief justice, on the ground of the obligation involved to tell a lie and write a lie every day, subscribing himself the humble servant of people he did not serve, and towards whom he felt no humility. Various eligible offers were made to him, but rejected for reasons which made it too probable that he could be brought to consent to nothing. The impractical notions he had of veracity are shown in an inscription written by him for his father's tombstone. He objected to the date 18—, because, unless it was added, *of the Christian era*, no one could know in which era his father had lived. His grossest absurdities, however, had often a basis of truth, which it was not difficult to detect. I conclude, for the present, with a sentiment that leaves an impression of kindness mingled with pity : " Had I two thousand a year, I would give one half for birds and flowers."

On the 4th of January the coroner's inquest was held ; Pollock and I attended. We did not, however, offer ourselves as witnesses, not being so ready as others were to declare our conviction that Elton Hamond was insane. To those who *think*, this is always a difficult question, and that because the question of sane or insane must always be considered with a special reference to the relation in which the character, as well as the act, is viewed.

The neighbors very sincerely declared their belief in Hamond's insanity, and related anecdotes of absurdities that would not have weighed with wise men. We did not fear the result, and were surprised when the coroner came to us and said : " The jury say they have no doubt this poor gentleman was insane, but they have heard there was a letter addressed to them, and

---

" It was on a Sunday, I think, just after morning church. I offered to join in paying one or two porters to help the woman, but what he insisted on was that we should *ourselves* do it." Sir Frederick adds : " Hamond had in the highest degree *one* mark of insanity, viz. an utter disregard of the opinion of all the rest of the world on any point on which he had made up his own mind. He was once on the Grand Jury at the Old Bailey, and presented *as from himself alone* (all the rest of the jury dissenting) the manner in which the witnesses were sworn. I was present, and became from that moment satisfied that he was insane." " Hamond's case is worth recording; it was not a commonplace malady."

* Of Norwich. *Vide* " Memoir of William Taylor of Norwich," Vol. II. p. 357.

they insist on seeing it." On this I went into the room, and told the jury that I had removed the letter, in order that they should not see it. This at first seemed to offend them, but I further said that I had done this without having read the letter. It had been sealed and given to relations, who would certainly destroy it rather than allow it to be made public. I informed them of the fact that a sister of Mr. Hamond had died in an asylum, and mentioned that his insanity manifested itself in a morbid hostility towards some of his relations. I reminded them of the probability that any letter of the kind, if read in public, would be soon in the papers; and I put it to them, as a serious question, what their feelings would be if in a few days they heard of another act of suicide. The words were scarcely out of my mouth before there was a cry from several of the jury, "We do not wish to see it." And ultimately the verdict of insanity was recorded. The coroner supported me in my refusal to produce the letter.

Gooch directed a cast of Hamond's face to be taken. It was one of the handsomest faces I ever saw in a cast. Afterwards it was given to me, and I gave it to Hamond's sister, Harriet. The same man who took this mask, an Italian, Gravelli, took a mask of a living friend, who complained of it as unsatisfactory. It was, in truth, not prepossessing. The Italian pettishly said, "You should be dead! — you should be dead!"

Southey to H. C. R.

My dear Sir, — I shall not easily get your letter out of my thought. Some years ago I dined with E. H. at Gooch's, and perfectly remember his quiet melancholy and meditative manner. The two letters which he addressed to me respecting his papers were very ably written, and excited in me a strong interest. Of course, I had no suspicion who the writer could be; but if I had endeavored to trace him (which probably would have been done had I been in town), Gooch is the person whom I should have thought most likely to have helped me in the inquiry.

The school which you indicate is an unhappy one. I remember seeing a purblind man at Yarmouth two-and-twenty years ago, who seemed to carry with him a contagion of such opinions wherever he went. Perhaps you may have known him. The morbific matter was continually oozing out of him, and where it passes off in this way, or can be exploded in paradoxes and freaks of intellect, as by William Taylor, the destructive effect upon the heart is lessened or postponed. But when it meets with strong feeling, and an introspective introactive mind, the Aqua Toffana is not more deadly.

Respecting the papers, I can only say, at present, that I will do nothing with them that can be injurious either to the dead or the living. When I receive any application upon the subject, I shall desire them to be deposited at my brother's, to await my arrival in town, where I expect to be early in March, and to continue about two months, some ten days excepted ; and it is better that they should be in London, where I can consult with you. You will see by the letter to me (which I will take with me to town) what his wishes were. Consistently with these wishes, with his honor, and with the feelings of his friends,.I hope it may be possible to record this melancholy case for wholesome instruction. He says to me : " You may perhaps find an interest in making a fair statement of opinions which you condemn, when quite at liberty, as you would be in this case, to controvert them in the same page. I desire no gilt frame for my picture, and if by the side of it you like to draw another, and call mine a Satyr and your own Hyperion, you are welcome. A *true* light is all that I require, — a *strong* light all that I wish."

Having no suspicion of his intentions, I supposed him to be in the last stage of· some incurable disease, and addressed him as one upon the brink of the grave. If one of the pencil readings which you have transcribed were written since February last, it would show that my last letter had made some impression upon him, for I had assured him of my belief in ghosts, and rested upon it as one proof of a future state. There was not the slightest indication of insanity in his annunciation to me, and there was an expression of humility, under which I should never have suspected that so very different a feeling was concealed. God help us ! frail creatures that we are.

As my second letter was not noticed by him, I had supposed that it was received with displeasure, and perhaps with contempt. It rather surprises me, therefore, that he should have retained the intention of committing his papers to my disposal, little desirous as I was of the charge. Nevertheless, I will execute it faithfully ; and the best proof that I can give of a proper feeling upon the subject is to do nothing without consulting you.

Believe me, dear sir, yours with much esteem,
ROBERT SOUTHEY.

KESWICK, January 20.

Southey came to me in the March of this year, when he visited London. I soon satisfied him that the MSS. had no literary value, and he willingly resigned them to me.* In May of this year I wrote : " The more I read, the more I am convinced that they contain nothing which can benefit the world. They are not valuable either as works of art or as discoveries of truth.† They are merely manifestations of an individual mind, revealing its weaknesses." Yet I must qualify this by saying that Hamond wrote with feeling, and, being in earnest, there was an attractive grace in his style. But it raised an expectation which he could not fulfil. Southey appears to have formed a high opinion of him ; he was, however, not aware that, though Hamond could write a beautiful sentence, he was incapable of continuous thought. Some extracts from Hamond's letters and papers I mean to annex to these Reminiscences as *pièces justificatives.*

NOTE.

The papers now in the hands of the executors consist of, — (A), " Life. Personal Anecdotes. Indications of Character." (B), " Letters of Farewell." (C), " Miscellaneous Extracts." (D), " Extracts from Journal, &c." (E), " Extracts. Scheme of Reforming the World, &c." (F), " On Education, Character, &c." (G), " Ethics." Also various letters by E. H. and others. Those by himself include the long one, finished only a few minutes before his death. Among the letters from others to him are several by Jeremy Bentham on business matters (1809 – 1819) and a larger number by Maria Edgeworth, on matters of personal interest, (1808 – 1811). As Mr. Robinson did not make the extracts he proposed, the following are given as among the most interesting : —

When I was about eight or ten I promised marriage to a wrinkled cook we had, aged about sixty-five. I was convinced of the insignificance of beauty, but really felt some considerable ease at hearing of her death about four years after, when I began to repent of my vow.

I always said that I would do anything to make another happy, and told a boy I would give him a shilling if it would make him happy ; he said it would, so I gave it him. It is not to be wondered at that I had plenty of such applications, and soon emptied my purse. It is true I rather grudged the money, because the boys laughed rather more than I wished them. But it would have been inconsistent to have appeared dissatisfied. Some of them were generous enough to return the money, and I was prudent enough to take it, though I declared that if it would make them happy I should be sorry to have it back again.

---

* These MSS. are now in the hands of H. C. R.'s executors. An account of them, and some extracts, will be found in a Note to this chapter.

† The scheme for the reformation of the world seems to consist in a number of moral precepts, and has in it no originality.

· At the age of eighteen I used to amuse myself with thinking on how many followers I could muster on a state emergency. I reckoned Abbot, Charles, Edward Deacon, Charles Mills, H. Jeffreys, and the Millers. I was then profuse of my presents, and indifferent to my comforts. I was shabby in my appearance, loved to mix with the lowest mob, and was sometimes impatiently desirous of wealth and influence. I remembered that Cæsar walked carelessly and part drunken along the streets, and I felt myself a future Cæsar. The decencies of life I laughed at. I was proud to recollect that I had always expected to be great since I was twelve years old.

I cannot remain in society without injuring a man by the tricks of commerce, or the force which the laws of honor sometimes require. I must quit it. I would rather undergo twice the danger from beasts and ten times the danger from rocks. It is not pain, it is not death, that I dread, — it is the hatred of a man; there is something in it so shocking that I would rather submit to any injury than incur or increase the hatred of a man by revenging it;· and indeed I think this principle is pretty general, and that, as Mr. Reynolds says: " No, I don't want to fight, but it is to please Mr. Jenkins and Mr. Tomkins that I must fight."

To H. C. ROBINSON.

SILVER STREET, 20 October, 1813.

MY DEAR ROBINSON, — I leave you all my papers, with entire liberty to preserve, destroy, lend, or publish all or any of them as you please; you will, I know, take care that no one suffers unjustly or improperly by anything that I have written about him. There are passages in some of my early journals which might, I think, be injurious to my brother in a manner that he never at all merited. Any expressions injurious to —— I have no wish that you should conceal; in general, I may say that I should like everybody of whom I have expressed any opinion to be acquainted with it. The chief philosophical value of my papers (most of them utterly worthless in every other respect) I conceive to be that they record something of a mind that was very near taking a station far above all that have hitherto appeared in the world. Rely upon this, I am quite certain of it, that nothing but my sister Harriet's confidence and sympathy,* and such things as are easily procured, was wanting to enable me to fulfil my early and frequent vow to be the greatest man that had ever lived. I never till last May saw my course clearly, and then all that I wanted to qualify me for it I was refused. I leave my skull to any craniologist that you can prevail upon to keep it. Farewell! my dear friend; you have thought more justly of me than anybody has; maintain your sentiments; once more, farewell! I embrace you with all my heart.

E. HAMOND.

June 29th, 1817. — It is provoking that the secret of rendering man perfect in wisdom, power, virtue, and happiness should die with me. I never till this moment doubted that some other person would discover it, but I now recollect that, when I have relied on others, I have always been disappointed. Perhaps none may ever discover it, and the human race has lost its only chance of eternal happiness.

Another sufficient reason for suicide is, that I was this morning out of temper with Mrs. Douglas (for no fault of hers). I did not betray myself in the

---

* She would have been willing to devote her life to him, but he required that she should implicitly adopt his opinions. — H. C. R.

least, but I reflected that to be exposed to the possibility of such an event once a year was evil enough to render life intolerable. The disgrace of using an impatient word is to me overpowering.

A most sufficient reason for dying is, that if I had to write to Sir John Lubbock or Mr. Davey, I should be obliged to begin "Dear Sir," or else be very uncomfortable about the consequences. I am obliged to compromise with vice. At present (this is another matter), I must either become less sensible to the odiousness of vice, or be entirely unfit for all the active duties of life. Religion does but imperfectly help a man out of this dilemma.

SOUTHEY TO ELTON HAMOND.

KESWICK, 5 February, 1819.

SIR, — I lose no time in replying to your extraordinary letter. If, as you say, the language of your papers would require to be recast, it is altogether impossible for me to afford time for such an undertaking. But the style of your letter leads me to distrust your opinion upon this point; and if the papers are written with equal perspicuity, any change which they might undergo from another hand would be to their injury. It appears, therefore, to me that they would only require selection and arrangement.

Now, sir, it so happens that I have works in preparation of great magnitude, and (unless I deceive myself) of proportionate importance. And there must be many persons capable of preparing your manuscripts for the press, who have time to spare, and would be happy in obtaining such an employment. There may possibly also be another reason why another person may better be applied to on this occasion. The difference between your opinions and mine might be so great, that I could not with satisfaction or propriety become the means of introducing yours to the public. This would be the case if your reasonings tended to confound the distinctions between right and wrong, or to shake the foundations of religious belief. And yet I think that if there had been a great gulf between us you would hardly have thought of making me your editor. Indeed, if there had not been something in your letter which seems to make it probable that I should feel a lively interest in the transcript of your thoughts and feelings, my answer would have been brief and decisive.

I should like to see a specimen of the papers, such as might enable me to form a judgment of them; more than this I cannot say at present. I cannot but admire the temper of your letter. You are looking wisely and calmly toward the grave; allow me to add a fervent hope that you may also be looking with confidence and joy beyond it.

Believe me, sir,
Yours with respect,
ROBERT SOUTHEY.

SOUTHEY TO ELTON HAMOND.

KESWICK, 2 March, 1819.

Your letter, my dear sir, affects me greatly. It represents a state of mind into which I also should have fallen had it not been for that support which you are not disposed to think necessary for the soul of man. I, too, identified my own hopes with hopes for mankind, and at the price of any self-sacrifice would have promoted the good of my fellow-creatures. I, too, have been disappointed, in being undeceived; but having learnt to temper hope with patience, and when I lift up my spirit to its Creator and Redeemer, to say, not with the lips alone but with the heart, Thy will be done, I feel that whatever afflictions I have endured have been dispensed to me in mercy, and am deeply and devoutly thankful for what I am, and what I am to be when I shall burst my shell.

O sir ! religion is the one thing needful, — without it no one can be truly happy: (do you not *feel* this?) with it no one can be entirely miserable. Without it, this world would be a mystery too dreadful to be borne, our best affections and our noblest desires a mere juggle and a curse, and it were better, indeed, to be nothing than the things we are. I am no bigot. I believe that men will be judged by their actions and intentions, not their creeds. I am a Christian, and so will Turk, Jew, and Gentile be in heaven, if they have lived well according to the light which was vouchsafed them. I do not fear that there will be a great gulf between you and me in the world which we must both enter: but if I could persuade you to look on towards that world with the eyes of faith, a change would be operated in all your views and feelings, and hope and joy and love would be with you to your last breath, — universal love, — love for mankind, and for the Universal Father into whose hands you are about to render up your spirit.

That the natural world by its perfect order displays evident marks of design, I think you would readily admit: for it is so palpable, that it can only be disputed from perverseness or affectation. Is it not reasonable to suppose that the moral order of things should in like manner be coherent and harmonious? It is so, if there be a state of retribution after death. If that be granted, everything becomes intelligible, just, beautiful, and good. Would you not, from the sense of fitness and of justice, wish that it should be so? And is there not enough of wisdom and of power apparent in the creation to authorize us in inferring, that whatever upon the grand scale would be best, therefore must be? Pursue this feeling, and it will lead you to the Cross of Christ.

I never fear to avow my belief that warnings from the other world are sometimes communicated to us in this, and that absurd as the stories of apparitions generally are, they are not always false, but that the spirits of the dead have sometimes been permitted to appear. I believe this because I cannot refuse my assent to the evidence which exists of such things, and to the universal consent of all men who have not *learnt* to think otherwise. Perhaps you will not despise this as a mere superstition when I say that Kant, the profoundest thinker of modern ages, came by the severest reasoning to the same conclusion. But if these things are, there is a state after death; and if there be a state after death, it is reasonable to presume that such things should be.

You will receive this as it is meant. It is hastily and earnestly written, — in perfect sincerity, — in the fulness of my heart. Would to God that it might find the way to yours! In case of your recovery, it would reconcile you to life, and open to you sources of happiness to which you are a stranger.

But whether your lot be for life or death, — dear sir, —

God bless you!

ROBERT SOUTHEY.

TO JOSEPH ———.

NORWOOD, 31st December, 7 o'clock, 1819.

MY DEAR JOSEPH, — I fear that my late letters have offended and perplexed you; but I am convinced you will forgive all that you have thought amiss in them, and in the author of them, when you are told that he is — don't be shocked, my dear Joseph — *no more*. I am somewhat disturbed, while I think of the pain which this may give you, as I shed tears over my poverty when I saw Pollock cry about it, although it was not, neither is the present moment, painful to me. I have enjoyed my dinner, and been saying "good by" to my poor acquaintance as I met them, and running along by moonlight to put a letter in the post-office, and shall be comfortable — not to say merry — to the last, if I don't oppress myself with farewell letters, of which I have several still to write. I have much indeed to be grateful to you for, but I dare not give way to tender feelings.

Your letters, as you know, will be offered to Southey, with all my other papers, to do the best he can and chooses with. . . . .

Good by to you!

E. H.

To H. C. R , UNDER THE NAME OF ROVISO.

NORWOOD, 31 December, 1819 (8 o'clock in the evening).

DEAR ROVISO, — I am stupefied with writing, and yet I cannot go my long journey without taking leave of one from whom I have received so much kindness, and from whose society so much delight. My place is booked for a passage in Charon's boat to-night at twelve. Diana kindly consents to be of the party. This is handsome of her. She was not looked for on my part. Perhaps she is willing to acknowledge my obedience to her laws by a genteel compliment. Good. The gods, then, are grateful. Let me imitate their example, and thank you for the long, long list of kind actions that I know of, and many more which I don't know of, but believe without knowing.

Go on, — be as merry as you can. If you can be religious, good; but don't sink the man in the Christian. Bear in mind what you know to be the just rights of a fellow-creature, and don't play the courtier by sacrificing your fellow-subjects to the imaginary King of heaven and earth. I say imaginary, — because he is known only by the imagination. He may have a real existence. I would rather he had. I have very little hopes of my own future fate, but I have less fear. In truth, I give myself no concern about it, — why should I? why fumble all through the dictionary for a word that is not there?

But I have some more good-bys to say.

I have left a speech for the gentlemen of the inquest. Perhaps the driver of the coach may be able to tell you what is going on. On Monday my landlord, Mr. Williams, of the Secretary's Office, E. I. House, will probably be in town at a little after nine. Mind you don't get yourself into a scrape by making an over-zealous speech if you attend as my counsel. You may say throughout, "The culprit's defence is this." Bear in mind, that I had rather be thrown in a ditch than have a disingenuous defence made.

I take the liberty of troubling you with the enclosed. The request it contains is the last trouble I shall ask of you. Once more, good by!

Yours gratefully and affectionately,

ELTON HAMOND.

To THE CORONER AND THE GENTLEMEN WHO WILL SIT ON MY BODY.

NORWOOD, 31st December, 1819.

GENTLEMEN, — To the charge of self-murder I plead not guilty. For there is no guilt in what I have done. Self-murder is a contradiction in terms. If the king who retires from his throne is guilty of high treason; if the man who takes money out of his own coffers and spends it is a thief; if he who burns his own hayrick is guilty of arson; or he who scourges himself of assault and battery, then he who throws up his own life may be guilty of murder, — if not, not.

If anything is a man's own, it is surely his life. Far, however, be it from me to say that a man may do as he pleases with his own. Of all that he has he is a steward. Kingdoms, money, harvests, are held in trust, and so, but I think less strictly, is life itself. Life is rather the stewardship than the talent. The king who resigns his crown to one less fit to rule is guilty, though not of high treason; the spendthrift is guilty, though not of theft; the wanton burner of his hayrick is guilty, though not of arson; the suicide who could have performed the duties of his station is perhaps guilty, though not of murder, not of felony. They are all guilty of neglect of duty, and all, except the suicide, of breach of trust. But I cannot perform the duties of my station. He who wastes his life in idleness is guilty of a breach of trust; he who puts an end to it resigns his trust, — a trust that was forced upon him, — a trust which I never accepted, and probably never would have accepted. Is this felony? I smile at the ridiculous supposition. How we came by the foolish law which considers suicide as felony I don't know; I find no warrant for it in Philosophy or Scripture. It is worthy of the times when heresy and apostacy were capital offences; when offences were tried by battle, ordeal, or expurgation;

when the fine for slaying a man was so many shillings, and that for slaying an ass a few more or less.

Every old institution will find its vindicators while it remains in practice. I am an enemy to all hasty reform, but so foolish a law as this should be put an end to. Does it become a jury to disregard it? For juries to disregard their oaths for the sake of justice is, as you probably know, a frequent practice. The law places them sometimes in the cruel predicament of having to choose between perjury and injustice: whether they do right to prefer perjury, as the less evil, I am not sure. I would rather be thrown naked into a hole in the road than that you should act against your consciences. But if you wish to acquit me, I cannot see that your calling my death accidental, or the effect of insanity, would be less criminal than a jury's finding a £ 10 Bank-of-England note worth thirty-nine shillings, or premeditated slaying in a duel simple manslaughter, both of which have been done. But should you think this too bold a course, is it less bold to find me guilty of being *felo de se* when I am not guilty at all, as there is no guilt in what I have done? I disdain to take advantage of my situation as culprit to mislead your understandings, but if you, in your consciences, think premeditated suicide no felony, will you, upon your oaths, convict me of felony? Let me suggest the following verdict, as combining liberal truth with justice: "Died by his own hand, but not feloniously." If I have offended God, it is for God, not you, to inquire. Especial public duties I have none. If I have deserted any engagement in society, let the parties aggrieved consign my name to obloquy. I have for nearly seven years been disentangling myself from all my engagements, that I might at last be free to retire from life. I am free to-day, and avail myself of my liberty. I cannot be a good man, and prefer death to being a bad one, — as bad as I have been and as others are.

I take my leave of you and of my country condemning you all, yet with true honest love. What man, alive to virtue, can bear the ways of the best of you? Not I, you are wrong altogether. If a new and better light appears, seek it; in the mean time, look out for it. God bless you all!

ELTON HAMOND.

CHAPTER XXIV.

FEBRUARY 6th. — Mrs. Flaxman died. A woman of great merit, and an irreparable loss to her husband. He, a genius of the first rank, is a very child in the concerns of life. She was a woman of strong sense, and a woman of business too, — the very wife for an artist. Without her, he would not have been able to manage his household affairs early in life. *Now*, his sister and the youngest sister of his wife will do this for him.

February 19th. — Went to Drury Lane for the first time this season. I was better pleased than usual. Though Braham is growing old, he has lost none of his fascination in singing two or three magnificent songs in " The Siege of Belgrade." But he shared my admiration with a new actress, or rather singer, who will become, I have no doubt, a great favorite with the public, — a Madame Vestris. She is by birth English, and her articulation is not that of a foreigner; but her looks, walk, and gesticulations are so very French, that I almost thought myself in some Parisian theatre. She has great feeling and *naïveté* in her acting, and I am told is a capital singer. I know that she delighted me.

March 4th. — Took tea at Flaxman's. I had not seen him since his loss. There was an unusual tenderness in his manner. He insisted on making me a present of several books, Dante's Penitential Psalms and [a blank in the Diary], both in Italian, and Erasmus's Dialogues, as if he thought he might be suddenly taken away, and wished me to have some memorial of him. The visit, on the whole, was a comfortable one. I then sat an hour with Miss Vardill, who related an interesting anecdote of Madame de Staël. A country girl, the daughter of a clergyman, had accidentally met with an English translation of "Delphine" and "Corinne," which so powerfully affected her in her secluded life as quite to turn her brain. And hearing that Madame de Staël was in London, she wrote to her, offering to become her attendant or amanuensis. Madame de Staël's secretary, in a formal answer, declined the proposal. But her admirer was so intent on being in her service in some way, that she came up to London, and stayed a few days with a friend, who took her to the great novelist, and, speaking in French, gave a hint of the young girl's mind. Madame de Staël, with great promptitude and kindness, administered the only remedy that was likely to be effectual. The girl almost threw herself at her feet, and earnestly begged to be received by her. The Baroness very kindly, but decidedly, remonstrated with her on the folly of her desire. "You may think," she said, "it is an enviable lot to travel over Europe, and see all that is most beautiful and distinguished in the world; but the joys of home are more solid; domestic life affords more permanent happiness than any that fame can give. You have a father, — I have none. You have a home, — I was led to travel because I was driven from mine. Be content with your lot; if you knew mine, you would not desire it." With such admonitions she dismissed the petitioner. The cure was complete. The young woman returned to her father, became more steadily industrious, and without ever speaking of her adventure with Madame de Staël, silently profited by it. She is now living a life of great respectability, and her friends consider that her cure was wrought by the only hand by which it could have been effected.

March 7th. — Dined with the Judge (Graham). Among the most eminent judges of the last generation was Mr. Justice Buller. He and Baron Graham were of the same standing at College. Graham said to-day, that though Buller was a great lawyer, he was ignorant on every subject but law. He actually believed in the obsolete theory that our earth is the centre of the universe.

April 7th. — Arrived at Bury before tea. My brother and sister were going to hear an astronomical lecture. I stayed alone and read a chapter in Gibbon on the early history of the Germans. Having previously read the first two lectures of Schlegel, I had the pleasure of comparison, and I found much in Gibbon that I had thought original in Schlegel. Their views differ slightly ; for the most part in the higher character given by Schlegel to the Germans, the correctness of which I had doubted. It seems absurd to ascribe great effects to the enthusiastic love of nature by a people otherwise so low in civilization. But probably he is justified in the opinion that the Goths were to no great degree the bringers of barbarism. He considers them the great agents in the renovation of society.

April 26th. — An invitation from Aders to join him in one of the orchestra private boxes at Drury Lane. There was novelty in the situation. The ease and comfort of being able to stand, sit, or loll, have rather the effect of indisposing the mind to that close attention to the performance which is necessary to full enjoyment. Kean delighted me much in Lear, though the critics are not satisfied with him. His representation of imbecile age was admirable. In the famous imprecation scene he produced astonishing effect by his manner of bringing out the words with the effort of a man nearly exhausted and breathless, rather *spelling* his syllables than forming them into words. "How sharp-er-than-a-serp-ent's-tooth-it-is," &c., &c. His exhibition of madness was always exquisite. Kean's defects are lost in this character, and become almost virtues. He does not need vigor or grace as Lear, but passion, — and this never fails him. The play was tolerably cast. Mrs. W. West is an interesting Cordelia, though a moderate actress. And Rae is a respectable Edgar. I alone remained of the party to see "The King and the Miller (of Mansfield)." But I heard scarcely any part, for the health of the King being drunk, a fellow cried out from the shilling gallery, "The Queen!" The allusion was caught up, and not a word was heard afterwards. The cries for the health of the Queen were uttered from all quarters, and as this demand could not be complied with, not a syllable more of the farce was audible.

June 2d. — At nine I went to Lamb's, where I found Mr. and Mrs. Wordsworth. Lamb was in a good humor. He read some recent compositions, which Wordsworth cordially praised. Wordsworth seemed to enjoy Lamb's society. Not much was said about his own new volume of poems. He himself spoke of " The Brownie's Cell " * as his favorite. It appears that he had heard of a recluse living on the island when there himself, and afterwards of his being gone, no one knew whither, and that this is the fact on which the poem is founded.

June 11th. — Breakfasted with Monkhouse. Mr. and Mrs. Wordsworth there. He has resolved to make some concessions to public taste in " Peter Bell." Several offensive passages will be struck out, such as, " Is it a party in a parlor," &c., which I implored him to omit before the book first appeared. Also the over-coarse expressions, " But I will bang your bones," &c. I never before saw him so ready to yield to the opinion of others. He is improved not a little by this in my mind. We talked of Haydon. Wordsworth wants to have a large sum raised to enable Haydon to continue in his profession. He wants £ 2,000 for his great picture. The gross produce of the exhibition is £ 1,200.†

June 19th. — Went to the British Gallery, where a collection of English portraits was exhibited.‡ Very interesting, both as

---

* Vol. III. p. 44. Edition 1857.

† Haydon exhibited his great picture of " Christ's Entry into Jerusalem " at the Egyptian Hall, in Piccadilly. It was opened to the public March 27th. Wordsworth's face was introduced, " A Bowing Head "; also " Newton's Face of Belief," and " Voltaire's Sneer." The exhibition continued open till November, by which time £ 1,547 8 s. had been received in shillings at the doors, and £ 212 19 s. 6 d. paid for sixpenny catalogues. The picture is now in America. During the exhibition in London a gentleman asked if £ 1,000 would buy it, and was told, " No." — *Autobiography of Haydon*, Vol. I. p. 337.

‡ This very interesting exhibition, and the first of its kind, was opened in May of this year at the British Institution, Pall Mall. It comprised 183 portraits of the most eminent historical characters, almost entirely British, and the catalogue, with a well-considered preface, contained biographical accounts of the persons represented. In the year 1846 another portrait exhibition was held at the same institution, but not with commensurate success. The pictures then amounted to 215 in number, and the catalogue was destitute of biographical notices. A more extensive and extremely well-organized collection of national portraits formed part of the great Art-Treasures Exhibition at Manchester, in 1857. These, exclusive of many choice portraits in other departments of the Exhibition, amounted to 386. Many of these paintings were of considerable size. These portrait gatherings have, however, been far distanced by the successive exhibitions of national portraits, under government auspices, at South Kensington, which extended over the last three years, and

works of art and as memorials of eminent persons. Certainly such a gallery is calculated to raise a passion for biography, though some of the portraits rather tend to produce historical scepticism than to confirm the impressions which have been handed down to us. I was really displeased to see the name of the hated Jeffreys put to a dignified and sweet countenance, that might have conferred new grace on some delightful character. This, however, was the most offensive violation of probability.

June 21st. —After taking tea at home I called at Monkhouse's, and spent an agreeable evening. Wordsworth was very pleasant. Indeed he is uniformly so now. And there is absolutely no pretence for what was always an exaggerated charge against him, that he could talk only of his own poetry, and loves only his own works. He is more indulgent than he used to be of the works of others, even contemporaries and rivals, and is more open to arguments in favor of changes in his own poems. Lamb was in excellent spirits. Talfourd came in late, and we stayed till past twelve. Lamb was at last rather overcome, though it produced nothing but humorous expressions of his desire to go on the Continent. I should delight to accompany him.

June 24th. — Took Miss Wordsworth to the British Gallery. A second contemplation of these historic portraits certainly adds to their effect. To-day there was an incident which somewhat gratified me. The Duke of Wellington was there, and I saw him looking at the portrait of the Duke of Marlborough. A lady was by his side. She pointed to the picture, and he smiled. Whether the compliment was to his person or to his military glory I cannot tell. Though Marlborough has the reputation of having been as distinguished in the ball-room as in the field of battle, the portrait is neither beautiful nor interesting. The Duke of Wellington's face is not flexible or subtle, but it is martial, that is, sturdy and firm. I liked him in dishabille better than in his robes at the chapel of his palace in the Rue St. Honoré.

June 27th. —- Went to Lamb's, found the Wordsworths there, and having walked with them to Westminster Bridge, returned

combined in the aggregate no fewer than 2,846 pictures. The greater part of these portraits were of the highest authenticity, and the catalogues were remarkable both for the conciseness and comprehensiveness of the information which they afforded. Mr. Robinson's words in the text above have been signally verified. The portrait of Lord Chancellor Jeffreys was painted by Riley, and contributed by the Earl of Winchelsea. That of John, Duke of Marlborough, was by Kneller, and contributed by the Marquis of Stafford.

to Lamb's, and sat an hour with Macready, a very pleasing man, gentlemanly in his manners, and sensible and well informed.

July 8th. — I rode early (from Hadleigh) to Needham in a post-chaise, to be taken on by the Ipswich coach to Bury. I had an agreeable ride, and was amused by perusing Gray's letters on the Continent, published by Mason.* His familiar epistolary style is quite delightful, and his taste delicate without being fastidious. I should gladly follow him anywhere, for the sake of remarking the objects he was struck by, but I fear I shall not have it in my power this year.

July 18th. — (At Cambridge on circuit.) After a day's work at Huntingdon, I had just settled for the evening, when I was agreeably surprised by a call from Miss Lamb. I was heartily glad to see her, and, accompanying her to her brother's lodgings, I had a very pleasant rubber of whist with them and a Mrs. Smith. An acceptable relief from circuit society.

July 20th. — I had nothing to do to-day, and therefore had leisure to accompany Lamb and his sister on a walk behind the colleges. All Lamb's enjoyments are so pure and so hearty, that it is an enjoyment to see him enjoy. We walked about the exquisite chapel and the gardens of Trinity.

July 31st, August 1st. — It is now broad daylight, and I have not been to bed. I recollected Lord Bacon's recommendation of occasional deviation from regular habits, and though I feel myself very tired (after making preparations for my journey on the Continent), and even sleepy at half past four, yet I shall recover, I trust, in the course of the day.

SWISS TOUR WITH THE WORDSWORTHS.

Rem.† — This account of my first tour in Switzerland may not improperly be compared to the often-cited performance of "Hamlet," with the character of Hamlet left out. The fact being that every place in Switzerland is known to every one, or may be, from the innumerable books that have been published, the names are sufficient, and I shall therefore content myself with relating the few personal incidents of the journey, and a very few particulars about places. What I have to say will probably disappoint the reader, who may be aware that the journey was made in the company of no less a person than

---

* " Works, containing his Poems and Correspondence. To which are added, Memoirs of his Life and Writings, by W. Mason, M. A." London, 1807. A new edition in 1820.

† Written in 1851·

the poet Wordsworth. [If there are fewer of Wordsworth's observations than might be expected, the clew may perhaps be in the fact stated elsewhere, that " he was *a still man when he enjoyed himself.*" — ED.]

He came to London with Mrs. and Miss Wordsworth in the month of June, partly to be present at the marriage of Mrs. Wordsworth's kinsman, Mr. Monkhouse, with Miss Horrocks, of Preston, in Lancashire, and to accompany them in a marriage tour. I was very much gratified by a proposal to be their companion on as much of the journey as my circuit would permit. It was a part of their plan to go by way of the Rhine, and it was calculated (justly, as the event showed) that I might, by hastening through France, reach them in time to see with them a large portion of the beauties of Switzerland.

Mr. Wordsworth published on his return a small volume, entitled " Memorials of a Tour on the Continent," one of the least popular of his works. Had it appeared twenty years afterwards, when his fame was established, the reception would have been very different.

I left London on the 1st of August, and reached Lyons on the 9th. On the journey I had an agreeable companion in a young Quaker, Walduck, then in the employ of the great Quaker chemist, Bell, of Oxford Street. It was his first journey out of England. He had a pleasing physiognomy, and was stanch to his principles, but discriminating. Walking together in one of the principal streets of Lyons, we met the *Host*, with an accompanying crowd. "You must pull off your hat, Walduck." — "I will die first!" he exclaimed. As I saw some low fellows scowling, and did not wish to behold an act of martyrdom, *I* pulled off his hat. Afterwards, passing by the cathedral, I said to him : "I must leave you here, for I won't go in to be insulted." He followed me with his hat off. "I thought you would die first!" — "O no ; here I have no business or right to be. If the owners of this building choose to make a foolish rule that no one shall enter with his hat, they do what they have a legal right to do, and I must submit to their terms. Not so in the broad highway." The reasoning was not good, but one is not critical when the conclusion is the right one practically. Passing the night of the 10th on the road, we reached Geneva late on the 11th. On the 13th we went to Lausanne, where Walduck left me. On the 14th I went to Berne. I rose before five, and saw the greater part of the town before breakfast. It is one of the most singular places I ever saw. It stands on a sort of peninsular elevation formed by the River Aare, and consists of two or three long streets, with a few others intersecting them. The houses are of freestone, and are built in part on arches, under which there is a broad passage, with shops within. No place, therefore, can be cooler in summer or warmer in winter. In the middle of the streets there is a channel with a rapid stream of water.

About the town there are fountains in abundance, crowned with statues of armed men, Swiss heroes. And there are gross and whimsical representations of bears * on several of the public buildings. Two living bears are kept in a part of the fosse of the town. I walked to the Enge Terrace, from which the view of the Bernese Alps is particularly fine. The people are as picturesque as the place. The women wear black caps, fitting the head closely, with prodigious black gauze wings : Miss Wordsworth calls it the butterfly cap. In general, I experienced civility enough from the people I spoke to, but one woman, carrying a burden on her head, said sharply, on my asking the way, "Ich kann kein Welsch" (I can't speak any foreign language). And on my pressing the question, being curious to see more of her, and at last saying, "Sie ist dumm" (She is stupid), she screamed out, "Fort, fort" (Go along).

On the 15th I went to Solothurn, and an acquaintance began out of which a catastrophe sprang. In the stage between Berne and Solothurn, which takes a circuit through an unpicturesque, flat country, were two very interesting young men, who I soon learned were residing with a Protestant clergyman at Geneva, and completing their education. The elder was an American, aged twenty-one, named Goddard. He had a sickly air, but was intelligent, and not ill-read in English poetry. The other was a fine handsome lad, aged sixteen, of the name of Trotter, son of the then, or late, Secretary to the Admiralty. He was of Scotch descent. They were both genteel and well-behaved young men, with the grace communicated by living in good company. We became at once acquainted, — I being then, as now, *young* in the facility of forming acquaintance. We spent a very agreeable day and evening together, partly in a walk to a hermitage in the neighborhood, and took leave of each other at night, — I being bound for Lucerne, they for

* The arms of the town.

Zürich. But in the morning I saw, to my surprise, my young friends with their knapsacks in their hands ready to accompany me. Goddard said, with a very amiable modesty : "If you will permit us, we wish to go with you. I am an admirer of Wordsworth's poems, and I should be delighted merely to see him. Of course I expect no more." I was gratified by this proposal, and we had a second day of enjoyment, and this through a very beautiful country. My expectations were not disappointed. I had heard of the Wordsworth party from travellers with whom we met. I found my friends at the Cheval Blanc. From them I had a most cordial reception, and I was myself in high spirits. Mrs. Wordsworth wrote in her journal : " H. C. R. was drunk with pleasure, and made us drunk too." My companions also were kindly received.

I found that there was especial good luck attending my arrival. Wordsworth had met with an impudent fellow, a guide, who, because he would not submit to extortion, had gone off with the ladies' cloaks to Sarnen. Now it so happened that one of our fellow-travellers this day was the Statthalter of Sarnen. I spoke to him before we went to bed, and we arranged to go to Sarnen the next day. We rose at four o'clock, had a delightful walk to Winkel, embarked there on the lake, sailed to Alpnach, and then proceeded on foot. The judge was not betrayed into any impropriety. He had heard Mr. Wordsworth's story, and on going to the inn, he, without suffering Mr. Wordsworth to say a word, most judiciously interrogated the landlord, who was present when the bargain was made. He confirmed every part of Mr. Wordsworth's statement. On this, the Statthalter said : " I hear the man has not returned, a fact which shows that he is in the wrong. I know him to be a bad fellow. He will be home this evening, you may rely on it, and you shall have the cloaks to-morrow." Next day the man came, and was very humble.

Wordsworth and I returned to dinner, and found my young friends already in great favor with the ladies. After dinner we walked through the town, which has no other remarkable feature than the body of water flowing through it, and the several covered wooden bridges. In the angles of the roof of these bridges there are paintings on historical and allegorical subjects. One series from the Bible, another from the Swiss war against Austria, a third called the Dance of Death. The last is improperly called, for Death does not force his partner to an involuntary waltz, as in the famous designs which go by

Holbein's name, but appears in all the pictures an unwelcome visitor. There are feeling and truth in many of the conceptions, but the expression is too often ludicrous, and too often coarsely didactic.*

August 18th. — Proceeded on our journey. I purchased a knapsack, and sent my portmanteau to Geneva. All the party were, in like manner, put on short commons as to luggage, and our plan of travelling was this : in the plains and level valleys we had a char-à-banc, and we *walked* up and down the mountains. Once only we hired mules, and these the guides only used. Our luggage was so small, even for five (Mrs. Monkhouse and Miss Horrocks did not travel about with the rest of the party), that a single guide could carry the whole.

We sailed on the lake as far as Küsnacht, the two young men being still our companions ; and between two and three we began to ascend the Righi, an indispensable achievement in a Swiss tour. We engaged beds at the Staffel, and went on to see the sun set, but we were not fortunate in the weather. Once or twice there were gleams of light on some of the lakes, but there was little charm of coloring. After an early and comfortable supper we enjoyed the distant lightning ; but it soon became very severe, and some of the rooms of the hotel were flooded with rain. Our rest was disturbed by a noisy party, who, unable to obtain beds for themselves, resolved that no one else should enjoy his. The whole night was spent by them in an incessant din of laughing, singing, and shouting. We were called up between three and four A. M., but had a very imperfect view from this "dread summit of the Queen of Mountains," — Regina montium. The most beautiful part of the scene was that which arose from the clouds below us. They rose in succession, sometimes concealing the country, and then opening to our view dark lakes, and gleams of very brilliant green. They sometimes descended as if into an abyss beneath us. We saw a few of the snow-mountains illuminated by the first rays of the sun.

My journal simply says : "After breakfast our young gentlemen left us." I afterwards wrote : "We separated at a spot well suited to the parting of those who were to meet no more. Our party descended through the valley of our 'Lady of the

* The XXXVIII. Poem of the "Memorials" was written while the work was in the press, and at H. C. R.'s suggestion that Mr. Wordsworth should write on the bridges at Lucerne. This will appear in a letter by Miss Wordsworth in 1822.

Snow,' and our late companions went to Arth.   We hoped to meet in a few weeks at Geneva."

· I will leave the order of time, and relate now all that appertains to this sad history.   The young men gave us their address, and we promised to inform them when we should be at Geneva, on our return.   But on that return we found that poor Goddard had perished in the lake of Zürich, on the third day after our leave-taking on the Rigi.

I heard the story from Trotter on the 23d of September. They had put themselves in a crazy boat ; and, a storm arising, the boat overset.   It righted itself, but to no purpose.   Trotter swam to the shore, but Goddard was not seen again. Trotter was most hospitably received by a Mr. Keller, near whose house the catastrophe took place.   The body was cast ashore next day, and afterwards interred in the neighboring churchyard of Küsnacht.   An inscription was placed near the spot where the body was found, and a mural monument erected in the church.   At the funeral a pathetic address was delivered by the Protestant clergyman, which I read in the Zürich paper.   We were all deeply impressed by the event.   Wordsworth, I knew, was not fond of drawing the subjects of his poems from occurrences in themselves interesting, and therefore, though I urged him to write on this tragic incident, I little expected he would.   There is, however, a beautiful elegiac poem by him on the subject.*   [To the later editions there is prefixed a prose Introduction.   This I wrote.   Mr. Wordsworth wrote to me for information, and I drew up the account in the first person.]

> " And we were gay, our hearts at ease ;
>   With pleasure dancing through the frame
>   We journeyed ; all we knew of care, —
>   Our path that straggled here and there ;
>   Of trouble, — but the fluttering breeze ;
>   Of Winter, — but a name.
>   If foresight could have rent the veil
>   Of three short days, — but hush, — no more !
>   Calm is the grave, and calmer none
>   Than that to which thy cares are gone,
>   Thou victim of the stormy gale ;
>   Asleep on Zürich's shore.
>   O Goddard ! — what art thou ? — a name, —
>   A sunbeam followed by a shade."

In a subsequent visit to Switzerland I called at Mr. Keller's, and saw some of the ladies of the house, who gave me full particulars.   I afterwards became acquainted, in Italy, with

---

* Poems of the Imagination, Vol. III. p. 169, Poem XXXIII.

Goddard's nearest surviving relative, a sister, then married to
a Mr. ——. The winter preceding I was at Rome, when a
Mrs. Kirkland, the wife of an American gentleman, once Principal of Harvard College, asked me whether I had ever known
a Mr. Goddard, her countryman. On my answering in the
affirmative, she said : " I am sorry to hear it, for there has
been a lady here in search of you. However, she will be here
again on her return from Naples." And in a few months I
did see her. It was Goddard's sister. She informed me that
Wordsworth's poem had afforded her mother great comfort,
and that she had come to Europe mainly to collect all information still to be had about her poor brother ; that she had
seen the Kellers, with whom she was pleased, and that she
had taken notes of all the circumstances of her brother's fate ;
that she had seen Trotter, had been to Rydal Mount, and
learned from Wordsworth of my being in Italy. She was a
woman of taste, and of some literary pretensions.

On my return to England, I was very desirous to renew my
acquaintance with Trotter, but I inquired after him in vain.
After a time, when I had relaxed my inquiries, I heard of him
accidentally, — that he was a stock-broker, and had married a
Miss Otter, daughter of the Bishop of Chichester. I had
learned this just before one of the balloting evenings at the
Athenæum, — when, seeing Strutt there, and beginning my
inquiries about his brother-in-law, he stopped them by saying,
" You may ask himself, for there he is. He has been a member of the Athenæum these twelve years ! " He called to
Trotter, " Here is a gentleman who wants to speak with you."
— " Do you recollect me ? " — " No, I do not." — " Do you
recollect poor Goddard ? " — " You can be no one but Mr.
Robinson." We were glad to see each other, and our acquaint-
ance was renewed. The fine youth is now the intelligent man
of business. He has written a pamphlet on the American
State Stocks. Many years ago he came up from the country,
travelling fifty miles to have the pleasure of breakfasting with
Mr. and Mrs. Wordsworth at my apartments.

To go back to the 19th of August, after parting from our
young companions we proceeded down the valley in which is
the chapel dedicated to our Lady of the Snow, the subject of
Wordsworth's nineteenth poem. The preceding eighteen have
to do with objects which had been seen before I joined the
party. The elegiac stanzas are placed near the end of the
collection, I know not for what reason. The stanzas on the

chapel express poetically the thoughts which a prosaic mind like mine might·receive from the numerous votive offerings hung on the walls. There are pictures representing accidents, — such as drowning, falling from a horse, and the Mother and the Child are in the clouds, — it being understood that the escape proceeded from her aid. Some crutches with painted inscriptions bear witness to the miracles wrought on the lame.

> "To thee, in this aërial cleft,
> As to a common centre, tend
> All sufferers that no more rely
> On mortal succor, — all who sigh
> And pine, of human hope bereft,
> Nor wish for earthly friend.
>
> Thy very name, O Lady! flings
> O'er blooming fields and gushing springs
> A tender sense of shadowy fear,
> And chastening sympathies!"

We passed the same day through Goldau, a desolate spot, once a populous village, overwhelmed by the slip from the Rossberg.

On the 20th at Schwyz, which Wordsworth calls the "heart" of Switzerland, as Berne is the "head."[*] Passing through Brunnen, we reached Altorf on the 21st, the spot which suggested Wordsworth's twentieth effusion.[†] My prose remark on the people shows the sad difference between observation and fancy. I wrote: "These patriotic recollections are delightful when genuine, but the physiognomy of the people does not speak in favor of their ancestors. The natives of the district have a feeble and melancholy character. The women are afflicted by goître. The children beg, as in other Catholic cantons. The little children, with cross-bows in their hands, sing unintelligible songs. Probably Wilhelm Tell serves, like Henri Quatre, as a name to beg by." But what says the poet ? —

> "Thrice happy burghers, peasants, warriors old,
> Infants in arms, and ye, that as ye go
> Home-ward or school-ward, ape what ye behold;
> Heroes before your time, in frolic fancy bold!"

> "And when that calm Spectatress from on high
> Looks down, — the bright and solitary moon,
> Who never gazes but to beautify ;
> And snow-fed torrents, which the blaze of noon
> Roused into fury, murmur a soft tune

[*] Poem XXI. of the "Memorials."
[†] "Effusion in Presence of the Painted Tower of Tell at Altorf."

That fosters peace, and gentleness recalls;
Then might the passing monk receive a boon
Of saintly pleasure from these pictured walls,
While, on the warlike groups, the mellowing lustre falls."

We next crossed the St. Gotthard. Wordsworth thinks this pass more beautiful than the more celebrated [a blank here]. We slept successively at Amsteg on the 22d, Hospenthal on the 23d, and Airolo on the 24th. On the way we were over-taken by a pedestrian, a young Swiss, who had studied at Heidelberg, and was going to Rome. He had his flute, and played the Ranz des Vaches. Wordsworth begged me to ask him to do this, which I did on condition that he wrote a son-net on it. It is XXII. of the collection. The young man was intelligent, and expressed pleasure in our company. We were sorry when he took French leave. We were English, and I have no doubt he feared the expense of having such costly companions. He gave a sad account of the German Universi-ties, and said that Sand, the murderer of Kotzebue, had many apologists among the students.

We then proceeded on our half-walk and half-drive, and slept on the 25th at Bellinzona, the first decidedly Italian town. We walked to Locarno, where we resisted the first, and indeed al-most the only, attempt at extortion by an innkeeper on our journey. Our landlord demanded twenty-five francs for a luncheon, the worth of which could scarcely be three. I ten-dered a ducat (twelve francs), and we carried away our luggage. We had the good fortune to find quarters in a new house, the master of which had not been spoiled by receiving English guests.

On the 27th we had a row to Luino, on the Lago Maggiore, a walk to Ponte Tresa, and then a row to Lugano, where we went to an excellent hotel, kept by a man of the name of Rossi, a respectable man.

Our apartments consisted of one handsome and spacious room, in which were Mr. and Mrs. Wordsworth (this room fronted the beautiful lake); a small back room, occupied by Miss Wordsworth, with a window looking into a dirty yard, and having an internal communication with a two-bedded room, in which Monkhouse and I slept. I had a very free conversation with Rossi about the Queen, who had been some time in his house. It is worth relating here, and might have been worth making known in England, had the trial then going on had another issue. He told me, but not emphatically, that when the Queen came, she first slept in the large room, but not

19 *

liking that, she removed to the back room. "And Bergami," said Rossi, " had the room in which you and the other gentleman sleep." — " And was there," I asked, "the same communication then that there is now between the two rooms ? " — " Of course," he replied. " It was in the power, certainly, of the Queen and Bergami to open the door : whether it was opened or not, no one can say." He added, " I know nothing ; none of my servants know anything." The most favorable circumstance related by Rossi was, that Bergami's brother did not fear to strike off much from the bill. He added, too, that the Queen was surrounded by *cattiva gente*.

On the 28th we took an early walk up the mountain San Salvador, which produced No. XXIV. of Wordsworth's Memorial Poems.[*] Though the weather was by no means favorable, we enjoyed a much finer view than from the Rigi. The mountains in the neighborhood are beautiful, but the charm of the prospect lies in a glimpse of distant mountains. We saw a most elegant pyramid, literally in the sky, partly black, and partly shining like silver. It was the Simplon. Mont Blanc and Monte Rosa were seen in parts. Clouds concealed the bases, and too soon also the summits. This splendid vision lasted but a few minutes. The plains of Piedmont were hardly visible, owing to the black clouds which covered this part of the horizon. We could, however, see in the midst of a dark surface a narrow ribbon of white, which we were told was the Po. We were told the direction in which Milan lay, but could not see the cathedral.

The same day we went on to Menaggio, on the Lake Como. This, in Wordsworth's estimation, is the most beautiful of the lakes. On the 29th and 30th we slept at Cadenabbia, and "fed our eyes"

> " In paths sun-proof
> With purple of the trellis roof,
> That through the jealous leaves escapes
> From Cadenabbia's pendent grapes." [†]

The beds in which Monkhouse and I slept at Menaggio were intolerable, but we forgot the sufferings of the night in the enjoyment of the morning. I wrote in my journal : " This day has been spent on the lake, and so much exquisite pleasure I never had on water. The tour, or rather excursion, we have

---

[*] Wordsworth speaks of the " prospect " as " more diversified by magnificence, beauty, and sublimity than perhaps any other point in Europe, of so inconsiderable an elevation (2,000 feet), commands." — *Introduction to Poem XXIV.*

[†] *Vide* Poem XXV. of the " Memorials."

been making, surpasses in scenery all that I have ever made ;
and Wordsworth asserts the same.   I write now from an inn
where we have been served with all the promptitude of an
English hotel, and with a neatness equal to that of Holland.
But the pleasure can hardly be recorded.   It consists in the
contemplation of scenes absolutely indescribable by words, and
in sensations for which no words have been even invented.   We
were lucky in meeting two honest fellows of watermen, who have
been attentive and not extortionate.   I will not enumerate the
points of view and villas we visited.   We saw nothing the guide-
books do not speak of."

On the 31st we slept at Como, and next day went to Milan,
where we took up our abode at Reichardt's Swiss Hotel.   We
were, however, sent to an adjacent hotel to sleep, there being
no bed unoccupied at Reichardt's.   We arrived just before
dinner, and were placed at the upper end of a table reserved
for the English, of whom there were five or six present, besides
ourselves.   Here we made an acquaintance with a character of
whom I have something to say.

A knot of young persons were listening to the animated conversation of a handsome young man, who was rattling away on
the topics of the day with great vivacity.   Praising highly the
German poets Goethe, Schiller, &c., he said : " Compared with
these, we have not a poet worth naming."   I sat opposite him,
and said : " Die gegenwärtige Gesellschaft ausgenommen " (The
present company excepted).   Now, whether he heard or understood me I cannot possibly say.   If so, the rapidity with which
he recovered himself was admirable, for he instantly went on :
" When I say no one, I always except Wordsworth, who is
the greatest poet England has had for generations."   The effect
was ludicrous.   Mrs. Wordsworth gave me a nudge, and said :
" He knows that 's William."   And Wordsworth, being taken
by surprise, said : " That 's a most ridiculous remark for you to
make.   My name is Wordsworth."   On this the stranger threw
himself into an attitude of astonishment, — well acted at all
events, — and apologized for the liberty he had taken.   After
dinner he came to us, and said he had been some weeks at Milan, and should be proud to be our cicerone.   We thought the
offer too advantageous to be rejected, and he went round with
us to the sights of this famous city.   But though I was for a
short time taken in by him, I soon had my misgivings ; and
coming home the first evening, Wordsworth said : " This Mr.
—— is an amusing man, but there is something about him I

don't like." And I discovered him to be a mere pretender in German literature, — he knew merely the names of Goethe and Schiller. He made free with the names of our English literary notabilities, such as Shelley, Byron, Lamb, Leigh Hunt; but I remarked that of those I knew he took care to say no more. One day he went to Mrs. Wordsworth with a long face, and said he had lost his purse. But she was not caught. Some one else must have paid the piper. At Paris we met the same gentleman again, and he begged me to lend him £15, as he had been robbed of all his money. I was enabled to tell him that I had that very morning borrowed £10. He was, however, more successful in an application to Monkhouse, who said : " I would rather lose the money than ever see that fellow again." It is needless to say he " lost his money and his friend," but did not, in the words of the song, "place great store on both." As usually happens in such cases, we learnt almost immediately after the money had been advanced, that Mr. —— was a universal borrower. His history became known by degrees. He was an American by birth, and being forced to fly to England, he became secretary to a Scotchman, who left him money, that he might study the law. This money he spent or lost abroad, and it was at this stage that we fell in with him. He afterwards committed what was then a capital forgery, but made his escape. These circumstances being told in the presence of the manager of a New York ·theatre, he said : " Then I am at liberty to speak. I knew that fellow in America, and saw him with an iron collar on his neck, a convict for forgery. He had respectable friends, and obtained his pardon on condition that he should leave the country. Being one day in a box at Covent Garden, I saw him. Perceiving that I knew him, he came to me, and most pathetically implored me not to expose him. ' I am a reformed man,' said he ; ' I have friends, and have a prospect of redeeming myself. I am at your mercy.' His appearance was not inconsistent with this account. I therefore said : ' I hope you are speaking the truth. I cannot be acquainted with you, but unless I hear of misconduct on your part in this country, I will keep your secret.' "

Some time afterwards we heard that this reckless adventurer had died on a bed of honor, — that is, was killed in a duel.

I remained a week at Milan, where I fell in with Mrs. Aldebert, and renewed my acquaintance with her excellent brother, Mr. Mylius, who is highly honored in very old age. Milan furnished Wordsworth with matter for three poems, on Leonardo da Vinci's "Last Supper," "The Eclipse of the Sun" (which Monkhouse and I saw on our journey from Milan), and "The Column," a memorial of Buonaparte's defeated ambition.[*] I have very little to say, as I abstain from a description of the usual sights. I may, however, remark, that at the picture gallery at the Brera, three pictures made an impression on me, which was renewed on every subsequent visit, — Guercino's "Abraham and Hagar," Raphael's "Marriage of the Virgin," and Albani's "Oak-Tree and Cupids."

At the Ambrosian Library we inspected the famous copy of Virgil which belonged to Petrarch. It has in the poet's own handwriting a note, stating when and where he first saw Laura. Wordsworth was deeply interested in this entry, and would certainly have requested a copy, if he had not been satisfied that he should find it in print. The *custos* told us that when Buonaparte came here first, and the book was shown him, he seized it, exclaiming, "This is mine." He had it bound, and his own *N.* marked on it. It came back when the other plunder was restored. Another curiosity was a large book by Leonardo da Vinci, full of mechanical studies. Wordsworth was much struck with the fact that a man who had produced works of so great beauty and sublimity had prepared himself by intense and laborious study of scientific and mathematical details. It was not till late that he ventured on beauty as exhibited in the human form.

Other objects of interest at Milan, which I never forgot, were the antique columns before the Church of St. Laurent; the exhibition of a grand spectacle, the siege of Troy, in the Amphitheatre, capable of holding 30,000 persons, which enabled me to imagine what Roman shows probably were; and the exquisite scenery of the Scala Theatre.

But the great attraction of this neighborhood is the celebrated picture of Leonardo da Vinci in the refectory of the Convent of Maria della Grazia. After sustaining every injury from Italian monks, French soldiers, wet, and the appropriation of the building to secular purposes, this picture is now protected by the public sense of its excellence from further injury. And more remains of the original than from Goethe's dissertation I expected to see. The face of our Saviour appears to have suffered less than any other part. And the countenance has in it exquisite feeling; it is all sweetness and dignity. Wordsworth says : —

[*] Poems XXVI., XXVII., and XXIX. of the "Memorials."

> "Though searching damps, and many an envious flaw,
> Have marred this work; the calm ethereal grace,
> The love deep-seated in the Saviour's face,
> The mercy, goodness, have not failed to awe
> The elements; as they do melt and thaw
> The heart of the beholder." *

Some of the apostles have a somewhat caricature expression, which has been far better preserved in the several copies existing, as well as in the engraving of Raphael Morghen. There is a sort of mawkish sentimentality in the copies of St. John, which always offended me. There is less of it in the original. That and St. Andrew are the best preserved, next to the face of Christ.

On the 5th of September the Wordsworths went back to the Lake of Como, in order to gratify Miss Wordsworth, who wished to see every spot which her brother saw in his first journey, — a journey made when he was young.

On the 7th, Monkhouse and I went to Varese. As we approached the town we drew nigh the mountains. Varese is most delightfully situated. There is on a mountain, 2,000 feet high, a church with fifteen appendant chapels. To this we found peasants were flocking in great numbers, it being the eve of the birthday of the Virgin. We resolved to witness this scene of devotion, and our walk afforded me more delight than any single excursion I have yet made. For two miles the mountain is very steep. The fifteen chapels are towards the top, and beautiful, containing representations of the Passion of Christ in carved and painted wood. The figures are as large as life, and at least very expressive. Though so closely resembling wax figures, they excited no disgust. On the contrary, I was highly pleased with the talent of the artists. The dragging of the cross, and the crucifixion, are deeply affecting. The spectator looks through iron grates, the apertures of which are purposely small. My view was imperfect, on account of the number of pious worshippers. Towards the top the crowd was immense. We sometimes had to jump over the bodies of men and women. The church I could scarcely enter. Hundreds of women were lying about with their provisions in baskets. The hats of the peasantry were covered with holy gingerbread mingled with bits of glass. Bands of people came up chanting after a sort of leader. This scene of devotion would have compensated for the walk ; but we had, in addition, a very fine prospect. On one side the plains of Lombardy, studded with

* Poem XXVI. of the "Memorials."

churches and villages; on another, five or six pieces of water. In another direction we saw a mass of Alpine hills and valleys, glens, rocks, and precipices. A part of the Lake of Lugano was prominently visible. To enjoy this view I had to ascend an eminence beyond the church. Our walk home, Monkhouse thought, was hardly less than six miles. We found our inn rather uncomfortable from the number of guests, and from the singing in the streets.

We rejoined the Wordsworths at Baveno on the 8th. Then we crossed the Simplon, resting successively on the 9th at Domo d'Ossola, 10th Simplon, 11th Turtman, and the 12th and 13th at the baths of Leuk. From this place we walked up the Gemmi, by far the most wonderful of all the passes of Switzerland I had ever, or have now ever crossed. The most striking part is a mountain wall 1,600 feet in perpendicular height, and having up it a zigzag path broad enough to enable a horse to ascend. The road is hardly visible from below. A parapet in the more dangerous parts renders it safe. Here my journal mentions our seeing men employed in picking up bees in a torpid state from the cold. The bees had swarmed four days before. It does not mention what I well recollect, and Wordsworth has made the subject of a sonnet, the continued barking of a dog *irritated by the echo of his own voice.* In human life this is perpetually occurring. It is said that a dog has been known to contract an illness by the continued labor of barking at his own echo. In the present instance the barking lasted while we were on the spot.

> " A solitary wolf-dog, ranging on
> Through the bleak concave, wakes this wondrous chime
> Of aëry voices locked in unison, —
> Faint, — far off, — near, — deep, — solemn and sublime! —
> So from the body of one guilty deed
> A thousand ghostly fears and haunting thoughts proceed! " *

On the 14th we slept at Martigny, having passed through the most dismal of all the valleys in Switzerland, — the valley of the Rhône, and Sion,† the most ugly of all the towns. A barren country, and a town of large and frightful edifices. An episcopal town too. It looked poverty-struck.

I say nothing of Chamouni, where we slept two nights, the 15th and 16th ; nor of the roads to it, but that the Tête Noire, by which we returned, is still more interesting than the Col de Balme, by which we went. Again at Martigny on the 17th.

---

* No. XXXI. of the " Memorials," " Echo upon the Gemmi."
† The painters, however, think it full of picturesque subjects.

I should not have omitted to mention that, to add to the sadness produced by the Valais, Wordsworth remarked that there the Alps themselves were in a state of decay, — crumbling to pieces. His is the line : —

> " The human soul craves something that endures."

On the 18th we were at Villeneuve, and on the 19th and 20th at Lausanne. In the latter place I saw some relations of Mrs. H. Mylius, the Minnets, an agreeable family.

At Geneva I became acquainted with a Scotch M. D., a Dr. Chisholm, a very estimable man, with four very agreeable daughters. The mother an English lady in the best sense of the word. At Dr. Chisholm's house I met the celebrated historian Sismondi, who reminded me of Rogers, the poet. On the 23d I sought out Mr. Pictet, to make what could not but be a melancholy call. I met Trotter on the road. He was affected when he saw me. We walked together to the city, and he gave me those details which I have already written. We had all been sincerely afflicted at Goddard's death. He was an amiable and interesting young man ; and we could not help recollecting that it was his rencontre with me, and his desire to see Wordsworth, which occasioned his being at the Lake of Zürich when the storm took place.

In the afternoon I called on Mrs. Reeve.* She, too, had a sad tale to tell. She witnessed the departure of the party for Mont Blanc, among whom were the three guides who perished.†

September 24th. — In the morning much time lost in running about. After dinner we went to a delightful spot at Petit-Saconnex, where Geneva, the lake, Mont Blanc, were all seen illuminated by the setting sun. A very magnificent scene which we all enjoyed.

On the 25th we left Geneva. On our way to Paris we visited Montbar, the residence of Buffon, a man of sufficient fame to render one curious to see the seat of his long retirement and study. We did not see the dwelling-house within, it being out of order, and his library and its furniture are dispersed ; but we walked in the garden, and ascended a tower of considerable height as well as antiquity. This belonged to the royal family, and was purchased by the celebrated Buffon, who had changed the military castle into a modern chateau.

---

* The widow of Dr. Reeve, of Norwich, and mother of Mr. Henry Reeve, the translator of De Tocqueville.

† In Dr. Hamel's well-known attempt to ascend Mont Blanc.

The garden is of small extent, and consists of several broad terraces with very fine trees in them. The prospect is not particularly fine. The view embraces several valleys, but the surrounding hills are all of one height, and the valleys are cold and somewhat barren. Near the tower there is a small column, which the son of Buffon raised to his father's memory. The inscription was torn off during the Revolution. I thought more of the unfortunate son than of the father, for the son left this retreat (which his father preferred to the court), to perish on the scaffold at Paris. The heroism with which he died, saying only to the people, "Je m'appelle Buffon," bespeaks an intense sense of his father's worth, and interests me more than the talents which gave the father celebrity.

We passed through the forest of Fontainebleau. The part through which we rode is in no way remarkable, — a mere collection of trees with avenues. No variety of surface. We alighted at the Ville de Lyon, where we were in all respects well satisfied with our entertainment. The chateau is a vast hunting-palace, built by a succession of French kings from Saint Louis downwards. Francis I. and Henry IV. are spoken of as having built the more prominent parts. It has no pretension to architectural beauty whatever. The apartments are curious, — some from their antiquity, with painted roofs exhibiting the taste of ancient times, — others from their splendor, with the usual decorations of satin hangings, gilt thrones, china tables, &c., &c. In a little plain room there is exhibited a table, which must be an object of great curiosity to those who are fond of associating the recollection of celebrated events with sensible objects. I have this feeling but feebly. Nevertheless I saw with interest the table on which Buonaparte signed his abdication in the year 1814. We were also shown the apartments in which the Pope was kept a prisoner for twenty months, for refusing to yield to Napoleon; from which apartments, the *concierge* assured us, he never descended. After an excellent dinner, we were shown some pleasing English gardens, laid out by Josephine.

On nearing Paris I answered the solicitations of a beggar by the gift of a most wretched pair of pantaloons. He clutched them, and ran on begging, which showed a mastery of the craft. When he could get no more from the second carriage, he sent after me kisses of amusing vivacity. Our merriment was checked by the information of the postilion that this beggar was an *ancien curé*. We came to another sight not to be

c c

found in England, — a man and woman actually yoked together, and harrowing. The sight was doubly offensive on Sunday, the day of rest, when we witnessed it. We cannot expect to make political economists of the peasantry, but professed thinkers ought to know that were the seventh day opened universally to labor, this would but lessen the value of the poor man's capital, — his limbs.

At Fontainebleau we were awakened by the firing of cannon. The waiter burst into our room, — " Voilà un Prince ! " It was the birth of the now Duc de Bordeaux, — perhaps one day the King of France.

At Paris I renewed my old acquaintance, and saw the old sights. On the 8th I left the Wordsworths, who were intending to prolong their stay. On the 9th I slept at Amiens ; on the 10th was on the road ; on the 11th reached Dover ; and on the 12th of October slept in my own chambers.

" And so," my journal says, " I concluded my tour in excellent health and spirits, having travelled farther, and seen a greater number and a greater variety of sublime and beautiful objects, and in company better calculated to make me feel the worth of these objects, than any it has been my good fortune to enjoy." Of that journal I must now say that it is the most meagre and defective I ever wrote, — perhaps from want of time. The most interesting details, and not the least true, have been written from memory, the journal giving me only the outlines. The fidelity of what I have written from recollection might be doubted ; but that would be unjust.

October 29th. — I was employed looking over law papers all the forenoon ; I then walked in the rain to Clapton, reading by the way the *Indicator.** There is a spirit of enjoyment in this little work which gives a charm to it. Leigh Hunt seems the very opposite of Hazlitt. He loves everything, he catches the sunny side of everything, and, excepting that he has a few polemical antipathies, finds everything beautiful.

November 8th. — Spent the afternoon with H. Mylius, and dined there with a large party, — English and foreign. Mr. and Mrs. Blunt, friends of Monkhouse, were there, — she a sensible, lively woman, though she ventured to ridicule the

---

* A weekly publication edited by Leigh Hunt. It consists of a hundred numbers, and forms two vols. London, 1819 – 21.

great poet. I suspect she has quarrelled with Monkhouse about him ; for she says : " All Wordsworth's friends quarrel with those who do not like him." Is this so ? And what does it prove ?

November 9th. — In the afternoon called on Wordsworth. He arrived yesterday night in town after a perilous journey. He was detained nine days at Boulogne by bad weather, and on setting off from the port was wrecked. He gave himself up for lost, and had taken off his coat to make an attempt at swimming ; but the vessel struck *within* the bar, and the water retired so fast that, when the packet fell in pieces, the passengers were left on land. They were taken ashore in carts.

November 13th. — In the evening I set out on a walk which proved an unlucky one. As I passed in the narrow part of the Strand, near Thelwall's, I entered incautiously into a crowd. I soon found myself unable to proceed, and felt that I was pressed on all sides. I had buttoned my great-coat. On a sudden I felt a hand at my fob. I instantly pressed my hands down, recollecting I had Mrs. Wordsworth's watch in my pocket. I feared making any motion with my hands, and merely pressed my waistband. Before I could make any cry, I was thrown down (how, I cannot say). I rose instantly. A fellow called out, " Sir, you struck me ! " I answered, " I am sorry for it, — I 'm robbed, and that is worse." I was uncertain whether I had lost anything, but it at once occurred to me that this was a sort of protecting exclamation. I ran into the street, and then remarked, for the first time, that I had lost my best umbrella. I felt my watch, but my gold chain and seals were gone. The prime cost of what was taken was about eight guineas. On the whole, I escaped very well, considering all circumstances. Many persons have been robbed on this very spot, and several have been beaten and ill-treated in the heart of the City, — and in the daytime. Such is the state of our police ! My watch-chain was taken from me, not with the violence of robbery, or the secrecy of theft, but with a sort of ease and boldness that made me for a moment not know what the fellow meant. He seemed to be decently dressed, and had on a white waistcoat.

I called at Lamb's, where the Wordsworths were. I was in good spirits telling my tale. It is not my habit to fret about what happens to me through no fault of my own. I did not reproach myself on this occasion ; and as the loss was not a serious inconvenience, it did not give me a moment's uneasiness.

I then went to a large party at Masquerier's. There were whist-tables, dancing, beautiful drawings by Lewis, made on Masquerier's late journey, and some interesting people there. I saw, but had no conversation with, Lawrence, whose medical lectures have excited much obloquy on account of the Materialism obtruded in them.*

November 18th. — The afternoon was agreeable. I dined with the Wordsworths, and Lambs, and Mr. Kenyon, at Monkhouse's. It was an agreeable company and a good dinner, though I could not help sleeping. Wordsworth and Monkhouse either followed my example, or set me one, and Lamb talked as if he were asleep. Wordsworth was in excellent mood. His improved and improving mildness and tolerance must very much conciliate all who know him.

November 20th. — I was glad to accompany the Wordsworths to the British Museum. I had to wait for them in the ante-room, and we had at last but a hurried survey of the antiquities. I did not perceive that Wordsworth much enjoyed the Elgin Marbles; but he is a still man when he does enjoy himself, and by no means ready to talk of his pleasure, except to his sister. We could hardly see the statues. The Memnon,† however, seemed to interest him very much. Took tea with the Lambs. I accompanied Mrs. and Miss Wordsworth home, and afterwards sat late with Wordsworth at Lamb's.

November 21st. — I went late to Lamb's, and stayed an hour there very pleasantly. The Wordsworths were there, and Dr. Stoddart. The Doctor was very civil. Politics were hardly touched on, for Miss Kelly ‡ stepped in, thus drawing our at-

---

* Lectures on Physiology, Zoölogy, and the Natural History of Man. By William Lawrence. London: John Callord. 1819. The author recalled and suppressed this edition; but the work has since been repeatedly reprinted.

† This formed no part of the Elgin Collection. It is the colossal Egyptian head of Rameses II., supposed to be identical with the Sesostris of the Greeks, and was known when first brought to the British Museum as the Memnon. This head, one of the finest examples of Egyptian art in Europe, was removed by Belzoni in 1815, and presented to the Museum by Messrs. H. Salt and Burckhardt, in 1817.

‡ Miss Kelly, born at Brighton in 1790, attained great popularity as an actress in performing characters of a domestic kind. She was twice shot at on the stage. Charles Lamb, in 1818, addressed her in the lines beginning:—

" You are not Kelly of the common strain."

One of her best performances was in the melodrama of " The Maid and the Magpie," subsequently referred to. Miss Kelly built the small theatre in Dean Street, Soho, and latterly devoted her time to preparing pupils for the stage.

tention to a far more agreeable subject. She pleased me much. She is neither young nor handsome, but very agreeable; her voice and manner those of a person who knows her own worth, but is at the same time not desirous to assume upon it. She talks like a sensible woman. Barry Cornwall, too, came in. Talfourd also there.

November 29th. — Being engaged all day in court, I saw nothing of the show of the day, — the Queen's visit to St. Paul's. A great crowd were assembled, which the *Times* represents as an effusion of public feeling, echoed by the whole nation in favor of injured innocence. The same thing was represented by the Ministerial papers as a mere rabble. I think the government journals on this occasion are nearer the truth than their adversaries; for though the popular delusion has spread widely, embracing all the lowest classes, and a large proportion of the middling orders, yet the great majority of the educated, and nearly all the impartial, keep aloof.

*Rem.** — The disgraceful end of the disgraceful process against the Queen took place while the Wordsworths were in town. Whilst the trial was going on, and the issue still uncertain, I met Coleridge, who said, "Well, Robinson, you are a Queenite, I hope?" — "Indeed I am not." — "How is that possible?" — "I am only an anti-Kingite." — "That's just what I mean."

On the 3d of December I dined with the Beneckes, and made an acquaintance, which still continues, with Mr. and Mrs. Sieveking.† · He is a merchant of great respectability, and related to my Hamburg acquaintance. A man of sense, though not a writer; he is highly religious, a believer in mesmerism, and with an inclination to all mystical doctrines. His eldest son is now a young M. D.,‡ and a very amiable young man. He was educated partly at our University College, and I can cite him as a testimony in its favor. After spending several years at Paris, Berlin, and at Edinburgh, where he took his degree, he gave his decided opinion that the medical school of our University College was the best in Europe.

December 8th. — I read a little of Keats's poems to the Aders's, — the beginning of "Hyperion," — really a piece of great promise. There are a force, wildness, and originality in

---

* Written in 1851.
† Resident for many years at Stamford Hill. Mr. Sieveking died at his son's residence in Manchester Square, November 29, 1868, aged 79.
‡ Now Physician in Ordinary to the Prince of Wales. He attended H. C. R. in his last illness.

the works of this young poet which, if his perilous journey to Italy does not destroy him, promise to place him at the head of the next generation of poets. Lamb places him next to Wordsworth, — not meaning any comparison, for they are dissimilar.

December 14th. — On my return from court, where I had gained a cause for H. Stansfeld, I met Esther Nash and walked with her. After dining at Collier's, I accompanied her to Drury Lane. "The English Fleet," a very stupid opera, but Braham's singing was delightful. Madame Vestris, though rather too impudent, is a charming creature, and Munden, as the drunken sailor, was absolutely perfect. Afterwards a mélodrama ("The Maid and the Magpie"), in which the theft of a magpie gives occasion to a number of affecting scenes, was rendered painfully affecting by Miss Kelly's acting. The plan well laid and neatly executed.

December 15th. — I spent the forenoon at home reading law, and went late to the Aders's, where I read Keats's "Pot of Basil," a pathetic tale, delightfully told. I afterwards read the story in Boccaccio, — each in its way excellent. I am greatly mistaken if Keats do not very soon take a high place among our poets. Great feeling and a powerful imagination are shown in this little volume.

December 20th. — Another forenoon spent at home over law-books. The evening I spent at Aders's. The Flaxmans there. They seemed to enjoy the evening much. Aders produced his treasures of engraving as well as his paintings, and Flaxman could appreciate the old masters. He did not appear much to relish Thorwaldsen's designs, and some anecdotes he related made us suppose that he was indisposed to relish Thorwaldsen's works of art. Flaxman greatly admired the head of Mrs. Aders's father,* and declared it to be one of the best of Chantrey's works. We supped, and Flaxman was in his best humor. I was not aware how much he loved music. He was more than gratified, — he was deeply affected by Mrs. Aders's singing. It was apparent that he thought of his wife, but he was warm in his praises and admiration of Mrs. Aders's.

December 26th. — After dining at Collier's I went to Flaxman, — took tea and had several interesting hours' chat with him. I read some of Wordsworth's poems and Keats's "Eve of St. Agnes." I was, however, so drowsy that I read this

---

* John Raphael Smith, the eminent engraver, who died in London, 1811. He was appointed engraver to the Prince of Wales.

poem without comprehending it. It quite affects me to remark the early decay of my faculties. I am so lethargic that
I shall soon be unable to discharge the ordinary business of
life ; and as to all pretensions to literary taste, this I must lay
aside entirely. How wretched is that state, at least how low
is it, when a man is content to renounce all claim to respect,
and endeavors only to enjoy himself ! Yet I am reduced to
this. When my vivacity is checked by age, and I have lost
my companionable qualities, I shall then have nothing left but
a little good-nature to make me tolerable, even to my old acquaintances.*

   December 31st. — Bischoff told me that when, some years
back, T——, the common friend of himself and Monkhouse,
was in difficulties, Bischoff communicated the fact to Monkhouse, who seemed strongly affected. He said nothing to Mr.
Bischoff, but went instantly to T—— and offered him £10,000,
if that could save him from failure. It could not, and T——
rejected the offer.

   After dining with W. Collier alone, and sitting in chambers
over a book, I went to Edgar Taylor's,† having refused to dine
with him. He had a party, and I stayed there till the old year
had passed. There were Richard and Arthur Taylor, E. Taylor's partner, Roscoe,‡ and a younger Roscoe § (a handsome and
promising young man, who is with Pattison the pleader,|| and
is to be called to the bar), and Bowring the traveller. His
person is mild and amiable, and his tone of conversation agreeable. He is in correspondence with the Spanish patriots, and
is an enthusiast in their cause.

   So passed away the last hours of the year, — a year which
I have enjoyed as I have the former years of my life, but which
has given me a deeper conviction than I ever had of the insignificance of my own character.

   * Written between forty-six and forty-seven years before H. C. R. died.
   † Mr. Edgar Taylor was a very eminent solicitor, and an accomplished man.
He translated the French metrical chronicle, by Wace, entitled "Roman de
Rou." He also wrote a "History of the German Minnesingers," with translated specimens; and prepared a version of some of the admirable fairy stories
of the brothers Grimm: illustrated by George Cruikshank. And it is well
known that he was the "Layman" whose revised translation of the New Testament was published by Pickering in 1840, shortly after his death. This
work was almost entirely prepared by him during a long and painful illness.
   ‡ Robert Roscoe. Like almost all William Roscoe's sons, an author and
poet. He died in 1850.
   § Henry Roscoe, author of "The Lives of Eminent Lawyers," &c., &c. He
died in 1836.
   || Afterwards a Judge.

CHAPTER XXV.

1821.

JANUARY 1st. — I dined at Collier's, and then went to Covent Garden, where I saw "Virginius." Macready very much pleased me. The truth of his performance is admirable. His rich mellow tones are delightful, and did he combine the expressive face of Kean with his own voice, he would far surpass Kean, for in judgment I think him equal. The scene in which he betroths his daughter is delightfully tender, but the catastrophe is too long delayed and wants effect, and the last act is an excrescence.

January 21st. — I looked over papers, and at twelve o'clock walked out. I called on the Colliers, and then went to Mrs. Barbauld's. She was in good spirits, but she is now the confirmed old lady. Independently of her fine understanding and literary reputation, she would be interesting. Her white locks, fair and unwrinkled skin, brilliant starched linen, and rich silk gown, make her a fit object for a painter. Her conversation is lively, her remarks judicious, and always pertinent.

January 30th. — This day being a holiday, I went to Kemble's sale. I met Amyot there, and we had a pleasant lounge together. Mr. and Mrs. Masquerier and Lewis took tea with me, and stayed several hours looking over my prints, and I enjoyed their pleasure. Is it vanity, sympathy, or good-nature, or a compound of all these feelings, which makes the owner of works of art enjoy the exhibition? Besides this, he learns the just appreciation of works of art, which is a positive gain, if anything appertaining to taste may be called so.

February 10th. — The evening was devoted to Talfourd's call to the bar, which was made more amusing by the contemporaneous call of the Irish orator, Phillips.* Talfourd had a numerous dinner-party, at which I was the senior barrister. We were so much more numerous than the other parties, — there being three besides Phillips's, — that we took the head-table and the lead in the business of the evening. Soon after we were settled, with the dessert on the table, I gave Talfourd's

* Afterwards Commissioner of the Insolvent Court.

health. He, after returning thanks, gave as a toast the Irish Bar, and in allusion to Phillips's call, said that what had just taken place was a great gain to England, and a loss to Ireland. This compliment called up the orator, and he spoke in a subdued tone and with a slowness that surprised me. I left the Hall for an hour and a half to take tea with Manning. When I returned Phillips was again on his legs, and using a great deal of declamation. He spoke five times in the course of the evening. Monkhouse came to the Hall, and at about twelve we adjourned to Talfourd's chambers, where an elegant supper was set out. In bed at half past two.

March 10th. — I took tea at Flaxman's, and enjoyed the two hours I stayed there very much. Of all the religious men I ever saw, he is the most amiable. The utter absence of all polemical feeling, — the disclaiming of all speculative opinion as an essential to salvation, — the reference of faith to the affections, not the understanding, are points in which I most cordially concur with him ; earnestly wishing at the same time that I was in all respects like him.

WORDSWORTH TO H. C. R.

12th March, 1821.

MY DEAR FRIEND, — You were very good in writing me so long a letter, and kind, in your own Robinsonian way. Your determination to withdraw from your profession in sufficient time for an autumnal harvest of leisure is of a piece with the rest of your consistent resolves and practices. Consistent I have said, and why not *rational?* The word would surely have been added, had not I felt that it was awkwardly loading the sentence, and so truth would have been sacrificed to a point of taste, but for this compunction. Full surely you will do well ; but take time ; it would be ungrateful to quit in haste a profession that has used you so civilly. Would that I could encourage the hope of passing a winter with you in Rome, about the time you mention, which is just the period I should myself select ! . . . . As to poetry, I am sick of it ; it overruns the country in all the shapes of the Plagues of Egypt, — frog-poets (the Croakers), mice-poets (the Nibblers), a class which Gray, in his dignified way, calls flies, the "insect youth," — a term wonderfully applicable upon this occasion. But let us desist, or we shall be accused of envying the rising generation. Mary and I passed some days at Cambridge, where, what with the company of my dear brother,* — our stately apartments, with all the venerable portraits there, that awe one into humility, — old friends, new acquaintance, and a hundred familiar remembrances, and freshly conjured up recollections, I enjoyed myself not a little. I should like to lend you a sonnet, composed at Cambridge; but it is reserved for cogent reasons, to be imparted in due time. Farewell! happy shall we be to see you.

WM. WORDSWORTH.

April 16th. — (On a visit to the Pattissons at Witham.) I walked to Hatfield † with William. Looked into the church, — the Vicar, Bennet, was our cicerone. He spoke of Goldsmith as a man he had seen. Goldsmith had lodged at Springfield, with some farmers. He spent his forenoons in his room, writing, and breakfasted off water-gruel, without bread. In his manners he was a bear. — "A tame one," I observed, and it was assented to. He dressed shabbily, and was an odd man. No further particulars could I get, except that while Goldsmith was there, a gentleman took down some cottages, which Bennet supposes gave rise to the "Deserted Village." Bennet pointed out to us the antiquities of his church; among them a recumbent statue, which every one believed was a woman, till Flaxman came and satisfied him that it was a priest.

April 17th. — Hayter, a painter in crayons,‡ dined with us. He is taking a likeness of Mr. Pattisson, and is certainly successful as a portrait-painter. In other respects he is a *character.* He is self-educated, but is a sensible man, and blends humor with all he says. And his affection for his children, one of whom is already a promising young artist, gives a kind of dignity to his character.

June 12th. — I accompanied my brother and sister to Covent Garden. We had a crowding to get there. It was Liston's benefit. He played delightfully Sam Swipes in "Exchange no Robbery," his knavish father passing him off as the foster-son of a gentleman who had run away after intrusting

---

* Dr. Christopher Wordsworth, Master of Trinity College, Cambridge.

† Hatfield Peverel, two miles from Witham.

‡ Mr. Charles Hayter, author of "A Treatise on Perspective," published in 1825, and generally considered successful in taking likenesses. He was the father of the present Sir George Hayter and Mr. John Hayter, both distinguished portrait-painters, still living. Charles Hayter lodged at Witham many months during 1821. His price for such crayon drawings was ten guineas. The picture above referred to is still in possession of the family.

him with the child.   The supposed father was admirably represented by Farren.   And these two performers afforded me
more pleasure than the theatre often gives me.

July 7th. — I was busied about many things this forenoon.
I went for a short time to the King's Bench.   Then looked
over Hamond's papers, and went to Saunders's sale.   Dined
hastily in Coleman Street, and then went to Mrs. Barbauld's,
where I was soon joined by Charles and Mary Lamb.   This
was a meeting I had brought about to gratify mutual curiosity.   The Lambs are pleased with Mrs. Barbauld, and
therefore it is probable that they have pleased her.   Mrs. C.
Aikin was there, and Miss Lawrence.   Lamb was chatty, and
suited his conversation to his company, except that, speaking
of Gilbert Wakefield, he said he had a peevish face.   When he
was told Mrs. Aikin was Gilbert Wakefield's daughter, he was
vexed, but got out of the scrape tolerably well.   I walked with
the Lambs by the turnpike, and then came home, not to go to
bed, but to sit up till the Norwich coach should call for me.
I had several letters to write, which with packing, drinking ·
chocolate, &c. fully occupied my time, so that I had no ennui,
though I was unable to read.

*Rem.** — One evening, when I was at the Aikins', Charles
Lamb told a droll story of an India-house clerk accused of
eating man's flesh, and remarked that among cannibals those
who rejected the favorite dish would be called *misanthropists.*

July 23d. — Finished Johnson's "Hebrides."   I feel ashamed
of the delight it once afforded me.   The style is so pompous,
the thoughts so ordinary, with so little feeling, or imagination,
or knowledge.   Yet I once admired it.   What assurance have
I that I may not hereafter think as meanly of the books I now
admire ?

August 12th. — (Bury.)   I went with Pryme † to see the jail,
which, notwithstanding its celebrity, I had not visited.   There I
saw neither a filthy assemblage of wretches brought together to
be instructed for future crimes rather than punished for past,
nor a place of ease and comfort, inviting rather than deterring
to the criminal.   The garden, yards, and buildings have an air
of great neatness ; but this can hardly be a recommendation
to the prisoners.   They are separated by many subdivisions,
and constantly exposed to inspection.   In the day they work

---

* Written in 1849.
† A fellow-circuiteer of H. C. R.'s, long M. P. for Cambridge.   He died Dec.
19, 1868.

at a mill, and at night all are secluded.   Each has his little cell.   The all-important thing is to avoid letting criminals be together in idleness.   To a spectator there is nothing offensive in this prison.   And certainly if its arrangements were followed universally, much misery would be prevented and good service rendered to morality.

[In the autumn of this year Mr. Robinson made a tour to Scotland of a little over a month.   The chief personal recollections are all that will be given here. — ED.]

August 29th. — Visited Dryburgh Abbey.   A day of interest, apart from the beauties of my walk.   Mrs. Masquerier had given me a letter of introduction to the well-known Earl of Buchan, — a character.   He married her aunt, who was a Forbes.   Lord Buchan, who was advanced in years, had, by a life of sparing, restored in a great measure the family from its sunken state ; but, in doing this, he had to endure the reproach of penurious habits, while his two younger brothers acquired a brilliant reputation : one was Lord Erskine, the most perfect of *nisi prius* orators, and one of the poorest of English Chancellors, — the other, Henry Erskine, the elder brother, enjoyed a higher reputation among friends, but, in the inferior sphere of the Scotch courts, could not attain to an equally wide-spread celebrity.   Lord Buchan had been a *dilettante* in letters.   He had written a life of Thomson the poet, and of the patriotic orator, Fletcher of Saltoun, the great opponent of the Scottish union.

Before I was introduced to the Earl, I saw in the grounds ample monuments of his taste and character.   He received me cordially.   He being from home when I called, I left my letter, and walked in the grounds.   On my return, he himself opened the door for me, and said to the servant : " Show Mr. Robinson into his bedroom.   You will spend the day here."

He was manifestly proud of his alliance with the royal house of the Stuarts, but was not offended with the free manner in which I spoke of the contemptible pedant James I. of England.   He exhibited many relics of the unfortunate Mary ; and (says my journal) enumerated to me many of his ancestors, " whom my imperfect recollections would have designated rather as infamous than illustrious."   But no man of family ever heartily despised birth.   He was a stanch Whig, but had long retired from politics.   He was proud of his brother, the great English orator, but lamented his acceptance of the Chancellorship.   " I wrote him a letter," said the Earl, " offering, if he would decline the office, to settle my estate on his eldest son. Unluckily, he did not receive my letter until it was too late, or he might have accepted my offer ; his mind was so confused when he announced the fact of the appointment, that he signed his letter ' Buchan.' "

The next day I left Dryburgh, furnished with a useful letter to the Scotch antiquary and bookseller, David Laing, who rendered me obliging offices at Edinburgh. I had also a letter to the famous Sir James Sinclair, the agriculturist, which I was not anxious to deliver, as in it I was foolishly characterized as a "really learned person," this being provably false. "The praises," says my journal, "usually contained in letters of the kind one may swallow, because they never mean more than that the writer likes the object of them." Lord Buchan offered me a letter to Sir Walter Scott, which I declined. I found that he had no liking for Sir Walter, and I was therefore sure that Sir Walter had no liking for him ; and it is bad policy to deliver such letters. I regretted much that a letter from Wordsworth to Scott reached me too late ; *that* I should have rejoiced to deliver.

My first concern at Edinburgh was to see Anthony Robinson, Jun. He showed me such of the curiosities of the place as were known to him. In his sitting-room I complained of an offensive smell, which he explained by opening a closet door, and producing some human limbs. He had bought these of the resurrection-men. He afterwards disappeared ; and on his father's death, a commission was sent to Scotland to collect evidence respecting Anthony Robinson, Jun.; from which it was ascertained that he had not been heard of for years. He had left his clothes, &c. at Perth, and had gone to Edinburgh to continue his studies ; and it was at Edinburgh that he was last heard of. This being just before the dreadful exposure took place of the murders effected by *burking*, my speculation was that poor Anthony was one of the victims.

2d September (Sunday). — Mr. David Laing took me to hear Dr. Thomson, a very eminent Scotch preacher, who had at Edinburgh the like pre-eminence which Dr. Chalmers had at Glasgow. But he appeared to me to be a mere orator, profiting by a sonorous voice and a commanding countenance. This, however, may be an erroneous judgment.

This same day originated an acquaintance of which I will now relate the beginning and the end. Walking with Laing, he pointed out to me a young man. "That," said he, "is James

Grahame, nephew of the poet of 'The Sabbath.'" I begged Laing to introduce me. His father's acquaintance I had made at Mr. Clarkson's. This produced a very cordial reception, and after spending a day (the 3d) in a walk to Roslin and Hawthornden (of which, if I said anything on such subjects, I should have much to say), I went to an evening party at Mr. Grahame's. Laing was there, and my journal mentions a Sir W. Hamilton, the same man, I have no doubt, who has lately been involved in a controversy with our (University College) Professor De Morgan on logic. My journal speaks of him as, according to Laing, a young lawyer of brilliant talents, a profound thinker, and conversant with German philosophy and literature.

On the 9th of September an incident occurred especially amusing in connection with what took place immediately afterwards. I rose very early to see a new place, and (it was between six and seven) seeing a large building, I asked a man, who looked like a journeyman weaver, what it was. He told me a grammar-school. " But, sir," he added, " I think it would become you better on the Lord's day morning to be reading your Bible at home, than asking about public buildings." I very quickly answered : " My friend, you have given me a piece of very good advice ; let me give you one, and we may both profit by our meeting. Beware of spiritual pride." The man scowled with a Scotch surliness, and, apparently, did not take my counsel with as much good-humor as I did his.

It was after this that I heard Dr. Chalmers preach. In the forenoon it was a plain discourse to plain people, in a sort of school. In the afternoon it was a splendid discourse, in the Tron Church, against the Judaical observance of the Sabbath, which he termed " an expedient for pacifying the jealousies of a God of vengeance," — reprobating the operose drudgery of such Sabbaths. He represented the whole value of Sabbath observance to lie in its being a *free* and *willing* service, — a foretaste of heaven. " If you cannot breathe in comfort here, you cannot breathe in heaven hereafter." Many years afterwards, I mentioned this to Irving, who was then the colleague of Chalmers, and already spoken of as his rival in eloquence, and he told me that the Deacons waited on the Doctor to remonstrate with him on the occasion of this sermon.

That I may conclude with Dr. Chalmers now, let me here say, that I was as much gratified with him as I was dissatisfied with Andrew Thomson ; that he appeared absorbed in his

subject, utterly free from ostentation, and forgetful of himself.
I admired him highly, ranking him with Robert Hall ; but I
heard him once too often. On my return from the Highlands,
I heard him on the 30th of September, in the morning, on the
sin against the Holy Ghost, which he declared to be no particular sin, but a general indisposition to the Gospel. "It
can't be forgiven," he said, " because the sinner can't comply
with the condition, — desire to be forgiven." But it was the
evening sermon which left a painful impression on my mind.
He affirmed the doctrine of original sin in its most offensive
form. He declined to explain it.

The elder Mr. Grahame was one of the leading members of
the Doctor's congregation. He is very much like his son, only
milder, because older. He had another son, still living, and
whom I saw now and then. This was Tom Grahame, an
incarnation of the old Covenanter, a fierce radical and ultra-
Calvinist, who has a warm-hearted, free way, which softens his
otherwise bitter religious spirit.

On September 16th I had a little adventure. Being on the
western side of Loch Lomond, opposite the Mill, at Inversnaid,
some women kindled a fire, the smoke of which was to be a
signal for a ferry-boat. No ferryman came ; and a feeble old
man offering himself as a boatman, I intrusted myself to him.
I asked the women who he was. They said, "That's old Andrew." According to their account, he lived a hermit's life in
a lone island on the lake ; the poor peasantry giving him meal
and what he wanted, and he picking up pence. On my asking
him whether he would take me across the lake, he said, " I
wull, if you 'll gi'e me saxpence." So I consented. But
before I was half over, I repented of my rashness, for I feared
the oars would fall out of his hands. A breath of wind would
have rendered half the voyage too much for him. There was
some cunning mixed up with the fellow's seeming imbecility,
for when his strength was failing he rested, and entered into
talk, manifestly to amuse me. He said he could see things
before they happened. He saw the Radicals before they came,
&c. He had picked up a few words of Spanish and German,
which he uttered ridiculously, and laughed. But when I put
troublesome questions, he affected not to understand me ; and
was quite astonished, as well as delighted, when I gave him
two sixpences instead of the one he had bargained for. The
simple-minded women, who affected to look down on him,
seemed, however, to stand in awe of him, and no wonder. On

my telling Wordsworth this history, he exclaimed, "That's my 'Brownie.'" His "Brownie's Cell"* is by no means one of my favorite poems. My sight of old Andrew showed me the stuff out of which a poetical mind can weave such a web.

After visiting Stirling and Perth, I went to Crieff. On my way I met a little Scotch girl, who exhibited a favorable specimen of the national character. I asked the name of the gentleman whose house I had passed, and put it down in my pocket-book. "And do you go about putting people's names in your book?"—"Yes."—"And what's the use of it?" Now this was not said in an impertinent tone, as if she thought I was doing a silly act, but in the real spirit of naïf inquiry.

On Saturday, the 22d of September, I went by Comrie to Loch Earn head. On Sunday, the 23d, by Killin to Kenmore. I put down names of places which I would gladly see again in my old age. This day I witnessed a scene which still rests on my eye and ear. I will abridge from my journal : "It was in the forenoon, a few miles from Kenmore, when, on the high-road, I was startled by a screaming noise, which I at first mistook for quarrelling ; till, coming to a hedge, which I overlooked, I beheld a scene which the greatest of landscape-painters in the historic line might have delighted to represent. The sombre hue cast over the field reminded me of Salvator Rosa. I looked down into a meadow, at the bottom of which ran a brook ; and in the background there was a dark mountain frowning over a lake somewhat rippled by wind. Against a tree on the river's bank was placed a sort of box, and in this was a preacher, declaiming in the Gaelic tongue to an audience full of admiration. On the rising hill before him were some two or three hundred listeners. Far the greater number were lying in groups, but some standing. Among those present were ladies genteelly dressed. In the harsh sounds which grated on my ear I could not distinguish a word, except a few proper names of Hebrew persons."

On September the 29th, from Lanark, I visited the Duke of Hamilton's palace, and had unusual pleasure in the paintings to be seen there. I venture to copy my remarks on the famous Rubens's "Daniel in the Lion's Den" : "The variety of character in the lions is admirable. Here is indignation at the unintelligible power which restrains them ; there reverence towards the being whom they dare not touch. One of them is

---

* See Wordsworth's "Memorials of a Tour in Scotland in 1814," Vol. III. p. 44.

consoled by the contemplation of the last skull he has been picking; one is anticipating his next meal; two are debating the subject together. But the Prophet, with a face resembling Curran's (foreshortened * so as to lose its best expression), has all the muscles of his countenance strained from extreme terror. He is without joy or hope; and though his doom is postponed, he has no faith in the miracle which is to reward his integrity. It is a painting rather to astonish than delight."

On the *1st of October* I passed a place the name of which I could not have recollected twelve hours but for the charm of verse : —

> " I wish I were where Ellen lies,
>   By fair Kirkconnel Lea."

On returning to England, a stout old lady, our coach companion, rejoiced heartily that she was again in *old* England, a mean rivulet being the insignificant boundary. This feeling she persisted in retaining, though an act of disobedience to the law which annihilated England as a state, and though our supper was worse than any lately partaken of by any of us in Scotland.

October 4th. — I went to Ambleside, and for four days I was either there or at Rydal Mount. My last year's journey in Switzerland had improved my acquaintance with the Wordsworth family, and raised it to friendship. But my time was short, and I have nothing to record beyond this fact, that Mrs. Wordsworth was then in attendance upon a lady in a fever, consequent on lying in, — Mrs. Quillinan, a lady I never saw, a daughter of Sir Egerton Brydges.

October 7th. — My journal mentions (what does not belong to my recollections, but to my obliviscences) an able pamphlet by Mr. De Quincey against Brougham, written during the late election, entitled, "Close Comments on a Straggling Speech," a capital title, at all events. All that De Quincey wrote, or

---

* Daniel's head is thrown back, and he looks upwards with an earnest expression and clasped hands, as if vehemently supplicating. The picture formerly belonged to King Charles I. It was at that time entered as follows in the Catalogue of the Royal Pictures: " A piece of Daniel in the Lion's Den with lions about him, given by the deceased Lord Dorchester to the King, being so big as the life. Done by Sir Peter Paul Rubens." Dr. Waagen very justly observes that, upon the whole, the figure of Daniel is only an accessory employed by the great master to introduce, in the most perfect form, nine figures of lions and lionesses the size of life. Rubens, in a letter to Sir Dudley Carleton (who presented the picture to the King), dated April 28, 1618, expressly states that it was wholly his own workmanship. The price was 600 florins. Engraved in mezzotint by W. Ward, 1789.

writes, is curious, if not valuable ; commencing with his best-known " Confessions of an English Opium-Eater," and ending with his scandalous but painfully interesting " Autobiography," in *Tait's Magazine.*

October 23d. — To London on the Bury coach, and enjoyed the ride. Storks, Dover, Rolfe, and Andrews were inside play-ing whist. I was outside reading. I read Cantos III., IV., and V. of "Don Juan." I was amused by parts. There is a gayety which is agreeable enough when it is playful and ironi-cal, and here it is less malignant than it is in some of Byron's writings. The gross violations of decorum and morality one is used to. I felt no resentment at the lines,

> " A drowsy, frowzy poem called ' The Excursion,'
> Writ in a manner which is my aversion," *

nor at the affected contempt throughout towards Wordsworth. There are powerful descriptions, and there is a beautiful Hymn to Greece. I began Madame de Staël's "Ten Years' Exile." She writes with eloquence of Buonaparte, and her egotism is by no means offensive.

October 26th. — Met Charles Aikin. I saw he had a hatband, and he shocked me by the intelligence of his wife's death. I saw her a few days before I set off on my journey. She then appeared to be in her usual health. The conversation between us was not remarkable ; but I never saw her without pleasure, or left her without a hope I should see her again. She was a very amiable woman. She brought to the family a valuable accession of feeling. To her I owe my introduction to Mrs. Barbauld. I have been acquainted with her, though without great intimacy, twenty-four years. She was Gilbert Wakefield's eldest daughter, and not much younger than myself.

November 2d. — Finished Madame de Staël's "Ten Years' Exile." A very interesting book in itself, and to me especially interesting on account of my acquaintance with the author. Her sketches of Russian manners and society are very spirited, and her representation of her own sufferings under Buonaparte's persecutions is as eloquent as her novels. The style is ani-mated, and her declamations against Napoleon are in her best manner.

November 7th. — Called on De Quincey to speak about the *Classical Journal.* I have recommended him to Valpy, who will be glad of his assistance. De Quincey speaks highly of

* "Don Juan," Canto III. v. 94.

the liberality of Taylor and Hessey, who gave him forty guineas for his " Opium Eater."

November 9th. — Dined at Guildhall. About five hundred persons present, perhaps six hundred. The tables were in five lines down the hall. Gas illumination. The company all well dressed at least. The ornaments of the hustings, with the cleaned statues, &c., rendered the scene an imposing one. I dined in the King's Bench, a quiet place, and fitter for a substantial meal than the great hall. I was placed next to Croly (newspaper writer and poet), and near several persons of whom I knew something, so that I did not want for society. Our dinner was good, but ill-served and scanty. As soon as we had finished a hasty dessert, I went into the great hall, where I was amused by walking about. I ascended a small gallery at the top of the hall, whence the view below was very fine ; and I afterwards chatted with Firth, &c. Some dozen judges and sergeants were really ludicrous objects in their full-bottomed wigs and scarlet robes. The Dukes of York and Wellington, and several Ministers of State, gave éclat to the occasion.

November 18th. — I stepped into the Lambs' cottage at Dalston. Mary, pale and thin, just recovered from one of her attacks. They have lost their brother John, and feel their loss. They seemed softened by affliction, and to wish for society.

Poor old Captain Burney died on Saturday. The rank Captain had become a misnomer, but I cannot call him otherwise. He was made Admiral a few weeks ago. He was a fine old man.* His whist parties were a great enjoyment to me.

December 11th. — Dined with Monkhouse. Tom Clarkson went with me. The interest of the evening arose from MSS. of poems by Wordsworth, on the subject of our journey. After waiting so long without writing anything, — so at least I understood when in Cumberland, — the fit has come on him, and within a short time he has composed a number of delightful little poems ; and Miss Hutchison writes to Mr. Monkhouse that he goes on writing with great activity.†

December 31st. — At Flaxman's, where I spent several hours very pleasantly. We talked of animal magnetism. Flaxman declared he believed it to be fraud and imposition, an opinion

* The circumnavigator of the world with Captain Cook, and historian of circumnavigation. A humorous old man, friend of Charles Lamb, son of Dr. Burney, and brother of Madame d'Arblay. Martin Burney was his son. — H. C. R.

† These poems have been referred to in connection with the tour which suggested them.

I was not prepared for from him. But the conversation led to some very singular observations on his part, which show a state of mind by no means unfit for the reception of the new doctrine. He spoke of his dog's habit of fixing her eye upon him when she wanted food, &c., so that he could not endure the sight, and was forced to drive her away : this he called an *animal* power ; and he intimated also a belief in demoniacal influence ; so that it was not clear to me that he did not think that animal magnetism was somewhat criminal, allowing its pretensions to be well founded, rather than supposing them to be vain. There is frequently an earnestness that becomes uncomfortable to listen to when Flaxman talks with religious feeling.

Rem. — My Diary mentions " John Wood, a lively genteel young man ! " Now he is a man of importance in the state, being the Chairman of the Board of Inland Revenue. He was previously the head of the Stamp Office and Chairman of Excise. In the latter capacity he lately effected great economical reforms. He is a rare example of independence and courage, not renouncing the profession of his unpopular religious opinions.

My practice this year was as insignificant as ever, even falling off in the amount it produced ; the fees being 572½ guineas, whereas in 1820 they were 663.

CHAPTER XXVI.

1822.

JANUARY 10th. — At twelve Monkhouse called. I walked with him and had a high treat in a call at Chantrey's, having to speak with him about Wordsworth's bust. What a contrast to Flaxman ! A sturdy, florid-looking man, with a general resemblance in character to Sir Astley Cooper, both looking more like men of business and the world than artists or students. Chantrey talks with the ease of one who is familiar with good company, and with the confidence of one who is conscious of his fame. His study is rich in works of art. His busts are admirable. His compositions do not in general please

* Written in 1851.

me. He has in hand a fine monument of Ellenborough. A good likeness too.*

January 22d. — I went into court on account of a single defence, which unexpectedly came on immediately, and having succeeded in obtaining an acquittal, I was able to leave Bury by the "Day" coach. I had an agreeable ride, the weather being mild. I finished "Herodotus," a book which has greatly amused me. The impression most frequently repeated during the perusal was that of the compatibility of great moral wisdom with gross superstition. It is impossible to deny that "Herodotus" encourages by his silence, if not by more express encouragement, the belief in outrageous fictions. The frequency of miracle in all ancient history is unfavorable to the belief of that affirmed in the Jewish history. This book inspires a salutary horror of political despotism, but at the same time a dangerous contempt of men at large, and an uncomfortable suspicion of the pretensions of philosophers and patriots.

February 25th. — I went to Aders's, and found him and his wife alone. An interesting conversation. Mrs. Aders talked in a tone of religion which I was pleased with. At the same time she showed a tendency to superstition which I could only wonder at. She has repeatedly had dreams of events which subsequently occurred, and sometimes with circumstances that rendered the coincidence both significant and wonderful. One is remarkable, and worth relating. She dreamed, when in Germany, that a great illumination took place, of what kind she was not aware. Two luminous balls arose. In one she saw her sister, Mrs. Longdale, with an infant child in her arms. On the night of the illumination on account of the Coronation (years after the dream), she was called by Miss Watson into the back drawing-room, to see a ball or luminous body which had been let off at Hampstead. She went into the room, and on a sudden it flashed on her mind with painful feelings, "This was what I saw in my dream." That same evening her sister died. ·She had been lately brought to bed. The child lived.

---

* Chantrey was an excellent bust-maker, and he executed ably. He wanted poetry and imagination. The Children in Lichfield Cathedral, which might have given him reputation with posterity, were the design of Stothard. It is to Chantrey's high honor that he left a large portion of his ample fortune, after the death of his widow, for the encouragement of fine art, and made for that purpose wise arrangements. Lady Chantrey gave all his casts, &c. to Oxford University, where they constitute a gallery. Asking Rogers its value lately, he said: "As a collection of historical portraits, they are of great value; as works of art, *that,*" snapping his fingers. — H. C. R.

H. C. R. TO MISS WORDSWORTH.

3 KING'S BENCH, 25th February, 1822.

I am indeed a very bad correspondent, but a long foolscap letter was written more than a fortnight back, when I met Mr. Monkhouse, and he told me what rendered my letter utterly inexpedient, for it was an earnest exhortation to you and Mrs. Wordsworth to urge the publication of the delightful poems, which is now done ; and the expression of a wish that one of the Journals might appear also, and that would be in vain. I am heartily glad that so many imperishable records will be left of incidents which I had the honor of partially enjoying with you. The only drawback on my pleasure is, that I fear when the book is once published, Mr. Wordsworth may no longer be inclined to meditate on what he saw and felt, and therefore much may remain unsaid which would probably have appeared in the Memorials, if they had been delayed till 1823. I hope I have not seen all, and I should rejoice to find among the unseen poems some memorial of those patriotic and pious bridges at Lucerne, suggesting to so *generative* a mind as your brother's a whole cycle of religious and civic sentiments. The equally affecting *Senate-house* not made by hands, at Sarnen, where the rites of modern legislation, like those of ancient religion, are performed in the open air, and on an unadorned grass-plat ! ! ! But the poet needs no prompter ; I shall be grateful to him for what he gives, and have no right to reflect on what he withholds. I wish he may have thought proper to preface each poem by a brief memorandum in prose. Like the great poet of Germany, with whom he has so many high powers in common, he has a strange love of riddles. Goethe carries further the practice of not giving collateral information : he seems to anticipate the founding of a college for the delivery of explanatory lectures like those instituted in Tuscany for Dante.

My last letter, which I destroyed, was all about the poems. I have not the vanity to think that my praise can gratify, but I ought to say, since the verses to Goddard were my suggestion, that I rejoice in my good deed. It is instructive to observe how a poet sees and feels, how remote from ordinary sentiment, and yet how beautiful and true ! Goethe says he had never an affliction which he did not turn into a poem. Mr. Wordsworth has shown how common occurrences are transmuted into poetry. Midas is the type of a true poet. Of the Stanzas, I love most — loving all — the " Eclipse of the Sun." Of the Sonnets, there is *one* remarkable as *unique ;* the humor and naïveté, and the exquisitely refined sentiment of the Calais fishwomen, are a combination of excellences quite novel. I should, perhaps, have given the preference after all to the Jungfrau Sonnet, but it wants unity. I know not which to distinguish, the Simplon Stone, the Bruges, or what else ? I have them not here. Each is the best as I recollect the impression it made on me. . . . .

MISS WORDSWORTH TO H. C. R.

3d March, 1822.

My brother will, I hope, write to Charles Lamb in the course of a few days. He has long talked of doing it ; but you know how the mastery of his own thoughts (when engaged in composition, as he has lately been) often prevents him from fulfilling his best intentions ; and since the weakness of his eyes has returned, he has been obliged to fill up all spaces of leisure by going into the open air for refreshment and relief of his eyes. We are very thankful that the inflammation, chiefly in the lids, is now much abated. It concerns us very much to hear so indifferent an account of Lamb and his sister ; the death of their brother, no doubt, has afflicted them much more than the death of any brother, with whom there had, in near neighborhood, been so little personal or family communication, would afflict any other minds. We deeply lamented their loss, and wished to write to them as soon as we heard of it ; but it not being the particular duty of any one of us, and a painful task, we put it off, for which we are now sorry, and very much blame ourselves. They are too good and too confiding to take it unkindly, and that thought makes us feel it the more. . . . . With respect to the tour poems, I am afraid you will think my brother's notes not sufficiently copious ; prefaces he has none, except to the poem on Goddard's death. Your suggestion of the Bridge at Lucerne set his mind to work ; and if a happy mood comes on he is determined even yet, though the work is printed, to add a poem on that subject. You can have no idea with what earnest pleasure he seized the idea ; yet, before he began to write at all, when he was pondering over his recollections, and asking me for hints and thoughts, I mentioned that very subject, and he then thought he could make nothing of it. You certainly have the gift of setting him on fire. When I named (before your letter was read to him) your scheme for next autumn, his countenance flushed with pleasure, and he exclaimed, " I 'll go with him." Presently, however, the conversation took a sober turn, and he concluded that the journey would be impossible; " And then," said he, "if you or Mary, or both, were not with me, I should not half enjoy it; and that is impossible." . . . . We have had a long and interesting letter from Mrs. Clarkson. Notwithstanding bad times, she writes in cheerful spirits and talks of coming into the North this summer, and we really hope it will not end in talk, as Mr. Clarkson joins with her ; and if he once determines, a trifle will not stop him. Pray read a paper in the *London Magazine*, by Hartley Coleridge, on the Uses of the Heathen Mythology in Poetry. It has pleased us very much. The style is wonderful for so young a man, — so little of effort and no affectation. . . . .

DOROTHY WORDSWORTH.

March 1st. — Came home early from Aders's to read " Cain." The author has not advanced any novelties in his speculations on the origin of evil, but he has stated one or two points with great effect. The book is calculated to spread infidelity by furnishing a ready expression to difficulties which must occur to every one, more or less, and which are passed over by those who confine themselves to scriptural representations. The second act is full of poetic energy, and there is some truth of passion in the scenes between Cain's wife and himself.

April 8th. — I had a very pleasant ride to London from Bury. The day was fine, and was spent in reading half a volume of amusing gossip, — D'Israeli on the literary character, in which the good and evil of that by me most envied character are displayed so as to repress envy without destroying respect. Yet I would, after all, gladly exchange some portion of my actual enjoyments for the intenser pleasures of a more intellectual kind, though blended with pains and sufferings from which I am free.

April 10th. — As I sat down to dinner, a young man introduced himself to me by saying, " My name is Poel." — " A son of my old friend at Altona ! " I answered ; and I was heartily glad to see him. Indeed the sight of him gave my mind such a turn, that I could scarcely attend to the rest of the company.

Poel was but a boy in 1807. No wonder, therefore, that I had no recollection of him. He, however, recognized me in a moment, and he says I do not appear in the slightest degree altered. I should have had a much heartier pleasure in seeing him had I not known that his mother died but a few months ago. She was a most amiable and a superior woman. The father is now advanced in years, but he retains, the son tells me, all his former zeal for liberty.*

April 13th. — Took tea with the Flaxmans, and read to them extracts from Wordsworth's new poems, "The Memorials." And I ended the evening by going to Drury Lane to see "Giovanni in London," a very amusing extravaganza. Madame Vestris is a fascinating creature, and renders the Don as entertaining as possible. And at the same time there is an air of irony and mere wanton and assumed wickedness, which renders the piece harmless enough. The parodies on well-known songs, &c. are well executed.

April 29th. — Walked to Hammersmith and back. On my way home I fell into chat with a shabby-looking fellow, a master-bricklayer, whose appearance was that of a very low person, but his conversation quite surprised me. He talked about trade with the knowledge of a practical man of business, enlightened by those principles of political economy which indeed are become common ; but I did not think they had alighted on the hod and trowel. He did not talk of the books of Adam Smith, but seemed imbued with their spirit.

May 7th. — I took tea with the Flaxmans. Flaxman related with undesigned humor some circumstances of the dinner of the Royal Academy on Saturday. He was seated between Cabinet Ministers ! Such a man to be placed near and to be expected to hold converse with Lord Liverpool and the Marquis of Londonderry, the Duke of Wellington, and Chateaubriand ! A greater contrast cannot be conceived than between an artist absorbed in his art, of the simplest manners, the purest morals, incapable of intrigue or artifice, a genius in his art, of pious feelings and an unworldly spirit, and a set of statesmen and courtiers ! The only part of the conversation he gave was a dispute whether *spes* makes *spei* in the genitive, which was referred to the Chief Justice of the King's Bench. Flaxman spoke favorably of the conversation and manners of Lord Harrowby.

May 18th. — Took tea with the Nashes, and accompanied

* See *ante*, p. 153.

Elizabeth and Martha to Mathews's Mimetic Exhibition. I was delighted with some parts. In a performance of three hours' duration there could not fail to be flat and uninteresting scenes; e. g. his attempt at representing Curran was a complete failure. I was much pleased with a representation of John Wilkes admonishing him, Mathews, when bound apprentice; Tate Wilkinson's talking on three or four subjects at once, and an Irish party at whist. I really do believe he has seen F——, so completely has he copied his voice and his words. These were introduced in a sort of biography of himself. In a second part of the entertainment, three characters were perfect, — a servant scrubbing his miserly master's coat, a French music-master in the character of Cupid in a ballet, and (the very best) a steward from a great dinner-party relating the particulars of the dinner. He was half drunk, and, I know not how, Mathews so completely changed his face that he was not to be known again. The fat Welshman, the miser, and the lover, were less successful.

May 22d. — I read a considerable part of Ritson's "Robin Hood Ballads," recommendable for the information they communicate concerning the state of society, rather than for the poetry, which is, I think, far below the average of our old ballads.

May 23d. — Visited Stonehenge, a very singular and most remarkable monument of antiquity, exciting surprise by the display of mechanical power, which baffles research into its origin and purposes, and leaves an impression of wonder that such an astonishing work should not have preserved the name of its founders. Such a fragment of antiquity favors the speculation of Schelling, and the other German metaphysicians, concerning a bygone age of culture and the arts and sciences.

June 1st. — Hundleby sent me, just before I went to dinner, papers, in order to argue at ten on Monday morning before the Lords (the Judges being summoned) the famous case of Johnstone and Hubbard, or, in the Exchequer Chamber, Hubbard and Johnstone, in which the Exchequer Chamber reversed the decision of the King's Bench, the question being on the effect of the Registry Acts on sales of ships at sea. This case had been argued some seven or eight times in the courts below, among others, by two of the Judges (Richardson and Parke), and had been pending fourteen years (the first action, indeed, against Hubbard was in 1803). And on such a case I was to prepare myself in a few hours, because Littledale, who had attended the Lords three times, could not prepare himself for want of time ! No wonder that I took books into bed, and was in no very comfortable mood.

June 3d. — I rose before five and had the case on my mind till past nine, when Hundleby called. He took me down to Westminster in a boat. There I found Carr in attendance. A little after ten I was called on, and I began my argument before the Chancellor, Lord Redesdale, one bishop, and nearly all the Judges. I was nervous at first, but in the course of my argument I gained courage, and Manning, who attended without telling me he should do so (an act of such kindness and friendship as I shall not soon forget), having whispered a word of encouragement, I concluded with tolerable comfort and satisfaction.

In the course of my argument I said one or two bold things. Having referred to a late decision of the King's Bench, which is, in effect, a complete overruling of the case then before the Lords (Richardson *v.* Campbell, 5 B. and A. 196), I said : "My learned friend will say that the cases are different. And they are different : the Lord Chief Justice, in giving judgment, says so. My Lords, since the short time that I have been in the profession, nothing has excited my admiration so much as the mingled delicacy and astuteness with which the learned Judges of one court avoid overruling the decisions of other courts. (Here Richardson, Parke, and Bailey smiled, and the Chancellor winked.) It would be indecorous in me to insinuate, even if I dared to imagine, what the opinion of the Judges of the King's Bench is ; but I beg your Lordships to consider whether the reasoning of Lord Chief Justice Abbott applies to that part of the case in which it differs from the case before the House, or to that in which the cases are the same." I afterwards commented on a mistake arising from confounding the words of the statute of W. and those of 34 George III., and said : "This mistake has so pervaded the profession, that the present reporters have put a false quotation into the lips of the Chief Justice," I knowing that the Chief Justice himself supplied the report.

After I had finished, Carr began his answer. But in a few minutes the Chancellor found that the special verdict was imperfectly framed, and directed a *venire de novo* (i. e. a new trial). Carr and I are to consent to amend it. Carr said to me very kindly : " on his honor, that he thought I had argued it better than any one on my side." Manning, too, said I had done it very well, and the Chancellor, on my observing how unprepared my client was to make alterations, said : "You have done so well at a short notice, that I have no doubt you will manage the rest very well." As Hundleby, too, was satisfied, I came away enjoying myself without being at all gay, like a man escaped from peril. I was, after all, by no means satisfied with myself, and ascribed to good-nature the compliments I had received.

June 4th. — Went for half the evening to Drury Lane. The few songs in the piece (the " Castle of Andalusia ") were sung by Braham, viz. " All 's Well," and " Victory," songs sung by him on all occasions and on no occasion, but they cannot be heard too often.

June 9th. — Went to the Lambs'. Talfourd joined me there. I was struck by an observation of Miss Lamb's, " How stupid those old people are ! " Perhaps my nephew's companions say so of my brother and me already. Assuredly they will soon say so. Talfourd and I walked home together late.

June 17th. — I went to call on the Lambs and take leave, they setting out for France next morning. I gave Miss Lamb a letter for Miss Williams, to whom I sent a copy of " Mrs. Leicester's School." * The Lambs have a Frenchman as their companion, and Miss Lamb's nurse, in case she should be ill. Lamb was in high spirits; his sister rather nervous. Her courage in going is great.

June 29th. — Read to-day in the Vienna *Jahrbücher der Literatur* a very learned and profound article on the history of the creation in Genesis. I was ashamed of my ignorance. Schlegel defends the Mosaic narrative, but understands it in a higher sense than is usually given to the history. His ideas are very curious. He supposes man to have been created between the last and last but one of the many revolutions the earth has undergone, and adopts the conjecture, that the Deluge was occasioned by a change in the position of the equation, which turned the sea over the dry land, and caused the bed of the ocean to become dry. He also supposes chaos not to have been created by God, but to have been the effect of sin in a former race of creatures ! Of all this I know nothing. Perhaps no man can usefully indulge in such speculations, but it is at least honorable to attempt them.

July 18th. — I finished " Sir Charles Grandison," a book of

* A set of Tales by Mary Lamb, with three contributed by her brother.

great excellence, and which must have improved the moral character of the age. Saving the somewhat surfeiting compliments of the good people, it has not a serious fault. The formality of the dialogue and style is soon rendered endurable by the substantial worth of what is said. In all the subordinate incidents Sir Charles is certainly a beau ideal of a Christian and a gentleman united. The story of Clementina is the glory of the work, and is equal to anything in any language.

[Mr. Robinson's tour this year was principally in the South of France. He kept a journal, as usual. A few extracts will be given, but no connected account of the journey.]

August 10th. — At 7 A. M. I embarked on board the *Lord Melville* steam-packet off the Tower Stairs, London. Our departure was probably somewhat retarded, and certainly rendered even festive, by the expected fête of the day. The King was to set out on his voyage to Scotland, and the City Companies' barges had been suddenly ordered to attend him at Gravesend. The river was therefore thronged with vessels of every description, and the gaudy and glittering barges of the Lord Mayor and some four or five of the Companies' gave a character to the scene. The appearance of unusual bustle continued until we reached Gravesend, near which the *Royal Sovereign* yacht was lying in readiness for his Majesty. The day was fine, which heightened the effect of the show. At Greenwich, the crowds on land were immense ; at Gravesend, the show was lost. Of the rest of the prospect I cannot say much. The Thames is too wide for the shore, which is low and uninteresting. The few prominent objects were not particularly gratifying to me. The most remarkable was a group of gibbets, with the fragments of skeletons hanging on them. A few churches, the Reculvers, and the town of Margate, were the great features of the picture.

August 20th. — (Paris.) Mary Lamb has begged me to give her a day or two. She comes to Paris this evening, and stays here a week. Her only male friend is a Mr. Payne, whom she praises exceedingly for his kindness and attentions to Charles. He is the author of " Brutus," and has a good face.

August 21st. — (With Mary Lamb.) When Charles went back to England he left a note for his sister's direction. After pointing out a few pictures in the Louvre, he proceeds : " Then you must walk all along the borough side of the Seine, facing the Tuileries. There is a mile and a half of print-shops and bookstalls. If the latter were but English ! Then there is a place where the Paris people put all their dead people, and bring them flowers, and dolls, and gingerbread-nuts, and sonnets, and such trifles ; and that is all, I think, worth seeing as sights, except that the streets and shops of Paris are themselves the best sight." I had not seen this letter when I took Mary Lamb a walk that corresponds precisely with Lamb's taste, all of whose likings I can always sympathize with, but not generally with his dislikings.

August 22d. — Aders introduced me to Devou, a very Frenchman, but courteous and amiable, lively and intelligent. He accompanied us to Marshal Soult's house. But the Marshal was not at home. He would have been a more interesting object than the Spanish pictures which were his plunder in the kidnapping war. Though the paintings by Murillo and Velasquez were very interesting, I omit all mention of them. But being taken to Count Sommariva's, I there saw what has never been equalled by any other work of Canova, though this was an early production, the Mary Magdalene sitting on a cross. The truth and homely depth of feeling in the expression are very striking.

On the *2d of September* I left Grenoble, and after a hot and fatiguing journey of two nights and three days, partly through a very beautiful country, I reached Marseilles.

This journey was rendered interesting by the companions I had in the diligence. A *religieuse* from Grenoble, and two professors of theology. One of them, Professor R——, especially an ingratiating man. He praised the lately published " Essai sur l'Indifférence en Matière de Religion," and offered me a copy. But I promised to get it.

Rem.* — This I did. It was the famous work of De Lamennais, of which only two volumes were then published. A book of great eloquence, by a writer who has played a sad part in his day. From being the ultramontanist, and exposing himself to punishment in France as the libeller of the *Eglise Gallicane,* he became the assailant of the Pope, and an ultra-radical, combining an extreme sentimental French chartism with a spiritualism of his own. He has of late years been the associate of George Sand. Her "Spiridion," it is said, was written when travelling with him.

September 4th. — It was during this night, and perhaps between two and three, that we passed the town of Manosque, where a new passenger was taken in, who announced his office as

---

* Written in 1851.

Procureur du Roi to the people in a tone which made me fear we should meet with an assuming companion. On the contrary, he contributed to render the day very agreeable.

I talked law with him, and obtained interesting information concerning the proceedings in the French administration of justice. It appears that within his district — there are about 500 *Procureurs du Roi* in the country — he has the superintendence of all the criminal business. When a robbery or other offence is committed, the parties come to him. He receives the complaint, and sends the *gendarmerie* in search of the offender. When a murder or act of arson has been perpetrated, he repairs to the spot. In short, he is a sort of coroner and high sheriff as well as public prosecutor, and at the public expense he carries on the suit to conviction or acquittal.

On inquiry of the steps he would take on information that a person had been killed in a duel, he said, that if he found a man had killed his adversary in the defence of his person, he should consider him as innocent, and not put him on his trial. I asked, " If you find the party killed in a *fair* duel, what then?" — " Take up my papers and go home, and perhaps play a rubber at night with the man who had killed his adversary." I am confident of these words, for they made an impression on me. But I think the law is altered now.

October 4th. — We had for a short distance in the diligence an amusing young priest, — the only lively man of his cloth I have seen in France. He told anecdotes with great glee ; among others the following : —

When Madame de Staël put to Talleyrand the troublesome question what he would have done had he seen her and Madame de Récamier in danger of drowning, instead of the certainly uncharacteristic and sentimental speech commonly put into his lips as the answer, viz. that he should have jumped into the water and saved Madame de Staël, and then jumped in and died with Madame de Récamier, — instead of this, Talleyrand's answer was, " Ah ! Madame de Staël sait tant de choses que sans doute elle peut nager ! "

October 13th. — At home. I had papers and letters to look at, though in small quantity. My nephew came and breakfasted with me. He did not bring the news, for Burch of Canterbury had informed me of his marriage with Miss Hutchison. I afterwards saw Manning ; also Talfourd, who was married to Miss Rachel Rutt during the long vacation.

October 14th. — I rode to Norwich on the " Day coach,"

and was nearly all the time occupied in reading the Abbé De Lamennais' "Essai sur l'Indifférence," an eloquent and very able work against religious indifference, in which, however, he advocates the cause of Popery, without in the slightest degree accommodating himself to the spirit of the age. He treats alike Lutherans, Socinians, Deists, and Atheists. I have not yet read far enough to be aware of his proofs in favor of his own infallible Church, and probably that is assumed, not proved; but his skill is very great and masterly in exposing infidelity, and especially the inconsistencies of Rousseau.

December 9th. — Heard to-day of the death of Dr. Aikin, — a thing not to be lamented. He had for years sunk into imbecility, after a youth and middle age of extensive activity. He was in his better days a man of talents, and of the highest personal worth, — one of the salt of the earth.

December 21st. — The afternoon I spent at Aders's. A large party, — a splendid dinner, prepared by a French cook, and music in the evening. Coleridge was the star of the evening. He talked in his usual way, though with more liberality than when I saw him last some years ago. But he was somewhat less animated and brilliant and ·paradoxical. The music was enjoyed by Coleridge, but I could have dispensed with it for the sake of his conversation.

"For eloquence the soul, song charms the sense."

December 31st. — The New Year's eve I spent, as I have done frequently, at Flaxman's. And so I concluded a year, like so many preceding, of uninterrupted pleasure and health, with an increase of fortune and no loss of reputation. Though, as has always been the case, I am not by any means satisfied with my conduct, yet I have no matter of self-reproach as far as the world is concerned. My fees amounted to 629 guineas.

CHAPTER XXVII.

1823.

JANUARY 8th. — Went in the evening to Lamb. I have seldom spent a more agreeable few hours with him. He was serious and kind, — his wit was subordinate to his judgment, as is usual in *tête-à-tête* parties. Speaking of Coleridge, he said : " He ought not to have a wife or children ; he should have a sort of diocesan care of the world, — no parish duty." Lamb reprobated the prosecution of Byron's " Vision of Judgment." Southey's poem of the same name is more worthy of punishment, for his has an arrogance beyond endurance. Lord Byron's satire is one of the most good-natured description, — no malevolence.

February 26th. — A letter from Southey. I was glad to find he had taken in good part a letter I had written to him on some points of general politics, &c., the propriety of writing which I had myself doubted.

SOUTHEY TO H. C. R.

KESWICK, 22d February, 1823.

MY DEAR SIR, — I beg your pardon for not having returned the MSS. which you left here a year and a half ago, when I was unlucky enough to miss seeing you. I thought to have taken them myself to London long ere this, and put off acknowledging them till a more convenient season from time to time. But good intentions are no excuse for sins of omission. I heartily beg your pardon, — and will return them to you in person in the ensuing spring.

I shall be at Norwich in the course of my travels, — and of course see William Taylor. As for vulgar imputations, you need not be told how little I regard them. My way of life has been straightforward, and — as the inscription upon Akbar's seal says — " I never saw any one lost upon a straight road." To those who know me, my life is my justification ; to those who do not, my writings would be, in their whole tenor, if they were just enough to ascertain what my opinions are before they malign me for advancing them.

What the plausible objection to my history * which you have repeated means, I cannot comprehend, — " That I have wilfully disregarded those changes in the Spanish character which might have been advantageously drawn from the spirit of the age in the more enlightened parts of Europe." I cannot guess at what is meant.

Of the old governments in the Peninsula, my opinion is expressed in terms of strong condemnation, — not in this work only, but in the " History of Brazil," wherever there was occasion to touch upon the subject. They are only not so bad as a Jacobinical tyranny, which, while it continues, destroys the only good that these governments left (that is, *order*), and terminates at last in a stronger despotism than that which it has overthrown. I distrust the French, because, whether under a Bourbon or a Buonaparte, they are French still; but if their government were upright, and their people honorable, in that case I should say that their interference with Spain was a question of expediency; and that justice and humanity, as well as policy, would require them to put an end to the commotions in that wretched country, and restore order there, if this could be effected. But I do not see how they can effect it. And when such men as Mina and Erolles are opposed to each other, I cannot but feel how desperately bad the system must be which each is endeavoring to suppress; and were it in my power, by a wish, to decide the struggle on one side or the other, so strongly do I perceive the evils on either side, that I confess I should want resolution and determination.

You express a wish that my judgment were left unshackled to its own free operation. In God's name, what is there to shackle it? I neither court preferment nor popularity; and care as little for the favor of the great as for the obloquy of the vulgar. Concerning Venice, — I have spoken as strongly as you could desire. Concerning Genoa, — instead of giving it to Sardinia, I wish it could have been *sold* to Corsica. The Germans were originally *invited* to govern Italy, because the Italians were too depraved and too divided to govern themselves. You cannot wish more sincerely than I do that the same cause did not exist to render the continuance of their dominion, — not indeed a good, but certainly, under present circumstances, the least of two evils. It is a bad government, and a clumsy one; and, indeed, the best foreign dominion can never be better than a necessary evil.

---

* The first volume of Southey's " History of the Peninsular War." The second volume was published in 1827, and the third in 1833.

Your last question is, what I think of the King of Prussia's utter disregard of his promises? You are far better qualified to judge of the state of his dominions than I can be. But I would ask you whether the recent experiments which have been made of establishing representative governments are likely to encourage or deter those princes who may formerly have wished to introduce them in their states? And whether the state of England, since the conclusion of the war, has been such as would recommend or disparage the English constitution, to those who may once have considered it as the fair ideal of a well-balanced government? The English Liberals and the English press are the worst enemies of liberty.

It will not be very long before my speculations upon the prospects of society will be before the world. You will then see that my best endeavors for the real interests of humanity have not been wanting. Those interests are best consulted now by the maintenance of order. Maintain order, and the spirit of the age will act surely and safely upon the governments of Europe. But if the Anarchists prevail, there is an end of all freedom; a generation like that of Sylla, or Robespierre, will be succeeded by a despotism, appearing like a golden age at first, but leading, like the Augustan age, to the thorough degradation of everything.

I have answered you, though hastily, as fully as the limits of a letter will admit, — fairly, freely, and willingly. My views are clear and consistent, and, could they be inscribed on my gravestone, I should desire no better epitaph.

Wordsworth is at Coleorton, and will be in London long before me. He is not satisfied with my account of the convention of Cintra; the rest of the book he likes well. Our difference here is, that he looks at the principle, abstractedly, and I take into view the circumstances.

When you come into this country again, give me a few days. I have a great deal both within doors and without which I should have great pleasure in showing you. Farewell! and believe me

Yours sincerely,

ROBERT SOUTHEY.

March 1st. — (On circuit.) We dined with Garrow. He was very chatty. He talked about his being retained for Fox, on the celebrated scrutiny in 1784 before the House of Commons, "To which," he said, "I owe the rank I have the honor to fill." He mentioned the circumstances under which he went first to the bar of the Commons. He was sent for on a sudden, without preparation, almost without reading his brief. He spoke for two hours; "And it was," he said, "the best speech I ever made. Kenyon was Master of the Rolls, hating all I said, but he came down to the bar and said, good-naturedly, 'Your business is done; now you'll get on.'" Garrow talked of himself with pleasure, but without expressing any extravagant opinions about himself.

April 2d. — An interesting day. After breakfasting at Monkhouse's, I walked out with Wordsworth, his son John, and Monkhouse. We first called at Sir George Beaumont's to see his fragment of Michael Angelo, — a piece of sculpture in bas and haut relief, — a holy family. The Virgin has the child in her lap; he clings to her, alarmed by something St. John holds towards him, probably intended for a bird. The expression of the infant's face and the beauty of his limbs cannot well be surpassed. Sir George supposes that Michael Angelo was so persuaded he could not heighten the effect by completing it, that he never finished it. There is also a very fine landscape by Rubens, full of power and striking effect. It is highly praised by Sir George for its execution, the management of its lights, its gradation, &c.

Sir George is a very elegant man, and talks well on matters of art. Lady Beaumont is a gentlewoman of great sweetness and dignity. I should think among the most interesting by far of persons of quality in the country. I should have thought this, even had I not known of their great attachment to Wordsworth.

We then called on Moore, and had a very pleasant hour's chat with him. Politics were a safer topic than poetry, though on this the opinions of Wordsworth and Moore are nearly as adverse as their poetic character. Moore spoke freely and in a tone I cordially sympathized with about France and the Bourbons. He considers it quite uncertain how the French will feel at any time on any occasion, so volatile and vehement are they at the same time. Yet he thinks that, as far as they have any thought on the matter, it is in favor of the Spaniards and liberal opinions. Notwithstanding this, he says he is disposed to assent to the notion, that of all the people in Europe, the French alone are unfit for liberty. Wordsworth freely contradicted some of Moore's assertions, but assented to the last.

Of French poetry Moore did not speak highly, and he thinks

that Chenevix has overrated the living poets in his late articles in the *Edinburgh Review*. Moore's person is very small, his countenance lively rather than intellectual. I should judge him to be kind-hearted and friendly.

Wordsworth and I went afterwards to the Society of Arts, and took shelter during a heavy rain in the great room. Wordsworth's curiosity was raised and soon satisfied by Barry's pictures.

Concluded my day at Monkhouse's. The Lambs were there.

April 4th. — Dined at Monkhouse's. Our party consisted of Wordsworth, Coleridge, Lamb, Moore, and Rogers. Five poets of very unequal worth and most disproportionate popularity, whom the public probably would arrange in a different order. During this afternoon, Coleridge alone displayed any of his peculiar talent. I have not for years seen him in such excellent health and with so fine a flow of spirits. His discourse was addressed chiefly to Wordsworth, on points of metaphysical criticism, — Rogers occasionally interposing a remark. The only one of the poets who seemed not to enjoy himself was Moore. He was very attentive to Coleridge, but seemed to relish Lamb, next to whom he was placed.

*Rem.** — Of this dinner an account is given in Moore's Life, which account is quoted in the *Athenæum* of April 23, 1853. Moore writes : " April 4, 1823. Dined at Mr. Monkhouse's (a gentleman I had never seen before) on Wordsworth's invitation, who lives there whenever he comes to town. A singular party. Coleridge, Rogers, Wordsworth and wife, Charles Lamb (the hero at present of the *London Magazine*) and his sister (the poor woman who went mad in a diligence on the way to Paris), and a Mr. Robinson, one of the *minora sidera* of this constellation of the Lakes ; the host himself, a Mæcenas of the school, contributing nothing but good dinners and silence. Charles Lamb, a clever fellow, certainly, but full of villanous and abortive puns, which he miscarries of every minute. Some excellent things, however, have come from him." Charles Lamb is indeed praised by a word the most unsuitable imaginable, for he was by no means a *clever* man ; and dear Mary Lamb, a woman of singular good sense, who, when really herself, and free from the malady that periodically assailed her, was quiet and judicious in an eminent degree, — this admirable person is dryly noticed as " the poor woman who went mad in a dili-

* Written in 1853.

gence," &c.   Moore is not to be blamed for this, — they were strangers to him.   The *Athenæum* Reviewer, who quotes this passage from Moore, remarks : " The tone is not to our liking," and it is added, " We should like to see Lamb's account." This occasioned my sending to the *Athenæum* (June 25, 1853) a letter by Lamb to Bernard Barton.*   " Dear Sir, — I wished for you yesterday.   I dined in Parnassus with Wordsworth, Coleridge, Rogers, and Tom Moore : half the poetry of England constellated in Gloucester Place !   It was a delightful evening !   Coleridge was in his finest vein of talk, — had all the talk ; and let 'em talk as evilly as they do of the envy of poets, I am sure not one there but was content to be nothing but a listener.   The Muses were dumb while Apollo lectured on his and their fine art.   It is a lie that poets are envious : I have known the best of them, and can speak to it, that they give each other their merits, and are the kindest critics as well as best authors.   I am scribbling a muddy epistle with an aching head, for we did not quaff Hippocrene last night, marry ! It was hippocrass rather."

Lamb was in a happy frame, and I can still recall to my mind the look and tone with which he addressed Moore, when he could not articulate very distinctly : " Mister Moore, will you drink a glass of wine with me ? " — suiting the action to the word, and hobnobbing.   Then he went on : " Mister Moore, till now I have always felt an antipathy to you, but now that I have seen you I shall like you ever after." Some years after I mentioned this to Moore.   He recollected the fact, but not Lamb's amusing manner.   Moore's talent was of another sort; for many years he had been the most brilliant man of his company.   In anecdote, small-talk, and especially in singing, he was supreme ; but he was no match for Coleridge in his vein.   As little could he feel Lamb's humor.

Besides these five bards were no one but Mrs. Wordsworth, Miss Hutchison, Mary Lamb, and Mrs. Gilman.   I was at the bottom of the table, where I very ill performed my part.

April 5th. — Went to a large musical party at Aders's, in Euston Square.   This party I had made for them.   Wordsworth, Monkhouse, and the ladies, the Flaxmans, Coleridge, Mr. and Mrs. Gilman, and Rogers, were *my* friends.   I noticed a great diversity in the enjoyment of the music, which was first-rate.   Wordsworth declared himself perfectly delighted and satisfied, but he sat alone, silent, and with his face covered,

* Lamb's Works, Vol. I. p. 204.

and was generally supposed to be asleep. Flaxman, too, confessed that he could not endure fine music for *long*. But Coleridge's enjoyment was very lively and openly expressed.

April 13th. — Dover lately lent me a very curious letter, written in 1757 by Thurlow to a Mr. Caldwell, who appears to have wanted his general advice how to annoy the parson of his parish. The letter fills several sheets, and is a laborious enumeration of statutes and canons, imposing an infinite variety of vexatious and burdensome duties on clergymen. Thurlow begins by saying: "I have confined myself to consider how a parson lies obnoxious to the criminal laws of the land, both ecclesiastical and secular, upon account of his character and office, omitting those instances in which all men are equally liable." And he terminates his review by a triumphant declaration: "I hope my Lord Leicester will think, even by this short sketch, that I did not talk idly to him, when I said that parsons were so hemmed in by canons and statutes, that they can hardly breathe, according to law, if they are strictly watched."

Scarcely any of the topics treated of have any interest, being for the most part technical; but after writing of the Statutes of Uniformity, especially 13th and 14th Ch. II. c. 64, he has this passage: "I have mentioned these severe statutes and canons, because I have known many clergymen, and those of the best character, followers of Eusebius, who have, in the very face of all these laws, refused to read the Athanasian Creed. Considering the shocking absurdity of this creed, I should think it a cruel thing to punish anybody for not reading it but those who have sworn to read it, and who have great incomes for upholding that persuasion."

> . . . . Neque enim lex est æquior ulla
> Quam necis artifices arte perire sua.

May 2d. — Having discharged some visits, I had barely time to return to dress for a party at Mr. Green's, Lincoln's Inn Fields. An agreeable party. Coleridge was the only talker, and he did not talk his best; he repeated one of his own jokes, by which he offended a Methodist at the whist-table; calling for her *last trump*, and confessing that, though he always thought her an angel, he had not before known her to be an archangel.

*Rem.** — Early in May my sister came to London to obtain surgical advice. She consulted Sir Astley Cooper, Cline, and

* Written in 1851.

Abernethy. Abernethy she declared to be the most feeling and tender surgeon she had ever consulted. His behavior was characteristic, and would have been amusing, if the gravity of the occasion allowed of its being seen from a comic point of view. My sister calling on him as he was going out, said, by way of apology, she would not detain him two minutes. "What! you expect me to give you my advice in two minutes? I will do no such thing. I know nothing about you, or your mode of living. I can be of no use. Well, I am not the first you have spoken to; whom have you seen? — Cooper? — Ah! very clever with his fingers; and whom besides? — Cline? — *why* come to me then? you need not go to any one after him. He is a sound man."

May 21st. — Luckily for me, for I was quite unprepared, a tithe case in which I was engaged was put off till the full term. Being thus unexpectedly relieved, I devoted great part of the forenoon to a delightful stroll. I walked through the Green Park towards Brompton; and knowing that with the great Bath road on my right, and the Thames on my left, I could not greatly err, I went on without inquiry. I found myself at Chelsea. Saw the new Gothic church, and was pleased with the spire, though the barn-like nave, and the slender and feeble flying buttresses, confirmed the expectation that modern Gothic would be a failure. Poverty or economy is fatal in its effects on a style of architecture which is nothing if it be not rich. I turned afterwards to the right, through Walham Common, and arrived at Naylor's at three. The great man whom we were met to admire came soon after. It was the famous Scotch preacher, the associate of Dr. Chalmers at Glasgow, Mr. Irving. He was brought by his admirer, an acquaintance of Naylor's, a Mr. Laurie,* a worthy Scotchman, who to-day was in the background, but speaks at religious meetings, Naylor says. There was also Tho. Clarkson, not in his place to-day. Irving on the whole pleased me. Little or no assumption, easy and seemingly kind-hearted, talking not more of his labors in attending public meetings (he was come from one) than might be excused; he did not obtrude any religious talk, and was not dogmatical.

Rem.† — Irving had a remarkably fine figure and face, and Mrs. Basil Montagu said it was a question with the ladies whether his squint was a grace or a deformity. My answer would have been, It enhances the effect either way. A better

* Afterwards Sir Peter. — *Rem.* 1851.   † Written in 1851.

saying of Mrs. Montagu's was, that he might stand as a model for St. John the Baptist, — indeed for any Saint dwelling in the wilderness and feeding on locusts and wild honey. Those who took an impression unpropitious to him might liken him to an Italian bandit. He has a powerful voice, feels always warmly, is prompt in his expression, and not very careful of his words. His opinions I liked. At the meeting he had attended in the morning (it was of a Continental Bible Society), he attacked the English Church as a persecuting Church, and opposed Wilberforce, who had urged prudent and *unoffending* proceedings. I told Irving of my Scotch journey. He informed me that the sermon I heard Dr. Chalmers preach against the Judaical spending of the Sabbath had given offence to the elders, who remonstrated with him about it.* He only replied that he was glad his sermon had excited so much attention. On my expressing my surprise that Dr. Chalmers should leave Glasgow for St. Andrew's, Irving said it was the best thing he could do. He had, by excess of labor, worn out both his mind and body. He ought for three or four years to do nothing at all, but recruit his health. We talked a little about literature. Irving spoke highly of Wordsworth as a poet, and praised his natural piety.

May 25th. — After reading a short time, I went to the Caledonian Chapel, to hear Mr. Irving. Very mixed impressions. I do not wonder that his preaching should be thought to be acting, or at least as indicative of vanity as of devotion. I overheard some old ladies in Hatton Garden declaring that it was not pure gospel ; they did not wish to hear any more, &c. The most unfavorable circumstance, as tending to confirm this suspicion, is a want of keeping in his discourse. Abrupt changes of style, as if written (and it *was* written) at a dozen different sittings. His tone equally variable. No master-feeling running through the whole, like the red string through the Royal Marine ropes, to borrow an image from Goethe. Yet his sermon was very impressive. I caught myself wandering but once. It began with a very promising division of his subject. His problem to show how the spiritual man is equally opposed to the sensual, the intellectual, and the moral man, but he expatiated chiefly on the sensual character. He drew some striking pictures. He was very vehement, both in gesticulation and declamation. To me there was much novelty, perhaps because I am less familiar with Scotch than English preaching.

* See *ante*, p. 462.

21 *

Basil Montagu and several young barristers were there. The aisles were crowded by the profane, at least by persons drawn by curiosity.

*Rem.** — One unquestionable merit he had, — he read the Scriptures most beautifully; he gave a new sense to them. Even the Scotch hymns, when he recited them, were rendered endurable. Of my own acquaintance with him I shall speak hereafter.

June 8th. — I attended Mrs. J. Fordham to hear Mr. Irving, and was better pleased with him than before. There was an air of greater sincerity in him, and his peculiarities were less offensive. His discourse was a continuation of last week's, — on the intellectual man as opposed to the spiritual man. He showed the peculiar perils to which intellectual pursuits expose a man. The physician becomes a materialist, — the lawyer an atheist, — because each confines his inquiries, the one to the secondary laws of nature, the other to the outward relations and qualities of actions. The poet, on the contrary, creates gods for himself. He worships the creations of his own fancy. Irving abused in a commonplace way the sensual poets, and made insinuations against the more intellectual, which might be applied to Wordsworth and Coleridge. He observed on the greater danger arising to intellectual persons from their being less exposed to adversity; their enjoyments of intellect being more independent of fortune. The best part of his discourse was a discrimination between the *three* fatal errors of, 1st, conceiving that our actions are bound by the laws of necessity; 2d, that we can reform when we please; and 3d, that circumstances determine our conduct. There was a great crowd to-day, and the audience seemed gratified.

June 17th. — I had an opportunity of being useful to Mr. and Mrs. Wordsworth, who arrived to-day from Holland. They relied on Lamb's procuring them a bed, but he was out. I recommended them to Mrs. ——, but they could not get in there. In the mean while I had mentioned their arrival to Talfourd, who could accommodate them. I made tea for them, and afterwards accompanied them to Talfourd's. I was before engaged to Miss Sharpe, where we supped. The Flaxmans were there, Samuel Rogers, and his elder brother, who has the appearance of being a superior man, which S. Sharpe reports him to be. An agreeable evening. Rogers, who knows all the gossip of literature, says that on the best authority he can affirm that

---

* Written in 1851.

Walter Scott has received £ 100,000 honorarium for his poems and other works, including the Scotch novels! Walter Scott is Rogers's friend, but Rogers did not oppose Flaxman's remark, that his works have in no respect tended to improve the moral condition of mankind. Wordsworth came back well pleased with his tour in Holland. He has not, I believe, laid in many poetical stores.

June 22d. — An unsettled morning. An attempt to hear Irving; the doors crowded. I read at home till his service was over, when by appointment I met Talfourd, with whom I walked to Clapton. Talfourd was predetermined to be contemptuous and scornful towards Irving, whom he heard in part, and no wonder that he thought him a poor reasoner, a commonplace declaimer, full of bad imagery. Pollock, with more candor, declares him to be an extraordinary man, but ascribes much of the effect he produces to his sonorous voice and impressive manner.

June 29th. — Thomas Nash, of Whittlesford, calling, induced me to go again to hear Mr. Irving. A crowd. A rush into the meeting. I was obliged to stand all the sermon. A very striking discourse; an exposition of the superiority of Christianity over Paganism. It was well done. His picture of Stoicism was admirably conceived. He represented it at the best as but the manhood, not the womanhood, of virtue. The Stoic armed himself against the evils of life. His system, after all, was but refined selfishness, and while he protected himself, he did not devote himself to others; no kindness, no self-offering, &c. Speaking of the common practice of infidels to hold up Socrates and Cato as specimens of Pagan virtue, he remarked that this was as uncandid as it would be to represent the Royalists of the seventeenth century by Lord Falkland, or the Republicans by Milton, or the courtiers of Louis XIV. by Fénélon, the French philosophers before the Revolution by D'Alembert, or the French Republicans after by Carnot! But neither in this nor in any other of his sermons did he manifest great powers of thought.

This week has brought us the certain news of the counter revolution in Portugal. But men still will not be convinced that the counter-revolution in Spain must inevitably follow.

June 30th. — I finished Goethe's fifth volume. Some of the details of the retreat from Champagne, and still more those of the siege of Mayence, are tedious, but it is a delightful volume notwithstanding. It will be looked back upon by a remote posterity as a most interesting picture from the hand of a master of the state of the public mind and feeling at the beginning of the Revolution. The literary and psychological parts of the book are invaluable. The tale of the melancholy youth who sought Goethe's advice, which, after a visit in disguise to the Harz, he refused to give, because he was assured he could be of no use, is fraught with interest. It was at that time Goethe wrote the fine ode, "Harz Reise im Winter." *

July 12th. — I met Cargill by appointment, but on calling at Mr. Irving's we received a card addressed to callers, stating that he had shut himself up till three, and wished not to be interrupted except on business of importance. How excellent a thing were this but a fashion !

I called on Murray, and signed a letter (which is to be lithographed, with a fac-simile of handwriting) recommending Godwin's case. It is written by Mackintosh.†

August 6th. — Went to the Haymarket. I have not lately been so much amused. In "Sweethearts and Wives," by Kenny, Liston plays a sentimental lover and novel-reader. A burlesque song is the perfection of farce : —

> " And when I cry and plead for marcy,
> It does no good, but wice warsy."

[This year Mr. Robinson made a tour in Germany, Switzerland, and the Tyrol ; but as he went over the same ground at other times, no selections will be given from the journal he wrote on this occasion.]

October 26th. — I met with Talfourd, and heard from him much of the literary gossip of the last quarter. Sutton Sharpe,‡ whom I called on, gave me a second edition, and lent me the last *London Magazine*,§ containing Lamb's delightful letter to Southey. ‖ His remarks on religion are full of deep feeling, and his eulogy on Hazlitt and Leigh Hunt most generous. Lamb must be aware that he would expose himself to

---

* See Vol. II. p. 49.

† The object of this letter was to obtain a sum of money to help Godwin out of his difficulties.

‡ Nephew of Samuel Rogers. Afterwards Q. C., and eminent at the equity bar.

§ See the Works of Charles Lamb, Vol. I. p. 322.

‖ Southey had said in a review of " Elia's Essays ": " It is a book which wants only a sounder religious feeling, to be as delightful as it is original." He did not intend to let the word *sounder* stand, but the passage was printed without his seeing a proof of it.

obloquy by such declarations. It seems that he and Hazlitt are no longer on friendly terms. Nothing that Lamb has ever written has impressed me more strongly with the sweetness of his disposition and the strength of his affections.

November 10th. — An interesting day. I breakfasted with Flaxman, by invitation, to meet Schlegel. Had I as much admiration for Schlegel's personal character as I have for his literary powers, I should have been gratified by his telling Flaxman that it was I who first named him to Madame de Staël, and who gave Madame de Staël her first ideas of German literature. Schlegel is now devoting himself to Indian learning, and hardly attends to anything else. Our conversation during a short breakfast was chiefly on Oriental subjects. He brought with him his niece, an artist, who has been studying under Girard at Paris. Flaxman had made an appointment with Rundle and Bridge. And we rode there, principally to see Flaxman's "Shield of Achilles," one of his greatest designs. Mr. Bridge said it is a disgrace to the English nobility that only four copies have been ordered, — by the King, the Duke of York, the Duke of Northumberland, and Lord Lonsdale.* Schlegel seemed to admire the work. It was Lord Mayor's Day, and we stayed to see the procession.

November 18th. — I spent the forenoon at home. Finished Mrs. Wordsworth's Journal. I do not know when I have felt more humble than in reading it; it is so superior to my own. She saw so much more than I did, though we were side by side during a great part of the time. Her recollection and her observation were alike employed with so much more effect than mine. This book revived impressions nearly dormant.

November 24th. — I walked out early. Went to the King's Bench, where one of Carlile's men was brought up for judgment for publishing blasphemy. A half-crazy Catholic, French, spoke in mitigation. "My Lords," he said, "your Lordships cannot punish this man, now that blasphemy is justified by Act of Parliament." This roused Lord Ellenborough. "That cannot be, Mr. French." — "Why, my Lord, the late Bill repealing the penalties on denying the Trinity justifies blasphemy!"† This was a very sore subject to Lord Ellenborough, on account of

---

* There is a fine cast of it in the Flaxman Gallery, University College. London, presented by C. R. Cockerell, R. A.

† See *ante*, p. 413.

the imputed heterodoxy of the Bishop of Carlisle, his father. French could only allege that this might have misled the defendant. He was put down after uttering many absurdities. On this the defendant said : " I should like to know, my Lords, if I may not say Christ was not God without being punished for it ? " This brought up Best, and he said : " In answer to the question so indecently put, I have no hesitation in saying that, notwithstanding the Act referred to, it is a crime punishable by law to say of the Saviour of the world that he was " — and then there was a pause — " other than he declared himself to be." He was about to utter an absurdity, and luckily bethought himself.

November 26th. — Took tea and supped at Godwin's. The Lambs there, and some young men. We played whist, &c. Mrs. Shelley there. She is unaltered, yet I did not know her at first. She looks elegant and sickly and young. One would not suppose she was the author of " Frankenstein."

November 27th. — I called early on Southey at his brother's ; he received me cordially ; we chatted during a short walk. He wishes me to write an article on Germany for the *Quarterly*, which I am half inclined to do. Southey talks liberally and temperately on Spanish affairs. He believes the King of Portugal will give a constitution to the people, but he has no hopes from the King of Spain. He has been furnished with Sir Hew Dalrymple's papers, from which he has collected two facts which he does not think it right at present to make public : one, that the present King of France * offered to fight in the Spanish army against Buonaparte ; the other, that of thirty-five despatches which Sir Hew sent to Lord Castlereagh, only three were answered. The Spanish Ministry have been very abstinent in not revealing this fact against Louis lately ; it would give new bitterness to the national feeling against him. No one now cares about Castlereagh's reputation.

December 3d. — I dined in Castle Street, and then took tea at Flaxman's. A serious conversation on Jung's " Theorie der Geisterkunde " † (" Theory of the Science of Spirits "). Flaxman is prepared to go a very great way with Jung, for though he does not believe in animal magnetism, and has a strong and very unfavorable opinion of the *art*, and though he does not believe in witchcraft, yet he does believe in ghosts, and he related the following anecdotes as confirming his belief : Mr. E—— ordered of Flaxman a monument for his wife, and

---

* Louis XVIII.   † This work has been translated into English.

directed that a dove should be introduced. Flaxman supposed it was an armorial crest, but on making an inquiry was informed that it was not, and was told this anecdote as explanatory of the required ornament. When Mrs. E—— was on her death-bed, her husband, being in the room with her, perceived that she was apparently conversing with some one. On asking her what she was saying, Mrs. E—— replied, " Do not you see Miss —— at the window ? " — " Miss —— is not here," said her husband. " But she is," said Mrs. E——. " She is at the window, standing with a dove in her hand, and she says she will come again to me on Wednesday." Now this Miss ——, who was a particular friend of Mrs. E——, resided at a dis-tance, and had then been dead three months. Whether her death was then known to Mrs. E——, I cannot say. On the Wednesday Mrs. E—— died. Flaxman also related that he had a cousin, a Dr. Flaxman, a Dissenting minister, who died many years ago. Flaxman, when a young man, was a believer in ghosts, the Doctor an unbeliever. A warm dispute on the subject having taken place, Mr. Flaxman said to the Doctor : " I know you are a very candid, as well as honest man, and I now put it to you whether, though you are thus incredulous, you have never experienced anything which tends to prove that appearances of departed spirits are permitted by Divine Providence ? " Being thus pressed, the Doctor confessed that the following circumstance had taken place : There came to him once a very ignorant and low fellow, who lived in his neighborhood, to ask him what he thought of an occurrence that had taken place the preceding night. As he lay in bed, on a sudden a very heavy and alarming noise had taken place in a room above him where no one was, and which he could not account for. He thought it must come from a cousin of his at sea, who had promised to come to him whenever he died. The Doctor scolded at the man and sent him off. Some weeks afterwards the man came again, to tell him that his cousin, he had learned, was drowned that very night.

*Rem.** — Let me add here, what I may have said before, that Charles Becher told me a story the very counterpart of this, — that one night he was awakened by a sound of his brother's voice crying out that he was drowning, and it afterwards ap-peared that his brother was drowned that very night. It should be said that there was a furious tempest at the time, and Becher was on the English coast, and knew that his brother was at sea on the coast of Holland.

* Written in 1851.

I should add to what I have said of Flaxman, that he was satisfied Jung had borrowed his theory from a much greater man, Swedenborg.

December 22d. — Dined with Southern in Castle Street, and then went to Flaxman's. I read to them parts of Jung's work, but Flaxman thought his system very inferior to Swedenborg's. Flaxman declared his conviction that Swedenborg has given the true interpretation of the Old and New Testaments, and he believes in him as an inspired teacher. He says, that till he read his explanations of the Scriptures, they were to him a painful mystery. He has lent me a summary of the Swedenborgian doctrines.

December 31st. — A year to me of great enjoyment, but not of prosperity. My fees amounted to 445 guineas. As to myself, I have become more and more desirous to be religious, but seem to be further off than ever. Whenever I draw near, the negative side of the magnet works, and I am pushed back by an invisible power.

END OF VOL. I.

University Press, Cambridge : Printed by Welch, Bigelow, & Co.

Printed in the United States
111577LV00001B/76/A